HISTORY AND GENEALOGY OF THE FAMILIES OF OLD FAIRFIELD

Compiled and Edited by
DONALD LINES JACOBUS

Volume II, Part 1

Reprinted
With Additions and Corrections

CLEARFIELD

Originally Published
Fairfield, Connecticut
1930-1932

Reprinted
Two Volumes in Three

With
*Additions and Corrections
to History and Genealogy of
the Families of Old Fairfield*
(originally published as a
Supplement to The American
Genealogist, October 1943)

Genealogical Publishing Co., Inc.
Baltimore, 1976, 1991

Reprinted for
Clearfield Company by
Genealogical Publishing Co.
Baltimore, Maryland
2007

Library of Congress Catalogue Card Number 76-3279

Volume II, Part 1 ISBN-13: 978-0-8063-1298-9
Volume II, Part 1 ISBN-10: 0-8063-1298-X
Set ISBN-13: 978-0-8063-0719-0
Set ISBN-10: 0-8063-0719-6

Made in the United States of America

HISTORY AND GENEALOGY

OF THE FAMILIES OF

OLD FAIRFIELD

VOLUME II

Part 1

Compiled and Edited by
DONALD LINES JACOBUS, M.A.

For
THE EUNICE DENNIE BURR CHAPTER
DAUGHTERS OF THE AMERICAN REVOLUTION
FAIRFIELD, CONNECTICUT
1932

GENEALOGICAL RESEARCH COMMITTEE

ANNIE BURR JENNINGS
LORETTA BRUNDIGE PERRY
HELEN TURNEY SHARPS, *Chairman*

THE TUTTLE, MOREHOUSE & TAYLOR COMPANY,
NEW HAVEN, CONN.

Respectfully Dedicated

to the memory of

Winthrop H Perry

and

Orlando P. Dexter

to whose comprehensive genealogical collections of Fairfield data,
the fruit of long, patient and accurate research,
the present volume is so largely indebted.

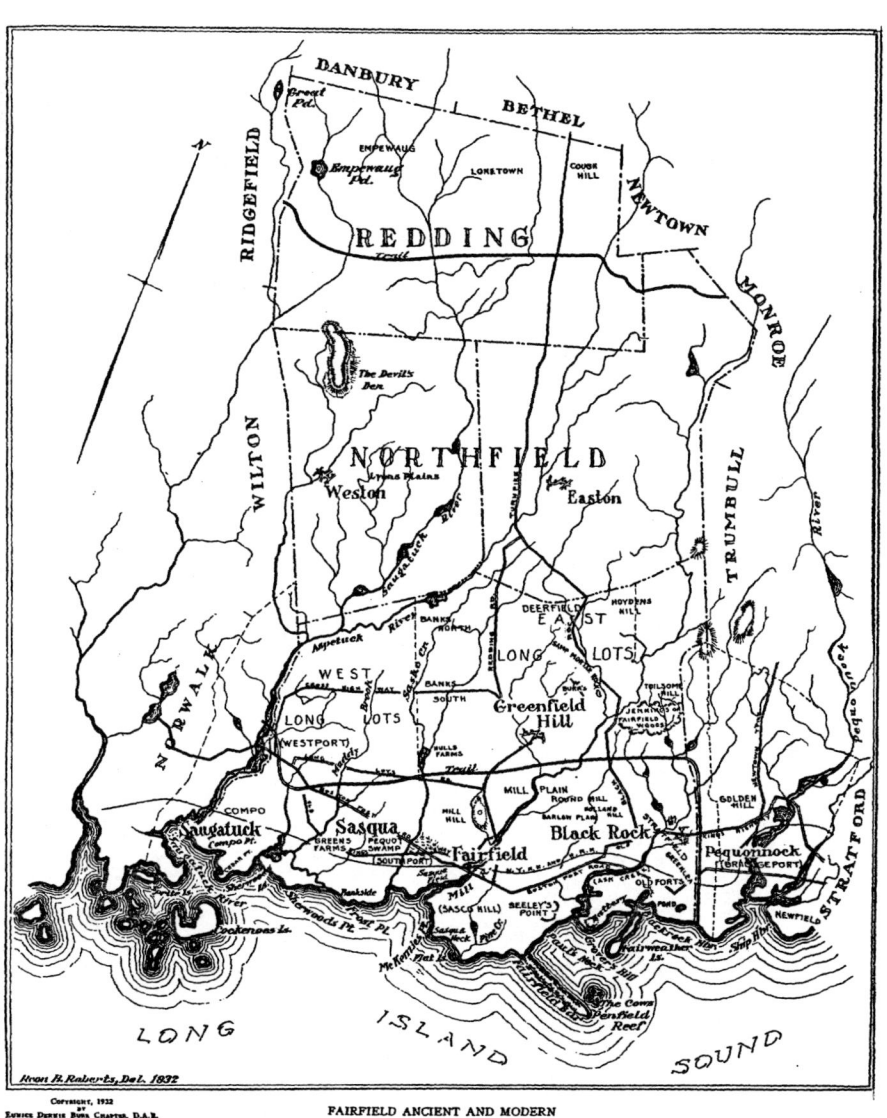

FAIRFIELD ANCIENT AND MODERN
From the original drawing made by Reon B. Roberts of Fairfield

PREFACE

As indicated by the dedication, this volume is indebted to the manuscript collections made by Mr. Winthrop H. Perry and Mr. Orrando P. Dexter much more largely than to any other private source. The task of the present compiler and editor has not been limited, however, to the classification and arrangement of the voluminous data copied and abstracted by them with infinite care from original sources.

Members of the Eunice Dennie Burr Chapter donated their time to visit many persons who possess old family Bibles and to copy the records contained therein. These have been incorporated in this volume, except when too recent in date; and the copies were then deposited at the State Library in Hartford, where they may be consulted by any who are interested.

Extensive data were also obtained from the manuscript diary of Peter Perry, which contains a mortuary list covering many years, through the kindness of Miss Loretta Brundige Perry of Fairfield; and from the large manuscript collections of Mr. Cyrus S. Bradley of Fairfield, to whose generosity our volume is considerably indebted.

We make a general acknowledgment to the many who have been helpful in supplying private records or the results of their personal research, regretting that the limitations of space forbid individual mention of each one. Special mention must be made of aid received from Mrs. Helen Turney Sharps of Fairfield, Conn., on several families, and from Mrs. Cornelia Penfield Lathrop of Bridgeport, Conn., on the Penfield and other families, as well as from the latter's fascinating and helpful book, *Black Rock* (1930). To Mrs. Nellie L. Elwood of Westport, Conn., and to Mr. Frederick Wood of Springfield, Penn., we are indebted for data on several families; to Mr. Clarence A. Torrey of Dorchester, Mass., for important additions to the Adams family; to Mrs. G. E. Fellows of Salt Lake City, Utah, for help on the Sherwood family; to Mrs. Thomas D. Watkins of Utica, N. Y., for Osborn data; and to Mrs. C. W. Nichols of New Britain, Conn., and Mrs. Walter Corbin of Florence, Mass., for Squire data.

Among printed histories utilized by the compiler, special mention should be made of those of Stratford (Orcutt) and Fairfield (Schenck); Trinity Church, Southport (Guilbert); the Commemorative Biographical Record of Fairfield County; Yale Biographies (Dexter); and also the Old Burying Ground of Fairfield (Perry). Many printed genealogies have been consulted, notably those of the Buckingham, Burr, Chapman, Hendrick, Higgins, Hubbell, Jessup, Middlebrook, Redfield, Sanford, Solley, Spalding, Sterling, Stratton, Trubee, Wakeman, Ward, and Whitney families; and the excellent typed Seeley genealogy. The printed Colonial and State records (eighteen volumes) were searched page by page for the appearance of Fairfield names.

Since prefaces are so seldom read, and the present volume should speak for itself, the compiler need say but little of his own labors. So far as possible, original record sources have been consulted. In addition to the copies of church records and gravestone inscriptions and the abstracts of probate and land records, contained in the collections of Mr. Dexter and Mr. Perry, the compiler has carried the search of the probate records in Fairfield to 1832, and has covered the records of the Danbury Probate District (chiefly for Redding families) from 1744 to 1830; besides gleaning much information from the land records of Stratford and Norwalk concerning intermarriages between the people of those towns and the people of Fairfield. Much has been obtained from other sources, such as the pension abstracts, the County Court records at Bridgeport, and the Connecticut Archives at Hartford.

A work so extensive as this, even though liberally financed, cannot hope to be perfect, either in completeness or in accuracy. The aim of the compiler has been to show what the records contain, and for this purpose we have usually indicated the source of vital entries, and have included very brief abstracts of wills and distributions. It is believed that errors in copying, clerical errors, and mistakes in judgment, will be rare; but they cannot entirely be avoided unless a lifetime be spent on such a compilation as this. It is estimated that upward of 50,000 vital entries of all kinds have been classified and entered, not to mention several thousand abstracts of probate and land records. The work has been compressed into the course of two years, and during the same period Volume III also was edited, pre-*pared for publication, and indexed. The compiler would have preferred to labor another year on the present volume; but the subscribers to the first volume have become impatient for the sequel, and the funds generously provided for the compilation are nearing exhaustion. With regret, and without further apology for such imperfections as may be found in the volume, the compiler lays down his pen, confident that he has accomplished the best that could be achieved within the necessary limits of time, cost, and labor.

EXPLANATORY NOTES

In order to aid the genealogical inquirer in tracing family lines from the present volume back through the generations recorded in Volume I, brief synopses of the early generations are given herein at the head of each family in small type; and heads of families have been assigned reference numbers.

Towns mentioned are in Connecticut unless otherwise specified or unless, like New York City, the place is too well known to require more definite identification.

*N.B. Volume III, dealing with the Revolutionary War records of Fairfield, has been omitted from the reprint edition because it is not strictly a compendium of genealogies. It may be issued separately at some later date.

Genealogical Publishing Co., Inc.

ABBREVIATIONS

abt.	about	Exec'r	Executor
adm.	admitted	Exec'x	Executrix
adm'n	administration	g. s.	gravestone
Adm'r	Administrator	Inv.	Inventory
Adm'x	Administratrix	Leg.	Legislature [General Assembly]
ae.	aged		
b.	born	m.	married
bapt.	baptized	mo.	month
bur.	buried	prob.	probably
Cong.	Congregational	rec.	recorded, records
d.	died		
dau.	daughter	rem.	removed
dec'd	deceased	res.	residence
Epis.	Episcopal	s.	son
Est.	Estate	yr.	year

PARISHES CONNECTED WITH TOWN OF FAIRFIELD

[This list was compiled by Miss Loretta B. Perry, to whom also we owe the suggestion of the map for a frontispiece, and was rearranged somewhat by the Editor. Readers are referred to the map for further information.]

(A) CONGREGATIONAL

I. FAIRFIELD SOCIETY. Church organized 1639. [Records of town and parish included to beyond 1800.]

II. BRIDGEPORT FIRST SOCIETY. Established 1691 as Pequonnock or Poquonock Society in Fairfield and Stratford, by division of the First Societies in those towns. Called Fairfield Village, 1699; name changed 1701 to Stratfield Society. Name formally changed 1847 to Bridgeport First Society. [Records included except for Stratford surnames.]

III. GREENS FARMS SOCIETY. Set off as the West Farms Society in 1711, and came to be called Greens Farms. The part of Fairfield including this Society was incorporated as Westport in 1835. [Records included to beyond 1800.]

IV. GREENFIELD HILL SOCIETY. Set off in 1725 as Northwest Society in Fairfield; name changed to Greenfield, 1727. [Records included to beyond 1800.]

V. REDDING SOCIETY. Established in 1729 as Redding Society in the town of Fairfield. This part of Fairfield was incorporated as the town of Redding, 1767. This region was early known as Lone town and Chestnut Ridge. [Records of town and parish included to beyond 1800.]

VI. WESTON SOCIETY. Established 1757 as Norfield Society in Fairfield and Norwalk by a division of the Societies of Greens Farms, Greenfield, and Wilton. Part of Fairfield (including that part of Norfield) was incorporated, 1787, as the town of Weston. The part of Norwalk which had been in Norfield Society was incorporated, 1802, as the town of Wilton. This parish is sometimes erroneously called Northfield, but the name, Nor-field, was formed from syllables of the names Norwalk and Fairfield. [Records of town and parish included to beyond 1800.]

VII. EASTON SOCIETY. Established 1762 as North Fairfield Society in Fairfield and Stratford, by a division of Greenfield, Stratfield and North Stratford Societies. The part of Fairfield which was included in this Society became the town of Weston in 1787. The part of Stratford which was included in North Fairfield was added, part to Trumbull in 1797, the rest to Bridgeport in 1821. The part of Weston which was in this Society was incorporated as the town of Easton, 1845. [Records included to 1800.]

VIII. BLACK ROCK SOCIETY. Set off from Fairfield, 1849.

(B) EPISCOPALIAN

I. TRINITY CHURCH. Organized at Fairfield, 1725; the church was located at Mill Plain until 1842, when it was voted to move to Southport. [Records partially included to beyond 1800.]

HISTORY AND GENEALOGY OF THE FAMILIES OF OLD FAIRFIELD

Abbott [*Unplaced*].

EBENEZER m. 15 Oct. 1781, Elizabeth Godfrey. [Weston Church]
THADDEUS m. 24 May 1788, Rebecca Marvin. Children: Polly, b. 8 Nov. 1788; Sarah, b. 15 Jan. 1792; Betsey, b. 1 Apr. 1794. [Redding rec.]
HANNAH m. 21 Nov. 1790, William Scofield. [Weston Church]
JOHN had a son Elijah, bapt. 6 July 1776. [Redding Church]

Abel, Elijah, Lt., 1st Co., Fairfield, May 1767; Capt., Oct. 1774; Capt. in Army, May 1776, Oct. 1776; Maj., 4th Regt., May 1777; appointed to enlist men into 4th Regt., June 1779; Brig.-Gen., Conn. Militia, 1794-97. Deputy for Fairfield, May and Oct. 1777, Jan. and Feb. 1778, May and Oct. 1782, May and Oct. 1785, May and Oct. 1786, Oct. 1787, May and Oct. 1788, May and Oct. 1789, May and Oct. 1790, May 1791, May and Oct. 1792, Oct. 1793, Oct. 1799. High Sheriff, Fairfield County, abt. 1774-1806.

Son of Samuel and Lydia (Gifford), b. at Bozrah, 18 Sept. 1738; grad. Yale Coll. 1760; settled in Fairfield; d. at Bozrah, 3 June 1809.

Of Norwich, m. 31 Dec. 1761, Grizzel Burr, dau. of Capt. Nathaniel, b. 15 Nov. 1741, d. 10 Oct. 1808 ae. 67.

Will 10 May 1809, proved 19 June 1809; two nephews Simeon Abel and Elijah Abel, Jr., of Bozrah; Nathaniel son of Isaac Burr; my emancipated negro servants, Amos and Philip; residue equally to Theophilus, Samuel, Simeon and Hezekiah Abel and Asa Baker, all of Bozrah, and Lydia wife of Daniel Kilbourn of Colchester; Sally wife of Nathaniel Burr; niece Rhoda Abel now with me at Fairfield.

Abrahams, George H.

His wife Hannah was bapt. at Weston, 23 July 1786, with children George and Abigail. Other children: Levi, bapt. 16 June 1788; Eunice, bapt. 3 July 1791; Hannah, bapt. 17 Feb. 1796.

Adair, James.

He m. 3 June 1744, Ann Carter; or by church record, 18 Oct. 1744, Ann McCarty, which is more accurate.

Will 21 Oct. 1766, proved 4 Nov. 1782; wife Ann; four daus. Mary, Esther, Ann, and Sarah; son Andrew.

Children, rec. Fairfield, bapt. Greenfield:

> Andrew, b. 23 Apr. 1745, bapt. 1745/6.
> Mary, b. 3 Jan. 1747, bapt. 12 Jan. 1746/7; [m. Epaphras Merwin, of Easton].
> Esther, b. 2 July 1749; m. 20 Dec. 1770, James Goodsell.
> Ann, b. 2 Feb. 1752.
> Sarah, b. 1 Mar. 1755.
> James, b. 26 Aug. 1757, d. y.

Adams [Vol. I, pp. 7-11].

```
1 Edward (    -1671) m. Mary ———.
  2 Samuel (    -1694) m. Mary Meeker.
     5 Daniel (1679-    ).
     6 David (1689-1723).
     7 John (1692-1727).
  3 Abraham (1650-1729) m. (1) ———; (2) Martha (Hobby) Morehouse.*
       No sons.
  4 Nathan (c. 1660-1749) m. (1) Mary James; (2) Jane (Blackman) (Russell)
       (Griffin) Clark; (3) Anna ———.
(By 1): 8 Nathan (1694-1724).
        9 Stephen (1708-1794).
```

5. Adams, Daniel, s. of Samuel.

Born 17 May 1679; m. (1) Rebecca, prob. dau. of John Cable, 2d; m. (2) Sarah Turney, dau. of Benjamin, 2d, b. perhaps 1681. Rebecca wife of Daniel renewed her Covenant, Fairfield Church, 30 Aug. 1702.

He conveyed 1733 to son-in-law and dau. William Stevens and Rebecca his wife of Fairfield, land bounded on heirs of my bro. David Adams.

Children [by first wife], bapt Fairfield:

> Rebecca, bapt. 30 Aug. 1702; m. William Stevens.
> Samuel, bapt. 19 Mar. 1703/4, d. at Danbury, 13 Feb. 1782; m.

---

* The identity of Martha as dau. of John Hobby of Greenwich and widow of Thomas Morehouse of Fairfield has been established by Fairfield County Court Records, Vol. I, pp. 132, 320.

Deborah [perhaps Meeker], b. [18 Mar. 1702], d. 2 Feb. 1794 ae. 91 yrs. 10 mos. 3 days (g. s., Danbury).
Daniel, bapt. 29 June 1707.*
Sarah, bapt. June 1711.

Child [by which wife?] :

10+Abraham.

Child [by second wife] :

Elizabeth, bapt. 2 June 1717; m. 15 Apr. 1735, John Mallory.

6. Adams, David, s. of Samuel.

Born 24 June 1689, d. in 1723; m. Abigail Silliman, dau. of Daniel; she m. (2) 22 Mar. 1737, John Hide, and d. at Westport in 1775.

Will 5 Feb. 1722/3, proved 22 Apr. 1723; wife Abigail; two children David, Anna; if both children die under age, a comfortable livelihood for my wife, and balance to my brethren and sisters.

Will of Abigail Hide, widow of Dea. John, 1 Mar. 1763, proved 30 June 1775; gr. son David Jennings, son of dau. Ann; son David Adams, Exec'r.

Children, bapt. Fairfield:

Abigail, bapt. 7 Mar. 1713/4, d. y.
Ann, bapt. 12 Feb. 1715/6, d. before 1743; m. Nathan Jennings.
11+David, bapt. 8 Feb. 1718/9.

7. Adams, John, s. of Samuel.

Born 6 Sept. 1692, d. at Greenwich in 1727; m. 5 Sept. 1717, Elizabeth Husted.

Blacksmith, of Greenwich, he conveyed land in Fairfield, 1717.

Adm'n granted to widow Elizabeth, 5 Sept. 1727. Nathaniel Husted of Greenwich was appointed guardian, 6 Oct. 1730, to Samuel, Jonathan and Sarah, children of John Adams, their mother and former guardian being dead.

---

* He m. Joanna Lane, dau. of Charles, b. [say 1714], d. before 1755; they had children, not positively identified. Among them were prob. Sarah, b. abt. 1747, d. at Pownal, Vt., 2 Mar. 1819, who m. (1) at Redding, 7 Sept. 1763, George Gage, and (2) Timothy Munson; and Daniel of Redding, who in Dec. 1762 chose John Mallory for guardian; and possibly Deborah who m. John Drew.

Children, rec. Greenfield:

Samuel, b. 10 June 1717; m. Abigail Lockwood; she m. (2) **David** Whelpley.
Jonathan, b. 6 Nov. 1719; living 1757.
Sarah, b. 6 Aug. 1721.
John, b. 22 Jan. 1724; d. in 1757; will, 12 Jan. 1757, proved 5 Apr. 1757, names uncle Joseph Husted of Stamford; bro. Jonathan of Greenwich; bro. John Peck of Greenwich; cousin Joseph Husted of Stamford.
Elizabeth, b. 17 Apr. 1727.

8. Adams, Nathan, s. of Nathan.

Bapt. 23 Dec. 1694, d. in 1724; m. abt. 1714, Rebecca Clapham, dau. of Peter. She m. (2) (rec. Christ Church, Stratford, 3 Feb. 1724/5), Joshua Jennings; and (3) Ebenezer Mead of Greenwich; and d. abt. 1759.

Inv. 6 Apr. 1724, presented 12 Feb. 1725/6 by widow Rebecca, now wife of Joshua Jennings.

Rebecca Mead with consent of her husband conveyed 1758 to son Nathaniel Adams a right in Clapham land, mentioning her other two sons, Nathan Adams and Joshua Jennings. Nathanel on 27 Mar. 1760 conveyed to Joshua Jennings the land from his mother Rebecca Mead dec'd.

Children:

12+Nathaniel, b. abt. 1716.
13+Nathan, b. abt. 1721.

9. Adams, Stephen, s. of Nathan.

Born abt. 1708; d. 4 Nov. 1794 "in one breath" (Perry Diary), bur. 5 Nov. 1794 ae. 86 (Trinity Church rec.); m. (1) at Fairfield, 17 Oct. 1727, Sarah Finch.

He m. (2) 9 May 1764, Esther, widow of John Hill, and dau. of Joseph Bulkley, bapt. 20 Dec. 1713, d. before 1793.

Will 23 Sept. 1793, proved 25 Nov. 1794; son Nathan; dau. Elizabeth Beardsley; gr. children Timothy, Daniel, and Ann Hubbell; dau. Ann Hubbell; gr. children (children of dau. Mary Hayes dec'd), Ann, John, Joseph, Stephen, Reney, Nehemiah, Sarah, Nathan, William, and Elizabeth; son Nathan and Timothy Hubbell, Exec'rs.

Children [by first wife], born Fairfield:
Mary, b. 18 Oct. 1728, d. by 1793; m. Abraham Hayes.
John, b. 9 Apr. 1732, d. 11 Mar. 1733.
Sarah, b. 15 Sept. 1733, d. y.
Nathan, b. 26 Oct. 1736; m. 11 Feb. 1756, Mary Hubbell; prob. dau. of Samuel, bapt. 4 Oct. 1741.*
Ann, b. 10 Aug. 1742; m. Timothy Hubbell.
Elizabeth, b. 9 Oct. 1744; m. ——— Beardsley.

10. **Adams, Abraham,** s. of Daniel.

He d. in the French and Indian War; reported dead 11 June 1761 in roll of Col. Smedley's Co.

He m. at Redding, 9 May 1740, Elizabeth Williams, b. 31 Aug. 1719; she m. (2) ——— Fillio, and d. in 1789.

Adm'n on Est. of Elizabeth Fillow, formerly Elizabeth Adams, of Redding, was granted to Joseph Adams of Redding, 8 Apr. 1789. Distribution, 8 Apr. 1791: eldest son Joseph Adams; 3d son Abel Adams; Anna wife of Samuel Jacocks; heirs of Elizabeth wife of Nathan Fillow; Benjamin Adams; Abraham Adams; Huldah wife of Zachariah Ferris; Asahel Adams; Lydia wife of Arnon Crow.

Children:

14+Joseph.
Anna, m. Samuel Jacocks [prob. Jacquith]; res. Harpersfield, N. Y.
15+Abraham, b. 2 Dec. 1745 (Pension record).
Abel, chose Timothy Lyon for guardian, 3 Feb. 1767; m. at Easton, 25 Nov. 1773, Lucretia Crane.
Elizabeth, m. Nathan Fillio.
Benjamin, m. (1) Chloe Hatch; m. (2) Sarah (Gridley) Morgan.
Huldah, b. abt. 1750, d. at Newtown, 18 Nov. 1833; m. 5 Apr. 1768, Zachariah Ferris.
Asahel, m. Deserta Cram.
Lydia, m. Arnon Crow.

11. **Adams, David,** s. of David.

Bapt. 8 Feb. 1718/9; d. 1 Dec. 1796 ae. 78 yrs. 1 mo.

He m. (1) abt. 1738, Susannah Lockwood, dau. of John; she d. 6 June 1747; m. (2) 2 Nov. 1748, Sarah Squire; dau. of Nathaniel, b. 9 Nov. 1731, d. 2 Jan. 1817 ae. 85.

---

* Probably they had children: Sarah, m. at Fairfield, 18 Oct. 1781, John Hayes; Stephen, called Jr., m. at Fairfield, 25 Oct. 1781, Ellen Burr, dau. of Nathan, bapt. 4 May 1760. Children of Stephen, Jr.: Samuel, bapt. 24 Feb. 1784; Ruth, bapt. 18 June 1786; Polly, bapt. 7 Oct. 1790.

Adm'n granted, 21 Feb. 1797, to Sarah Adams, with Squire Adams surety.

David, Jr., and Squire Adams, were accused of being inimical to the U. S., May 1778.

Child [by first wife]:

16+David.

Children [by second wife]:

    Abigail, m. at Weston, 9 Nov. 1768, Michael Lockwood.
    Squire, d. at Weston, 29 Nov. 1826; m. at Weston, 24 Jan. 1779, Mary Godfrey; dau. of David, b. 24 Feb. 1752.*
    Sarah, b. 24 Aug. 1756, d. 19 Jan. 1857 ae. 100 yrs. 5 mos.; m. at Weston, 31 Jan. 1779, Joshua Adams.

17+Silliman, b. abt. 1763.

    Lucy, bapt. 5 Oct. 1765, living at Redding, 1851; m. 26 Nov. 1788, Joshua Chapman.
    Mary, m. 15 Jan. 1792, Daniel Mallory, Jr.

12. Adams, Nathaniel, s. of Nathan, 2d.

Born abt. 1716, d. at Westport, 29 Mar. 1784 ae. 68 (g. s.); m. 3 Oct. 1739, Ann Silliman; dau. of Capt. John, bapt. 1 Nov. 1719, d. at Westport, 14 Nov. 1748 ae. 29 yrs. 16 days (g. s.).

Nathaniel was appointed guardian to his five children, 28 Dec. 1752.

Will, proved 2 Oct. 1784; children, Nathaniel, Mary wife of Stephen Wakeman, Abigail wife of Joseph Hanford, Ann wife of Gideon Wakeman, Rebecca wife of Joseph Wakeman.

Children, rec. Fairfield:

    Ann, b. 19 Feb. 1740 [1740/1]; m. 24 Oct. 1759, Gideon Wakeman.
    Rebecca, b. 3 June 1742, d. at Westport, 16 Apr. 1772; m. 28 July 1762, Joseph Wakeman.
    Mary, b. 1 Feb. 1744, d. 18 Oct. 1812; m. 3 Feb. 1763, Stephen Wakeman.

18+Nathaniel, b. 19 Feb. 1746.

    Abigail, b. 2 Nov. 1748; m. (1) 25 June 1767, Stephen Bradley; m. (2) 20 Sept. 1772, Joseph Hanford.

---

* Adm'n on Est. of Squire Adams was granted, 7 Dec. 1826, to Mary Adams of Weston and Samuel B. Sherwood of Fairfield. Distribution 1827: widow Mary; bro. Silliman Adams; sisters Sarah wife of Joshua Adams, Mary Mallery, Lucy wife of Joshua Chapman, and Abigail Lockwood.

13. Adams, Nathan, s. of Nathan, 2d.

Born [9 Jan. 1721], d. at Westport, 17 Aug. 1782; m. Mary Burr, dau. of Daniel, bapt. 31 July 1721, d. 15 Mar. 1806 ae. 84.

Nathan of Norwalk conveyed, 1770, to Nathaniel Adams; and 1781, to Joshua Adams of Fairfield, land in Fairfield.

Children, b. prob. at Norwalk:

>Peter, m. (1) at Wilton, 23 Nov. 1769, Rebecca Dunning; m. (2) at Westport, 17 Mar. 1784, Milicent Hurlbut.
>Molly, b. abt. 1743, d. 3 Apr. 1771 in 29 yr.; m. Barnabas Marvin.
>Nathan, b. 4 May 1745, d. at South Salem, Westchester County, N. Y., 14 Apr. 1812; rem. to South Salem, 1790; m. Rhoda Scribner, b. 18 Oct. 1748, d. 3 Apr. 1812.*
>Sarah, b. abt. 1747, d. 29 Apr. 1813 ae. 66; m. Obadiah Wright.
>Joshua, b. 19 June 1750, d. 19 Sept. 1836 (Pension rec.); m. 31 Jan. 1779, Sarah Adams, b. 24 Aug. 1756, d. 19 Jan. 1857 ae. 100 yrs. 5 mos. Joshua's will, 19 Aug. 1831, proved 4 Oct. 1836; wife Sarah; to dau. Rebecca Belden, land in Wilton; gr. children (children of son Joshua dec'd) Charles A., Strong C., Burr M., Caroline-Agnes and Mary-Elizabeth Adams.†
>Betsey, m. Sept. 1776, Phineas Hanford, Jr.
>Jabez, a loyalist; Peter Adams appointed Adm'r, 6 Dec. 1784.
>Aaron, b. 9 Apr. 1759, d. 21 Feb. 1836 ae. 77; m. (1) 4 Mar. 1784, Rhoda Hanford, dau. of Phineas, b. abt. 1763, d. 22 Feb. 1802 in 39 yr.; m. (2) Hannah Morehouse, b. abt. 1781, d. 28 Oct. 1869 ae. 88.
>Stephen, b. 3 Aug. 1762, d. 10 Mar. 1854; rem. to Pawling, Dutchess County, N. Y.; m. at Westport, 13 Nov. 1783, Abigail Gorham, dau. of Joseph, bapt. 24 May 1767, d. 26 July 1850 ae. 83.‡
>Anna, b. abt. 1766, d. 23 Sept. 1835 ae. 69; m. 21 Nov. 1791, John Hurlbut.
>Daniel, living 1777, d. s. p.

14. Adams, Joseph, s. of Abraham.

He m. 9 Sept. 1761, Joanna Disbrow; dau. of Nathan, b. 6 Jan. 1739/40.

---

* Children, bapt. Weston: Susa and Esther, bapt. 21 June 1779; Hosea, bapt. 29 Jan. 1781; Rhoda, bapt. 30 June 1782; Moses-Scribner, bapt. 11 Feb. 1784; Sarah, bapt. 19 Mar. 1786; Susa, bapt. 14 Sept. 1788; Amarinda, bapt. 23 Oct. 1790.

† Children, rec. Weston: Rebecca, b. 2 May, bapt. 8 July 1781; m. at Weston, 16 Aug. 1801, William Belden, of Wilton. Joshua, b. 30 Sept. 1787, bapt. 4 May 1788, d. 16 July 1831 in 44 yr.; m. Catherine C. ———, who d. 12 Mar. 1878 ae. 94 (g. s.).

‡ Children, bapt. Westport: Peter, b. 15 Sept. 1784, bapt. 17 Apr. 1785; Stephen, bapt. 1 Apr. 1787; Samuel, bapt. 8 Aug. 1791; Charles, bapt. 23 June 1793; Polly, bapt. 21 Feb. 1796; there were four younger children.

Children, rec. and bapt. Redding:

    Stephen, b. 15 July, bapt. 15 Aug. 1762, d. [in the Revolution].
    Hezekiah, b. 14 Aug., bapt. 30 Sept. 1764, d. at Redding, 25 Dec. 1819 ae. 55-4-11 (g. s.); m. 11 Sept. 1788, Betty Parsons, bapt. 17 Mar. 1771, d. 23 May 1849 in 79 yr. (g. s.).*
    Ellen, b. 30 Aug., bapt. 10 Nov. 1765, living at Westport, 1848; m. at Redding, 23 Jan. 1783 (Pension Rec.), Josiah Gregory of Norwalk.
    Abigail, b. 1 Oct. 1767, bapt. 6 Mar. 1768.
    Joseph, b. 27 Aug. 1770, bapt. 28 Apr. 1771.
    Israel, b. 5 Sept. 1772, bapt. 10 Jan. 1773, d. at Redding, 27 Sept. 1838 ae. 66 (g. s.); m. 28 Mar. 1796, Abigail Stow, b. 11 Apr. 1776.†
    Aaron, b. 22 Feb., bapt. 16 July 1775.
    Nathan, b. 27 Jan., bapt. 6 Sept. 1778.

15. Adams, Abraham, s. of Abraham.

Born 2 Dec. 1745.
He m. (1) Deborah ———, who d. 24 June 1766.
He m. (2) Sarah ———.

Child [by first wife], bapt. Redding:

    Molly, bapt. 10 Nov. 1765.

Children [by second wife], bapt. Redding:

    Ani, bapt. 6 Mar. 1768.
    Deborah, bapt. 28 Apr. 1771.
    Abraham, bapt. 15 Dec. 1771, d. y.
    Sarah, bapt. 31 July 1774.
    Abraham, bapt. 20 Oct. 1776; ? m. 5 Apr. 1798, Sarah Hull, dau. of Eliphalet.
    Eli, bapt. 30 Jan. 1780.

16. Adams, David, s. of David.

He m. at Westport, 10 Nov. 1757, Adrea Couch. It is said that he m. (2) Hannah Cummings, and rem. abt. 1800 to Butternuts, N. Y.

Children [by first wife], bapt. Weston:

    Elizabeth, bapt. 15 Feb. 1759, d. y.
    Adrea, bapt. 27 July 1760.

---

* Adm'n granted, 6 Mar. 1820, to Lemuel Adams of Redding. Distribution: widow Betty; children, Betsey, Stephen, Lemuel, Aaron, Eleanor, Jedediah. Children, rec. Redding: Betty, b. 6 July 1789; Stephen, b. 22 Jan. 1791; Lemuel, b. 18 Dec. 1792; Aaron, b. 21 July 1795; Ellen, b. 10 Apr. 1799; Jedediah, b. 26 Oct. 1805.

† Children, rec. Redding: Philo, b. 12 May 1797; Lynda, b. 18 Nov. 1798.

Elizabeth, b. 18 June, bapt. 27 July 1760; m. 10 Jan. 1793, Salmon Starr, of Butternuts, N. Y.
Susannah, bapt. 17 May 1762; m. (rec. Danbury) 28 Sept. 1788, Timothy Foster.
Jared, bapt. 10 Feb. 1765, d. in 1847; rem. to Butternuts abt. 1800; m. Jemima Ruscoe.
Deborah, bapt. 6 Mar. 1768.
David, bapt. 26 Nov. 1769; m. ———.*
Isaac, bapt. 23 Aug. 1772.
Mary, bapt. 9 Oct. 1774.
Lockwood, bapt. 11 Aug. 1776; m. at Weston (rec. Fairfield Church), 26 Oct. 1800, Mary Gray.
Eunice, bapt. 12 Sept. 1779.

Child [by second wife] :

Samuel, b. 10 Jan. or 14 Aug. 1790, d. 24 Dec. 1865; Capt.; res. Painted Post, N. Y., and had a family.

17. **Adams, Silliman,** s. of David.

Born about 1763; d. at Weston, 9 Aug. 1830 ae. 67 (g. s.) ; m. (1) at Weston, 19 Sept. 1782, Rhoda Taylor, b. abt. 1762, d. 26 Feb. 1825 ae. 63 (g. s.) ; m. (2) Olive ———.

Will 3 Aug. 1830, proved 23 Aug. 1830; Olive, "my second wife"; children of dec'd dau. Sally wife of David St. John; sons Squire, John, David; daus. Susan wife of Anson Gray, Aritta widow of late Samuel Fairchild, Nancy wife of John Crossman, Mary wife of David S. Gray, and Polly Adams.

Children, bapt. Weston:

Sally, bapt. 25 Apr. 1784; m. David St. John.
John, bapt. 19 Mar. 1786, d. y.
Squire, bapt. 27 July 1788; m. Pamela Waterbury, b. [6 May 1797], d. at Weston, 26 Nov. 1868 ae. 71-6-20 (g. s.).
Susan, bapt. 27 Mar. 1791; m. Anson Gray.
John, bapt. 7 June 1795, d. at Weston, 25 Mar. 1869 ae. 74 yrs. 5 days (g. s.) ; m. Eunice ———, who d. 5 Feb. 1865 ae. 66 yrs. 15 days (g. s.).
Nancy, b. [17 Sept. 1797], ba᠆ 18 Mar. 1798, d. at Weston, 30 Jan. 1880 ae. 82-4-13 (g. s.) ; n.. John Crossman.
Mary, bapt. 28 June 1801; m. David S. Gray.
David.
Aretta, m. Samuel Fairchild.
Polly.

---

* Child, bapt. Weston: Samuel, bapt. 10 Jan. 1790.

18. Adams, Nathaniel, s. of Nathaniel.

Born 19 Feb. 1746; d. at Westport, 8 Oct. 1801 in 56 yr.; m. 21 Dec. 1775, Salome Hide, b. 30 Aug. 1757, d. 15 May 1802 ae. 44-8-15 (g. s.).

Will 23 June, proved 2 Nov. 1801; wife Saloma; sons Joseph, Nathaniel; daus. Saloma, Anna, Abigail, Myrinda (under 21); dau. Rebecca Ogden [wife of Jonathan by distribution].

Children, bapt. Westport:

    Rebecca, bapt. 26 Jan. 1777, d. at Westport, 1 Sept. 1848 ae. 72 (g. s.); m. 27 Aug. 1797, Jonathan Ogden.
    Joseph, bapt. 11 Apr. 1779, d. at Westport, 15 Dec. 1872 ae. 93-9-27 (g. s.); m. Sarah Banks, dau. of Ebenezer, bapt. at Weston, 17 Mar. 1782, d. 22 Oct. 1853 in 73 yr. (g. s.).
    Salome, bapt. 30 Mar. 1783; m. 31 Jan. 1808, David Banks, of Greenfield.
    Ann, bapt. 28 Jan. 1787, d. at Greenfield, 7 June 1820 in 34 yr. (g. s.); m. 22 Sept. 1816, William Nichols. Her will, 26 May 1820, proved 22 Mar. 1822, named bro. Nathaniel Adams and sister Abigail Adams.
    Nathaniel, b. 24 Sept. 1789 (g. s.), bapt. 6 Dec. 1789, d. 7 Apr. 1837 (g. s.); grad. Yale Coll.; m. Jerusha Bull, dau. of Henry, b. 27 Mar. 1798 (g. s.), d. 4 Mar. 1835 (g. s.).
    Abigail, bapt. 16 Sept. 1792.
    Dorcas, bapt. 4 Aug. 1793, d. y.
    Miranda, bapt. 21 Sept. 1794, d. 11 Aug. 1795.
    Miranda, bapt. 15 Feb. 1798; m. 24 Dec. 1818, Walter Banks, of Weston.

Adams [*Unplaced*].

    EZRA of Fairfield; adm'n granted, 28 Oct. 1765, to David Middlebrook of Stratford.
    JOHN m. at Weston, 31 Aug. 1765, Sarah Coley, dau. of Jonathan, b. 8 June 1743.
    CLARA m. 19 Jan. 1794, David Silliman, Jr. [Weston rec.]
    EPHRAIM of Fairfield, d. 1823; adm'n granted, 13 June 1823, to David Adams of Fairfield and Eli Adams of Weston, with John Staples as surety. Distribution made to children, 1824: Ezra, David, Eli, Clarissa wife of David Silliman, Azubah wife of Andrew Wood, Eleanor wife of Andrew Lyon, Sally wife of Samuel Lyon, Eliza Adams, and Ruth wife of John Wakeman. Of these, Clarissa, b. abt. 1774, m. 19 Jan. 1794, David Silliman. Eli, b. abt. 1784, d. at

THE FAMILIES OF OLD FAIRFIELD 15

Easton, 19 Feb. 1861 ae. 77 (g. s.); m. Huldah ———, b. abt. 1792, d. 29 Dec. 1862 ae. 70 (g. s.). Ezra m. Oct. 1792, Elizabeth Beardsley.
FRANCIS m. 5 Mar. 1778, Sabra Parsons. [Redding rec.]

Alderman [*Unplaced*].

GAD, of Simsbury, m. 1 May 1783, Happy Bulkley. [Greens Farms Church]

ALLEN FAMILY (MILFORD-FAIRFIELD)

Allen [Vol. I, pp. 13-15].

1 George (-1648) m. Catherine ———.
2 Gideon (-1693) m. Sarah Prudden.
   3 Gideon (1671-1751) m. (1) Anna Burr;* (2) Jane (———) (Hill) Dimon.
(By 1) 4 *John* (1710-1798).
     5 *David* (1714-1777).

4. **Allen, (Dr.) John,** s. of Lt. Gideon. Justice, 1774.

Born 1 Dec. 1710; d. at Sherman, 21 Dec. 1798 ae. 88 yrs. 10 days; m. 17 Jan. 1750/1, Abigail Jessup; dau. of Edward, b. 9 May 1731, d. 4 July 1773 in 43 yr. (g. s.).
Graduated from Yale Coll., 1729.

Children, rec. Fairfield, bapt. Fairfield Church:

  Gideon, b. 19 Oct. 1751, bapt. 27 Oct. 1751, d. at Sherman, 22 Nov. 1824; unm. Representative in State Leg. for New Fairfield, 1779-90, 1794, and for Sherman, 1806.
  Abigail, b. 13 Mar. 1753, bapt. 18 Mar. 1753.
  Martha, b. 1 Apr. 1755, bapt. 6 Apr. 1755; m. 17 Feb. 1773, John Fairchild.
  Ann, b. 19 Jan. 1757, bapt. 30 Jan. 1757, d. 14 Jan. 1776 ae. 19 yrs. wanting 4 days; m. 22 Sept. 1774, William Silliman.
  John, b. 14 Aug. 1759, bapt. 19 Aug. 1759; m. 29 Nov. 1803,† Elizabeth Maltby.

---

* Their eldest son Gideon (1703-1748) was Ens., 2d Co., Fairfield, May 1745. He d. unmarried (see Vol. I, p. 15). Their youngest son George, bapt. 14 May 1721, d. unmarried by 1770, and his estate was distributed, 7 Nov. 1770, to John Allen, heirs of Anne Burr dec'd, David Allen, Sarah Keeler, Abigail Wakeman, Mary wife of Peter Penfield, and Hannah Gibbs.

† Or 6 Dec. by Fairfield Church rec.

James, b. 14 July 1762, bapt. 18 July 1762; Representative for Sherman, 1814; m. 25 Mar. 1804, Abigail Dimon, dau. of William, bapt. 26 Feb. 1775.*
Samuel, b. 3 Aug. 1765, bapt. 4 Aug. 1765, d. at Sherman, 27 Nov. 1837; unm. Representative in State Leg. for New Fairfield, 1791-92, 1801-02, and for Sherman, 1803-04.
Sarah, b. 25 Dec. 1768, bapt. 1 Jan. 1769, d. at Sherman, 15 May 1847; unm.

5. **Allen, David,** s. of Lt. Gideon. Ens., 1st Co., Fairfield, May 1748; Lt., Oct. 1752.

Bapt. 4 July 1714; Lt. David d. at Fairfield, 8 Sept. 1777 in 64 yr. (g. s.); m. 11 Oct. 1739, Sarah Gold, dau. of John, bapt. 1 June 1718, d. Feb. 1778 in 60 yr. (g. s.).

Will 11 Apr., proved 6 Oct. 1777; wife Sarah; two sons David and George; five daus. Ann, Sarah, Hannah, Elizabeth, Marah.

Inv. of Widow Sarah Allen proved 4 Jan. 1779.

Distributions of estates of David and Widow Sarah Allen, approved 20 Jan. 1812: eldest son David; 2d son George; eldest dau. Ann widow of Col. David Dimon; 2d dau. Sarah; 3d dau. Hannah wife of Andrew Wakeman; 4th dau. Elizabeth wife of Jonathan Maltbie; 5th dau. Mary wife of Abijah Morehouse.

Children, rec. Fairfield, bapt. Fairfield Church:

Sarah, bapt. 13 Oct. 1740, d. y.
Ann, b. 28 Sept. 1741, bapt. 4 Oct. 1741, d. at Fairfield, 9 Mar. 1812 ae. 70 (g. s.); m. 15 Nov. 1762, David Dimon.
6+David, b. 13 Nov. 1743, bapt. 20 Nov. 1743.
Sarah, b. 23 July 1745, bapt. 28 July 1745; ? m. 11 July 1776, Peter Hendrick.
Hannah, b. 29 May 1747, bapt. 31 May 1747, d. at Fairfield, 8 Sept. 1787 in 41 yr. (g. s.); m. 14 Apr. 1773, Andrew Wakeman.
Elizabeth, b. 13 Apr. 1749, bapt. 23 Apr. 1749, d. at Fairfield, 14 Mar. 1799 ae. 50 (g. s.); m. 23 Oct. 1768, Jonathan Maltby.
Mary, b. 6 May 1752, bapt. 10 May 1752; m. 1 Nov. 1770, Abijah Morehouse.
Ellen, b. 19 Nov. 1754, bapt. 1 Dec. 1754, d. 4† Sept. 1775 ae. 20 yrs. 9 mos. 15 days (g. s.).
Edward, b. 7 Feb. 1757, bapt. 20 Feb. 1757, d. 8 Nov. 1774 ae. 17 yrs. 9 mos. (g. s.).
7+George, b. 26 July 1760, bapt. 8 Aug. 1760.

---
* A child, Harriet-Dimon, bapt. 9 June 1805.
† 7, by Perry Diary.

6. **Allen, David,** s. of David.

Born 13 Nov. 1743, d. at Fairfield, 20 Jan. 1812 in 69 yr. (g. s.).
He m. (1) 10 Nov. 1768, Sarah Hull, dau. of Cornelius, b. 15 Apr. 1745, d. 30 Aug. 1804 in 60 yr. (g. s.).
He m. (2) Martha ———.
Will 15 Jan., proved 4 Feb. 1812; wife Martha; children living here, viz.: John G., Stephen, Joseph, Abigail; daus. Ellen Warren and Abigail Allen; four sons John G., Stephen, David and Joseph.
John G. Allen was appointed Adm'r on the estate of his mother, Sarah Allen, 4 July 1812.

Children [by first wife], rec. Fairfield, bapt. Fairfield:

> John-Gold, b. 22 Jan. 1771, bapt. 27 Jan. 1771, d. at Fairfield, 8 Oct. 1842 in 73 yr.; m. 5 Nov. 1795, Elizabeth Nichols, dau. of Hezekiah, bapt. 23 Mar. 1777.*
> Gideon, b. 1 Mar. 1772, bapt. 8 Mar. 1772, d. 8 Dec. 1805 ae. 34 (g. s.).
> David, b. 22 Sept. 1773, bapt. 3 Oct. 1773.
> Ellen, b. 27 July 1775, bapt. 6 Aug. 1775; m. 13 Feb. 1798, Jonathan Warren, of Troy, N. Y.
> Edward, b. 22 June 1778, bapt. 12 July 1778, d. 2 Oct. 1794 ae. 16 yrs. 3 mos. 10 days (g. s.).
> Stephen, b. 23 Nov. 1782, bapt. 1 Dec. 1782.
> Joseph, b. 25 Dec. 1784, bapt. 9 Jan. 1785, d. 3 July 1812 in 28 yr. (g. s.); will 4 Feb., proved 14 July 1812; m. at Westport, 25 Mar. 1807, Sarah Nichols, dau. of Hezekiah, bapt. 14 Apr. 1782, d. 19 June 1843 ae. 61 (g. s.).
> Sarah, bapt. 8 July 1787, d. 16 Oct. 1805 in 19 yr. (g. s.).
> Abigail, bapt. 1 July 1792.

7. **Allen, George,** s. of David.

Born 26 July 1760; d. at Fairfield, Apr. 1822 ae. 62.
He m. at Fairfield, 24 July 1782, Huldah Knapp; dau. of James.

Children, bapt. Fairfield:

> Esther, bapt. 27 Feb. 1785.
> John, bapt. 31 Aug. 1788.
> George, bapt. 26 Dec. 1790.
> Gold, bapt. 20 Mar. 1793.

---

* Children, bapt. Fairfield: Albert, bapt. 14 July 1805; Edward and Maria, bapt. 15 Dec. 1805.

ALLEN FAMILY (WESTPORT)

Allen [Vol. I, pp. 15, 16].

1 Gideon (-) m. (1) Mary Wright; (2) Phebe (———) Bennett.
(By 1): 2 *Joseph* (1702-1776).
        3 *Ebenezer* (1704-1780).
(By 2): 4 *John* (1714-1791).

2. Allen, Joseph, s. of Gideon.

Born 25 June 1702, d. at Westport between Mar. and Oct. 1776; m. 26 Mar. 1724, Rachel Bennett, dau. of John, b. Mar. 1702/3, d. in 1776.

Hannah Baker and Rachel Couch conveyed, 1779, to Benjamin Allen, their portions from their father.

Children, rec. Fairfield:

    Joseph, b. 6 Feb. 1725.
    Hannah, b. 20 Sept. 1727; m. 10 June 1770, Avery Baker.
    Rachel, b. 28 July 1728, d. at Westport, 23 Feb. 1817 ae. 87 yrs. 7 mos.; m. 22 Feb. 1756, Samuel Couch.
5+Elnathan, b. 23 June 1729.
    Mary, b. 24 Aug. 1732, d. y.
6+Thomas, b. 2 July 1733.
    Mary, b. 2 July 1733, bur. 10 May 1811 ae. 77 (Trinity Church rec.); m. 18 Oct. 1756, Daniel Nichols; they res. Stamford, 1780.
    John, b. 16 June 1736; rem. to Stamford, and conveyed 1780 to bro. Benjamin.
7+Benjamin, b. 4 Oct. 1743, bapt. 9 Nov. 1746.

3. Allen, Ebenezer, s. of Gideon.

Born 9 Oct. 170[4], d. at Westport, 24 Mar. 1780; m. (1) 12 Nov. 1731, Deborah Bennett, dau. of John. She d. 15 Feb. 1757. He m. (2) 27 Apr. 1760, Tabitha Phillips [a widow]. She d. 31 Jan. 1802 ae. 86.

On 15 Feb. 1759, Ebenezer Allen and Martha his wife of Fairfield, and William Jenkins and Sarah his wife of Norwalk, conveyed to Joseph Disbrow. This would indicate that Ebenezer had a wife between Deborah and Tabitha.

In 1769 (deed recorded 1792), Ebenezer Allen, Jr., and Moses Allen, of Fairfield, and Stephen Scribner and Deborah his wife, and Peter Moseman and Thankful his wife, of Bedford, conveyed right in homestead of father Ebenezer Allen which belongs to us by our mother Deborah Allen dec'd.

Children, rec. Fairfield, bapt. Westport :*

> Sarah, b. 3 Aug. 1732; m. Nehemiah Nichols, of Norwalk, with whom she conveyed 1770 to John Phillips, right in house in Compo of our father Ebenezer Allen that belongs to us by our mother Deborah Allen dec'd.

8+Samuel, b. 10 Aug. 1734.

> Martha, b. 19 Aug. 1737.

9+Ebenezer, b. 21 July 1739.

10+Moses, b. 27 Sept. 1742, bapt. 3 Oct. 1742.

> Deborah, b. 8 Oct. 1744, bapt. 28 Oct. 1744; m. 22 Mar. 1768, Stephen Scribner, of Norwalk; they res. 1769, Bedford, N. Y.; 1772, Norwalk.
>
> Thankful, b. 20 July 1748, bapt. 25 Sept. 1748; m. at Weston, 26 Aug. 1766,† Peter Moseman; they res. 1769, Bedford, N. Y.

4. Allen, John, s. of Gideon.

Bapt. 31 Oct. 1714, d. at Westport, 30 Dec. 1791; m. (1) 23 Mar. 1739, Sarah Bennett, dau. of Deliverance; b. 8 Apr. 1716, d. 18 Apr. 1761 (parentage, birth and death, all on g. s.). He m. (2) 12 Apr. 1768, Martha (Hurlbut), widow of David Lyon. She d. 30 July 1796.

Adm'n granted, 20 Feb. 1792, to George Moyer, Deliverance Bennet surety. Dower set to widow Martha, 1792. Distribution 18 Mar. 1793; Ann Crossman, Mary Hilton, Sarah Allen, Martha Lockwood, Rhoda Allen, heirs of Eunice Grey dec'd, Rebecca Lockwood, Phebe Dean, Asenah Moyer. Dower set to widow Martha.

Children [by first wife], rec. Fairfield, all but first two bapt. Westport :‡

> Ann, b. 20 Dec. 1739, d. at North Salem, N. Y., 27 Apr. 1806 (Bible rec.); m. 15 Dec. 1756, John Crossman, of Dartmouth.
>
> Mary, b. 1 Sept. 1742, bapt. at Greenfield, 4 Oct. 1741; m. Adkinson Hilton, of Weston.
>
> Sarah, b. 6 July 1744, bapt. 7 Aug. 1743; m. 16 Feb. 1764, Ebenezer Allen, Jr.
>
> Martha, b. 4 July 1746, bapt. 6 Oct. 1745; m. 22 Feb. 1767, Gershom Lockwood.

---

* The births of the first four children, rec. Greens Farms, are all exactly one yr. earlier than in town rec.

† She was erroneously called Ellen in marriage record.

‡ Some of the birth records are a year too late; the baptismal record is to be preferred where town and church records disagree.

20 HISTORY AND GENEALOGY OF

> Eunice, b. 4 May 1748, bapt. 5 June 1748; m. 27 Nov. 1766, Elias Gray.
> Rhoda, b. 1 Sept. 1750, bapt. 23 Sept. 1750, d. 10 Oct. 1814 ae. 64; m. 25 Feb. 1770, Benjamin Allen.
> Rebecca, b. 17 Oct. 1752, bapt. 19 Nov. 1752; m. 22 Oct. 1772, Stephen Lockwood, of Norwalk.
> Phebe, b. 5 Sept. 175[5], bapt. 19 Oct. 1755; m. (1) 15 Jan. 1775, Daniel Seymour, of Norwalk; m. (2) ——— Dean.
> Asenath, bapt. 2 Sept. 1759, d. at Westport, 19 Sept. 1806 ae. 47; m. 24 Feb. 1780, George Moyer.

5. **Allen, Elnathan**, s. of Joseph.

Born 23 June 1729, d. at Westport, 26 May 1816 ae. 85; m. 28 Dec. 1751, Salome Nott; dau. of John, b. 10 July 1735.

> Children, bapt. Westport:
>
> Honour, bapt. 22 July 1753, d. 21 Aug. 1753.
> Gershom, bapt. and d. 9 Sept. 1753.
> 11+Gabriel, b. 23, bapt. 26 Jan. 1755.
> Temperance, bapt. 20 Feb. 1757, d. 4 Mar. 1757.
> Mercy, b. 12, bapt. 25 Dec. 1757, d. 14 Mar. 1759.
> Elnathan, bapt. and d. 9 Oct. 1759.
> Salome, bapt. and d. 27 Oct. 1761.
> Joseph, bapt. 27 Feb. 1763, d. 21 July 1773.
> 12+William, b. Jan. 1765 (Pension record), bapt. 28 Apr. 1765.
> Olive, bapt. 15 May 1768; m. 15 May 1788, Charles Wilson of Norwalk.
> Gershom, bapt. 22 Apr. 1770, d. 19 Feb. 1799 ae. 29; m. 18 May 1788, Ann Crossman, dau. of John, b. 19 Jan. 1769.*
> Nathan, bapt. 24 Apr. 1774.
> Honour, bapt. 28 Apr. 1776.
> Hezekiah, b. 5 Sept. 1780 (g. s.), bapt. 1 July 1781, d. 6 Sept. 1849 (g. s.);† m. 21 Oct. 1804, Deborah Comstock, b. 26 July 1782 (g. s.), d. 1 Jan. 1855 (g. s.).

6. **Allen, Thomas**, s. of Joseph.

Born 2 July 1733, d. at Westport, Aug. 1779; the Greens Farms rec. of death calls him a "continental soldier." He m. at Greenfield, 16 June 1763, Phebe Rogers; dau. of Robert, b. 22 June 1742; Widow Phebe d. 30 Oct. 1779.

---

* Children, bapt. Westport: Abigail, bapt. 23 Aug. 1789; Lydia, bapt. 2 Oct. 1791; James-Hervey and Ann, bapt. 16 Sept. 1797.

† Hung himself at Westport (Miss Treadwell's book).

Children, bapt. Westport:

> Thomas, bapt. 6 May 1764.
> David-Osborn, bapt. (as son of Thomas Allen dec'd) 1 July 1781.
> Amelia, bapt. (as dau. of Thomas Allen dec'd, offered by G. and Ellen Morehouse), 22 July 1781.

7. **Allen, Benjamin,** s. of Joseph.

Born 4 Oct. 1743, d. at Westport, 27 Mar. 1827 ae. 80 (g. s.); m. at Weston, 25 Feb. 1770, Rhoda Allen, dau. of John; b. 1 Sept. 1750, d. 10 Oct. 1814 ae. 64 years 1 mo. 8 days (g. s.)

Will 25 Mar. 1826, proved 26 Apr. 1827; dau. Polly wife of Abraham Gregory of Warwick, Orange County, N. Y.; wife Mary; son Benjamin for life, then to his children and gr. children; son Delancy; son Jeremiah; Rhoda wife of Hezekiah Fairchild; Huldah wife of Daniel Murray.

Children, bapt. Westport:

> Gideon, bapt. 28 June 1772.
> Benjamin, bapt. 20 June 1773, d. at Westport, 16 Feb. 1848 ae. 75 (g. s.); m. Deborah Disbrow, who d. 7 Apr. 1840 ae. 68-10-7 (g. s.).*
> John, bapt. 11 Aug. 1776; m. at Danbury, 12 July 1799, Eunice Corbin.
> Rhoda, bapt. 13 July 1777, d. at Westport, 20 Sept. 1854 ae. 77 (g. s.); m. 25 Mar. 1801, Hezekiah Fairchild.
> Polly, bapt. 3 Oct. 1779, d. at Westport, 18 Oct. 1870 ae. 90 yrs. 10 mos. (g. s.); "Polly 2d" m. 10 Apr. 1798, Abraham Gregory, Jr., of Norwalk.
> Delancy, bapt. 26 Oct. 1783, d. at Westport, 17 Nov. 1833 ae. 50-8-24 (g. s.); m. Chloe ———, who d. 17 Nov. 1870 ae. 84 yrs. 7 days (g. s.).
> Jeremiah, bapt. 2 Aug. 1789, d. 4 May 1843 ae. 57 (g. s.); m. Lydia ———.
> Huldah, m. Daniel Murray.

8. **Allen, Samuel,** s. of Ebenezer.

Born 10 Aug. 1734.

He m. 17 Jan. 1757, Eunice Nichols, dau. of Benjamin, b. 16 Dec. 1738.

---

* Children of Benjamin, bapt. Westport: Benjamin, bapt. and d. 4 Sept. 1794; Gideon, bapt. 17 July 1796, d. 14 Dec. 1829 in 35 yr. (g. s.); Polly, bapt. 21 July 1799; Alanson, bapt. 12 Mar. 1801; Charles and Henrietta, bapt. 29 Jan. 1806.

Child, rec. Fairfield, bapt. Westport:

> Samuel, b. 3 Oct., bapt. 27 Nov. 1757; res. 1784, Salem, Westchester County, N. Y., and conveyed a right inherited from gr. mother Deborah Allen.

9. Allen, Ebenezer, s. of Ebenezer.

Born 21 July 1739.

He m. 16 Feb. 1764, Sarah Allen; dau. of John, b. 6 July 1744.

Children, bapt. Westport:

> Benjamin, bapt. 13 Oct. 1765; m. (1) Sarah ———, who d. 9 Dec. 1788; m. (2) at Weston, 19 May 1791, Ruamah Bulkley, dau. of Talcott, bapt. 26 Apr. 1767.*
> Stephen, b. 14 May 1764 (Pension record), bapt. 13 Oct. 1765; rem. 1817 to Danbury, living 1841 at Ridgefield; m. 31 Dec. 1788, Wait Thorp.†
> Samuel, bapt. 27 Dec. 1767.‡
> Sarah, bapt. 8 July 1770, d. 3 Oct. 1839; m. 26 Oct. 1786, John Batterson.
> Joseph, bapt. 1 May 1774, d. in 1812; will 4 Feb., proved 14 July 1812, named wife Sarah, son Joseph-Gideon, and dau. Sarah-Ann; m. (1) 18 Aug. 1793, Molly Nichols; m. (2) 15 Apr. 1798, Patty Thorp, who d. 30 Mar. 1809 ae. 26; m. (3) 16 Sept. 1811, Sally Street.§
> John, bapt. 6 June 1777, d. 5 July 1777.
> William, bapt. 16 Sept. 1781.
> John, bapt. 22 Sept. 1782.
> James, bapt. 4 July 1793.

10. Allen, Moses, s. of Ebenezer.

Born 27 Sept. 1742.

He m. 2 Nov. 1772, Ann Hendrick, dau. of David, bapt. 30 Mar. 1746.

---

* Children of Benjamin, Jr., and Sarah: Child, d. 6 Apr. 1782; Isaac, bapt. 22 June 1783; Betsey, bapt. 23 Oct. 1785 (at Norfield, rec. Westport), d. 28 July 1791. Child of Benjamin: Huldah, bapt. 18 Sept. 1791. Children, rec. Weston Church: Child, bapt. by Rev. Mr. Ripley, 5 Oct. 1794; Ruamah and Eunice, bapt. 31 Jan. 1798; Bradley, bapt. 18 June 1800.

† Children, bapt. Westport: Lyman, bapt. 9 May 1790; Barnabas, bapt. 18 Nov. 1792; Elijah, bapt. 3 May 1795; Henry, bapt. 16 July 1797, d. 19 Aug. 1800 ae. 3-11; Lucinda, bapt. 27 Oct. 1799; Alba, bapt. 23 Dec. 1801, d. 14 Apr. 1803 ae. 2; Louisa, bapt. 29 Jan. 1806; Noah, bapt. 24 Feb. 1808, d. 23 June 1808 ae. 9 mos.

‡ Samuel had John, bapt. 14 Apr. 1796; Chary, bapt. 16 Feb. 1798; Delia, bapt. 12 Mar. 1801; Betsey, bapt. 6 Sept. 1804; Sarah-Jackson, bapt. 29 Jan. 1806.

§ Child, bapt. Westport: Burr-Nichols, bapt. 12 Oct. 1794, drowned on shore of N. B., Dec. 1809.

Children, bapt. Westport:
> David, bapt. 27 Dec. 1772; m. 24 Jan. 1797, Hannah Sherwood.*
> Aaron, bapt. 3 July 1775.

11. Allen, Gabriel, s. of Elnathan. Capt.

Born 23 Jan. 1755; d. in 1838; m. Sarah ———, who d. 20 Oct. 1827 in 73 yr.

Children, bapt. Westport:
> Joseph, bapt. 29 July 1793; perhaps m. at Ridgebury (called of Fairfield), 8 Nov. 1795, Phebe Seymour.†
> James-Hull, b. [15 Apr. 1777], d. 6 Aug. 1792 ae. 15-3-21 (g. s.).
> Esther, bapt. 29 July 1793, d. 30 July 1793.
> Salome, bapt. 18 Aug. 1793.
> Martha, bapt. 18 Aug. 1793; "Patty" m. 12 Oct. 1802, Lewis Raymond.
> Gabriel, b. abt. 1787, bapt. 18 Aug. 1793, d. at New Orleans, 26 Oct. 1810 ae. 23.
> Elizabeth, bapt. 18 Aug. 1793.
> Edward, bapt. 18 Aug. 1793.
> James H., bapt. 29 July 1793, d. at Westport, 9 Sept. 1874 ae. 81 (g. s.).
> William, bapt. 18 Oct. 1795.
> Hull, bapt. 24 Dec. 1799.

12. Allen, William, s. of Elnathan.

Born Jan. 1765 (Pension record); d. at Westport, 3 Oct. 1845; m. 24 Mar. 1785, Rebecca Green, b. abt. 1765, living 1849.

Children, bapt. Westport:
> Abraham, bapt. and d. 28 Apr. 1787.
> Polly, bapt. 5 Apr. 1789; m. 3 Dec. 1807, James Allen.
> Charity, bapt. 27 Mar. 1791; m. 4 Sept. 1808, James Hurlbut.
> Rebecca, b. [say 1793], bapt. 24 Aug. 1797; m. 28 Oct. 1810, John Hurlbut.
> Esther, b. [say 1795], bapt. 24 Aug. 1797.
> Tammy, bapt. 24 Aug. 1797.

Allen [*Unplaced*].
> JOHN m. 5 July 1789, Anna Seeley. [Weston Church]
> ELIPHALET m. 21 Sept. 1788, Abigail Monroe.‡ [Greens Farms Church]

---
* Child, bapt. Westport: David-Sherwood, bapt. 16 Nov. 1800.

† This Joseph was called "Jr.," in distinction from his cousin, the son of Ebenezer (9). Child, bapt. Westport: Alfred, bapt. 21 July 1799, d. 3 May 1802.

‡ Children, bapt. Westport: Thomas, bapt. 6 Sept. 1789; Sarah, bapt. 5 Feb. 1792.

POLLY m. 8 May 1798, William-Johnson Nash of Norwalk. [Greens Farms Church]
MERCY, a child offered for baptism by Avery Baker and wife. [Weston Church]
WILLIAM m. 30 Sept. 1798, Polly Nichols. [Trinity Church]

1. Alvord, Elisha. Ens., Greenfield company, 4th Regt., May, 1761; Lt., Oct. 1765; Capt., Oct. 1767.

Born at Northampton, Mass., 19 June 1717, son of Thomas and Mary (Strong); rem. to Durham; m. (1) Abigail Finch, who d. 15 Nov. 1743 in 25 yr.; rem. to Fairfield; m. (2) at Greenfield, 11 May 1745, Hannah Goodsell, b. 9 Aug. 1726, d. 20 May 1757; ae. 31 yrs. lacking 3 mos. (g. s.). He m. (3) in 1758, Mary Hanford, dau. of Eleazer, b. abt. 1718; she m. (2) 23 Nov. 1778, Thomas Sherwood. He d. at Greenfield, 28 Jan. 1776 in 57 yr.

Elisha Alvord of Durham on 25 Apr. 1744 sold interest in homestead of father-in-law Nathaniel Finch of Norwalk which was given to Abigail and Mary Finch, daus. of Nathaniel. [Fairfield Deeds.]

His wife Mary was adm. to church at Greenfield, Apr. 1758, by recommendation from Norwalk.

Inv. 20 Apr. 1776. Distribution of Est. of Capt. Elisha made 3 May 1778 to widow; John and Elihu Alvord; Molly wife of Jonathan Knapp; Hannah wife of David Nichols. The part of the Est. which was set to his widow as dower, was distributed 6 Dec. 1811 to his heirs: son John Alvord; heirs of son Elihu Alvord dec'd; heirs of dec'd dau. Hannah, wife of David Nichols; and dau. Molly, wife of Jonathan Knapp.

Children by second wife, rec. Fairfield, bapt. Greenfield:

Abigail, b. 26 June 1746, bapt. in infancy, d. in 1766.* Adm'n granted to Elisha Alvord, 17 Dec. 1766.
Hannah, b. 9 Mar. 1748, bapt. in infancy, d. 13 July 1793 ae. 46 (g. s.); m. 11 Aug. 1768, David Nichols.
2+John, b. 11 July 1751 [1750 by Greenfield rec.], bapt. 15 July 1750.
3+Elihu, b. 23 July 1753, bapt. in infancy.
Mary, b. 26, bapt. 28 Apr. 1757; m. 7 Sept. 1772, Jonathan Knapp.

---

* Sarah Perry, dau. of Abigail Alvord (by Peter Perry), bapt. at Greenfield, 15 Jan. 1764.

2. **Alvord, John,** s. of Elisha. Sergt., Rev. War.

Born 11 July 1750; d. at Greenfield, 3 July 1845 ae. 95 (g. s.).
He m. (1) 11 Nov. 1772, Sarah Wakeman, b. 24 Jan. 1754, d. 29 Apr. 1779 ae. 25-5-5 (g. s.).
He m. (2) Nov. 1779, Abigail Banks; dau. of Nehemiah, b. in 1752, d. 2 Mar. 1831 ae. 79 (g. s.).
Will of Abigail, 23 Aug. 1827, proved 2 Apr. 1831; five children, Joseph Alvord, Nehemiah B. Alvord, Morris Alvord, Sarah W. Higgins, and son Elisha Alvord dec'd's children.

Children [by first wife], bapt. Greenfield:
> John, bapt. 8 Jan. 1775 (ae. abt. 9 mos.); m. 5 Feb. 1797, Elizabeth Bulkley, dau. of Gershom, b. abt. 1777.
> David, bapt. 21 July 1776; m. 2 Dec. 1800, Abigail Jennings, who d. at Westport, 20 Nov. 1857 ae. 78 (g. s.).

Children [by second wife], bapt Greenfield:
> Joseph.
> Sarah W., m. ———— Higgins.
> Elisha, bapt. Aug. 1784; m. 3 Feb. 1807, Betsey Bradley; dau. of Daniel, b. abt. 1786, d. 7 Aug. 1864 ae. 78 (g. s., Westport).
> Morris, m. at Westport, 7 Sept. 1817, Elizabeth Burr.
> Nehemiah-Banks, m. Rana Sherwood, dau. of Abel, bapt. 12 May 1793.
> Talcott, b. [Feb. 1792], d. 19 Sept. 1792 ae. 7 mos. (g. s.).

3. **Alvord, Elihu,** s. of Elisha.

Born 23 July 1753; d. abt. 1778.
He m. 20 Jan. 1773, Mary Beers, dau. of David, b. 9 July 1754. She m. (2) 15 June 1785, Joseph Perry, and d. 2 Jan. 1845 in 91 yr. (g. s.)
Inv. 2 Nov. 1778.

Children:
> ?Eleazer, d. at Greenfield, 24 Sept. 1777.
> Others?

Alvord, Bela.
He m. Sarah ————.

Children, bapt. Greenfield:
> Aaron, bapt. 27 Mar. 1774.
> Abigail, bapt. 14 Jan. 1776.

Andrews [Vol. I, pp. 18-21].

1 Francis (-1663) m. Anna ———.
2 John (1646-1683) m. Bethia Kirby.
   3 John (1679-1728) m. (1) Eleanor Burr; (2) Abigail (Sturges) Couch.
(By 1): 4 *John* (1707-1771).
     5 *Daniel* (1714-1800).
     6 *Ebenezer* (1720-   ).

4. Andrews, John, s. of John, 2d.

Born 6 Aug. 1707; Dea. John d. at Westport, 28 Mar. 1771 ae. 63 yrs. 7 mos. 11 days (g. s.); m. 28 Oct. 1730, Sarah Couch, dau. of Simon; b. 30 Mar. 1706, d. 9 Mar. 1783 in 77 yr. (g. s.).

Will 5 May 1769, proved 2 Apr. 1771; wife Sarah; eldest son John; sons Abraham, Samuel, Simon; daus. Sarah, Ellen, Abigail, Isabel.

Sarah Andrews conveyed for love, 1783, to son Abraham and daus. Sarah and Abigail.

Adm'n on Est. of Widow Sarah of Fairfield granted, 5 Dec. 1785, to Daniel Sherwood.

Abraham Andrews, and Daniel Sherwood and Abigail his wife, conveyed 1790 to Nathan Godfrey and Sarah his wife, right in Greens Farms, bounded on said Sarah Godfrey and on heirs of Ellen wife of Ebenezer Jessup.

Children, rec. Fairfield:*

   Sarah, b. 6 Aug. 1731, d. at Ridgefield in 1810; m. (1) 14 Mar. 1754, Jonathan Nash; m. (2) 24 Jan. 1764, Nathan Godfrey, Sr.
7+John, b. 17 Mar. 1734.
8+Abraham, b. 23 Aug. 1735.
   Abigail, b. 13 Dec. 1736, d. at Greenfield, 27 Dec. 1793 ae. 57 yrs. 14 days (g. s.); m. 27† Jan. 1760, Daniel Sherwood.
   Eleanor, b. 4 Aug. 1738, d. at Westport, 7 May 1772 ae. 34 (g. s.); m. 6 May 1764, Ebenezer Jessup.
9+Samuel, b. 23 Feb. 1740.
   Isabel, b. 20 Sept. 1742, bapt. at Greenfield, 4 Oct. 1741, d. at Westport, 26 May 1772 in 29 yr. (g. s.); m. 24 Dec. 1766, Nathan Godfrey, Jr.
10+Simon, b. 28 Oct. 1744, bapt. at Westport, 30 Nov. 1743.
   Seth, bapt. at Westport, 5 Aug. 1750, d. Oct. 1751.

---

* Some of the recorded births are evidently a year too late.
† 28 Jan., by town record.

5. **Andrews, Daniel,** s. of John, 2d. Ens., west parish, Fairfield, May 1752; Lt., Oct. 1753.

Born 20 Feb. 1714; d. 10 Jan. 1800 (Bible rec.)

He m. 8 Feb. 1741, Sarah Silliman, dau. of John; bapt. 23 Mar. 1717/8, d. Aug. 1795. Deacon, Weston Church.

Children, rec. Fairfield, all but eldest bapt. Westport (and youngest two bapt. Weston):

> 11+John-Silliman, b. 16 Apr. 1741, bapt. at Fairfield, 26 Apr. 1741.
> Rebecca, bapt. 19 June 1743, d. y.
> Ann, b. 15 June 1743, bapt. 19 June 1743; ?m. at Weston, 26 Jan. 1768, John Olmstead.
> Rachel, b. 28 Mar. 1748, bapt. 10 Apr. 1748; m. at Weston, 3 Oct. 1771, Joseph Ogden.
> Daniel, bapt. 29 July 1750, "child" d. 13 Oct. 1751.
> Child (infant), d. Sept. 1751.
> 12+Daniel, b. 27 Apr., bapt. 5 May 1754.
> Mabel, b. 2 Apr. 1756, bapt. 16 May 1756; m. 21 Sept. 1777, Samuel Rowland.
> Ephraim, bapt. 6 Aug. 1758, [d. 26 Feb. 1829 (Bible rec.)].
> Naomi, bapt. 29 Apr. 1761.

6. **Andrews, Ebenezer,** s. of John, 2d.

Born 12 May 1720.

He m. Jan. 1746, Sarah Sturgis, dau. of Peter, bapt. 15 May 1726, d. at Redding in 1793.

Will of Sarah of Redding, 31 Mar. 1792, proved 3 Jan. 1794; gr. dau. Sarah Andrews, dau. of my dec'd son Stephen; gr. dau. Lydia, dau. of my son Francis; four sons, Ebenezer, Francis, Jonathan, Seth; three daus. Molly, Eunice, Ellen; son Jonathan's three children, Abigail, Rue, and Peter. Distribution, 2 May 1795: sons Seth, Francis, Jonathan, Ebenezer; daus. Mary wife of John Hull, Eleanor wife of Isaac Munson, Eunice wife of Ezekiel Fairchild:

> Children, rec. Fairfield, bapt. Westport:
> Molly, b. 15 June 1746, bapt. 10 May 1748; m. at Redding, 3 Feb. 1763, John Hull.
> Stephen, b. 21 Dec. 1747, bapt. 10 May 1748; m. at Redding, 27 Dec. 1773, Lois Osborn; dau. of William, b. 20 Dec. 1751.*
> Eunice, b. 31 Aug. 1750, bapt. 5 Aug. 1750; m. 8 Jan. 1767, Ezekiel Fairchild.

---

* A child, Sarah, bapt. 15 Jan. 1775.

Ebenezer, b. 9 Dec. 1752, bapt. 17 Dec. 1752, d. at Redding in 1803; m. at Redding, June 1781, Hannah Wheeler. She was widow of Lazarus Wheeler, and dau. of Isaac Gorham, b. 15 Nov. 1752; she m. (3) James Hubbell and d. 1826. His will, 8 Aug. 1801, proved 5 Mar. 1803; wife Hannah; nephews Peter Andrews (who now lives with me), and Ebenezer, son of my bro. Seth; mentioned land distributed to me and my bro. Francis from mother Sarah Andrews dec'd; two bros. Jonathan of Ridgefield and Seth of Redding, Exec'rs.

Francis, b. 8 July 1754, bapt. 13 July 1754; res. Redding; m. (1) Amelia Prince, bapt. 3 June 1750; they had one child, Lydia; m. (2) at Redding, 5 Mar. 1778, Sabra Parsons, dau. of Timothy, bapt. 5 Mar. 1758.

Peter, b. 12 Aug. 1757, bapt. 11 Sept. 1757, d. y.

Jonathan, bapt. 13 Apr. 1760; res. Ridgfield, 1801; m. at Greenfield, 7 Dec. 1779, Rhue Hull, dau. of Cornelius, b. 16 Dec. 1751, d. 19 May 1784 (Perry Diary).*

Seth, b. 16 May 1763, d. at Redding, 25 Nov. 1838 ae. 75 (g. s.); m. at Redding, 1 May 1782, Rachel Fairchild, b. 2 Feb. 1761.† [Mabel, widow of Seth, d. 25 Sept. 1841 ae. 50 (g. s.); was she second wife of this Seth?].

Eleanor, m. Isaac Munson.

7. Andrews, John, s. of John, 3d. Ens., west parish, Fairfield, May 1767; Lt., Oct. 1769; Capt., May 1774.

Born 17 Mar. 1734; Capt. John d. at Westport, 19 Nov. 1777 ae. 46 yrs. 9 mos. (g. s.); m. 28 Mar. 1758, Temperance Cable, dau. of George. She m. (2) 22 Sept. 1779, Ens. Ebenezer Morehouse. She was b. 16 Jan. 1739, d. 18 Mar. 1819 ae. 79 (g. s.).

Children, bapt. Westport:

John, b. abt. 1759, d. at Westport, 29 May 1825 in 66 yr. (g. s.); Lt.; m. 9 Oct. 1783, Lydia Gorham, who d. 7 Sept. 1851 ae. 87-5-14 (g. s.).‡

---

* She left children Abigail, Peter, and Rue, named in her father's will. Peter, b. [31 Dec. 1782], d. at Redding, 13 Nov. 1839 ae. 56-10-13 (g. s.); his wife Molly d. 6 Aug. 1845 ae. 65-11-19 (g. s.).

† Children, rec. Redding: Ebenezer, b. 17 Feb. 1783 (g. s.), d. at Redding, 22 Feb. 1847 (g. s.); m. at Weston, 19 Mar. 1801, Sarah Coley, dau. of Eliphalet, b. 17 Sept. 1779, d. 7 Mar. 1854 in 74 yr. (g. s.). Eleanor, b. 17 Oct. 1789.

‡ Children, bapt. Westport: Temperance, bapt. 18 July 1783, d. at Southport, 9 Nov. 1870 ae. 86-5-9 (g. s.); m. 12 Sept. 1802, William-Burr Dimon. Ellen, bapt. 7 Jan. 1787; m. 4 Feb. 1816, Ebenezer B. Sherwood. Shubael, bapt. 5 Apr. 1789, d. 29 June 1818 in 30 yr. (mariner at Richmond, Va.). Ebenezer, b. 30 Apr., bapt. 5 July 1795, d. 28 Apr. 1864 (g. s.); m. Rachel Hide, b. 13 June 1802, d. 13 Aug. 1881 (g. s.). John's will, 24 May 1825, proved 23 June 1825; wife Lydia; three children, Temperance, Eleanor, Ebenezer. Distribution signed by Temperance Dimon, Eleanor and Ebenezer B. Sherwood, Ebenezer Andrews, and Lydia Andrews.

Thomas, b. [26 May 1761], d. at Westport, 30 July 1801 ae. 40-2-4 (g. s.); m. Abigail Davis, bapt. 6 Feb. 1763, d. at Westport, 6 Dec. 1831 ae. 69 (g. s.); she m. (2) 14 Feb. 1808, Jeremiah Rowland. Will 12 Oct 1796, proved 16 Nov. 1801; wife Abigail; Thomas St. John, $100; four sons, Thomas, John, Benjamin, George; wife and father-in-law Ebenezer Morehouse, Exec'rs.*
George, bapt. 5 Aug. 1764, d. at Westport, 9 Apr. 1791 ae. 26-9-24 (g. s.).

8. **Andrews, Abraham,** s. of John, 3d. Justice, 1777-82.

Born 23 Aug. 1735; d. at Westport, 25 Feb. 1811 in 74 yr.

He m. 14 Feb. 1765, Catherine Wakeman, dau. of Samuel, b. 23 Aug. 1740, d. 26 June 1780.

Children, bapt. Westport:

> Abraham, bapt. 21 Oct. 1770; m. at Weston, 5 Apr. 1798, Sally Hull, dau. of Dr. Eliphalet.
> Wakeman, bapt. 21 Oct. 1770, d. 7 Mar. 1772.
> Isaac, bapt. 4 Jan. 1772, d. 4 Jan. 1772.
> Samuel-Wakeman, bapt. 19 Sept. 1773.
> Catherine, bapt. 26 Feb. 1775, d. at Easton, 1 Sept. 1846 ae. 70-7-16 (g. s.); m. at Weston, 8 Sept. 1799, Wakeman Bradley.
> Elizabeth, bapt. 3 June 1780.

9. **Andrews, Samuel,** s. of John, 3d.

Born 23 Feb. 1740; Capt. Samuel "undoubtedly perished at sea" 1772.

He m. 24 May 1767, Hannah Wakeman; dau. of Samuel, b. 18 Oct. 1741, d. 2 Dec. 1772.

Children, one bapt. Westport:

> Joseph, d. 6 Nov. 1773.
> William, bapt. 27 Sept. 1772, d. 28 Sept. 1772.
> Samuel, bapt. at Fairfield, 21 Nov. 1773 (son of Samuel and Hannah dec'd, offered for baptism by his gr. mother, the widow Ruth Wakeman).

---

* Children, bapt. Westport: Thomas, bapt. 5 Sept. 1784, d. 26 Mar. 1815 ae. 31 (g. s.); m. 8 May 1809, Mary Banks, dau. of Talcott, who d. 19 Dec. 1820 ae. 30 (g. s.). John, bapt. 9 Apr. 1786, m. 17 Jan. 1808, Laurinda Morehouse. Benjamin, b. 22 Mar., bapt. 18 May 1788, d. 19 Jan. 1850 (g. s.), m. Eliza Hobby, b. 19 Mar. 1792, d. 26 Jan. 1867 (g. s.). Aletheia, bapt. 19 Feb. 1792, d. 28 Nov. 1793. George, bapt. 19 Apr. 1795, drowned going to Europe, Spring 1812 ae. 17.

30 HISTORY AND GENEALOGY OF

10. **Andrews, Simon,** s. of John, 3d. Ens., Greens Farms Co., May 1774.

Born 28 Oct. 1744; d. between 15 Mar. and 7 Oct. 1776 (Greens Farms rec.).

He m. 16 May 1771, Elizabeth Hanford, who d. between 15 Mar. and 7 Oct. 1776 (Greens Farms rec.).

Child, bapt. Westport:

> Joseph, bapt. 18 July 1773 (offered by Abraham Andrews, Esq.).

11. **Andrews, John-Silliman,** s. of Daniel.

Born 16 Apr. 1741; d. at Weston, 9 Oct. 1826 (Bible rec.); m. (1) 8 Feb. 1764, Eunice Lyon, dau. of Ephraim. She d. 1 June 1806 (Bible rec.). He m. (2) 14 Mar. 1807, Elizabeth Downs [possibly widow of William].

Will 11 June 1825; proved 26 Sept. 1826; wife Elizabeth; Elisa-Ann dau. of my son Samuel; heirs of son Hezekiah dec'd; four children, Rachel, Eleanor, Daniel, Samuel; representatives of son Silliman dec'd. The distribution calls Rachel wife of Daniel S. Godfrey, and Eleanor wife of Ebenezer Godfrey.

Will of Elizabeth Andrews, 25 Jan. 1842, proved 26 Apr. 1843; to Rhoda wife of Samuel Andrews and her children Elizabeth-Ann, Harriet-Agnes, and Samuel-Silliman. The distribution shows that Elizabeth-Ann was wife of David R. Hoyt, and Harriet-Agnes wife of Daniel S. Godfrey.

Children [by first wife], rec. and bapt. Weston:

> Silliman, b. 30 Oct. 1766 [1765], bapt. 18 Jan. 1766, d. at Weston, 4 Mar. 1817 ae. 51-4-5 (g. s.); m. 23 Sept. 1790, Mary Thorp, b. 10 Mar. 1770, d. 14 Feb. 1833 ae. 63 (g. s.).*
> Hezekiah, b. 24 Sept. 1768 [1767], bapt. 10 Oct. 1767; m. 5 Aug. 1790, Sarah Beers.
> Rachel, b. 28 Aug. 1775 [1774], bapt. 16 Oct. 1774, d. at Weston, 30 Dec. 1861 in 88 yr. (g. s.); m. Daniel-Silliman Godfrey.
> Eleanor, b. 11 Aug. 1778 [1777], bapt. 31 Aug. 1777, d. 15 Nov. 1867 (Bible rec.); m. 22 Jan. 1800, Ebenezer Godfrey.

---

* Distribution ordered, 1819, to Widow Mary and children, John S., 2d, Joseph B., and Ebenezer B. The children, John-Silliman, Joseph-Bradley, and Ebenezer-Burr, were bapt. at Weston, 9 Apr. 1807.

Daniel, b. 19 Apr. bapt. 10 Aug. 1783, d. at Weston, 13 Mar. 1844 ae. 60-10-24 (g. s.); m. (1) Sarah ———, who d. 15 May 1818 ae. 34 (g. s.); m. (2) Esther ———, who d. 6 Oct. 1854 ae. 67-5-7 (g. s.).*

Samuel, b. 27 July, bapt. 20 Aug. 1786, d. at Weston, 21 Dec. 1866 ae. 79-4-27 (g. s.); m. Rhoda ———, who d. 29 July 1860 ae. 67-3-25 (g. s.).

12. Andrews, Daniel, s. of Daniel.

Born 27 Apr. 1754; d. at Weston, 4 Jan. 1805 ae. 51.

He m. 27 May 1778, Betsy Hide, dau. of Joseph, b. 15 Dec. 1753.

Distribution, 21 Dec. 1805: widow Elizabeth; daus. Anna, Sarah, Elizabeth, and Mabel Andrews; sons Ephraim, Joseph, Selleck, and Daniel Andrews.

Children, births from Bible rec., bapt. Weston:

Anna, b. 18 Nov. 1779, bapt. 30 Jan. 1780.†
Sarah, b. 1 Sept., bapt. 7 Oct. 1781, d. 18 Feb. 1857 ae. 75 yrs. 5 mos. (Bible rec.); m. 6 Mar. 1808, Azariah Coley.
Ephraim, b. 9 Apr., bapt. 6 July 1783, d. at Weston, 27 Jan. 1825 ae. 41 (g. s.); adm'n granted, 14 Feb. 1825, to Lydia Andrus, with Squire Adams as surety; dower set to widow Lydia; m. Lydia Thorp, d. 31 Aug. 1862 ae. 72 (g. s.).
Joseph-Hide, b. 20 Mar. 1785, bapt. at Westport, 19 June 1785, d. 8 Sept. 1851 ae. 66-5-18 (g. s.); m. 30 May 1810, Clary Thorp, b. 21 Sept. 1788, d. 12 Feb. 1866 ae. 77-4-23 (g. s.).
Selleck-Silliman, b. 14 Jan., bapt. 25 Mar. 1787, d. 19 Mar. 1866 ae. 79-1-20 (g. s.); m. ———, b. 10 June 1795 (g. s.), d. 5 July 1874 (g. s.).
Elizabeth, b. 11 Jan., bapt. 21 Mar. 1790.
Daniel, b. 27 Oct., bapt. 25 Dec. 1791.‡
Mabel, b. 27 June, bapt. 21 July 1795.

Andrews [*Unplaced*].

Adm'n on Est. of Mary Andrews of Fairfield granted, 23 Dec. 1820, to Ebenezer Beers, with Talcott Banks as surety. Distribution

---

* Adm'n on Daniel's estate granted 1 Apr. 1844. Distribution to widow Esther, sons Elias S., John S., William E., dau. Catherine A. wife of Andrew Jackson, and heirs of dec'd dau. Eunice Sturges. Adm'n on Esther's estate was granted, 23 Nov. 1854; distribution made to sons Elias S., John S., and William E.

† Anna, b. [7 Oct. 1779], d. 28 Aug. 1848 ae. 68-10-21 (g. s.); m. Silliman Godfrey.

‡ One Daniel m. at Westport, 16 July 1820, Kezia Pearsall. Daniel's wife d. 25 Dec. 1829 (Miss Treadwell's book). See also Daniel son of John-Silliman (11).

ordered to her children; and made 1822 to Mathar (?), Mary and Thomas.

MARY m. (1) 12 Jan. 1773, Daniel Chapman; m. (2) 6 Nov. 1777, Benjamin Darling.

JOSEPH of Fairfield chose Sarah Andrews for guardian, 21 Apr. 1755.

CLARA of Wilton m. 19 Feb. 1801, Uriah Beers. [Weston Church]

Annable, Anthony.

He m. 16 Jan. 1748/9, Sarah Middlebrook, dau. of Jonathan, bapt. 7 Mar. 1724/5, d. 4 Aug. 1775 (Perry Diary).

Adm'n granted, 6 Dec. 1797, to David Allen, with Daniel Osborn surety.

Distribution 5 Sept. 1798: dau. Nancy; son Ebenezer; dau. Sarah wife of Levi Mallory; son David; dau. Mary wife of Hezekiah Burr.

Children, rec. and bapt. Fairfield:

> Samuel, b. 29 June, bapt. 7 July 1751.
> David, b. 19 Jan. 1753.
> Sarah, b. 25 Dec. 1754, d. at Fairfield, 12 July 1807 ae. 53; m. 3 Aug. 1772, Levi Mallory.
> Ebenezer, b. 16 July 1756, d. at Sharon, Washtenaw County, Mich., 23 Sept. 1842; res. Manlius, Onondaga County, N. Y.; m. at Watertown, Conn., 5 Feb. 1789, Ann Merriam, b. 6 June 1768.
> Mary, b. 3 June 1759, bapt. 8 Mar. 1778, d. 8 Jan. 1848 ae. 88 yrs. 7 mos. (g. s.); m. 5 Dec. 1784, Hezekiah Burr.
> Ann, b. 3 Oct. 1761, bapt. 24 Sept. 1786.

Arthing, James.

He m. 12 May 1767, Hannah Squire. She, dau. of Nathaniel Squire, Jr., divorced him in 1775, stating that she had seen nothing of him for five years, that he was of the Province of New York, and that he had two children by another woman. Hannah m. (2) 29 Aug. 1775, Jacob Rescoe.

Children, bapt. Weston:

> Betty, bapt. 15 May 1768.
> James, bapt. 12 Aug. 1770.

Arthur [Unplaced].

REV. THOMAS, of New Brunswick, m. 16 Sept. 1746, Miss Sarah Burr.

Atwell [*Unplaced*].

JOSEPH m. 9 Nov. 1791, Hannah Lyon. [Easton Church]

Atwood, Jesse.

He m. 20 Oct. 1784, Lois Wheeler, and had children: Polly, b. 8 Sept. 1785; James-Lovel, b. 10 July 1787; Wheeler, b. 30 June 1791, d. 28 Feb. 1794; Roxana, b. 3 June 1793. [Weston rec.]

Austin [*Unplaced*].

JOHN P., of New Haven, m. 10 Sept. 1797, Susan Rogers. [Greens Farms Church]

Avery [*Unplaced*].

MARY m. 14 Aug. 1718, Benjamin Baker. [Fairfield rec.]
REV. JOHN m. 3 Apr. 1782, Anne Hazard. [Greens Farms Church]
CHARLES, son of Rev. John, d. 29 Dec. 1807 in 20 yr. (Kingston, Jamaica). [Greens Farms Church]

Aylwood [*Unplaced*].

THOMAS and Susanna had: Jacob, bapt. 7 May 1783. [Fairfield Church]

Babbitt [*Unplaced*].

ABIEL, of North Stratfield, m. 25 Dec. 1789, Abigail Sturges. [Greens Farms Church]

Bailey, Thomas.

He m. by 1716 Deborah, widow of Samuel Smith, and dau. of Moses Jackson, b. 8 Feb. 1678.

Removed to Elizabeth, N. J., where he resided 1729 when he conveyed Fairfield land to John Bedient.

Child, bapt. Fairfield:

Thomas, bapt. 20 Apr. 1718.

Bailey [*Unplaced*].

JOHN d. 9 Mar. 1769 ae. (as was supposed) near 90. [Greenfield Church]

HISTORY AND GENEALOGY OF

1. Baker, Benjamin.

He m. (rec. Fairfield) 14 Aug. 1718, Mary Avery.

He sold (with wife Mary) to Obadiah Platt of Huntington, L. I., his homelot, 1725.

He d. at Westport, 27 Sept. 1779.

He conveyed, 1762, to sons Joshua, Ebenezer and Avery.

Children, rec. Fairfield:

2+James, b. 30 June 1722.
3+Samuel, b. 28 Mar. 1724.
  Benjamin, b. 10 May 1728.
  Mary, b. 24 Apr. 1732; m. at Westport, 5 Nov. 1750, Samuel Turney.
  Avery, b. 22 Oct. 1734, prob. d. before 1779; m. 10 June 1770, Hannah Allen, b. 20 Sept. 1727.
4+Ebenezer, b. 9 Dec. 1736.
5+Joshua, b. 22 Apr. 1740.

2. Baker, James, s. of Benjamin.

Born 30 June 1722; d. at Fairfield by 1771.

He m. 13 Mar. 1755, Thankful Coley; dau. of Andrew, bapt. 11 Nov. 1733.

Children, first rec. Fairfield:

  Benjamin, b. 9 Jan. 1756; chose Joshua Baker for guardian, 14 Oct. 1771.
  Andrew, bapt. at Redding, 5 Mar. 1758.

3. Baker, Samuel, s. of Benjamin.

Born 28 Mar. 1724; bur. 23 Apr. 1803 ae. 85(?) (Trinity Church rec.).

He m. 28 Feb. 1754, Sarah Barlow; dau. of George, b. 28 Mar. 1732.

Distribution, Est. of Mrs. Sarah Baker of Weston, 1 Nov. 1799; David Baker, eldest son; dau. Mary wife of Nathaniel Whitehead; dau. Eunice Whitehead; son Avery Baker.

Distribution, Est. of Samuel Baker of Weston, 7 Apr. 1804; Mary wife of Nathaniel Whitehead; Eunice wife of Phineas Sly; David Baker; heirs of Avery Baker dec'd.

Children, two rec. Fairfield:

Mary, b. 2 Nov. 1755; m. 20 Dec. 1778, Nathaniel Whitehead.
David, b. 16 Oct. 1757; m. at Easton, 1 Mar. 1789, Lucia Squire.*
Eunice, m. (1) John Whitehead; m. (2) Phineas Sly.
Avery, in 1786 called himself late of Fairfield, now of Dutchess County, N. Y.

4. Baker, Ebenezer, s. of Benjamin.

Born 9 Dec. 1736; d. at Westport, 1 Oct. 1817 in 81 yr.; m. 8 Aug. 1765, Mabel Lockwood, dau. of Gershom. She d. 14 Mar. 1797.

Children, bapt. Westport:

Molly, bapt. 27 Mar. 1768; m. 17 Oct. 1788, John Barnes.
Lockwood, bapt. 10 Dec. 1769; m. 12 Mar. 1794, Betty Raymond.†
Ebenezer, bapt. 8 Sept. 1771; m. 1 Aug. 1793, Rebecca Batterson, dau. of William, bapt. 30 Apr. 1775.‡
Daniel, bapt. 12 Dec. 1773.
James, bapt. 7 Apr. 1776.
Mabel (twin), bapt. 7 Apr. 1776.
Damaris, bapt. 14 June 1778; m. 25 Sept. 1801, Justus Disbrow, Jr.
Salome, bapt. 14 June 1778; m. 26 Mar. 1795, William Forbes.
Joseph, bapt. 11 Aug. 1782.
Lewis, bapt. 26 Feb. 1786.

5. Baker, Joshua, s. of Benjamin.

Born 22 Apr. 1740; d. in army at Canada, 15 Mar. 1776; m. 15 Mar. 1769, Abigail Sturges; dau. of Jeremiah, b. 29 Nov. 1743. She m. (2) 19 Nov. 1780, Nehemiah Couch, and d. 9 Aug. 1791.

Inv. 4 Jan. 1777. Distribution 3 Sept. 1787; Widow Abigail, now wife of Nehemiah Couch; eldest son Abraham; youngest son Joseph. On 3 Oct. 1785, Joseph chose Nehemiah Couch for guardian; the latter becoming incompetent, Joseph chose Wills Clift, 6 Aug. 1787.

---

* Child, bapt. Trinity Church: Sarah, bapt. 19 Sept. 1790.

† Children, bapt. Westport: Samuel, bapt. 3 May 1795; Elijah, bapt. 3 July 1796; John, bapt. 24 June 1798; Abigail-Hendrick, bapt. 20 Apr. 1800; Henry, bapt. 15 May 1803; Rachel, bapt. 24 July 1804; Angeline, bapt. 21 Jan. 1807.

‡ Children, bapt. Westport: Bradley, bapt. 17 Aug. 1794; Betsey, bapt. 5 June 1796; Florilla, bapt. 26 Nov. 1797; William, bapt. 15 Sept. 1799; Lewis, bapt. 17 Jan. 1802; Hezekiah, bapt. 4 Sept. 1803; Ebenezer, bapt. 6 Oct. 1805; Sally-Ann, bapt. 13 Apr. 1808, d. 2 May 1810 ae. 2 yrs. 10 mos.

Children, bapt. Westport:

> Abraham, bapt. 4 Mar. 1769; res. 1794, Lansingburgh, N. Y.; m. Mary Coley, b. 2 Jan. 1780.
> Joseph, bapt. 29 Sept. 1771; m. 27 July 1797, Sarah Jessup, dau. of Ebenezer, b. 14 May 1776, d. at Westport, 2 Jan. 1837.
> Joshua, bapt. 26 May 1776, d. y.

Baker [*Unplaced*].

> SARAH wife of NATHAN d. 22 Feb. 1816 ae. 43.* [Greens Farms Church]
> JOHN d. 23 June 1803 ae. 23. [Greens Farms Church]

Baldwin, Dudley.

Son of Michael and Lucy (Dudley) Baldwin, b. at Guilford, Conn., 17 Apr. 1753, d. at New Haven, 29 Mar. 1794 ae. 41 (g. s., Greenfield); m. 1787, Sarah (Bradley) Wakeman, b. 18 Nov. 1758, d. 3 Dec. 1795 ae. 37 (g. s.).

Will 28 Mar. 1794, proved at New Haven, 1 Apr. 1794; wife Sarah; son Abraham; codicil, 29 Mar. 1794, gave half of the double portion received from father's estate to his bros. and sisters.

Graduated from Yale Coll. 1777.

His bro. Abraham, b. 22 Nov. 1754, d. 4 Mar. 1807 ae. 52 (g. s., Greenfield), grad. Yale Coll. 1772, was Pres. of Univ. of Georgia and U. S. Senator; his sister Ruth, b. 13 Sept. 1756, m. Joel Barlow; and his bro. Henry was Judge of U. S. Supreme Court, 1829-44.

Adm'n on estate of Sarah Baldwin granted, 7 Dec. 1795, to Walter Bradley.

Child:

> Abraham-Dudley, b. abt. 1788, d. at Greenfield, 8 June 1862 ae. 74 (g. s.); grad. Yale Coll. 1807; m. (1) at Westport, 2 Nov. 1810, Mary Grant, b. [Apr. 1791], d. 6 Sept. 1814 ae. 23 yrs. 5 mos. (g. s.); m. (2) Henrietta Jennings, b. abt. 1787, d. 4 June 1867 ae. 80 (g. s.).

---

* Abba-Jane, dau. of Widow Sarah Baker, bapt. 15 May 1803, d. 29 Oct. 1802 ae. 10 mos.

THE FAMILIES OF OLD FAIRFIELD 37

Baldwin, John.

Born 19 Nov. 1768; d. at Easton, 7 July 1840 ae. 73 (g. s.); m. 30 Dec. 1790, Naomi Brinsmade; dau. of Josiah, b. 17 Feb. 1769, d. 16 Dec. 1812 ae. 43 (g. s.).

Children, rec. Weston, bapt. Easton:
- Eli, b. 30 July, bapt. 27 Nov. 1791.
- Josiah-Brinsmade, b. 28 Feb., bapt. June 1793.
- Clara, b. 14 Feb., bapt. June 1795.
- Esther, b. 16 Apr. 1797.

Baldwin, (Dr.) Gabriel, s. of Jared.

Son of Jared and Damaris (Booth) Baldwin; Jared, b. at Milford, 30 Jan. 1732 (Easton rec.), d. at Easton, 19 Apr. 1817 in 87 yr. (g. s.); Damaris was dau. of Abel and Rebecca Booth, b. at Newtown, 7 Sept. 1733, d. in Luzerne County, Pa., Aug. 1816.

Gabriel was b. at Brookfield, 29 Jan. 1766, and d. at Easton, 1 Sept. 1825 ae. 60 (g. s.).

He m. 2 May 1788, Sarah Summers, dau. of Zechariah, b. 14 Nov. 1767, d. 9 June 1852 ae. 84 (g. s.).

Adm'n granted, 29 Sept. 1825, to James Baldwin; estate insolvent.

Children, rec. Fairfield, bapt. Easton:
- Burr, b. 19 Jan. 1789, bapt. May 1789.
- Anna, b. 28 July 1790, bapt. Jan. 1791.
- David, b. 10 Mar. 1792, bapt. 12 Aug. 1792.
- Summers, b. 24 Jan. 1794.
- Stephen, b. 18 Sept. 1795.
- Charles, b. 4 July 1797.
- Ira, b. 8 Apr. 1799.
- Alonzo, b. 5 Jan. 1801.
- James, b. 27 Aug. 1802.
- Eliza, b. 7 Dec. 1804.
- Morris, b. 16 Sept. 1806.
- Sarah Maria, b. 4 Jan. 1811.

Bangs, Lemuel. Lt., 9th Co., 4th Regt., May 1778.

He m. Hannah Hall, dau. of Richard, bapt. 30 Jan. 1742/3, d. by 1785.

In 1785, for £66.13.4 received from sale of estate of wife

Hannah Bangs dau. of Richard Hall now dec'd, and for love, he conveyed to his (and her) children, Richard, Lemuel-Hamblin, Eliakim, and Phebe Bangs.

Children:

> Richard, m. Dec. 1793, Elizabeth Bulkley, dau. of James, bapt. 2 Aug. 1772, d. at Fairfield, 5 Apr. 1847 ae. 74 (g. s.); she m. (2) **Levi Perry**.
> Phebe, m. 3 Apr. 1796, Amos Wilson.
> Lemuel-Hamlin.
> Eliakim.

Child [by second wife]:

> Herman, bapt. at Trinity Church, 20 June 1790.

Banks [Vol. I, pp. 25-27].

> 1 John (-1685) m. (1) ──── Taintor; (2) Mary (────) Sherwood.
> (By 1): 2 John (-1699) [Greenwich branch].
> 3 Benjamin (-1692) m. Elizabeth Lyon.
> 4 *Benjamin* (1682-1760).
> 5 *Joseph* (1690-1766).

4. Banks, Benjamin, s. of Benjamin.

Born at Fairfield, 30 Oct. 1682; d. at Greenfield, 13 Jan. 1760 in 78 yr. (g. s.). He m. (1) Ruth Hyatt, dau. of Thomas, b. May 1684;* d. 20 May 1751 in 66 yr. (g. s.), or May 1750 ae. 67 (church rec.). He m. (2) Elizabeth ────, who d. 27 Dec. 1758 in 63 yr. (church rec.). He m. (3) at Greenfield, 23 July 1759, "Widow Whitney"; she was Ann (Laborie), widow of Samuel Whitney of Stratford.

Children [by first wife], rec. Greenfield:

> 6+Benjamin, b. 8 Aug. 1706, bapt. 7 Feb. 1713/4.
> 7+Thomas, b. 13 Nov. 1707, bapt. 7 Feb. 1713/4.
> John, b. 8 Sept. 1710, d. ae. abt. 4.
> 8+Gershom, b. 1 May 1712, bapt. 7 Feb. 1713/4.
> Joanna, b. 28 Feb. 1714/5, bapt. 10 Apr. 1715, d. 23 June 1767; m. 29 Mar. 1737, Joseph Banks, Jr.
> 9+John, b. 7 Nov. 1717, bapt. 2 Mar. 1717/8.
> Nehemiah, b. 27 Apr. 1720, d. y.
> Mary, b. 18 Mar. 1721/2, bapt. 29 Apr. 1722, d. 1736.

---

* 18 May 1683, by Greenfield record.

5. **Banks, Joseph,** s. of Benjamin.

Born 30 Dec. 1690; d. at Greenfield, 4 Jan. 1766 ae. 75 (g. s.); ae. 75 wanting 5 days (church rec.); m. 25 June 1712, Mary Sherwood; dau. of Benjamin, b. 8 Jan. 1692/3, d. 15 June 1770 ae. 77 (g. s.).

He was bapt. at Fairfield Church, 13 Apr. 1712.

Children, rec. Greenfield:
- 10+Joseph, b. 12 Apr. 1713, bapt. 19 Apr. 1713.
- Sarah, b. 1 Feb. 1715/6, bapt. 4 Mar. 1715/6, d. 7 May 1791 in 76 yr. (g. s.); m. 17 May 1736, Gershom Bulkley.
- 11+David, b. 22 Apr. 1718, bapt. 25 May 1718.
- Mindwell, b. 6 Oct. 1720, bapt. 9 Oct. 1720.
- 12+Nehemiah, b. 28 Feb. 1722, bapt. 27 May 1722.
- 13+Ebenezer, b. 9 Dec. 1724, bapt. 31 Jan. 1724/5.
- Mary, b. 19 July 1731, bapt. 25 July 1731, d. 28 July 1815 ae. 85 (g. s.); m. 8 Aug. 1751, Daniel Bradley, Jr.

6. **Banks, Benjamin,** s. of Benjamin, 2d.

Born 8 Aug. 1706 [7 Aug. 1703 by g. s.]; d. at Greenfield, 19 May 1805 (g. s.); m. (1) Nov. 1729, Mary Treadwell; dau. of Edward, bapt. 27 Feb. 1708/9.

He m. (2) 20 June 1744, Ellen Bradley; b. 7 Oct. 1725, d. 29 May 1812 (g. s.).

He conveyed for love, 1782, to dau. Rhoda Sturges; and in 1779 to daus. Ellen and Ann Banks.

Will 2 Jan. 1789, proved 27 Jan. 1806; sons Jonathan, Hezekiah; wife Ellen; portions advanced to other children; son Benjamin Exec'r with other two sons.

Children [by first wife], rec. Greenfield:
- Mercy, b. Sept. 1730, bapt. 21 Sept. 1730; m. 23 Mar. 1748/9, Abel Platt.
- Mary, bapt. 18 Apr. 1736; m. (1) 27 June 1754,* Samuel Ogden; m. (2) at Weston, 7 Jan. 1779, John Finch; m. (3) at Weston, 21 Jan. 1801, Shubael Gorham.
- Hezekiah, bapt. 2 July 1738, d. July 1742.
- Rhoda, bapt. 11 Oct. 1741, d. in 1811; m. (1) 27 Aug. 1761, Isaac Sturges; m. (2) Thomas Goodsell.

---
* Or 19 June 1753, by town record.

Children [by second wife]:

>Molly, bapt. 7 Apr. 1745, d. 5 Aug. 1847 ae. 102 (g. s.); m. 17 Nov. 1763, Moses Ogden.
>14+Benjamin, bapt. 21 Dec. 1746.
>15+Hezekiah, bapt. 1748/9.
>Mabel, bapt. 13 Oct. 1751; prob. m. Moses Burr.
>Ruth, b. Apr. 1755; m. 20 Apr. 1774, Gershom Banks, Jr.
>Esther, b. 5 Feb. 1757.
>16+Jonathan, b. 4 Dec. 1760, bapt. 1 Feb. 1761.
>Ellen, bapt. 6 Feb. 1763.
>Ann, b. 11 June 1768, bapt. 19 June 1768; m. Adad Bradley.

7. Banks, Thomas, s. of Benjamin, 2d.

Born 13 Nov. 1707, d. at Greenfield, 30 Apr. 1747 in 40 yr. (g. s.); m. (1) Esther ———, who d. 12 Apr. 1732; m. (2) Sarah Osborn, bapt. 29 Nov. 1713, living 1778. She m. (2) 19 Sept. 1751, Samuel Odell.

Will 18 Apr. 1747, proved 8 May 1747; wife Sarah; dau. Hester, a chest of drawers, etc., that were my first wife's; daus. Ruth, Sarah; sons Seth, Thaddeus, the latter committed to the care of my Father and Mother Banks; wife and bros. Benjamin, Jr., and Gershom, Exec'rs.

Sarah Odell conveyed, 1778, to son Thaddeus Banks, farm set to her as dower in estate of former husband, Thomas Banks.

Children [by second wife], rec. Greenfield:

>Esther, b. 15 Apr. 1735; m. 11 June 1752, John Bates.
>Ruth, b. 13 Apr. 1736.
>17+Seth, b. 13 July 1738, bapt. 27 July 1738.
>18+Thaddeus, b. May 1740, bapt. 17 June 1740; chose John Banks for guardian, Mar. 1756.
>Sarah, b. Mar. 1745/6, bapt. 9 Mar. 1745/6.

8. Banks, Gershom, s. of Benjamin, 2d.

Born 1 May 1712; d. at Greenfield in 1795; grad. Yale Coll. 1732.

He m. (1) May 1739, Mary Bradley, dau. of Francis; b. 13 Sept. 1719, d. 24 May 1741 ae. 21 yrs. 6 mos. 9 days (g. s.).

He m. (2) 14 Oct. 1743, Hannah Bradley, dau. of John; b. 14 Oct. 1726, d. 24 Oct. 1749 ae. 23 (g. s.).

He m. (3) Jan. 1751 [or by Greenfield record, 14 Feb. 1752], Mary Perry, dau. of Joseph; bapt. 28 Mar. 1725, d. at Greenfield, 3 Jan. 1807 ae. 82.

He conveyed, 1788, to dau. Jane wife of David Burr, 2d; and 1792 to sons Gershom, Elijah, Hyatt, and Isaac.

Adm'n granted to Ebenezer Wakeman, 4 May 1795.

Child [by first wife], rec. Greenfield and Fairfield:

19+Daniel, b. 5 Dec. 1739, bapt. 6 Dec. 1739.

Children [by second wife]:

    Marianna, b. 22 Dec. 1745, bapt. 29 Dec. 1745, d. 5 [June or July] 1770 (Perry Diary); m. 7 Nov. 1765, Samuel Whitney, Jr.
20+Thomas, b. 14 Oct. 1747, bapt. 18 Oct. 1747.
    Jane, b. 30 Sept. 1749, bapt. 15 Oct. 1749, d. 26 Oct. 1749 ae. 28 days.

Children [by third wife]:

21+Gershom, b. 31 Aug. 1752.
22+Joseph, b. 2, bapt. 10 Nov. 1754.
    Jane, b. 8 Aug. 1757, bapt. 14 Aug. 1757, d. at Westport, 17 Aug. 1838 ae. 80 yrs. 9 mos. (g. s.); m. (1) 3 Nov. 1776, David Burr; m. (2) 22 Jan. 1814, David Sherwood.
    Noah, b 1 June 1760, bapt. 8 June 1760.
23+Elijah, b. 7 Aug. 1762, bapt. 15 Aug. 1762.
24+Hyatt, b. 7 Mar. 1764, bapt. 11 Mar. 1764.
25+Isaac, b. 26 May 1766, bapt. 1 June 1766.

9. **Banks, John,** s. of Benjamin, 2d.

Born 7 Nov. 1717; d. 4 Sept. 1784 (Perry Diary).

He m. 14 May 1740, Elizabeth Bradley, b. 30 Aug. 1721; d. 1808.

Will 27 July, proved 20 Sept. 1784; wife Elizabeth; sons John, Moses, Peter, Nathan; heirs of son Aaron; daus. Rachel, Elizabeth; children of dau. Ellen.

A distribution of the part of the estate that had been the widow's dower was made, 1 Nov. 1820, to Mary Banks, dau. of his dec'd dau. Eleanor Banks [*sic*], and his son John. An undated distribution was made to widow Elizabeth, eldest son John, second son Moses, heirs of Aaron dec'd, heirs of Peter dec'd, Rachel wife of Francis Bradley, Jr., Nathan Banks, and Elizabeth wife of Daniel Nichols.

Will of Elizabeth, 2 Dec. 1803, proved 27 June 1808; son Nathan; dau. Elizabeth wife of Daniel Nichols; gr. dau. Betsey wife of Joseph Cable; Daniel Banks, Exec'r.

Children, rec. Fairfield and Greenfield:

Elizabeth, b. 11 Feb. 1741, bapt. 23 Feb. 1740/1, d. 23 Apr. 1760 ae. 18 yrs. 2 mos.; m. 14 Mar. 1759, Peter Osborn.

Eleanor, b. 14 Oct. 1743, bapt. in infancy, d. before 1779; m. 21 Oct. 1765, Reuben Beers.

26+John, b. 23 Aug. 1746, bapt. 24 Aug. 1746.

27+Moses (twin), b. 25 Sept. 1749, bapt. 15 Oct. 1749.

28+Aaron, b. 25 Sept. 1749, bapt. 15 Oct. 1749.

29+Peter, b. 9 Nov. 1751, bapt. 17 Nov. 1751.

Nathan, bapt. 31 Mar. 1754, d. y.

Hannah, b. 6 May 1756; called "Eunice," d. Apr. 1765 ae. abt. 9.

Rachel, b. and bapt. 16 Apr. 1758, d. 27 Feb. 1800; m. 27 Apr. 1780, Francis Bradley, Jr. Her will, 15 Oct. 1799, proved 17 Mar. 1800, mentioned her husband, her dec'd father John Banks, and her mother (living).

30+Nathan, bapt. 11 May 1760.

Elizabeth, bapt. 17 July 1763; m. Daniel Nichols.

10. Banks, Joseph, s. of Joseph.

Born 12 Apr. 1713; d. at Redding, 8 July 1802 ae. 89-2-15 (g. s.).

He m. (1) 29 Mar. 1737, Joanna Banks, dau. of Benjamin; b. 28 Feb. 1714/5, d. at Redding, 23 June 1767 ae. 52 yrs. 3 mos. (g. s.).

He m. (2) 29 Nov. 1767, Ann Morehouse, widow of Stephen Morehouse and previously of George Holloway, and dau. of John Eliot.

He m. (3) Sarah ———.

Will 2 June 1801, proved 6 Aug. 1802; wife Sarah; son Jesse; gr. son Jesse Sherwood who lives with me; my other heirs, Jesse Banks, Joanna wife of John Morgan of Norwalk, and Sarah wife of Lewis Goodsell of Fairfield; Sarah, dau. of said Jesse Sherwood; Peter Lyon, son of gr. dau. Sarah late wife of Andrew Lyon; Sener, dau. of said Sarah.

Children [by first wife], rec. Fairfield and Greenfield:

Gershom, b. 18 Dec. 1737, bapt. Dec. 1737, d. at Redding, 23 Dec. 1773 ae. 36 (g. s.).

Joanna, b. 11 Dec. 1739, bapt. 23 Dec. 1739, [? d. 28 Apr. 1804]; m. 5 Jan. 1758, John Morgan, of Norwalk.

31+Jesse, b. 14 Oct. 1742, bapt. 17 Oct. 1742.
Sarah, b. 26 Dec. 1743, bapt. 8 Jan. 1743/4, d. at Greenfield, 11 July 1809 ae. 67 (g. s.); m. (1) 13 Nov. 1763,* Noah Sherwood; m. (2) 1 June 1780, Lewis Goodsell.
Mary, bapt. at Westport, 28 Jan. 1750, as dau. of Joseph of Redding; d. y.

11. Banks, David, s. of Joseph. Ens., 5th Co., Fairfield, May 1747.

Born 22 Apr. 1718; Capt. David d. at Greenfield, 19 Sept. 1791 in 73 yr. (g. s.).

He m. (1) 1 Nov. 1738, Widow Sarah Hull; widow of Eliphalet Hull, and dau. of John Barlow, b. 27 Feb. 1703/4, d. 28 Nov. 1767.

Capt. David m. (2) at Westport, 2 June 1768, widow Sarah Wakeman. She was widow of Stephen Wakeman, and dau. of Edward Jessup, b. 14 July 1726, d. in 1805 in 78 yr.

David and Sarah his wife conveyed 1787 to son Stephen Wakeman, right from her late husband, Stephen Wakeman.

Will 17 Apr. 1790, proved 12 Oct. 1791; wife Sarah; Ruth wife of Francis Bradley; Mary wife of James Redfield; Miriam dau. of Mary dec'd wife of Joseph Rumsey; daus. of Sarah dec'd wife of Ebenezer Bradley; two sisters Sarah Bradley [should be Mary] and Mary Bulkley [should be Sarah]; two bros. Joseph and Nehemiah Banks; David Banks, son of Joseph and gr. son of my dec'd bro. Ebenezer; Ebenezer, son of my dec'd bro. Ebenezer.

Child [by first wife], rec. Greenfield:

Eliphalet, b. 25 July, bapt. 4 Aug. 1740, d. 18 Feb. 1784 in 45 yr. (g. s.); B.A. (Yale Coll. 1758).

12. Banks, Nehemiah, s. of Joseph.

Born 28 Feb. 1722; d. at Greenfield, 16 Nov. 1807 ae. 86 (g. s.), or 18 Nov. (church rec.).

He m. (1) Abigail Bradley, b. 25 Apr. 1725, d. 19 Mar. 1785 in 59 yr. (g. s.).

* The *Hist. of Redding* states that Noah Hull m. Sarah Banks on this date; but I can find no Noah Hull for the marriage, and the date is right for the proved marriage of Sarah Banks to Noah Sherwood.

He m. (2) Mindwell (Sherwood), widow of David Osborn; b. 31 Jan. 1727/8, d. 7 Aug. 1805 in 78 yr. (g. s.).

Will 30 May 1799, codicil 30 Oct. 1806, proved 29 Feb. 1808; sons Nehemiah, Talcott; wife Mindwell, mentioning jointure before marriage; children of dau. Esther dec'd,—Aaron, Daniel, Bradley and David Lee, Polly Edmonds, Esther Edmonds, Mary and Betsey Lee; daus. Amelia Burritt, Mindwell Burr, Abigail Alvord, Clarina Wakeman.

> Children [by first wife], rec. Greenfield:
>> Hester, b. 30 Nov. 1744, bapt. 2 Dec. 1744, d. before 1799; m. 16 Nov. 1768, Daniel Lee, of Ridgefield.
>> Amelia, b. July 1747, bapt. 1 Aug. 1747; m. (1) 29 Dec. 1768, Jessup Wakeman; m. (2) Wakeman Burritt.
>> Mindwell, b. in 1750, d. at Westport, 23 July 1827 ae. 77 (g. s.); m. 15 Nov. 1770, Talcott Burr.
>> Abigail, b. in 1752, d. at Greenfield, 2 Mar. 1831 ae. 79 (g. s.); m. Nov. 1779, John Alvord.
>> 32+Nehemiah, b. Oct. 1754, bapt. 20 Oct. 1754.
>> Mary, b. [June 1757], d. 25 Sept. 1776 ae. 19 yrs. 3 mos. (g. s.).
>> 33+Talcott, bapt. 17 June 1759.
>> Clarina, b. 10 Mar. 1761 (family rec.), bapt. 15 Mar. 1761; m. 21 June 1781, Jabez Wakeman.
>> Bradley, b. 22 June 1766, bapt. 26 June 1766, d. 9 Dec. 1776 ae. 10 yrs. 5 mos. 16 days (g. s.).

13. Banks, Ebenezer, s. of Joseph. Capt., Greenfield Co., Oct. 1757. Justice, 1774, '75, '76.

Born 9 Dec. 1724; d. at Greenfield, 22 Mar. 1777 in 53 yr. (g. s.).

He m. 17 [18 by Greenfield rec.] June 1746, Sarah Hide, b. 27 Nov. 1727, d. 20 Mar. 1796 in 69 yr. (g. s.).

Will 12 Mar., proved 19 Dec. 1777; wife Sarah; children, Ebenezer, Joseph, Eunice, Ann, Sarah. Agreement, 1 May 1797, of heirs of Ebenezer and Sarah Banks: Ebenezer and Joseph Banks, Eunice wife of Elisha Bradley, Ann wife of Ebenezer Wakeman, 2d, and Sarah wife of John Willson, Jr.

> Children, rec. Fairfield and Greenfield:
>> Eunice, b. 21 Mar. 1747, bapt. 22 Mar. 1746/7, d. 16 Jan. 1820 ae. 73 (g. s.); m. 13 Feb. 1770, Elisha Bradley.
>> Ann, b. 5 Aug. 1749, bapt. 13 Aug. 1749, d. at Ballston, N. Y., 27 June 1827; m. at Weston, 17 Nov. 1771, Ebenezer Wakeman.

34+Ebenezer, b. 19 Oct. 1752 [1753 by Bible record].
35+Joseph, b. 7 Nov. 1756.
    Jesse, b. and bapt. 8 Dec. 1759,* d. 10 Mar. 1777 ae. 17 (g. s.).
    David, b. and bapt. 8 Dec. 1759,* d. 10† Mar. 1777 ae. 17 (g. s.).
    Sarah, b. 27, bapt. 30 June 1765, d. at Fairfield, 3 Apr. 1814 ae. 48-9-7 (g. s.); m. John Wilson, Jr.

14. Banks, Benjamin, s. of Benjamin, 3d.

Bapt. 21 Dec. 1746; d. at Greenfield, 7 Mar. 1835 ae. 88 yrs. 1 mo. 13 days (g. s.); m. at Westport, 11 Oct. 1770, Sarah Wakeman, bapt. 10 Aug. 1746, d. 28 July 1828 ae. 82 (g. s.).

Adm'n on Sarah's estate granted, 21 Apr. 1835, to Abraham D. Baldwin. Distribution to children: Sarah Ogden; Cynthia Hill; Deborah wife of Burr Middlebrooks; Clarina wife of Robert Fanton.

Children, rec. Greenfield:

    Sarah, b. [28 Apr. 1771], bapt. 16 Aug. 1772, d. at Easton, 29 Apr. 1852 ae. 81 yrs. 1 day (g. s.); m. abt. 1790, Albee Ogden.
    Cynthia, b. 16 Nov. 1772, bapt. 14 Jan. 1773, d. at Easton, 3 Jan. 1839 ae. 66 (g. s.); m. (rec. Weston) 26 Oct. 1793, Seth Hill.
    Charity, b. [Dec. 1774], bapt. 19 Mar. 1775, d. at Westport, 14 Nov. 1818 ae. 43 yrs. 11 mos. (g. s.); m. 6 Mar. 1796, Silas Burr.
    Deborah, bapt. 2 Apr. 1780, d. at Greenfield, 10 Dec. 1861 ae. 82 (g. s.); m. Burr Middlebrook.
    Betsey, b. abt. 1782; d. at Greenfield, 20 June 1821 ae. 39.
    Clarina, m. Robert Fanton.

15. Banks, Hezekiah, s. of Benjamin, 3d.

Bapt. 1748/9; d. at Easton, 31 Mar. 1812 in 64 yr. (g. s.); m. at Westport, 14 Oct. 1772, Sarah Couch; dau. of Thomas, b. 30 Mar. 1754, d. 24 Feb. 1815 ae. 62.

Will 17 Sept. 1811, proved 25 Apr. 1812; wife Sarah; sons Sturges, Hezekiah, Jesup; daus. Sarah, Patty, Mary, Arette. Distribution, June 1812: widow; dau. Mary wife of Sherwood Seeley; dau. Patty wife of John Staples; dau. Arita Banks; eldest son Sturges; Hezekiah, Jesup, and Walter; Sarah wife of Joseph Hill.

---

* 1760, by Bible record.
† 8 Mar., by Bible record.

46   HISTORY AND GENEALOGY OF

Distribution of dower set to Sarah Banks from Est. of Hezekiah, to the heirs, 25 Apr. 1815; son Hezekiah; dau. Arita wife of William Nichols; dau. Patty wife of John Staples; dau. Sarah wife of Joseph Hill; son Walter; dau. Mary; son Sturges; son Jessup.

Children, bapt. Easton:

> Sturges, bapt. 9 Jan. 1774, d. at Easton, 24 Aug. 1817 in 44 yr. (g. s.); m. ——— Gold.
> Sarah, b. abt. 1776, d. at Liberty, Sullivan County, N. Y., 8 Sept. 1868 in 93 yr.; m. Joseph Hill.
> Hezekiah, b. 12 Dec. 1777 (g. s.), d. at Easton, 6 Oct. 1872 ((g. s.); m. 30 Dec. 1806, Ruhamah Betts, dau. of Moses, b. [4 Sept. 1785], d. 12 Feb. 1875 ae. 89-5-8 (g. s.).
> Patty, b. abt. 1780, d. at Greenfield, 15 Apr. 1858 ae. 78 (g. s.); m. 1798, John Staples.
> Mary, b. [July 1782], d. at Easton, 4 Jan. 1879 ae. 96 yrs. 6 mos. (g. s.); m. Sherwood Seeley.
> Arette, bapt. 12 Apr. 1789, d. at Easton, 10 July 1815 in 27 yr. (g. s.); m. William Nichols.
> Jesup, bapt. 11 June 1791, d. at Bridgeport, 2 Feb. 1863 ae. 72; J. P.; m. at Trinity Church, 7 May 1818, Laura Sherwood; dau. of Philemon.
> Walter, b. 3 June 1793 (g. s.), bapt. 9 Jan. 1794, d. at Easton, 19 Mar. 1887 (g. s.); m. (1) Marinda Adams, dau. of Nathan, who d. 12 Dec. 1829 ae. 32 (g. s.); m. (2) Hannah Betts, dau. of Moses, who d. at Greenfield, 16 Apr. 1879 ae. 81 (g. s.).

16. Banks, Jonathan, s. of Benjamin, 3d.

Born 4 Dec. 1760; d. at Greenfield, 29 Nov. 1820 ae. 60 (g. s.). He m. 20 Dec. 1781, Molly Wakeman, b. 4, bapt. 21 July 1765, d. 22 Nov. 1839 ae. 74 (g. s.).

Distribution, 3 Apr. 1822: widow Molly; dau. Sally; dau. Sophia; children of Jonathan, Jr. (son of Jonathan, Sr.); 2d son Zalmon; 3d son Abraham.

Children, from family record (Pension Files):

> Jonathan, b. 24 Mar. 1783, d. 19 Oct. 1820 ae. 37 (g. s.); m. 23 June 1805, Abigail Wakeman, b. 20 Nov. 1786, d. 20 Oct. 1841 ae. 54-10-23 (g. s.).
> Zalmon, b. 2 June 1785, d. 12 Mar. 1855 [12 Mar. 1854 ae. 68-9-20 (g. s.)]; m. 19 Dec. 1809, Fanny Sherwood, dau. of Gershom, who d. 27 Dec. 1875 ae. 87 yrs. 5 mos. (g. s.).

Abraham, b. 11 Mar. 1788, d. 24 Jan. 1870;* m. 11 Mar. 1810, Eunice Banks, b. 1 July 1789, d. 15 Aug. 1883 ae. 94-1-15 (g. s.).
Molly, b. 16 Apr. 1790, d. 15 Feb. 1794.
Sally, b. 22 Apr. 1793, d. 6 Dec. 1843;† m. 7 July 1811, Zalmon Bradley.
Polly W., b. 10 Sept. 1795, d. 5 Sept. 1859; m. 11 Jan. 1815, Charles Nichols.
Sophia, b. 13 Apr. 1798, d. 22 Dec. 1800.
Sophia, b. 24 Mar. 1802, d. 20 Sept. 1822 ae. 20 (g. s.); m. 6 Feb. 1822, Medad Bradley. Adm'n on Est. of Sophia Bradley, late dau. of Jonathan Banks, dec'd, granted to Zalmon Banks and Medad Bradley, 10 Feb. 1823. Distribution: Jonathan, Aaron-Wakeman, Anne-Caroline, Catharine and Polly, children of Jonathan Banks, Jr., bro. of Sophia; bro. Zalmon Banks; bro. Abram Banks; sister Sally Bradley; sister Polly Nichols.

17. Banks, Seth, s. of Thomas.

Born 13 July 1738.

He m. at Redding, 20 Nov. 1766, Sarah Platt.

Children, rec. Redding:
Mehitabel, b. 15 Jan. 1768.
Thomas, b. 17 May 1770; m. 21 Jan. 1792, Sarah Wood.‡
Josiah P., b. 5 July 1774, d. 19 Sept. 1775.
Sally, b. 25 Feb. 1782.
Esther, b. 3 July 1785.

18. Banks, Thaddeus, s. of Thomas.

Born May 1740.

He m. 1 Nov. 1759, Olive Bradley; dau. of David, b. 21 Sept. 1738.

Children, bapt. Greenfield:
Elizabeth, bapt. 28 Dec. 1760; m. 4 Nov. 1781, Nathan Winton.
Thomas, bapt. 27 Feb. 1763.
David, bapt. 6 Oct. 1765; res. Delaware, N. Y.; m. at Weston, 18 Jan. 1798, Lois Lyon; dau. of Ephraim, bapt. 23 June 1773.
Molly, bapt. 1 Oct. 1769; m. at Weston, 23 Nov. 1800, Francis Bradley.
Justus, b. 14 June, bapt. 30 Aug. 1772.
Bradley, bapt. 17 May 1778.

* 24 Jan. 1871 ae. 82-10-13 (g. s.).
† 16 Dec. 1842 ae. 49 (g. s.).
‡ Children, rec. Redding: Laura, b. 6 Apr. 1794, d. 27 May 1796; Platt, b. 24 Feb. 1796; Morgan, b. 31 May 1797.

48 HISTORY AND GENEALOGY OF

19. **Banks, Daniel,** s. of Gershom. Ens., 8th Co., 4th Regt., May 1777.

Born 5 Dec. 1739; Dea. Daniel d. at Greenfield, 16 Jan. 1839 in 100 yr. (g. s.); m. 26 Nov.* 1761, Hannah Thorp, dau. of Nathan; b. 29 July 1739, d. 27 Mar. 1813 in 73 yr. (g. s.), or 25 Mar. 1813 ae. 72 yrs. 8 mos. (church rec.).

Children, rec. Greenfield and Fairfield:

    Mary, b. 16 Nov. 1762, bapt. 18 Nov. 1762, d. at Fairfield, 13 Feb. 1854 ae. 91 yrs. 3 mos. (g. s.); m. 31 Mar. 1790, Abel Sherwood.
    Daniel, b. 18 July 1764, bapt. 29 July 1764, d. at Greenfield, 1 June 1840 ae. 76 (g. s.); m. 25 Sept. 1785, Eunice Ogden, dau. of Moses, b. 18 Oct. 1764, d. 29 June 1855 ae. 91 (g. s.).†
    Samuel, b. 2 July 1766, bapt. 13 July 1766, d. at Greenfield, 13 Jan. 1849 in 83 yr. (g. s.); m. 15 Feb. 1787, Deborah Bradley, dau. of Francis, b. 27 Dec. 1760, d. 19 Feb. 1851 ae. 90-1-23 (g. s.).‡
    Lyman, b. 17 May 1768, bapt. 29 May 1768, d. at Greenfield, 1 Nov. 1849 ae. 81 yrs. 5 mos. (g. s.); m. 7 Jan. 1798, Charity Sherwood, b. 21 Oct. 1772, d. 25 Jan. 1842 ae. 69-3-4 (g. s.).§
    Hannah, b. 14 Oct. 1770.
    Justice, b. 14 Oct. 1770, d. 21 Nov. 1770.

20. **Banks, Thomas,** s. of Gershom.

Born 14 Oct. 1747; d. at Weston, 1 July 1819.

He m. 25 Nov. 1773, Sarah Dean; dau. of Benjamin, b. 31 Jan. 1754, d. 24 Sept. 1820.

He gave wife Sarah all movables, by will 11 Feb. 1818; she refused and took legal dower, 26 July 1819. Distribution 20 June 1820: Thomas, Benjamin, and Zalmon Banks; heirs of Joseph Banks; heirs of Laurana Nickols; and part set to widow Sarah as dower ordered distributed to same heirs, 16 Oct. 1820.

Children, rec. Weston:

    Bradley, b. [23 Mar. 1774], bapt. 21 May 1774, d. at Weston, 12 Oct. 1779 ae. 5-6-20 (g. s.).
    Mary-Anna, bapt. 12 July 1778, d. y.
    Bradley, b. 4 Nov., bapt. 31 Dec. 1780.

---

* 10 Dec. by town record.

† Children, rec. and bapt. Weston: Daniel, b. 3 June, bapt. 29 Oct. 1786, d. Aug. 1827. Moses, b. 14 Mar., bapt. 8 June 1788, d. 12 Aug. 1858 ae. 70 (Miss Treadwell's book); m. Amelia Nichols. Eunice, b. 28 Nov. 1793, bapt. 27 Apr. 1794. Marinda, b. 18 July, bapt. 2 Oct. 1796; Polly-Ogden, bapt. 26 June 1803.

‡ Fanny, dau. of Samuel of Greenfield, bapt. at Weston, 23 Nov. 1800.

§ Lyman-Sherwood, son of Lyman of Greenfield, bapt. at Weston, 24 Aug. 1804.

Thomas, b. 21 Sept., bapt. 10 Nov. 1782, d. at Easton, 30 July 1848 ae. 66 (g. s.); m. (1) Abigail Merwin, dau. of Nathan, b. 5 Feb. 1786, d. 22 Feb. 1835 ae. 49 yrs. 17 days (g. s.); m. (2) Betsey ———.*

Benjamin, b. 15 Oct. 1784, bapt. at Norfield, 30 Jan. 1785 (rec. Westport), d. (found in the river) 29 Sept. 1852 (Miss Treadwell's book); m. Rachel ———, d. at Easton, 4 Jan. 1827 ae. 40 (g. s.).

Esther, b. 17 Sept. 1788 [1787], bapt. at Weston, 4 Nov. 1787.

Joseph-Squire, b. 23 Dec. 1791, bapt. at Weston, 18 Mar. 1792, d. at Weston, 18 Nov. 1817.†

Zalmon, b. 7 Aug. 1794, bapt. at Weston, 26 Aug. 1794, d. at Weston, 23 Apr. 1830; adm'n granted, 28 Apr. 1830, to Ezra P. Bennett, of Danbury, with Roxy M. Banks of Weston as surety.‡

Laurana, m. ——— Nichols.

21. Banks, Gershom, s. of Gershom.

Born 31 Aug. 1752; d. at Greenfield, 11 Jan. 1835 (Pension record), ae. 82 (church rec.).

He m. at Greenfield, 20 Apr. 1774, Ruth Banks; dau. of Benjamin, b. Apr. 1755.

Children, bapt. Greenfield:
Ruth, bapt. 19 Feb. 1775.
Huldah, bapt. 15 Aug. 1777.
Noah, bapt. 23 July 1780, d. at Greenfield, 26 May 1855 ae. 75 (g. s.); m. Sally ———, who d. 28 Mar. 1855 ae. 72 (g. s.).
Cynthia, bapt. 13 Nov. 1795 (at Greenfield, rec. Weston).

22. Banks, Joseph, s. of Gershom.

Born 2 Nov. 1754; d. at Easton, 15 July 1830 ae. 75 (g. s.).

He m. 16 Oct. 1776, Esther Williams, b. 13 Dec. 1760, d. 2 Nov. 1844 ae. 84 (g. s.).

Children, first bapt. Greenfield; from Bible record (Pension files):§
Esther, b. 19 Feb., bapt. 6 July 1777; m. (1) by 1794, Lockwood Lyon; m. (2) ——— Burr.
Joanna, b. 1 May 1779.

---

* The will of Thomas, 29 July, proved 8 Aug. 1848; wife Betsey; son Thomas; dau. Sarah Banks.

† Will Nov. 1817, proved 16 Dec. 1817, named his wife and "our little children." Another Joseph d. in 1830, adm'n being granted to Joseph Silliman of Weston and George A. Raymond of Norwalk; unless this refers to the same estate after the widow's death.

‡ Distribution made to widow Roxy M. and dau. Adeline Loiza.

§ Weston records differ slightly in year dates of the children.

Rachel, b. 15 Aug. 1782, bapt. at Weston, 19 Jan. 1783; m. 8 Apr. 1802, Isaac Fairchild.
Pamela, b. 6 Nov. 1786, bapt. at Weston, 27 May 1787.
Lucinda, b. 3 Feb. 1792, bapt. at Weston, 13 Feb. 1792.
Jane, b. 23 June 1794, bapt. at Weston, 26 Aug. 1794.

23. Banks, Elijah, s. of Gershom.

Born 7 Aug. 1762; d. at Greenfield, 3 Mar. 1816 ae. 53 yrs. 7 mos.; m. abt. 25 Nov. 1784, Mabel Ogden; dau. of Samuel, b. 29 Nov. 1765, d. 20 Mar. 1847 ae. 81 yrs. 3 mos. 20 days (g. s.).

Will 29 Mar. 1815, proved 26 Mar. 1816; wife Mabel; two daus., Mary wife of Peter Winton, Anna wife of Robert Turney; son Elijah; son Samuel Ogden Banks (minor); son William; etc. Distribution, 1 May 1817, named the nine children.

Children, from Bible record (Pension Office):

Mary, b. 22 June 1785; m. Peter Winton.
Anna, b. 8 Sept. 1787, d. 2 May 1865 ae. 78 (g. s.); m. Robert Turney.
Elijah, b. 11 May 1790, d. at Greenfield, 22 Apr. 1840 in 50 yr. (g. s.).
Harriet, b. 15 Nov. 1792; m. (by 1 May 1817, date of distribution of Elijah's estate), Walter Perry, Jr.
Samuel, b. 7 Nov. 1795.*
Finetta, b. 28 Mar. 1798.
William, b. 6 Feb. 1801, d. at Greenfield, 15 Nov. 1845 ae. 44-9-11 (g. s.).
Marietta, b. 31 Oct. 1803.
Julia, b. 21 Jan. 1807; m. Benjamin Williams.

24. Banks, Hyatt, s. of Gershom.

Born 7 Mar. 1764; d. at Greenfield, 14 Apr. 1847 ae. 83 (g. s.); m. Elizabeth Wakeman, bapt. 23 June 1765, who d. 4 June 1835 ae. 70 (g. s.).

Children:

Milly, b. [8 Feb. 1794], d. at Greenfield, 16 Apr. 1875 ae. 81-2-8 (g. s.); m. Anson Wheeler.
Eben W., b. abt. 1796, d. at Greenfield, 12 Nov. 1869 ae. 73 yrs. 18 [days?] (g. s.); m. Mercy Ann ———, b. abt. 1799, d. at Greenfield, 21 Jan. 1836 ae. 36 (burned to death).

---

* Samuel-Ogden Banks d. 12 Sept. 1832 (Miss Treadwell's book).

Emily, m. Charles Winton.
Albert.
Noah, m. Sally Gould.
Charles.

25. Banks, Isaac, s. of Gershom.

Born 26 May 1766; d. at Greenfield, 24 Dec. 1840 ae. 74 (g. s.); m. Eleanor Sturges, bapt. 16 June 1765, d. 19 Feb. 1847 ae. 81 yrs. 9 mos. (g. s.).

Will 16 Dec. 1840, proved 18 Jan. 1841; wife Eleanor; dau. Charlotte wife of Bradley H. Nicholls; heirs of dec'd dau. Eleanor wife of Wakeman Couch; dau. Charity wife of Walter Nicholls; Isaac B. Nicholls, son of my dau. Charity; son Horace.

Children:

> Eleanor, b. [2 Sept. 1787], d. at Westport, 14 Mar. 1823 ae. 35-6-12 (g. s.); m. Wakeman Couch.
> Charity, m. at Trinity Church, 15 Aug. 1810, Walter Nichols.
> Charlotte, m. Bradley-Hull Nichols.
> Horace, b. 31 Jan. 1806 (g. s.), d. at Greenfield, 8 Mar. 1860 (g. s.); Col.; m. Eleanor ———, b. 11 Sept. 1819 (g. s.), d. 24 June 1857 (g. s.).

26. Banks, John, s. of John.

Born 23 Aug. 1746; d. at Greenfield, 3 Sept. 1814 ae. 78 (!) (church rec.).

He m. 16 June 1768, Mary Sturges; dau. of Daniel, b. 13 Sept. 1750; perhaps the Widow Mary who d. at Greenfield, 8 May 1820 ae. 66.

Will 31 Aug., proved 22 Sept. 1814; wife Mary; son John, Jr.; gr. children Eunice-Banks Gilbert, Burr Gilbert, Bradley Gilbert, and Charlotte Gilbert, children of dau. Mary dec'd; dau. Eleanor; Gideon Tomlinson, Exec'r.

Children, rec. Greenfield:

> Mary, b. 4 Sept. 1768, bapt. 5 Sept. 1768 (twins, untimely), d. Nov. 1768.
> Hannah, b. 4 Sept. 1768, bapt. 5 Sept. 1768, d. 19 Sept. 1768 ae. 15 days.
> John, b. 12 Jan. 1773, bapt. 28 Feb. 1773; m. Betsey ———, who d. at Greenfield, 4 Jan. 1864 ae. 83 (g. s.).

Mary, m. ——— Gilbert.
Eleanor, d. 6 Mar. 1818. Her will, 5 Feb. 1818, proved 31 Mar. 1819, mentioned Est. of father John Banks and dower interest of her mother Mary, and gave all to "my own beloved daughter of my body Mary Banks (so called)."

27. Banks, Moses, s. of John.

Born 25 Sept. 1749; d. by 1798.
He m. (1) Hannah Downs, b. in 1755, d. in 1777.
He m. (2) 9 Dec. 1778, Abigail Wakeman; dau. of Gershom, b. 10 Mar. 1758, d. at Greenfield, 3 Dec. 1835 ae. 78. She m. (2) Jehiel Thorp.
Distribution, 26 May 1798: widow; sons Wakeman, Timothy, Aaron; daus. Hannah wife of Isaac Hoyt, Eunice, Tammy, and Elizabeth.

Child [by first wife], bapt. Greenfield:

> Hannah, b. abt. 1777, bapt. 5 Mar. 1780 (ae. abt. 2); m. (rec. Redding) 8 Oct. 1796, Isaac W. Hoyt.

Children [by second wife], bapt. Greenfield:

> Wakeman, bapt. 5 Mar. 1780, d. 16 Jan. 1781 ae. 1 yr. 7 mos.
> Timothy, d. at Greenfield, 11 Nov. 1827; adm'n granted, 4 Dec. 1827, to Bradford Winton of Weston and Eleanor Banks of Fairfield;* m. at Trinity Church, 3 Apr. 1808, Eleanor Ogden; dau. of Moses, b. 17 July 1780, d. 18 Dec. [1831] ae. 51 (Bible rec.).
> Eunice, ? m. 7 Jan. 1806, David Fanton.
> Tammy.
> Aaron, d. 4 Oct. 1808 (Miss Treadwell's book).
> Elizabeth.

28. Banks, Aaron, s. of John.

Born 25 Sept. 1749; d. at Fairfield in 1785.
He m. at Easton, Nov. 1772, Sarah Dimon; prob. dau. of Benoni, b. 27 June 1750.†
Adm'n granted, 5 Sept. 1785, to Samuel Wakeman.

---

* Estate insolvent; realty subject to life use of Abigail wife of Jehiel Thorp as dower in estate of her husband Moses Banks. Eleanor, dau. of Timothy, d. at Greenfield, 15 Oct. 1823. Moses, son of Timothy, d. 25 Jan. 1828 (Miss Treadwell's book).

† Sarah wife of Aaron Banks d. at Greenfield, 28 Dec. 1828 ae. 44 (g. s.); if age is a misreading for 77, she could have been this Sarah.

THE FAMILIES OF OLD FAIRFIELD 53

29. Banks, Peter, s. of John.

Born 9 Nov. 1751; d. in 1787.

He m. 19 Jan. 1774, Elizabeth Bradley, bapt. 13 Feb. 1758, d. in 1791.

Adm'n granted to Nathan Banks, 2 July 1787. Order of distribution, 5 Apr. 1790: eldest son Reuben-Bradley; Pamela Banks; Betsey Banks. Nathan Banks to be guardian of the son and of Pamela.

Adm'n on Elizabeth's Est. was granted to Nathan Banks, 5 Apr. 1791; Daniel Banks to be guardian of Betsey.

Children, rec. Greenfield:
> Elizabeth, bapt. June 1775 (sick), d. June 1775.
> Betsey, bapt. 8 Dec. 1776.
> Reuben-Bradley, bapt. 21 Feb. 1779; m. at Weston, 8 Oct. 1801, Huldah Whitney, dau. of Samuel, who d. 20 Sept. 1831.
> Pamela.
> Gershom, bapt. 25 May 1784, d. y.

30. Banks, Nathan, s. of John.

Bapt. 11 May 1760; d. at Greenfield, 10 Mar. 1847 ae. 87 (g. s.).

He m. 1 Apr. 1781, Mabel Bradley; dau. of Reuben, bapt. 6 Feb. 1763; d. 15 June 1858 ae. 95 yrs. 6 mos. (g. s.).

Will 17 Aug. 1841, proved 23 Mar. 1847; wife Mabel; children Medad, Bradley, Aaron, Clarissa widow of Elijah Nichols, Marilda wife of Charles Wakeman, Betsey wife of Hezekiah Ogden, Pamela Banks; children of dec'd dau. Mabel; children of dec'd gr. dau. Charlotte wife of Willys Nichols. The distribution after his widow's death named the same, except that Bradley Banks' children received his share; the representatives of Mabel Sherwood were named as Eli Sherwood, Mabel Oakley, and the heirs of Charlotte Nichols dec'd.

Children:
> Mabel, b. 3 Oct. 1781, d. 20 May 1805; m. at Weston, 2 Aug. 1798, Hezekiah Sherwood.
> Medad, b. [26 Apr. 1788], d. at Easton, 6 June 1871 ae. 83-1-10 (g. s.); m. Polly Betts, dau. of Moses, b. [4 Nov. 1792], d. 10 July 1879 ae. 86-8-6 (g. s.).
> Clarissa, b. 6 Sept. 1791; m. at Trinity Church, 25 Feb. 1812, Elijah Nichols.

HISTORY AND GENEALOGY OF

Bradley, b. abt. 1794, d. at Greenfield, 26 Nov. 1855 ae. 61 (g. s.); m. Polly Banks, dau. of Daniel, b. abt. 1802, d. 22 Mar. 1892 ae. 89.
Aaron, [b. [July 1797], d. at Greenfield, 13 Sept. 1859 ae. 62 yrs. 2 mos. (g. s.); m. Polly-Ann Sherwood, dau. of Hezekiah, b. [May 1807], d. 3 Oct. 1885 ae. 78 yrs. 5 mos (g. s.)].*
Merilda, b. abt. 1798, d. at Greenfield, 6 Oct. 1873 ae. 75 (g. s.); m. Charles Wakeman.
Betsey, m. Hezekiah Ogden.
Pamela, b. abt. 1802, d. at Greenfield, 12 Feb. 1854 ae. 51 (g. s.); m. William Banks.

31. Banks, Jesse, s. of Joseph.

Born 14 Oct. 1742; d. at Redding, 1 Nov. 1826 ae. 84 (g. s.); m. at Redding, 11 June 1764, Mabel Wheeler, bapt. 12 Feb. 1744, d. 2 June 1822 ae. 78 yrs. 4 mos. (g. s.).

Will 5 July 1823, proved 6 Nov. 1826; sons Hyatt, Jesse, Jr.; daus. Mary Burr, Mabel Foot; to gr. dau. Joanna Judson and gr. child Josiah Brinsmade, the share of their dec'd mother, my dau. Joanna; gr. children Fanny Morgan, Willis Burr, Wakeman Burr, Eli Burr, Emaline Burr, to have share of their mother Mary Burr.

Children, rec. and bapt. Redding:

Hyatt, b. 9 Dec. 1764, bapt. 31 Jan. 1765, d. at Redding, 7 Apr. 1836 ae. 72 (g. s.); adm'n granted 19 Apr. 1836; m. 1 Dec. 1785, Sarah Summers, dau. of Nathan, b. 3 May 1769, d. 23 Oct. 1860 ae. 91-5-20 (g. s.).†
Jesse, b. 29 Oct., bapt. 11 Nov. 1766, d. at Redding, 31 July 1833 ae. 67 (g. s.); adm'n granted 3 Aug. 1833; m. 14 Dec. 1787, Martha Summers, dau. of Zechariah, b. [28 Feb. 1769], d. 17 Sept. 1821 ae. 52-6-17 (g. s.).‡
Joanna, b. 27 July, bapt. 18 Sept. 1768, d. at Easton, 15 Apr. 1804 ae. 36 (g. s.); m. abt. 1794, Cyrus Brinsmade.
Mabel, b. 2 Oct. 1772, bapt. 2 May 1773, d. 27 Nov. 1774 ae. 2.
Mary, b. 23 June, bapt. 21 Oct. 1774; m. ——— Burr.
Mabel, b. 17 Nov. 1778, bapt. 10 Feb. 1779; m. 29 Aug. 1797, Ebenezer Foote.

---

* There was also an Aaron, son of Moses.

† Children, rec. Redding: Nathan-Summers, b. 21 May 1786, d. 18 Feb. 1795. Joseph, b. 3 May 1788. Ebenezer, b. 15 Apr. 1790, d. 29 Mar. 1794. Gershom, b. 7 Apr. 1792, d. 15 Feb. 1795. Jeremiah, b. 18 Mar. 1794, d. 12 Mar. 1851 ae. 56 (g. s.); his wife Fanny d. 5 Sept. 1856 ae. 56 yrs. 6 mos. (g. s.). Laura, b. 21 July 1796. Sally, b. 15 Apr. 1798. Jesse, b. 15 Mar. 1800, d. 3 Mar. 1886 ae. 86 (g. s.); his wife Sally d. 21 June 1845 ae. 40 (g. s.). Mabel, b. 3 May 1802.

‡ Children, rec. Redding: Sarah, b. 22 June 1788, d. 29 Apr. 1791. David, b. 1 May 1792. Eli, b. 22 June 1794. Anna, b. 8 Nov. 1798.

32. Banks, Nehemiah, s. of Nehemiah.

Born Oct. 1754; d. at Greenfield, 19 Apr. 1835 ae. 81 (g. s.); m. 21 Jan. 1779, Sarah Sherwood, b. abt. 1757, d. 4 Nov. 1823 ae. 66 (g. s.).

Adm'n granted, 29 Apr. 1835, to Zalmon B. Banks of Redding and John Banks of Fairfield.

Children, rec. Ridgefield, first two bapt. Greenfield:

>Zalmon-Bradley, b. 9 Nov. 1779, bapt. Jan. 1780, d. 17 Mar. 1864 ae. 84; m. 10 Apr. 1802, Martha Jackson, b. Oct. 1778, d. 3 Nov. 1862 ae. 84.
>Burr, b. 17 Aug. 1781, bapt. 23 Sept. 1781.
>Samuel, b. 2 May 1784.
>Nehemiah, b. 10 Oct. 1786.
>Sarah, b. 10 Oct. 1786.
>Anna, b. 11 May 1789.
>Abigail, b. 8 Dec. 1790.
>Mary, b. 23 Feb. 1793.
>Eliphalet, b. 6 Apr. 1795.

33. Banks, Talcott, s. of Nehemiah.

Bapt. 17 June 1759; buried at Westport, 25 June 1812 ae. 53 (g. s.); d. 24 June 1812 ae. 53 yrs. 2 mos. (church rec.); m. 4 Jan. 1781, Eunice Chapman, dau. of Dennie, bapt. 30 Nov. 1760, buried 26 Mar. 1831 ae. 70 (g. s.).

Will 13 Mar., proved 7 July 1812; wife Eunice; sons Daniel-Chapman, Lyman, Talcott; dau. Mary wife of Thomas Andrews. The part set to the widow Eunice as dower was administered 20 Sept. 1831, when the younger Talcott was appointed Adm'r; he died and Lyman Banks was appointed Adm'r, 9 Nov. 1831.

Children, bapt. Westport:

>Mary, bapt. 28 Sept. 1783, d. 21 Jan. 1791 ae. 7-6-1 (g. s.).
>Daniel-Chapman, b. [say 1785]; B.A.; m 24 Sept. 1805, Martha-Ann Silliman.
>Talcott, bapt. 20 May 1787, d. 6 Sept. 1792 ae. 6-9-17 (g. s.).
>Eunice, bapt. 6 Sept. 1789, d. 17 Oct. 1795 ae. 6-3-22 (g. s.).
>Mary, bapt. 28 May 1791, d. 19 Dec. 1820 ae. 30 (g. s.); m. 8 May 1809, Thomas Andrews.
>Abigail, bapt. 21 July 1793, d. 18 Mar. 1802 ae. 9 yrs. 24 days (g. s.).
>Talcott, bapt. 3 May 1795, d. 16 Apr. 1796.
>Lyman, bapt. 30 Apr. 1797, d. at Westport, 21 Jan. 1859 ae. 62 (g. s.); m. (1) 12 Jan. 1817, Mary Morehouse, dau. of Abraham, bapt. 3

Mar. 1799, d. 30 June 1828 ae. 29 (g. s.); m. (2) Esther, widow of Abraham Morehouse, and dau. of Abijah Gray, b. 1803, d. 13 June 1853 ae. 50 (g. s.).

Talcott, bapt. 24 Mar. 1799, d. at Westport, 3 Nov. 1831 ae. 32 (g. s.); Dr.; m. Martha Burr, d. 10 Dec. 1893 ae. 94 (g. s.).

34. Banks, Ebenezer, s. of Ebenezer. Ens., 7th Co., 5th Regt., Army, 1775; 2d Lt., 2d Co., 1st Batt., Army, June 1776; 2d Lt., Oct. 1776.

Born 19 Oct. 1752; d. at Greenfield, 1 July 1838 ae. 85, Officer in Revolution (g. s.).

He m. at Weston, 27 Dec. 1778, Huldah Sherwood; dau. of Rev. Samuel; she d. 1 Mar. 1833 in 78 yr. (g. s.).

Will 3 Feb. 1838, proved 29 Aug. 1838; dau. Eunice; dau. Sally Adams; gr. son Ebenezer B. Belden and Mariah L. Belden; son-in-law Capt. Joseph Adams and dau. Eunice Banks, Exec'rs.

Children, first bapt. Greenfield:

Ebenezer, bapt. 7 Jan. 1780, d. 28 Jan. 1780 ae. 16 days (g. s.).
Sarah, bapt. at Weston, 17 Mar. 1781, d. at Westport, 22 Oct. 1853 in 73 yr. (g. s.); m. Joseph Adams.
Eunice, b. abt. 1783, d. at Greenfield, 29 Apr. 1854 ae. 71 (g. s.). Will 26 Dec. 1844, proved 10 May 1854; nephew Ebenezer B. Adams; niece Harriet L. Hyde; nephew Ebenezer B. Belden; niece Maria L. Belden.
Rachel, b. abt. 1787, d. at Greenfield, 12 Mar. 1827 ae. 39 (g. s.); m. Dr. Lewis B. Belden, who d. 30 Mar. 1832 ae. 45 (g. s.). A child, Eunice-Banks, d. 10 Apr. 1827 ae. 13 mos. 29 days (g. s.); two children survived.

35. Banks, Joseph, s. of Ebenezer. Sergt., Rev. War.

Born 7 Nov. 1756; d. at Greenfield, 4 Sept. 1836 in 80 yr. (g. s.).

He m. (1) 19 Nov. 1778, Eleanor Hull; dau. of John, b. 14 Jan. 1761 (Bible record), d. 16 Nov. 1791 in 31 yr. (g. s.).*

He m. (2) at Easton, Feb. 1792, Abigail Bradley, dau. of Francis; b. 24 Mar. 1757 (Bible record), d. 18 May 1835 ae. 78 yrs. 2 mos. (g. s.).

Children [by first wife], births from Bible record:

David, b. 9 Sept. 1780, bapt. at Greenfield, 21 Jan. 1781, drowned 11 Dec. 1809 ae. 29; m. at Westport, 31 Jan. 1808, Salome Adams, bapt. 30 Mar. 1783. Adm'n granted, 20 Feb. 1810, to Joseph Banks,

---

* Died in childbed (Perry Diary).

with Increase Bradley as surety. Dower ordered set to David's widow Salome, 29 Mar. 1814.

Jesse, b. 5 Aug. 1782, d. at Greenfield, 29 Feb. 1868 ae. 85-6-24 (g. s.); m. (1) at Trinity Church, 25 Sept. 1806, Jerusha Sherwood, dau. of Benjamin, b. [Sept. 1786], d. 19 Apr. 1813 ae. 26 yrs. 7 mos. (g. s.); m. (2) Sally Dimon, dau. of Samuel, b. abt. 1790, d. 9 Dec. 1834 ae. 44 in Ballston, N. Y. (g. s., Greenfield).

Joseph, b. 1 Feb. 1784, bapt. at Westport, 21 Sept. 1788; m. at Trinity Church, 8 Nov. 1807, Sally Sherwood.

Eliphalet, b. 7 Feb. 1786, bapt. at Westport, 21 Sept. 1788, d. at Greenfield, 5 Mar. 1830 in 35(?) yr.;* Capt.; adm'n granted, 18 Mar. 1830, to Mary C. Banks and Abraham D. Baldwin; m. Mary G. Hull, who m. (2) Wyllys Nichols and d. 30 May 1887 ae. 88 (g. s.).

Charity, b. 14 Apr. 1789.

Children [by second wife], births from Bible record:

Eleanor, b. 26 Aug. 1792.
Caroline, b. 19 Dec. 1800; m. Henry Wakeman.

Banks [*Unplaced*].

HANNAH, b. 7 July 1739; m. at Weston, 12 Jan. 1758, Joseph Morehouse.
SARAH m. 24 Dec. 1797, Isaac Scudder. [Weston Church]
PHILEMA m. 3 Nov. 1777, Samuel Raymond.
HANNAH m. 18 Aug. 1795, Joseph Johnson. [Weston Church]
ESTHER d. 16 July 1802. [Miss Treadwell's book]
WIDOW BETTY d. 29 Apr. 1808. [Miss Treadwell's book]
EMELIA d. 4 May 1798. [Miss Treadwell's book]
WIDOW RACHEL d. 18 June 1828. [Miss Treadwell's book]

Barlow [Vol. I, pp. 27-31].

1 John (-1674) m. Ann ———.
  2 John (-1691) m. Abigail Lockwood.
    3 John (1668-1715) m. Ruth (Sherwood) Drake.
      5 *Samuel* (1695-1734).
      6 *Joseph* (1701-).
      7 *Francis* (1702-).
  4 Samuel (1682-1745) m. Elizabeth Rumsey.
    8 *Joseph* (1707-).
    9 *Samuel* (1710-1773).
    10 *David* (1719-1795).
Ancestry unknown:
  George (-1706) m. Mary Stilson.
    11 *John* (1688-1755).
    12 *George* (1701-).

---

* Was there not a second Eliphalet, by the second wife, b. abt. 1795?

5. **Barlow, Samuel,** s. of John, 3d.

Born 14 Nov. 1695; d. at Fairfield in 1734; m. Sarah, widow of Benajah Strong, and dau. of Capt. David Sherman. She m. (3) Samuel Rowland.

Adm'n granted, 8 Dec. 1734, to Sarah Barlow.

Children:

13+Jabez, bapt. 8 Nov. 1719.
14+Benajah, b. by 1724; chose guardian, 14 Feb. 1738/9.
  Mary, m. Jan. 1746/7, James Burr.
15+John, b. by 1728; chose guardian, 9 Mar. 1741/2; he conveyed 1763, a seventh of nearly 30 acres which was the right of Mrs. Mercy Sherman (wife of Capt. David) and came to her from her father Dea. Isaac Wheeler.

6. **Barlow, Joseph,** s. of John, 3d.

Born 14 Apr. 1701.

He m. (1) Sarah Bradley, dau. of Joseph. She was bapt. 3 Feb. 1705/6, and adm. to Fairfield Church, 5 Jan. 1723/4. Greenfield rec. say first wife of Joseph died (without name or date).

He m. (2) Experience Davis, dau. of Samuel. She renewed her Covenant at Greenfield, 3 Aug. 1728.

In 1740, he was of "Wostershear," N. Y.

John son of Joseph chose his uncle Francis Barlow of Danbury for guardian, 15 Apr. 1762.

Child [by first wife], bapt. Fairfield:

Nehemiah, bapt. 1 Nov. 1724.

Children [by second wife], bapt. Greenfield:

Sarah, bapt. 22 Sept. 1728; ? m. 2 Feb. 1748/9, Ichabod Gorham?
Grace, bapt. 9 Aug. 1730.
Peter, bapt. July 1734.
Seth, bapt. July 1736.
Experience, bapt. 4 Nov. 1738.
John, b. after 1741.

7. **Barlow, Francis,** s. of John, 3d.

Born 11 July 1702.

Deeds show him at Norwalk 1726, Stratford 1730, Newtown 1746; and he was of Danbury in 1747 and 1762.

He m. Elizabeth Mitchell, b. 9 Sept. 1703; with whom he conveyed 1747 land in Stratford, mentioning our dec'd father Mr. Daniel Mitchell.

Children, rec. Stratford:
> Susannah, b. 18 Dec. 1727.
> Mary, b. 21 June 1731; ? m. 20 July 1748, Josiah Burritt, of Newtown.
> Daniel, b. 20 Mar. 1734.
> Ruth, b. 8 May 1736.
> Silas, b. Jan. 1738, d. at Danbury, 1780; will 29 Apr., proved 8 May 1780, named dau. Amarillis Barlow and son Mitchell Barlow; Ezekiel Bradley, Albert Barlow, and Hezekiah Stevens, Jr., Exec'rs. Albert Barlow was appointed guardian of the two children; and distribution was made to them, 1786.
> Nehemiah, b. May 1740.
> ? Albert, d. at Danbury, early in 1788; will 7 Jan., proved 19 Feb. 1788; wife Ruth; daus. Polly, Lois, and Lucy (all under age).

8. Barlow, Joseph, s. of Samuel.

Bapt. 16 Mar. 1706/7; d. before date of his father's will (29 Apr. 1743); m. ⸺.

Only child:
> Eunice, d. in 1768; m. at Weston, 27 Aug. 1758, Thomas Downs.

9. Barlow, Samuel, s. of Samuel.

Bapt. 22 Jan. 1709/10; d. at Redding, 20 Dec. 1773 ae. 63 (g. s.).

He m. (1) 2 Aug. 1731, Eunice Bradley, dau. of Daniel, bapt. 30 May 1708.

He m. (2) 7 Aug. 1744, Esther Hull, dau. of Nathaniel, b. 11 June 1721, d. 28 Aug. 1775 ae. 54 (g. s.).

He conveyed, 1767, to sons James and Jabez and dau. Ruhamah wife of John Gray, referring to former wife Eunice.

Will 20 Dec. 1773, proved 4 Jan. 1774; wife Esther; children James, Jabez, Nathaniel, Aaron, Samuel, Joel, Ruhamah, Huldah; "whereas I expect my son Joel will have a Liberal Education and therefore may need his portion Before he Arives to the Age of Twenty-One Years my will is that his portion of my Estate be Divided Out to him at the Discresson of the person that may Be his Guardian"; wife Esther and son Jabez, Exec'rs.

Will of Esther, 28 Aug., proved 6 Sept. 1775; son Joel, Exec'r; children James, Jabez, Nathaniel, Aaron, Samuel, Joel, Ruamah, Huldah.

Children [by first wife]:
>   Daniel, b. 24 Nov. 1734, d. at Redding, 2 Dec. 1759 ae. 25.
>   Ruhamah, b. 22 Jan. 1737, d. at Redding, 2 June 1813 ae. 74 (g. s.); m. 7 Aug. 1759, John Gray.
>   James, b. 29 Jan. 1739, d. at Redding, 1803; m. Abigail [perhaps dau. of Ithamar Gregory]. Adm'n granted, 14 Mar. 1803, to Joel Marchant and Moses Hubbell of Redding. Distribution: son Samuel; children, Betsey, Lewis, James; widow Abigail.
>   Jabez, b. 21 Mar. 1742.

Children [by second wife]:

16+Nathaniel, b. 13 May 1745.
17+Aaron, b. 11 Feb. 1750.
>   Samuel, b. 3 Apr. 1752, d. at Rhinebeck, 26 Jan. 1776 ae. 23, in service of country after return from St. John and Montreal (g. s.).
>   Joel, b. 24 Mar. 1754, d. at Zarniwica, Poland, 24 Dec. 1812; grad. Yale Coll. 1778; m. 26 Jan. 1781, Ruth Baldwin, dau. of Michael; she d. at Washington, D. C., 29 May 1818 in 62 yr. Chaplain, 4th Mass. Brigade, 1780; Consul, Algiers, 1795-97; Minister to France, 1811; journalist; poet.
>   Huldah, b. 11 July 1760; m. 3 Dec. 1778, Nathan Bennett; of Malta, N. Y.

10. **Barlow, David,** s. of Samuel.

Bapt. 1 Mar. 1718/9; bur. 7 Oct. 1795 ae. 76 (Trinity Church rec.).

He m. (1) 27 Dec. 1743, Susannah Hubbard, dau. of Zechariah, who d. 15 Oct. 1745 in 19 yr. (g. s.); m. (2) 29 Nov. 1750, Esther Sturges, dau. of Jeremiah, b. 29 May 1722. Perhaps she was the "Graney Barlow" who d. 3 Feb. 1791 (Perry Diary).

In 1785, David of Fairfield mortgaged land to David of New Fairfield.

Child [by first wife], rec. Fairfield:
>   David, b. 10 Jan. 1745; prob. res. 1785, New Fairfield; m. at Greenfield, 9 Aug. 1764, Sarah Bradley; dau. of Gershom, bapt. 13 Jan. 1744/5.*

---

* Among their children prob. were the following, who all m. at Fairfield Church: Anna, m. 18 Mar. 1782, Talcott Gold. Abigail, m. 4 May 1788, Robert Jennings. David, m. 16 Aug. 1789, Hannah Patchen. The younger David may have been the man who had these children bapt. Trinity Church: Eunice and Betsey, 30 Jan. 1791; Sarah, 13 Oct. 1793; Betsey, 18 Oct. 1795.

Children [by second wife], rec. Fairfield:

>Joseph, b. 24 Aug. 1751, d. at Stamford, Delaware County, N. Y., 1803; m. Esther Osborn.*
>Suse, b. 10 Dec. 1752, d. 17 Feb. 1753.
>Susannah, b. 2 Feb. 1754; m. 16 Oct. 1777, Thomas Elwood.
>Benjamin, b. 23 Oct. 1755.
>Elizabeth, b. 14 Jan. 1758.

11. Barley, John, s. of George.

In this generation, the name was often spelled Barlow, though Barley is still found.

Born [say 1688]; d. at Stratford in 1755; m. at Stratford, 10 Jan. 1716/7, Mary Sykes.

Will 1 Aug. 1748, proved 1 Sept. 1755; wife Mary; son David; son Joseph; son Samuel, dwelling house; dau. Elizabeth wife of William Cone; dau. Sarah wife of Thomas Stratton, Jr; dau. Mary Barley. Samuel Barley was appointed Adm'r, 18 Mar. 1756, and gave bond with George Beard of Stratford.

Children, rec. Stratford:

>John, b. 16 Oct. 1718.†
>Elizabeth, m. William Cone.
>Sarah, bapt. at Stratford, 31 Mar. 1723, d. June 1770 ae. 47; m. 6 May 1746, Thomas Stratton, Jr.
>David, bapt. at Stratford, 18 Apr. 1725.‡
>Joseph.
>Samuel.
>Mary.

12. Barley, George, s. of George.

Bapt. 5 Jan. 1700/1; d. at Fairfield in 1769.

He m. 1 Apr. 1722, Mehitabel Staples; dau. of John, b. abt. 1695.

---

* Children, b. in Conn., living 1850: Benjamin, b. abt. 1778; Burr, b. abt. 1782. Benjamin son of Joseph Barley was bapt. July 1780 by the Derby Epis. Rector (in a group of Fairfield baptisms).

† Adm'n on Est. of John Barlow of Stratford granted, 18 July 1786, to Benjamin Barlow. [Stratford Pro. Rec.]

‡ David was prob. father of Benjamin, David Jr., Huldah, Polly, Anna, Abiah, Elizabeth, and William. Benjamin d. in 1791, and his estate was distributed between his brothers and sisters. Huldah m. Justus Plumb, 2d; and one of the older daus., Polly or Anna, m. John Curtis, 3d. David, Jr., may be the man, b. abt. 1761, bur. 6 Oct. 1820 ae. 59, m. 1 Nov. 1789, Lucy Sherwood, dau. of Samuel, and had children: Lucia, bapt. 5 Dec. 1790; John; Edwin, bapt. 4 June 1797 [Trinity Church Records].

Adm'n granted to Azariah Odell, 5 Aug. 1769. Deed of partition, 23 Aug. 1769, between Nehemiah Barlow and Samuel Baker and Sarah his wife, children and heirs of George Barlow of Fairfield.

Children, rec. Fairfield:
 18+Nehemiah, b. 11 May 1723 [1724], bapt. at Stratford, 26 May 1724.
 Hezekiah, b. 19 Dec. 1725, bapt. at Stratford, 26 Dec. 1725, d. 1¾ yrs. after.
 Mary, b. Mar. 1730, d. 8 mos. after.
 Sarah, b. 28 Mar. 1732; m. 28 Feb. 1754, Samuel Baker.

13. **Barlow, Jabez,** s. of Samuel. Lt. for Cape Breton Expedition, May 1745.

He m. at Fairfield, 1 Mar. 1743/4, Elizabeth Hunt.

He d. 23 Nov. 1750.

Children, rec. Fairfield:
 John, b. 22 Oct. 1744, bapt. 11 Nov. 1744; res. Ridgefield, 1784 and 1791; rem. abt. 1802 to Ballston, N. Y.; m. 10 Jan. 1769, Sarah Whitney, of Greenfield; dau. of Samuel, b. 16 May 1751.*
 Jabez, b. 21 Feb. 1746/7; chose John Barlow for guardian, Apr. 1763.
 Edmund, b. 4 May 1749; m. at Greenfield, 29 Nov. 1769, Salome Middlebrook; dau. of Jonathan, b. 27 Sept. 1752.†

14. **Barlow, Benajah,** s. of Samuel.

He m. Anne ———.

Children, first two bapt. Greenfield, two others at Trumbull:
 Mehitabel, bapt. 1 Apr. 1744.
 Child, bapt. 12 Jan. 1745/6.
 Lucy, b. 2, bapt. 7 Jan. 1750.
 Phebe, bapt. 14 June 1752.

15. **Barlow, John,** s. of Samuel.

Born by 1728; living at Stratfield, 1763.

He m. at Stratfield, 10 Nov. 1749, Beulah Bennett; dau. of Isaac, bapt at Stratfield, 19 Sept. 1731.

---

* Children (rec. Ridgefield): John, b. 13 July 1769; Jabez, b. 16 July 1771; Mansfield, b. 17 Aug. 1773; Samuel-Whitney, b. 22 June 1775; Abigail, b. 13 Aug. 1778; Nehemiah, b. 23 Dec. 1781; Elizabeth, b. 23 Oct. 1783; Edmund; Amy; Amelia; Polly; Anna.

† Their "oldest girl" d. 29 Aug. 177[2?] (Perry Diary). Jesse and Jonathan, sons of Edmund, bapt. at Trinity Church, 30 Oct. 1791.

Children, one bapt. Stratfield:

> Stephen, bapt. 10 Mar. 1755; m. at Easton, 12 Aug. 1773, Phebe Jackson.

16. **Barlow, Nathaniel,** s. of Samuel.

Born 13 May 1745, d. at Redding, 26 Dec. 1782 in 41 (?) yr. (g. s.); m. at Easton, 24 Apr. 1765, Jane Bradley, dau. of Gershom, b. 22 May 1747, d. 12 Feb. 1829.

Will 15 Nov. 1782, proved 1 Feb. 1783; wife Jane; children, Gershom, Esther, Sarah, Betsey, Huldah; wife and son, Exec'rs.

Sarah, dau. of Nathaniel, chose Andrew Bradley of Redding for guardian, 23 June 1783; and Jane Barlow was appointed guardian of Betsey and Huldah.

Children:

> Gershom, b. 21 Oct. 1765, d. 28 Sept. 1794 in 30 yr. (g. s.); unm. Will 22 Sept., proved 18 Oct. 1794; mother Jane Barlow; two loving sisters, Sarah Hill and Betsey Barlow; Methodist Society.
> Esther, b. 30 Sept. 1767, d. 10 May 1783, unm. On 5 Mar. 1795, order to distribute Ests. of Esther and Huldah Barlow, daus. of Nathaniel, to their two surviving sisters, Sarah wife of Ebenezer Hill and Betsey.
> Sarah, b. 16 Jan. 1770 (rec. Redding), d. 11 Apr. 1845; m. May 1791, Ebenezer Hill.
> Jonathan, b. 14 Apr. 1772, d. 28 Aug. 1775.
> Betsey, b. 2 Aug. 1778 (rec. Redding), bapt. 24 Oct. 1778, d. 9 Sept. 1864; m. William Hill.
> Huldah, b. 3 Apr. 1780, d. 29 Aug. 1787.

17. **Barlow, Aaron,** s. of Samuel. Ens., 9th Co., 4th Regt., Jan. 1778; Lt., June 1780; Capt., Oct. 1781. Deputy for Redding, May and Oct. 1794, May 1795.

Born 11 Feb. 1750, d. at Norfolk, Va., 12 Aug. 1800, of yellow fever; m. 17 Dec. 1772, Rebecca Sanford; dau. of Elnathan, b. [say 1752], d. 15 Apr. 1839.

Children:

> Elnathan, b. 14 Oct. 1773, bapt. 2 Jan. 1774, d. 31 Aug. 1774 ae. 10 mos. 18 days (g. s.).
> Elnathan, b. 8 May, bapt. 16 July 1775, d. at Detroit, Mich., 14 Jan. 1815; res. Gallia County, Ohio; m. at Weston, 23 Mar. 1802, Anna Morehouse.

64 HISTORY AND GENEALOGY OF

Samuel, b. 8 Mar., bapt. 4 May 1777; res. 1803, "Galipoli, Galia County, Ohio"; m. Betsey Bradley, dau. of Lyman.
Stephen, b. 19 Apr., bapt. 13 June 1779, d. at Meadville, Pa.
Daniel, b. 19 Feb. 1781, perhaps d. at Redding, 15 May 1850 (Miss Treadwell's book).
Aaron, b. 25 Dec. 1782, d. at Savannah, Ga., unm.
Deborah, m. Peter Oakley, of Wappinger's Peek, near Peekskill, N. Y.
Esther, b. 19 Aug. 1786, d. at Norfolk, Va., 10 Aug. 1800, of yellow fever.
Rebecca, b. 12 Oct. 1788; m. Zalmon Olmstead.
Joel, b. 14 Sept. 1790, d. 28 Mar. 1799.
Thomas, b. 12 Oct. 1793; m. Amelia Preble, of Washington, Pa.

18. **Barlow, Nehemiah,** s. of George.

Born 11 May 1723; d. at Fairfield, 3 Nov. 1787 (Perry Diary).
He m. (1) 25 Jan. 1751, Jemima Turney, dau. of Thomas, who d. by 1759.
He m. (2) Ann Jennings, dau. of John, bapt. 1 Aug. 1725.
Will 4 Oct. proved 17 Dec. 1787; wife Ann; two gr. children, Zalmon and Jabez Jennings, sons of Nathaniel Jennings; son Nehemiah; dau. Esther wife of Edmund Jennings; son George.

Children [by first wife], rec. Fairfield:

Jemima, b. 25 Sept. 1752, d. before 1787; m. Nathaniel Jennings.
Mabel, b. 16 Feb. 1757.

Children [by second wife]:

Esther, b. in 1764, d. at Easton, 13 June 1826 ae. 63 (g. s.); m. (rec. Weston) 10 Nov. 1782, Edmund Jennings.
Nehemiah, b. (rec. Weston) 1 June 1766, d. at Easton, 24 May 1822 ae. 56 (g. s.); m. Rebecca ———, b. 16 Apr. 1767, d. 4 Apr. 1847 ae. 80 (g. s.).*
George.

Barlow [*Unplaced*].

ABIGAIL had a child, Joseph, bapt. 31 Oct. 1736. [Fairfield Church]
DANIEL had dau. Mehitabel, bapt. at Easton, 19 June 1774. Daniel and Abigail had dau. Hannah, bapt. at Fairfield, 21 Mar. 1791.

---

* Adm'n on Est. of Nehemiah was granted, 15 July 1822, to Turney Foot of Weston. Distribution 1823 to widow Rebecca and daus. Anna wife of William Corning, Nabby wife of Isaac Silliman, Jemima wife of Turney Foot, and Huldah, Eliza and Rebecca Barlow. Children, rec. Weston: Anna, b. 2 Nov. 1787, d. 2 May 1788; Anna, b. 20 July 1788; Nabby, b. 20 June 1791; Jemima, b. 18 Dec. 1793; Huldah, b. 27 Feb. 1796. Adm'n on Rebecca's estate was granted 11 May 1847.

SAMUEL, of Stratford, chose John Turney for guardian, Aug. 1762; m. Ann Hawley, dau. of Daniel, b. 10 June 1753.
STEPHEN of Saugatuck m. 9 Dec. 1804, Abigail Sturges. [Fairfield Church]
EUNICE m. 17 July 1808, Joseph Lockwood. [Greens Farms Church]
BENAJAH and wife renewed covenant, and had son Stephen bapt., May 1790. [Easton Church]

Barnes [Unplaced].

JOHN m. 17 Oct. 1788, Molly Baker. [Greens Farms Church]

Bartlett, (Rev.) Nathaniel. Minister at Redding, 1753-1810. Chaplain, Gen. Putnam's Division encamped at Redding, 1778-79.

Son of Daniel and Ann (Collins), b. at Guilford, 22 Apr. 1727; d. at Redding, 11 Jan. 1810 in 83 yr. (g. s.); Yale Coll. 1749.

He m. 13 June 1753, Mrs. Eunice Russell, of Branford; dau. of Jonathan and Eunice (Barker). She d. at Redding, 12 Aug. 1810 in 84 yr. (g. s.).

Will 11 Apr. 1809, proved Jan. 1810; wife Eunice; dau. Anna for life (my son Jonathan to be her trustee with Jonathan R. Sanford), then to her dau. Sally; son Russell; children of son Daniel-Collins by his late wife Esther; dau. Eunice wife of Ezekiel Jackson; son Jonathan; dau. Lucretia wife of James-John Davies.

Will of Eunice, 8 Feb., proved Aug. 1810; gr. gr. son Jonathan-Collins Bartlett, the children of my son Daniel-Collins by his late wife Esther, and gr. son William Bartlett; sons Russell, Daniel-Collins; dau. Anna, referring to her "simplicity and inexperience in worldly affairs"; son Jonathan.

Children, rec. Fairfield, bapt. Redding:

> Russell, b. 3, bapt. 9 June 1754; m. [at Danbury], 28 Feb. 1776, Rachel Taylor.*
> Daniel-Collins, b. 12, bapt. 16 Jan. 1757, d. at Amenia, N. Y., 13 Dec. 1837 ae. 82 (g. s.); m. 7 Jan. 1778, Esther Read, bapt. 11 Jan. 1761, d. 30 Mar. 1809 ae. 48 yrs. 3 mos. (g. s.).†

---

* Children, rec. and bapt. Redding: Clare, b. 7 Feb., bapt. 30 Mar. 1777; Flora, bapt. 29 Aug. 1779.
† Child, rec. Redding: Abigail, b. 26 June, bapt. 23 Aug. 1778.

Ann, bapt. 25 Feb. 1759.*
Eunice, bapt. 26 Apr. 1761; m. 26 Dec. 1806, Ezekiel Jackson.
Jonathan, bapt. 14 Oct. 1764; Rev.; m. (1) 16 Aug. 1795, Rhoda Sanford, dau. of Lemuel, b. 4 Mar. 1773, d. 23 Dec. 1796 ae. 23-9-19 (g. s.); m. (2) 10 Sept. 1798, Betsy Marvin, of Wilton, who d. 12 Mar. 1811 in 39 yr. (g. s.); m. (3) 6 Apr. 1812, Abigail Sanford, dau. of Lemuel, b. 18 Apr. 1784, d. 24 July 1854.
Lucretia, b. 4 Jan., bapt. 27 Mar. 1768; m. James-John Davies.

Bartram [Vol. I, p. 34].

```
1 John (    -1675) m. Sarah ———.
  2 John (    -1740) m. Sarah ———.
    3 John (1694-1747).
    4 Ebenezer (1699-1769).
    5 David (1702-1768).
```

3. Bartram, John, s. of John, 2d.

Born 9 Jan. 1693/4; d. at Greenfield, 11 Dec. 1747.

He m. abt. 1718, Sarah, widow of Francis Bradley, and dau. of Joseph Jackson; she d. Mar. or Apr. 1753. As wife of John, Jr., she joined Greenfield Church, 1726.

Adm'n granted, 17 Dec. 1747, to Benjamin Sherwood and Joseph Rumsey.

Child:

Sarah, b. 14 May 1719, bapt. 28 June 1719; m. (1) 16 Aug. 1738, Joseph Rumsey; m. (2) 20 Sept. 1768, Hezekiah Bulkley.

4. Bartram, Ebenezer, s. of John, 2d.

Born 29 Apr. 1699; d. at Fairfield, 7 Dec. 1769 ae. 71 (g. s.).

He m. 15 May 1728, Elizabeth Williams; dau. of John, bapt. 23 Apr. 1704, d. 5 Dec. 1769 ae. 69 (g. s.).

Children, rec. and bapt. Fairfield:

6+Joseph, b. 21, bapt. 23 Feb. 1728/9.
Hannah, bapt. 4 July 1731.
7+Ebenezer, b. 13, bapt. 18 June 1732.
8+Job, b. 20, bapt. 30 Mar. 1735.
Eulalia, b. 24 June, bapt. 3 July 1737, d. 5 Dec. 1785; m. at Westport, 25 Mar. 1774, Rev. Robert Ross, of Stratfield.

---

* Sally, dau. of Anna Bartlett, b. 18 Feb. 1784; certified by Nathaniel Bartlett. Sally Bartlett d. 25 Mar. 1813 in 29 yr. (g. s.).

Barnabas, b. 20, bapt. 30 Sept. 1739, d. in 1771; Capt.; adm'n granted, 5 Nov. 1771. Distribution 11 Nov. 1773; Ebenezer Bartram; Job Bartram; Eulalia Bartram; heirs of bro. Joseph Bartram, viz. Elizabeth and Eulalia Jr. Barnabas d. on his passage from the West Indies, four days "after they sot out" to come home; news received 15 Oct. 1771 (Perry Diary).

5. **Bartram, David,** s. of John, 2d.

Bapt. 13 Dec. 1702; d. at Redding, 7 Feb. 1768; m. 14 Dec. 1730, Mabel Johnson, dau. of Moses.

Adm'n granted, 9 May 1768, to John and Paul Bartram.

Children, rec. and bapt. Fairfield:
9+John, b. 17, bapt. 24 Oct. 1731.
    Hannah, b. 18, bapt. 25 Nov. 1733; m. 26 Dec. 1762, Elnathan Bradley.
10+David, b. 18, bapt. 25 May 1735.
11+Paul, b. 12, bapt. 17 Oct. 1736.
12+James, b. 18, bapt. 23 Apr. 1738.
    Isaac, b. 7, bapt. 25 Jan. 1740/1, d. June 1747.
    Elizabeth, b. 6, bapt. 11 Sept. 1743; m. William Tigsby.
    Sarah, b. 6, bapt. 11 Sept. 1743; m. 21 Dec. 1763, Samuel Olmstead.
13+Daniel, b. 23, bapt. 27 Oct. 1745.
    Isaac, b. 24 July 1748, bapt. at Redding, 28 Aug. 1748.

6. **Bartram, Joseph,** s. of Ebenezer.

Born 21 Feb. 1728/9; d. at Fairfield, 28 Mar. 1759 ae. 30 yrs. 24 days.

He m. 7 Nov. 1754, Rebecca Squire, dau. of Samuel; b. abt. 1725, d. 15 June 1776 ae. 51.

Adm'n granted, 31 July 1759, to Rebecca Bartram, John Squire surety. Elizabeth chose Rebecca Bartram for guardian, 15 Dec. 1772, and she was appointed for William.*

Children, rec. and bapt. Fairfield:
    Elizabeth, b. 6, bapt. 12 Oct. 1755; m. 18 Apr. 1779, John Wasson.
    Eulalia, b. 1, bapt. 4 Dec. 1757, d. 1 May 1777 in 20 yr. (g. s.).

7. **Bartram, Ebenezer,** s. of Ebenezer. 1st Lt., Brig. *Defence,* Mar. 1776; called Capt., Nov. 1777.

Born 13 June 1732; d. at Fairfield, 3 Jan. 1783 in 52 yr. (g. s.); m. 1 Nov. 1759, Mary Burr, dau. of Capt. John, b. 7 Apr. 1732, d. 15 Mar. 1806 in 75 yr. (g. s.).

* Misreading for Eulalia?

Thomas Bartram chose Mary Bartram for guardian, 15 Mar. 1788.

Children, bapt. Fairfield:

    Joseph, bapt. 28 Sept. 1760, d. at sea on return from West Indies, Dec. 1787 in 28 yr. (g. s.); Capt.
    Ebenezer, bapt. 15 Aug. 1762; ? m. 9 Jan. 1803, Abigail Jennings, dau. of Isaac, b. 12 Jan. 1776; a child, Ebenezer, bapt. 13 Aug. 1803.
    Thomas, b. 22 Feb., bapt. 3 June 1764, d. 28 July 1764 ae. 5 mos. 6 days (g. s.).
    Mary, bapt. 6 Oct. 1765; m. (1) 7 Apr. 1787, Daniel Osborn, Jr.; m. (2) 29 Apr. 1804, Gershom Bulkley, of Harrison, N. Y.
    Job, bapt. 17 May 1767, drowned 28 Oct. 1817 ae. 50 yrs. 6 mos. (g. s.); m. 6 Nov. 1796, Ruth Holberton; dau. of Thomas.*
    Jerusha, bapt. 6 Aug. 1769; m. 2 Dec. 1792, Nathan Lewis, of Derby.
    Thomas, bapt. 5 May 1771; m. 16 Nov. 1797, Sarah Burr; dau. of Nehemiah, b. 29 Mar. 1771.†
    Barnabas, bapt. 30 May 1773, d. of yellow fever in West Indies, 1805 (Wheeler Journal); m. 23 Jan. 1803, Deborah Squire, dau. of Ebenezer, bapt. 6 Sept. 1778, d. by 1813.‡
    Sarah, bapt. 28 July 1776.

8. Bartram, Job, s. of Ebenezer. Capt., 1st Co., 4th Regt., Alarm List, Aug. 1777.

Born 20 Mar. 1735.

He m. (1) 18 Nov. 1762, Jerusha Thompson, dau. of David; b. 25 Dec. 1729, d. 24 Nov. 1773 ae. 44 yrs. wanting 43 days (g. s.).

He m. (2) at Danbury, 7 Nov. 1774, Abigail, widow of Daniel Starr, Jr., and dau. of Wakefield Dibble of Danbury; b. 5 Sept. 1748, d. 14 Jan. 1776 ae. 27 yrs. 4 mos. wanting 2 days (g. s.).

He m. (3) 27 Aug. 1776, Elizabeth Scudder, dau. of Isaac of Norwalk.

Child [by second wife], rec. and bapt. Fairfield:

    Daniel-Starr, b. 2, bapt. 7 Jan. 1776.

---

* Children, bapt. Fairfield: Mary-Burr, bapt. 12 May 1799; William, bapt. 20 Sept. 1801; John, bapt. 21 June 1803; George-Wakeman, bapt. 2 Sept. 1804.

† Children, bapt. Fairfield: Sally, bapt. 22 Jan. 1798; Joseph, bapt. 21 Dec. 1800; Thomas-Burr, bapt. 30 Oct. 1803.

‡ Adm'n on Est. of Deborah was granted, 8 June 1813, to Mary Squire, formerly of Fairfield, now a resident of New York; William W. Squires, surety. Mary-Wheeler, dau. of Barnabas, bapt. 2 Sept. 1804.

Children [by third wife], rec. Norwalk, bapt. Fairfield:
> Isaac, b. 27 (?) Mar. 1777, bapt. 23 Mar. 1777, d. 28 Mar. 1777.
> John, b. 27 Dec. 1778, bapt. 27 Dec. 1778, d. 12 Feb. 1779.
> Isaac-Scudder, b. 2 July 1780, d. 12 Feb. 1783.
> Eulalia, b. 22 Dec. 1782.
> Betsey, b. 10 July 1785.

9. **Bartram, John,** s. of David.

Born 17 Oct. 1731; d. at Danbury, 1777.

He m. at Redding, 19 Mar. 1757, Charity Bulkley, dau. of Daniel, bapt. 13 May 1733.

Adm'n granted to James Bartram, 25 June 1777.

Children, bapt. Redding:
> Mabel, b. 15, bapt. 16 Oct. 1757.
> Joseph, bapt. 10 June 1759.

10. **Bartram, David,** s. of David.

Born 18 May 1735.

He m. at Redding, 30 Apr. 1762, Phebe Morehouse; dau. of Jonathan, bapt. 27 Mar. 1744. She m. (2) ——— Morehouse.

Will of Phebe Morehouse of Brookfield, 3 July 1804, proved 31 July 1806; two eldest sons Joel and David Bartram; two youngest sons John and Jonathan Bartram; daus. Hepe wife of Ezra Congo, Huldah wife of Noah Bartram, Phebe wife of Elijah Thayre, Matilda wife of James Morehouse, Lucy (single).

11. **Bartram, Paul,** s. of David.

Born 12 Oct. 1736.

He m. at Redding, 19 Sept. or 9 Nov. 1756, Mary Hawley; dau. of Joseph, b. 2 Feb. 1742.

Children, rec. and bapt. Redding:
> Twins, b. and d. 12 Jan. 1757 [1758?].
> Joseph, b. 28, bapt. 31 Jan. 1759, d. 2 Feb. 1759 ae. 4 days.
> Mary, b. 12 May, bapt. 8 June 1760; m. 12 Feb. 1778, Jabez Burr; rem. to Clarendon, Vt.
> Sarah, b. 6 Aug., bapt. 3 Oct. 1762; m. 26 Sept. 1790, Milo Palmer; rem. to Clarendon, Vt.

Eunice, b. 3 Jan. 1765; m. 15 Mar. 1783, Daniel Parsons.
Eli, b. 30 Mar., bapt. 3 May 1767; m. 9 Sept. 1794, Dolly Lyon; rem. to Delaware County, N. Y.*
Ruth, b. and bapt. 17 June 1769, d. 18 June 1769 ae. 11 hours.
Ezekiel, b. 9 July, bapt. 2 Sept. 1770; m. 26 Jan. 1793, Esther Parsons, bapt. 9 Apr. 1775.†
Ezra, bapt. 9 May 1773; m. Eleanor Marchant; dau. of Chauncey, b. 13 May 1781.
Joseph, bapt. 10 Mar. 1776; rem. to Vt. and Tioga County, N. Y.
Olive, m. Justus Stillson; rem. to Groton, N. Y.

12. Bartram, James, s. of David.

Born 18 Apr. 1738; d. at Danbury, after Aug. 1832.
He m. Hannah Morehouse.

Children, bapt. Redding:

Isaac, b. Nov. 1758, bapt. 20 Dec. 1758, d. at (Sherman?), 13 Sept. 1843; m. Molly Hamilton, b. abt. 1764.
Noah, b. 8 Feb. 1759 (his own statement, prob. error for 1761); res. Sherman, 1788-1832; m. Huldah Bartram, dau. of David, 2d.
Ruth, bapt. 15 May 1763; ? m. 9 Mar. 1780, William Darrow.
Lucy.
Hannah.
Betsey.
James, b. 1770.
Irena, bapt. 29 May 1779.
Anna.
Aaron, b. 21 Feb. 1784; m. Eunice Jenkins.

13. Bartram, Daniel, s. of David.

Born 23 Oct. 1745.
He m. at Redding, 10 Oct. 1769, Ann Merchant; dau. of Gurdon, b. 31 Jan. 1749.

Children, rec. Redding:

Esther, b. 16 Apr., bapt. 1 July 1770.
Gurdon, b. 25 Dec. 1771, bapt. 26 Jan. 1772, d. 20 Mar. 1772.
Anna, b. 21 Jan., bapt. 28 Feb. 1773, d. 27 Sept. 1777.
Eleanor, b. 1 Nov., bapt. 4 Dec. 1774, d. 21 Sept. 1777.

---

* Children, rec. Redding: William, b. 3 May 1795; Belinda, b. 24 Nov. 1798.
† Children, rec. Redding: Mary, b. 18 Aug. 1792 (?); Jared, b. 25 Dec. 1794; Milo, b. 8 Sept. 1797.

Gurdon, b. 21 Sept., bapt. 20 Oct. 1776, d. at Redding, 12 Apr. 1845 ae. 68-6-21 (g. s.); m. 1 Jan. 1804, Lorrain Sanford, d. 3 Dec. 1871 ae. 84 yrs. 3 mos. (g. s.).
Anna, b. 18 Aug. bapt. 20 Sept. 1778.
Eleanor, b. 4 Feb., bapt. 26 Mar. 1780, d. 24 May 1781.
Uriah, b. 9 Jan. 1782.
Eleanor, b. 28 Oct. 1783.
Ulilla, b. 12 Nov. 1785.
Levi, b. 26 Nov. 1787.
Phebe, b. 19 Sept. 1790.
David, b. 5 June 1795.

Bartram [*Unplaced*].

EULALIA m. 10 Apr. 1804, Rev. Henry Whitlock. [Trinity Church rec.]

Bassett [*Unplaced*].

JOHN m. 17 Nov. 1799, Urane Thorp of Greenfield. [Weston Church]

1. **Bates, Nicholas.**

He m. (1) Martha ———.
He m. (2) Abigail ———.
Of Danbury, and owned property in Ridgefield.

Will 17 June, proved 7 Dec. 1741; wife Abigail; three sons Elias, John, Henry; only dau. Mary wife of Jonathan Pierson of Derby; bro. Henry Bates of Wallingford and Lt. Ebenezer Hickock of Danbury, Exec'rs.

Henry, son of Nicholas Bates of Danbury, chose Jonathan Pierson of Derby for his guardian, 4 Nov. 1745. [New Haven Pro. Rec.]

Children [by first wife], rec. Ridgefield:

Mary, b. 31 Aug. 1720, d. at Derby, 16 Feb. 1755; m. 5 Mar. 1739, Jonathan Pierson.
2+Elias, b. 3 Apr. 1722.
3+John, b. 2 May 1724.
Henry, b. 15 June 1730.

2. **Bates, Elias**, s. of Nicholas. Ens., west company, Redding, Oct. 1757.

Born 3 Apr. 1722; m. (1) 17 Jan. 1734 [error for 1744], Sarah Platt, dau. of Obadiah, b. 25 June 1725.

He m. (2) at Redding, 25 Feb. 1759, Tabitha Read. She was widow of John Read, Jr., and dau. of Joseph Hawley, b. at Stratford, 5 Apr. 1730, d. at Redding, in 1783.

Ens. Elias d. at Redding, 30 Apr. 1761.

Receipt of Tabitha, widow of Elias Bates, to Gurdon Merchant, Adm'r, Dec. 1762; also of John Read as guardian for John, Mary, and Abigail, children of John Read; also of Tabitha Bates as guardian for two children, Walker and Elias; also of Obadiah Platt as guardian of Martha and Sarah; and of John Bates as guardian of Justus.

Adm'n on Tabitha's Est. granted, 4 Feb. 1783, to William Hawley, Esq.

Children [by first wife], rec. Fairfield, bapt. Redding:

> Justus, b. 5 Feb. 1736 [1746], d. 8 Feb. 1736 [1746].
> Justus, b. 20 July 1737 [1747], bapt. 26 July 1747; m. 23 May 1771, Hannah Coley.*
> Martha, b. 20 July 1739 [1749], d. at Berne, Albany County, N. Y., in 1836; m. at Easton, 10 Dec. 1767, Joseph Bradley.
> Sarah, b. 7 Nov. 1741 [1751], bapt. 2 Feb. 1752.

Children [by second wife], bapt. Redding:

> Walker, bapt. 6 Jan. 1760.
> Elias, bapt. 16 Feb. 1761; res. 1834, Windham, Green County, N. Y.; m. 9 Nov. 1793, ――――.†

3. **Bates, John,** s. of Nicholas.

Born 2 May 1724; d. at Redding in 1778; m. 11 June 1752, Esther Banks, dau. of Thomas, b. 15 Apr. 1735.

Inv. 1778. Distribution 29 July 1782; eldest son Ezra; 2d son John; Ruth wife of Enos Lee; Sarah Bates; Esther Bates; Aaron; Nathan.

---

* Children, recorded at Redding: Justus, b. 19, bapt. 16 (?) Aug. 1771; Elias, b. 29 Aug., bapt. 4 Oct. 1772. Abigail, wife of Elias, d. at Weston, 6 Nov. 1873 ae. 93-10-28 (g. s.). Elias was granted adm'n, 27 Apr. 1827, on the estate of Stephen Diteman of Weston, whose widow Abigail he had married.

† Child, rec. Redding: Walker, b. 4 June 1796; m. Matsy Bradley, dau. of Gershom, b. 29 Jan. 1800, d. 5 June 1851 (Miss Treadwell's book).

Children, rec. Fairfield, bapt. Redding:

Ezra, b. 20 July, bapt. 26 Aug. 1753, d. 15 Mar. 1754.
Mary, b. 14 Mar., bapt. 13 Apr. 1755; m. 20 Mar. 1774, John Pickett.
Ruth, b. 1 Nov. (?) bapt. 4 Sept. 1757; m. 22 Apr. 1778, Enos Lee.
Ezra, b. 11 Mar. 1758 (his own statement, in error), bapt. 23 Mar. 1760; res. 1832, Redding; m. 11 Mar. 1785, Huldah Platt, dau. of Isaac, b. 12 Nov. 1769, d. 7 May 1835.
John, bapt. 25 July 1762; m. Esther ———.
Sarah, bapt. 5 May 1765; m. 3 Apr. 1786, Daniel Olmstead.
Esther, bapt. 22 Aug. 1767.
Nathan, bapt. 25 Mar. 1770; m. Ruth Taylor, dau. of Preserved, b. 19 Jan. 1776.
Aaron, bapt. 5 July 1772; m. Eunice Taylor, dau. of Preserved, b. 22 July 1773.
Martha, bapt. 25 Jan. 1778.
Slawson, bapt. 25 Jan. 1778.

Bates [*Unplaced*].

LOIS m. 26 Feb. 1786, Ebenezer Mills, Jr. [Weston rec.]
ELIZABETH m. 2 Jan. 1791, Samuel Watkins. [Easton Church]

1. Batterson, Anthony.

He first appears as resident in Norwalk in 1723, when he purchased land on the Saugatuck River from John Beers. [Norwalk Deeds.]

Of Norwalk in 1725, he conveyed any pretense of right he might have in lands or other estate of Simon Couch of Fairfield dec'd, but it is not clear what claim he had.

In 1743, his wife was Abigail.

Children, youngest bapt. Westport:*

2+? James.
3+? George.
4+? Zachary.
Esther, bapt. 29 May 1743.

2. Batterson, James, [s. of Anthony?].

He d. at Westport, 7 Dec. 1796 ("found dead in morning").
He m. Elizabeth ———.

---
* Jemima, dau. of ——— *Paterson*, bapt. at Redding, 7 Apr. 1734, may perhaps belong to Anthony.

Children, bapt. Westport:

    Joseph, bapt 13 May 1744, killed on a privateer, 15 July 1759.
5+William, bapt. 13 May 1744.
? Ann, m. 23 Nov. 1768, John Elwood.
John, bapt. 4 Feb. 1750; m. Marianne ———.*
Stephen-Powell, bapt. 17 Dec. 1752, d. 22 Apr. 1756.
Mary, bapt. 13 Apr. 1755; m. 18 Aug. 1774, Ichabod Canfield.
Elizabeth, bapt. 24 June 1759, living 1820 at Scipio, N. Y.; m. 9 Mar. 1781, Isaac Batterson.
Joseph, bapt. 18 Apr. 1762; m. 5 Mar. 1779, Tammy Hendricks.
? Powell, b. abt. 1766; res. 1841, Wilton; m. Grace Jackson.

3. **Batterson, George,** [s. of Anthony?].

He m. 1 Dec. 1752, Elizabeth Oysterbanks; dau. of Jacob.

Children, one rec. Fairfield; bapt. Westport:

    Naomi, b. 19 Mar., bapt. 15 Apr. 1753; living 1837, Fairfield, Vt.; m. 3 Oct. 1771, Joseph Elwood
George, bapt. 13 Aug. 1758, d. at Warren, 11 May 1837; m. 23 May 1779, Mary Seeley.†
Stephen, bapt. 20 Sept. 1761; m. (1) (rec. Norwalk), 20 Oct. 1784, Sarah Wardwell; m. (2) Amy ———, b. abt. 1757.‡
William, bapt. 11 July 1762.
Betty, bapt. 18 Mar. 1764; living 1841 at Westport; m. 2 Mar. 1780, Stephen Elwood.
Selleck, bapt. 10 July 1768; res. 1840, Catskill, Greene County, N. Y.; m. 13 Dec. 1795, Molly Batterson; dau. of William, bapt. 5 July 1772.§
Samuel, bapt. and d. 20 June 1770.
Grace, bapt. 11 Aug. 1771, d. 5 Sept. 1771.
Eliakim, bapt. 15 Nov. 1772, d. 7 Aug. 1795. Adm'n granted, 16 Nov. 1795, to John Andrews.
Data, bapt. 26 Mar. 1775;‖ m. (1) Oct. 1797, Joseph Squire, of

---

* Children, bapt. Westport: Molly, bapt. 12 Apr. 1778. John, bapt. 27 Sept. 1782, d. young. John, bapt. 25 Apr. 1784, prob. the John Batterson, 3d, who d. at sea, June 1808. Anne, bapt. 16 Nov. 1789, d. 2 Jan. 1790. Morris, bapt. 27 Nov. 1790. Anna, bapt. 21 June 1795. Susanna, bapt. 2 July 1797.

† Children, bapt. Trinity Church: Polly, bapt. 10 Sept. 1786; Anna and Nathan, bapt. 22 Sept. 1792.

‡ Children, bapt. Westport: Abigail, bapt. 20 Nov. 1785; Sally, bapt. 26 Aug. 1787. Recorded Norwalk (Hall, p. 271): Abigail, b. 31 July 1785; William, b. 10 July 1787; Isaac, b. 10 June 1791; Stephen, b. 12 July 1796.

§ Children, bapt. Westport: Molly, bapt. 16 Apr. 1797; Lucy, bapt. 15 July 1798, d. 21 July 1798; Selleck, bapt. 5 Apr. 1801; Joel, bapt. 12 June 1803; Legrand, bapt. 1 May 1805.

‖ Cyndarilla Hull, dau. of Data Batterson, bapt. 26 July 1795, d. 9 Dec. 1795.

Weston; prob. as Data Squire of Trumbull m. (2) at Westport, 2 Feb. 1807, Nathan Gilbert of Huntington.

Roxy, bapt. 29 Mar. 1778; m. 25 Apr. 1802, Joel Nichols, of Wilton.

4. **Batterson, Zachary,** [s. of Anthony?].

He m. Naomi ———.

Children, bapt. Redding:

> Hezekiah, bapt. 20 Nov. 1763.
> Mary, bapt. 26 May 1765.

5. **Batterson, William,** s. of James.

Bapt. 13 May 1744; d. at Ravenna, Ohio, in 1825 ae. 83 (a soldier of the Revolution; death so reported in newspaper issue of 25 July 1825).

He m. 16 Apr. 1764, Grissel Jacocks; dau. of William, b. 5 Apr. 1743.

He and wife Grissel lived 1823 in Portage County, Ohio.

Children, bapt. Westport:

> Ruhamah, b. 23 Oct. 1764 (family rec.), bapt. 17 Mar. 1765, d. 9 July 1845; m. 30 May 1792, Libbeus Sword.
> Zadoc, bapt. 18 Oct. 1767.
> Anna, bapt. 2 June 1770; m. 21 Aug. 1788, John Monroe.
> Molly, bapt. 5 July 1772; m. 13 Dec. 1795, Selleck Batterson.
> Rebecca, bapt. 30 Apr. 1775; m. 1 Aug. 1793, Ebenezer Baker.
> Samuel, bapt. 2 Nov. 1779.
> Lewis, bapt. 2 Nov. 1779.
> Rhoda, bapt. 30 June 1782.
> Grissel, bapt. 26 Sept. 1784.
> William, bapt. 3 Feb. 1788.

Batterson, James, Jr.

He m. 16 May 1754, Rachel Oysterbanks; dau. of Jacob.

Children, bapt. Westport:

> Patience, bapt. 2 Feb. 1755, d. 24 May 1799 ae. 45; m. 21 Feb. 1782, Samuel Brotherton.
> Joseph, bapt. 15 May 1757, d. in Otsego County, N. Y., 30 Apr. 1838; res. 1818, Bradford County, Pa.; m. at Orange, N. J., 25 Mar. 1781, Rebecca Dodd, b. 11 May 1762, living at Unadilla, N. Y., 1839.*

---

* Children, bapt. Westport: Rachel, bapt. 18 May 1783; Seymour, bapt. 25 Sept. 1785.

76   HISTORY AND GENEALOGY OF

Rachel, bapt. 31 Dec. 1758, d. 1 June 1760.
Tamason, d. 29 Nov. 1760.
James, bapt. 22 Feb. 1761; m. at Weston, 29 Nov. 1787, Nancy Williams, of Wilton, b. abt. 1770.
Tamason, bapt. 4 Apr. 1762; m. 15 Mar. 1787, Samuel Green. She res. 1832, Chemung, Tioga County, N. Y.
Abijah, b. 24 Oct., bapt. 27 Nov. 1763; res. 1832, Chemung, Tioga County, N. Y.
Rachel, bapt. 2 June 1765; m. 5 Sept. 1782, Daniel Brotherton.
? John, called "Jr."; d. at Westport, 17 Mar. 1831; m. 26 Oct. 1786, Sarah Allen; dau. of Ebenezer, bapt. 8 July 1770, d. 3 Oct. 1839.*

Batterson [Unplaced].

HEZEKIAH m. 24 Sept. 1764, Mary Sherwood. [Redding Church]
JEREMIAH m. 12 Nov. 1777, Betty Clugston. [Redding Church]
MARGARET d. 2 Dec. 1781. [Greens Farms Church]
MRS. killed by lightning, 16 July 1831. [Miss Treadwell's book]
MARY m. 8 May 1791, Lockwood Monroe. [Greens Farms Church]
SALOME m. 2 Nov. 1808, Aaron Smith. [Greens Farms Church]

Baxter [Unplaced].

DAVID m. 26 Apr. 1750, Rhoda Lyon.

Beach, (Rev.) John, s. of Isaac [Vol. I, p. 43].

Born at Stratford, 6 Oct. 1700, d. at Newtown, 19 Mar. 1782.
Grad. Yale Coll. 1721; Congregational minister at Newtown, 1724-32; ordained in Eng. 1732; Episcopal minister at Newtown and Redding, 1732-82.

He m. (1) Sarah Beach, dau. of Nathaniel, b. 12 Nov. 1699, d. 1 Aug. 1756 in 57 yr. (g. s.).

He m. (2) Abigail, widow of John Holbrook, and dau. of Abel Gunn.

Will 11 May 1772, proved 3 Apr. 1782; wife Abigail; son John, lands in Newtown; son Lazarus, lands in Redding; dau. Lucy Townsend; gr. son Abel Hill; my Congregations at Newtown and Redding, £10 for settling another minister.

---

* Children, bapt. Westport: Abraham, bapt. 30 Dec. 1787; Joseph, bapt. 23 Aug. 1789, m. 11 Mar. 1815, Salome Mills.

Children:

> Joseph, b. 26 Sept. 1727, d. y.
> Phebe, b. 1729, d. 9 May 1751 in 22 yr. (g. s.); m. 31 Oct. 1748, Daniel Hill.
> John, b. 1734, d. at Newtown, 15 May 1791 in 57 yr. (g. s.); m. Phebe Curtis, who d. 4 Dec. 1815 ae. 78 (g. s.).
> +Lazarus, b. abt. 1736.
> Hannah, b. abt. 1740, d. at Redding, 7 Jan. 1759 ae. 18 (g. s.).
> Lucy, b. 8 Oct. 1746; m. Rev. Townsend.

Beach, Lazarus, s. of John.

Born abt. 1736; d. at Redding, 20 Jan. 1800 in 64 yr. (g. s.); m. 20 June 1756, Lydia Sanford, b. 19 May 1738, d. 28 Nov. 1796 in 59 yr. (g. s.).

Imprisoned as a Tory, Jan. 1777; discharged on parole next month.

Will 11 May 1787, proved 13 Feb. 1800; wife Lydia; children, Lazarus, Lemuel, Sarah Sanford, Hannah Lyon, Eunice Beach Isaac, Abigail Beach.

Children, rec. Redding:

> Sarah, b. 27 Sept. 1758, d. 21 Nov. 1759 in 2 yr. (g. s.).
> Lazarus, b. 1 Dec. 1760, d. 28 June 1816; m. (1) Mary Morgan, dau. of James, b. abt. 1760, bur. 10 Nov. 1795 ae. 35 (Trinity Church rec.); m. (2) at Trinity Church, 19 Aug. 1797, Polly Hall.
> Lemuel, b. 31 Mar. 1763.
> Sarah, b. 19 Nov. 1764, d. 10 May 1828 ae. 63-5-21 (g. s.); m. 1780, James Sanford.
> Hannah, b. 14 Apr. 1767, d. at Redding, 25 Jan. 1814 ae. 47 (g. s.); m. Philo Lyon.
> Eunice, b. 23 Nov. 1769, d. 19 Sept. 1822; m. Jonathan Hull.
> Isaac, b. 19 May 1773, d. at Redding, 20 July 1822 ae. 49-2-1 (g. s.); m. (1) 7 Dec. 1794, Elizabeth Silliman, b. 11 Dec. 1769, d. 14 Feb. 1796 in 26 yr. (g. s.); m. (2) 26 Sept. 1797, Hannah Hill, b. 7 Jan. 1776, d. 30 Jan. 1846 ae. 71 (g. s.).*
> Abigail, b. 13 Sept. 1778, d. 17 Dec. 1837 ae. 59-3-4 (g. s.).

Beach [Unplaced].

> ELIZABETH m. 7 Jan. 1741/2, Benjamin Fairweather. [Fairfield Church]

---

* Children by second wife, rec. Redding: Betsey, b. 12 Nov. 1798; Lydia, b. 27 Feb. 1800; Charles, b. 27 Nov. 1801; Wyllys, b. 20 Aug. 1803.

RHODA m. 9 Dec. 1795, John Saltmarsh. [Weston rec.]
ANNE m. 2 Nov. 1783, Ezra Winton. [Weston rec.]
STEPHEN, of Vermont, m. 19 Oct. 1801, Anne Penfield, of Trumbull. [Fairfield Church]
MR. d. 18 Jan. 1809. [Miss Treadwell's book]
JOSEPH had: Molly, bapt. 15 Jan. 1764, m. 23 Apr. 1789, Philemon Jennings; Anne, bapt. 10 June 1764; Rebecca, bapt. 31 May 1767; Thomas, bapt. Feb. 1770. [Easton Church]
JEMIMA m. 20 Mar. 1771, James Rowell. [Easton Church]

Beadle, William, s. of Samuel.

Son of Samuel of Parish of Great Bursted, co. Essex, Eng.
He m. 15 Apr. 1770, Lydia Lothrop, dau. of Ansell of Plymouth, New England.

Child, rec. Fairfield:

Ansell-Lothrop, b. 2 Feb. 1771.

Beardsley, Benjamin.

Born 12 May 1739; son of Benjamin; d. at Easton, 9 Mar. 1827 in 88 yr. (g. s.); m. at Stratford, 2 June 1766, Elizabeth Hinman; dau. of Justus; b. 22 Jan. 1742; d. 24 Oct. 1821 in 80 yr. (g. s.).

Children, rec. Weston:*

Molly, b. 16 June 1768, d. 27 Apr. 1773.
Hannah, b. 15 Jan. 1770, d. 25 Dec. 1814 ae. 44 (g. s.).
Joseph, b. 2 Nov. 1771, d. 1 Mar. 1773.
Justus, b. 13 June 1773.
Betty, b. 6 May 1775; "Elizabeth" m. at Easton, Oct. 1792, Ezra Adams.
Joseph, b. 3 Feb. 1778, d. at Easton, 18 Dec. 1827 ae. 49-10-15 (g. s.); m. Eunice ———, who d. 1 Jan. 1878 ae. 87-11-12 (g. s.).
Benjamin, b. 3 Feb. 1778.
Sarah, b. 18 Dec. 1779.
Judson, b. 17 May 1782.

Beardsley, Jesse, s. of William.

He m. 26 Nov. 1760, Ruth Lyon, dau. of Daniel.
Will 16 July 1798, proved 5 Oct. 1799: wife Ruth; sons Daniel, Levi, Jabez, Jesse, Aaron, William; dau. Miriam.

---

* Recorded also at Stratford, with some differences of date.

Children, first rec. Fairfield:

> Daniel, b. 16 Oct. 1761.
> Levi.
> Jabez.*
> Jesse, d. at Redding in 1801. Adm'n granted, 31 Dec. 1801, to Ebenezer Mallory.
> Aaron.
> William, m. at Redding, 28 July 1798, Molly Sanford of Newtown.†
> Miriam.

Beardsley, Josiah.

He, of Greenfield, m. at Fairfield, 28 Jan. 1779, Abigail Bulkley; dau. of James, bapt. 14 Dec. 1760.

Rem. to Butternuts, Otsego County, N. Y.

Child, bapt. Fairfield:

> Daniel, bapt. 26 Mar. 1780.

Beardsley [Unplaced].

> ANN m. 6 Mar. 1787, Nehemiah Curtiss. [Weston rec.]
> MARY m. 4 July 1774, Samuel French. [Weston rec.]

Beaty, James.

Born abt. 1725; bur. 19 Sept. 1811 ae. 86 (Trinity Church rec.).
He m. (1) in 1748, Ruhamah Sturgis, who d. 9 Mar. 1797; and (2) Jan. 1798, Elizabeth Northrop of Ridgefield.

Will 26 Mar., proved 25 Nov. 1811; "late of Danbury, now residing in Fairfield"; sons James, Daniel; daus. Ruhama wife of Nathan Hawley, Caty widow of Nathaniel Selleck; four gr. children, Alfred, Nathan, Daniel, and Dennis, children of late dau. Sarah Dikeman dec'd.

Children [by first wife], rec. Danbury:

> James, b. 2 Sept. 1749; m. at Norwalk, 25 Jan. 1775, Peggy Whitney.
> Ann, b. 30 Aug. 1754, d. 12 Dec. 1751 [sic].

---

* Jabez Beardsley, Jr., b. 19 Feb. 1770, m. (rec. Weston) 18 Sept. 1791, Eunice Summers. Children: Abijah, b. 11 Oct. 1793; Nathan, b. 24 Jan. 1796; Sally, b. 2 Mar. 1798.

† Children, rec. Redding: Lois, b. 4 Apr. 1799; Lydia, b. 21 Nov. 1800; Jesse, b. 9 July 1802; Polly-Ann, b. 19 May 1804; Ruth, b. 16 Feb. 1806; William, b. 12 Feb. 1808; Aaron T., b. 8 Aug. 1809.

Ruhamah, b. 17 Oct. 1758; m. Nathan Hawley.
Catherine, b. 20 Jan. 1761; m. Nathaniel Selleck.
Daniel, b. 23 Aug. 1767.
Sarah, b. 23 Aug. 1767; m. at Danbury, 14 Dec. 1786, Daniel Dikeman.

Beden [*Unplaced*] (perhaps Bedient).

ELIZABETH m. 27 June 1776, Samuel Price.

Bedient [Vol. I, pp. 53, 54, 705].

1 Mordecai?
    2 Thomas (-1699) m. Mary Osborn.
      3 John (-).

3. Bedient John, s. of Thomas.

He m. 28 May 1723, Mary Morehouse; dau. of Thomas, 3d, bapt. 16 May 1702. They rem. to Wilton. John conveyed, 1758, to sons Adoniram and Azariah. He conveyed, 1759, to son Thomas of Norwalk. John, Jr., and Mordecai, conveyed 1761 to father John Bedient. John conveyed to son Gilead, 1763. Gilead of Norwalk conveyed to his father John, 1767. Azariah conveyed to father John, 1759.

Children, rec. and bapt. Fairfield:

Thomas, b. 11 Nov. 1724, bapt. 10 Dec. 1727, d. in 1760; adm'n granted, 2 Sept. 1760, to Azariah Bedient; m. at Greenfield, 30 May 1751, Susan ———.
Mary, b. 23 Feb. 1727, bapt. 10 Dec. 1727; m. 19 Apr. 1753, Abraham Betts, of Norwalk.
John, b. 4 June 1730 [1729], bapt. 22 June 1729.
Elizabeth, b. 30 Oct. 1731, bapt. 27 Feb. 1731/2; m. 14 Apr. 1757, Luke Guire.
4+Azariah, b. 9 Apr. 1734, bapt. 6 Apr. 1735.
Adoniram, b. 9 Apr. 1734, bapt. 6 Apr. 1735.
Mordecai, bapt. 25 July 1736, d. y.
5+Mordecai, b. 7 Oct. 1737, bapt. 15 Jan. 1737/8.
Eunice, b. 9 Mar. 1740, bapt. 27 July 1740.
Gilead, b. Jan. 1743 [1742], bapt. 24 Jan. 1741/2; m. at Wilton, 13 June 1770, Abigail Hurlbut.
Jesse, b. 13 Jan. 1745, bapt. 9 June 1745; m. at Wilton, 25 Nov. 1772, Sarah Whitney.

THE FAMILIES OF OLD FAIRFIELD 81

4. **Bedient, Azariah,** s. of John.

   Born 9 Apr. 1734.

   He m. 28 Mar. 1756, Phebe Hurlbut.

   Children, bapt. Greenfield:
   > Molly, bapt. 29 Jan. 1758.
   > Azariah, bapt. 1 July 1759 (premature birth).

5. **Bedient, Mordecai,** s. of John.

   Born 7 Oct. 1737.

   He m. at Fairfield, 26 Apr. 1761, Abigail Raymond.

   Children, bapt. at Wilton:*
   > Eleazer, bapt. 8 Apr. 1764, d. at Danbury, 16 Apr. 1827 ae. 63 (g. s.); m. Rachel ———, who d. 9 Feb. 1828 ae. 58 (g. s.).
   > Abigail, bapt. 23 Jan. 1766.
   > William, bapt. 1 July 1770.
   > Isaac, bapt. Oct. 1772; m. at Weston, 6 Jan. 1799, Hannah Bennett.
   > Samuel, bapt. 10 July 1774.
   > Ann, bapt. 1 June 1777.

Beebe [*Unplaced*].

> GIDEON m. 10 May 1769, Betty Sherwood. [Fairfield Church]
> GIDEON m. 23 Apr. 1772, Rebecca Gray. [Greens Farms Church]
> ANNA m. 26 Mar. 1803, Joseph Mills. [Greens Farms Church]

Beebe, Jonathan.

Son of Jonathan of East Haddam.

He m. Hannah Coley, dau. of Peter, bapt. 4 Aug. 1700.

In 1735, Peter Coley, Simon Coley, and Jonathan Beebe and Hannah his wife, all of Fairfield, sold land from our father Peter Coley. In 1771, Jonathan and Hannah were of East Haddam, and conveyed land from dec'd brother Ebenezer Coley.

Children, bapt. Fairfield:
> Jonathan, bapt. 4 Sept. 1726.
> David, bapt. 4 Sept. 1726.
> Samuel, bapt. 4 Sept. 1726.

---

* Was an older child that Mordecai, b. 1762/3, d. at Gilbertsville, Otsego County, N. Y., 12 Oct. 1855? See pension abstracts in Vol. III.

Hannah, bapt. 4 Sept. 1726.
Daniel, bapt. 17 Nov. 1728.
Rachel, bapt. 4 Apr. 1731.
Joshua, bapt. 16 Sept. 1733.
Elizabeth, bapt. 11 July 1736.

Beecher [Unplaced].

ELIZABETH [of New Haven] m. Nov. 1746, John Clinton. [Fairfield Rec.]

BEERS FAMILY (ANTHONY)

Beers [Vol. I, pp. 55-57].

1 Anthony (-1679) m. (1) ———; (2) Mary (———) Adams.
(By 1): 2 Ephraim (1648-   ) m. ———.
         3 *Ephraim* (-1759).

3. Beers, Ephraim, s. of Ephraim.

He d. at Westport, 15 June 1759; m. Susanna Meeker, dau. of John, bapt. 29 Mar. 1696.

He conveyed to his sons, land in Fairfield.

Adm'n granted, 12 Dec. 1759, to David and Daniel Beers. Distribution 17 Jan. 1760: Widow Susanna; Elizabeth Elou(?); Eunice Beers; Sarah Guire; Abigail Blackman; Deborah Monroe; the sons had rec'd their portions.

On 16 Jan. 1784, Ephraim, Nathan, Daniel, and Nehemiah Beers, and Abigail Blackman, of Fairfield, and Joseph and Deborah "Rowe" of Salem, Westchester County, N. Y., conveyed to Fanton Beers of Fairfield, right from late mother Susanna Beers' estate, mentioning deed of sisters Elisabeth Elis and Sarah Guire. Elizabeth Elis and Sarah Guire of Fairfield had conveyed to the others previously.

Children:

Elizabeth, m. ——— Elis.
Eunice.
Sarah, b. abt. 1719, bur. 5 May 1807 ae. 88 (Trinity Church rec.); m. 20 Apr. 1742, Ebenezer Guire.
4+Ephraim.

Abigail, d. in 1791; m. 18 Oct. 1746, Peter Blackman.
5+Nathan.
6+Daniel, b. abt. 1726.
Deborah, m. Joseph Monroe, of Salem, N. Y.
7+Nehemiah.

4. Beers, Ephraim, s. of Ephraim.

He m. 24 Dec. 1745, Mary Fanton, dau. of Jonathan, b. [say 1728], d. at Weston, abt. 1813.

Adm'n on estate of Mary of Weston was granted, 27 Sept. 1813, to Jared Beers, with Rowland Fanton as surety. Distribution to children 1814: Jonathan; Ephraim; Mary wife of James Fairchild, late of Newtown; Lois wife of Philo Fairchild; David; Ezra; Jared; Amy wife of James Piersons; Ellen wife of Thaddeus Bradley; Joseph; Zalmon Beers, son of Hezekiah dec'd; Levi and Eliphalet B., sons of Eliphalet dec'd.

Children, rec. Fairfield, five bapt. Westport, nine at Weston:

8+Jonathan, b. 22 Dec. 1746, bapt. 22 Feb. 1747.
9+Ephraim, b. 23 Dec. 1748, bapt. 19 Mar. 1749.
Mary, b. 16, bapt. 25 Aug. 1751; m. 23 June 1777, James Fairchild, of Newtown.
Hezekiah, b. 16, bapt. 21 Apr. 1754; m. ———.*
10+David, b. 27 Apr. 1757 [1756], bapt. 9 May 1756.
Lois, b. 12, bapt. 15 Jan. 1759; m. 12 June 1783, Philo Fairchild, of Newtown.
Ezra, b. 15, bapt. 28 Aug. 1761; m. 16 Sept. 1787, Lucretia Squire; prob. dau. of Thaddeus, bapt. 16 Feb. 1764. Children, bapt. Weston: Betsey, bapt 23 Nov. 1788; Laura, bapt. 4 July 1790; Ezra-Fitch, bapt. 9 June 1793.
Ellen, b. 11 Feb., bapt. 9 Apr. 1764; m. 12 June 1783, Thaddeus Bradley.
Eliphalet, bapt. 27 Apr. 1766, d. at Weston, 18 Aug. 1809; will 3 May, proved 4 Sept. 1809, gave estate to wife Anna for life, then to lawful heirs; m. 30 Sept. 1795, Anna Cable; dau. of Nehemiah, bapt. 11 May 1772. Eliphalet's realty was distributed, 14 Mar. 1825, to his two sons, Levi and Eliphalet B.
Jared, bapt. 8 Sept. 1768; m. 3 Apr. 1796, Sarah Parsons.
Sarah, bapt. 17 Jan. 1771.
Susannah, bapt. 17 Jan. 1771.
Amy [Ruamah], bapt. 19 Apr. 1772;† m. 20 Aug. 1795, James Parsons.

---
* A child, Zalmon, bapt. at Weston, 8 Mar. 1778.
† Demila Guire, dau. of Ruhamah Beers, bapt. at Weston, 13 Nov. 1791.

Joseph, bapt. 28 Nov. 1775; m. 19 Aug. 1798, Betty Morehouse, who d. 16 May 1856 ae. 76-4-5 (g. s.). A child Esther, b. 11 Mar. 1799 (Weston rec.).

5. Beers, Nathan, s. of Ephraim.

He d. at Weston, 1795/6.

He m. 16 Jan. 1749/50, Ann Burr, dau. of Peter, bapt. 10 Apr. 1726.

Will 24 Aug. 1795, proved 17 Jan. 1796; wife Ann; five children, Pinkney, Esther, Abigail, Anna, Elizabeth; son-in-law Daniel Rowland.

Children, rec. Fairfield, bapt. Westport:

> Pinkney, b. 8, bapt. 17 Nov. 1751, d. at Weston, in 1841; will 25 Sept. 1830, proved 11 Aug. 1841, named wife Eunice and son Humphrey; m. at Weston, 19 Nov. 1778, Eunice Ogden; dau. of Humphrey, b. 28 Dec. 1756.*
> Esther, b. 24 Apr., bapt. 6 May 1753; m. 21 Oct. 1772, Daniel Rowland.
> Abigail, b. 20, bapt. 29 Dec. 1754, d. 3 Mar. 1847 ae. 94 (g. s.); m. (1) 8 June 1780, Seth Meeker, Jr.; m. (2) 25 Dec. 1796, David Jennings.
> Ann, b. 17, bapt. 21 Nov. 1756; ? m. at Greenfield, 27 Jan. 1777, David Goodsell.
> Elizabeth, bapt. 11 May 1766.

6. Beers, Daniel, s. of Ephraim.

Born abt. 1726; d. at Salem, Westchester County, N. Y., 1 Apr. 1801 ae. 75.

He m. 3 Sept. 1760, Abigail Dikeman, dau. of Cornelius.

Daniel of Norwalk conveyed, 1774, to Nehemiah Beers of Fairfield, land undivided between me and my brother, which our father gave us by gift.

Daniel and Abigail Beers of Salem, Westchester County, N. Y., conveyed land in Fairfield, 1784.

---

* Child, bapt. Westport: Anne, bapt. 11 June 1780; prob. m. 25 Apr. 1804, Joseph Rowland, and d. at Weston, 8 Nov. 1809 ae. 29 (g. s.). Children, bapt. Weston: Nathan, bapt. 31 Oct. 1784; m. 19 Jan. 1806, Rachel Smith. Aaron, bapt. 22 Mar. 1789. Humphrey, bapt. 4 Mar. 1792.

Children, rec. Fairfield, bapt. Westport:

Huldah, b. 12 Sept., bapt. 1 Nov. 1761.
Rebecca, bapt. 17 Oct. 1762.
Ann, bapt. 8 Apr. 1764.
Daniel, bapt. 15 Feb. 1766.
Edmund, bapt. 3 July 1768.
Abigail, bapt. 8 Apr. 1770.
Elias, bapt. 26 June 1774.
Silas, bapt. 15 June 1777.
Cornelius-Dikeman, bapt. 22 Aug. 1779.
Mary, bapt. 27 May 1781.

7. **Beers, Nehemiah,** s. of Ephraim.

He d. at Weston in 1793.

He m. 27 June 1753, Eunice Fanton; dau. of Jonathan, b. [say 1735], d. after 1793.

Will 18 May 1793, proved 7 Jan. 1794; wife Eunice; four sons, Fanton, Isaac, Uriah, Nehemiah; five daus. Sarah, Rhoda, Zillah, Hannah, Rachel. Uriah was appointed guardian of Nehemiah, 1795.

Children, rec. Fairfield, first bapt. Westport, others at Weston:

Sarah, b. 3 Feb., bapt. 5 May 1754, d. at Weston, 10 Jan. 1817 ae. 63 (g. s.); m. 19 May 1777, David Bulkley.
Fanton, b. 11 Jan. 1756; m. Sarah ———, b. abt. 1760.*
Isaac, b. 20 Feb., bapt. 16 Apr. 1758; m. 16 Apr. 1786, Rhuhamah Fountain [Fanton]; dau. of Gershom, bapt. 13 Apr. 1760.†
Eunice, b. 15 Apr. 1760, d. 22 June 1781.
Rhoda, b. 27 Apr., bapt. 5 June 1762.
Uriah, b. 20 July, bapt. 11 Sept. 1764; m. (1) in 1798, Charry-Ann Goodsell; dau. of John; m. (2) 19 Feb. 1801, Clara Andrews, of Wilton.
Zillah, b. 23 Oct. 1766, bapt. 15 Feb. 1767.
Hannah, b. 24 Feb., bapt. 7 May 1769; ? m. 22 May 1797, Jabez Gorham.

---

* Child, bapt. Westport: Hezekiah, bapt. 14 Sept. 1783, d. at Redding, 14 July 1855 ae. 72 (g. s.); m. 27 Mar. 1806, Lucy Lockwood, who d. 19 Sept. 1859 ae. 72 yrs. 7 mos. (g. s.). Children, bapt. Weston: Jerusha, bapt. 19 Mar. 1786, m. 20 Apr. 1806, Hezekiah Cole; Philo-Fairchild, bapt. 18 Nov. 1787; Molly, bapt. 23 May 1790; Benjamin, bapt. 3 June 1792; Sarah, bapt. 1 Oct. 1797; Eunice, bapt. 7 July 1799; Betsey, bapt. 4 Oct. 1801.

† Children, rec. Weston: Isaac, b. 21 Sept. 1787; Jane, b. 1 Nov. 1790, bapt. 8 May 1791; Anne, b. 20 June 1795, bapt. 25 Oct. 1795; Lewis, b. 20 Mar. 1798, bapt. 23 May 1798; Lyman, bapt. 9 Jan. 1800; Kate, bapt. 27 June 1802.

Nehemiah, b. 23 Dec. 1771, bapt. 24 May 1772, d. 13 Mar. 1775.
Rachel, b. 12 Aug., bapt. 18 Oct. 1778, d. at Weston, 12 Mar. 1859 ae. 80 yrs. 6 mos. (g. s.); m. at Weston, 8 Apr. 1800, Reuel Sherwood.
Nehemiah, b. 11 July 1781, bapt. 6 Jan. 1782.

8. Beers, Jonathan, s. of Ephraim, 2d.

Born 22 Dec. 1746; d. at Weston, 23 Sept. 1814 (Miss Treadwell's book); m. at Westport, 20 Sept. 1772, Olive Calhoun; dau. of Nathaniel, bapt. 22 Apr. 1753, d. 12 Aug. 1820 (Miss Treadwell's book).

Will 9 Sept., proved 21 Nov. 1814; wife Olive; son Jonathan, Jr., daus. Eunice, Abigail, Urania, Clara, Mary, Lydia, and Olive had had their "setting out"; daus. Nancy and Marinda left to their mother's care, "trusting that she will do justice by them."

Olive's will, 29 May, proved 22 Sept. 1820; son Jonathan; gr. dau. Miranda wife of Walter Treadwell; gr. son Dimon French, son of John French, Jr.; residue equally to children.

Children, bapt. Weston:

Eunice, bapt 28 Mar. 1773; m. 9 June 1799, Samuel Lord.
Abigail, bapt. 19 Feb. 1775.
Urana, bapt. 9 Feb. 1777, d. 6 July 1867 ae. 91 (g. s.); m. 21 Dec. 1796, Aaron Dimon.
Clara, bapt. 9 May 1779; m. 31 Oct. 1802, Pinkney Dimon.
Mary, bapt. 18 Mar. 1781, d. y.
Mary, bapt. 3 Aug. 1782.
Lydia, bapt. 31 Oct. 1784.
Olive, bapt. 26 Aug. 1787.
Jonathan, bapt. 26 Apr. 1789.
Lucinda, bapt. 9 June 1793, d. y.
Nancy, bapt. 2 Oct. 1796.
Miranda, bapt. 27 Dec. 1797.

9. Beers, Ephraim, s. of Ephraim.

Born 23 Dec. 1748.
He m. at Greenfield, 21 Feb. 1769, Abigail Thorp.

Children, bapt. Weston:

Salome, bapt. 17 June 1769.
Abel, bapt. 19 May 1771.
Hezekiah, bapt. 19 Feb. 1775.
Betsey, bapt. 8 June 1777.

Ephraim, bapt. 10 Oct. 1779.
Abigail, bapt. 19 May 1782.
David, bapt. 1 Aug. 1784.
Lois, bapt. 17 Sept. 1786.
Jonathan, bapt. 9 Oct. 1788.

10. Beers, David, s. of Ephraim.

Born 27 Apr. 1756; d. 11 July 1838 (Pension rec.).

He m. (1) Eunice Burr, dau. of Ephraim, bapt. 1 July 1764, d. 16 June 1791.

He m. (2) at Westport, 18 Jan. 1792, Molly Ogden; dau. of Ebenezer, bapt. 6 June 1773, living 1855.

He lived in Redding, 1818; his widow was of Wilton, 1838.

Children [by first wife], bapt. Westport:

Ephraim-Burr, bapt. 7 May 1786.
Wakeman, bapt. 22 June 1788.
Wilson, bapt. 19 Sept. 1790, d. 13 June 1791.

Children [by second wife]:

Polly, bapt. 14 July 1793.
David, bapt. 10 May 1795.
Hezekiah, bapt. 3 June 1798.
Ellen, bapt. 26 Oct. 1800.
Bradley, bapt. 27 Feb. 1805, d. [28 Feb.?] 1807 ae. 3.
Eunice, bapt. 21 Jan. 1807.
Areta, b. abt. 1809.
A daughter.

BEERS FAMILY (JAMES)

Beers [Vol. I, pp. 57-59].

```
1 James (    -1694) m. Martha Barlow.
  2 James (    -1691) m. ———.
     Only daus. survived.
  3 Joseph (    -1696) m. Abigail Norton.
     4 Joseph (1689-    ).
     5 James (1694-1772).
```

4. Beers, Joseph, s. of Joseph.

Born 18 Mar. 1688/9.

He m. 1 Mar. 1711, Hannah Whitlock, b. abt. 1685, d. 10 Mar. 1771 in 86 yr. (Perry Diary).

He conveyed for love to his son David in 1769.

Children, rec. and bapt. Fairfield:

6+Joseph, b. 19 Dec. 1711, bapt. 2 Mar. 1711/2.
Sarah, b. 12 Nov. 1714, bapt. 9 Jan. 1714/5; perhaps m. David Bulkley.
7+David, b. 27 Apr., bapt. 9 June 1717.
Abigail, b. 11 Oct. 1721, bapt. 28 Jan. 1721/2; m. 10 Nov. 1743, Abraham Pulling.

5. **Beers, James,** s. of Joseph. Ens., 2d Co., Fairfield, May 1741; Lt., May 1745.

Bapt. 21 Oct. 1694; Lt. James d. at Fairfield, 29 Apr. 1772 in 79 yr. (g. s.); m. (1) 20 Jan. 1716, Hannah Rumsey, dau. of Isaac, bapt. 30 Aug. 1696, d. 17 Mar. [1724?]; m. (2) 5 Aug. 1725, Olive Bulkley, dau. of John, bapt. 30 Aug. 1696, d. 5 Oct. 1774.

Will 14 Jan. 1771, proved 11 May 1772; wife Olive; daus. Mary, Hannah, Abigail; sons Samuel, Nathan, James. Distribution 18 Mar. 1773: Mary wife of Daniel Sturgis, Hannah wife of Nathan. Persons, Abigail wife of James Hall, Samuel, James, and Nathan.

Children by first wife, rec. and bapt. Fairfield:

8+Samuel, b. 2, bapt. 8 June 1718.
Mary, b. 29 Nov., bapt. 2 Dec. 1722, d. in 1811; m. (1) 5 Nov. 1741, Daniel Sturges; m. (2) 9 July 1775, John Burr.

Children by second wife, rec. and bapt. Fairfield:

Hannah, b. 8, bapt. 12 June 1726, d. 8 Mar. 1794 (Perry Diary); m. 14 Oct. 1746, Nathaniel Pierson [Parsons].
9+James, b. 4, bapt. 7 July 1728.
Abigail, b. 2, bapt. 4 Apr. 1731; m. 3 Apr. 1755, James Hall.
10+Nathan, b. 6, bapt. 20 Oct. 1734.

6. **Beers, Joseph,** s. of Joseph, 2d.

Born 19 Dec. 1711; d. 6 June 1795 (Perry Diary), bur. 7 June 1795 ae. 83 (Trinity Church).

He m. 21 Sept. 1738, Elizabeth Livesay; dau. of James and Eunice of Stratford, b. 31 Mar. 1715; bur. 6 July 1798 ae. 84 (Trinity Church).

Adm'n granted, 5 Aug. 1795, to Reuben Beers.

Children, rec. Fairfield:

11+Reuben, b. 21 Nov. 1739.
Sarah, b. 19 Sept. 1743.
Isabel, b. 14 July 1745, d. at Fairfield, 16 Mar. 1836 ae. 91 (g. s.); m. 17 Dec. 1769, Ansel Trubee.
Abigail, b. 24 Apr. 1747; m. 25 Dec. 1771, Josiah Bulkley.
Elizabeth, b. 28 Apr. 1752; m. 26 Jan. 1775, Nicholas Darrow.
Joseph, b. 28 May 1754, d. at Fairfield, 3 Apr. 1826 ae. abt. 70; m. 2 Feb. 1786, Mary Buddington; "wife of Joseph" d. between Aug. and Nov. 1811 (Episcopalian; recorded Fairfield Church).*

7. Beers, David, s. of Joseph, 2d.

Born 27 Apr. 1717; d. at Fairfield, 9 May 1808 in 92 yr. (g. s.).

He m. 10 Nov. 1743, Mary Livesay, doubtless dau. of James and Eunice of Stratford. David Beers' wife d. 23 Aug. 1785 (Perry Diary).

In 1793, David Beers conveyed to David, Jr., Aaron and Jonathan Beers.

Children, rec. Fairfield:

Eunice, b. 14 Aug. 1744, d. at Greenfield, 29 Nov. 1843 in 100 yr. (g. s.); m. 24 Dec. 1767, Hezekiah Price, of Greenfield.
12+David, b. 17 Mar. 1746.
Abel, b. 18 May 1748.
Aaron, b. 14 Aug. 1750, d. 11 June 1813 ae. 63 (g. s.). Adm'n granted, 23 June 1814, to David Beers, with Hezekiah Nichols as surety.
Mary, b. 9 July 1754, d. at Fairfield, 2 Jan. 1845 in 91 yr. (g. s.); m. (1) 20 Jan. 1773, Elihu Alvord; m. (2) 15 June 1785, Joseph Perry.
Jonathan, b. abt. 1759, d. 7 June 1813 ae. 54 (g. s.). Adm'n granted, 8 June 1814, to David Beers, with Edmund Burr as surety.

8. Beers, Samuel, s. of James.

Born 2 June 1718; d. at Fairfield, 11 Mar. 1793 ae. 74 yrs. 9 mos. 19 days (g. s.).

He m. 10 Nov. 1743, Thankful Osborn, dau. of John, bapt. 2 May 1725, d. 13 Apr. 1812 ae. 87 (g. s.).

---

* Hannah and Walter, children of Joseph, bapt. at Trinity Church, 13 Jan. 1807.

Will 24 June 1790, proved 15 Apr. 1793; wife Thankful; son Samuel; dau. Mary. In 1795, Samuel Beers, David Osborn and Mary his wife, and Thankful Beers, conveyed together.

Children, rec. and bapt. Fairfield:

13+Samuel, b. 4, bapt. 9 Sept. 1744.
 Mary, b. 15, bapt. 17 July 1748, d. at Fairfield, 13 Mar. 1814 ae. 66 (g. s.); m. 11 July 1771, David Osborn.
 Daniel, b. and bapt. 22 July 1753, d. 31 Oct. 1777 ae. 23 yrs. 3 mos. 9 days (g. s.).

9. Beers, James, s. of James.

Born 4 July 1728; d. at New Milford in 1796.

He m. at Westport, 18 Mar. 1756, Hannah Burr; dau. of Peter, bapt. Dec. 1731.

Will 4 Sept. 1787, proved 15 June 1796; wife Hannah; sons James, Ezra; daus. Distribution 20 Jan. 1798: Ezra; Esther wife of Thomas Brooks; Olive wife of Ira Cannon; Abigail wife of Czar Stevens.

Children, bapt. Fairfield:

Ebenezer, bapt. 16 Jan. 1757, d. y.
James, bapt. 5 Aug. 1759, d. at New Milford in 1790; will 15 Jan. 1790, proved 7 Sept. 1790, named: wife Abiah; bro. Ezra; sisters Olive, Abigail, Esther. His widow Abiah m. 28 Sept. 1791, Samuel Stevens.
Hezekiah, bapt. 9 Nov. 1760, d. y.
Ezra, bapt. 14 Apr. 1765.
Esther, bapt. 14 Apr. 1765; m. Thomas Brooks.
Burr, bapt. 4 Oct. 1767, d. y.
Olive, bapt. at New Milford, 4 Aug. 1771; m. 10 Oct. 1793, Ira Cannon, of Lee, Mass.
Abigail, m. 10 Oct. 1793, Czar Stevens, of Lee, Mass.

10. Beers, Nathan, s. of James.

Born 6 Oct. 1734; d. at Fairfield, 22 Jan. 1813 ae. 78 (g. s.).

He m. 22 July 1756, Widow Abigail Squire. She was dau. of Joseph Osborn, and widow of Daniel Squire. She d. 12 Sept. 1815 ae. 90 (g. s.).

Will 24 Nov. 1812, proved 1 Feb. 1813; wife Abigail; son Nathan, Jr.; dau. Esther Oysterbanks. Distribution 5 Dec. 1815: son Nathan; dau. Esther wife of Ezekiel O. Banks.

Will of Abigail, widow of Nathan, 20 Feb. 1813, proved 13 Nov. 1815; gr. daus. Abigail Beers and Priscilla Beers, daus. of son Nathan Beers; sons Nathan Beers and Daniel Squire.

Children, rec. Fairfield and Greenfield:
14+Nathan, b. 3 June 1757.
    Esther, b. 25 [June 1763?], bapt. 3 July 1763, d. at Greenfield, 13 Oct. 1822 ae. 69 [60?] (g. s.); m. 20 June 1782, Ezekiel Oysterbanks.

11. Beers, Reuben, s. of Joseph.

Born 21 Nov. 1739; bur. 23 July 1806 ae. 66 (Trinity Church).

He m. (1) at Greenfield, 21 Oct. 1765, Eleanor Banks; dau. of John, b. 14 Oct. 1743.

He m. (2) by 1779, Mary, widow of Benjamin Osborn, and dau. of Ebenezer Dimon, bapt. 26 June 1737, d. in 1816; unless she was the Widow Beers who d. 28 June 1815 ae. 80.

Distribution 31 Oct. 1807: widow; eldest son Reuben; son Gershom; son David D.; dau. Clarina.

Will of Mary, 21 June 1804, proved 27 June 1816; husband Reuben Beers; son David Dimon Beers; children of son Samuel* dec'd,—Benjamin, Seth, Samuel, James-Stuart. Witnesses: (Capt.) David Beers, Jr., Aaron Beers, Jonathan Beers.

Children [by first wife]:
    Reuben.
    Gershom, b. abt. 1771, d. at Richmond, Va., 7 Aug. 1832; m. 10 Nov. 1793, Sarah White, dau. of Jacob; "wife of Gershom" d. 29 Sept. 1813.†
    Clarina.‡

Child [by second wife]:
    David-Dimon.§

12. Beers, David, s. of David.

Born 17 Mar. 1746; Capt. David d. 3 May 1826 ae. 81 (g. s.); m. at Trinity Church, 20 Sept. 1789, Mary Gray; dau. of Elisha, bapt. 30 Dec. 1768, d. at Southport, 8 Sept. 1851 ae. 82 (g. s.).

---

* Samuel Osborn.

† Children, bapt. Trinity Church: Jonathan-White, bapt. 1 Mar. 1795; Sally, bapt. 17 July 1796; Elizabeth, bapt. 4 Aug. 1799; William, bapt. 14 Feb. 1802; Susannah and Mary, bapt. 24 Oct. 1812.

‡ Clara Beers, d. Jan. 1841 ae. abt. 70 (Fairfield Church rec.).

§ David D. had children, bapt. Trinity Church: Munson-Hoyt, Sally-Osborn, and Dimon, bapt. 22 Feb. 1809.

Will 9 Feb. 1814, proved 7 July 1826; wife Mary; my children (son Abel and dau. Mary mentioned).

Distribution 9 May 1827: Widow; son Abel; dau. Mary wife of Than[1] P. Beers; dau. Sarah wife of Nehemiah Bulkley; son Sturges; son Isaac; dau. Eunice Beers; dau. Abigail Beers; son David.

Children, bapt. Trinity Church:*

>Abel, b. [19 Jan. 1790], d. at Southport, 10 Mar. 1874 ae. 94-1-18 (g. s.); sea capt.; m. (1) 24 Dec. 1808, Elizabeth Whitney, b. 21 June 1789, d. 21 June 1828; m. (2) Lucretia Dimon, b. [18 Apr. 1796], d. 4 July 1873 ae. 77-2-16 (g. s.).
>Mary, b. abt. 1791, d. at Southport, 2 Sept. 1864 ae. 73; m. Nathaniel-Perry Beers.
>Sarah, b. 18 Jan. 1794, d. 28 Mar. 1867 ae. 73-2-10 (g. s.); m. Nehemiah-Beers Bulkley.
>Sturges, b. [Aug. 1796], d. at Southport, 27 Oct. 1877 ae. 81 yrs. 2 mos. (g. s.); m. ———, who d. 11 Sept. 1877 ae. 72 yrs. 6 mos. (g. s.).
>Eunice.
>Isaac.
>Abigail.
>David.

13. **Beers, Samuel,** s. of Samuel. Ens., 4th Co., 4th Regt., May 1779.

Born 4 Sept. 1744; Capt. Samuel d. 1 Sept. 1813 ae. 69 (g. s.).

He m. at Greenfield, 12 Feb. 1766, Sarah Perry; prob. dau. of Samuel, b. abt. 1747.

She m. (2) at Trinity Church, 23 Mar. 1817, Capt. Andrew Bulkley, and d. 5 Aug. 1828 ae. 81 (g. s.).

Will 7 Aug., proved 17 Sept. 1813; wife Sarah; four sons, Noah, Abel, Stephen, and Samuel, Jr., of whom the last received the homestead.

Children, bapt. Fairfield:

>Noah, bapt. 30 Nov. 1766; ? m. 10 Mar. 1785, Elizabeth Lewis.†
>Abel, bapt. 23 July 1769; m. Elizabeth ———.‡

---

* The first six children were bapt. together, 13 Jan. 1807.

† Child, bapt. Westport: Daniel, bapt. 15 Apr. 1787. Child, bapt. Fairfield: Ebenezer, bapt. 31 May 1789.

‡ Children, bapt. Fairfield: William, bapt. 11 Oct. 1795; Deborah, bapt. 4 Mar. 1798; Ebenezer, bapt. 2 Nov. 1800; Elizabeth, bapt. 7 Nov. 1802; Aretie, bapt. 18 Nov. 1804.

Ebenezer, b. 7 Oct. 1771 (Perry Diary), bapt. 10 Nov. 1771, d. 8 Apr. 1772.
Stephen, bapt. 4 June 1775; m. 21 Dec. 1796, Lydia Hobart; dau. of Justin, b. 12 Mar. 1774.*
Samuel, bapt. 29 Oct. 1780, d. at Fairfield, 1 Aug. 1832 ae. 52 (g. s.); m. Hannah ———.† Adm'n on Samuel's estate granted, 25 Aug. 1832, to Hannah Beers and Charles Thorp of Fairfield, Henry T. Beers of New York surety; estate insolvent; dower set to widow Hannah.

14. **Beers, Nathan,** s. of Nathan.

Born 3 June 1757; d. at Fairfield, 15 Dec. 1835 ae. 78 (g. s.).

He m. 27 Nov. 1777, Mehitabel Perry; b. 26 Mar. 1753 (Bible rec.), d. 9 May 1824 ae. 71 yrs. 1 mo. 13 days (g. s.).

Will 16 July 1835, proved 11 Jan. 1836; dau. Abigail Perry; dau. Polly wife of David Perry; dau. Priscilla wife of Ebenezer Osborn; four sons, Ebenezer, Nathaniel P., Nathan, James.

Children, bapt. Fairfield:
Priscilla, bapt. 31 Jan. 1779, d. at Southport, 31 Dec. 1848 ae. 69 (g. s.); m. Ebenezer Osborn.
Ebenezer, bapt. 9 July 1780, d. at Westport, 26 June 1868 ae. 83 [88?] (g. s.); m. at Westport, 15 Feb. 1803, Clarina Burr; dau. of Talcott, b. 6 June (g. s.), bapt. 28 July 1782.
Abigail, bapt. 3 Nov. 1782, d. 20 Nov. 1841 ae. 50 (60?) (g. s.); m. 15 Aug. 1813, Joseph Perry.
Nathan, bapt. 24 Oct. 1784.
Polly, bapt. 25 Mar. 1787, d. 29 Aug. 1849 ae. 62 (g. s.); m. 15 Jan. 1810, David Perry.
Nathaniel-Perry, bapt. 6 July 1788, d. at Southport, 5 July 1868 ae. 80 (g. s.); m. Mary Beers, dau. of David, b. abt. 1791, d. 2 Sept. 1864 ae. 73 (g. s.).
James, b. 17 Apr., bapt. 29 May 1791; m. 18 Dec. 1812, Maria Sturges, b. 28 June 1794, d. 2 Mar. 1840.

Beers [*Unplaced*].

SARAH, wife of Nathan, d. 12 Sept. 1796. [Greens Farms Church]
SARAH m. 5 Aug. 1790, Hezekiah Andrews. [Weston Church]
GERSHOM m. 13 Nov. 1783, Mary Parsons. Children: Cyrus, b. 13 June 1784; Eli, b. 12 Apr. 1789; Simeon, b. 1 July 1792; Eunice, b. 15 Feb. 1796; Asenath, b. 3 Mar. 1798. [Redding rec.]
ABIGAIL m. 26 Feb. 1797, Levi Fanton. [Redding rec.]

---
* Children, bapt. Fairfield: George-Hobart, bapt. 14 Jan. 1798; Sarah, bapt. 21 July 1799; John-Sloss. bapt. 5 July 1801; Mary, bapt. 13 May 1804.

† Children, bapt. Fairfield: Paulina, bapt. 18 Oct. 1801; Almira, bapt. 21 Aug. 1803.

Rachel m. 4 Mar. 1787, Joseph Fairweather. [Weston rec.]
James m. Feb. 1780, Eunice Waterbury. [Weston Church]
Sally m. 16 May 1800, Jared Partrick. [Weston Church]
Isaac, b. abt. 1762, d. at Easton, 9 Oct. 1829 ae. 67 (g. s.); m. 2 Mar. 1794, Jemima ———, who d. 17 June 1832 ae. 56 (g. s.). Children, rec. Weston: William, b. 13 Dec. 1795; Burton-Mills, b. 15 Oct. 1796; Oliver, b. 7 Mar. 1799.
Lucy, of Stratford, m. 4 Oct. 1781, George Smith, of Smithfield, L. I. [Greens Farms Church]
William-Pitt, son of Samuel and Sarah (Wetmore), b. at Stratford, 12 Apr. 1766; grad. Yale Coll. 1785; lawyer, of Albany, N. Y.; Clerk of City and County of Albany, 1810; d. at Fairfield, 13 Sept. 1810 ae. 44 (g. s.); m. at Fairfield, 9 June 1793, Anna Sturges; dau. of Jonathan, bapt. 14 Apr. 1765.
John-Benjamin m. 3 Feb. 1793, Harriet Hurd. Children, rec. Weston: Roswell-Newton, b. 20 Nov. 1793; Betsey-Antoinette, b. 16 Jan. 1796; Polly-Ann, b. 4 Dec. 1797.
John had a child who d. 3 Jan. 1789. [Greens Farms Church; possibly the surname should be Barnes instead of Beers.]
Anne m. 5 Jan. 1798, Nehemiah Turrell.
Sherwood m. 3 Dec. 1791, Rachel Burr. [Easton Church]
David, of Stratford, m. 12 Oct. 1783, Hannah Porter. Children, rec. Weston: Lois, b. 27 Apr. 1784; Ephraim, b. 3 Feb. 1786; Elijah, b. 3 July 1788; Benjamin, b. 3 June 1790; Ruth, b. 29 Jan. 1794.
Widow Eleanor had child, Samuel, bapt. 20 Oct. 1793. Mary, dau. of Eleanor, bapt. 30 Dec. 1792.* [Greens Farms Church]
Mary bur. 11 Aug. 1811 ae. 55. [Trinity Church rec.]
Sarah bur. 1 Oct. 1813 ae. 44. [Trinity Church rec.]
Sarah m. Jan. 1792, Silvester Booth. [Easton Church]

Belden [*Unplaced*].

Eunice m. 4 Mar. 1784, Zalmon Hull. [Redding rec.]

Bell, John.

He m. 10 June 1736, Elizabeth Hide, dau. of John.
Of Fairfield, conveyed 1783.
John Bell d. 22 Jan. 1790 (Perry Diary); Old Mrs. Bell d. 6 May 1789 ae. 96 (Perry Diary).

Benedict, Jesse.

He m. (1) at Redding, 25 Dec. 1777, Molly Ward; called Polly, she d. at Fairfield, 3 May 1808 in 54 yr. (g. s.).

---

* This entry *may* be Eleanor *Burr* instead of *Beers*.

He m. (2) Huldah ———.

Of Fairfield, will 7 Mar., proved 14 Nov. 1815; residue equally to wife Huldah, son Aaron-Jackson, and my natural son Jesse Wheeler; sister Deborah Wildman; nephew Ward Benedict, son of bro. Peter; Jesse Benedict, son of bro. Elihu.

Children [by first wife]:

>   Samuel-Ward, b. [8 June 1778], bapt. 23 Aug. 1778, d. at Fairfield, 12 Jan. 1796 ae. 17-7-4 (g. s.).
>   Polly, b. abt. 1781, d. at Fairfield, 22 Jan. 1802 in 20 yr. (g. s.).
>   Jesse, b. abt. 1784, bapt. 25 Sept. 1795, d. at Fairfield, 27 Sept. 1795 ae. 11 (g. s.).

Child [by second wife]:

>   Aaron-Jackson.

Benedict, Thaddeus. Justice, 1783, 1784, 1790, 1794, and 1795; Representative for Redding to Conn. Leg., May 1783, May 1784, May and Oct. 1790, May and Oct. 1794, and May 1795. Town Clerk, Redding.

Son of Thaddeus and Abigail (Starr), b. at Danbury, 14 Apr. 1749, d. at Redding, 6 Oct. 1799 [but bur. 7 Sept. 1799 ae. 50 by Trinity Church rec.].

He m. at Redding, 12 July 1775, Deborah Read; dau. of John, b. 5 Apr. 1756.

Grad. from Yale Coll. 1773; lawyer, of Redding and Bridgeport; probate clerk, 1776; selectman, 1777.

Children, rec. and bapt. Redding:

>   Sarah, b. 13 Mar., bapt. 5 May 1776, d. at Danbury, 1836, unmarried.
>   William, b. 14 Feb. 1778, "Billy" bapt. 12 Apr. 1778, d. at Bridgeport, 1819, unmarried; grad. Yale Coll. 1797.
>   Hiram, b. 21 Nov. 1779, bapt. 26 Mar. 1780; m. ———.
>   Charles, b. 22 Aug. 1783, d. at Danbury, 1828; m. 1803, Triphene Husted, b. 1784, d. 1842.
>   Henry, b. 8 July 1785, d. before 1819, unmarried.
>   Thaddeus, b. 29 July 1791.

Benedict [*Unplaced*].

>   EZRA m. 2 Nov. 1775, Mabel Morehouse. [Weston Church]
>   ABIJAH [later of Pompey, N. Y.] m. 17 Jan. 1781, Amelia Bulkley. [Family rec.]

ELIHU m. Martha Burr, dau. of Nathan, bapt. 25 June 1775.
WILLIAM m. 20 Feb. 1782, Nancy Fitch, of Norwalk. [Greens Farms Church]
DANIEL m. 16 Mar. 1786, Rebecca Meeker. Children: Michael, b. 14 Feb. 1787; Sarah, b. 20 Mar. 1789, d. 27 Mar. 1794; Betty, b. 6 Mar. 1791; Jared-Meeker, b. 22 Mar. 1795; Mabel, b. 13 Nov. 1798. [Redding rec.]

BENNETT (FAIRFIELD FAMILY)

Bennett [Vol. I, pp. 65-74].

1 James (-1659) m. Hannah Wheeler.
  2 Thomas (1642-1704) m. Elizabeth Thompson.
    5 Thomas (1665-   ) m. Sarah Hubbard.
      14 *Deliverance* (1688-1761).
      15 *Thomas* (1693-1781).
    6 John (1670-1713) m. Phebe ———.
      16 *Edmund* (1696-1754).
    7 James (1675-1725) m. Deborah Adams.
      [Ridgefield branch.]
    8 Peter (1685-   ) m. Elizabeth Rowland.
      [New Fairfield branch.]
  3 James (1645-1736) m. (1) ——— Joy; (2) Mary (Osborn) Booth; (3) Rebecca ———.
(By 1): 9 James (1668-1707) m. Sarah Lewis.
      17 *James* (1694-1750).
      18 *Stephen* (1702-1739).
    10 Thomas (1669-1739) m. Mary Booth.
      [Newtown branch.]
    11 Joseph (-before 1736) m. Elizabeth Whidden.
      [Hanover, N. J., branch.]
    12 Isaac (1685-after 1762) m. (1) Martha ———; (2) Sarah ———.
(By 1): 19 *William* (1708-1788).
      20 *Isaac* (1711-1791).
(By 2): 13 Jeremiah (1696-1773).
  4 John (1648-   ) m. Mary Thompson.
    [Fairfield, N. J., branch.]

14. Bennett, Deliverance, s. of Thomas.

Born 25 Dec. 1688; d. at Westport, 18 Apr. 1761 ae. 72 yrs. 3 mos. 13 days (g. s.); m. 5 Mar. 1708, Mary Bigg; b. abt. Oct. 1688, d. 14 Apr. 1761 ae. 72 yrs. and abt. 6 mos. (g. s.).

Will 29 Aug. 1759, proved 5 May 1761; wife Mary; sons Benjamin, Samuel; youngest son Moses; sons William, Daniel; daus. Sarah, Eunice, Rachel.

Children, rec. Fairfield:

21+William, b. 8 Jan. 1708 [1708/9].
22+Daniel, b. 11 Nov. 1711.
    Sarah, b. 8 Apr. 1716, d. in 1761; m. 23 Mar. 1739, John Allen.

Eunice, b. 24 Oct. 1718; m. Stephen Gray.
23+Benjamin, b. 2 July 1721.
24+Samuel, b. 24 Aug. 1723.
25+Moses, b. 8 Apr. 1727.
   Rachel, b. 11 Oct. 1729, living 1793; m. 21 Jan. 1746/7, Eleazer Godfrey.

15. Bennett, Thomas, s. of Thomas.

Born abt. 1693; d. at Westport, 5 June 1781 in 88 yr. (g. s.); m. (1) 17 Mar. 1717, Mary Rowland, dau. of Israel, bapt. 10 Mar. 1694/5, d. 17 Apr. 1733, and he m. (2) 14 Oct. 1741, Mercy Scofield. She d. 8 June 1771.

Children by first wife, rec. Fairfield:
   Tabitha, b. Apr. 1718.
   Hannah, b. Oct. 1721; m. 22 Oct. 1743, Humphrey Ogden.
26+Nathan, b. 4 Mar. 1725.
27+Thomas, b. 8 Mar. 1727.

Child by second wife, rec. Fairfield, bapt. Westport:
28+James, b. 15 July, bapt. 7 Aug. 1743.

16. Bennett, Edmund, s. of John.

Bapt. 24 May 1696; d. at Westport, 15 July 1754; m. Elizabeth, prob. dau. of Stephen Pierson of Derby. She m. (2) at Westport, 22 Sept. 1755, Jonathan Mallory of Redding.

Adm'n granted, 14 Apr. 1755, to William Bennett. Distribution, 21 Aug. 1770: Elizabeth, late wife of Edmund, now wife of Jonathan Mallory of Redding; daus. Betty and Thankful.

Children:
   Betty, b. [say 1741]; chose Jonathan Mallory for guardian, Sept. 1755; d. before 30 May 1777, when Inv. was presented, calling her Betty of Redding; and prob. d. before her sister. In 1770 she was *non compos mentis,* and Daniel Sanford of Redding as her conservator conveyed to James Bennett.
   Thankful, d. at Westport, 2 Jan. 1777; will 1 Jan., proved 3 Feb. 1777, gave estate to friend Joseph Bennett.

17. Bennett, James, s. of James, 3d.

Born abt. 1694, d. abt. 1750; mariner, of Stratfield.

He m. (1) Elizabeth Wakeman, dau. of Capt. John, b. 1 June 1695.

He m. (2) Tabitha Hubbell, dau. of Samuel, Sr., b. 24 Dec. 1700, living 1771.

James and wife Tabitha conveyed Hubbell land in Stratford, 13 July 1749.

Tabitha Bennett conveyed land in Stratford in 1751 to son James, and in 1761 to sons Ebenezer, David, Charles, Lewis, and Daniel. Nehemiah Hubbell gave bond 1 Mar. 1761, as guardian of David Bennett of Stratford. Tabitha conveyed 1771 to son Stephen of Fairfield. Daniel Bennett of Stratford conveyed 1765 to Stephen of North Fairfield, right in farm of my mother Mrs. Tabitha Bennett, formerly the wife of Capt. James Bennett.

Children [by second wife]:

29+James.
30+Charles.
    Elizabeth, bapt. 26 Sept. 1731.
    Lewis, bapt. 27 May 1733; chose James Bennett of Stratford for guardian, 15 Apr. 1751; m. Content ———.*
    Ebenezer, bapt. 22 Aug. 1736; m. Experience ———.†
    ? Naomi, of Stratford, chose Amos Hinman for guardian, 12 May 1752.
31+Stephen, b. abt. 1740.
    Daniel, b. [say 1741], d. at Huntington, by 1804; chose Stephen Hubbell for guardian, Apr. 1755; m. 4 Jan. 1773, Rhoda Hubbell; dau. of Andrew.‡
    David, b. [say 1744], d. in Revolution, 1776; m. at Trumbull, 6 Oct. 1764, Bethia Burton, bapt. 19 Aug. 1750, d. at Trumbull, 14 Oct. 1788 ae. 39; she m. (2) David Mallett.§

18. Bennett, Stephen, s. of James, 3d.

Bapt. 21 June 1702; d. at Stratfield in 1739; m. 8 Oct. 1724, Abigail French, dau. of Sergt. Samuel, bapt. Jan. 1701/2.

Adm'n granted to Gamaliel French of Stratfield, 6 Mar. 1738/9. His son Philip chose Zephaniah Hull his guardian, 1740. Philip Bennett of Fairfield was appointed guardian to Samuel, 1750. Abigail chose Gamaliel French her guardian.

---

* They had children, Elijah, Lewis, Daniel, John, and Polly, bapt. at Huntington Epis. Church, 29 Feb. 1764.

† They had children bapt. at Huntington Epis. Church: Joseph, 4 Aug. 1765; Daughter, bapt. in 1769.

‡ A child, Daniel-Hubbell, bapt. 14 Mar. 1781.

§ Children, bapt. Trumbull; John, b. Oct. [1765], bapt. 27 Feb. 1766; Phebe, b. 14 Nov., bapt. 27 Dec. 1767; Mary, b. June, bapt. 17 July 1769.

Children, rec. Stratfield:

> Philip, b. 19 Mar. 1726, d. at Stratfield, 1807 ae. 80; sold house at Clapboard Hill, 1780; m. Sarah Knapp, dau. of Daniel, b. 26 May 1726.*
> Prudence, b. 14 July 1728; ? m. at Weston, 3 Dec. 1760, Reuben Salmon.
> Stephen, b. 8 Apr. 1730.†
> Ebenezer, b. 23, bapt. 30 Jan. 1731/2.
> Samuel, bapt. 24 Mar. 1734; [Ens., 12th Co., 4th Regt., May 1780].‡
> Gershom, bapt. 16 May 1736.
> Abigail.

19. Bennett, William, s. of Isaac. Lt., Stratfield company, Oct. 1751.

Bapt. 26 Dec. 1708; d. at Easton, 16 Feb. 1788 in 80 yr. (g. s.); m. (1) 26 July 1731, Hannah Seeley, dau. of James, b. 23 May 1713, d. 27 Nov. 1743, or 28 Nov. in 31 yr. (g. s., Stratfield); m. (2) 3 Dec. 1744, Katharine Hawley, dau. of Thomas, b. 17 Feb. 1721/2, d. 22 July 1809 in 88 yr. (g. s., Easton).

Deacon, Easton Church, elected 3 May 1764.

Will 19 Sept. 1778, proved 17 Mar. 1788; wife Katharine; two sons Samuel and Thomas (minors); daus. Eunice wife of Benjamin Pickett, Rebecca wife of Peter Coley, Damaris wife of Francis Jackson, Hannah wife of Ebenezer Gilbert, Martha wife of Ezra Jennings, Mary wife of Joseph Lacy, Katharine wife of Eliphalet Wakeman, Mercy wife of Elijah Hawley; children of dec'd dau. Ann, formerly wife of Timothy Hubbell; eldest son Daniel Bennett.

Will of Katharine, (not dated), proved 14 Aug. 1809; daus. Mary, Mercy, Hannah; gr. son Ezra Gilbert; dau. Martha; dau. Catherine; sons Samuel, Thomas; gr. dau. Gulielma Bradley; gr. dau. Betty Platt; gr. son Eliphalet Hawley; son Joseph Lacy and gr. son Hull Bradley,§ Exec'rs.

---

* A son, Daniel, bapt. 6 Jan. 1751. On 7 June 1798, Samuel, Philip, Gershom, Abijah, Sarah, and Lyman, children of a Philip Bennett, were bapt. at Trinity Church. Sarah, wife of Philip, bur. 20 June 1798 ae. 43.

† Adm'n on Est. of one Stephen Bennett of Norwalk was granted, 2 Oct. 1797, to Margery and Stephen Bennett, with William Sterling surety.

‡ See the unplaced records.

§ His wife was Gulielma Wakeman, gr. dau. of Mrs. Bennett.

Children by first wife, rec. Fairfield:

32+Daniel, b. 26 Apr. 1732, bapt. at Stratfield, 30 Apr. 1732.
Eunice, b. 17 Dec. 1734, bapt. 22 Dec. 1734; m. Benjamin Pickett.
Rebecca, b. 14 Jan. 1736/7; m. Peter Coley.
Ann, b. Nov. 1738; m. Timothy Hubbell.
Damaris, b. 15 Dec. 1741; m. 24 Aug. 1758, Francis Jackson.
William, b. 11 Nov. 1743, d. 12 May 1744; or d. 10 May 1744 ae. 6 mos. (g. s.).

Children by second wife, rec. Fairfield:

Hannah, b. 11 Dec. 1745; m. 23 Sept. 1766, Ebenezer Gilbert.
Martha, b. 5 Nov. 1747; m. at Easton, 23 Nov. 1769, Ezra Jennings.
Mary, b. 6 Aug. 1749; m. 3 Feb. 1772, Joseph Lacey.
Katharine, b. 7 Apr. 1751, bapt. at Stratfield, 11 May 1751; m. (1) 11 Mar. 1773, Eliphalet Wakeman; m. (2) 6 July 1779, Samuel Hawley; she divorced him.
Mercy, b. 1 Jan. 1753; m. 27 Feb. 1772, Dea. Elijah Hawley, of Stratford; rem. to Ohio.
William, b. 29 Aug. 1756, d. 15 Sept. 1757.
Samuel, b. abt. 1759. Children, bapt. Easton: William-Hawley, bapt. 15 June 1783; Clarissa, bapt. 7 Mar. 1790; Willis, bapt. Aug. 1792; Henry, bapt. Mar. 1795.
Thomas, b. abt. 1761, living 1832, Rome, Oneida County, N. Y., and 1836, Stratford, N. Y.

20. **Bennett, Isaac,** s. of Isaac. Lt., north company, Stratfield and Stratford, Oct. 1754.

Bapt. 4 Mar. 1711; d. at Easton, 10 Dec. 1791 in 82 yr. (g. s.).

He m. (1) abt. 1734, Mary, widow of Isaac Wheeler, 3d, and dau. of Jonathan Wakelee, b. 10 June 1708 (g. s.), d. 5 July 1768 (g. s.); m. (2) Eunice, widow of James Hawley, and dau. of Henry Jackson, b. 7 Aug. 1715, d. 6 Sept. 1796 in 82 yr. (g. s., Stratfield).

Adm'n granted, 19 Dec. 1791, to Najah Bennett. On 29 Mar. 1792, the Adm'r received acknowledgment of portions from the heirs,—James Johnson and wife Abiah, Nathaniel Seeley, Jr., and wife Rhoda, Isaac Bennett, Cyrus Brinsmade, Ezbon Hall and wife Rhoda, Daniel Silliman and wife Sarah, William Bennett and wife Mary, John Baldwin and wife Naomi. [Of these, Isaac Bennett was son of Nathan; Cyrus, Rhoda (Hall), Sarah, Mary, and Naomi, were children of Naomi (Brinsmade).] The widow Eunice was also mentioned.

Children [by first wife]:
> Naomi, bapt. at Stratfield, 3 Oct. 1736, d. at Easton, 21 Sept. 1776 in 42 yr. (g. s.); m. Josiah Brinsmade.
> Abiah, b. 8 June 1739, d. at Easton, 14 Jan. 1822 in 83 yr. (g. s.); m. Rev. James Johnson, first Minister at North Fairfield.

33+Najah, b. 31 Sept. 1742.
34+Nathan, b. abt. 1744.
> Rhoda, b. abt. 1746; m. at Easton, July 1768, Nathaniel Seeley, Jr.
> Justice, b. abt. 1748, d. at Easton, 23 Nov. 1772 in 25 yr. (g. s.).

21. Bennett, William, s. of Deliverance.

Born 8 Jan. 1708/9; d. at Westport, 16 Sept. 1772 ae. 62 yrs. 7 mos. 26 days (g. s.).

He m. Aug. 1733, Abigail Hickok, dau. of Benjamin; b. abt. 1718, d. 30 Dec. 1800 in 83 yr.; she m. (2) 24 Oct. 1773, Thaddeus Morehouse.

Will 5 Aug. 1772, proved 6 Oct. 1772; wife Abigail; sons Thaddeus, Deliverance, Joseph, Stephen; daus. Sarah, Abigail. Receipts from Samuel and Abigail Smith, and Jabez and Sarah Lockwood, for portions from their father's estate, 31 Dec. 1776.

Will of Abigail Morehouse, 16 Feb. 1797, proved 1 Feb. 1801; sons Thaddeus and Deliverance Bennett, land in Wilton; dau. Abigail Smith.

Children, rec. Fairfield, bapt. Westport:
> Sarah, b. 17 Mar. 1734; m. 17 Oct. 1754, Jabez Lockwood.

35+Thaddeus, b. 22 June 1736.
36+Deliverance, b. 27 Feb. 1738.
> William, b. 5 July 1741, d. on way from Canada, 15 Oct. 1760.
> Mary, b. 25, bapt. 28 Aug. 1743, d. 4 Oct. 1754.

37+Joseph, b. 17, bapt. 22 Sept. 1745.
38+Stephen, b. and bapt. 18 Dec. 1747.
> Abigail, b. 30 Dec. 1749, bapt. 4 Feb. 1750; m. 28 Aug. 1768, Samuel Smith.

22. Bennett, Daniel, s. of Deliverance.

Born 11 Nov. 1711.

He m. Sarah Trowbridge, dau. of Samuel, bapt. 19 Feb. 1715/6.

Child, bapt. Westport:
> Trowbridge, bapt. 23 June 1745, d. at Ridgefield, 4 Sept. 1804; m. at Ridgefield, 20 Aug. 1767, Sarah Hine, dau. of Josiah.
> Others?

23. **Bennett, Benjamin,** s. of Deliverance.

Born 2 July 1721; d. at Ridgefield in 1760; m. (1) Mary ———, who d. at Westport, 27 Nov. 1745.

He m. (2) by 1747, Mary Lobdell, dau. of Joshua and Mary (Reynolds), b. at Ridgefield, 6 Dec. 1725.

His widow Mary was appointed guardian to the six children, 1 July 1760, and gave bond with Ebenezer Lobdell. The son Benjamin chose Caleb Lobdell for guardian, 13 May 1771.

Children,* first two bapt. at Westport, and two at St. John's, Stamford:

> Elias, bapt. 9 Nov. 1746, d. Feb. 1746/7.
> Mary, bapt. in 1748.
> David, bapt. 30 Dec. 1750; perhaps m. Eunice Olmstead, dau. of Reuben.
> Susannah, b. [say 1753].
> Benjamin, b. [say 1755].
> Martha, perhaps the dau. bapt. 24 Jan. 1757; prob. m. at Ridgefield, 18 Nov. 1781, John Jackson
> Hannah, b. [say 1759].

24. **Bennett, Samuel,** s. of Deliverance.

Born 24 Aug. 1723.

He m. Abigail Sherwood, dau. of Thomas.

Children, first bapt. Westport, the rest rec. Ridgefield:

> Ellen, bapt. 4 July 1742.
> Ebenezer, b. 30 May 1743.
> Abigail, b. 2 Apr. 1746, d. 10 Jan. 1770.
> Sarah, b. 6 Dec. 1751; prob. m. at Ridgebury, 16 Nov. 1769, **Ezekiel** Osborn.
> Samuel, b. 23 Aug. 1755, d. 8 Dec. 1776.
> John, b. 10 May 1759;† ? m. at Westport, 4 Dec. 1783, Grissel Chapman; dau. of Phineas, b. 16 Apr. 1755.
> Ezekiel, b. 23 Aug. 1761; perhaps m. at Westport, 23 July 1783, Sarah Perry.‡

---

* All by second wife except the eldest child.

† One John d. at Westport, 4 Dec. 1805 ae. 52. The John who m. Grissel Chapman was of Huntington, L. I., in 1787.

‡ Ezekiel had children, bapt. Trinity Church: Nabby, bapt. 2 Oct. 1785; child, bapt. 3 Feb. 1790; [perhaps Jesse, son of ——— Bennett, bapt. 13 Nov. 1791, belongs here]; Sarah, bapt. 26 Apr. 1795.

25. Bennett, Moses, s. of Deliverance.

Born 8 Apr. 1727; d. at Westport, 20* Dec. 1796 ae. 69 (g. s.); m. 17 June 1746, Eunice Hurlbut, dau. of Gideon; she d. 19 Mar. 1796 ae. 70 yrs. 2 mos. 25 days (g. s.).

Children, rec. Fairfield, bapt. Westport:

Molly, b. 5 June, bapt. 5 July 1747; m. 15 Oct. 1773, John Phillips.
Lydia, b. 10, bapt. 19 Feb. 1749; m. at Weston, 24 Sept. 1766, Elias Scribner.
Eunice, b. 21, bapt. 27 Jan. 1751; m. 28 Oct. 1767, Samuel Nash, of Norwalk.
Rachel, bapt. 25 Feb., d. 12 Mar. 1753.
39+Moses, b. 12, bapt. 14 Apr. 1754.
Hannah, b. 11, bapt. 15 Aug. 1756, perhaps d. 29 July 1821 ae. 65 (Westport Church). Adm'n on estate of Hannah Bennett, "widow," granted 28 Aug. 1821 to John Phillips and Jabez Bennett.†
Sarah, bapt. 3 Dec. 1758; ? m. 14 Mar. 1781, Silas Gregory, of Norwalk.
40+Jabez, b. [28 Feb. 1761], bapt. 8 Mar. 1761.
Rhoda, bapt. 8 May 1763; m. 27 Feb. 1782, John Couch.
Jesse, bapt. 30 Sept. 1765, d. at Westport, 21 Feb. 1806 ae. 41.
David, bapt. 19 Jan. 1772; m. (1) Jan. 1793, Charity Disbrow; m. (2) at Weston, 17 Apr. 1803, Polly Waterbury.‡

26. Bennett, Nathan, s. of Thomas.

Born 4 Mar. 1725; d. at Westport, 5 Oct. 1792.

He m. at Westport, 7 June 1746, Hannah Sturgis; dau. of John, b. abt. 1728, d. 19 Apr. 1809 ae. 81.

Children, rec. Fairfield, bapt. Westport:§

41+Nathan, b. 30 Nov. 1747.
42+Andrew, b. 11 Mar., bapt. 22 Apr. 1750.
43+Elias, b. 10 May, bapt. 14 June 1752.
44+Daniel, b. 1 Apr., bapt. 5 May 1754.
Hezekiah, b. 7 Apr., bapt. 9 May 1756, d. 11 July 1777.
Hannah, b. 20 May, bapt. 25 June 1758; m. 24 June 1779, Gilbert Fairchild, of Norwalk.

---

* Prob. a misreading; the church record says 29 Dec.
† This Hannah was sister of Jabez, and sister-in-law of Phillips; but the record may refer to the widow of Moses (39).
‡ Children, bapt. Westport: Myrinda, bapt. 2, d. 3 Apr. 1795; Henry, bapt. 27 Mar. 1796; Lucinda, bapt. 4 Mar. 1798; Betsey, bapt. 20 Apr. 1800.
§ Only the first five children are recorded in the Vital Records; the other births are from family records.

Sarah, b. 2 Mar., bapt. 4 May 1760; m. 6 May 1781, Moses Oysterbanks.

Ruth, b. 10 Mar., bapt. 11 July 1762;* m. 28 May 1786, Ebenezer Monroe.

Naomi, b. 15 Apr., bapt. 27 May 1764; m. 7 Feb. 1782, Thomas Squire, of Weston.

Josiah, b. 28 Apr. 1766; rem. 1816 to Danbury; m. at Weston, 13 Sept. 1789, Mary Hilton. Children, bapt. Westport: Eli, bapt. 17 Oct. 1790; Nathan, bapt. 13 Apr. 1794.

Thomas, b. 21 July, bapt. 2 Oct. 1768; res. Sherman, 1810; m. 24 Aug. 1788, Sarah Stratton, dau. of Cornelius, bapt. 12 Feb. 1769.†

Esther, b. 1 Mar., bapt. 1 Sept. 1771; m. Eliphalet Stevens.

27. Bennett, Thomas, s. of Thomas.

Born 8 Mar. 1727; d. at Westport, 26 Jan. 1797.

He m. 1 Apr. 1754, Mary Couch, dau. of Samuel; b. 28 Mar. 1729, d. 27 July 1788.

Children, bapt. Westport:
Thomas, bapt. 17, d. 18 Jan. 1758.
Others?

28. Bennett, James, s. of Thomas.

Born 15 July 1743; d. at Westport, 1 June 1799 ae. 56.

He m. (1) 7 Apr. 1762, Sarah Read dau. of Thomas; she d. 28 Oct. 1779 ae. 39 yrs. 9 mos. (g. s.).

He m. (2) at Weston, 7 June 1780, Anne Godfrey; she d. 30 Oct. 1816 ae. 74 yrs. 6 mos. (g. s.).

Will 21 Dec. 1798, codicil 13 May 1799, proved 19 June 1799; wife Anne; children James, Thomas, Gershom, Abigail wife of Jabez Bennett, Mercy wife of Seymour Taylor, and Gillen wife of Jabez Platt of Norwalk.

Children [by first wife], bapt. Westport:
Abigail, bapt. 9 Sept. 1764, d. at Westport, 12 Jan. 1851 ae. 86 yrs. 5 mos. (g. s.); m. 27 June 1784, Jabez Bennett.
Gillen, m. 5 Feb. 1786, Jabez Platt, of Norwalk.

---

* Elizabeth Reed, dau. of Ruth Bennett, bapt. 25 Apr. 1784.

† Perhaps he d. 20 Jan. 1853; perhaps the Mrs. Sarah Bennett who d. at Sherman, 23 Aug. 1843 ae. 73 yrs. 8 mos., was his wife. Children (from family record, four bapt. Westport): Charity, b. 12 Apr., bapt. 23 Aug. 1789. Deborah, b. 18 June, bapt. 9 Oct. 1791· perhaps m. at Sherman, 4 Feb. 1806, Daniel Putnam. Abigail, b. 11 June 1792 [1793], bapt. 15 Dec. 1793, d. at Spring Hill, Pa., 29 May 1864; m. 13 Mar. 1813, Harry Ackley. Sarah, b. 26 July 1795, bapt. 21 Feb. 1796. Charles, b. [say 1798]. Ferris, b. 31 May 1801. Hester, b. 5 June 1805.

Sarah, bapt. 6 Dec. 1767, d. 29 Sept. 1773 ae. 5 yrs. 10 mos. (g. s.).
Gershom, b. [31 Dec. 1769], bapt. 14 Jan. 1770, d. 11 Nov. 1773 ae. 3 yrs. 10 mos. 11 days (g. s.).
James, b. [11 Dec. 1771], bapt. 19 Jan. 1772, d. 25 Sept. 1773 ae. 1 yr. 9 mos. 14 days (g. s.).
Mercy, b. [6 Feb. 1774], bapt. 13 Mar. 1774, d. at Westport, 21 Jan. 1854 ae. 79-11-15 (g. s.); m. 11 Dec. 1793, Seymour Taylor.
Sarah, bapt. 26 May 1776, d. 11 Apr. 1785.
James, b. [20 Mar. 1779], bapt. 9 May 1779, d. 24 Jan. 1848 ae. 68 yrs. 10 mos. 4 days (g. s.); m. 4 July 1799, Mary Burr; dau. of David, b. 30 July 1783, d. 15 Mar. 1826 ae. 42 (g. s.).*

Children [by second wife], bapt. Westport:

Mary, bapt. 1 July 1781, d. 10 Feb. 1782.
Thomas, b. [18 Mar. 1783], bapt. 5 May 1783, d. 28 Sept. 1863 ae. 80 yrs. 6 mos. 10 days (g. s.); m. 30 May 1804, Betsey Moyer, b. [28 Aug. 1784], d. 8 Nov. 1856 ae. 72-2-11.
Gershom, bapt. 14 Aug. 1785; m. 19 May 1806, Salome Wilson.

29. Bennett, James, s. of James, 4th.

He lived in Stratford and d. abt. 1780; m. ———.

On 28 Feb. 1745/6, Daniel Curtiss of Stratford conveyed land to James Bennitt, late of Stonington, but now residing in Stratford.

Distribution, 27 Nov 1780 [in Stratford Deeds], names his children: James Aaron, Tabitha wife of Ebenezer Beach, Abigail wife of Timothy Beach, Jr., Sarah wife of Ebenezer Jennings, and Esther.

Children:

James, m. (rec. Weston) 4 Apr. 1776, Anna Cable; dau. of John, b. 4 Nov. 1750, d. at Trumbull, 13 Sept. 1826 in 77 yr. (g. s.).†
Aaron, b. 11 Mar. 1755 (Pension rec.), living 1832; rem. 1799 to Sugar Creek, Bradford County, Pa.; rem. 1810 to Catherine, Tioga County, N. Y.

---

* Children, bapt. Westport: Sarah-Reed, bapt. 26 Oct. 1800; David-Burr, bapt. 3 Apr. 1803: James, bapt. 28 June 1807.

† Children, rec. Weston, three bapt. Huntington Epis. Church: Abigail, b. 8 June 1774; James, b. 8 May 1777, bapt. 24 Mar. 1778; John, b. 8 Sept. 1779, d. in 1822; Aaron, b. 7 Mar. 1782, bapt. 27 Sept. 1782, prob. m. Mabel Wheeler; Ann, b. 30 July 1784; Ruth, bapt. 27 Nov. 1788; Walker, b. 25 Feb. 1795. [The Abigail entered at Weston was Abigail Sanford, dau. of Anna Cable, bapt. 14 Aug. 1774.] Adm'n on estate of Anna Bennet of Weston was granted, 1 Mar. 1830, to Calvin Wheeler, Jr. of Weston. Distribution: Abigail Brisco; gr. children Polly Beach, Aaron Bennet, Ruth Bennet, John Bennet, and Burr Bennet; gr. children Bennet Rowland and Abba Gray; gr. dau. Sally Beardsley. Adm'n on estate of John Bennett of Weston granted, 24 June 1822, to Jeremiah Burton, with James Bennett as surety; dower set to widow Charity.

Tabitha, m. Ebenezer Beach.
Abigail, m. Timothy Beach, Jr.
Sarah, m. at Easton, Mar. 1772, Ebenezer Jennings.
Esther.

30. Bennett, Charles, s. of James, 4th.

This family lived in the Trumbull section of Stratford and were members of the Huntington Epis. Church. He m. Sarah Adams, prob. dau. of Abraham of Newtown.*

Charles, called "late of Stratford, but now with ye Enemy of the United States," is referred to in Conn. State Rec., Mar. 1781; and Solomon Booth, who was appointed Adm'r, sold his property to Capt. John Sherwood, reserving use of part to his wife and children.

In 1785 Charles of Stratford sold land in Blanket Meadow, bounded south on land which was set off to Sarah Bennitt, said Charles' wife, for her Thirds in said Charles' Estate, the other part having been confiscated to the Use of this State. Sarah petitioned 1786 for reversal of the confiscation for the benefit of herself and crippled son, she having nine children; but it was negatived.

It seems certain that Charles was father of the family group named in the will of Ephraim, as follows:

Charles, bought land in 1773 as Charles, Jr.
Ephraim, b. abt. 1751, d. at Huntington, 1 June 1799 in 49 yr. (g. s.). Will 31 May, proved 1 July 1799; eldest bro. Charles; bros. Samuel, Silas, Ezra, Francis; sisters, Ruth Husted, Deborah Wheeler.
Ruth, b. [say 1753]; m. at Easton, 23 Nov. 1773, James Husted.
Samuel, b. 17 Oct. 1755 (family rec.), d. at Perrinton, Monroe County, N. Y., 28 Aug. 1819; m. Paulina Jennings, b. 21 Mar. 1760; had 7 children.†
Silas.
Ezra.

---

* A letter written by a dau. of their son Samuel states that Samuel was son of Charles and Sarah (Adams).

† Children: Clarissa, b. 8 Sept. 1782 (at Weston), d. at Hamilton, N. Y., 26 Aug. 1859, m. 27 Nov. 1803, Abraham Spear; Betsey, b. 15 Apr. 1784, m. Lyman Tripp; Charles B., b. 30 Apr. 1786, d. 24 Jan. 1832, m. ———; Frances, b. 3 Nov. 1788, m. in 1809, Richard Treadwell; Lydia, b. 11 July 1791, m. in 1811, Benjamin Slocum; Sarah, b. 28 Oct. 1793, d. at Maple Rapids, Mich., 21 Nov. 1885, m. 21 Feb. 1813, Ezra-Ide Perrin; Susan, b. 23 Oct. 1798, m. 9 Mar. 1817, Giles Holden, of Charlotte, N. Y.

Deborah, m. —— Wheeler.
Francis, bapt. at Huntington, 11 Feb. 1766.*
Son (youngest child), a cripple from birth, living 1786, prob. d. before 1799.

31. Bennett, Stephen, s. of James, 4th.

Born abt. 1740; d. at Easton, 3 Mar. 1773 in 34 yr (g. s.); m. at Easton, 20 June 1765, Ann Seeley; widow of Ephraim. She was dau. of Zachariah Sanford, b. 6 Feb. 1739/40; and m. (3) James Crofut.

Will 31 Dec. 1772, proved 20 Apr. 1773; wife Ann; youngest son Stephen; other son Seeley; bro. Daniel Bennett, Exec'r.

Distribution of Est. of Ann Crofut of Weston, 14 Aug. 1802: dau. Abigail wife of Samuel Crofut; eldest son Seeley Bennett; son Stephen Bennett; daus. Rachel, Ann and Olive Crofut.

Children, bapt Huntington Episcopal Church:
Seeley.
Olive, bapt. 18 Mar. 1771, d. young.
Stephen, bapt. 15 Dec. 1772.

32. Bennett, Daniel, s. of William. Ens., east company of North Fairfield and North Stratford, Oct. 1771.

Born 26 Apr. 1732; d. at Cornwall, 27 Nov. 1824 ae. 93; m. at Trumbull, 27 Mar. 1758, Lois (Hawley), widow of Nathan Burton; dau. of Nathan Hawley, b. at Stratford, 28 Feb. 1731/2.

Children, bapt. Easton:
William, bapt. 9 Dec. 1764; m. 16 Oct. 1785, Mary Brinsmade, bapt. 2 Aug. 1761.†
Daniel, bapt. 24 May 1767.‡
Abraham, bapt. 5 Sept. 1769; m. Dec. 1790, Kate Hubbell.§
Lois, b. 2 Nov. 1772 [1771], bapt. 26 Apr. 1772; m. Feb. 1787, Jesse Seeley.

---

* By a copy of Huntington Epis. Church rec., this was a dau. Frances.
† Children, rec. Weston: Naomi, b. 2 May 1789, bapt. Aug. 1790; Daniel, b. 8 Jan. 1792, bapt. June 1792, d. at Cornwall, 9 Apr. 1876 ae. 84; Nathan-Burton, b. 23 May 1794, d. at Easton, 13 Aug. 1795 ae. 15 yrs. 8 mos. (g. s.); Marshall-D.-Warville, b. 30 Mar. 1798.
‡ Mary, wife of Daniel, d. at Cornwall, 2 Aug. 1829 ae. 66; Delia, wife of Daniel, d. there 10 Aug. 1835 ae. 62.
§ Child, bapt. Easton: Fanny, bapt. June 1792.

33. **Bennett, Najah,** s. of Isaac. Ens., 12th Co., 4th Regt., May 1775; Capt., Oct. 1777.

Born 31 Sept. 1742; d. at Easton, 26 Aug. 1821 in 80 yr. (g. s.). He m. (1) at Easton, Aug. 1768, Sarah Gilbert; dau. of Joseph, b. 29 Mar. 1745.

He m. (2) 15 Jan. 1777, Mary ———, b. 9 June 1744; d. 21 Feb. 1827 ae. 83 (g. s.).

Will 1 July, proved 2 Oct. 1821; sons Joseph, Justus, Nathan; daus. Hannah, Sarah, Eunice, Mary; wife Mary. Three of the daus. with their husbands gave receipts.

Children [by first wife]:

Mary, bapt. 6 Aug. 1769, d. y.
Joseph, b. 27 Apr. 1772, d. 30 May 1844 in 73 yr. (g. s.); m. 10 Mar. 1791, Naomi Gregory, b. 5 Sept. 1772, d. 30 Jan. 1845 ae. 72 (g. s.).*
Justus, b. 17 Aug. 1773, bapt 26 Sept. 1773, d. 6 Nov. 1847 ae. 74 (g. s.); m. 24 Dec. 1795, Eunice Mallett, b. 2 Dec. 1777, d. 20 Sept. 1833 (g. s.).†
Hannah, b. 23 Jan. 1775; m. Sherwood Leavitt.

Children [by second wife]:

Sarah, b. 10 Dec. 1777; m. Jesse Jennings, of Salisbury.
Eunice, b. 31 Aug. 1780.
Mary, b. 17 Sept. 1782; m. Seth B. Sherwood, of Stratford.
Nathan, b. 22 Mar. 1785, d. 14 Nov. 1878 ae. 93 yrs. 8 mos. (g. s.); m. Sarah ———, who d. 10 Sept. 1864 ae. 76 yrs. 8 mos. (g. s.).

34. **Bennett, Nathan,** s. of Isaac.

Born abt. 1744; d. at Easton, 20 Sept. 1777 in 34 yr. (g. s.); m. 25 June 1767, Abigail Sherwood, dau. of Thomas, bapt. 25 Mar. 1750, d. at Westport, 7 Aug. 1805 ae. 56 (g. s.). She m. (2) 1786, Capt. Joseph Bennett.

Children, bapt. Easton:

Isaac. bapt. 8 Oct. 1769, d. 2 May 1860 ae. 90 yrs. 9 mos. (g. s.); m. 24(?) Dec. 1790, Polly Johnson, b. 20 Dec 1770, d. 16 May 1841 ae. 71 (g. s.).‡
Thomas, bapt. 1 Mar. 1772, d. before 1789.

---

* No issue. Joseph's estate was distributed to widow Naomi, bro. Justus Bennett, and heirs of sister Hannah dec'd wife of Sherwood Leavitt (Joseph B., Anson S., David and Oramel Leavitt, Polly-Ann Brown, Eliza Leavitt, Hannah M. Banta, and the heirs of Justus B. Leavitt dec'd).

† A child, rec. Weston: Sarah-Collins, b. 29 Oct. 1799, d. at Easton, 24 Sept. 1833 ae. 34 (g. s.).

‡ Children, bapt. Easton: Nathan-Johnson, bapt. Apr. 1792; Anson, bapt. 1 June 1794.

THE FAMILIES OF OLD FAIRFIELD 109

35. Bennett, Thaddeus, s. of William. Lt., Stratfield company, May 1772; Capt., 3d Co., 4th Regt., May 1775.

Born 22 June 1736; d. at Easton, 20 Jan. 1823 in 88 yr. (g. s.). He m. 15 Apr. 1761, Mary Platt, dau. of Ebenezer, b. abt. 1741, d. 21 Oct. 1819 ae. 78 (g. s.).

Children, rec. and bapt. Weston:
> Jabez, b. 31 Mar., bapt. 22 Apr. 1762; m. (1) 23 Nov. 1786, Rebecca Wakeman, b. [say 1767], d. 12 Feb. 1790; m. (2) 16 Sept. 1790, Mary Bennett; m. (3) 14 Jan. 1795, Nancy Outhouse.
> Mary, bapt. 24 Jan. 1764, d. y.
> Sarah, bapt. 24 Jan. 1764, d. y.
> Abigail, bapt. 3 Feb. 1766; ? m. at Weston, 26 Oct. 1791, Isaiah Mallory.
> Hannah, b. 4 July, bapt. 14 Aug. 1768, d. 29 Jan. 1840; m. (rec. Weston) 23 July 1786, Calvin Wheeler, Jr.
> Platt, b. 28 July, bapt. 16 Sept. 1770; m. at Redding, 29 July 1792, Martha Wheeler; dau. of Calvin, b. 15 Mar. 1771.*
> Mary, b. 6 July, bapt. 6 Aug. 1773.
> Sarah, b. 17 Nov. 1775, d. at Salisbury, 25 July 1845; m. at Trinity Church, 29 Apr. 1797, Seth Wakeman.
> Ezra, b. 10 Sept. 1778.†
> Irena, b. 28 Oct. 1780.

36. Bennett, Deliverance, s. of William.

Born 27 Feb. 1738; d. at Westport, 7 Mar. 1808 ae. 69 yrs. 11 mos. 28 days (g. s.); m. Mary Benedict, dau. of Nathaniel and Mary (Lockwood), b. 21 Oct. 1741, d. 23 Apr. 1835 ae. 93 yrs. 5 mos. 22 days (g. s.).

Will 9 July 1806, proved 28 Mar. 1808; wife Mary; five sons, William, Haynes, Nathaniel, Isaac, Joseph; four daus. Mary, Esther, Betty, Albert.

Children, bapt. Westport:
> William, b. 9 Feb., bapt. 4 Apr. 1762, d. at Westport, 22 Oct. 1833; Lt.; m. at Norwalk, 25 Feb. 1786, Elizabeth Marvin, b. 24 Nov. 1766, living 1855.‡

---

* Children, rec. Redding, bapt. Trinity Church: Elousia, b. 16 Dec. 1792, bapt. 27 Jan. 1793; Lucinda, b. 20 Feb. 1795, bapt. 17 May 1795; Fanny, b. 20 Nov. 1798, bapt. 23 Mar. 1799.

† One Ezra m. at Weston, 9 Sept. 1796, Esther Godfrey; a child, Moses-Prince, b. 19 Apr. 1798; Ziba, bapt. 19 Apr. 1801. Ezra d. 30 Nov. 1831 (Miss Treadwell's book). See also Ezra son of Charles (30).

‡ Children, bapt. Westport: Polly, bapt. 31 Dec. 1786, d. 30 Aug. 1788; Ozias-Merwin, bapt. 18 May 1788; Lorry, bapt. 26 June 1790; Esther, bapt. 13 Apr. 1794; Eliza, bapt. 19 Feb. 1800. William's will, 30 Apr., proved 10 Nov. 1832, named wife Elizabeth, son Ozias M., and daus. Laury wife of Joseph S. Bennett, Esther wife of Samuel Johnson [called Jackson in distribution], and Eliza Bennett.

Haynes, bapt. 27 May 1764; m. 23 Dec. 1784, Kezia Wright.*
Mary, bapt. 5 Apr. 1767; m. 23 Feb. 1786, Ozias Marvin.
Nathaniel, bapt. 27 Aug. 1769; m. (1) ———; m. (2) 25 May 1800, Betsey Lobdell.†
Esther, b. 30 Aug., bapt. 1 Sept. 1771, d. 5 Jan. 1853; m. 22 Mar. 1789, John Taylor, of Norwalk.
Betty, bapt. 10 Apr. 1774; m. 5 Dec. 1793, Taylor Hurlbut.
John-Benedict, bapt. 25 Aug. 1776.
Isaac, bapt. 21 Mar. 1779; m. 20 Dec. 1798, Lydia Wood.‡
Joseph, b. [23 Apr. 1781], bapt. 24 June 1781, d. 16 July 1830 ae. 49 yrs. 2 mos. 23 days (g. s.); m. Hetta ———, b. 28 Feb. 1783, d. 21 Apr. 1833 ae. 50-1-21 (g. s.).§
Alethea, bapt. 18 Apr. 1784.

37. Bennett, Joseph, s. of William. Lt., 6th Co., 4th Regt., Jan. 1778; Capt., Nov. 1780.

Born 17 Sept. 1745; d. at Westport, 19 Nov. 1819 ae. 74 (g. s.); m. (1) 21 Dec. 1763, Sarah Lyon, b. 30 June 1748, d. 6 Jan. 1786 ae. 38 yrs. 5 mos. and a few days (g. s.); m. (2) in 1786, Abigail (Sherwood), widow of Nathan Bennett, bapt. 25 Mar. 1750, d. at Westport, 7 Aug. 1805 ae. 56 (g. s.); m. (3) at Weston, 29 Sept. 1805, Sarah Gorham; widow of Stephen Gorham and dau. of Jeremiah Sturges, bapt. 5 June 1748, d. 16 June 1812 ae. 64; m. (4) Elizabeth ———, b. abt. 1762, d. 5 Dec. 1852 ae. 90 (g. s.).

Will 21 June, proved 29 Nov. 1819; three sons, Joseph-Sherwood, Thomas-Burr, and Stephen; children of dec'd dau. Sarah wife of Zophar Brush; dau. Rhoda widow of Robert Taylor; children of dec'd dau. Lydia wife of Thomas Lockwood; daus. Charity wife of David Judah, Priscilla wife of Isaac Sears, Martha wife of Samuel Sears, Anna wife of Jabez Adams, Nabby wife of Zalmon Hanford; Wife; gr. son William, son of Joseph-Sherwood Bennett.

Adm'n on Est. of Abigail Bennett granted, 24 Nov. 1813, to Isaac Bennett of Weston, with Joseph Bennett as surety.

---

* Children, bapt. Westport: Lotta-Williams, bapt. 2 Oct. 1785; Uriah-Wright, bapt. 18 Mar. 1787; Sarah, bapt. 27 Mar. 1791; John-Hervey, bapt. 17 Mar. 1793; Mary, bapt. 11 Sept. 1796.

† Children, bapt. Westport: Philander and Harriet, bapt. 10 May 1798.

‡ Children, bapt. Westport: John-Benedict, bapt. 16 Nov. 1800; Mary, bapt. 16 June 1805.

§ Joseph's estate was distributed, 1832, to widow Hetty, Edwin Bennett, and Elethea wife of Edwin Hurlbutt.

THE FAMILIES OF OLD FAIRFIELD 111

Distribution order, estate of Abigail Bennett, 3 Dec. 1813: children,—Isaac, Joseph S., and Thomas B. Bennett, Anna wife of Jabez Adams, Abigail wife of Zalmon Hanford, and Stephen Bennett. [Isaac was her son by first husband.]

Children [by first wife], bapt. Westport:

Sarah, bapt. 18 Nov. 1764; m. 4 May 1780, Zophar Brush.
Rhoda, bapt. 2 Apr. 1769; m. 19 Dec. 1787, Robert Taylor.
Lydia, bapt. 12 May 1771; m. 8 Mar. 1789, Thomas Lockwood, of Norwalk.
Priscilla, bapt. 7 Aug. 1774, d. 19 Jan. 1777.
Joseph, bapt. 11 Aug. 1776, d. 17 Jan. 1777.
Priscilla, bapt. 7 Feb. 1779; m. 26 Nov. 1799, Isaac Sears, of Easton.
Charity, bapt. 26 May 1782;* m. David Judah.
Martha, bapt. 18 July 1784; m. 2 Oct. 1803, Samuel Sears.

Children [by second wife], rec. Fairfield, bapt. Westport:

Joseph-Sherwood, b. 26 Apr. 1787, bapt. 1 July 1787; m. 12 July 1812, Laura Bennett; dau. of William, bapt. 26 June 1790.
Thomas-Burr, b. 24 July 1789, bapt. 11 Oct. 1789; [m. Polly (Allen?)].
Anna, b. 17 Apr. 1791, bapt. 10 July 1791; m. Jabez Adams.
Nabby, b. 23 Dec. 1793, bapt. 13 Apr. 1794; m. Zalmon Hanford.
Stephen, b. 11 Nov. 1795, bapt. beginning of Apr. 1796; m. 31 Dec. 1815, Eleanor Thorpe.

38. Bennett, Stephen, s. of William.

Born 18 Dec. 1747; d. at Ridgefield, 5 Sept. 1802 ae. 54 (g. s.); m. (1) Elizabeth ———; m. (2) abt. 1776, Mary ———, who d. 25 July 1789; m. (3) abt. 1790, Lucy [Barnum?], b. abt. 1755, d. 13 Sept. 1840 ae. 82 (g. s.).

Physician.

Will 7 July 1802, proved 27 Sept. 1802. Son Eliphalet had had portion. Distribution to widow Lucy; sons Abel, Eli; Nancy; son John; Betsey.

Children [by first wife], two bapt. Westport, one Wilton:

John-Satterly, bapt. 23 July 1769, d. 2 Aug. 1773.
Eliphalet, bapt. 31 Aug. 1772; m. at Ridgebury, 16 June 1791, Hannah Mead, dau. of Joseph.
Nancy, bapt. 10 July 1774, d. y.

---

* Did she m. (1) 16 Nov. 1802, Noah-Wakeman Bradley?

Children [by second wife], rec. Ridgefield:
> Betty, b. 1 Mar. 1777; perhaps m. at Ridgebury, 18 Jan. 1797, Ambrose Millard, of Milton.
> John, b. 20 July 1780.
> Abel, b. 7 Apr. 1782, d. at Leroy, N. Y., 7 Aug. 1857 ae. 74 yrs. 4 mos. (g. s., Ridgefield); Dr.; m. Mary B. Bulkley, b. abt. 1806, d. 18 Nov. 1884 ae. 78.
> Nancy, b. 15 May 1785.

Child [by third wife]:
> Eli-Barnum, b. 6 June 1792.

39. Bennett, Moses, s. of Moses.

Born 12 Apr. 1754.

He m. Hannah ———.*

Children, bapt. Westport:
> Phineas, bapt. 23 July 1775, d. 16 Oct. 1776.
> Hezekiah, bapt. 14 June 1778.
> Moses, bapt. 14 June 1778.
> Phineas, bapt. 11 June 1780.
> Philip, bapt. 25 May 1783.
> Lewis, bapt. 6 Mar. 1785.
> Fanny, bapt. 15 Apr. 1787.
> Polly, bapt. 8 Aug. 1791.
> Phebe, bapt. 17 Aug. 1794.

40. Bennett, Jabez, s. of Moses.

Born 28 Feb. 1761; d. at Westport, 23 Feb. 1831 ae. 69 yrs. 11 mos. 23 days (g. s.); m. 27 June 1784, Abigail Bennett, dau. of James, b. [Aug. 1764], d. 12 Jan. 1851 ae. 86 yrs. 5 mos. (g. s.).

Children, bapt. Westport:
> Sarah, bapt. 26 June 1785, d. at Westport, 10 Apr. 1832 ae. 47 (g. s.); m. Selleck Burr.
> John, bapt. 15 Apr. 1787.
> Lydia, bapt. 9 Nov. 1789, d. at Westport, 29 Aug. 1849 ae. 59-11-7 (g. s.); m. 9 Mar. 1811, Eliakim Elwood.
> Charles, bapt. 25 Dec. 1791.
> Edward, bapt. 27 Aug. 1797; m. Mary ———, who d. 14 May 1822 ae. 23 (Fairfield Church rec.).

---

* One Hannah Bennett d. 29 July 1821 ae. 65 (Greens Farms rec.); but see the dau. of Moses (25).

THE FAMILIES OF OLD FAIRFIELD 113

41. Bennett, Nathan, s. of Nathan.

Born 30 Nov. 1747.

He m. Mary Beers, dau. of Anthony.

Children, one bapt. Westport:

> Abijah, bapt. 15 Nov. 1767.
> Mary.
> Rebecca, ? m. at Weston, 27 Nov. 1792, Samuel Guire.
> Joseph.
> Harriet.
> Daniel.

42. Bennett, Andrew, s. of Nathan.

Born 11 Mar. 1750; d. at Westport, 6 Jan. 1805 ae. 55; m. 15 Dec. 1776, Elizabeth Couch, b. 20 Aug. 1756, d. 25 Apr. 1799 ae. 43.

Children, bapt. Westport:

> Kezia, bapt. 21 Sept. 1777; m. Jan. 1797, Stephen Patrick, of Norwalk.
> Elizabeth, bapt. 25 Apr. 1779.
> Stephen.
> Joshua.

43. Bennett, Elias, s. of Nathan.

Born 10 May 1752.

He m. (1) 25 Feb. 1776, Abigail Crossman, b. 25 Nov. 1756, d. 19 Apr. 1798.

He m. (2) 19 May 1798, Elizabeth Squires; [dau. of Jonathan, bapt. 19 Jan. 1772].

Children [by first wife], first two bapt. Westport:

> Abigail, bapt. 10 Aug. 1777, d. at Weston, 10 Sept. 1844 ae. 67 (g. s.); m. 9 Nov. 1797, Burr Rowland.
> Elias, bapt. 25 Dec. 1778, d. at Redding, 7 May 1863 ae. 84 yrs. 6 mos. (g. s.); m. at Weston, 20 Mar. 1805, Mary Perry, dau. of Thaddeus, b. [Feb. 1789], d. 26 Apr. 1863 ae. 74 yrs. 2 mos. (g. s.).
> John, bapt. at Weston, 31 Dec. 1780; m. at Weston, 8 Apr. 1800, Ruamah Finch; dau. of John, b. at Norwalk, 1 Sept. 1779.
> Lewis.
> Ann, bapt. at Weston, 24 June 1787; m. ——— St. John.
> Esther, bapt. at Weston, 11 July 1790.

Children [by second wife], two bapt. Weston:
Molly-Jackson, bapt. 8 Sept. 1799.
Charles, bapt. 24 Oct. 1802.
Minot.
William, b. 1807; m. Eliza Robinson.
Daniel.
Josiah.

44. Bennett, Daniel, s. of Nathan.

Born 1 Apr. 1754.

He m. 7 Oct. 1778, Mary Monroe; dau. of Ebenezer, b. 22 May 1757.

Children, bapt. Westport:
Dolly, bapt. 30 Oct. 1779; m. 14 Apr. 1805, Allen Hilton.
Isabel, bapt. 28 Apr. 1782; m. 26 Oct. 1800, Solomon Disbrow.
Silas, bapt. 21 Nov. 1784, d. at Westport, 26 Sept. 1815 ae. 31 yrs. 8 days; m. 28 Feb. 1810, Betsey Hilton of Weston.
Hezekiah, bapt. 18 Feb. 1787, d. at Westport, 19 Dec. 1813 ae. 27 yrs. 2 mos. (g. s.).
Mary, bapt. 2 Aug. 1789.
Ebenezer, bapt. 8 Jan. 1792; m. 26 Mar. 1815, Alvira Eells.
Daniel, bapt. 28 Sept. 1794.
Maccabees, bapt. 12 Feb. 1797; of Danbury, m. at Westport, 24 Aug. 1817, Polly Eells.
Miranda, bapt. 27 Oct. 1799.

BENNETT ("SHIPWRIGHT" FAMILY)

Bennett, Benjamin, s. of James "Shipwright" [Vol. I, p. 75].

Bapt. at Stratfield, 4 Apr. 1697; m. at Stratford, 28 Jan. 1724/5, Hannah Curtis; dau. of Jonathan, b. 24 Aug. 1705.

Children, rec. and bapt. Stratford:
+Thaddeus, b. 4 July 1725, bapt. 20 Nov. 1725.
Mary, bapt. Jan. 1726/7; m. David Beardsley.
Hannah, b. Feb. 1728/9, d. soon.
Benjamin, bapt. Aug. 1731.
James, bapt. Apr. 1734, d. before 1771.
Hannah, bapt. Feb. 1736/7, d. before 1771.
Sarah, bapt. Apr. 1741, d. y.
Eunice, bapt. Apr. 1745, d. before 1771.
Sarah, bapt. Sept. 1747; m. Solomon Plant.
Ann, b. [say 1750].

Bennett, Thaddeus, s. of Benjamin. Lt., Stratfield company, May 1772; Capt., 3d Co., 4th Regt., May 1775.

Born 4 July 1725; d. at Stratfield, 21 Jan. 1777.

He m. at Stratfield, 14 May 1751, Elizabeth Wilson; dau. of Joseph, bapt. 2 Apr. 1732; she m. (2) abt. 1780/1, Ebenezer Hall, and d. in 1815.

Will of Elizabeth Hall of Fairfield, 6 May 1806, proved at Stratford, Dec. 1815; three sons and two daus., Joseph-Wilson, Thaddeus Bennett, Silas Bennett, Grissel wife of Isaac Odle, Sarah wife of Nathan Fairchild.

Children:

> Joseph-Wilson, b. abt. 1751/2, d. at Stratfield, 1813; m. 1778, Sarah ———.
>
> Thaddeus, b. 23 Aug. 1758 [1753?] (Pension rec.), bapt. at Stratfield, 17 Mar. 1754, d. at Newtown, 8 Jan. 1831; m. at Stratford, 28 Feb. 1782, Martha Hall; dau. of David, b. at Weston, 3 Dec. 1760. He lived in Weston, 1789, and was then known as Jr. to distinguish him from Thaddeus (35).
>
> Grizell, b. 25 May 1761; m. 25 Apr. 1781, Isaac Odell.
>
> Sarah, m. Nathan Fairchild.
>
> Silas, b. abt. 1767, d. at Southford, 24 Apr. 1853 ae. 86 (g. s.); m. Betty-Ann ———, b. abt. 1768, d. 25 Jan. 1854 ae. 85 (g. s.).*

Bennett, Walcott.

He d. at Lincklaen, Chenango County, N. Y.

He m. at Stratfield, 17 Feb. 1777 (Pension rec.), Joanna Patchen, dau. of David, b. abt. 1756.

Children, bapt. Fairfield:†

> Joseph, b. in 1777, bapt. 7 Oct. 1790.
> David, bapt. 7 Oct. 1790.
> Ellen, bapt. 7 Oct. 1790.
> Esther, bapt. 22 Oct. 1789.
> Rufus, b. abt. 1799; m. Clarissa ———.

Bennett [*Unplaced*].

> ANNE m. Feb. 1791, Thomas Gilbert. [Easton Church]
> ASENATH m. Oct. 1792, Brown Whitehead. [Easton Church]

---

* Silas of Huntington conveyed, 1791, land in Stratfield in Hall's Neck, Joseph W. Bennett being a witness.

† First three bapt. at house of David Patchen.

116   HISTORY AND GENEALOGY OF

MARY m. 20 Mar. 1788, Augustus Lyon. [Redding rec.]
SHUBAEL m. 17 Feb. 1767, Rebecca Pickett. [Redding rec.]
LOIS, b. 13 Oct. 1767 (Pension rec.), m. (1) Jan. 1786, Jose Lyon of Weston; m. (2) 15 Oct. 1821, Elisha Morris of Stratfield.
SAMUEL, m. (rec. Weston) 3 Aug. 1773, Elizabeth Jackson. Children, rec. Weston: Zalmon, b. 4 June 1777; Ann, b. 27 Dec. 1778, d. 7 Mar. 1779; Ebenezer, b. 9 Nov. 1781; Elias, b. 11 Oct. 1785; Enos, b. 11 Apr. 1789; Lamson, b. 11 Apr. 1795. Adm'n on the estate of one Samuel [of Weston] was granted, 26 Aug. 1811, to Isaac Bennett.
MARY m. 16 Sept. 1790, Jabez Bennett. [Weston Church]
——— m. by 1777, Mary-Wheeler Jackson, dau. of Isaac, b. [say 1750].
——— m. by 1795, Eunice Westcott, dau. of Richard, b. [say 1760].
ANNE m. 24 Feb. 1785, Walker Sherman. [Weston rec.]
NATHAN had children bapt. Trinity Church: Nathan-Platt, bapt. 11 Sept. 1785; Sally, bapt. 23 July 1786.
HANNAH m. 6 Jan. 1799, Isaac Bedient. [Weston Church]
TIMOTHY had child, William-Ward, bapt. 22 Sept. 1793. [Greens Farms Church]

Benson [Unplaced].

ABRAHAM m. (1) 16 May 1802, Esther Jarvis; m. (2) 6 May 1804, Grizzel Burr. [Fairfield Church]

Bertine [Unplaced].

ISAAC of New York m. 17 Mar. 1805, Lydia Putnam. [Fairfield Church]

Betts, Stephen, Jr., s. of Stephen. Deputy for Redding, Oct. and Nov. 1776, May and Oct. 1782, May and Oct. 1783.

[Ruth wife of Mr. Stephen, d. at Redding, 18 Oct. 1764 ae. 61 yrs. 7 mos. (g. s.).]*

Stephen, Esq., d. at Redding, 24 Jan. 1826 ae. 87-9-9.

He m. at Danbury, Sarah Clark, b. [10 Feb. 1751], d. 31 Dec. 1821 ae. 70-10-21 (g. s.).

---

* But Ruth, dau. (?) of Stephen, d. 14 Oct. 1760 ae. 54, by the church record. Stephen, Sr., was living in Redding, 1766. Mary, dau. of Stephen Betts, m. (rec. Fairfield) 2 Nov. 1748, Daniel Hull. Hannah Betts m. (rec. Fairfield) 7 Nov. 1751, Peter Fairchild.

THE FAMILIES OF OLD FAIRFIELD 117

Children, rec. Redding:

Hannah, b. 19 Dec. 1773, d. 13 Apr. 1777.
Daniel, b. 19 Feb., bapt. 22 Sept. 1776; m. 25 Nov. 1798, Abigail Rogers.*
Sarah, b. 23 Nov. 1779, bapt. 19 Mar. 1780, d. at Redding, 3 May 1832 ae. 54 (g. s.); m. Samuel Whiting, who d. 29 Jan. 1832 ae. 71 (g. s.).
Polly, b. 19 Apr. 1786, d. 29 Feb. 1788 ae. 1 yr. 10 mos. (g. s.).
Polly, b. 29 May 1789.

Betts, Moses.

Born abt. 1755; d. at Greenfield, 19 Feb. 1818 ae. 63 (g. s.); m. Mary ———, b. [July 1763], d. 4 Mar. 1861 ae. 97 yrs. 8 mos. Moses of Wilton m. at Westport, 7 Mar. 1776, Ann Sturgis. Wife of Moses d. 20 Sept. 1835 (Miss Treadwell's book).

Distribution, 18 June 1818; widow Mary; eldest son Joseph P.; son Samuel; dau. Ruhamah wife of Hezekiah Banks; dau. Polly wife of Medad Banks; dau. Hannah Betts; son Moses G.

Children (Abigail and Moses bapt. at Westport as children of Moses of Wilton):

Joseph P.
Ruhamah, b. [4 Sept. 1785], d. at Easton, 12 Feb. 1875 ae. 89-5-8 (g. s.); m. Hezekiah Banks.
Polly, b. [4 Nov. 1792], d. at Easton, 10 July 1879 ae. 86-8-6 (g. s.); m. Medad Banks.
Samuel, b. abt. 1790, d. 21 May 1874 ae. 84 (g. s.); m. Sally Merwin, dau. of Abijah, b. abt. 1797, d. 30 June 1855(?) ae. 58(?) (g. s.).
Abigail, bapt. 26 Nov. 1791.
Moses G., bapt. 26 Nov. 1791.
Hannah, b. abt. 1798, d. at Greenfield, 16 Apr. 1879 ae. 81 (g. s.); m. Walter Banks.

Betts [*Unplaced*].

ELIJAH, JR., m. 19 Dec. 1792, Betty Patchen, at Wilton. [Weston Church]
MARY m. 12 Nov. 1793, Lewis Hanford, at Wilton. [Weston Church]
WIDOW MARTHA m. 25 Jan. 1759, Theophilus Hull, both of Redding. [Redding Town and Church]

---

* Children, rec. Redding: Julia, b. 19 Sept. 1799, d. 27 Dec. 1804 ae. 5-3-8 (g. s.), Eliza, b. 26 Apr. 1802.

PETER m. 15 Oct. 1786, Bathsheba Wright, of Norwalk. [Greens Farms Church]
RUTH m. 19 Sept. 1756, Ebenezer Hull. [Redding Church]
ABIGAIL m. 13 Dec. 1758, Hezekiah Booth. [Redding Church]
SARAH m. 25 Oct. 1764, Ephraim DeForest. [Redding Church]
ENOCH m. 27 June 1775, Mary Coley.* [Redding Church]
JOSEPH m. 29 Nov. 1749, Abigail Whitney. [Greens Farms Church]
MR. THADDEUS, of Ridgefield, m. 8 Nov. 1752, Miss Mary Gold. [Fairfield Church]
ABRAHAM, of Norwalk, m. 19 Apr. 1753, Mary Bedient. [Fairfield Church]
THADDEUS m. 3 Dec. 1760, Anna Patchen. [Weston Church]
MARY of Norwalk m. 15 Apr. 1781, Daniel Platt of L. I. [Greens Farms Church]

Bibbins, Israel.

Son of Arthur Bibbins of Windham; b. abt. 1747, d. at Fairfield, 15 June 1822 ae. 75 (g. s.).

He m. 9 Nov. 1769, Hannah Silliman, dau. of Capt. Nathaniel, b. 23 Jan. 1744/5, d. 7 Aug. 1819 ae. 75 (g. s.).

Called late of Windham, now of Fairfield, he bought a house in 1770 in the latter place.

Will 2 Aug. 1802, proved 19 June 1822; wife Hannah; children, Elijah, Betsey wife of David Wilson, Billy, Nathaniel Willson (?), Abigail wife of Ethan Sherwood, Hannah and Sally Bibbins. In the distribution, Sally was called widow of Stephen Morehouse.

Children, rec. and bapt. Fairfield:

Elijah, b. 25 Aug., bapt. 14 Oct. 1770, d. 3 Oct. 1843 ae. 73 (g. s.); Dea.; m. (1) 22 Sept. 1796, Lucretia Jennings, bapt. 17 Sept. 1769, d. 1 July 1819 ae. 49-9-26 (g. s.); m. (2) 25 Feb. 1821, Eunice Burr Eliot, b. 16 Aug. 1778, d. 28 Apr. 1862 ae. 83 (g. s.).†

Betsey, bapt. 5 Sept. 1773, d. 9 Apr. 1852 ae. 79 (g. s.); m. 20 Mar. 1800, David Wilson.

Billy, bapt. 18 Feb. 1776, d. 25 Apr. 1842 ae. 67 (g. s.); m. (1) 22 Sept. 1802, Anna Morehouse, dau. of William, bapt. 27 Oct. 1782, d. 6 Aug. 1825 ae. 42 yrs. 11 mos. (g. s.); m. (2) 11 Dec. 1825, Sarah Morehouse, bapt. 29 Aug. 1784, d. 30 Jan. 1862 ae. 77 yrs. 6 mos. (g. s.).‡

---

* Children of Enoch of Wilton, bapt. at Weston: Enoch, bapt. 24 Aug. 1787; Calvin, bapt. 16 May 1789.
† Children, bapt. Fairfield: Susan, bapt. 3 Feb. 1798; Anson, bapt. 7 July 1799.
‡ Child, bapt. Fairfield: William-Henry, bapt. 7 Apr. 1805.

THE FAMILIES OF OLD FAIRFIELD 119

Nathaniel-Silliman, bapt. 18 Jan. 1778, d. 18 Dec. 1841 ae. 64 (g. s.);
m. (1) Susan ———, who d. 16 Nov. 1814 in 34 yr. (g. s.); m.
(2) Ruth ———, who d. 20 Apr. 1874 ae. 84 (g. s.).
Abigail, bapt. 29 Apr. 1781; m. 4 Nov. 1798, Ethan Sherwood.
Hannah, b. abt. 1783, bapt. 26 Feb. 1786, d. at Fairfield, 23 Mar. 1824 ae. 42 (g. s.).
Sally, b. [Oct. 1785], bapt. 26 Feb. 1786, d. at Fairfield. 23 Nov. 1865 ae. 80 yrs. 1 mo. (g. s.); m. Stephen Morehouse.

Biggs [Unplaced].

MARY m. 15 Mar. 1708, Deliverance Bennett. [Fairfield Rec.]

1. Bixby, Elias.

He m. Eleanor Andrews, dau. of Ens. John, b. 9 Oct. 1711.

Children:

2+Jonathan.
3+? Ebenezer.
    Abigail, bapt. 11 Apr. 1742, d. 16 Sept. 1760.
    David, bapt. 18 May 1746.
    Elias, bapt. at Redding, 27 Mar. 1748; m. at Wilton, 28 Apr. 1771, Grace Sterling.
    ? Ellen, d. 6 Aug. 1774; m. at Redding, 27 Mar. 1770, Seth Meeker.
    ? Mabel, m. at Redding, 15 Nov. 1770, Nathan Coley.

2. Bixby, Jonathan, s. of Elias.

He m. 4 July 1752, Martha Hull, dau. of George, bapt. 22 Sept. 1731.

Children, first four rec. Fairfield:

Lydia, b. 19 Feb. 1753.
Sarah, b. 9 Feb. 1755.
Daniel, b. 15 May 1757.
John, b. 15 May 1757.

3. Bixby, Ebenezer, s. of Elias.

He m. at Weston, 1 Jan. 1767, Mary Morehouse; dau. of Nathan, b. 14 Nov. 1747.

Children, bapt. Weston:

Eleanor, bapt. 17 Nov. 1768; m. 24 Jan. 1788, Joseph Morehouse.
Alban, bapt. 14 July 1771; m. 29 Mar. 1790, Mary Sturges.

Black [*Unplaced*].

CATY m. 15 July 1787, Samuel Wakeman, Jr. [Weston rec.]

Blackman, John, s. of John [Vol. I, p. 87].

Born abt. 1705; d. at Fairfield in 1737.

He m. Anna Jackson, dau. of Joseph, bapt. 2 July 1710, d. at Oxford, 17 July 1777 ae. 68. She m. (2) Samuel Chatfield, of Redding and Oxford.

Children (incomplete record):

Gershom, d. at Derby, 14 Sept. 1751.
Anna, d. at Oxford, 9 May 1781; m. (1) at Derby, 12 Oct. 1756, Thomas Silby; m. (2) at Oxford, 7 Aug. 1761, Richard Smith.

Blackman, Peter, s. of John [Vol. I, p. 87].

Born abt. 1725; d. by 1780; m. at Westport, 14 Oct. 1746, Abigail Beers; dau. of Ephraim. She d. in 1791.

Est. distributed 4 Apr. 1780 to widow Abigail; only son John; eldest dau. Eunice wife of John Downing; youngest dau. Nabby wife of Hezekiah Bulkley.

Children, rec. Fairfield, bapt. Greenfield:

Eunice, b. 10, bapt. 22 June 1747; m. John Downing.*
John, b. 15(?), bapt. 9 July 1749.
Abigail, b. 16 Feb. 1755; m. 23 Feb. 1775, Hezekiah Bulkley.

Blackman [*Unplaced*].

EUNICE m. 26 July 1771, Alexander Russique. [Weston Church]
ABRAHAM, had son John, bapt. 17 Aug. 1735. [Greenfield Church]
EDWARD [of Stratford] m. 10 Oct. 1747, Eunice Odell.† [Greenfield Church]
MARY of Fairfield m. 1 Feb. 1802, David Monroe of Ripton. [Greens Farms Church]
DANIEL m. 1 July 1773, Mary Hubbell. Children: William, b. 26 Dec. 1773, d. 25 Nov. 1795; Thomas, b. 2 Aug. 1777; Elizabeth, b. 12 Jan. 1780; Abigail, b. 2 Nov. 1782, d. 14 June 1796; Mary, b. 25 Oct. 1786; Ebenezer-Hubbell, b. 11 Aug. 1789; Daniel, b. 9 Aug. 1792, bapt. at Easton, 30 Dec. 1792. [Weston rec.]

---

* Eunice Downing m. at Trinity Church, 7 Jan. 1798, Daniel Monroe.
† Edward had Eunice, bapt. at Easton, 17 Nov. 1765.

NEHEMIAH S., b. 21 Sept. 1763; m. 25 Feb. 1788, Olly ———. Children: Edward, b. 7 Dec. 1788; James, b. 23 Oct. 1790; John, b. 15 Sept. 1792; Elizabeth, b. 15 Aug. 1794; Abigail, b. 7 June 1796; Nathaniel, b. 17 Mar. 1798. [Weston rec.]

STEPHEN, b. 26 Nov. 1769; m. 28 Nov. 1792, Charity Wheeler, b. 2 Nov. 1773. Children: Israel, b. 26 Aug. 1793; Wheeler, b. 5 Jan. 1795, bapt. at Easton, May 1795; Eli, b. 28 Jan. 1797. [Weston rec.]

ALICE, b. 28 Sept. 1767; m. 8 Nov. 1786, Wildman Hall. [Weston rec.]

TIMOTHY m. 21 Mar. 1764, Rhoda Risden. [Easton Church]

NEHEMIAH m. 25 July 1764, Abiah Booth. They owned the Covenant at Easton Church, Sept. 1766. Children, bapt. Easton: Alla, bapt. 1 Nov. 1767; Stephen, bapt. 28 Jan. 1770.

Blair Archibald.

Son of James, bapt. at Fairfield Church, Sept. 1726.

He d. at Greenfield, 1 Apr. 1766.

He m. Feb. 1754, Abigail Goodsell; dau. of Rev. John, b. 8 Jan. 1737/8, d. 5 Apr. 1776 ae. abt. 40. She m. (2) 28 June 1768, William Hicks.

Phebe Blair chose Epaphras Goodsell for guardian, 5 Mar. 1767; and he was appointed for Hannah Blair.

Children, bapt. Greenfield:

> Phebe, b. 29 Sept., bapt. 6 Oct. 1754; m. 24 Mar. 1776, Peter Morehouse, of Fairfield.
> Abigail, bapt. 19 Aug. 1759, d. 21 July 1762 ae. abt. 3.
> Hannah.
> James, bapt. Feb. 1764, d. 11 Feb. 1764 ae. 5 days.
> Abigail, bapt. 16 June 1765.

Blatchley [*Unplaced*].

> EUNICE, of Norwalk, m. 10 Aug. 1788, Trowbridge Crossman. [Greens Farms Church]
> MARTHA d. 5 Jan. 1809 ae. 94. [Greens Farms Church]

Booth, Ebenezer, s. of Ebenezer [Vol. I, p. 89].

Born (at Stratford, but rec. Newtown), 11 Mar. 1686; d. at Newtown, 11 Feb. 1726/7; m. at Stratford, 8 Sept. 1709, Mary Clark; dau. of James, b. 10 Jan. 1686/7.

Inv. 29 June 1727; adm'n granted to widow Mary, 3 Oct. 1727. She was appointed guardian, 4 June 1728, to five of her children,

Abner, Mary, Ebenezer, Abiah, and Eunice. Distribution was made to the widow and eight children.

Nathaniel Booth of Redding, Abner Booth of Newtown, Ebenezer Booth of Stratford, John Fabrique and Deborah his wife of Newtown, Ebenezer Sanford and Ann his wife of Newtown, Peter Mallet and Mary his wife of Stratford, Joseph Summers and Abiah his wife of Stratford, and Eunice Booth of Newtown, conveyed 1744 to Nathaniel Nichols of Newtown. [Newtown Deeds.]

Children, rec. Newtown:

Deborah, b. 6 July 1710; m. John Fabrique, of Newtown.
Ann, b. 6 Dec. 1711; m. 10 June 1731, Ebenezer Sanford, of Newtown.
+Nathaniel, b. 10 Mar. 1713.
Abner, b. 16 July 1714.
Mary, b. 22 Feb. 1716/7; m. Peter Mallett.
Ebenezer, b. 1 Apr. 1718; m. 6 Dec. 1739, Rachel Sanford, dau. of Samuel of Milford and Newtown.
Abiah, b. 11 Feb. 1719/20; m. Joseph Summers.
Eunice.

Booth, Nathaniel, s. of Ebenezer.

Born 10 Mar. 1713; d. in Redding, 1761; m. 4 Oct. 1739, Mary Foote; dau. of Solomon, bapt. 29 Oct. 1721.

Will of Nathaniel of Redding, 26 Oct., proved 1 Dec. 1761; sons and daus.; son Solomon for his birthright.

Inv. of Nathaniel of Fairfield, 3 Feb. 1762. Distribution of Est. of Nathaniel of Redding, 26 Apr. 1763: Nathaniel, Mary, Abner, Solomon, Sarah, Abner [*sic,* for Admar], Eunice Booth.

Children, rec. Fairfield:

Solomon, b. 13 Oct. 1740, bapt. at Redding, 9(?) Oct. 1740.
Mary, b. 23 Sept. 1742, d. at Redding, 1764. Will of Mary of Fairfield, 14 Mar., proved 17 May 1764; sisters Sarah and Eunice Booth; bros. Solomon, Admar, Nathan; neighbor, Gurdon Merchant, Exec'r.
Abner, b. 25 Feb. 1745/6, bapt. 10 Mar. 1745; will dated 20 Feb. 1767, named wife Mercy and only son Nathaniel; m. at Weston, 2 Dec. 1764, Mercy Olmstead.
Sarah, b. 24 Feb. 1748/9.
Eunice, b. 27 Jan. 1751.
Nathaniel, b. 22 May 1755.
Admar.

THE FAMILIES OF OLD FAIRFIELD

Booth, Josiah.

Born 26 Mar. 1748; d. at Easton, Feb. 1812 in 64 yr. (g. s.); m. 20 May 1768, Sarah ———, b. 23 June 1749, d. 20 Sept. 1804 in 55 yr. (g. s.). Children, rec. Weston: Ebenezer-Hoyt, b. 1 Jan. 1769; Silvester, b. 1 Oct. 1771, drowned 15 Oct. 1784 (?); Lydia, b. July 1772; Mary, b. 11 Sept. 1774; Abiah, b. 15 Nov. 1776; Daniel-Bronson, b. 25 Oct. 1778; Mary, b. 4 Dec. 1780; John, b. 28 Dec. 1782; Sarah, b. 23 Sept. 1784; Justice, b. 8 Mar. 1787; Joseph, b. 25 May 1789; Sylvina, b. 3 Nov. 1794.

Booth [Unplaced.]

> MARY, b. 19 July 1741; m. 4 Nov. 1756, Thomas Gilbert. [Weston rec.]
> ABIAH m. 14 Aug. 1796, Samuel Treadwell. [Weston rec.]
> ABIAH m. 25 July 1764, Nehemiah Blackman. [Easton Church]
> LYDIA m. 26 Oct. 1791, Ebenezer Hall. [Easton Church]
> SILVESTER m. Jan. 1792, Sarah Beers. [Easton Church]

Bostwick, David, s. of Zechariah [Vol. I, p. 94].

Born 26 Oct. 1693, d. in 1758.

He m. (1) 26 Feb. 1719/20, Sarah Nichols.

He m. (2) 3 Sept. 1726, Elizabeth MacKenzie, dau. of Dougal; bapt. 29 Sept. 1706.

Will 8 Oct. 1752, proved 8 July 1758; wife Elizabeth; children Henry, William, Samuel, Augustus, Sarah Bates, Elizabeth Bostwick, Anna Bostwick.

Child [by first wife]:
> David, b. 24 Apr. 1721.

Children [by second wife]:
> Sarah, bapt. July 1727; m. ——— Bates.
> John, bapt. Aug. 1728, d. Aug. 1728.
> Henry.
> William.
> +Samuel.
> Elizabeth.
> Anna.
> Augustus.

Bostwick, Zechariah, s. of Zechariah [Vol. I, p. 94].

He m. Elizabeth Rumsey, dau. of Robert, bapt. 13 Sept. 1713. She m. (2) 30 Aug. 1744, Joseph Jennings, 3d.

Child, bapt. Fairfield:

>Mary, bapt. 29 May 1739, d. at Ridgefield, 8 Aug. 1768 in 30 yr.; m. 22 Apr. 1762, Philip-Burr Bradley.

Bostwick, Samuel, s. of David.

He m. Mar. 1756, Sarah Jennings, dau. of Isaac, bapt. 14 May 1732.

Children, rec. Fairfield:

>Esther, b. 20 Aug. 1756.
>Elizabeth, b. 8 Jan. 1758.
>Sarah, b. 14 Aug. 1759.
>Abigail, b. 25 Sept. 1761.
>David, b. 27 Sept. 1763.
>Henry, b. 28 Nov. 1767.
>William, b. 27 Feb. 1771.

Bosworth [*Unplaced*].

>MARY of New Milford m. 5 Nov. 1772, Elijah Couch. [Redding rec.]

Botsford [*Unplaced*].

>FRANCIS m. 29 May 1796, Ruth Nichols, of Stratfield. [Fairfield Church]

Boughton [*Unplaced*].

>ANNIS m. 1 Nov. 1792, Stephen Gray. [Redding Rec.]
>ORRIN m. 9 Jan. 1810, Sally Gray, and had dau. Fanny, b. 7 Mar. 1810. [Redding Rec.]
>JOSHUA had child John, bapt. 1 Dec. 1797. [Greens Farms Church]

Bradley [Vol. I, pp. 97-100].

1 Francis (-1689) m. Ruth Barlow.
  2 John (-1703) m. Hannah Sherwood.
      6 *Joseph* (1702-1770).
  3 Francis (-1716) m. Sarah Jackson.
      7 *Francis* (1699-1786).
      8 *Samuel* (1701-1772).
      9 *Ephraim* (1703-1748).
     10 *John* (1705-1776).
     11 *Peter* (1710-1768).
     12 *Gershom* (1712-1795).
  4 Daniel (-1713) m. Abigail Jackson.
     13 *Daniel* (1704-1765).
     14 *James* (1712-1784).
  5 Joseph (-1714) m. Ellen ———.
     15 *David* (1708-1772).
     16 *Joseph* (1711-1776).

6. **Bradley, Joseph,** s. of John.

Bapt. 14 June 1702, d. at Fairfield in 1770; m. 20 June 1724, Olive Hubbell, dau. of Samuel; bapt. 15 Feb. 1707/8.

Will 7 Feb. 1770, proved 5 Mar. 1770; wife Olive; four sons, Onesimus, Nathan, Joseph, Benjamin; daus. Ruth, Martha. The two daus. with their husbands conveyed in 1770 to their four brothers.

    Children, rec. Fairfield, bapt. Greenfield:

      Thaddeus, b. 25 May, bapt. 18 June 1727, d. y.
  17+Onesimus, b. 17, bapt. 20 July 1730.
      Eunice, b. 2 Jan., bapt. 18 Mar. 1732/3; m. at Westport, 19 Dec. 1752, Obadiah Platt.
      Ruth, b. 24 Feb., bapt. 11 May 1735, d. 25 Sept. 1811 in 77 yr. (g. s., Easton); m. Thomas Treadwell.
      Martha, b. 2 Sept. 1737; m. at Weston, 22 Feb. 1759, Nehemiah Cable.
  18+Nathan, b. 20 July 1740, ["daughter" bapt. 15 June 1740].
      Isaac, b. 15 Jan. [1742/3?], d. y.
  19+Joseph, b. 22 Oct. 1746, bapt. 15 Feb. 1746/7.
  20+Benjamin, b. 1 Apr., bapt. 9 May 1749.

7. **Bradley, Francis,** s. of Francis, 2d.

Born 29 May 1699; d. at Greenfield in 1786; m. 29 Apr. 1719, Mary Sturgis, dau. of John, b. 8 Aug. 1699. "Old Graney Bradley" d. 8 Apr. 1794 in 95 yr. (Perry Diary).

Will 23 Feb. 1786, proved 3 Apr. 1786; wife Mary; children of son Ebenezer dec'd, viz., two gr. sons Eliphalet and Ebenezer, and four gr. daus.; sons Elnathan and Francis; gr. dau. Hannah Nichols; gr. son Daniel Banks; dau. Elizabeth Banks; gr. dau.

Jane Bulkley; daus. Eleanor Banks, Esther Wakeman, Abigail Davis, Mary Lyon; gr. son Joseph Burr; son-in-law Seth Lyon.

Children, rec. Fairfield and Greenfield:
>Mary, b. 13 Sept. 1719, bapt. 22 May 1720, d. 24 Apr. 1741 ae. 21 yrs. 6 mos. 9 days; m. May 1739, Gershom Banks.
>Elizabeth, b. 30 Aug. 1721, d. in 1808; m. 14 May 1740, John Banks.
>21+Ebenezer, b. 5 Oct., bapt. 1 Dec. 1723.
>Eleanor, b. 7 Oct., bapt. 26 Dec. 1725, d. 29 May 1812 (g. s.); m. 20 June 1744, Benjamin Banks, Jr.
>22+Francis, b. 11, bapt. 28 Jan. 1727/8.
>23+Elnathan, b. 21, bapt. 24 Jan. 1729/30.
>Jane, b. 21, bapt. 22 Apr. 1733, d. 17 Feb. 1768 in 35 yr.; m. 3 Jan. 1753, Increase Burr.
>Esther, b. 2, bapt. 7 Sept. 1735, d. 20 Dec. 1808 ae. 73 (g. s.); m. 3 Oct. 1754, John Wakeman, Jr.
>Abigail, b. 20, bapt. 21 May 1737; m. 21 Mar. 1758, Joseph Davis.
>Nehemiah, b. 20, bapt. 21 May 1737, d. 22 May 1737 ae. 2 days.
>Mary, b. [say 1741]; m. 7 Mar. 1764, Seth Lyon.

8. Bradley, Samuel, s. of Francis.

Born 29 Sept. 1701; d. at Greenfield, 12 Oct. 1772 ae. 71 (g. s.); m. Nov. 1724, Sarah Whelpley; dau. of Joseph, b. 17 Jan. 1707,* d. 12 Sept. 1777 (g. s.).

Will 14 Oct. 1757, proved 11 Nov. 1772; wife Sarah; five children, Samuel, Hezekiah, Sarah, Mabel, Huldah.

Distribution of Mrs. Sarah's Est., 10 Oct. 1778; eldest son, Samuel Esq.; Hezekiah; heirs of Sarah dec'd wife of Col. John Read; dau. Mabel Osborn; Huldah wife of Capt. Zalmon Read.

Children, rec. Fairfield and Greenfield:
>Sarah, b. 27 Nov., bapt. 25 Dec. 1726, d. at Redding, 8 May 1774 ae. 47 (g. s.); m. 19 Dec. 1750, John Read.
>Mabel, b. 1, bapt. 11 May 1729, d. at Fairfield, 13 June 1807 ae. 77 (g. s.); m. 21 May 1761, Seth Osborn.
>24+Samuel, b. 4, bapt. 13 Jan. 1733/4.
>25+Hezekiah, b. 28 July, bapt. 3 Aug. 1735.
>Huldah, b. 22, bapt. 29 Jan. 1740/1, d. at Redding, 24 Feb. 1824 ae. 83 (g. s.); m. Zalmon Read.

9. Bradley, Ephraim, s. of Francis.

Bapt. 19 Sept. 1703; d. at Westport, 5 Oct. 1748 ae. 45 (g. s.); m. Sarah Scribner, dau. of Thomas. She m. (2) Mar. 1749, Daniel Bradley, and d. abt. 1783.

---
* By gravestone and Fairfield town rec., or 18 Jan. 1705/6 by Greenfield rec.

Distribution 5 Apr. 1749: Widow Sarah; eldest dau. Sarah wife of John Goodsell, Jr.; 2d dau. Molly Bradley; 3d dau. Betty Bradley; youngest dau. Ruth Bradley; only son Stephen.

Jonathan Coley, 5 Mar. 1771, had land undivided with heirs of Ephraim Bradley; there were also minor heirs, John, Sarah and Molly Goodsell, children of Sarah (dec'd), under guardianship of their father John Goodsell.

Unrecorded will of Sarah, 14 Feb. 1783; eldest dau. Betty; 2d dau. Ruth; 3d dau. Eunice; son-in-law Eliphalet Coley, Exec'r.

In 1784, Daniel and Betty Hull, Ebenezer and Ruth Ogden, Silliman and Molly Godfrey, all of Fairfield, and Silas and Sarah Fairchild of Newtown, conveyed to Jonathan Hanford and Stephen-Bradley Hanford, sons of Joseph Hanford of Fairfield, the homestead which lately belonged to Stephen Bradley dec'd.

Children, last two bapt. Westport:

> Sarah, b. Mar. 1730, d. at Westport, 27 Aug. 1755: m. at Greenfield, 18 Jan. 1748/9, John Goodsell.
> Molly, b. [say 1731], d. at Westport, 19 Sept. 1753 in 5 [misreading?] yr. Adm'n was granted, 1 Jan. 1754. Adm'n granted, 1 Dec. 1772, to Daniel Hull and Ebenezer Ogden.
> Betty, b. abt. 1733, d. at Greenfield, 3 May 1809 in 77 yr. (g. s.); m. 11 Apr. 1759, Daniel Hull.
> Ruth, b. [say 1736], d. at Westport [say 1742], ae. 6 (g. s.).
> Ruth, bapt. 30 Oct. 1743; m. 17 Mar. 1763, Ebenezer Ogden.
> 26+Stephen, b. 15 Aug. 1745, bapt. 6 Oct. 1745; chose Daniel Bradley for guardian, June 1763.

10. **Bradley, John,** s. of Francis. Lt., 5th Co., Fairfield, May 1747.

Born Nov. 1705, d. at Greenfield, Oct. 1776 (death entered under Dec. by the minister as occurring during his absence). He m. (1) 13 Jan. 1725/6, Sarah Gilbert, b. 12 Feb. 1705/6, d. 14 Apr. 1767 ae. 61; m. (2) 11 Oct. 1768, Widow Mary Silliman. She was widow of Robert Silliman and formerly of Abijah Morehouse; prob. dau. of Henry Summers, Jr.*

Will 4 Oct. 1776, proved 4 Nov. 1776; wife Mary; son Isaac; two daus. Lois wife of Joseph Gilbert and Miriam wife of Thomas Goodsell; gr. children Thomas Banks and Maranie Banks; gr. son

---

* She could not have been the Mary who d. at Greenfield, 18 May 1776 in 58 yr.; this is prob. a variant record for the death of the wife of Joseph (16) who by gravestone d. 24 May 1776 in 61 yr.

Adad; all my sons (I have heretofore given my son Ephraim); sons John and Seth, Exec'rs.

Distribution 4 Apr. 1778: Widow Mary Bradley; eldest son John; sons Seth, Enos, Ephraim, Moses, Abel, Isaac; daus. Lois wife of Joseph Gilbert and Miriam wife of Thomas Goodsell; gr. son Adad Bradley; gr. dau. Marany wife of Samuel Whitney; gr. son Thomas Banks.

Children [by first wife], rec. Greenfield:*

    Hannah, b. and bapt. 14 Oct. 1726, d. 24 Oct. 1749 ae. 23 (g. s.); m. 12 Oct. 1743, Gershom Banks.

    Lois, b. 25 June, bapt. 18 July 1729, d. at Easton, 28 Dec. 1801 ae. 72 (g. s.); m. 3 Oct. 1744, Joseph Gilbert.

27+John, b. 14 Apr., bapt. 15 May 1731.
28+Reuben, b. 17 Jan., bapt. 18 Feb. 1732/3.
29+Seth, b. 5 Apr., bapt. 4 May 1735.

    Miriam, b. 5 Feb., bapt. 6 Mar. 1736/7, d. 11 Dec. 1781; m. Thomas Goodsell.

30+Enos, b. 14 Sept., bapt. 14 Oct. 1739.

    Lockwood, b. 19, bapt. 23 May 1742, d. 24 June 1745.

31+Ephraim, b. 10, bapt. 16 Dec. 1744.
32+Moses, b. 3, bapt. 7 Dec. 1746.
33+Abel, b. 10, bapt. 12 Aug. 1750.
34+Isaac, b. 19 Dec. 1754.

11. Bradley, Peter, s. of Francis.

Bapt. 17 Dec. 1710; d. at Greenfield, 2 Aug. 1768 in 59 yr.; m. (1) 5 Nov. 1735, Damaris Dimon, b. Sept. 1714.

He m. (2) Oct. 1756, Sarah Price; widow of Lemuel Price and dau. of Joseph Middlebrook, bapt. 8 Feb. 1712/3.

Will 4 June 1760, proved 23 Sept. 1768; wife Sarah; daus. Hannah wife of Enos Wheeler, Grizzel wife of Ichabod Burr, and Grace wife of Joseph Burr; son William Bradley; daus. Jane, Damaris, Ruamah Bradley. William chose Joseph Burr of Redding for guardian, 25 Aug. 1768. John Hubbell was appointed Adm'r, 1 Nov. 1768.

Adm'n on Est. of Damaris was granted, 10 Aug. 1768, to Ichabod Burr. Distribution 2 Jan. 1769 of Est. of Damaris wife of Peter Bradley: William Bradley; Hannah wife of Enos Wheeler; Grace wife of Joseph Burr; Grizel wife of Ichabod Burr; heirs of Ruamah late wife of Calvin Wheeler; Jane wife of Epaphras Goodsell; Damaris wife of John Murwin.

---

* Bible record of this family furnished by Mrs. Nellie L. Elwood of Westport.

Children by first wife, rec. Greenfield:
> Hannah, b. 6, bapt. 10 Oct. 1736; m. 15 May 1760, Enos Wheeler.
> Grace, b. 31 Mar., bapt. 2 Apr. 1738; m. 28 May 1758, Joseph Burr, Jr.
> Grissell, b. 22 Oct., bapt. 25 Nov. 1739, d. at Greenfield, 20 June 1825 ae. 86 (g. s.); m. Ichabod Burr.
> Aaron, b. and bapt. 20 Sept. 1741, d. 6 Jan. 1759 ae. 17 yrs. 4 mos.
> Ruamah, b. 25, bapt. 26 June 1743, d. at Redding, 5 Dec. 1762; m. 5 July 1762, Calvin Wheeler.
> Jane, b. 22, bapt. 24 Mar. 1744/5; m. 5 Dec. 1765, Epaphras Goodsell.
> Damaris, b. 17, bapt. 21 Dec. 1746, d. at Greenfield, 8 Oct. 1777 in 32 yr.; m. 13 Aug. 1767, John Merwin, Jr.
> Peter, b. Nov., bapt. 20 Nov. 1748, d. 4 Sept. 1750 ae. 1 yr. 10 mos.

35+William, b. 2, bapt. 26 Aug. 1750.

12. Bradley, Gershom, s. of Francis. Lt., 7th Co., Fairfield, May 1753.

Bapt. 7 Dec. 1712; d. at Easton, 15 Jan. 1795 in 83 yr. (g. s.); m. (1) Sarah Sherwood, dau. of Benjamin, Sr., bapt. 12 Aug. 1711*; m. (2) Elizabeth Osborn, bapt. 28 June 1719; m. (3) Dec. [1741], Jane Dimon, dau. of Moses, b. 11 Aug. 1722, d. 3 Feb. 1755 ae. 32 yrs. 5 mos. 12 days (g. s., Greenfield); m. (4) Deborah Dimon, dau. of Ebenezer, bapt. 27 Apr. 1735, d. at Easton, 3 Sept. 1832 in 99 yr. (g. s.).

Will proved 5 Feb. 1795; wife Deborah; to children equally; son Gershom.

Gershom conveyed, 1786, to son Gershom, 3d, as part of his portion; and the same year to dau. Molly-Burr Bradley, a negro girl Dorcas, aged abt. 9, reserving said negro girl to himself and wife during their lives.

Child by second wife, bapt. Greenfield:†
> Sarah, b. 29 Mar. 1739, bapt. 24 Mar. 1739, d. y.

Children by third wife, rec. Greenfield:†
> Gershom, b. 19 Nov. 1742, bapt. Nov. 1742, d. in 1767.
> Sarah, b. 27 Dec. 1744, bapt. 13 Jan. 1744/5; m. 9 Aug. 1764, David Barlow, Jr.

---

* Greenfield rec. give 20 Feb. 1725/6 as date of baptism of Sarah, first wife of Gershom Bradley. This was the date of baptism of Sarah Sherwood, dau. of Benjamin, Jr.; but as she was too young to be Bradley's wife and furthermore is known to have died at age of nine, it seems obvious that the minister copied in this baptism by error, mistaking it for that of Sarah Sherwood, dau. of Benjamin, Sr.

† The births of all the children are from the family Bible (printed Edinburgh, 1752), now owned by Mrs. Wesley Burr, Greenfield Hill, Fairfield, Conn. According to the Bible, Jane was b. 21 May 1747, and Jonathan 22 Mar. 1749, differing from the Greenfield record.

Jane, b. 22, bapt. 24 May 1747, d. 12 Feb. 1829; m. 24 Apr. 1765, Nathaniel Barlow, of Redding.

Jonathan, b. 23, bapt. 26 Mar. 1749, perhaps d. Dec. 1824 (Miss Treadwell's book); m. at Redding, 8 Dec. 1772, Grace Jackson; dau. of Joseph, b. at Ridgefield, 12 Jan. 1754.*

Dimon, b. 14 Apr. 1752, d. 17 Nov. 1785; m. Charity Wheeler, dau. of Enoch of New Fairfield.†

Andrew, b. 31 Jan. 1754, bapt. 31 Mar. 1754, d. at Fairfield, Vt., 1832; res. Redding, 1783, and New Fairfield, 1787; m. Ruth Wakeman, dau. of William, b. 3 June 1757, d. 25 May 1793.

Children by fourth wife, rec. Greenfield:‡

Deborah, b. 22 May 1757, bapt. at Fairfield, 11 Sept. 1757, d. at Easton, 24 Jan. 1846 ae. 89 (g. s.); m. 1 Feb. 1775, David Bradley.

Molly-Burr, b. 18, bapt. 20 Nov. 1766 (ae. abt. 2 days), d. 9 Dec. 1766.

Gershom, b. 13 Feb., bapt. 27 Mar. 1768, d. at Easton, 27 Aug. 1855 in 86 yr. (g. s.); will 16 Nov. 1850, proved 13 Sept. 1855; m. (1) 10 Dec. 1786, Mary Scudder, b. 6 Dec. 1770, d. 1 June 1824 in 55 yr. (g. s.); m. (2) Betsey ———, who d. 29 Aug. 1856 (Miss Treadwell's book); had seven children rec. Weston. Children (Bible rec.), two bapt. Easton: Elizabeth, b. 10 Aug. 1788, bapt. 5 Apr. 1789; m. Daniel Platt, d. 23 Dec. 1852; Deborah-Dimon, b. 20 May 1790, m. Uriah Parruck, d. 17 Jan. 1864; Sarah, b. 19 Sept. 1791, m. Enos B. Williams, d. 1 Apr. 1885; Burr, b. 19 July 1793, bapt. 9 Jan. 1794, d. 20 Sept. 1822; Scudder, b. 10 Mar. 1795; Lewis, b. 6 Aug. 1796, d. 22 Mar. 1799; Harry, b. 9 Jan. 1798, d. 7 Nov. 1822; Matsy, b. 29 Jan. 1800, m. Walker Bates, d. 5 June 1851; Mariah, b. 18 Sept. 1801, d. 6 Nov. 1803; Gershom, b. 11 Mar. 1803, d. 21 Jan. 1846; Mariah, b. 15 Feb. 1805, m. (1) 15 Feb. 1825, Frederick-Augustus Sanford; m. (2) Lyman Spears; Moses, b. 8 Feb. 1808, d. 25 Dec. 1834; Lewis, b. 15 Nov. 1810, d. 13 Apr. 1869.

Molly-Burr, b. 12 Mar. 1777 (Bible rec.), d. at Redding, 29 Nov. 1860 ae. 83-8-17 (g. s.); m. 22 Dec. 1795, Ephraim Sanford.

13. Bradley, Daniel, s. of Daniel. 1st Lt. of Regt. of Foot, Cape Breton Expedition, Feb. 1745; Capt., 5th Co., Fairfield, May 1747.

Bapt. 11 June 1704; d. at Ridgefield, 23 Apr. 1765.

---

* Child, Sarah, bapt. at Easton, 8 May 1774. Jonathan was appointed guardian, 1784, for his children Philip-Jackson and Sarah. Children of Jonathan, bapt. Trinity Church: Anna, bapt. 3 Feb. 1789; Charity, bapt. 20 May 1792.

† Children: Anna, m. Thaddeus Barnum; and Huldah, d. unm.

‡ See second footnote on preceding page.

He m. (rec. Fairfield) June 1724, Esther Burr, bapt. 31 Jan. 1702/3, d. 29 Dec. 1741 ae. 39 (g. s.).

He m. (2) (rec. Fairfield) Mar. 1743, Mary Fitch, who d. 21 Oct. 1746 (church rec.) or Dec. 1747 (town rec.).

He m. (3) Mar. 1748/9, Sarah Bradley; widow of Ephraim Bradley, and dau. of Thomas Scribner; she d. abt. 1783.

Daniel Bradley was appointed guardian to his children, Abigail, Jabez, Daniel, Hester, Stephen, Philip, and Elizabeth as they had realty which descended to them from Hannah Burr of Fairfield dec'd.

Will 5 Apr., proved 7 May 1765; wife Sarah; daus. Abigail Banks, Esther Bulkley, Elizabeth Bradley, Ruhamah Bradley, Eunice (unmarried); sons Daniel, Philip-Burr (educated), Stephen; he gave Ruhamah extra because he had sold her land in Canaan [New Canaan, prob. an inheritance from her mother].

Children by first wife, rec. Fairfield, bapt. Greenfield:

>Abigail, b. 25 Apr. 1725, d. 19 Mar. 1785 in 59 yr. (g. s.); m. Nehemiah Banks.
>Jabez, b. 20, bapt. 26 Feb. 1726/7, d. y.

36+Daniel, b. 20, bapt. 25 May 1729.
>Esther, b. 30 Mar. 1733, bapt. at Redding, 9 Apr. 1733, d. 18 Aug. 1770 (Perry Diary); m. 19 June 1753, Talcott Bulkley.

37+Stephen, b. 14 Dec. 1734, bapt. at Redding, 15 Dec. 1734.
38+Philip-Burr, b. 26 Mar., bapt. 9 Apr. 1738.
>Elizabeth, b. 22 Dec. 1741, bapt. in infancy.

Child by second wife, rec. Fairfield, bapt. Greenfield:

>Ruhamah, b. 31 July, bapt. 4 Aug. 1745, d. 23 Dec. 1767 ae. 22 yrs. 4 mos (g. s.); m. 21 Nov. 1765, Seth Sherwood.

Child by third wife, rec. Fairfield, bapt. Greenfield:

>Eunice, b. 22 July 1752, d. 25 June 1837 (g. s.); m. 13 Feb. 1770, Eliphalet Coley.

14. Bradley, James, s. of Daniel.

Bapt. 11 May 1712, d. at Ridgefield, 1784.

He m. at Redding, 4 Dec. 1735, Abigail Sanford; dau. of Ezekiel, bapt. 29 Aug. 1714.

Inv. 19 Mar. 1787; Samuel Bradley, Adm'r; estate insolvent.

In 1761, Ezekiel Bradley, and Ebenezer Lobdell, Jr., and Eunice his wife, all of Ridgefield, conveyed to Samuel Barlow a right at the rear end of Joshua Knowles' long lot. James Bradley, Jr., conveyed his interest, 1762.

Children, bapt. Redding:

> Ezekiel, bapt. 14 Aug. 1737; Ens., Newbury company, Oct. 1769; Lt.; m. (1) Ruth Lobdell, dau. of John, b. at Ridgefield, 26 Mar. 1745, d. at Brookfield, 7 June 1777 in 33 yr. (g. s.); m. (2) at Ridgebury, 23 Apr. 1778, Martha Wood.
> Eunice, bapt. 4 Mar. 1739; m. Ebenezer Lobdell, Jr.
> James, bapt. 24 May 1741; m. at Ridgefield, Mar. 1762, Olive Bennett.*
> Nathan, bapt. 21 Aug. 1743, d. May 1744.
> Abigail, bapt. 7 July 1745.

15. Bradley, David, s. of Joseph.

Bapt. 2 May 1708; d. at Greenfield, 13 May 1772 ae. 64.

He m. 25 Apr. 1731, Damaris Davis, bapt. 5 Sept. 1714, d. 15 July 1784 (Perry Diary).

Adm'n granted, 15 Sept. 1776, to David Bradley and Nathan Bradley, Jr.

Children, rec. Fairfield, bapt. Greenfield:

> Eunice, b. 15, bapt. 18 Mar. 1731/2, d. at Sherman, 6 Feb. 1790; m. 13 Nov. 1753, John Hendrick, Jr. [A Eunice Bradley had a dau. Dorothy Williams bapt. at Greenfield in 1753; who, called Dorothy Bradley, m. at Easton, 18 Feb. 1773, Seth Bradley, and d. at Greenfield, 14 Dec. 1843 ae. 90 (g. s.).]
> Justus, b. 7, bapt. 24 Mar. 1734/5, d. 1 Feb. 1745/6.
> Ellen, b. 16 June 1736, d. 4 Apr. 1775 in 39 yr.
> Olive, b. 21, bapt. 24 Sept. 1738; m. 1 Nov. 1759, Thaddeus Banks.
> David, b. 12 Sept. 1740, bapt. 1740.
> Damaris, b. 2 Dec. 1742, bapt. at Westport, 5 Dec. 1742; m. at Greenfield, 28 May 1761, Squire Wakeman.
> Justus, b. 22 Oct. 1745, bapt. at Westport, 24 Nov. 1745, d. at Greenfield, 14 Jan. 1778 in 33 yr.; m. at Westport, 9 Nov. 1773, Mabel Bradley, dau. of Joseph, b. 30 Mar. 1753, d. 6 Nov. 1822 ae. 69.†
> Nathan, b. 5 Feb. 1747/8 [16 Feb. by Pension record,—New Style], d. at Greenfield, 24 Dec. 1836 ae. 89; m. at Greenfield, 17 May 1775, Amelia Osborn; dau. of David, b. abt. 1755, d. 15 Apr. 1838 ae. 83.‡

---

* They had children rec. Ridgefield; see Rockwell's *Hist. of Ridgefield,* p. 503.

† Children, bapt. Greenfield: Justus, bapt. 6 Nov. 1774; David, bapt. Dec. 1776, d. at Greenfield, 17 Nov. 1820 ae. 44. A Justus of New York City, will 4 Nov. 1823, proved 1 Oct. 1827, left all to wife Frances.

‡ Children, bapt. Greenfield: Noah-Wakeman, bapt. 5 May 1776; Samuel, bapt. 17 May 1778. Noah W. m. at Westport, 16 Nov. 1802, Charity Bennett.

Mary, b. 28 [——] 1750, bapt. at Redding, 25 Jan. 1751; "Molly" m. 3 Dec. 1772, Noah Wakeman.
Betty, b. 9 July 1753, d. 16 Sept. 1778 ae. 26; "Elizabeth" m. at Fairfield, 18 July 1776, Moses Sturges.
Peter, b. 1 Apr. 1756; m. 20 Nov. 1777, Phebe Stratton.*

16. Bradley, Joseph, s. of Joseph.

Bapt. 8 Apr. 1711; d. at Greenfield, 26 June 1776 in 66 yr. (g. s.); Deacon; m. (1) 9 Nov. 1732, Jerusha Turney, dau. of Robert, bapt. 17 May 1713, d. 16 Jan. 1746 [1746/7] in 34 yr. (g. s.); m. (2) 11 Apr. 1747, Mary Squire, dau. of Lt. Samuel, b. abt. 1716, d. 24 May 1776 in 61 yr. (g. s.).

Will 1 Jan. 1774; proved 1 July 1776; wife Mary; sons Elisha and Increase (their late mother Jerusha had land); dau. Jerusha; sons Increase, Elisha, Joseph; daus. Jerusha, Ann, Naomy (these three already had received £60 apiece), Ruth, Mabel (had received £60), Sarah, Charity; friend David Williams, Exec'r.

Sarah Bradley conveyed, 1782, to sister Mary Winton, right from father Joseph Bradley dec'd.

Children by first wife, rec. Fairfield, bapt. Greenfield:

Mary, b. 21 June 1733, bapt. at Fairfield, July 1733, d. 23 Feb. 1756; m. 10 July 1755, Gershom Hubbell.
Jerusha, bapt. 1 Dec. 1734, d. y.
Increase, b. 29 May, bapt. 6 June 1736, d. 18 Dec. 1787 in 52 yr. (g. s.); Justice, 1777-82. Will 15, proved 19 Dec. 1787; sisters Mabel Bradley, Ruth Dimon; bro. Elisha Bradley, Exec'r.
Jerusha, b. 19, bapt. 22 Apr. 1739, d. 11 Oct. 1777; m. 26 June 1766, John Mills.

39+Elisha, b. 20, bapt. 26 May 1745.

Children by second wife, rec. Fairfield, bapt. Greenfield:

Ann, b. 11, bapt. 13 Jan. 1747/8; m. 16 Jan. 1766, Peter Sturges.
Naomi, b. and bapt. 22 Nov. 1749; m. 21 Oct. 1767, Daniel Sturges, Jr.
Ruth, b. 17, bapt. 21 July 1751; m. 11 May 1779, Col. Jonathan Dimon.
Mabel, b. 30 Mar., bapt. 10 June 1753, d. at Greenfield, 6 Nov. 1822 ae. 69; m. at Westport, 9 Nov. 1773, Justus Bradley.
Sarah, b. 17 Dec. 1754.
Mary, b. 6 Feb. 1757, d. at Easton, 2 July 1825 in 69 yr. (g. s.); "Molly" m. 11 Mar. 1778, Joseph Winton.

40+Joseph, b. 4, bapt. 7 Jan. 1759.

Charity, b. 14 Apr., bapt. Apr. 1761.

---

* Children, bapt. Greenfield: Oliver, bapt. 21 Mar. 1779; David, bapt. 6 Feb. 1780, perhaps d. 6 Dec. 1819 (Miss Treadwell's book).

17. Bradley, Onesimus, s. of Joseph.

Born 17 July 1730.

He m. at Greenfield, 8* Aug. 1754, Emitt Cable; dau. of John, b. 28 June 1734.

Children, first rec. Fairfield:
> Asa, b. 26 June 1756.
> Prob. others.

18. Bradley, Nathan, s. of Joseph.

Born 20 July 1740; d. at Greenfield, 31 July 1817 ae. 76 (church rec.), or 8 Aug. 1817 (Miss Treadwell's book).

He m. at Greenfield, 26 Apr. 1764, Mary Meeker of "Greens Farms"; dau. of Samuel, b. 28 Sept. 1743; the widow of Nathan, d. 4 Feb. 1820, of old age.

Children:
> Esther, b. 28 Mar. 1765, d. 12 or 13 Mar. 1847 ae. 82 (Bible rec.; 12 Mar. by g. s., Weston).†
> Samuel, d. in West Indies, Oct. 1802.
> Stephen, b. [Feb. 1774], d. at Greenfield, 6 Oct. 1861 ae. 87 yrs. 8 mos. (g. s.); m. at Westport, 6 Oct. 1799, Betty Downs, b. abt. 1777, d. (as "Elizabeth") at Greenfield, 10 Jan. 1820 ae. 42 (g. s.); m. (2) Lucy ———, b. abt. 1782, d. 6 Feb. 1824 ae. 42 [20 Feb. ae. 41 by g. s.]; m. (3) Lucinda ———, b. abt. 1781, d. 7 Aug. 1847 ae. 66 (g. s.).‡
> Charity, [? m. (rec. Weston) 30 Sept. 1797, Levi Wheeler]; m. [2?] ——— Roberts.
> Olive, m. at Westport, 8 Oct. 1797, Thaddeus Folliot, of Ridgefield.
> Sarah, m. at Westport, 28 Apr. 1796, Benjamin Merchant, of Redding.
> Eunice, m. at Westport, 20 Aug. 1797, John Merchant, of Redding.
> Happy, b. abt. 1787, d. at Greenfield, 14 Apr. 1867 ae. 80 (g. s.). Adm'n on her estate was granted, 8 May 1867, to Franklin Smith of Fairfield. Distribution, 1868: sister Charity Roberts; heirs of Samuel Bradley dec'd; heirs of Stephen Bradley dec'd; heirs of Esther Bradley dec'd; heirs of Eunice Merchant dec'd; heirs of Sarah Merchant dec'd; heirs of Olive Follett dec'd.

---

* 1 Aug., by town record.

† Her son, William Bradley, b. 28 Mar. 1789, d. 27 Feb. 1862; m. 3 Oct. 1813, **Sarah Treadwell**, b. 17 May 1791, d. 18 Oct. 1860.

‡ Stephen's will, 2 Oct. 1861, proved 16 Oct. 1861; dau. Elizabeth Wakeman; Larindia Nichols and Sylvester Turney, children of my dau. Mary M. Turney dec'd; sister Happy Bradley; son-in-law Charles Wakeman, Exec'r.

19. Bradley, Joseph, s. of Joseph. Justice, 1775, '76.

Born 22 Oct. 1746; d. at Berne, Albany County, N. Y., 1828.
He m. at Easton, 10 Dec. 1767, Martha Bates; dau. of Elias, b. 20 July 1749, d. 1836.
Rem. to Albany County, N. Y., 1791.

Children:

    Isaac, b. 1769, d. at Weston, 5 Apr. 1792; Inv. 5 Apr. 1792; m. at Easton, Sept. 1791, Sarah Williams.
    Joseph, b. 1771; m. Mary Wheeler, dau. of Calvin, b. 25 Aug. 1775.
    Daniel, b. 1773.
    Thankful, b. 1775; m. Sherwood Fanton, of Danbury.
    Sarah, b. 1777; m. Daniel Holmes, of Danbury.

20. Bradley, Benjamin, s. of Joseph.

Born 1 Apr. 1749; d. at Easton, in 1789.
He m. at Easton, 1 Feb. 1770, Abigail Dimon, b. 26 Apr. 1752, d. at Easton, 3 Oct. 1783 ae. 32 (g. s.).
Adm'n granted to Nathan Wheeler of Weston, 6 July 1789. Estate insolvent. Benoni Dimon was made guardian of Gold Bradley, 20 July 1789.

Children?:

    Jesse, b. 8 Feb. 1772; rem. 1802 to Thompson, Sullivan County, N. Y.; living there 1818; m. at Westport, 28 Feb. 1798, Abigail Bulkley, b. 31 Oct. 1778, d. at Greenfield, 31 Oct. 1851 ae. 73 (g. s.); called widow of Jesse of Sullivan County.*
    Gold.

21. Bradley, Ebenezer, s. of Francis.

Born 5 Oct. 1723; d. at Greenfield 26 Jan. 1782 (Perry Diary).
He m. (1) Sarah Hull, dau. of Eliphalet, b. 10, bapt. 29 May 1726, d. 20 Nov. 1770 (Perry Diary).
He m. (2) 6 June 1773, Mary Burr; dau. of Andrew, b. 22 May 1730, d. in 1784.
Inv. 3 June 1782. Distribution 28 Mar. 1786: widow Mary; sons Eliphalet, Ebenezer; daus. Sarah wife of Peter Perry, Lois wife of Daniel Dimon, Hannah wife of John Sherwood, Miriam

---

* In Weston records, under the births of Jesse Bradley and his wife Abigail, appear Ebenezer, b. 12 Apr. 1791, and Maryan, b. 13 Jan. 1794.

wife of Ephraim Nichols; gr. son Bradley Hull, son of dec'd dau. Ellen.

Children [by first wife], rec. Greenfield:

    Nehemiah, b. 16, bapt. 21 Oct. 1744, d. 18 Aug. 1762 ae. near 18.
    Ellen, b. Feb., bapt. 9 Feb. 1745/6, d. 3 Mar. 1775 (Perry Diary); m. 25 Dec. 1765, Silas Hull.
    Sarah, b. Jan., bapt. 17 Jan. 1747/8, d. 6 Apr. 1821; m. 6 Nov. 1763, Peter Perry.
    Eliphalet, b. 1749, bapt. 21 Nov. 1749, d. at Weston, 10 Apr. 1802; res. 1787, Newtown; m. 18 Dec. 1775, Sarah Price; prob. dau. of Samuel.* A widow Sarah Bradley d. June 1831 (Miss Treadwell's book).
    Lois, b. Sept., bapt. 8 Sept. 1751, living 1808; m. 6 Dec. 1770, Daniel Dimon.
    Hannah, b. abt. 1755, d. 19 Feb. 1830 ae. 74 (g. s.); m. 14 Jan. 1779, John Sherwood, Jr.
    Ebenezer, bapt. 8 Oct. 1758 (ae. 1 week), d. 26 Feb. 1759 ae. abt. 5 mos.
    Miriam, b. 20, bapt. 23 Mar. 1760 (ae. 5 days), d. 7 Oct. 1841 ae. 81 (g. s.); m. 15 Oct. 1780, Ephraim Nichols.
    Ebenezer, b. 8, bapt. 12 July 1767.

22. Bradley, Francis, s. of Francis, 3d.

Born 11 Jan. 1727/8; d. at Easton, 2 July 1809 in 83 yr. (g. s.); m. at Greenfield, 21 Feb. 1749/50, Ruth Hull, dau. of Eliphalet; b. 27 Mar. 1730, d. 6 Jan. 1806 ae. 76 (g. s.).

Will 16 Mar. 1808, proved 31 July 1809; to son Nehemiah, land in Weston; gr. dau. Naby, dau. of son Gershom dec'd; dau. Ruth Merwin; daus. Mary, Abigail, Ruth, Deborah, Sarah, Jemima, Lucinda; heirs of son Thaddeus dec'd. Distribution, 1810: son Nehemiah; Sarah wife of Hezekiah Hall; Deborah wife of Samuel Banks; Ruth wife of Abijah Merwin; Abigail wife of Joseph Banks; heirs of Thaddeus Bradley dec'd; Mary wife of Jabez Thorp; Tamason wife of Aaron Burr; Lucinda wife of Joseph Burr.

---

* Children, bapt. Greenfield: Eliphalet-Banks, bapt. 15 Feb. 1778 (ae. abt. 1 yr.); Hull, bapt. 20 June 1779, d. 20 Feb. 1813; a son, b. Feb. 1781 ae. 5 weeks. His will, 18 Jan., proved 5 June 1802; wife Sarah; two sons, Eliphalet and Hull; friend Calvin Wheeler, Exec'r. Adm'n on estates of Hull and Damaris Bradley was granted, 12 July 1822, to Calvin Wheeler, Jr.; her estate insolvent, his ordered distributed to his children. The estate of Hull Bradley of Weston was distributed, June 1823, to Matilda Gilbert, Hiram Bradley, Aaron B. Bradley, and Eliphalet H. Bradley. But one Hull Bradley d. 2 Sept. 1850 (Miss Treadwell's book).

THE FAMILIES OF OLD FAIRFIELD 137

Children, four rec. Fairfield; bapt. Greenfield; also Bible record:

> Mary, b. 11,* bapt. 19 May 1751, d. 6 Feb. 1825; m. 16 Aug. 1769, Jabez Thorp.
> Francis, b. 25† Oct. 1753, bapt. 14 Apr. 1754, d. 9 July 1807 in 54 yr. (g. s., Easton); m. (1) 27 Apr. 1780, Rachel Banks, b. 16 Apr. 1758, d. 27 Feb. 1800; m. (2) 23 Nov. 1800, Mary Banks, bapt. 1 Oct. 1769. His will, 16 June, proved 7 Aug. 1807; wife Mary; father Francis; nephew Francis Bradley, of Saratoga County, N. Y., son of Thaddeus dec'd.
> Thaddeus, b. 14 May 1755, drowned at Lake George, 14 July 1798 [10 July 1797, by Bible record]; m. 12 June 1783, Ellen Beers, b. 11 Feb. 1764.‡
> Abigail, b. 24 Mar. 1757, d. 18 May 1835 ae. 78 yrs. 2 mos. (g. s.); m. Feb. 1792, Joseph Banks.
> Ruth, b. 20 Dec. 1758, bapt. 18 Mar. 1759 ae. 2 or 3 mos., d. 18 Apr. 1826 ae. 68 (g. s.); m. 26 Oct. 1779, Abijah Merwin.
> Deborah, b. 27 Dec. 1760, bapt. 1 Mar. 1761, d. at Greenfield, 19 Feb. 1851 ae. 90-1-23 (g. s.); m. Samuel Banks.
> Sarah, b. 18 Apr., bapt. 11 Sept. 1763; m. Hezekiah Hall.
> Tamison, b. 7 Feb. 1765; m. 7 Apr. 1799, Aaron Burr.
> Nehemiah, b. 28 Jan. 1767, bapt. at Easton, 5 Sept. 1767; m. at Weston, 13 Sept. 1792, Esther Cable, [? dau. of William, bapt. 31 Aug. 1766].
> Gershom, bapt. at Easton, 5 Sept. 1767, d. y. [not in Bible record].
> Gershom, b. 21 Jan. 1769; m. 22 Apr. 1789, Sarah Davis.
> Lucinda, b. 26 Apr. 1773, d. 17 Feb. 1797; m. 8 Apr. 1795, Joseph Burr.

23. Bradley, Elnathan, s. of Francis.

Born 21 Jan. 1729/30; d. (by private rec.) 31 Jan. 1805.

He m. (1) at Greenfield, Oct. 1754, Sarah Goodsell; dau. of Rev. John, b. 4 Mar. 1734/5, d. 11 Apr. 1762 ae. 28 (g. s.).

He m. (2) 26 Dec. 1762, Hannah Bartram, of Redding; dau. of David, bapt. 18 Nov. 1733.

Children by first wife, bapt. Greenfield:

> Esther, b. 28 Feb. 1754 (family record; 1755?), bapt. 13 July 1755, d. 25 June 1827 ae. 72; m. at Westport, 23 Dec. 1771, Ebenezer Buckingham.
> Sarah, bapt. 8 Apr. 1759; m. 18 Jan. 1781, Moses Sturges; rem. to Ballston, N. Y.

---

* 22, by Bible record [New Style].
† 24, by Bible record.
‡ Child of Thaddeus, bapt. Trinity Church: Mary, bapt. 19 Sept. 1790.

Children by second wife, bapt. Greenfield:

Mabel, bapt. 16 Oct. 1763 (ae. abt. 2 mos.); res. 1841, Ballston Spa, Saratoga County, N. Y.; m. ―――― Hopps.

Sturges, bapt. 19 May 1765 (ae. abt. 10 days), d. 1849; rem. to Bradford, Steuben Company, N. Y.; m. ――――.

Ellen, bapt. 26 Apr. 1767 (ae. abt. 5 weeks); res. 1841, Otisco, Onondaga County, N. Y.; [prob. m. (1) 21 Nov. 1782, Thomas Perry]; m. (2) Squire Sherwood.

Jane, bapt. 19 Mar. 1769; res. 1841, Ballston, Saratoga County, N. Y.; m. Elijah Raymond.

Peter, perhaps m. at Fairfield, 9 June 1803, Nancy McRay.

Elnathan ["call'd Nathan, part idiot and ugly," wrote Uriah Bulkley (b. 1782)]; perhaps the Nathan who d. 1 Apr. 1793 of smallpox (Perry Diary).

Hannah, bapt. 14 Jan. 1776; m. ―――― Rumsey.

24. Bradley, Samuel, s. of Samuel. Justice, 1769-82.

Born 4 Jan. 1733/4; d. at Greenfield, 29 Aug. 1804 ae. 70 (g. s.); m. 10 Sept. 1751, Sarah Wakeman; dau. of Jabez, b. 15 Apr. 1732, d. 20 Feb. 1803 (g. s.).

He was a Universalist in religion.

Will 1 Mar. 1803, proved 4 Sept. 1804; daus. Lucy, Huldah; two sons, Zalmon, Walter; gr. son Abraham D. Baldwin, son of dau. Sarah dec'd.

Children, rec. Greenfield:

Zalmon, b. 10, bapt. 15 Feb. 1752, d. y.

Zalmon, b. 31 Dec. 1754, d. at Greenfield, 6 Oct. 1813 ae. 59 (g. s.); m. 20 Mar. 1776, Betty Wakeman, bapt. 1 June 1755, d. 20 Apr. 1805 ae. 50 (g. s.). His will, 4 Sept., proved 12 Oct. 1813; nephew William Bradley; bro. Walter.

Samuel, b. 9 Sept. 1756, d. 4 Dec. 1777 in 22 yr.

Sarah, b. 18, bapt. 23 Nov. 1758, d. at Greenfield, 3 Dec. 1795 ae. 37 (g. s.); m. (1) 4 June 1776, Thomas-Hanford Wakeman; m. (2) Dudley Baldwin.

Priscilla, b. and bapt. 10 Feb. 1760, d. s. p. 23 Nov. 1787 (Perry Diary); m. 8 Apr. 1778, Sturges Lewis.

Clarina, b. 16, bapt. 21 Nov. 1762, d. 23 Dec. 1787 (g. s.).

Walter, b. 15, bapt. 26 Aug. 1764, d. 7 Mar. 1842 in 78 yr. (g. s.); Deputy for Fairfield, May 1796, May and Oct. 1798, Oct. 1802, May and Oct. 1804, May 1805, May 1806, Oct. 1807; m. (1) at Trinity Church, New Haven, 6 Dec. 1783, Sarah Bradley, b. at Guilford, 22 Jan. 1765, d. at Greenfield, 6 May 1799 ae. 34 (g. s.); m. (2) 19 Jan. 1803, Nancy Abernathy, b. 12 July 1779, d. 25 Feb. 1833 ae. 53 (g. s.).

THE FAMILIES OF OLD FAIRFIELD 139

Lucy, b. 18, bapt. 24 Jan. 1768, d. 26 Mar. 1823 (g. s.). Will 30 Nov. 1818, proved 8 July 1823; sister Huldah Bradley.
Urania, b. 22, bapt. 26 Mar. 1769, d. 1 Sept. 1777 (g. s.).
Ulilla, b. 22, bapt. 26 Mar. 1769, d. 3 Sept. 1777 (g. s.).
Oliver, b. 10 Nov. 1771, bapt. in infancy, d. 27 Jan. 1775 (g. s.).
Huldah, b. 10, bapt. 11 Sept. 1773, d. 14 Dec. 1842 ae. 69 yrs. 3 mos. (g. s.).

25. Bradley, Hezekiah, s. of Samuel.

Born 28 July 1735; d. at Greenfield, 15 Nov. 1818 ae. 83 (g. s.). He m. (1) 1 Jan. 1756, Abigail Sherwood, dau. of Samuel, b. 10 May 1736, d. 9 July 1803 ae. 67 yrs. 2 mos. (g. s.). He m. (2) at Trinity Church, 25 July 1805, Ann Sherwood, widow of Capt. Samuel. She was dau. of Theophilus Nichols, b. at Stratford, 19 May 1738, d. 26 Dec. 1822 (g. s., Stratfield).

Will 14 Nov. 1816, proved 23 Nov. 1818; wife Anna, referring to prenuptial agreement; son Medad; gr. son Hezekiah S. Bradley.

Children [by first wife], rec. Fairfield and Greenfield:

Hezekiah, b. 23 June 1757, bapt. at Westport, 28 Aug. 1757, d. 15 Sept. 1780 ae. 23 yrs. 3 mos. (g. s.); m. Lydia Bradley, dau. of Reuben, bapt. 22 June 1760; she m. (2) John Wakeman.*
Abigail, b. 23, bapt. 24 Feb. 1760, d. 1 Sept. 1777 in 18 yr. (g. s.).
Medad, b. 30 Oct., bapt. 1 Nov. 1761, d. 23 Feb. 1830 ae. 67 (g. s.); m. (1) Charity ———, b. [21 Apr. 1765], d. 1 Sept. 1794 ae. 29-4-10 (g. s.); m. (2) at Trinity Church, 12 Apr. 1812, Anna Curtis, who d. 14 Oct. 1834 ae. 63 (g. s.).† Medad's will, 1 Feb. 1828, proved 18 Mar. 1830; gr. children Aaron-Burr, Charity, Samuel-Sherwood, William, and Hezekiah Bradley.
Charlotte, b. 15 July 1764, d. y.
Aaron-Burr, b. 22, bapt. 30 Apr. 1769, d. 18 Feb. 1814 (g. s.), ae. 56(!) by church rec. (but ae. 45 by Trinity Church entry); Dr.
Sarah, b. abt. 1771, d. 20‡ Feb. 1775 in 5 yr. (g. s.).
Abigail, bapt. 28 Mar. 1779, d. 10 Oct. 1779 ae. 1 yr. (g. s.).

26. Bradley, Stephen, s. of Ephraim.

Born 15 Aug. 1745; d. at Westport, 3 Mar. 1772 ae. 26 yrs. 6 mos. 17 days (g. s.); m. 25 June 1767, Abigail Adams, b. 2 Nov. 1748. She m. (2) 20 Sept. 1772, Joseph Hanford.

---
* Child, bapt. Greenfield: Hezekiah, bapt. 16 Jan., d. July 1780.
† Only child: Hezekiah (1794-1826), m. 1813 Amelia Burr (1796-1862), dau. of Ebenezer 3d. Adm'n on Hezekiah's estate granted, 8 Mar. 1826, to Timothy Burr.
‡ 30, by Perry Diary.

Adm'n granted, 21 Apr. 1772, to Abigail Bradley. Adm'n granted, 6 Nov. 1772, to Daniel Hull in right of wife Betty and Ebenezer Ogden in right of wife Ruth, sisters of Stephen and daus. of Ephraim. The dau. Molly had d. without issue, and Stephen's widow, now wife of Joseph Hanford, claimed to be next of kin to Molly.

Child, bapt. Westport:
> Molly, bapt. 18 June 1769, d. 4 Mar. 1772 ae. 2 yrs. 10 mos. (g. s.).

27. Bradley, John, s. of John.

Born 14 Apr. 1731; d. at Greenfield, 3 Aug. 1817 in 87 yr. (g. s.); m. (1) 13 Dec. 1750, Abigail Merwin; dau. of Samuel, bapt. 9 Aug. 1730, d. 19 Dec. 1787 in 58 yr. (g. s.); m. (2) 26 Mar. 1791, Esther Sherwood, dau. of Joseph, b. 6 May 1763, d. at Greenfield, 19 Aug. 1847 ae. 84 yrs. 3 mos. 13 days (g. s.). She m. (2) Ezekiel O'Banks.

Will 3 Jan. 1817, proved 25 Aug. 1817; wife Esther; sons Zalmon H., Medad; daus. Hannah wife of Wm. Wakeman, Clarina wife of Nathan Wheeler.

Children by first wife, bapt. Greenfield (births from Bible record):

41+David, b. 10, bapt. 25 Jan. 1752.
42+Lyman, b. 16 Feb., bapt. 17 Mar. 1754.
> Hannah, b. 3 Mar., bapt. 15 Apr. 1759, d. in 1833; m. William Wakeman.

43+John, b. 5(?) Sept. 1764, bapt. 2 Sept. 1764.
> Abigail, b. 18 Mar., bapt. 19 Apr. 1778, d. 5 Feb. 1798.

Children by second wife (births from Bible record):
> Clarina, b. 18 Mar. 1792, d. at Greenfield, 28 Mar. 1875 ae. 83 (g. s.); m. Nathan Wheeler.
> Zalmon H., b. 26 May 1793, bapt. at Easton, Nov. 1794, d. at Greenfield, 5 Jan. 1871 ae. 77-7-17 (g. s.); m. 7 July 1811, Sally Banks, dau. of Jonathan, Sr., b. 22 Apr. 1793, d. 16 Dec. 1842 ae. 49 (g. s.).
> Abigail, b. 26 Mar. 1798, d. y.
> Medad, b. 9 Dec. 1803, d. 23 Feb. 1830 (Miss Treadwell's book); m. (1) 6 Feb. 1822, Sophia Banks, dau. of Jonathan, b. 24 Mar. 1802, d. 20 Sept. 1822 ae. 20 (g. s.); m. (2) 14 Apr. 1824, Catherine-Maria Bradley, b. 28 Nov. 1801.

28. **Bradley, Reuben,** s. of John. Ens., North Fairfield Company, May 1768.

Born 17 Jan. 1732/3; d. 2 Feb. 1771 (Perry Diary).

He m. at Westport, 13 Apr. 1757, Elizabeth Nash; dau. of Thomas, b. 23 Aug. 1734. She m. (2) 24 Oct. 1773, John Hubbell.

Adm'n granted, 5 Mar. 1771, to Elizabeth Bradley. Distribution 17 Feb. 1774: widow, Adad, Elizabeth, Lydia, Mabel. Peter Banks and Elizabeth his wife conveyed, 1784, to Adad Bradley, right in house, etc., of father Reuben Bradley, dec'd; Nathan Banks and Mabel his wife conveyed the same, 1790.

Children, bapt. Greenfield:

>Elizabeth, bapt. at Westport, 13 Feb. 1758, d. in 1791; m. 19 Jan. 1774, Peter Banks.
>Lydia, bapt. 22 June 1760 (ae. abt. 1 mo.); m. (1) Hezekiah Bradley; m. (2) John Wakeman.
>Mabel, bapt. 6 Feb. 1763, d. at Greenfield, 15 June 1858 ae. 95 yrs. 6 mos. (g. s.); m. 1 Apr. 1781, Nathan Banks.
>Adad, bapt. 4 Aug. 1765 (ae. abt. 1 mo.); m. Ann Banks, dau. of Benjamin, b. 11 June 1768.

29. **Bradley, Seth,** s. of John. Ens., West Company, North Fairfield, May 1774; Ens., Army, Nov. 1776 (resigned).

Born 5 Apr. 1735; d. at Greenfield, 29 May 1798 ae. 63 (g. s.).

He m. (1) 8 Sept. 1755, Eunice Hull, b. 6 Mar. 1734/5, d. at Greenfield, 28 Sept. 1770 ae. 36 yrs. 7 mos. 22 days (g. s.); m. (2) at Easton, 18 Feb. 1773, Dorothy Bradley, who d. 14 Dec. 1843 ae. 90 (g. s.).*

Will 18 May 1798, proved 5 June 1798; wife Dorothy; children, Levi, Eliphalet, Alban, Hull, Alton, Selleck, Frederick, daus. Sarah, Eunice, Matilda, Stella. Distribution 30 May 1799: widow Dorothy; eldest dau. Sarah wife of Joseph Sherwood; eldest son Levi Bradley; 2d son Eliphalet Bradley; 3d son Albon Bradley; 4th son Hull Bradley; 2d dau. Eunice wife of Ebenezer Wakeman 3d; 5th son Alton Bradley; 3d dau. Matilda wife of Capt. Hezekiah Wakeman; 6th son Selleck Bradley; 7th son Frederic Bradley; 4th dau. Stella Bradley.

---

* Dorothy was also known as *Williams;* see under DAVID BRADLEY.

Will of Dorothy, 27 Mar. 1834, proved 8 Jan. 1844; gr. dau. Dorothy Burr; gr. dau. Mary Bradley; daus. Eunice and Stella; son Alton; codicil, 12 Mar. 1840, named gr. s. Wilsey Bradley, son of my son Frederic dec'd.

Children [by first wife], bapt. Greenfield:

Sarah, b. [say 1757], d. at Franklin, N. Y., 7 Apr. 1806; m. 26 Feb. 1778, Joseph Sherwood.
Levi, b. 5 Nov. 1758, bapt. 14 Jan. 1759 (ae. abt. 2 mos.), d. at Easton, 8 May 1829 in 71 yr. (g. s.); m. 25 Jan. 1781, Mary Wakeman, b. 15 July 1758, d. 20 Jan. 1849 ae. 90 yrs. 6 mos. (g. s.). His will, 14 Feb. 1825, proved 4 June 1829; wife Mary; sons Aljah, Woolsey; dau. Clarissa Treadwell.*
Seth, bapt. 4 May 1760 (at home, untimely born and sick), d. y.
Eliphalet, bapt. 9 May 1761 (at home, sick), d. 10 Aug. 1813; m. Eunice ———.†
Alban, bapt. 15 Nov. 1767, d. at Greenfield, 17 Feb. 1832 ae. 65 (g. s.); Capt.; m. Rhoda Burr, bapt. 10 Sept. 1769, d. 9 June 1845 ae. 77 (g. s.).‡
Hull, b. [19 Mar. 1770], d. 2 Sept. 1850 ae. 80-5-14 (g. s.); m. Julia-Alma Wakeman, bapt. 19 Jan. 1777, d. 29 May 1844 ae. 67 (g. s.). Their dau. Maria, bapt. at Easton, Nov. 1795.

Children [by second wife], bapt. Greenfield:

Eunice, b. 14 Aug., bapt. 6 Nov. 1774, d. at Greenfield, 27 Mar. 1861 ae. 86 yrs. 8 mos. (g. s.); m. Ebenezer Wakeman, 3d.
Alton, bapt. 21 June 1778, d. at Roxbury, 21 Oct. 1838 ae. 60; m. 11 Dec. 1796, Jane Nichols, dau. of Peter, b. abt. 1777, d. 29 Nov. 1853 ae. 76.
Matilda, m. Capt. Hezekiah Wakeman.
Selleck, d. 10 Apr. 1833 (Miss Treadwell's book).
Frederick, d. Sept. 1825 (Miss Treadwell's book).
Stella.

---

*Children, rec. Weston: Alja, b. 9 Oct. 1782, d. 2 Dec. 1861; m. Elizabeth Dimon, dau. of John. Clarissa, b. 21 Oct. 1786. Eunice, b. 1 May 1791, d. at Easton, 18 Feb. 1806 ae. 14-9-18 (g. s.). Wolsey, b. 5 Dec. 1794, d. at Easton, 14 Sept. 1848 ae. 54 (g. s.).

† Children: Eli (1786-1826), m. Hannah Fanton; Alba (1789-1829); Sally (1794-1868); Tolman (1797-1843); Morris S. (1799-1872). Will of Eliphalet of New Fairfield, 3 Oct. 1811, proved 3 Sept. 1813; wife Eunice; sons Eli (eldest), Alba, Talman-Hull, Morris; dau. Sally Barnum; son Eli and son-in-law Azor Barnum, Exec'rs. Alba was bapt. at Easton, Jan. 1790.

‡ Adm'n on Alban's estate granted, 8 Mar. 1832, to Gershom W. Sherwood. Distribution to widow Rhoda, eldest dau. Marietta Burr, and dau. Charlotte B. Sherwood. Children of Alban, bapt. Trinity Church: Burritt, bapt. 18 Mar. 1792; Marietta, bapt. 27 Oct. 1793; Charlotte-Burr, bapt. 20 July 1800.

THE FAMILIES OF OLD FAIRFIELD

30. Bradley, Enos, s. of John.

Born 14 Sept. 1739; d. at Easton, 23 July 1814 in 76 yr. (g. s.).

He m. at Greenfield, 10 Dec. 1761, Mary Merwin, dau. of Samuel, bapt. 4 July 1742, d. 15 Dec. 1825 ae. 82 (g. s.).

Adm'n granted, 28 Nov. 1814, to Nathan Wheeler, with Joseph Winton as surety. Dower set to widow Mary, 29 Apr. 1815.

Children, two bapt. Greenfield:
> Huldah, bapt. 13 May 1764.*
> Abigail, b. [19 Dec. 1765], bapt. 11 May 1766, d. at Easton, 5 May 1837 ae. 71-4-17 (g. s.); m. 28 Sept. 1783, Elnathan Williams, Jr.

31. Bradley, Ephraim, s. of John.

Born 10 Dec. 1744.

He m. at Greenfield, 22 Feb. 1764, Damaris Dimon; dau. of Moses, b. 23 Mar. 1744/5.

Ephraim and Damaris his wife, of New Fairfield, conveyed 1777 land in Fairfield.

Children, two bapt. at Greenfield:
> Aaron, b. 7, bapt. 9 Apr. 1766 (at home sick), d. 1 Jan. 1767 ae. almost 9 mos.
> Hannah, bapt. 1 Nov. 1767, d. 9 Nov. 1767 ae. 8 weeks wanting 2 days.
> Lloyd, bapt. at Easton, 8 July 1770.

32. Bradley, Moses, s. of John.

Born 3 Dec. 1746; d. at Redding in 1797; m. at Westport, 2 Sept. 1770, Molly Chapman; dau. of Phineas, b. 10 June 1752, d. in 1821. She m. (2) John Hull.

Moses Bradley and his wife owned the Covenant at Easton, 5 May 1771; they res. New Milford, 1787. Adm'n on his estate was granted, 27 Nov. 1797, to Joshua Chapman of Danbury; insolvent.

Will of Mary wife of John Hull of Redding, 20 July 1811, proved 25 July 1821; dau. Polly wife of Phineas Lockwood; dau. Cinderilla; four daus. Sarah, Polly, Priscilla, Cinderilla; bro. John Chapman, Exec'r. The distribution called Cinderilla wife of Daniel Sanford.

---
* Was she Huldah-Ann Bradley who m. Jonathan Godfrey?

Children:
>
> Child, bapt. at Easton, 5 May 1771.
> Sarah, b. 23 Feb. 1775, d. at Redding, 25 Apr. 1813 ae. 38 (g. s.); m. 20 Sept. 1795, Jesse Sherwood.
> Polly, m. Phineas Lockwood.
> Priscilla, m. at Redding, 3 Nov. 1795, Daniel Chapman.
> Cinderilla, b. 24 June 1783, d. at Redding, 19 Dec. 1867; m. 1814, Capt. Daniel Sanford.

33. Bradley, Abel, s. of John.

Born 10 Aug. 1750; Capt. Abel d. at Salisbury, N. Y., Mar. 1814 in 64 yr. (g. s.).

He m. at Weston, 28 Nov. 1772, Hannah Morehouse; dau. of Jabez, b. 2 May 1750, d. June 1812.

Children, bapt. Greenfield:
>
> Betsey, b. 11 Sept., bapt. 6 Nov. 1774, d. at Weston, 11 May 1845 ae. 70 (g. s.); m. 27 Jan. 1792, Robert Downs.
> Anna, bapt. 11 Feb. 1776.
> Aaron, bapt. 18 Oct. 1778.
> Huldah, bapt. 12 Mar. 1781, d. 12 Mar. 1781 ae. 4 weeks.

34. Bradley, Isaac, s. of John.

Born 19 Dec. 1754; d. at Weston in 1791.

He m. Esther Wakeman, dau. of John, b. 15 Aug. 1756, d. 4 Mar. 1820.

Adm'n granted, 16 Jan. 1792, to Esther Bradley of Weston and John Wakeman, 3d, of Fairfield.

Will of Esther of Weston, 25 Jan., proved 16 Mar. 1820; son Uriah; dau. Eleanor wife of William Lyon; gr. children Timothy, Eleanor, Marina, Horace, Harry and Harriet, children of late dau. Urania Nichols; bro. Zalmon Wakeman, Exec'r. Distribution of the part of Isaac's Est. set to Esther, made Nov. 1820, named the same, calling the gr. dau. Eleanor Nichols wife of Anson Lyon.

Children, first bapt. Greenfield:
>
> Urana, bapt. 2 Apr. [1780], d. at Easton, 9 Oct. 1813 in 34 yr. (g. s.); m. Peter Nichols.
> Uriah, d. 21 June 1826; m. ———, who d. 23 Nov. 1822.

Isaac, d. 30 Apr. 1819 (Miss Treadwell's book). Estate distributed, 18 May 1814 [1819?] to bro. Uri; sister Eleanor wife of William Lyon; Timothy, Eleanor, Marina, Horace, Harry, and Harriet, children of dec'd sister Urana Nichols.

Eleanor, b. abt. 1785, d. at Easton, 31 Oct. 1829 ae. 44 yrs. 5 mos. (g. s.); m. William Lyon.

35. Bradley, William, s. of Peter.

Born 2 Aug. 1750; d. at Weston, in 1812; m. at Redding, 22 Feb. 1773, Mary Westcott, dau. of Richard, b. 12 Oct. 1749, perhaps d. in 1797.

Adm'n on estates of William and Mary was granted, 10 Dec. 1812, to Aaron Bradley, with Hull Bradley as surety.

Distribution of estates of William and Mary Bradley of Weston, 18 Oct. 1813: children, Peter, Aaron, and Damaris Bradley.

Children:

> Peter, b. abt. 1775, d. at Weston, 11 Sept. 1838; m. Mary Merwin, b. abt. 1776, d. at Bridgeport, 12 Apr. 1869.*
> Aaron.
> Damaris. [Inventory of estate of Damaris Bradley of Weston taken 25 July 1822; insolvent.]

36. Bradley, Daniel, s. of Daniel.

Born 20 May 1729; d. at Greenfield, 8 Jan. 1780 ae. 51 (g. s.); m. 8 Aug. 1751, Mary Banks; dau. of Joseph, b. 19 July 1731, d. 28 July 1815 ae. 85 (g. s.).

David Banks in 1791 conveyed land in Greenfield to his sister Mary Bradley, widow of Daniel, reserving life use. The same property was conveyed 1795 by Mary to her three sons, Daniel, David, and Wakeman, reserving life use.

Children, five bapt. Greenfield:

> Esther, b. abt. 1752, d. at Greenfield, 22 Nov. 1823 ae. 71 (g. s.); m. 10 Nov. 1772, Thaddeus Wakeman.
> Amelia, b. abt. 1754, d. at Greenfield, 1 Nov. 1848 ae. 94 (g. s.); m. 16 Mar. 1774, Gershom Bulkley.

---

* Adm'n on Peter's estate granted to Walter Bradley of Redding; insolvent; dower set to widow Polly. But Miss Treadwell's book gives a Capt. Peter who d. 2 Mar. 1839. Peter and Mary (Merwin) Bradley have stones in Bridgeport.

Daniel, b. abt. 1756, d. at Fairfield, 1837; Ens., Jan. 1777, 2d Lt., Jan. 1778, 1st Lt., July 1780, Rev. War; m. Elizabeth (Stratton), prob. widow of Peter Winton, bapt. 27 Jan. 1760.*

Mary, b. 2 Sept., bapt. 15 Oct. 1758, d. 10 Oct. 1852 ae. 94-1-8 (Bible record); m. 23 Feb. 1783, Samuel Morehouse.

Sarah, bapt. 1760; ? m. 23 Apr. 1782, John Hayes.

Sybil, b. 22, bapt. 28 Nov. 1762, d. at Greenfield, 25 Dec. 1828 ae. 66 (g. s.); m. 13 Dec. 1781, Gershom Wakeman.

Burr, bapt 2 Dec. 1764, d. at Westport, 24 Apr. 1778.

Abigail, bapt. 14 June 1767, d. 29 May 1769 ae. 2.

David, bapt. at Westport, 25 July 1773, d. at Fairfield, 5 May 1858 ae. 84 (g. s., West Cemetery); Capt.; m. (1) at Westport, 14 Oct. 1804, Eunice Perry; dau. of Nathan, bapt. 24 Sept. 1780, d. 11 (?) Nov. 1814; m. (2) 31 Dec. 1815, Sarah Bulkley; dau. of Joseph, b. 9 July 1784, d. 12 Sept. 1838 ae. 54 (g. s.).

Wakeman, bapt. at Westport, 28 Oct. 1775, d. at Easton, 1 Apr. 1863 ae. 86 yrs. 6 mos. (g. s.); chose Daniel Bradley for guardian, 14 June 1791; m. at Weston, 8 Sept. 1799, Katharine Andrews, bapt. 26 Feb. 1777, d. 1 Sept. 1846 ae. 70-7-16 (g. s.).

37. Bradley, Stephen, s. of Daniel.

Born 14 Dec. 1734.

Probable child:
Daniel, of Ridgefield.

38. Bradley, Philip-Burr, s. of Daniel. Deputy for Ridgefield, May and Oct. 1769, May and Oct. 1770, Oct. 1771, May and Oct. 1772, May and Oct. 1773, Jan., May and Oct. 1774, Mar., Apr., Oct. and Dec. 1775, May 1776, May 1780, May and Oct. 1782, May and Oct. 1783, May and Oct. 1784, May and Oct. 1785, May and Oct. 1786, May and Oct. 1787, May and Oct. 1788, May and Oct. 1789, May and Oct. 1790, May and Oct. 1791. Justice, 1769-82. Lt.-Col., 16th Regt., Oct. 1771; Lt.-Col. in Army, Jan. and May 1776; Col., Oct. 1776. Member of Convention to ratify Constitution of U. S., 1788; U. S.

---

* Children, bapt. Westport: Betsey and Ruhamah, bapt. 5 Oct. 1788. Betsey, b. abt. 1786, d. 7 Aug. 1864 ae. 78 (g. s.); m. Elisha Alvord. Ruhamah, b. [29 Apr. 1788], d. 1 May 1874 ae. 86 yrs. 2 days (g. s.). Burr, b. 17 Feb. 1790, bapt. 20 June 1790, d. at Warsaw, Ill., 1 July 1849; grad. Yale Coll. 1808; Dr.; m. at Marietta, Ohio, 4 June 1818, Esther Williams Plumer, dau. of Jonathan and Esther (Williams) Plumer. Daniel-Banks, bapt. 6 Mar. 1796, d. at Westport, 21 Feb. 1872 ae. 76-2-20 (g. s.), m. Cynthia Sherwood, dau. of Gershom, who d. 24 Aug. 1861 ae. 70 yrs. 3 days (g. s.).

Marshal for District of Conn., 1789-1802; Judge of Fairfield County Court, 1782-1806.

Born 26 Mar. 1738; d. at Ridgefield, 4 Jan. 1821; m. (1) 22 Apr. 1762, Mary Bostwick, dau. of Zechariah, bapt. 29 May 1739, d. 8 Aug. 1768 in 30 yr. He m. (2) 11 Mar. 1770, Ruth Smith, dau. of Samuel, b. abt. 1746, living 1836.

Grad. Yale Coll. 1758.

Will 23 Dec. 1808, proved 10 Apr. 1820 (?); wife Ruth; son Jabez (an annuity for life); sons Philip, Jesse S.; dau. Ruth; gr. children Delia, Philo, Charlotte, Burr, and Samuel Dauchy, children of dau. Molly dec'd; dau. Esther; gr. children Harriet and Sally Dauchy, children of dau. Sally dec'd; niece Amelia wife of Abijah Benedict; nephew Daniel Bradley of Ridgefield, the house where he lives, with life use of one-half to his mother; son Philip to have land I bought of Benjamin and Hannah Sherwood, whereon my store stands. The distribution mentions children of dau. Ruth dec'd, and calls Sally Dauchy the only surviving heir to the dec'd dau. Sally.

Children [by first wife], rec. Ridgefield:

Molly, b. 3 Sept. 1766, d. 1805; m. Samuel Dauchy.
Jabez-Burr, b. 18 Feb. 1768.

Children [by second wife], rec. Ridgefield:

Philip, b. 17 Sept. 1770; m. Polly ———.
Ruth, b. 16 Oct. 1771; m. at Ridgefield, 13 Nov. 1794, Nathan Dauchy, Jr.
Esther, b. 7 May 1773.
Betsey, b. 12 Feb. 1775.
Sally, b. 11 July 1780; m. ——— Dauchy.
Jesse S., b. 17 Aug. 1782; m. Elizabeth ———.

39. Bradley, Elisha, s. of Joseph.

Born 20 May 1745; d. at Greenfield, 7 May 1828 ae. 83 (g. s.).

He m. 13 Feb. 1770, Eunice Banks; dau. of Ebenezer, b. 21 Mar. 1747, d. 16 Jan. 1820 ae. 73 (g. s.).

Will 25 May 1820, proved 26 May 1828; three sons, Jesse, Increase, Henry; two daus. Sally and Betsey; son Jesse Bradley and Abraham Sherwood to have allowance for improvements they have made on my lands in Thompson, Sullivan County, N. Y.

Adm'n on estate of Eunice Bradley of Fairfield was granted to Henry Bradley, 2 June 1828. Distribution: sons Jesse, Eli, Increase; dau. Betsey wife of Jonathan Mead; dau. Sally Madden; son Henry.

>Children, bapt. Greenfield:
>
>Jesse, bapt. in infancy [1770/1]; m. 18 Mar. 1790, Mary Morehouse; [? dau. of Abijah, b. 16 Nov. 1771].*
>Eli, b. 31 Oct., bapt. 6 Dec. 1772, d. 25 Jan. 1820 ae. 45 (g. s.). Will 1 Nov. 1819, proved 22 Mar. 1820, named father Elisha Bradley.†
>Eunice, b. 1 Apr., bapt. 8 May 1775, d. 20 Aug. 1814 ae. 39 (g. s.).
>Sarah, b. 2 Apr., bapt. 1 June 1777, d. at Greenfield, 27 Feb. 1854 ae. 77 (g. s.); m. (1) 7 Sept. 1800, Justus Sherwood; m. (2) ——— Madden.
>Increase, bapt. June 1780; Capt.; m. Grissel Osborn, dau. of Gershom, bapt. 4 Sept. 1785, d. 24 July 1813 ae. 27-11-7 (g. s.).
>Betsey, bapt. May 1784; m. Jonathan Mead.
>Susannah, bapt. 21 Aug. 1785, d. 20 May 1819 ae. 34 (g. s.).
>Henry.

40. Bradley, Joseph, s. of Joseph.

Bapt. 7 Jan. 1759; d. at Greenfield, 27 Feb. 1794 ae. 35 (g. s.). He m. at Westport, 18 Jan. 1784, Rachel Burr, dau. of Ichabod, b. abt. 1760, d. 25 June 1832 ae. 72 (g. s.).

Adm'n granted, 15 Dec. 1794, to Rachel Bradley.

>Child:
>
>? Grizzel, b. [Dec. 1784?], d. at Greenfield, 22 Sept. 1871 ae. 87 yrs. 9 mos. (g. s.).

41. Bradley, David, s. of John. Ens., 13th Co., 4th Regt., Jan. 1778; Capt.

Born 10 Jan. 1752; d. at Easton, 23 Feb. 1821 ae. 68 (g. s.); m. 1 Feb. 1775, Deborah Bradley, b. 22 May 1757, d. 24 Jan. 1846 ae. 89 (g. s.).

Adm'n granted, 11 Apr. 1821, at request of widow Deborah and son David, to Seth Hill of Weston and Hull Bradley of Fairfield.

---

* Children, bapt. Weston: Ebenezer-Banks, bapt. 14 Aug. 1791; Mary-Ann, bapt. 3 Aug. 1794; Charity, bapt. 11 Aug. 1799.
† An Eli Bradley m. at Westport, 24 Dec. 1795, Eleanor Sherwood.

THE FAMILIES OF OLD FAIRFIELD   149

Children, rec. Weston, two bapt. Easton:

> David, b. 11 Feb. 1777, perhaps d. 20 Jan. 1823 (Miss Treadwell's book); ? m. at Weston, 27 June 1804, Sarah Squire.
> Priscilla, b. 3 Apr. 1782, d. at Weston, 25 May 1851 in 69 yr. (g. s.); m. Eliphalet Coley.
> Abigail-Merwin, b. 12 Jan. 1789, bapt. 20 June 1789, d. at Easton, 21 May 1807 ae. 19 (g. s.).
> Harriet, bapt. Oct. 1792.

42. Bradley, Lyman, s. of John.

Born 16 Feb. 1754; d. at Easton, 8 Sept. 1822* ae. 67; m. (1) Abigail Wakeman, dau. of William, b. 4 Oct. 1755, d. 2 Sept. 1786; m. (2) Grizzel, widow of Moses Dimon, and dau. of Nathan Thorp, b. 18 Apr. 1756, d. 24 Dec. 1821 in 65 yr. (g. s.).

Adm'n granted, 18 Sept. 1822, to Simeon Fanton and Enos B. Williams. Distribution, 1823: son Daniel; son Samuel; dau. Betsey wife of Samuel Barlow; son Wakeman; dau. Charity wife of Levi Wheeler; son Nathan; son Lyman; dau. Salina wife of Ebenezer N. Treadwell; son Walter; dau. Abigail wife of David Willson.

Adm'n on Grizzel's estate granted, 16 Sept. 1822, to Thomas Dimon. Distribution to her sons Thomas Dimon, Daniel Bradley, Nathan Bradley, Walter Bradley, Moses Dimon, and daus. Abigail Thorp, Sarah Barlow, Selina Treadwell.

Children by first wife:

> Lyman, d. Jan. 1851 (Miss Treadwell's book); his wife Hannah d. "to the Lakes," Sept. 1850 (Miss Treadwell's book).†
> Samuel.
> Wakeman, m. at Easton, 10 Oct. 1796, Sarah Wheeler.‡
> Betsey, m. Samuel Barlow.
> Charity, m. 30 Sept. 1797, Levi Wheeler.
> Abigail, m. David Wilson.

Children by second wife:

> Daniel.
> Nathan-Thorp, bapt. at Easton, 11 June 1791.
> Walter, bapt. at Easton, 25 July 1793.

---

* Hung himself (Miss Treadwell's book).
† Abigail-Wakeman, dau. of Lyman, bapt. at Trinity Church, 1 Apr. 1798, is prob. an error for the child of his bro. Wakeman, *q. v.*
‡ Child: Abigail W., b. 14 Dec. 1797 (Weston rec.).

Selina, b. abt. 1796, hung herself 31 Mar. 1824 (Miss Treadwell's book), bur. 1 Apr. 1824 ae. 28 (suicide, Trinity Church rec.); m. Ebenezer N. Treadwell.

43. Bradley, John, s. of John.

Born 5(?) Sept. 1764; d. at Easton, 15 May 1840 in 76 yr. (g. s.); m. Hannah Nichols, dau. of David.

Will 3, proved 18 May 1840; wife Hannah; children, Murwin, Jesse, Wright, Lewis, and David N. Bradley, and Lucy wife of John H. Birdsall of Newburgh, N. Y.

Children:

Murwin.
Jesse.
Wright.
Lucy, m. John H. Birdsall.
Lewis.
David N.

Bradley [*Unplaced*].

ELI d. at Greenfield, 25 Jan. 1820.
ESTHER [of New Haven] m. 7 Dec. 1716, Samuel Gold. [Fairfield Rec.]
────── m. Ruth Lee of Redding, b. [say 1740].
ABEL b. abt. 1776, d. at Greenfield, 7 Aug. 1842 ae. 66 (g. s.); m. at Trinity Church, 17 Feb. 1799, Sybil Wheeler, b. abt. 1780, d. at Easton, 25 Dec. 1855 ae. 75 (g. s.).
MARY m. 14 Jan. 1798, Oliver Middlebrook. [Greens Farms Church]
NATHAN d. 27 Nov. 1784 (Perry Diary).
AMELIA of Greenfield, b. 4 Feb. 1781, m. at Westport, 27 Sept. 1801, Elihu Nichols; his sister Hannah m. John Bradley.
MARY Bradley, dau. of Sarah Sturges, bapt. 9 May 1784. [Greens Farms Church]
MARY m. 23 Mar. 1805, Benjamin Meeker, Jr. [Greens Farms Church]
MARY,—adm'n granted, 30 June 1797, to Josiah Lacey, with David Burr, Jr., as surety.
ELIPHALET d. 2 Mar. 1805. [Miss Treadwell's book]
LEWIS d. 22 Mar. 1799. [Miss Treadwell's book]
ABIGAIL d. 20 July 1802. [Miss Treadwell's book]
HEZEKIAH d. 9 July 1803. [Miss Treadwell's book]
MORIAH d. 6 Nov. 1803. [Miss Treadwell's book]

EUNICE d. 18 Feb. 1806. [Miss Treadwell's book]
DORCAS d. 4 Oct. 1807. [Miss Treadwell's book]
MABEL d. 15 Dec. 1832. [Miss Treadwell's book]
PRISCILLA d. 25 Oct. 1823. [Miss Treadwell's book]

Brewster, Caleb. Capt.

From Brookhaven, L. I.; b. abt. 1748, d. at Fairfield, 13 Feb. 1827 ae. 79 (Revolutionary soldier) (g. s.).

He m. 18 Apr. 1784, Anna Lewis, b. 17 Oct. 1760 (g. s.), d. 30 Aug. 1834 (g. s.).

Will 25 Feb. 1825, proved 17 Feb. 1827; wife Ann; dau. Sally; gr. son Caleb B. Brewster; son Sturges; gr. son Caleb B. Harkley; dau. Ann wife of Robert Anderson; son Jonathan, etc.

Will of Anna Brewster, 14 July 1828, proved 11 Sept. 1834; gr. son Caleb Brewster Hackley; dau. Sally Brewster; sons Sturges, Jonathan-Lewis; dau. Anna wife of Robert Anderson.

Children, rec. and bapt. Fairfield:

> Sarah, b. 5 Mar., bapt. 1 May 1785, d. 18 May 1875 (g. s.).
> Jonathan-Lewis, b. 5 Nov., bapt. 17 Dec. 1786, d. 27 Oct. 1837 ae. 49 (g. s.); m. at Trinity Church, 30 Dec. 1810, Clarissa Bradley.
> Sturges, b. 20 Jan., bapt. 8 Mar. 1789.
> Anna, b. 22 July, bapt. 8 Aug. 1790; m. Robert Anderson.
> Elizabeth-Burr, b. 11 July 1792 (g. s.), bapt. 12 Aug. 1792, d. 25 June 1796 (g. s.).
> Racilia, b. 17 Apr., bapt. 8 June 1794.
> Benjamin, b. 17 Aug., bapt. 25 Sept. 1796.
> Daniel, bapt. 14 Apr. 1802.

Brinsmade, Josiah.

Son of Zechariah and Sarah (Cobbitt), b. at Stratford, 17 Feb. 1727/8; d. at Easton, Apr. 1809 ae. 83.

He m. Naomi Bennett, dau. of Isaac, bapt. at Stratfield, 3 Oct. 1736, d. at Easton, 21 Sept. 1776 in 42 yr. (g. s.).

Will 19 Dec. 1808, proved 26 June 1809; four daus. Rhoda, Sarah, Mary, Naomi; son Cyrus.

Children:

> Rhoda, b. 9 Apr. 1755, d. at Easton, 5 Apr. 1850 ae. 95 (g. s.); m. 4 May 1775, Ezbon Hall.
> Sarah, b. 12 Nov. 1756; m. Daniel Silliman.
> Mary, bapt. 2 Aug. 1761; m. 16 Oct. 1785, William Bennett.

Cyrus, m. (1) by 1788, Ann ———; m. (2) abt. 1794, Joanna Banks, dau. of Jesse, b. 27 July 1768, d. 15 Apr. 1804 ae. 36 (g. s.).*
Naomi, b. 17 Feb., bapt. Mar. 1769, d. at Easton, 16 Dec. 1812 ae. 43 (g. s.); m. 30 Dec. 1790, John Baldwin.

Brinsmade [*Unplaced*].

SARAH m. 22 Nov. 1750, John Guire. [Fairfield Rec.]
JOSEPH m. 19 Oct. 1748, Ruth Winton. [Greenfield Church]
RHODA m. 16 Oct. 1768, Increase Burr. [Greenfield Church]

Bristol [*Unplaced*].

JERUSHA m. 27 June 1793, John R. Wheeler. [Redding rec|]

Brotherton, Daniel.

He m. at Westport, 5 Sept. 1782, Rachel Batterson, dau. of James, bapt. 2 June 1765; and he d. there 20 Mar. 1813 ae. 50.

Of Fairfield; adm'n granted, 29 Mar. 1813, to James Beaty, with Elkanah Brotherton as surety. Distribution, 30 Mar. 1814: widow; children, Elkanah, Israel, Joel, Eli, Abel, Hannah, Susannah, Clarina, Jerusha, Sally, Abigail.

Children, bapt. Westport:

Hannah, bapt. 18 May 1783; m. 17 Dec. 1804, David Brotherton.
Lydia, bapt. 11 June 1786, d. 10 Aug. 1793.
Elkanah, bapt. 24 Aug. 1788.
Susannah, bapt. 21 Nov. 1790.
Israel, bapt. 16 June 1793; m. 22 Sept. 1816, Harriet Allen.
Joel, bapt. 4 Oct. 1795.
Eli, bapt. 3 Sept. 1797.
Abel, bapt. 17 Dec. 1804.
Clarina, bapt. 17 Dec. 1804.
Jerusha, bapt. 17 Dec. 1804.
Sally-Ann, bapt. 21 Jan. 1807.
Abigail.

Brotherton, Samuel.

He m. at Westport, 21 Feb. 1782, Patience Batterson, bapt. 2 Feb. 1755, d. 24 May 1799 ae. 45.

---

* His wife Ann renewed Covenant with him at Easton, 11 Oct. 1789. Their dau. Fanny, bapt. 11 Oct. 1789, d. 31 Dec. 1793 in 5 yr. (g. s.). By the second wife, he had Joanna, bapt. June 1795, m. ——— Judson; and Josiah.

Children, bapt. Westport:

    Sarah, bapt. 27 July 1783, d. 15 Apr. 1794.
    David, bapt. 25 July 1784; m. 17 Dec. 1804, Hannah Brotherton.
    Nathaniel, bapt. 16 July 1786.
    Jerusha, bapt. 4 May 1788, d. 17 Apr. 1794.
    Samuel, bapt. 23 Sept. 1792.
    Zalmon, bapt. 23 Sept. 1792.

Brotherton [Unplaced].

DANIEL of Weston m. 18 Oct. 1808, Laurena Allen.

Brothwell, Joseph.

"From Yorkshire, England, being impressed as a soldier, he, while at West Indies, jumped overboard and swam six miles to the shore; came to New York and thence to Black Rock in Fairfield."

Born abt. 1727; d. at Stratfield, 27 Jan. 1811 in 84 yr. (g. s.).

He m. Hannah Fairweather, b. 30 Nov. 1731, d. 4 June 1815 in 85 yr. (g. s.).

Children:

    Elizabeth, b. 2 Feb. 1751, d. 13 Mar. 1840 in 90 yr. (g. s.); m. John Hubbell.
    Abigail, b. 1 Aug. 1753 (Pension rec.), d. at Danbury, 5 June 1841; m. Stephen Lyon.
    William, b. abt. 1756, d. 13 Apr. 1828 ae. 72 (g. s.); unm.
    Joseph-Fairweather, b. 30 Mar. 1758 (Pension rec.); res. Woodbury, 1832; m. Molly Lacy, dau. of Benjamin.
    Benjamin, b. abt. 1760; m. Anna Beach.
    Charlotte, m. James Knapp.
    Grizell, d. at Weston, 17 Aug. 1785; m. Jose Lyon.
    Thomas, b. 19 Aug. 1766, d. at Stratfield, 14 Apr. 1842 in 76 yr. (g. s.); m. (1) Hannah French, dau. of John, b. 17 May 1766, d. 1 Nov. 1829 ae. 63 yrs. 5 mos. (g. s.); m. (2) 1 May 1830, Nancy Webb.

Brown [Unplaced].

MARY m. 17 Dec. 1782, James Knapp. [Fairfield Church]

SAMUEL, b. 28 Dec. 1775; m. 29 Dec. 1796, Polly Whinkler, b. 22 Feb. 1779; their dau. Marietta, b. 14 Sept. 1798. [Weston rec.]

SAMUEL d. 19 Jan. 1845 ae. 70 (g. s.); his wife Polly d. 29 Oct. 1859 in 83 yr. (g. s.).

154   HISTORY AND GENEALOGY OF

  Lebbeus m. 29 July 1793, Hannah Godfrey. [Fairfield Church]
  Elisha d. 24 Oct. 1826 (Miss Treadwell's book); m. 7 July 1777, Abigail Sturges. [Weston Church]
  Betsey m. 25 Apr. 1799, Jesse Crossman. [Weston Church]

Brush [*Unplaced*].

  Zophar m. 4 May 1780, Sarah Bennett. Zophar of L. I. had dau. Sarah, bapt. 27 Nov. 1785. Zophar of Ridgebury had children: Joseph-Bennet, bapt. 24 Sept. 1786; Zophar, bapt. 25 Jan. 1789. Zophar had: Priscilla, bapt. 30 Oct. 1796; Polly, Betsey, and Lockwood, bapt. 16 Feb. 1798; Charles, bapt. 20 Sept. 1799. [Greens Farms Church]

Bryan [*Unplaced*].

  Ruth had son David, bapt. 9 Mar. 1746. [Greens Farms Church]
  John m. Oct. 1761, the woman brought up by Mr. Stewart. [Weston Church]
  Widow Sarah had son Stratton, bapt. 17 Aug. 1777. [Greens Farms Church]
  Sarah m. 16 May 1765, Daniel Glover. [Weston rec.]
  Sally* m. 17 Dec. 1793, Lewis Cable. [Greens Farms Church]

Buckhust, Richard.

Now resident in Fairfield, will 13 Oct. 1735, proved 18 Mar. 1736; Richard, son of bro. Stephen Buckhust, now in Great Britain; three children of bro. Stephen,—Mary, Stephen and Richard; Mr. Henry Caner and Mr. Jonathan Cutler of Fairfield, Exec'rs, to have £5 apiece. Witnesses: Elizabeth Bostwick, Abraham Pullen, Moses Dimon.

Buckingham, (Rev.) Daniel.

Son of Gideon and Sarah (Hunt), b. at Milford, 27 Oct. 1712; d. at Westport, 25† May 1766 in 55 yr. (g. s.); m. Mary Harpin, dau. of Dr. John, b. at Milford, 2 Aug. 1719, d. 6‡ June 1766 ae. 47 (g. s.). No issue.

---
* Called gr. dau. in will of Widow Mary Raymond, 1794.
† 23, by church rec.
‡ 7, by church rec.

THE FAMILIES OF OLD FAIRFIELD 155

Grad. Yale Coll. 1735; installed as minister at Greens Farms, 17 Mar. 1742, and served until his death.

Will 16 June 1761, proved 30 May 1766; wife Mary; mentioned father Gideon and land in Milford; John and Daniel, sons of my bro. John Buckingham of Milford; bros. and sisters, John Buckingham, Josiah Buckingham, Clemence Treat, Alice Treat.

Buckingham, Stephen.

Son of Daniel and Sarah (Lee) Buckingham, b. 4 Aug. 1703, supposed lost on sea voyage, 1762. He came to live at Norwalk with his uncle Rev. Stephen Buckingham; rem. by 1754 to Chesterfield, N. J.

He m. (rec. Norwalk) 24 Feb. 1728/9, Elizabeth Sherwood, dau. of Lt. Isaac of Fairfield; b. abt. 1708, d. at Cooperstown, N. Y., Aug. 1792 ae. 84.

Children:

> Solomon, b. 1 Feb. 1731.
> Temperance, b. 14 Jan. 1733; m. Solomon Sherwood.
> Daniel, b. 21 Aug. 1735, d. at Westport, 29 Oct. 1754.
> Ann, b. 3 July 1737, d. at Greenfield, 8 Nov. 1822 ae. 85 (g. s.); m. Albert Sherwood.
> Elizabeth, m. ——— Stackhouse, of Pittsburgh, Pa.
> Rachel, b. abt. 1746, bapt. at Greenfield, 13 Apr. 1766 (ae. abt. 18), d. 13 Sept. 1771 (Perry Diary); m. at Westport, 13 June 1771, Gershom Gilbert.
> +Ebenezer, b. 1 Nov. 1748, bapt. at Greenfield, 29 Mar. 1767 (in 18 yr.); chose Albert Sherwood for guardian, 13 Dec. 1764.

Buckingham, Ebenezer, s. of Stephen.

Born 1 Nov. 1748; d. at Carthage, Athens County, Ohio, 24 Oct. 1824 ae. 76.

He m. at Westport, 23 Dec. 1771, Esther Bradley; dau. of Elnathan, b. 28 Feb. 1754, d. 25 June 1827 ae. 72 and bur. at Zanesville, Ohio.

Children, rec. Greenfield:

> Ebenezer, b. 21 Mar. 1772, bapt. 7 Feb. 1773.
> Rachel, bapt. 27 Mar. 1774.
> Ten more children; see *Buckingham Family*.

Buddington, Edward.

Son of Walter and Joanna (Tubbs), b. at Groton, 15 Sept. 1708.

He m. Martha ———, who d. 7 Apr. 1759 in 55 yr. (g. s.).

He conveyed, 1773, to William and Nehemiah Buddington, a dwelling house and joiner's shop.

"Widow Buttonton" d. at Joseph Beers', 4 Aug. 1792 (Perry Diary).

Children, bapt. Fairfield:
- Joseph, bapt. 6 Dec. 1730.
- William, bapt. 1 Feb. 1732/3, d. at Fairfield, 27 Nov. 1811 ae. 79; Ens., 1st Co., Fairfield, Oct. 1768.
- Nehemiah, bapt. 26 Jan. 1734/5, bur. 5 Dec. 1805 ae. 70 (Trinity Church rec.); m. Elizabeth Hawley, dau. of Ephraim, b. at Stratford, 13 Nov. 1742.
- Irene, bapt. 16 July 1738.
- Grace, bapt. 14 Dec. 1740; m. 3 Mar. 1762, Noah Lane, of Killingworth.
- +Walter, bapt. 26 Aug. 1744.
- Martha, bapt. 25 Jan. 1746/7.

Buddington, Ozias.

Son of Walter and Joanna (Tubbs), b. at Groton, 7 Dec. 1712; d. at Fairfield abt. 1759.

He m. Mary Coley, dau. of Peter, bapt. 18 June 1721 (vol. I, p. 156).

Of Fairfield, with wife Mary conveyed to Peter Coley, Mar. 1741/2.

Adm'n granted, 12 Apr. 1759, to Jeremiah Jennings.

Ebenezer Buddington of Fairfield chose Mary Buddington for guardian, 1 Oct. 1760.

Children (incomplete):
- Ebenezer.

Buddington, Walter, s. of Edward.

Bapt. 26 Aug. 1744; d. at Milford, 22 July 1826 ae. 82 (g. s.); m. Ruth Couch, who d. 17 Aug. 1829 ae. 79 (g. s.).

THE FAMILIES OF OLD FAIRFIELD   157

Children, bapt. Fairfield:*

    Jonathan, bapt. 15 Aug. 1779, d. at New Haven, 21 Jan. 1823 ae. 42; m. at New Haven, 13 June 1820, Sarah Peck, dau. of Jesse S., b. 3 July 1799.
    Walter, bapt. 17 Dec. 1780.
    Edward, b. 12 Jan., bapt. 7 Dec. 1783, d. at Fairfield, 20 Sept. 1868 ae. 85 yrs. 8 mos. (g. s.).
    Samuel, b. 31 Mar., bapt. 15 May 1785, d. at Stratford, 15 Jan. 1849 ae. 62; m. 2 Sept. 1810, Amy Reynolds, dau. of Philemon and Hannah (Mead), b. 17 Sept. 1788, d. 7 Feb. 1861/2; had 10 children.
    Ruth, bapt. 2 Aug. 1787, d. at Fairfield, 28 Sept. 1864 ae. 77 (g. s.); m. Stephen Turney.
    William, bapt. 4 July 1790, d. at New Haven, 14 Aug. 1876 ae. 87 (g. s.); m. Lydia Ives, dau. of Dr. Levi, b. abt. 1795, d. 22 Nov. 1873 ae. 78 (g. s.).
    Rufus, bapt. 16 Feb. 1794.

Buddington [*Unplaced*].

    MARY m. 2 Feb. 1786, Joseph Beers. [Fairfield Church]

Buffet [*Unplaced*].

    PHEBE m. 21 Nov. 1782, Samuel Gorham. [Greens Farms Church]

Bulkley [Vol. I, pp. 109-115].

  1 Rev. Peter (1583-1659) m. (1) Jane Allen; (2) Grace Chetwood.
(By 1): 2 Thomas (1617-1658) m. Sarah Jones.
      4 John (-1707) m. Esther [Burr?]. No sons.
      5 Joseph (1648-1719) m. Martha Beers.
         8 *Joseph* (1682-1750).
         9 *Peter* (1684-1752).
        10 *Daniel* (1689-after 1762).
        11 *Thomas* (1691-1756).
        12 *John* (1702-1751).
(By 2): 3 Peter (1643-1691) m. Margaret ———.
      6 Gershom (1676-1753) m. (1) Eunice Hanford; (2) Rachel Talcott.
    (By 2): 13 *Gershom* (1709-1802).
         14 *Hezekiah* (1713-1788).
         15 *Peter* (1716-1804).
         16 *Talcott* (1724-1810).
      7 Peter (1683-1753) m. (1) Hannah Bulkley; (2) Abigail ———.
    (By 2): 17 *Jonathan* (1732-1789).

---

* Supplemented by information contributed by Miss Ruth L. Buddington of New Haven, Conn.

8. Bulkley, Joseph, s. of Joseph.

Born 9 May 1682; d. at Fairfield, 6 May 1750 ae. 68 (g. s.); m. (1) Esther Bulkley, dau. of John, b. 30 Jan. 1683/4, d. 18 Mar. 1725/6 ae. 42 yrs. 1 mo. 19 days (g. s.); m. (2) Ruth Jennings, bapt. 11 Apr. 1708, d. abt. 1787; she m. (2) 14 Mar. 1754, Capt. Seth Samuel Burr.

Adm'n granted to Nathan and Ruth Bulkley, 5 June 1750. Distribution 1750: Widow Ruth; John; Nathan; Samuel; Ebenezer; Esther wife of John Hill; Sarah wife of Ebenezer Middlebrook. Ebenezer chose his mother Ruth his guardian, 1750.

On 2 Apr. 1787, distribution was ordered of the estate of Ruth Burr, which was her dower in the estate of Joseph Bulkley.

Children [by first wife], rec. and bapt. Fairfield:

> John, b. 14 Sept. 1711, bapt. 9 Mar. 1711/2, d. at Fairfield, 25 July 1784; Inv. 21 Mar. 1785 showed very small estate; m. 8 Jan. 1756, Martha Hubbell. She was prob. widow of David Hubbell, and dau. of Nathan Gold, bapt. 24 May 1730, d. by 1761.
> Esther, bapt. 20 Dec. 1713; m. (1) 27 Jan. 1729 [1729/30], John Hill; m. (2) 9 May 1764, Stephen Adams.

18+Nathan, b. 16, bapt. 19 Jan. 1717/8.
> Joseph, bapt. 22 Nov. 1719, d. in 1744. Adm'n granted to Nathan Bulkley, 20 Dec. 1744. Distribution: John, Jr.; Esther Hill; Nathan; Samuel; Sarah; Ebenezer.

19+Samuel, b. 1, bapt. 6 Mar. 1725/6.

Children [by second wife], rec. and bapt. Fairfield:

> Sarah, bapt. 23 Feb. 1728/9, d. at Fairfield, 21 Jan. 1811 ae. 84; m. 20 Sept. 1749, Ebenezer Middlebrook.

20+Ebenezer, b. 3, bapt. 5 Dec. 1731.

9. Bulkley, Peter, s. of Joseph.

Born 21 May 1684; d. at Fairfield, 15 Oct. 1752 in 69 yr. (g. s.); m. [perhaps at Stratfield, 25 Oct. 1709], Hannah Ward, dau. of Samuel, who d. abt. 1772.

He was a weaver, and was called "Second" or "Jr." to distinguish ·him from his father's first cousin Peter, who was five months older than himself.

Adm'n granted, 9 Dec. 1752, to Hannah and James Bulkley. Distribution 16 Feb. 1754: Widow; David; Peter; Jabez; Moses;

James; Olive; Mary; Sarah Perry and Hannah wife of Eleazer Osborn had received portions.

The widow's dower was distributed to the heirs, 15 Dec. 1772: David; Peter; heirs of Jabez; Moses; James; Mary wife of Howes Osborn; Olive Bulkley; Sarah Wheeler; Hannah Osborn.

Children, bapt. Fairfield:

21+David, bapt. 9 Mar. 1711/2.
    Sarah, bapt. 14 Dec. 1712, d. y.
    Sarah, bapt. 29 Nov. 1713, d. at Greenfield, 22 Apr. 1789 in 76 yr. (g. s.); m. (1) 11 Nov. 1736, Joseph Perry; m. (2) at Greenfield, 17 Apr. 1760, Thomas Wheeler.
22+Peter, bapt. 9 Oct. 1715.
    Andrew, bapt. 6 Oct. 1717, d. in 1744. Adm'n granted to David Bulkley, 20 Dec. 1744.
    Hannah, b. 29 Aug. 1719 (Bible rec.), d. at Fairfield, 19 Nov. 1812 ae. 93 (g. s.); m. 29 June 1738, Eleazer Osborn.
    Gershom, bapt. 13 Aug. 1721, d. y.
23+Jabez, bapt. 4 Aug. 1723.
    Olive, bapt. July 1725, d. at Fairfield, 28 Aug. 1812 ae. 87, unm.
24+Moses, bapt. 9 July 1727.
25+James, bapt. 3 Aug. 1729.
    Mary, bapt. 17 Oct. 1731, d. at Fairfield, 25 Nov. 1812 ae. 81 (g. s.); m. 6 Feb. 1755, Howes Osborn.

10. Bulkley, Daniel, s. of Joseph.

Born abt. 1689; living in Redding, 1762.

He m. (1) Hannah ———,* who d. between 1724 and 1727; m. (2) 21 May 1728, Hannah Johnson, dau. of Moses.

The will of Moses Johnson of Newtown, 1753, bequeathed to children of his dec'd dau. Hannah wife of Daniel Bulkley of Fairfield, viz.: Jabez, Hannah, Charity, Miriam, and Sarah.

Daniel and Hannah his [first] wife renewed their Covenant at Fairfield Church, 25 May 1718. Daniel of Redding conveyed to Benjamin Hamilton, 27 Nov. 1762.

Children [by first wife], bapt. Fairfield:

26+Daniel, bapt. 15 June 1718.
    Jabez, bapt. 28 Feb. 1719/20, d. y.

---

* She was a Bartram according to her gr. gr. son Uriah Bulkley, but this is doubtful. It may be noted that the second wife, Hannah Johnson, had a sister Mabel Johnson who m. David Bartram. Hannah's children did not receive Bartram names; but she could have been sister of David and dau. of John and Sarah Bartram (Vol. I, p. 34).

Martha, bapt. 2 July 1721; m. Ephraim Wheeler, of Redding.
Nehemiah, bapt. 15 Nov. 1724, prob. d. s. p.

Children [by second wife], first bapt. Fairfield, others Greenfield:

> 27+Jabez, bapt. 16 Mar. 1728/9.
> Hannah, bapt. 21 Nov. 1731; m. 6 Apr. 1754, Benjamin Hamilton.
> Charity, bapt. 13 May 1733; m. 9 Mar. 1757, John Bartram.
> Daughter, bapt. in 1736, d. y.
> Miriam, bapt. 11 June 1738.
> Sarah, bapt. 19 July 1741.

11. Bulkley, Thomas, s. of Joseph.

Born abt. 1691; d. at Westport, 25 May 1756; m. Abigail ———, who d. at Westport, 15 Apr. 1765.

On 15 Mar. 1755, Thomas Bulkley conveyed to his son-in-law John Osborn "and my daughter Abigail his wife" his property, Osborn agreeing to maintain Bulkley and his wife for life. No probate.

Children:

> Abigail, b. [say 1719], d. at Westport, 7 May 1796; m. 15 Apr. 1741, John Osborn.
> Mary, b. abt. 1721, d. at Easton, 10 May 1801 in 81 yr. (g. s.); m. 25 Apr. 1745, Gershom Lyon.

12. Bulkley, John, s. of Joseph.

Bapt. 22 Mar. 1701/2; d. at Fairfield, between 2 Oct. and 5 Nov. 1751; m. Martha [perhaps Morehouse, bapt. 7 Sept 1712], who d. in 1759, having m. (2) 1 Nov. 1752, Gershom Whitehead.

Will 2 Oct., proved 5 Nov. 1751; wife Martha; children, Seth, Josiah, Joseph, Rebecca, Martha, Hester. Seth chose the widow Martha his guardian, and she was appointed for the other children. Distribution, 20 Apr. 1758; Widow Martha Whitehead, formerly widow of John Bulkley, and the same six children. Josiah chose William Raymond his guardian, 5 Apr. 1759, and Esther chose Ezekiel Hull.

Adm'n on Martha Whitehead's estate was granted, 29 Mar. 1759, and distribution made to the Bulkley children.

Samuel Mann and Rebecca his wife conveyed 1768 to Josiah Bulkley, who the same year purchased from Esther Bulkley, and from Martha Bulkley one-sixth of the dwelling house of her father John Bulkley dec'd.

Children, bapt. Fairfield:

28+Seth, bapt. 9 Nov. 1735.
    Rebecca, bapt. 11 Dec. 1737, d. y.
    Rebecca, bapt. 23 Mar. 1739/40; m. Samuel Mann.
    Martha, bapt. 14 Mar. 1741/2.
29+Josiah, bapt. 18 Mar. 1743/4.
    Esther, bapt. 29 June 1746; m. 24 Dec. 1772, Nathan Lewis.
30+Joseph, bapt. 31 Dec. 1749.

13. **Bulkley, Gershom,** s. of Gershom.

Bapt. 27 Mar. 1709; d. at Greenfield, 27 Sept. 1802 in 96 yr. (g. s.); m. 17 May 1736, Sarah Banks, b. 1 Feb. 1715/6, d. 7 May 1791 in 76 yr. (g. s.).

Will 11 Apr. 1797, proved 25 Oct. 1802; Amelia widow of my late son Gershom, and her children; gr. children Gershom, Timothy, and Amelia, children of son Gershom. Distribution 1 Apr. 1828: widow of Gershom, Jr., and the children of Gershom, Jr.,—Gershom and Timothy Bulkley and Amelia Hull dec'd late wife of Lyman Hull dec'd.

Children, rec. Fairfield, bapt. Greenfield:

    Amelia, b. 19, bapt. 20 Oct. 1738, d. 9 May 1754 in 16 yr. (g. s.) [29 May by town rec.].
    Joseph, b. 2 Nov., bapt. Nov. 1741, d. 22 Apr. 1742.
31+Gershom, b. 19 Sept., bapt. Sept. 1750 [1751 by town rec.].

14. **Bulkley, Hezekiah,** s. of Gershom.

Bapt. 29 Nov. 1713; d. at Fairfield, 24 Oct. 1788 (Perry Diary); m. (1) 4 Jan. 1739, Catherine Hill, bapt. 2 June 1717; m. (2) at Redding, 20 Sept. 1768, Sarah Rumsey, widow of Joseph Rumsey, and dau. of John Bartram, b. 14 May 1719.

Will 9 Sept., proved 22 Dec. 1788; wife Sarah, referring to her property before marriage; dau.-in-law Abigail, widow of son Hezekiah dec'd; son-in-law David Oysterbanks; gr. children

Zalmon, Clarina and Abigail Bulkley, children of son Hezekiah; Ezekiel, David, Nathan, Simeon, and Levi Oysterbanks, Ama Mann, and Huldah Redfield, the children of dau. Ann dec'd; friend Gershom Bulkley, son of Gershom, Exec'r, with my son-in-law David Oysterbanks.

Children [by first wife], rec. Fairfield:

> Ann, b. 15 Sept. 1739, d. 12 July 1788 (Perry Diary); m. David Oysterbanks.
> 32+Hezekiah, b. 17 Oct. 1749.

15. Bulkley, Peter, s. of Gershom.

Bapt. 5 Feb. 1715/6; d. at Westport, 12 May 1804 in 89 yr. (g. s.); m. 9 Apr. 1740, Ann Hill, bapt. 28 Feb. 1719/20, d. 11 Apr. 1795 ae. 76 (g. s.).

Children, rec. Fairfield:

33+William, b. 17 Sept. 1741.
> Abigail, b. 12 Apr. 1743, d. at Westport, 28 Jan. 1827 ae. 83 (g. s.); m. at Westport, 20 Apr. 1769, Daniel Burr.
> Grace, b. 7 Apr. 1745, d. at Westport, 7 Apr. 1766 in 21 yr. (g. s.).
> Elizabeth, b. 13 Dec. 1746, d. 6 Nov. 1775 (Perry Diary); m. Peter Morehouse.

34+Gershom, b. 9 May 1748.
> Rachel, b. 30 Mar. 1750; m. 31 July 1785, Robert Scudder.

35+Jonathan, b. 15 Nov. 1751.
> Eunice, b. 11 Apr. 1753, d. at Greenfield, 12 Apr. 1842 ae. 90 (g. s.); m. Daniel Meeker.

36+Abraham, b. 15 June 1755.
> Jerusha, b. 26 June 1757, d. at Fairfield, 6 Nov. 1847 ae. 90 (g. s.); m. 16 Mar. 1780, John Osborn.
> Eleanor, b. 24 July 1759, d. at Westport, 25 July 1808 ae. 48; m. 30 Dec. 1779, Lovel Chapman.
> Ann, b. 17 Aug. 1761 (family rec.); m. at Weston, 12 Oct. 1783, Increase Burr, Jr.

16. Bulkley, Talcott, s. of Gershom. Ens., 2d Co., Fairfield, May 1759; Lt., May 1765.

Born 21 Aug. 1724; d. at Westport, 26 Apr. 1810 ae. 86; m. 19 June 1753, Esther Bradley, dau. of Daniel, b. 30 Mar. 1733, d. 18 Aug. 1770 (Perry Diary).

Children, rec. and bapt. Fairfield:

> Esther, b. 6, bapt. 10 Feb. 1754.
> Molly, b. 5, bapt. 20 Sept. 1755; "Mary" m. at Westport, 19 Dec. 1773, Joseph Morehouse; rem. to Ballston, N. Y.
> Amelia, bapt. 12 June 1757, d. Aug. 1837; m. 17 Jan. 1781, Abijah Benedict; rem. to Pompey, N. Y.
> Talcott, bapt. 11 Feb. 1759.
> Abigail, bapt. 2 Aug. 1761.
> Happy, bapt. 19 June 1763 [b. 31 May 1764, by Simsbury rec.]; m. at Westport, 1 May 1783, Gad Alderman, of Simsbury.
> Bradley, bapt. 20 Jan. 1765, d. y.
> Ruhamah, bapt. 26 Apr. 1767;* m. at Weston, 19 May 1791, Benjamin Allen.
> Bradley, bapt. 7 May 1769, d. at Ridgefield, 6 May 1825 ae. 56 (g. s.); m. 13 July 1797, Molly Burr, bapt. 9 Jan. 1780, d. 11 June 1866 ae. 87 (g. s.).†

17. Bulkley, Jonathan, s. of Peter.

Born 3 Oct. 1732; d. at Fairfield, 13 Apr. 1789‡ in 57 yr. (g. s.); m. 21 Jan. 1762, Hannah Hoyt, dau. of James, b. abt. 1741, d. 4 Mar. 1817 ae. 76 (g. s.).

Taken prisoner by British, July 1779, liberated on parole Jan. 1780.

Will 8 Apr., proved 21 July 1789; wife Hannah; children, Peter, Jonathan, Abigail, Thomas, Hannah, Harry, James; mother living; son Peter's education at college.

Children, rec. and bapt. Fairfield:

> Peter, b. 3 Apr., bapt. 9 June 1765; grad. Yale Coll. 1785; res. 1819, Rhinebeck, N. Y.
> Jonathan, b. 9, bapt. 29 Mar. 1767, d. at Fairfield, 24 Mar. 1830 ae. 63 (g. s.).
> Abigail, b. 30 Aug., bapt. 3 Sept. 1769, d. at Fairfield, 13 Sept. 1847 ae. 77 (g. s.). Will 1 Jan. 1838, proved 3 Oct. 1847; all estate to sister Hannah.
> Thomas, b. 23 Nov., bapt. 1 Dec. 1771, d. at Fairfield, 30 May 1836 ae. 63 (g. s.).
> Hannah, b. 1, bapt. 5 Sept. 1773, d. at Fairfield, 30 Mar. 1851 ae. 77 yrs. 7 mos. (g. s.). Adm'n granted to bro. Henry S. Bulkley, 13 May 1851.

---

* Talcott, son of "Amy" Bulkley, bapt. at Weston, 20 Sept. 1790.
† Children, bapt. Westport: Harriet, bapt. 10 June 1798; Abigail, bapt. 1 Sept. 1803; Mary-Bradley, bapt. 20 Oct. 1805.
‡ But Jonathan was bur. 1 Mar. 1790 (Trinity Church rec.).

Henry-Stanley, b. 18 Mar., bapt. 9 Apr. 1776, d. at Fairfield, 30 Oct. 1855 ae. 80 (g. s.); is said to have m. (1) Sally Durrin, and (2) Mary Zeller; m. (3) Nancy ———, who d. 22 Mar. 1856 ae. 62 (g. s.).

James-Chester, b. 24 May, bapt. 6 June 1779.

18. Bulkley, Nathan, s. of Joseph. Deputy for Fairfield, Oct. 1765; Justice, 1774-78.

Born 16 Jan. 1717/8; d. at Fairfield, 6 Apr. 1793 in 76 yr. (g. s.); m. 15 Apr. 1756, Sarah Perry, dau. of Joseph, b. 30 Jan. 1727/8, d. 27 Dec. 1798 ae. 72 (g. s.).

Grad. Yale Coll. 1737. Town Clerk, Fairfield, 32 yrs.; deacon, Christ Church, 1768-93.

Adm'n granted, 23 Sept. 1793, to David Judson. Inv. included a library of Greek, Latin, and English books.

Children, rec. and bapt. Fairfield:

Esther, b. 1, bapt. 7 Aug. 1763, d. at Fairfield, 6 Sept. 1843 in 81 yr. (g. s.); m. 13 Nov. 1783, David Judson; no issue.

Sarah, b. 26 Jan., bapt. 7 Feb. 1768, d. at Fairfield, 7 Mar. 1839 ae. 71 (g. s.).

19. Bulkley, Samuel, s. of Joseph.

Born 1 Mar. 1725/6; d. at Fairfield, 27* Aug. 1772; m. 2 Sept. 1754, Beulah Henry, dau. of Samuel; she d. at Weston abt. 1813.

Adm'n granted to Beulah, 6 Oct. 1772. Distribution, 1786: widow; eldest dau. Esther wife of John Williams, Jr.; 2d dau. Deborah Bulkley; 3d dau. Hannah Bulkley; 4th dau. Mindwell Bulkley.

Adm'n granted 15 Nov. 1813 on the unadministered part of the estate of Samuel Bulkley, to David Davis of Southbury. Distribution: Esther widow of Dr. John Williams; Deborah wife of David Davis; Hannah wife of Daniel Parsons; Mindwell wife of John Davis.

Children, rec. Fairfield:

Esther, b. 7 Dec. 1755; m. Dr. John Williams.

Samuel, b. 19 Dec. 1757, bapt. at Greenfield, 9 Feb. 1758, d. y.

Deborah, b. 26 Jan. 1761; m. David Davis.

---

* 17, by Perry Dairy.

Hannah, b. 4 Apr. 1763; m. at Easton, 2 Jan. 1792, Daniel Pearsal [called Parsons in Pro. rec.].
Mindwell, b. 22 Aug. 1765, d. at Weston, 21 Dec. 1834 ae. 70 (g. s.); m. John Davis.

20. **Bulkley, Ebenezer,** s. of Joseph.

Born 3 Dec. 1731; d. at Fairfield, 22 Sept. 1786 ae. 54-9-8; m. 11 Dec. 1765, Hannah Maltby, dau. of Jonathan of Stamford, b. 5 Oct. 1741, d. 3 Oct. 1820 ae. 79; she m. (2) Seth Morehouse.

Adm'n granted, 20 Nov. 1786, to John Squire, Jr.; estate insolvent; dower set to widow. In 1790, Seth Morehouse and Hannah his wife of Fairfield conveyed to Nathan Bulkley her right as dower in estate of her former husband Ebenezer Bulkley dec'd.

Children, rec. Fairfield, five bapt. Fairfield:

Ebenezer, b. 19 Nov. 1766; m. Diana Williams; "wife of Ebenz" d. at Fairfield, 24 Apr. 1817 ae. 52.
Hannah, b. 14 Oct. 1768, living (1820) in Patterson, N. Y.; m. 15 Mar. 1789, Elijah Morehouse.
Maltby, b. 3 Dec. 1770, d. 12 Feb. 1845 ae. 75 (g. s.); m. Parthenia Morehouse, bapt. 19 Mar. 1780, d. 18 Feb. 1847 ae. 67 (g. s.).
Sarah, b. 2 May 1773, bapt. 13 Apr. 1788; m. 3 Feb. 1791, Abraham Morehouse, Jr.
Mary, b. 14 May 1775, bapt. 13 Apr. 1788; m. Silas Beach.
John, b. 28 Oct. 1778, bapt. 13 Apr. 1788.
Abigail, b. 16 Mar. 1781, bapt. 30 Mar. 1788, d. 7 Apr. 1788.
George, b. 3 Aug. 1784, bapt. 13 Apr. 1788, d. in Ohio ae. 80; m. Ruth Barnes.

21. **Bulkley, David,** s. of Peter.

Bapt. 9 Mar. 1711/2; d. at Weston in 1804; m. (1) Sarah [perhaps Beers, bapt. 9 Jan. 1714/5]; m. (2) 11 May 1760, Deborah, widow of Solomon Couch, and dau. of Daniel Silliman, b. by 1717, d. in 1766; m. (3) 17 Mar. 1767, Abigail, widow of Benjamin Davis, and dau. of Capt. Thomas Hill, b. 9 May 1718, d. at Amenia, N. Y., 20 June 1807 ae. 89 (g. s.).

He was a deacon; rem. by 1780 to "Little Nine Partners," Dutchess County, N. Y., but returned to Conn. and settled in Weston.

Children [by first wife], bapt. Fairfield:
37+Isaac, bapt. 10 Nov. 1735.
Amy, bapt. 28 Aug. 1737.

Eunice, bapt. 5 Oct. 1740, d. at Weston, 6 Mar. 1831 ae. 91 (g. s.);
m. at Weston, 22 Mar. 1759, Daniel Godfrey.

Sarah, bapt. 6 June 1742; m. at Westport, 15 Nov. 1764, Benjamin Whittier; res. 1774, Sharon.

38+David, bapt. 1 July 1744.

Hannah, bapt. 15 June 1746, d. at Weston, 10 Feb. 1789; m. at Weston, 14 Feb. 1769, William Downs.

Ward, bapt. 13 Mar. 1747/8.

Lois, bapt. 27 May 1750, d. before 1774; m. at Fairfield, 15 May 1770, Jonathan Cole.

Grace, bapt. at Westport, 22 Apr. 1753, d. at Redding, 19 Sept. 1829 ae. 76 (g. s.); m. at Greenfield, 19 Jan. 1774, Thaddeus Perry.

39+Joseph, bapt. at Westport, 18 May 1755.

22. Bulkley, Peter, s. of Peter.

Bapt. 9 Oct. 1715; d. at Fairfield in 1801; m. (1) 1 Jan. 1741, Sarah Turney, dau. of Thomas; she d. abt. 1757, and he m. (2) 14 Feb. 1760, Hannah Sherwood, dau. of John of Newtown, who d. by 1794.

Thomas Turney conveyed, 7 June 1759, to his gr. children, Elizabeth, Andrew, Peter, Aaron, Sarah, Gershom, Turney, and Nathan Bulkley, children of his dec'd dau. Sarah.

John Sherwood of Newtown, in his will 6 Sept. 1783, proved 7 Oct. 1783, gave £10 to dau. Hannah wife of Peter Bulkley.

In 1794, David Whitehead and Abigail his wife, Hezekiah Whitehead and Olive his wife, William Jennings and Hannah his wife, of Fairfield, conveyed to Nathan Bulkley land which our mother Hannah wife of our father Peter Bulkley bought of Peter Bulkley, Jr., of Redding. In 1795, Andrew Bulkley conveyed to Nathan Bulkley, land from dec'd mother Sarah wife of Peter Bulkley of Redding. In 1775, Peter of Newtown conveyed to bro. Gershom of Redding, and in 1786 to Hannah wife of Peter Bulkley. Aaron and Turney Bulkley also conveyed right inherited from mother Sarah. In 1800, John Bulkley of Sharon, Thomas Bulkley of New Milford, and William Tanner of Sharon and Eleanor his wife, conveyed to Nathan Bulkley.

Children [by first wife], rec. and bapt. Fairfield:

Elizabeth, b. 27 Aug., bapt. 27 Sept. 1741.

40+Andrew, b. 27 Aug., bapt. 27 Nov. 1743.

41+Peter, b. 13, bapt. 19 May 1745.

42+Aaron, b. 22, bapt. 28 Feb. 1747/8.
    Sarah, b. 29, bapt. 30 Dec. 1750; m. at Redding, 1 Nov. 1770, Joseph Lyon.
    Gershom, b. 6, bapt. 18 Feb. 1753; loyalist.
43+Turney, b. 9 June 1755.
    Nathan, b. 16 Feb. 1757, d. at Danbury, 9 June 1837 ae. 80 yrs. 3 mos. (g. s.); Baptist minister; will 2 Sept. 1833, proved 12 June 1837; m. (1) Anna Jennings, bapt. 28 Aug. 1763; m. (2) 12 May 1817, Jerusha (Barnum), widow of Timothy Benedict, b. [26 May 1762], d. 2 Dec. 1856 ae. 94-6-6 (g. s.).

Children [by second wife], one rec. Fairfield; bapt. Greenfield:

    Hannah, b. 12 Jan., bapt. 22 Feb. 1761, d. at Greenfield, 30 Mar. 1836 ae. 75 (g. s.); m. William Jennings.
    Abigail, bapt. 6 June 1762; m. David Whitehead.
    John, bapt. 9 Sept. 1764; m. (1) Serissa Edwards, who d. at New Milford, 18 Dec. 1797 in 32 yr. (g. s.); rem. to Sharon by 1800, living there 1808, and prob. m. again.
    Thomas, bapt. 21 June 1767, d. at Vergennes, Vt., 24 July 1845 ae. 78; m. Mary Marsh, b. at New Milford, 10 Jan. 1773, d. at Vergennes, 17 Jan. 1827.
    Olive, b. abt. 1771, d. at New Milford, 26 Dec. 1867 ae. 96 (g. s.); m. (1) Hezekiah Whitehead, of Kent; m. (2) in 1813, William Hallock, of New Milford.
    Eleanor,* m. William Tanner, of Sharon.

23. Bulkley, Jabez, s. of Peter.

Bapt. 4 Aug. 1723; d. at Fairfield in 1758; m. 5 Nov. 1747, Elizabeth Osborn, bapt. 28 May 1727. She m. (2) 9 Dec. 1761, Jonathan Darrow, Sr.

Adm'n granted, 27 Apr. 1758, to Elizabeth Bulkley, John Osborn surety. Jonathan Darrow was appointed guardian, 22 Dec. 1761, to Elizabeth, Lydia, and Sarah Bulkley.

Children, bapt. Fairfield:

    Elizabeth, bapt. 25 Nov. 1750, d. before 1778; m. 31 Jan. 1771, Jonathan Darrow, Jr.
    Lydia, bapt. 18 Mar. 1753, d. at Sherman, 31 Aug. 1805 ae. 52 (g. s.); m. 12 Dec. 1776, Jonathan Bulkley.
    Jabez, bapt. 28 Jan. 1755, d. y.
    Mary, bapt. 28 Jan. 1755, d. y.
    Sarah, bapt. 2 Apr. 1758; m. 4 July 1776, Ebenezer Sturgis.

---

* Eleanor, dau. of Peter, bapt. at Trinity Church, 24 Sept. 1786.

24. Bulkley, Moses, s. of Peter. Capt.

Bapt. 9 July 1727; d. at North East, N. Y., 3 June 1812 ae. 85 (g. s.); m. 29 Aug. 1758, Abigail Sturges, b. 7 Mar. 1737, d. 11 Apr. 1828 ae. 91 (g. s.).

Fairfield Deeds describe Moses as of Ridgefield, 1770 and 1774; of Fredericksburg, N. Y., 1776, and of "Little Nine Partners,"N. Y., 1782. Elnathan Sturges of Ridgefield conveyed 1763, to dau. Abigail wife of Moses Bulkley.

Children, bapt. Fairfield:

> Jabez, bapt. 12 Aug. 1759, d. at Schaghticoke, Rensselaer County, N. Y., in 1827; m. Phebe ———. Will 13 Apr. 1826, proved 19 Apr. 1827; three oldest sons, Joel, Tertullus, and Moses, a farm at Easton, Washington County; four youngest sons, Stephen, David, Ezra, and Samuel, the homestead farm at death of my wife Phebe, their mother; three daus. Abigail Deyo, Lois and Sally Bulkley, a third farm at Easton.*
> Ellen, bapt. 30 May 1762.
> Elizabeth, bapt. 25 Nov. 1764, d. at North East, N. Y., 15 May 1783 ae. 19 (g. s.); m. David Rood.
> Sturgis, bapt. 14 June 1767; m. Sally ———.
> Moses, bapt. 20 Aug. 1769.
> Others?

25. Bulkley, James, s. of Peter.

Bapt. 3 Aug. 1729; d. at Fairfield, 13 Feb. 1803 ae. 73 (g. s.); m. 8 Apr. 1756, Elizabeth Whitehead, b. abt. 1738, d. 27 June 1809 ae. 71 (g. s.).

He was a weaver.

Children, first rec. Fairfield, second bapt. Greenfield, others bapt. Fairfield:

> Mary, b. 3 Apr. 1757, d. at Fairfield in 1779 ae. 22 (g. s.); ? m. 26 Oct. 1775, Robert Harris, of Weston.
> Eunice, bapt. 17 June 1759; ? m. at Weston, 4 May 1780, Nathan Grey.

---

* For an abstract of this will, we are indebted to Mr. Conklin Mann, of New York City. Note that another Jabez, son of Jabez, was bapt. at Redding, 22 June 1760. The identity of the maker of the will has not been positively established, but it is believed that he was the son of Moses above.

Abigail, bapt. 14 Dec. 1760; m. 28 Jan. 1779, Josiah Beardsley; rem. to Butternuts, Otsego County, N. Y.
Eleazer, b. 2, bapt. 6 Feb. 1763, d. at Fairfield, 5 Feb. 1843 (g. s.); m. 22 Dec. 1785, Mary Ogden, b. 2 May 1770, d. 19 July 1839.*
Mabel, bapt. 14 July 1765, d. at Fairfield, 14 Dec. 1827 ae. 62 (g. s.); m. Nathan Wheeler.
James, b. 29 Aug., bapt. 11 Sept. 1768, d. at Norfolk, Va., 15 Sept. 1805 ae. 37 (g. s., Fairfield); m. 16 Dec. 1790, Sarah Smith, 2d, of Norwalk, b. 13 Feb. 1769, d. 5 Sept. 1849.†
Howkin, bapt. 27 May 1770, d. at Fairfield in 1819; m. (1) Catherine Judson; m. (2) Elizabeth Lee.
Elizabeth, bapt. 2 Aug. 1772, d. at Fairfield, 5 Apr. 1847 ae. 74 (g. s.); m. (1) Dec. 1793, Richard Bangs; m. (2) Levi Perry.
Andrew, bapt. 30 Oct. 1774, d. at Fairfield in 1788 ae. 14 (g. s.); d. 25 Aug. 1788 (Perry Diary).
Moses, bapt. 27 Oct. 1776, d. at Fairfield in 1796 ae. 20 (g. s.).
Mary, bapt. 15 Aug. 1779; m. 31 July 1800, Joab Squire; rem. by 1816 to Jesupville, Huron County, Ohio.

26. Bulkley, Daniel, s. of Daniel.

Soldier in French War, and at capture of Louisburg 1757 [autobiography of his gr. son Uriah Bulkley].

Bapt. 15 June 1718; d. at Greenfield, 9 June 1797 in 79 yr. (g. s.); m. 18 Mar. 1759, Hannah (Hill), widow of David Meeker, Jr., b. 25 June 1728, d. 7 Dec. 1809 ae. 82 (g. s.).

Will 16 Aug. 1793, proved 16 June 1797; wife Hannah; son Joseph; daus. Mabel, Esther, Ruth.

In 1797 his widow was residing in Newtown, and in 1799 in Redding. On 6 Sept. 1797, Jesse Nichols and Mabel his wife of Fairfield, Chapman Hull and Esther his wife of Redding, and William H. Peabody and Ruth his wife of Stratford, conveyed to Joseph Bulkley, Jr., their right in the homestead in Greenfield that formerly belonged to Daniel Bulkley dec'd.

Children, bapt. Greenfield:

Joseph, b. 21 Aug. 1759 (g. s.), bapt. 28 Oct. 1759 (ae. abt. 2 mos.), d. at Greenfield, 17 Oct. 1848 (g. s.); m. 2 June 1779, Ellen

---

* Children, bapt. Fairfield: Jonathan, bapt. 26 Nov. 1786; Andrew, bapt. 13 Dec. 1789, m. 11 Aug. 1816, Sally Dimon; Lot, bapt. 13 July 1794; Moses, bapt. 18 Sept. 1796; George, bapt. 29 June 1800.
† Children (from Bible rec.): Ruth, b. 28 Oct. 1791; Stephen, b. 12 Aug. 1794; Julian, b. 13 Nov. 1796; James, b. 29 Dec. 1799; George J., b. Jan. [———]; Rosalie, b. [———]. The name Ruth is apparently a misreading of the Bible record, and should be *Walter*.

Hubbell, bapt. 11 Apr. 1762, d. at Poughkeepsie, N. Y., 18 Jan. 1819 ae. 56.*
Mabel, bapt. 27 Dec. 1761 (ae. abt. 1 mo.), d. at Greenfield, 17 Jan. 1828 ae. 66 (g. s.); m. 22 Nov. 1778, Jesse Nichols.
Hill, bapt. 1 Apr. 1764 (ae. 5 or 6 weeks), d. 30 Oct. 1766 ae. 2 yrs. 8 mos.
Abel, bapt. 20 Apr. 1766 (ae. abt. 16 days), d. y.
Esther, bapt. 17 Dec. 1769; m. (1) Chapman Hull, of Redding; m. (2) Gould Nichols, of Weston.
Ruth, bapt. 6 June 1773; m. William Henry Peabody, of Bridgeport.

27. Bulkley, Jabez, s. of Daniel.

Bapt. 16 Mar. 1728/9; d. at Newtown in 1774; m. Mary Waring, dau. of Richard and Eunice (Lyon).

Will 22 June, proved 2 Aug. 1774; all estate to wife Mary except £2, which is to be divided equally among the children, Jabez, Hannah, Eunice, Calvin, Luther, Daniel, Peter and Billy; wife and Amiel Peck, Exec'rs. Est. insolvent.

Children, two bapt. Redding:

Eunice, b. [say 1757], d. at Newtown, 18 Jan. 1820 ae. 62 (g. s.); m. Peter Fairchild, b. 12 Mar. 1756, d. 20 Sept. 1833 ae. 77-6-8 (g. s.).
Hannah, bapt. 26 Aug. 1758.
Jabez, bapt. 22 June 1760.
Calvin, b. [say 1764], of Kent, 1780, when he enlisted.
Luther, b. [say 1766]; res. Liberty, Sullivan County, N. Y.; m. Lucinda Baldwin, b. 11 June 1769.
Daniel, b. [say 1768].
Peter, b. [say 1770]; res. Cornwall; m. Dorothy ———.
Billy, b. [say 1772]; res. Albany, N. Y., 1810; m. Mary Turner.

28. Bulkley, Seth, s. of John.

Bapt. 9 Nov. 1735.

Possibly his wife was the Hannah who was bur. 6 Mar. 1817 ae. 77 (Trinity Church rec.).

He was of Stratford in 1782, when he conveyed realty in Fairfield, and was listed at Stratford in the 1790 Census. Lived in "Mutton Lane" 1797, wrote Uriah Bulkley.

---

* Children: Ellen, b. 3 Oct. 1779, d. 25 Feb. 1865; m. at Fairfield, 21 July 1799, Philo Ruggles, of New Milford, Conn., Poughkeepsie, N. Y., and New York City. Uriah, b. 12 Aug. 1782, d. at Dobb's Ferry, N. Y., 23 July 1874; m. Jane Sayre, b. 20 Apr. 1788, d. 10 Feb. 1831. William-Samuel, b. 7 Oct. 1786, d. 1797. William-Henry, b. Oct. 1796, d. at New York City, 1840.

Children:
> Stephen.
> John, d. 17 Mar. 1859; m. 25 Feb. 1813, Lucinda Elwood, b. 4 Mar. 1795, d. 22 June 1820.
> Daniel, bapt. at Trinity Church, 4 Sept. 1785, d. at New Milford, 31 Oct. 1860 ae. 76 (g. s.); m. Sarah ———, b. 2 Mar. 1786, d. 11 Nov. 1868 ae. 83 (g. s.).
> Josiah, bapt. at Trinity Church, 21 Dec. 1785.
> Sally, bapt. at Trinity Church, 7 Sept. 1788.

29. **Bulkley, Josiah,** s. of John.

Bapt. 18 Mar. 1743/4.

He m. 25 Dec. 1771, Abigail Beers, dau. of Joseph, b. 24 Apr. 1747.

His wife testified regarding the burning of Fairfield by the British.

Children, last four bapt. Southport:
> Abel, bapt. June 1780 (rec. St. James', Derby).
> ? Josiah, m. at Rye, 7 Dec. 1809, Ann Brundage.
> Abigail, bapt. 20 May 1787.
> Abel, bapt. 25 Oct. 1789; m. at Rye, 13 Feb. 1813, Elizabeth Brundage.
> Lucretia, bapt. 18 Sept. 1791.
> Polly, bapt. 13 July 1794.

30. **Bulkley, Joseph,** s. of John.

Bapt. 31 Dec. 1749; bur. at Fairfield, 1 Mar. 1796 ae. 50 (Trinity Church rec.); m. 14 Mar. 1776, Elizabeth Lewis. She was perhaps the Betsey Bulkley bur. 10 Oct. 1824 ae. 74 (Trinity Church rec.).

A one-eyed man, lived on bank of Mill River below Nehemiah Jennings.

Children:
> Esther, b. [say 1778]; m. at Trinity Church, 9 July 1797, John Patchen.*
> Elizabeth, b. 12 June 1780, bapt. June 1780 (rec. St. James', Derby), d. 1 Mar. 1871; m. 7 Oct. 1804, David Penfield.
> Joseph, bapt. at Fairfield, 18 June 1783, d. at Fairfield, 3 Feb. 1832 ae. 49 yrs. 8 mos. (g. s.); m. at Trinity Church, 27 Apr. 1812, Chloe Hubbell, who d. abt. 1852.

---

* *The Bulkeley Family* states that Esther m. David Patchen, but the church entry is believed to be correct. Note that Turney Bulkley (43) had a dau. Esther of proper age for this marriage.

Morehouse (twin), bapt. at Fairfield, 18 June 1783, d. 20 Mar. 1829 (Wheeler Journal).
Adad, bapt. at Fairfield, 4 June 1786; m. Harriet (Hubbell), widow of Lewis Page.
Medad (twin), bapt. at Fairfield, 4 June 1786.
Nancy, bapt. at Trinity Church, 3 May 1789, d. 6 Mar. 1797 ae. 8.
Eben, bapt. at Trinity Church, 11 Nov. 1792.

31. Bulkley, Gershom, s. of Gershom.

Born 19 Sept. 1750; d. at Greenfield, 25 May 1791 ae. 41 (g. s.); m. 16 Mar. 1774, Amelia Bradley, dau. of Daniel, b. abt. 1754, d. 1 Nov. 1848 ae. 94 (g. s.).

Adm'n on estate of Amelia was granted to Timothy Bulkley, 29 Oct. 1849.

Children, bapt. Greenfield:

Amelia, bapt. 24 Mar. 1776, d. at Greenfield, 19 Aug. 1815 ae. 39 (g. s.); m. at Westport, 22 Oct. 1797, Lyman Hull.
Gershom, bapt. 28 June 1778, d. 18 Jan. 1785 ae. 6-8-13 (g. s.).
Bradley, bapt. 24 Sept. 1780, d. 5 Oct. 1781.
Gershom, b. abt. Dec. 1783, d. at Greenfield, 23 June 1830 ae. 46 yrs. 6 mos. (g. s.); m. at Westport, 10 Dec. 1808, Esther Morehouse, dau. of Samuel, b. 9 Mar. 1788, d. 24 Jan. 1871 ae. 82 yrs. 10 mos.*
Timothy, b. 23 Sept. 1787, d. at Greenfield, 11 Oct. 1857 ae. 70 (g. s.); m. (1) at Fairfield, 19 Oct. 1823, Susanna Osborn, bapt. 29 Apr. 1796, d. 8 Jan. 1828 ae. 33 (g. s.); m. (2) 23 Jan. 1830, Abigail Bulkley.†

32. Bulkley, Hezekiah, s. of Hezekiah.

Born 17 Oct. 1749; bur. at Fairfield, 9 Oct. 1786 (Trinity Church rec.); m. at Westport, 23 Feb. 1775, Abigail Blackman, b. 16 Feb. 1755.

Children:

Clarina, b. [6 Mar. 1776], d. at Westport, 4 Jan. 1849 ae. 72-9-29 (g. s.); m. 3 Sept. 1794, Squire Disbrow.

---

* By Bible record, Gershom was b. 23 Dec. 1784, d. 23 June 1830 ae. 45 yrs. 6 mos.; m. 25 Dec. 1807, Esther Morehouse, b. 9 Mar. 1788, d. 24 Jan. 1871 ae. 82 yrs. 10 mos. Children: Gershom, b. 17 Aug. 1809, d. 31 July 1827; Mary, b. 10 Oct. 1811, m. Jesup Sherwood; Sarah B., b. 10 Mar. 1814, m. Daniel Crossman; William T., b. 13 May 1817, d. 24 July 1818; Amelia B., b. 29 June 1819, m. Seth M. Bulkley; Emily, b. 31 Mar. 1822, m. Isaac Chidsey; Gershom B., b. 14 Oct. 1827, [m. Mary E. Griffeth].

† Timothy's will, 6 Apr. 1855, proved 11 Dec. 1857; wife Abigail; sons Timothy-Wakeman, Sereno-Bradley.

Abigail, b. 31 Oct. 1778, d. at Greenfield, 31 Oct. 1851 ae. 73 (g. s.); m. 28 Feb. 1798, Jesse Bradley.
Zalmon, b. abt. 1781, d. at Westport, 3 Mar. 1842 ae. 60 (g. s.); m. 24 Nov. 1801, Eleanor Meeker, dau. of Seth, bapt. 14 Jan. 1787, d. 24 Apr. 1872 ae. 88 (g. s.).

33. Bulkley, William, s. of Peter.

Born 17 Sept. 1741; d. at Westport, 4 Mar. 1787 ae. 45-5-17 (g. s.); m. at Greenfield, 4 Sept. 1766, Elizabeth Burr, b. 16 Sept. 1743, bur. 17 Sept. 1805 ae. 62 (Trinity Church rec.).

Will 24 Feb., proved 3 Apr. 1787; wife; eldest son William; sons Burr, Talcott, Hill; daus. Grace, Eunice, Anna Hill, Elizabeth; father Peter and bro. Gershom, Exec'rs. On 2 July 1788, Gershom Bulkley, 2d, was made guardian of Elizabeth, Talcott, and Hill; Peter Bulkley, 2d, of Anna-Hill and Eunice; Abraham Bulkley, of Burr.

Children:

> William, b. abt. 1768, bur. 2 Sept. 1808 ae. 40 (Trinity Church rec.); m. at Westport, 25 Oct. 1789, Sarah Redfield, bapt. 1 Sept. 1765, d. 15 June 1842 ae. 76. Adm'n on his estate was granted, 19 Sept. 1808, to Barnabas L. Sturges, with Ansel Trubee as surety.*
> Grace, b. abt. 1770, d. at Fairfield, 7 Oct. 1820 ae. 51 (g. s.); m. (1) 27 Apr. 1788, Capt. Peter Whitney; m. (2) 2 Sept. 1792, Ephraim Robbins.
> Eunice, b. abt. 1775, bur. 1 Feb. 1798 ae. 22 (Trinity Church rec.).
> Burr, b. 24 July 1777, d. 2 Oct. 1828; m. Sarah Conklin, b. 28 Mar. 1783, d. 17 Feb. 1867.
> Anna-Hill, bapt. July 1780 (rec. St. James', Derby); res. 1804, New Fairfield.
> Talcott, res. 1805, Harrison, Westchester County, N. Y.; m. Elizabeth ———.
> Hill, res. 1804, Harrison, N. Y.
> Elizabeth, b. 28 Mar. 1785, d. at Spencertown, N. Y., 23 Oct. 1866; m. 21 Sept. 1804, Samuel Higgins.

34. Bulkley, Gershom, s. of Peter.

Born 9 May 1748; d. at Rye, N. Y., 22 Feb. 1820 ae. 72 (g. s.); m. (1) at Westport, 3 June 1773, Elizabeth Chapman, b. 12 Aug. 1751, bur. at Fairfield, 26 May 1795 (Trinity Church rec.); m.

---

* Children, bapt. Trinity Church: William, bapt. 12 May 1790; Polly, bapt. 16 July 1792; Mathea (?), bapt. 15 Oct. 1794; Henrietta, bapt. 3 Dec. 1797.

(2) at Trinity Church, 9 Apr. 1797, Hannah (Raymond), widow of Jesse Platt, b. 1747, d. at Rye, 20(?) Dec. 1803 in 57 yr. (g. s.); m. (3) at Fairfield, 29 Apr. 1804, Mary (Bartram), widow of Daniel Osborn, Jr., bapt. 6 Oct. 1765, d. at Rye, 15 Apr. 1843 ae. 77-9-15 (g. s.).

Children [by first wife] :*

Peter, b. 25 Nov. 1774, d. 27 June 1840.
Elizabeth, b. abt. 1777; m. at Fairfield, 5 Feb. 1797, John Alvord.
Mary, d. 29 Oct. 1826; m. at Trinity Church, 27 May 1802, Abijah Wakeman.
Lovel, confirmed at Trinity Church, 18 Oct. 1798, with his bro. Peter and sisters Betsey Alvord and Polly Bulkley; was a sailor, bur. at Rye, unm.
Charles, bapt. 5 Apr. 1786, d. 1794/5.
William, b. 16 May 1787, bapt. 14 Oct. 1787, d. at Rye, N. Y., 29 Aug. 1860 ae. 73 (g. s.); m. at Rye, 26 Nov. 1809, Mary Bartram Osborn, b. 27 Mar. 1790, d. 10 Jan. 1850 (g. s.).
Gershom, b. 20 Oct. 1789, bapt. 12 May 1790; m. at Rye, 7 Sept. 1823, Mary G. Brush.

Children [by second wife]:

Caroline, bapt. 20 May 1798; m. at Rye, 23 Jan. 1820, John-Hull Osborn.
Abby-Jane, bapt. 7 Mar. 1802, d. at Rye in 1838; m. Henry M. Carpenter.

Child [by third wife]:

Ann-Hall, bapt. at Rye, 13 June 1807, d. at Babylon, L. I.; m. Rev. Ebenezer Platt.

35. Bulkley, Jonathan, s. of Peter. Representative for New Fairfield, 1809.

Born 15 Nov. 1751; d. at Sherman, 4 Nov. 1815 (g. s.); m. at Fairfield, 12 Dec. 1776, Lydia Bulkley, bapt. 18 Mar. 1753, d. 31 Aug. 1805 ae. 52 (g. s.).

Adm'n on Est. of Jonathan of New Fairfield granted, 15 Nov. 1815, to Jonathan Bulkley and William Josephus Bulkley.

---

* There was a Kezia dau. of Gershom bur. at Rye, 26 July 1820; if not a dau. of Gershom, Sr., she may have been dau. of the younger Gershom by a possible first marriage.

Children:

> Barzillai, bapt. June 1780 (rec. St. James', Derby); Rev.; first minister (Prot. Epis.) at Fairfield, Vt., 1806; m. Mary Gunn, who d. at New Milford, 21 July 1866 ae. 81 (g. s.).
> Lydia, b. 2 Feb. 1782, d. at Sherman, 21 May 1806 ae. 24 (g. s.); m. 8 Dec. 1799, David Leach.
> Elizabeth, b. abt. 1782, d. at Sherman, 19 Mar. 1804 ae. 22 (g. s.).
> Jonathan, b. 28 Aug. 1783, d. at Huntington, 24 Nov. 1869 (g. s.); m. Anna Osborn, bapt. 20 Sept. 1789, d. at Fairfield, 23 Aug. 1869 ae. 80 yrs. 1 mo. (g. s.).
> Anna, b. 12 Nov. 1785, d. at Sherman, 17 Feb. 1863; m. (1) Daniel Lane; m. (2) David Leach.
> William-Josephus.
> Priscilla, b. abt. 1790, d. at New Milford, 13 Sept. 1815 ae. 25 (g. s.); m. Asa Nichols.
> Sarah, b. 27 Nov. 1792, d. 5 Feb. 1851; m. 29 May 1816, Hanford-Martin Kellogg.
> Clarissa.

36. Bulkley, Abraham, s. of Peter.

Born 15 June 1755; d. at Westport, 26 Dec. 1838 in 84 yr. (g. s.); m. Jane Burr, bapt. 15 Mar. 1761, d. 4 Nov. 1838 in 78 yr. (g. s.).

Will 12 Apr. 1838, proved 21 Jan. 1839; wife; dau. Esther Downs; dau. Charlotte Jennings; gr. children Alanson, Eliza and Morris Osborn, children of dau. Rachel Osborn; sons Francis and Joel B.

Children, bapt. Trinity Church:

> Rachel, b. 25 May 1784, d. at Fairfield, 21 Oct. 1819 ae. 35 yrs. 5 mos. (g. s.); m. at Trinity Church 9 Nov. 1802, Stephen Osborn.
> Francis, b. 30 Jan. 1787, bapt. 5 Apr. 1786, d. at Fairfield, 17 Sept. 1868 ae. 81-7-17 (g. s.); m. at Trinity Church, 25 Feb. 1816, Sarah B. Morehouse, b. 17 Jan. 1792, d. 22 Dec. 1833 ae. 41-11-5 (g. s.).
> Esther, b. 13 July 1789, bapt. 25 Oct. 1789, d. 28 Nov. 1861; m. at Trinity Church, 14 Jan. 1816, Levi T. Downs.
> Charlotte, b. 24 Oct. 1791, bapt. 25 Mar. 1792, d. May 1874; m. in 1832, David Jennings.
> Joel-Burr, b. 7 July 1798, bapt. 2 Sept. 1798, d. at Fairfield, 12 Mar. 1887 ae. 88 yrs. 8 mos. (g. s.); m. Priscilla Sturges, b. 1801, d. 5 Apr. 1887 ae. 85 yrs. 5 mos. (g. s.).

37. Bulkley, Isaac, s. of David.

Bapt. 10 Nov. 1735; d. at Westport, 18 July 1770; m. 18 Nov. 1762, Deborah Couch, b. abt. 1738, d. at Fairfield, 31 Oct. 1816 ae. 78.

Deborah Bulkley was allowed guardian to Levi, 8 Mar. 1787. Adm'n on Deborah's estate was granted to Abel Turney, 2 Nov. 1816.

Children, bapt. Westport:

> Deborah, bapt. 24 July 1763, d. at Fairfield, 5 Jan. 1829 ae. 65 (g. s.); m. 26 Dec. 1784, Abel Turney.
> Mary, bapt. 24 June 1764; m. (1) 23 Feb. 1806, Aaron Cable; m. (2) Abel Turney.
> Isaac, b. abt. 1766; m. 13 July 1797, Abigail Turney.
> Levi, bapt. 29 May 1768, d. y.
> David, b. 23 May, bapt. 1 July 1770, d. at Waterbury, 11 Oct. 1860; m. at Weston, 7 Apr. 1798, Mercy Sturges, b. 31 Dec. 1775, d. 26 Mar. 1861.

38. Bulkley, David, s. of David.

Bapt. 1 July 1744; d. at Weston, 2 Aug. 1819 ae. 75 (g. s.); m. at Weston, 19 May 1777, Sarah Beers, b. 3 Feb. 1754, d. 10 Jan. 1817 ae. 63 (g. s.).

Will 3 Nov. 1818, proved 31 Aug. 1819; daus. Lois wife of Stephen Perry, Sarah wife of David B. Godfrey, and Eunice wife of John Gilbert; sons Moses (a minor), Aaron, Nehemiah Beers.

Children, rec. and bapt. Weston:

> Lois, b. 21 Dec. 1777, bapt. 8 Mar. 1778, d. at Redding, 18 Nov. 1863 ae. 86 (g. s.); m. 27 Oct. 1796, Stephen Perry.
> Sarah, b. 23 Dec. 1780, bapt. 18 Feb. 1781, d. at Weston, 8 Feb. 1869 ae. 88 (g. s.); m. 4 Oct. 1801, Capt. David-Bulkley Godfrey.
> David-Ward, b. 4 Apr., bapt. 15 June 1783, d. at Weston, 10 Jan. 1854 ae. 70 yrs. 9 mos. (g. s.); m. Rebecca Gregory, b. abt. 1789, d. 13 May 1881 ae. 92 (g. s.).
> Eunice-Beers, b. 29 Mar., bapt. 27 May 1787; m. John Gilbert.
> Aaron, b: 26 Feb., bapt. 4 July 1790, d. at Weston, 11 Jan. 1864 ae. 73 yrs. 11 mos. (g. s.); m. 28 Nov. 1816, Anna Bulkley, b. 1 Mar. 1793, d. in 1837.
> Nehemiah-Beers, b. 3 Aug. 1793, bapt. 1 Mar. 1794, d. at Weston, 22 Oct. 1880 ae. 87-2-19 (g. s.); m. (1) 1819, Sarah Beers, b. 18

Jan. 1794, d. 28 Mar. 1867 ae. 73-2-10 (g. s.); m. (2) 1872, Ellen (Odell) Fillow, b. 1792, d. 29(?) Feb. 1875.

Moses, bapt. 16 Dec. 1801, d. at Weston, 20 June 1881 ae. 79-10-5 (g. s.); m. Rebecca ———, b. [6 Oct. 1801], d. 7 Jan. 1881 ae. 79-3-1 (g. s.).

39. **Bulkley, Joseph,** s. of David.

Bapt. 18 May 1755; d. at Fairfield, 4 June 1813 ae. 58 (church rec.) or 2 June 1815 ae. 60 (g. s.); m. 27 July 1778, Grizzel Thorp, dau. of Jabez, bapt. 25 June 1758, d. 20 Oct. 1837 ae. 80 (g. s.).

Children, bapt. Fairfield, births from *Bulkeley Family:*

Isaac, b. 13 Nov. 1778, bapt. 6 June 1779, d. at Newburg, N. Y., 16 Nov. 1861; m. 1799, Mehitabel Simmons, b. 18 Mar. 1779, d. 9 Apr. 1869.

Clarina (twin), b. 13 Nov. 1778, bapt. 6 June 1779; m. 7 July 1799, Peter Sturges.

Ward, b. 29 Dec. 1782, bapt. 6 Apr. 1783, d. at Fairfield, 5 Mar. 1862 ae. 80 yrs. 3 mos. (g. s.); m. at Trinity Church, 5 June 1808, Mary Beers, b. 7 Dec. 1786, d. 27 Jan. 1848 ae. 61-1-20 (g. s.).

Sarah, b. 9 July 1784, bapt. 12 Sept. 1784, d. at Fairfield, 12 Sept. 1838 ae. 54 (g. s.); m. 31 Dec. 1815, David Bradley.

Eunice, b. 3 July 1786, bapt. 24 Sept. 1786; m. at Westport, 25 Oct. 1807, Aaron Morehouse.

Anna, b. 22 Dec. 1787, bapt. 22 June 1788, d. y.

Anna, b. 30 Oct. 1789, bapt. 13 June 1790, d. y.

David, b. 1 Aug. 1791, bapt. 6 Nov. 1791; m. Deborah ———.

Anna, b. 1 Mar. 1793, bapt. 9 June 1793, d. in 1837; m. 28 Nov. 1816, Aaron Bulkley.

Joseph, b. 13 July 1795, d. at Fairfield, 2 May 1837 ae. 43 (g. s.); m. 7 June 1829, Charlotte Mason.

Benjamin (twin), b. 13 July 1795, d. at Southport in 1872; m. 15 Mar. 1818, Rebecca Davis, b. abt. June 1799, d. 24 Feb. 1863 ae. 63 yrs. 8 mos.

Lois, b. 31 Oct. 1797; m. Ebenezer Morehouse.

40. **Bulkley, Andrew,** s. of Peter. Capt.

Born 27 Aug. 1743; d. at Fairfield in 1830; m. (1) at Westport, 15 Feb. 1769, Abigail Darrow, b. 3 Jan. 1749/50, d. 26 Sept. 1772 (Perry Diary). He m. (2) Jane, widow of Isaac Sterling, who was bur. 12 Nov. 1815 ae. 76 (Trinity Church rec.); m. (3) at Trinity Church, 23 Mar. 1817, Sarah (Perry), widow of Capt. Samuel Beers, b. abt. 1747, d. 5 Aug. 1828 ae. 81 (g. s.).

Child [by first wife]:

> Sarah, bapt. at Fairfield, 3 Nov. 1771, d. there 2 Nov. 1841; m. 20 Sept. 1792, Nathaniel-Lewis Sturges.

41. Bulkley, Peter, s. of Peter.

Born 13 May 1745; d. at Redding in 1813.

He m. at Redding, 2 Oct. 1768, Mary Green, dau. of Ebenezer, b. 8 Aug. 1751.

He was a member of the Redding Loyalist Association.

Adm'n granted, 10 Mar. 1813, to Mary Bulkley; estate insolvent.

Children, rec. Redding:

> Peter, b. 7 July 1769; perhaps m. at Easton, 25 Nov. 1789, Eunice Lyon.
> Mary, b. 6 June 1772; m. 16 Feb. 1794, Joseph Joyce.
> Sarah, b. 7 May 1774.
> Phebe, b. 9 Feb. 1776.
> Gershom, b. 30 July 1779, d. 28 Nov. 1849; res. Danbury; m. Damaris Wheeler, b. 30 Dec. 1777, d. 1 July 1865.
> Elizabeth, b. 8 Sept. 1781.
> Lucy, b. 14 Nov. 1783, d. 9 Nov. 1864.
> Andrew, b. 14 Oct. 1785, d. at Corning, Steuben County, N. Y., in 1860; m. Sarah Mallory.
> Ebenezer-Green, b. 30 Dec. 1787, d. at Rockford, Ill., 11 Feb. 1871; m. (1) Nov. 1814, Sophia Green, b. Oct. 1793, d. 28 Mar. 1833; m. (2) Emilie Tone.
> Daniel-Starling, b. 27 Dec. 1790, d. 28 Aug. 1872; m. 13 Apr. 1834, Miriam Peck.

42. Bulkley, Aaron, s. of Peter.

Born 22 Feb. 1747/8.

He m. Elizabeth Wakelee, dau. of Ebenezer, bapt. 29 July 1750.

Children, three bapt. North Stratford, one Huntington, one Trinity Church:

> Ebenezer-Wakelee, b. Jan., bapt. 26 Aug. 1770; m. at Trinity Church, 2 Oct. 1791, Hannah Davis.

James-Morehouse, bapt. 27 June 1773; m. Clara Hall, dau. of Abel.*
Noah-Summers, b. July, bapt. 8 Oct. 1775; m. ———.
Jemima, bapt. 31 Aug. 1788.
Helena, bapt. 6 Apr. 1792.
Others?

43. Bulkley, Turney, s. of Peter.

Born 9 June 1755; d. 2 Dec. 1826 [Pension Record].
He m. at Greenfield, 15 Mar. 1775, Esther Johnson, b. abt. 1756, d. at Greenfield, 20 Feb. 1838 ae. 82.

Children, four bapt. Greenfield:

Sarah, bapt. 31 Mar. 1776, d. 24 Sept. 1777.
Esther, bapt. 6 July 1777.
Sarah, bapt. 21 Mar. 1779; prob. d. at Greenfield 27 Mar. 1849 ae. 70 (g. s.); m. (1) 24 Nov. 1803, David Burr; m. (2) [prob. Phineas] Taylor.
Eunice, bapt. 1 Oct. 1780; Eunice Bulkley wife of Aaron Gray, b. 1780, d. 1869 (g. s., Greenfield); ? m. (1) at Westport, 25 Oct. 1807, Aaron Morehouse; m. Aaron Gray.
Lucy, b. [say 1782]; m. David Lyon.
Lois, b. [say 1784], d. abt. 1855; m. George-Washington Hall, of Newtown.
William, b. 7 June 1787, d. Apr. 1869; m. Jane S. Morehouse.
Eliza, m. Nov. 1824, Eli Hawley, of Bethel.
David, b. abt. 1792, d. at Greenfield, 24 Jan. 1823 ae. 30 (g. s.); m. Lucy Banks, b. abt. 1791, d. 2 Oct. 1856 ae. 65 (g. s.).†
Arrety, b. [Aug. 1794], d. 13 June 1881 ae. 86 yrs. 10 mos. (g. s.); m. Morris Burr.
Amelia, b. abt. 1801, d. at Bethel, 9 Sept. 1832; m. Oct. 1831, Marcus Noble.

Bully(?) [Unplaced].

WILLIAM m. 16 Oct. 1783, Isabel Raymond. [Greens Farms Church]

Bulmore, Patrick.

He m. Mary Godfrey, dau. of Christopher.

Child:

? Mary, m. 11 Oct. 1742, Thomas Chambers, of Newtown.

---

* Wife of Morehouse Bulkley d. at Stratfield, 10 Oct. 1826.
† Distribution: Widow; son David B.; son Nathan; dau. Lucy A. Bulkley; dau. Clarissa Bulkley.

HISTORY AND GENEALOGY OF

Bunnell, Gershom, s. of Benjamin.

Born at New Haven, 1 May 1707 [or 1708 by New Milford rec.]; d. at Danbury in 1758; m. at Stratford, 1 Jan. 1728/9, Margaret Johnson, dau. of George, b. at Stratford, 22 Sept. 1706.

Children, first six rec. Milford, next five bapt. Redding:

Margot, b. 15 June 1729, d. 2 July 1729 ae. 17 days (g. s.).
Hannah, b. 15 June 1729; m. Francis Bouton.
Rebecca, b. 28 Dec. 1730, bapt. 3 Jan. 1730/1.
Gershom, bapt. 30 Apr. 1732; res. Danbury 1790.
Joseph, bapt. 16 Dec. 1733; res. Woodbury and Milton; m. a dau. of Roger Kirby.
Margaret, bapt. 16 Nov. 1735; m. (rec. Waterbury) 4 Aug. 1755, Benjamin Warner.
Elizabeth, b. abt. 1737, d. at Redding, 29 Jan. 1740 ae. 2 or 3.
Solomon, bapt. 5 Aug. 1739.
Noah, bapt. 31 Jan. 1742, d. abt. 1791; res. Derby, Clinton, N. Y., and New Milford; m. Mary ———.
Nathaniel, bapt. 17 Oct. 1743; m. at Newtown, 18 Sept. 1768, Sarah Parsons.
Isaac, bapt. 21 July 1745; of Newtown; prob. m. Jerusha Sherwood, dau. of John.
John, of Woodbury.
Job, res. Brookfield 1790; m. at Newtown, 10 Sept. 1772, Rachel Bradley.

Bunnell [*Unplaced*].

JOSEPH m. 7 Apr. 1793, Esther Gilbert. [Weston Church]

Burchan [*Unplaced*].

POLLY, of Norwalk, m. 24 May 1780, Joseph Guire, of Redding. [Greens Farms Church]

Burnham [*Unplaced*].

CAPT. JOSIAH, of Kensington, m. 14 Apr. 1763, Mrs. Mary Smith [née Hill]. [Fairfield Church]

Burn, Ralph.

He, called of Milford, m. at Westport, 27 July 1800, Polly Morehouse of Weston. Child, bapt. at Fairfield: Esther-Maria, bapt. 18 Oct. 1801.

THE FAMILIES OF OLD FAIRFIELD 181

Burr [Vol. I, pp. 116-131].

1 Jehu (-   ).
    2 Jehu (1625-1692) m. (1) Esther [Ward?] Boosey; (2) Elizabeth Prudden.
    (By 1): 6 Daniel (1660-1727) m. (1) Hannah Banks; (2) Mary Sherwood; (3) Elizabeth Pinkney.
    (By 2): 14 *Jehu* (1687-1757).
    (By 3): 15 *Stephen* (1697-1778).
            16 *Peter* (1699-1777).
    (By 2): 7 Peter (1668-1724) m. (1) Abigail ———; (2) Sarah (Osborn) Sturges.
    (By 1): 17 *Thaddeus* (1700-1755).
    3 John (1633-1694) m. Sarah Fitch.
        8 John (1673-1705) m. Elizabeth Hanford.
        18 *Andrew* (1696-1763).
    4 Nathaniel (-1712) m. (1) Sarah Ward; (2) Hannah (Goodyear) Wakeman.
    (By 1): 9 Nathaniel (1664-1701) m. Susanna Lockwood.
        19 *Nathaniel* (1698-1761).
        20 *Ephraim* (1700-1776).
       10 John (1672-1750) m. (1) Deborah Barlow; (2) Elizabeth (Hawley) Wakeman.
    (By 1): 21 *John* (1698-1752).
        22 *William* (1711-1769).
      11 Daniel (1677-1722) m. (1) Abigail Stratton; (2) Mary Jennings.
    (By 1): 23 *Nathaniel* (1707-1784).
        24 *James* (1709-1782).
    (By 2): 25 *John* (1713-1783).
        26 *David* (1719-1792).
    5 Daniel (1642-1695) m. (1) Abigail Brewster; (2) Abigail Glover.
    (By 1): 12 Daniel (1670-1748) m. (1) Esther Perry; (2) Abigail ———.
        (By 1): 27 *Joseph* (-   ).
            28 *Timothy* (1702-1772).
        (By 2): 29 *James* (-   ).
            30 *Jabez* (-1770).
    (By 2): 13 Seth-Samuel (1694-1773) m. (1) Elizabeth Wakeman; (2) Ruth (Jennings) Bulkley.
    (By 1): 31 *Samuel* (1727-1791).
        32 *Daniel* (1730-1811).
        33 *Ebenezer* (1732-1767).
        34 *Nehemiah* (1734-1815).
        35 *Charles* (1741-1800).

14. **Burr, Jehu,** s. of Daniel.

Born [say 1687]; d. at Fairfield in 1757. He m. (1) Hannah ———.

He m. (2) Sarah ———, who was adm. to Greenfield Church, 1726.

Will 28 Sept. 1757, proved 1 Nov. 1757; wife Sarah; sons Jehu, Daniel; residue equally to daus. Hannah, Esther, Catherine, Patience, Prudence, Comfort, and children of Sarah dec'd, Mary dec'd, Abigail dec'd; two sons-in-law Ebenezer Gilbert and Elnathan Griffin; wife, bro. Stephen Burr, and son Jehu, Exec'rs.

Martin Keeler and Esther his wife of Ridgefield conveyed 1760 to Ebenezer Gilbert, right from father Jehu Burr dec'd. Elnathan Griffith and Patience his wife of Redding conveyed 1761, the same.

Children by first wife, rec. Newtown:

Sarah, b. 24 Jan. 1711 [1711/2]; possibly m. Gershom Whitehead.
Mary, b. 15 June 1713; m. ———.
36+Daniel, b. [say 1715].
Abigail, b. [say 1718]; m. at Trumbull, 15 Feb. 1739/40, Samuel Sherwood (both called of Redding).

Children [by second wife], two bapt. Fairfield, five Greenfield:

Hannah, bapt. 25 Aug. 1723.
Hester, bapt. 11 Apr. 1725; m. Martin Keeler, of Ridgefield.
Catherine, bapt. 17 Apr. 1727; m. at Redding, 20 Aug. 1745, Benjamin Meeker.
Patience, bapt. 9 Mar. 1728/9; m. 26 Nov. 1750, Elnathan Griffin.
Prudence, bapt. 12 Jan. 1731/2; m. 12 May 1756, Ebenezer Gilbert.
Comfort, bapt. 12 Jan. 1731/2; ? m. at Redding, 11 Jan. 1774, Joseph Truesdale.
37+Jehu, bapt. 23 Aug. 1734.

15. Burr, Stephen, s. of Daniel. Lt., Redding Co., Oct. 1739.

Bapt. 3 Oct. 1697; d. at Redding in 1778; m. (1) 8 June 1721, Elizabeth Hull, dau. of Cornelius; bapt. 15 Oct. 1699, d. at Redding, 26 Nov. 1760 ae. 62; m. (2) at Redding, 12 Apr. 1761, Abigail Hall, of New Jersey; prob. widow of Burgis.

Deacon, Redding Church, Mar. 1733.

Will 20 Aug. 1776, proved 1 Oct. 1778; wife Abigail (marriage covenant dated 12 Apr. 1761); son Hezekiah; dau. Elizabeth wife of Reuben Squire; gr. sons Stephen and Samuel Gold; three daus. Sarah wife of Joseph Jackson, Martha wife of Zach: Summers, and Esther wife of Anthony Angevine; eleven of my gr. children,—Abigail wife of Richard Nichols, Esther wife of Nathaniel Northrop, Sarah wife of David Turney, Mary wife of Seth Price, and Elizabeth Gold, all children of my dau. Grace Gold late of Redding dec'd; children of dau. Rebecca Sanford late of Redding dec'd, viz. Elias, Ebenezer, Joel, Elijah, Samuel and Seth Sanford. Distribution 10 Nov. 1779, shows that Elizabeth dau. of Grace Gold was then wife of Abel Gold, Jr., and that Elizabeth Squire was dec'd.

Children [by first wife], rec. Fairfield, first bapt. Fairfield, two Greenfield, last three Redding:

>Grace, b. 12 Dec. 1724, bapt. 17 Jan. 1724/5, d. by 1776; m. Daniel Gold.
>Philip, bapt. 22 Oct. 1726, d. at Redding, 26 Apr. 1740 ae. 13 to 14.
>Elizabeth, b. 17 Jan. 1728, d. abt. 1779; m. (1) at Redding, 7 June 1750, William Burritt; m. (2) 11 Oct. 1759, Alexander Bryant; m. (3) 19 May 1761, Reuben Squire.
>Hezekiah, b. 1 Sept., bapt. 3 Oct. 1730, d. 1785, unm. Distribution, 21 Aug. 1786: sister Sarah Jackson; heirs of sister Rebecca, late wife of Seth Sanford; heirs of sister Grace Gold, dec'd; sister Martha wife of Zachariah Summers; sister Esther wife of Anthony Angevine; heirs of sister Elizabeth Squire.
>Sarah, b. 9 Nov. 1732; m. Joseph Jackson.
>Martha, b. 24, bapt. 30 Mar. 1735, d. at Easton, Apr. 1820 in 87 yr. (g. s.); m. 15 Jan. 1765, Zechariah Summers.
>Rebecca, b. 2, bapt. 11 Nov. 1739, d. at Redding, 10 Sept. 1775 ae. 36 (g. s.); m. 18 Apr. 1759, Seth Sanford.
>Esther, b. 5, bapt. 12 Feb. 1743/4; m. 23 Dec. 1761, Anthony Angevine.

16. Burr, Peter, s. of Daniel.

Bapt. 23 July 1699; d. at Greenfield, 4 Mar. 1777 in 76 yr.; m. (1) Abigail ———, who d. at Redding, 19 Mar. 1736.

He m. (2) at Redding, 7 May 1736, Rebecca Ward, dau. of Moses, bapt. 1 Apr. 1716.

Inv. 7 Aug. 1779.

Children [by first wife], two bapt. Fairfield, three Greenfield, two Redding:

>Jane, bapt. 22 Dec. 1723.
>Ann, bapt. 10 Apr. 1726, living 1795; m. at Westport, 16 Jan. 1749/50, Nathan Beers.
>Peter, bapt. 29 Oct. 1727.
>Abigail, bapt. 7 Dec. 1729, d. 13 Apr. 1779 ae. abt. 50; m. at Greenfield, 2 May 1749, Nathan Gold.
>Hannah, bapt. Dec. 1731, d. after 1787; m. at Westport, 18 Mar. 1756, James Beers, Jr.
>Esther, bapt. 29 Nov. 1734, d. at Westport, 12 May 1819 ae. 85 (g. s.); m. 24 Dec. 1754, Joshua Jennings.
>Sarah, bapt. 21 Feb. 1736, [d. at Easton, 29 Aug. 1807 ae. 71 (g. s.); m. abt. 1753, Jeremiah Oakley].

184 HISTORY AND GENEALOGY OF

Children [by second wife], first bapt. Redding, last three Fairfield:

> Ezra, bapt. 2 Jan. 1737, d. at Fairfield, 9 Apr. 1810 ae. 73.
> Mary, b. abt. 1738, d. at Fairfield, 9 Nov. 1810 in 73 yr. (g. s.); m. 5 Feb. 1761, Seth Sturgis.
> Rebecca, b. abt. 1740; m. at Westport, 21 Feb. 1764, Stephen Guire.
> Martha, b. 24 Feb. 1744, d. by 1781; m. at Westport, 26 Mar. 1767, Ebenezer Redfield.
> Elizabeth, b. abt. 1745, d. at Fairfield, 28 Dec. 1808 in 64 yr. (g. s.); m. at Westport, 16 Nov. 1777, Jonathan Lewis. Her will, 4 Mar. 1808, proved 12 Jan. 1809, gave entire estate to niece Elizabeth Redfield.
> ? Aaron, b. 8 Feb. 1748.
> ? Eunice, b. abt. 1751; [? m. Daniel Meeker, of Greenfield].
> Miriam, bapt. 1 June 1755; [? m. ―――― Freeman].
> Philip, bapt. 10 Apr. 1757.
> Edmund, bapt. 28 Sept. 1760; rem. 1815 to Fredericksburg, Va.; res. 1829, Stafford County, Va.; m. Olive Meeker, dau. of Benjamin.*

17. Burr, Thaddeus, s. of Peter. Deputy for Fairfield, May 1730, May 1744, May 1745, May 1747, May 1748, Oct. 1749, May 1751. Quarter-Master, Fairfield County Troop, May 1726. Justice, 1744-55.

Bapt. 8 Sept. 1700; d. at Fairfield, 28 Mar. 1755 in 55 yr. (g. s.); m. 26 Nov. 1725, Abigail Sturges, dau. of Jonathan; b. 8 Sept. 1704, d. 26 June 1753 in 49 yr. (g. s.).

Children, rec. Fairfield:

> Sarah, b. 5 Sept. 1726; ? m. 16 Sept. 1746, Rev. Thomas Arthur, of New Brunswick.
> Abigail, b. 24 Mar. 1729, d. 8 July 1753; m. 20 May 1752, Lyman Hall.
> Peter, b. 27 Apr. 1731, d. 13 Sept. 1745 in 15 yr. (g. s.).
> 38+Thaddeus, b. 22 Aug. 1735.
> 39+Gershom, b. 10 June 1744, bapt. 7 Nov. 1756; chose Thaddeus Burr for guardian, May 1760.

---

* Children, bapt. Fairfield: Peter, bapt. 4 May 1783, drowned off Branford, 25 Oct. 1814 ae. 30; Laura, bapt. 9 June 1793. Another son, Ezra, was mentioned in pension records. Adm'n on estate of Peter was granted, 19 Nov. 1814, to Ezra Burr, with Edmund Burr as surety. Ezra, called "Jr.," m. at Westport, 23 Dec. 1798, Abigail Burr, and had a dau. Caroline, bapt. 11 Aug. 1799. Ezra, son of Ezra Burr, bapt. at Fairfield, 6 Sept. 1804.

18. **Burr, Andrew**, s. of John. Deputy for Fairfield, Oct. 1727, Oct. 1729, Oct. 1731 to Oct. 1733 inclusive, May 1735, May 1736, May 1737, May 1738, Oct. 1738 (Clerk), May and Oct. 1739, May 1740 (Clerk), July 1740 (Clerk), Oct. and Nov. 1740, May 1741, Oct. 1741 to Mar. 1745 inclusive (Speaker), Oct. 1745 (Speaker); Assistant, 1746-63. Sheriff, Fairfield County, 1726. Lt., 2d Co., Fairfield, Oct. 1731; Capt., May 1733; Major, Oct. 1739; Col., Cape Breton Expedition, Feb. 1745; Col., 4th Regt., Oct. 1750; Commissary, July 1740, May 1746; Committee of War, 1746, 1755, 1756. Justice, 1727-45; Judge, Fairfield County Court, 1745-63; Judge, Fairfield Probate Court, 1749-63.

Born 27 Sept. 1696; d. at Fairfield, 9 Nov. 1763 ae. 67; m. (1) 30 Apr. 1719, Sarah Sturges, dau. of Jonathan; b. 22 Dec. 1701, d. 9 Dec. 1745 ae. 45 yrs. wanting 13 days (g. s.); m. (2) 6 Aug. 1747, Sarah Stanley of Hartford, who d. 29 Aug. 1769 ae. 61 (g. s.).

Will 24 Nov. 1760, proved 20 Feb. 1764; children David, Andrew, John, George, Oliver, Elizabeth, Mary, Sarah, Jerusha; to first-born son David, law books, being in partnership with Gov. Fitch, etc.

Children by first wife, rec. and bapt. Fairfield:

    Ann, b. 6, bapt. 14 Feb. 1719/20, d. 17 Apr. 1775 in 56 yr. (g. s.); m. 17 Jan. 1739/40, Samuel Sturges.
40+David, b. 5, bapt. 8 July 1722.
41+Andrew, b. and bapt. 24 July 1724.
    Elizabeth, b. 22, bapt. 26 June 1726, d. 5 Oct. 1815 in 90 yr. (g. s.); m. 19 Jan. 1758, Daniel Osborn.
    Lucretia, b. 23 May, bapt. 9 June 1728, d. y.
    Mary, b. 22, bapt. 24 May 1730, d. in 1784; m. 6 June 1773, Ebenezer Bradley, as his second wife. Her will, 21 Sept., proved 6 Dec. 1784, named bro. George Burr.
42+John, b. 11, bapt. 12 Mar. 1731/2.
    Susannah, b. 29 Apr., bapt. 6 May 1734, d. y.
43+George, b. 26 May, bapt. 4 July 1736.
    Josiah, b. 15, bapt. 16 July 1738, d. y.
    Walter, b. 9 Sept. 1740, bapt. 15 Mar. 1740/1, d. y.
    Sarah, b. 23, bapt. 26 Sept. 1742.
    Oliver, b. and bapt. 10 Nov. 1745, d. at Danbury, 31 Jan. 1797 ae. 51 (g. s.); res. Salisbury, 1774; m. (1) 23 Apr. 1770, Elizabeth

Smith, who d. at Salisbury, 21 Feb. 1775;* m. (2) 14 June 1775, Mary Hubbard. She m. (2) Ebenezer White, and d. 3 Jan. 1845 ae. 90.

Child by second wife, rec. and bapt. Fairfield:

Jerusha, b. 3, bapt. 10 Dec. 1749; m. 21 Sept. 1767, Hezekiah Fitch.

19. **Burr, Nathaniel,** s. of Nathaniel, 2d.

Bapt. 15 May 1698; d. at Fairfield in 1761; m. 10 Nov. 1726, Martha Silliman, bapt. 24 Aug. 1701, d. 18 Mar. 1753.

Will 25 May, proved 21 Aug. 1761; household goods to daus. Sarah and Martha; west end of house to daus. Ruth, Rebecca, Mary, and Martha, and east end to son Nathan. Distribution agreement of the heirs, 11 Feb. 1771: Nathan Burr, Aaron Hubbell and Mary his wife, and Ruth, Sarah, Rebecca, and Martha Burr.

Children, rec. and bapt. Fairfield:

Ruth, b. 20, bapt. 24 Sept. 1727.
Sarah, b. 19, bapt. 20 Apr. 1729, d. abt. Jan. 1803. Her will, 23 Sept. 1800, proved 31 Jan. 1803; nephew Gideon Burr; brother Nathan; two sisters Rebecca and Martha Burr.
44+Nathan, b. 19, bapt. 24 Sept. 1732.
Rebecca, b. 13 Apr., bapt. 9 May 1736, d. in 1804. Her will, 26 Sept. 1804, proved 27 Nov. 1804; bro. Nathan, life use of realty, then to sister Martha Burr.
Martha, b. 13, bapt. 15 June 1740, d. in 1806. Her will, 13 Aug. 1806, proved 24 Nov. 1806; bro. Nathan; niece Martha wife of David Seeley; nephew Hezekiah Burr of Fairfield, Exec'r.
Mary, b. 13, bapt. 15 June 1740, d. 9 Sept. 1775 (Perry Diary); m. 29 Nov. 1761, Aaron Hubbell.

20. **Burr, Ephraim,** s. of Nathaniel, 2d.

Born 5 Apr. 1700; d. at Fairfield, 29 Apr. 1776 ae. 76 yrs. 13 days (g. s.); m. 7 Jan. 1724/5, Abigail Burr, dau. of Maj. Peter, bapt. 25 Oct. 1702, d. 8 July 1780 ae. 78 (g. s.).

Will 18 Aug. 1769, codicil 6 Apr. 1776, proved 6 May 1776; wife Abigail; daus. Eunice, Ellen, Abigail, Sarah, Ann; sons Ephraim, Ebenezer, Peter.

---

* Son, William, b. at Salisbury, 6 Feb. 1775.

On 11 Jan. 1810, action was taken on estate of Abigail widow of Ephraim Burr who d. abt. 27 yrs. since, will dated 1 Feb. 1777, partly intestate, but under incumbrance during life of her dau. Abigail Burr who lately dec'd; distribution ordered to: heirs of Lyman Jennings, only child of her dec'd dau. Eunice; Silas Burr, Anna, Catherine, heirs of Eunice, heirs of Abigail, and Sally,— the heirs of her eldest son Ephraim Burr dec'd; James Penfield, David, Thaddeus, heirs of Ephraim Penfield dec'd, Ellen, Mary, Eunice, and Anna,—heirs of her dec'd dau. Ellen Penfield; Sally wife of Samuel Wakeman, only heir of her dec'd dau. Abigail Burr; her dau. Sarah wife of Eleazer Osborn; her son Peter Burr. The distribution called the gr. dau. Anna (dau. of her son Ephraim) wife of Gershom Osborn, Jr.

Children, rec. and bapt. Fairfield:
Ebenezer, bapt. 10 Mar. 1727/8, d. y.
Eunice, b. and bapt. 8 Feb. 1729/30; m. 10* Dec. 1752, Daniel Jennings, Jr.
Ann, b. 16, bapt. 30 Jan. 1731/2; m. 10 Oct. 1752, Sturges Lewis.
Ellen, b. 23, bapt. 24 Feb. 1733/4, d. at Fairfield, 12 Mar. 1803 in 70 yr. (g. s.); m. 23 Apr. 1758, James Penfield.
45+Ephraim, b. 5 Dec. 1735,† bapt. 14 Mar. 1735/6.
46+Ebenezer, b. 23, bapt. 28 May 1738.
Abigail, b. 14, bapt. 22 Feb. 1740/1, d. 28 Nov. 1809 ae. 69 (g. s.). Will 13 Nov. 1794, proved Nov. 1810; all estate to beloved dau. Sally; bro. Ebenezer Burr, Exec'r.‡
Sarah, b. 5, bapt. 31 July 1743, d. at New Fairfield, 3 Mar. 1813 ae. 70 (g. s.); m. 3 June 1764, Eleazer Osborn, Jr.
47+Peter, b. 2, bapt. 3 Nov. 1745.

21. **Burr, John,** s. of Col. John. Deputy for Fairfield, Oct. 1737, May 1748; Justice, 1740-47. Lt., Stratfield Co., Oct. 1731; Capt., May 1734.

Bapt. 28 Aug. 1698; d. at Stratfield, 13 Sept. 1752 in 55 yr. (g. s.); m. 18 Oct. 1722, Katherine Wakeman, bapt. 21 Apr. 1700, d. 25 Sept. 1753 in 53 yr. (g. s.).

Will of Capt. John, 20 July 1752, proved 3 Oct. 1752; wife Catherine; daus. Katherine wife of Robert Wilson, Sarah wife of Daniel Silliman, Ann wife of Thomas Sherwood, Deborah wife of

---
* Or 21 [New Style].
† Or 5 Mar. 1736 (Bible rec.).
‡ Her dau. Sally, bapt. 19 Jan. 1783, d. 6 Mar. 1857 ae. 76 (g. s.); m. 18 Dec. 1800, Samuel Wakeman.

Ichabod Wheeler, Elizabeth, Mary, Abigail; son John; three sons Justus, Ozias, Wakeman; honored father Col. John Burr dec'd; provides for maintenance of bro. Joseph Burr; bro. William Burr, Exec'r.

 Children, rec. Fairfield:
  Katherine, b. 26 Oct. 1723, d. 1 Oct. 1810 in 87 yr. (g. s.); m. 7 Sept. 1741, Robert Wilson.
  Sarah, b. 7 Feb. 1724/5; m. 13 Mar. 1746, Daniel Silliman.
  Ann, b. 7 Sept. 1726, d. at Easton, 3 Dec. 1777 in 52 yr. (g. s.); m. Thomas Sherwood.
  48+John, b. 12 June 1728.
  Deborah, b. 14 May 1730, d. 5 May 1799 in 69 yr. (g. s.); m. 1 Jan. 1752, Ichabod Wheeler.
  Elizabeth, b. 7, bapt. 9 Apr. 1732, d. 5 Sept. 1815 in 84 yr. (g. s.); m. 1 Jan. 1754, Abraham Gold.
  Mary, b. 7, bapt. 9 Apr. 1732, d. 15 Mar. 1806 in 75 yr. (g. s.); m. 1 Nov. 1759, Ebenezer Bartram, Jr.
  49+Justus, b. 2, bapt. 8 Sept. 1734.
  Abigail, b. 27 July, bapt. 1 Aug. 1736, d. 18 Apr. 1794 in 58 yr. (g. s.); m. 11 Oct. 1759, Moses Jennings.
  50+Ozias, b. 1 May 1739.
  Amos, b. 8 Sept. 1741, d. 27 Sept. 1743.
  51+Wakeman, b. 3 Oct. 1743.

22. **Burr, William**, s. of Col. John. Deputy for Fairfield, Oct. 1754, Jan., Mar., May, Aug., and Oct. 1755, Jan. and Mar. 1756, Oct. 1758, Mar. and May 1759. Justice, 1747-69.

Born 9 Dec. 1711; d. at Stratfield, 5 May 1769 in 58 yr. (g. s.); grad. Yale Coll. 1732; m. (1) 4 Aug. 1736, Mary Wakeman, dau. of Capt. Joseph; bapt. 23 July 1710, d. 19 Mar. 1742/3 in 33 yr. (g. s.); m. (2) 16 May 1744, Charity, widow of Joseph Strong, and dau. of John Welles, Jr., of Stratford; b. 14 Oct. 1721, d. 2 Oct. 1769 in 48 yr. (g. s.).

Adm'n granted, 9 Oct. 1769, to Eliphalet Hull and Thomas Nash. Distribution, 12 June 1770; heirs of Charity, late widow; Charity wife of Eliphalet Hull; Mary wife of Thomas Nash; Deborah Burr. Joseph Strong was appointed guardian for Deborah, 3 Oct. 1769.

Will of Charity Burr, widow of William, 2 Aug., proved 16 Oct. 1769; dau. Charity wife of Dr. Eliphalet Hull; dau. Mary wife of Thomas Nash, Jr.; youngest dau. Deborah; son Joseph Strong.

Children [by first wife]:

> William, b. [May-June 1738], d. 20 June 1739 in 13 mo. (g. s.).
> William, b. 23 July 1740.

Children [by second wife], rec. Fairfield:

> Charity, b. 4 Mar. 1744/5, d. at Greenfield, 16 Sept. 1795 in 51 yr. (g. s.); m. Dr. Eliphalet Hull.
> Mary, b. 23 Mar. 1749, d. at Westport, 20 May 1784 in 34 yr. (g. s.); m. Capt. Thomas Nash.
> Deborah, b. after 1755.

23. **Burr, Nathaniel,** s. of Daniel. Ens., 2d Co., Fairfield, Oct. 1748; Lt., May 1756; Capt., May 1759.

Bapt. 1 June 1707; d. at Fairfield, 8 Nov. 1784; m. 23 Nov. 1732, Mary Turney, dau. of Robert, bapt. 26 Oct. 1712, d. by 1785, and prob. before him.

Watchmaker and jeweller.

Inv. 11 Dec. 1784. Distribution ordered, double share to Hezekiah Burr, single share to Isaac Burr and to Grizel wife of Col. Elijah Abel. The estate of Mary Burr, late his wife, was distributed to the same.

Children, rec. and bapt. Fairfield:

> Isaac, b. 13, bapt. 23 Dec. 1733, d. 28 Mar. 1738.
> Hezekiah, b. 28 Feb., bapt. 5 Mar. 1737/8, d. 7 Jan. 1787; ? m. at Easton, 15 Sept. 1773, Esther Downs.
> Grissel, b. 15, bapt. 22 Nov. 1741, d. at Fairfield, 10 Oct. 1808 ae. 67; m. 31 Dec. 1761, Elijah Abel.
> Isaac, b. 11, bapt. 15 Apr. 1744, d. at Fairfield, 21 May 1811 ae. 67; Lt. of Co. of 25 men at Fairfield, Jan. 1777; m. Abigail Beardsley.*

24. **Burr, James,** s. of Daniel.

Bapt. 23 Jan. 1708/9; d. in 1782; m. Deborah Turney, dau. of Robert, bapt. June 1711, d. in 1786.

Inv. 19 July 1783. Adm'n on his estate and that of his widow Deborah granted, 22 Aug. 1786, to Noah and Jehu Burr.

---

* Adm'n on Isaac's Est. granted, 2 Apr. 1813, to Nathaniel Burr, Jr., with Nathaniel Burr, Sr., as surety.

Children, bapt. Fairfield:

Deborah, bapt. 1 Jan. 1737/8, d. y.
Stratton, bapt. 4 Feb. 1738/9, d. in 1777, unm.
Benjamin, bapt. 20 Apr. 1740; m.
Noah, bapt. 22 Nov. 1741, d. at Huntington in 1802; m. ―――.*
James, bapt. 31 July 1743, d. at Monroe, 31 Mar. 1820 ae. 77 (g. s.); m. Justina ―――, b. abt. 1750, d. 19 Oct. 1824 ae. 74 (g. s.).
Deborah, bapt. 25 Nov. 1744.
Hosea, bapt. 27 Apr. 1746, d. at Huntington in 1798; adm'n granted, 20 Mar. 1798, to Elnathan Hurd; m. Hephzibah Hurd.†
Jerusha, bapt. 7 June 1747.
Josiah, bapt. 20 Jan. 1750/1, d. at Monroe, 22 July 1821 ae. 70 (g. s.); m. ―――.
Jehu, bapt. 5 Apr. 1752, d. 4 Aug. 1833; res. Andes, N. Y.; m. Mary Hawley, b. 25 Nov. 1756, d. 14 Mar. 1850.

25. Burr, John, s. of Daniel.

Bapt. 1 Feb. 1712/3; d. at Westport, 9 Apr. 1783 ae. 70 yrs. 3 mos. (g. s.); m. (1) 14 Oct. 1735, Elizabeth Nash, dau. of Thomas, b. 3 Mar. 1717, d. 29 Mar. 1740; m. (2) 9 Nov. 1741, Grace Bulkley, dau. of Gershom, bapt. 12 Feb. 1720/1, d. 21 Feb. 1772 in 52 yr. (g. s.).

He m. (3) 9 July 1775, Mary Sturges [widow of Daniel], and dau. of James Beers, b. 29 Nov. 1722, d. in 1811.

Distribution 1783: Daniel Burr; Talcott Burr; John Burr; Elizabeth wife of William Bulkley; Grace wife of Thaddeus Whitlock; Eunice wife of David Jennings.

Children [by first wife], rec. Fairfield:

52+Daniel, b. 5 Mar. 1737; he conveyed his interest, 1759, to the children and heirs of Jonathan Nash dec'd.
John, b. 9 Oct. 1739, d. 9 or 10 Oct. 1749.

Children [by second wife], rec. Fairfield, bapt. Westport:

Elizabeth, b. 16, bapt. 18 Sept. 1743, bur. 17 Sept. 1805 ae. 62 (Trinity Church rec.); m. 4 Sept. 1766, William Bulkley.
53+Talcott, b. 20, bapt. 26 Oct. 1746.

---

* Noah's will, 3 May 1802, proved 8 June 1802, named daus. Grisilia Mallet and Anthy Burr, and sons Elisha, David and Asaph Burr. David Burr's will, 28 Oct. 1819 (Inventory 22 Nov. 1819), named bro. Elisha Burr and his sons Zalmon, Munson, Ozias, Elizur, and Baldwin; Antha Burr, dau. of Asaph; and two sisters, Grissel and Antha.

† Children: Stratton, of Monroe, m. Huldah Northrup; Desire, b. 19 Feb. 1782, m. 1 July 1804, Justin Hobart; Anna, m. Anson Judson; Hephzibah, m. Albert Sherman.

54+John, b. 9, bapt. 10 Feb. 1751.
Grace, b. 2, bapt. 4 Feb. 1753; m. 2 Apr. 1775, Thaddeus Whitlock.
Eunice, b. 24 Sept., bapt. 5 Oct. 1755, d. Nov. 1795 ae. 42 (g. s.); m. 6 Apr. 1775, David Jennings.

26. Burr, David, s. of Daniel. 2d Lt., Capt. Josiah Starr's Co., Expedition to Canada, June 1746.

Bapt. 8 Mar. 1718/9;* d. at Westport, 29 Aug. 1792 ae. 73 yrs. 4(?) mos. 5 days (g. s.); m. 8 Apr. 1741, Abigail Silliman, dau. of John, b. 31 Oct. 1721 (Bible rec.), living 1817.

Will 23 Apr. 1781, proved 6 Sept. 1792; wife; son David; daus. Mary, Abigail; son Moses. The distribution 1800 called the widow Abigail, and the dau. Abigail wife of Benjamin Meeker.

Children, rec. Fairfield, bapt. Westport:†

    Ann, b. 24 Feb., bapt. 16 May 1742. [An Ann Burr m. at Westport, 18 Jan. 1776, John Fanton, of Easton.]
55+Moses, b. 5, bapt. 8 Apr. 1744.
    Abigail, b. 8, bapt. 19 Apr. 1747, d. in 1822; m. at Greenfield, 3 Feb. 1765, Benjamin Meeker.
    Aaron, b. 6 Oct., bapt. 29 Nov. 1749, d. s. p.
56+David, b. 29 Sept., bapt. 3 Nov. 1751.
    Silliman, b. 12, bapt. 19 Aug. 1753, d. 29 Jan. 1754.
    Mary, b. 2, bapt. 13 Apr. 1755. [A Mary Burr m. at Westport, 22 Dec. 1793, Amos Gray.]
    Child, stillborn 27 Oct. 1757.
    Infant, d. 4 Apr. 1760.
    Child, stillborn 7 Nov. 1762.
    Child, stillborn 3 Mar. 1764.

27. Burr, Joseph, s. of Daniel.

Bapt. at Greenfield as an adult, 20 Feb. 1725/6.
He m. 3 Mar. 1725, Hannah Hide, bapt. 14 Mar. 1707/8.

Children, rec. Fairfield, bapt. Greenfield:

57+Increase, b. 26 Dec. 1726, bapt. 1 Jan. 1726/7.
58+Abel, b. 8 Sept., bapt. 6 Oct. 1728.
    Rachel, b. 23 Sept., bapt. Sept. 1730, d. 20 Nov. 1766 in 36 yr. (g. s.).

---

* Born 15 Apr. 1719, by Bible record.
† The births of the surviving children (identical with the town record) are given in the Bible (printed 1793) which apparently belonged to his son David, Jr.

192   HISTORY AND GENEALOGY OF

 Joseph, b. 22, bapt. 28 Oct. 1733; perhaps the Joseph who d. 1 Nov. 1783 (Perry Diary); he m. 28 May 1758, Grace Bradley, dau. of Peter, b. 31 Mar. 1738.*
59+Ichabod, b. 1, bapt. 8 May 1736.
60+Eliphalet, b. 11 Jan., bapt. 3 Feb. 1738/9.
61+Moses, b. 22 Aug., bapt. 6 Sept. 1741.
62+Samuel, b. 9, bapt. 16 Mar. 1745/6.

28. **Burr, Timothy,** s. of Daniel.

Born abt. 1702; d. at Greenfield, 27 July 1772 in 69 yr. (g. s.); m. 6 Mar. 1728, Sarah Rowland, b. abt. 1705, d. 27 Sept. 1788 in 83 yr. (g. s.).

Will 21 July 1772, proved 15 Sept. 1772; wife; three daus. Hester, Sarah, Mabel (married); six gr. children, John, Ezekiel, Rachel, Eleanor, Esther, Hannah, children of John Hubbell by my dau. Eleanor; youngest son Timothy; son Ebenezer.

Children rec. Greenfield:

Ebenezer, b. and bapt. Jan. 1729/30, d. y.
Esther, b. 18, bapt. 21 Sept. 1730, d. in 1810; m. 7 Feb. 1749/50, David Williams, Jr.
Sarah, b. 16, bapt. 18 Mar. 1732/3, living 1795; m. 2 Nov. 1758, Ezekiel Hull.
63+Ebenezer, b. 16, bapt. 18 Mar. 1732/3.
Timothy, b. 23, bapt. 26 Jan. 1734/5, d. at Greenfield, 27 July 1802 in 69 yr. (g. s.). His will, 24 Apr. 1798, proved 30 Aug. 1802; nephew Ebenezer, 3d, and Zalmon, sons of bro. Ebenezer.
Ellen, b. 30 July, bapt. 28 Oct. 1738, d. at Greenfield, 20 May 1773 in 35 yr.; m. 30 Mar. 1758, John Hubbell.
Mabel, b. 17, bapt. 25 Jan. 1740/1, d. 19 June 1818; m. 8 May 1760, Samuel Wakeman.

29. **Burr, James,** s. of Daniel.

He. m. (1) 12 Dec. 1731, Hannah Osborn, Widow [prob. Hannah Hubbell, widow of Joseph Osborn, bapt. 19 May 1695]. She d. 11 Aug. 1743. He m. (2) Jan. 1746/7, Mary Barlow; dau. of Samuel.

---

 * Children, rec. and bapt. Redding: Joseph, b. 26 July, bapt. 6 Sept. 1772; m. 8 Apr. 1795, Lucinda Bradley. Aaron, b. 1 Sept. 1777; m. 7 Apr. 1799, Tamison Bradley.

Children [by first wife], rec. Fairfield, bapt. Greenfield:

> Isabel, b. 8 Jan. 1733, bapt. 12 Jan. 1734/5; m. 8 Jan. 1758, Eliphalet Hill.
> Isaac, b. 18, bapt. 21 May 1738, d. at Greenfield, 4 Aug. 1816 ae. 79.

Children [by second wife], rec. Fairfield, bapt. Greenfield:

> Mary, b. July, bapt. 16 Aug. 1747.
> Daniel, b. 25 Dec. 1748, bapt. 21 Jan. 1748/9.
> James, b. 25 May, bapt. 2 June 1751.
> Sarah, b. 17 Dec. 1753.
> Abigail, b. 18 Aug., bapt. 8 Sept. 1755.
> Benajah, b. 2 Sept. 1759, bapt. ae. abt. 2 mos.

30. **Burr, Jabez,** s. of Daniel.

Bapt. at Greenfield as an adult, 4 Nov. 1739; d. at Redding, 29 Apr. 1770; m. Elizabeth Hull, b. 2 Aug. 1719, d. 16 Nov. 1760 ae. 41 (g. s.).

Will 17 Apr. 1770, proved 1 May 1770; children, Elijah, Nathan, Jabez, Ezekiel, Stephen, Joel, Eunice, Huldah, Hannah. Ezekiel Hull was appointed guardian for Stephen and Joel, June 1770; and Ezekiel Burr chose the same guardian. Jabez of Redding chose Daniel Sanford, 21 Aug. 1771.

Children, five bapt. Redding:

> Eunice, bapt. at Greenfield, 16 Dec. 1739; m. at Redding, 22 Dec. 1762, Onesimus Coley.
> Elijah, bapt. 15 May 1743; m. (1) at Redding, 2 Apr. 1767, Rhoda Sanford, dau. of Lemuel, b. 20 Feb. 1748/9, d. 11 Jan. 1773; m. (2) 27 Apr. 1773, Eunice Hawley, dau. of Joseph, b. 6 Sept. 1750.*
> Nathan, b. 1 Jan. 1745 [*Burr Gen.*]; rem. 1792 to Pawling, Dutchess County, N. Y.; m. (1) Esther ———, who d. 5 Feb. 1775 ae. 21; m. (2) Phebe ———. They had children, Hannah and Esther, bapt. at Redding, 24 Oct. 1778.
> Huldah, bapt. 10 Apr. 1747, d. at Redding, 20 Apr. 1774 ae. 27; m. at Redding, 5 Nov. 1767, Abijah Fairchild.

---

* Children by first wife: Lemuel, bapt. 11 Dec. 1768; m. 7 Dec. 1793, Anna Hull; dau. of Timothy, b. 7 Dec. 1771. Elizabeth, bapt. 5 May 1771; m. 6 Jan. 1793, Jonathan Middlebrook. Children by second wife: Joseph, bapt. 4 Sept. 1774. Rhoda, bapt. 13 Oct. 1777. Children of Lemuel: Sarah, b. 15 Jan. 1794; Joseph, b. 7 Sept. 1796.

Hannah, bapt. at Redding, 15 Oct. 1749 (Trumbull Church rec.); m. 26 July 1769, Henry Hopkins, "a stranger."

Jabez, b. [say 1751]; rem. 1786 to Fairfield, Vt., where he d. 28 June 1825 [Pension Rec.]; m. 12 Feb. 1778 [or 1777], Mary Bartram, b. 12 May 1760.

Ezekiel, bapt. 23 Mar. 1755, d. at Redding, in 1794; m. Huldah Merchant(?), of Redding.*

Stephen, bapt. 16 Jan. 1757, d. at Redding in 1820; adm'n granted, 8 June 1820, to Jonathan R. Sanford and Stephen Burr; m. 19 Feb. 1787, Molly Griffin, dau. of John, bapt. 31 Aug. 1766.†

Joel, b. 23 Aug. 1758 [Pension Rec., prob. error for 1759], bapt. 9 Sept. 1759; rem. to Galway, N. Y., 1796, and lived there, insane, 1841; m. 13 Apr. 1786, Elizabeth Gold.

31. Burr, Samuel, s. of Capt. Samuel. Justice, 1779.

Bapt. 24 Sept. 1727; d. at Fairfield, 20 Mar. 1791; m. 31 May 1753, Eunice Sturgis, dau. of Solomon, b. 18 Feb. 1730/1. She d. ae. 75 (g. s.).

Will 30 Dec. 1790, proved 20 June 1791; wife; son-in-law John Squire, Jr., Exec'r.

Child, bapt. Fairfield:

Elizabeth, bapt. 7 July 1754, d. 6 June 1811 ae. 57 (g. s.); m. John Squire, Jr.

32. Burr, Daniel, s. of Capt. Samuel.

Born 2 July 1730; d. at Fairfield, 22 Jan. 1811 ae. 81.

He m. 22 Jan. 1756, Ann Silliman, dau. of Nathaniel, b. 29 Aug. 1730.

Children, rec. and bapt. Fairfield:

Ann, b. 9, bapt. 12 Dec. 1756, d. at Fairfield, 13 May 1843 ae. 86 yrs. 5 mos. (g. s.); m. 6 Dec. 1781, William Morehouse.

Abigail, b. 6, bapt. 8 Oct. 1758.

Seth, b. 2, bapt. 15 Mar. 1761; according to *Burr Gen.* served in Revolution, and later under Cornwallis in India; d. unm.

---

* Adm'n on Ezekiel's estate granted, 25 Nov. 1794, to widow Eleanor. Distribution: Widow; eldest dau. Huldah; 2d dau. Raney; eldest son Aaron; 2d son Billy; youngest son Ammon. Adm'n on Est. of Rana Burr granted, 19 Jan. 1804, to Eleanor Burr. The dau. Huldah m. 12 Oct. 1806, Daniel Mallory, Jr.

† Children, rec. Redding: Clara, b. 8 June 1788; Molly, b. 10, d. 15 July 1793; Stephen, b. 28 Dec. 1795.

Esther, bapt. 11 Sept. 1763; m. (1) at Fairfield, 24 Nov. 1789, Abijah Knapp; m. (2) Joseph Davis.
Isaac, bapt. 23 Mar. 1766; rem. to New York City; Port Warden and Harbor Master; m. Catherine Buchanan, dau. of John.
Hannah, bapt. 29 Jan. 1769, d. 24 Nov. 1819 ae. 52 (g. s.). Will 13 Nov. 1819, proved 29 Apr. 1820; George Morehouse, son of Stephen dec'd; sister Ann wife of William Morehouse; sister Elizabeth wife of Josiah B. Hall, and her dau. Sarah M. Hall; Sally dau. of Wm. Morehouse, Sr.; sister Esther wife of Joseph Davis, and Sally dau. of Joseph Davis; bro. Daniel Burr; Miriam Bibbins, dau. of Billy; Sarah Ann Morehouse, dau. of Wm., Jr.; Mary B. Morehouse, dau. of Stephen; Elijah Bibbins, Exec'r.
Daniel, b. abt. 1772, bapt. 17 Sept. 1775, d. 8 Aug. 1843 ae. 71 (g. s.).
Elizabeth, b. 24 July 1775 (Weston rec.), bapt. 17 Sept. 1775, d. at Easton, 24 Jan. 1848 ae. 72 yrs. 6 mos. (g. s.); m. 13 Nov. 1794, Josiah B. Hall.

33. Burr, Ebenezer, s. of Capt. Samuel.

Born Oct. 1732; d. in 1767 ae. 35 (g. s.); m. 26 Feb. 1759, Amelia Silliman, dau. of Ebenezer, b. 30 Oct. 1736, d. in 1794 ae. 58 (g. s.). She m. (2) 18 Jan. 1778, Abel Gold.

Adm'n on Est. of Ebenezer, 2d, granted to Amelia Burr, 13 Apr. 1767. Distribution ordered 1771 to widow, eldest son Samuel, son William, and dau. Amelia. Hezekiah Silliman was appointed guardian of the two boys, 3 July 1770.

Children, bapt. Fairfield:

Mabel, bapt. 17 Oct. 1761, d. y.
Samuel, bapt. 5 July 1767, d. at Bridgeport, 25 Oct. 1825; m. (1) 21 June 1781, Abigail Jennings, bapt. 13 Sept. 1761, d. 13 June 1790 ae. 28 yrs. 11 mos. (g. s.); m. (2) at Woodbridge, 16 June 1795, Jemima Darling, b. [June 1762], d. 19 Dec. 1822 ae. 60 yrs. 6 mos. (g. s., New Haven).*
William, bapt. 5 July 1767; res. Philadelphia, Pa.; m. 6 Mar. 1782, Eunice Thorp, dau. of Eliphalet, bapt. 19 June 1763.†
Amelia, bapt. 5 July 1767; m. 11 Dec. 1783, Joseph Noyes, Esq.

---

* Children of Samuel, Jr., and Abigail, bapt. Fairfield: Clarissa and Lucretia, bapt. 27 June 1784; Josiah, bapt. 10 Apr. 1785; Nabby, bapt. 23 Mar. 1788; Henry, bapt. 2 May 1790.

† Children of William and Eunice, bapt. Fairfield: Ebenezer, b. 8 Nov. 1783 (g. s.), bapt. 16 Apr. 1784, d. 8 Apr.(?) 1784 ae. 6 mos. (g. s.); Amelia, bapt. 12 June 1785; Eunice, bapt. 5 Aug. 1787; Susanna, bapt. 3 Jan. 1790; William, bapt. 24 Nov. 1791; Jenetta, bapt. 12 Oct. 1794; Charles-Sylvester, bapt. 22 July 1797; Elizabeth, bapt. 28 Sept. 1800; Lucretia, bapt. 15 Oct. 1802.

34. **Burr, Nehemiah,** s. of Capt. Samuel. Ens. in 3d Regt., Army, May 1759.

Born 18 Apr. 1734; d. at Fairfield, 5 July 1814 ae. 80 (Wheeler Journal); m. 21 Apr. 1763, Sarah Osborn, dau. of Eleazer, b. 27 May 1741, perhaps the Mrs. Burr who d. 6 Oct. 1819 ae. 79 (Wheeler Journal).

Adm'n granted, 5 Dec. 1814, to Ebenezer Burr, 4th, with Thomas Bartram as surety.

Children, rec. and bapt. Fairfield:

> Thomas, b. 2 Feb., bapt. 17 June 1764, d. at sea, Oct. 1789 (Perry Diary); m. Polly ———. Perhaps she m. (2) 30 Dec. 1792, Rowland Fanton. Adm'n granted, 28 Dec. 1789, to Ebenezer Burr, 4th. Distribution ordered, half to widow Polly; half to bros. and sisters, Ebenezer, 4th, Nehemiah, Sarah, Eleazer, Noah, and Hannah Burr.
> Nehemiah, b. 2 Aug., bapt. 13 Oct. 1765, d. 5 June 1766.
> Ebenezer, b. 31 Dec. 1766, bapt. 11 Jan. 1767, d. at Fairfield, 31 Dec. 1848 ae. 82; m. (1) 5 June 1794, Sarah Dimon, bapt. 26 June 1774, d. 22 May 1795; m. (2) 18 Dec. 1803, Eunice Ogden, bapt. 14 Dec. 1783, d. 12 Mar. 1855 ae. 71.*
> Nehemiah, b. 16 Feb., bapt. 23 Apr. 1769; returned home 1794 after an absence of 2½ yrs. (Wheeler Journal); prob. the son who d. in West Indies, 1796 (see Wheeler Journal).
> Sarah, b. 29 Mar., bapt. 12 May 1771; m. 16 Nov. 1797, Thomas Bartram.
> Eleazer, b. 8 Jan., bapt. 6 June 1773; d. at New York, 14 Sept. 1794 (Perry Diary).
> Noah, bapt. 26 Mar. 1775, d. y.
> Noah, bapt. 9 Sept. 1777, d. at Fairfield, 25 Dec. 1859 ae. 77(?); m. Anna Jennings, b. 22 July 1785, d. 17 Mar. 1830 ae. 45 (g. s.).
> Hannah, bapt. 16 Dec. 1780.

35. **Burr, Charles,** s. of Capt. Samuel.

Born Aug. 1741; d. at Fairfield, 15 Mar. 1800 ae. 58 (g. s.); m. Elizabeth Sturges, dau. of Benjamin, b. abt. 1744, d. 10 July 1813 ae. 69.

In 1789, Charles and Elizabeth his wife sold land to Benjamin Sturges [eldest nephew of Elizabeth, son of her brother Seth].

---

* Child by first wife, bapt. Fairfield: Sarah-Dimon, bapt. 24 May 1795.

Will 15 Mar. 1800, proved 15 Apr. 1800; wife Elizabeth; Elizabeth wife of James Johnson; children Wakeman, Mabel, Ellen, David, Andrew, and Priscilla Burr.

Children:
>   Sturges, b. abt. 1767, d. 4 July 1796 ae. 29 (g. s.).
>   Mabel, b. abt. 1769, d. 1778 ae. 9 (g. s.).
>   Aaron, b. abt. 1772, d. Aug. 1798 ae. 26 (g. s.).
>   Elizabeth, b. [June 1774], d. at Easton, 12 Oct. 1849 ae. 75 yrs. 4 mos. (g. s.); m. 23 May 1797, James Johnson, Jr.
>   Ellen, d. 19 Oct. 1863; m. David Wakelee, of Fairfield.
>   Wakeman, b. abt. 1776, d. 4 Aug. 1812 ae. 36 (g. s.).
>   Andrew, d. at Mackinaw, Mich.; an Indian agent.
>   David, b. abt. 1781, d. 10 Oct. 1803 ae. 22 (g. s.).
>   Mehitabel, b. [May 1778], bapt. at Fairfield, 4 Sept. 1778, d. 1 Dec. 1849 ae. 71 yrs. 6 mos. (g. s.).
>   Priscilla, d. in 1855; m. ——— Ditmas.

36. **Burr, Daniel,** s. of Jehu.

Born [say 1715]; m. at Redding, 22 Dec. 1737, Abigail Sherwood, dau. of Dr. Thomas, b. at Stratford, 28 Dec. 1714.

Child:
>   Silas, bapt. at Greenfield, 8 Dec. 1739.
>   Others?

37. **Burr, Jehu,** s. of Jehu.

Bapt. 23 Aug. 1734.

He m. at Redding, 22 Nov. 1755, Sarah Griffin, dau. of John, bapt. 9 May 1736.

Children, bapt. Redding:
>   Ephraim, bapt. 22 Aug. 1756.
>   Abigail, bapt. 2 July 1758.

38. **Burr, Thaddeus,** s. of Thaddeus. Deputy for Fairfield, Oct. 1769, Oct. 1771, Oct. and Dec. 1775, May, Oct. and Nov. 1776, May and Oct. 1778, Jan. 1779, May 1781, May and Oct. 1784, Oct. 1788; Sheriff, Fairfield County, May 1771. Commissioner to N. Y. and N. J., May 1775; member of Council of Safety, 1777, '78, '79; Justice, 1777, '78.

Born 22 Aug. 1735; d. at Fairfield, 19 Feb. 1801 ae. 65 (g. s.); m. 22 Mar. 1759, Eunice Dennie, dau. of James, b. abt. 1732, d. 14 Aug. 1805 in 76 yr. (g. s.).

Will 27 Sept. 1799, proved 20 Mar. 1801; wife Eunice; two sons of niece Abigail Capers,—Charles William and Nathaniel Lothrop; niece Eunice Dennie Hedge; niece Priscilla Lothrop Sturges; nephew Gershom Burr; negro man Cato.

Will of Eunice Burr, 6 Mar., proved 17 Aug. 1805; John, Francis, Jane, Eunice, Esther, James, and Dennie Sayre, children of my dec'd sister Sarah Sayre; real estate that came from my father James Dennie dec'd; Elizabeth wife of Gershom Burr; Gershom Burr; Eunice Hedge; Charles Capers; Nathaniel Lothrop Capers; Priscilla L. Sturges; Lewis B. Sturges.

39. Burr, Gershom, s. of Thaddeus.

Born 10 June 1744; d. at Fairfield, 12 Mar. 1774 ae. 30; m. 12 Dec. 1765, Priscilla Lothrop.

Children, bapt. Fairfield:

> Thaddeus, b. 14, bapt. 22 Feb. 1767, d. 9 Oct. 1776 in 10 yr. (g. s.). Adm'n granted, 26 Sept. 1789, to Thaddeus Burr, Esq., and distribution ordered to bros. and sisters.
> Gershom, bapt. 15 May 1768, d. at New York, 19 Mar. 1828; Brig.-Gen.; will 19 Feb., proved 18 Apr. 1828, gave all to wife Elizabeth; m. (1) at Fairfield, 10 Sept. 1789, Susanna Young of Stratfield,* who d. 12 Feb. 1797 in 24 yr. (g. s.); m. (2) 15 Oct. 1801, Elizabeth Eliot, dau. of Rev. Andrew, b. 29 Oct. 1776.†
> Isaac-Lothrop, bapt. 3 Sept. 1769.
> Abigail, bapt. 9 Sept. 1770; m. 9 Sept. 1789, William Henry Capers, of St. Helena, S. C.
> Eunice-Dennie, bapt. 11 Oct. 1772; m. 9 Sept. 1789, Barnabas Hedge, of Plymouth, Mass.
> Priscilla-Lothrop, bapt. 10 July 1774; m. (1) 12 Aug. 1793, Jonathan Sturges, Jr.; m. (2) John Bulkley, of New Haven.

---

* Sukey Young, only dau. of Daniel of Newfield, by Conn. Journal, issue of 28 Sept. 1789.

† Children, rec. Fairfield. By first wife: Thaddeus, b. 13 Nov. 1790, bapt. 2 Jan. 1791, drowned 15 July 1811 ae. 21; Susanna, b. 7, bapt. 27 Jan. 1793, d. 4 Feb. 1797; Isaac-Lothrop, b. 12, bapt. 27 July 1794. By second wife: Andrew-Eliot, b. 9 Aug., bapt. 5 Sept. 1802; Jonathan-Sturges, b. 6 Mar., bapt. 1 Apr. 1804; Priscilla-Lothrop, b. 6 July 1806; Susanna-Young, b. 6 Feb. 1808.

40. **Burr, David,** s. of Andrew. Deputy for Fairfield, Oct. 1760, Mar., May and Oct. 1761, May 1762 to Oct. 1765 inclusive, Oct. 1766 to Oct. 1771 inclusive, Oct. 1772. Capt., 2d Co., Fairfield, May 1764; Major, 4th Regt., May 1772; Lt.-Col., 4th Regt., Oct. 1772. Justice, 1762-73.

Born 5 July 1722; Col. David d. 3 Dec. 1773 in 52 yr. (g. s.); m. 11 Dec. 1751, Eunice Osborn, dau. of Samuel, b. 16 Feb. 1727/8, d. 1 Dec. 1789 ae. 63 (g. s.).

Grad. Yale College 1743.

Distribution 27 Oct. 1783; widow Eunice; eldest son Walter; 2d son David; 3d son William; 4th son Andrew; eldest dau. Ellen; 2d dau. Abigail; 3d dau. Sarah; heirs of Lucretia Burr dec'd; heirs of Eunice Burr dec'd.

In 1774, Walter of Fairfield, entitled to double portion of estate of dec'd father Col. David Burr, conveyed half of his share for love to bro. Andrew and sisters Ellen, Abigail and Sarah Burr.

Children, rec. and bapt. Fairfield:

Walter, b. 25, bapt. 31 Dec. 1752; res. Sharon; m. Mabel St. John.
Lucretia, b. 10, bapt. 17 Mar. 1754, d. at Sharon, 16 Nov. 1776 in 23 yr. (g. s.).
Eunice, b. 29 Dec. 1755, bapt. 4 Jan. 1756, d. at Sharon, 28 Sept. 1776 in 21 yr. (g. s.).
David, b. 8, bapt. 14 Aug. 1757, d. at Danbury, 18 Feb. 1825 ae. 67 (g. s., Fairfield); Deputy for Fairfield, Oct. 1790, May and Oct. 1791, May and Oct. 1793, Oct. 1795, Oct. 1796, May and Oct. 1797, Oct. 1798, May and Oct. 1799, May and Oct. 1800, May and Oct. 1801, May 1802, May and Oct. 1803, Oct. 1805, Oct. 1806, May 1807, Oct. 1809, May and Oct. 1811, May 1812; Clerk of County Court; m. 3 Oct. 1782, Sarah-Ann Beers, dau. of Samuel and Sarah (Huntington) (Wetmore) Beers, b. 20 June 1762, d. 4 May 1842 ae. 80 (g. s.). Only child: Julia-Ann, b. 1 May 1800, bapt. 2 Sept. 1804, d. 5 Feb. 1819 in 19 yr. (g. s.). David's will, 30 Mar. 1819, proved 5 Mar. 1825; wife Sarah-Anna; sister Abigail Nichols; heirs of dec'd bro. Walter Burr, late of Sharon.
William, b. 27, bapt. 29 July 1759, d. at Fairfield, in 1822; m. Huldah ———.
Ellen, b. 12, bapt. 16 Aug. 1761.
Abigail, b. 29 Sept., bapt. 9 Oct. 1763, d. at Fairfield, 18 Oct. 1830 ae. 67 (g. s.); m. at Westport, 19 May 1794, Hezekiah Nichols.
Sarah, b. 21, bapt. 27 Apr. 1766, d. 2 June 1787.
Andrew, b. 7, bapt. 10 Apr. 1768, perhaps d. Nov. 1815 (Miss Treadwell's book).

41. Burr, Andrew, s. of Andrew.

Born 24 July 1724.

He m. Jan. 1751, Lydia Smith of Norwalk. About 1755 he sailed from New Haven as master of a vessel to the West Indies; she divorced him for desertion in 1759 and m. (2) Nehemiah Strong of New Haven. In May 1761 he petitioned the Legislature, calling himself late of New Haven, now of Fairfield, and proved that his absence from his family was not desertion; his wife's divorce was set aside. She d. 10 Jan. 1794 ae. 64 (Trinity Church, New Haven).

Josiah son of Andrew Burr was one of the heirs named in distribution of the Est. of Matthew Smith of Norwalk, 1771.

Children:

>Josiah, b. abt. 1751, bur. 31 Oct. 1795 ae. 44 (Trinity Church rec., New Haven); m. Mary Burr, his first cousin.
>Sarah, b. abt. 1764, d. at New Haven, 27 Sept. 1766 ae. 2 (g. s.).

42. Burr, John, s. of Andrew. 2d Lt., 2d Co., 4th Regt., Army, Mar. 1758.

Born 11 Mar. 1731/2; d. at Fairfield in 1767; m. Elizabeth (Isaacs) Kerr.

He was called "of St. Croix now residing in Fairfield" in a deed in 1765.

Will 9 May, proved 2 July 1767; two children, Sturges and Mary; bro. Oliver Burr, Exec'r. Distribution of Est. of John, 3d, 1 Apr. 1774: Sturges Burr; Mary Burr.*

Children:

>Sturges, b. 1760, d. at Newtown, 1796; m. Elizabeth Sherman, b. at New Haven, 31 Dec. 1765; she m. (2) Simeon Baldwin. In 1784, Sturges, of Newtown, conveyed land distributed from my father John Burr's estate, bounded on land of uncle Andrew Burr and of uncle George Burr.
>Mary, b. 1763; m. Josiah Burr.

---

* David Judson, late of Kinderhook, N. Y., now on way to New Haven, Conn., made will 16 Oct., proved 18 Dec. 1790; sons Philander and David; Exec'rs, bro.-in-law Ebenezer R. White, Oliver Burr (both of Danbury), and bro.-in-law Sturgis Burr of New Haven [*N. Y. Calendar of Wills*]. Just how related to the Burrs, does not appear.

43. Burr, George, s. of Andrew. Ens., 7th Co., 5th Regt., Army, Apr. 1775 (resigned); Ens., 8th Co., 4th Regt., Oct. 1775; Lt., Nov. 1776 (refused). Justice, 1777-82. Deputy for Fairfield, May 1779.

Born 26 May 1736; d. in 1813.

He m. 30 Dec. 1762, Mabel Wakeman, dau. of Jabez, b. 24 May 1742, d. at Greenfield, 2 Aug. 1822 ae. 80.

Will 9 Mar. 1812, proved 26 July 1813; wife Mabel, all estate; David Burr and Lewis B. Sturges, Exec'rs.

Will of Mabel, 5 June, proved 9 Sept. 1822; dau. Eunice wife of Eliphalet Hull; four daus. Priscilla, Elizabeth, Eunice, and Debbee. Distribution 1825: daus. Eunice wife of Eliphalet Hull, Elizabeth wife of Moses Beers, and Debby Moyer; children of her daus. Priscilla, viz. Susannah wife of Abraham Purdy, Samuel Sherwood, Jr., Sarah B. wife of James L. Coggswell, Priscilla Sherwood, Fanny wife of Almon Smith, and Albert, Oliver B., Clarina, Marietta, Delia, and George B. Sherwood.

Children, rec. Fairfield, bapt. Greenfield:

> Priscilla, b. 26 Sept., bapt. 16 Oct. 1763; m. at Westport, 13 Aug. 1786, Samuel Sherwood.
> Ann, b. 3 Apr., 1765, bapt. 1 June 1766, d. 7 Nov. 1778 in 12 yr.
> Sarah, b. 15 May 1770, d. y.
> Child, stillborn May 1772.
> Elizabeth, b. 24 May, bapt. 11 July 1773; m. Moses Beers.
> Deborah, b. 4 Feb., bapt. 8 May 1775, d. 24 Apr. 1779 in 5 yr.
> Eunice, bapt. Mar. 1777, d. 14 Aug. 1845 ae. 67 (g. s.); m. 16 Feb. 1800, Eliphalet Hull.
> Debby, bapt. 25 May 1783;* m. 30 Jan. 1810, George Moyer.
> Mary, bapt. at Westport, 7 Apr. 1785, d. y.

44. Burr, Nathan, s. of Nathaniel.

Born 19 Sept. 1732; d. at Fairfield, 7 Aug. 1811 ae. 79.

He m. Ruth Jennings, dau. of Jeremiah, b. 13 Nov. 1735.

Children, bapt. Fairfield:

> Hezekiah, bapt. 22 Mar. 1759, d. y.
> Ellen, bapt. 4 May 1760; m. 25 Oct. 1781, Stephen Adams, Jr.

---
* She had a dau. Sally Marvin.

Hezekiah, b. 27 Aug., bapt. 12 Sept. 1762, d. 24 Apr. 1840 ae. 78 (g. s.); Maj.; m. 5 Dec. 1784, Mary Annable, b. 3 June 1759, d. 8 Jan. 1848 ae. 88 yrs. 7 mos. (g. s.).*
Grissel, bapt. 10 Nov. 1765, d. at Greenfield, 22 June 1846 in 81 yr. (g. s.); m. 22 Nov. 1795, Joseph Hayes.
Nathaniel, bapt. 14 Feb. 1768, d. 20 Dec. 1834 ae. 67 (g. s.); m. 3 Jan. 1801, Betsey Jennings, dau. of Jeremiah, bapt. 2 Aug. 1778, d. 4 Jan. 1833 ae. 55 (g. s.).
Gideon, bapt. 7 Apr. 1775, d. at Fairfield, by 1808. Distribution order 23 Oct. 1808: bros. and sisters,—Hezekiah Burr, Nathaniel Burr, Ellen wife of Stephen Adams, Grissel wife of Joseph Hayes, and Martha wife of Elihu Benedict.
Martha, bapt. 25 June 1775; m. Elihu Benedict.

45. Burr, Ephraim, s. of Ephraim.

Born 5 Dec. 1735; d. at Westport, 19 Nov. 1779 (church rec.), or Dec. 1779 ae. 43 (g. s.); m. 12 Aug. 1762, Eunice Wilson, dau. of Robert, b. 11 June 1743, d. May 1793 ae. 49 (g. s.).

Children, bapt. Westport:

Eunice, bapt. 1 July 1764, d. at Westport, 16 June 1791; m. David Beers.
Catherine, b. abt. 1766, d. at Westport, 2 Sept. 1835 ae. 69 (g. s.); m. 21 Mar. 1787, Daniel Sherwood.
Abigail, bapt. 4 Sept. 1768, d. at Westport, 3 June 1797 in 29 yr.; m. 20 Oct. 1793, Abraham Sherwood.
Silas, bapt. 19 May 1771, d. at Westport, 8 Sept. 1810 ae. 39 (g. s.); adm'n granted, 22 Dec. 1810, to Charity Burr and Samuel Meeker, with Daniel Sherwood, Jr., as surety; m. 6 Mar. 1796, Charity Banks; dau. of Benjamin, bapt. 19 Mar. 1775, d. 14 Nov. 1818 ae. 43 yrs. 11 mos. (g. s.).†
Sarah, bapt. 23 Jan. 1774.
Ann, bapt. 16 Mar. 1777, d. 9 July 1831 in 54 yr. (g. s.); m. 13 Dec. 1808, Gershom Osborn.
Ephraim, bapt. 25 Sept. 1779, d. 25 Mar. 1781.

46. Burr, Ebenezer, s. of Ephraim.

Born 23 May 1738; d. at Fairfield, 8 Jan. 1823 in 85 yr. (g. s.); m. 9 Jan. 1766, Hannah Morehouse, widow of James, and dau. of Peter Bulkley, bapt. 16 Oct. 1726, d. 23 July 1818 ae. 91 (g. s.).

---

* Children, bapt. Fairfield: Ephraim, bapt. 4 Nov. 1787, d. y. James, bapt. 4 Nov. 1787, d. 6 Nov. 1826; m. Sally Penfield, d. 19 Mar. 1870. Silliman, bapt. 12 June 1791. John, bapt. 22 Feb. 1800. Ephraim.

† Charity's dower was set to the daus. of Silas: Catherine wife of Morris Ketchum, Angeline Burr, and Charity Burr.

He was known as Ebenezer, Jr.; will 13 Apr. 1820, proved 16 Jan. 1823; niece Esther wife of William Morehouse, Jr.; nephews Ephraim and Ebenezer, sons of Peter Burr; niece Mary dau. of Peter Burr; niece Sarah wife of Joseph Sturges; niece Ellen Field of Harpersfield, N. Y.; Mary Willey, dau. of niece Mary Willey; Elijah Middlebrook, illegitimate son of niece Ruthy wife of John Jennings; Lois Jennings, dau. of "Abaj^h Jennings" dec'd.

47. Burr, Peter, s. of Ephraim.

Born 2 Nov. 1745; d. at Fairfield, 4 July 1816 in 71 yr. (g. s.); m. 17 Nov. 1776, Esther Jennings, b. 2 Mar. 1755, d. 2 Oct. 1837 ae. 82 yrs. 7 mos. (g. s.).

Will 30 Apr. 1812, proved 8 July 1816; wife Esther; sons Thaddeus, Ephraim, Ebenezer; daus. Sarah wife of Joseph Sturges, Eunice wife of Seth Osborn, Anna wife of A. G. Jennings, Esther wife of William Morehouse, Jr., and Abigail and Mary (unmarried); land in Ohio.

Children, bapt. Fairfield (births from Bible rec.):

Thaddeus, b. 17 Aug., bapt. 2 Nov. 1777, d. 21 Feb. 1858 ae. 80 yrs. 6 mos. (g. s.); m. Rhoda Meeker, bapt. 9 May 1779, d. 28 Aug. 1834 ae. 55 yrs. 7 mos. (g. s.).

Sarah, b. 6 Oct., bapt. 9 Dec. 1779, d. 24 Mar. 1855 ae. 75-5-20 (g. s.); m. 16 Apr. 1801, Joseph Sturges.

Eunice, b. 4 Feb., bapt. 2 Mar. 1783, d. 30 Apr. 1866 ae. 83 (g. s.); m. 15 Jan. 1804, Seth Osborn.

Anna, b. 9 Mar., bapt. 4 Apr. 1784, d. 8 Jan. 1855 ae. 70-9-29 (g. s.); m. 7 Sept. 1807, Abraham-Gould Jennings.

Esther, b. 10 Mar., bapt. 26 Mar. 1786, d. 29 Oct. 1855 ae. 69-7-19 (g. s.); m. 23 Mar. 1809, William Morehouse, Jr.

Abigail, b. 28 Oct., bapt. 22 Nov. 1789; m. ―――― Lyon.

Mary, b. 9 Sept. 1791, bapt. 18 Sept. 1791, d. at Fairfield, 18 Oct. 1864 ae. 73-1-9 (g. s.).

Ephraim-Hull, b. 7, bapt. 12 Oct. 1794, d. at Southport, 19 Sept. 1885 ae. 90-11-12 (g. s.); m. Eunice Sherwood, dau. of Daniel.

Ebenezer, b. 23 Dec. 1798, d. at Fairfield, 28 Nov. 1873; m. 24 Apr. 1825, Hannah Osborn, dau. of Daniel.

HISTORY AND GENEALOGY OF

48. **Burr, John,** s. of Capt. John. Lt., Stratfield Co., Oct. 1762; Capt., Oct. 1764. Justice, 1769-71.

Born 12 June 1728; d. at Stratfield, 28 July 1771 in 44 yr. (g. s.); m. 2 Apr. 1750, Eunice Booth, dau. of Joseph, who d. by 1786.

He was killed by lightning at Pequonnock when the church steeple was struck (Perry Diary).

Adm'n granted to Eunice, 12 Aug. 1771; she appointed guardian to John and William.

Distribution 20 Dec. 1771: widow Eunice; Jesse, John, William, Catherine Burr; Eunice Holberton. Ozias Burr appointed guardian of John, Jesse, and William, 3 Dec. 1772.

The widow's dower was set to the heirs 1786: eldest son Jesse; son William; dau. Eunice wife of William Holburton; son John; dau. Catherine wife of John Duncomb.

Children, rec. Fairfield:

> Eunice, b. 5, bapt. 7 Oct. 1750, d. 1837; m. Dec. 1770, William Holburton.
> Catherine, b. 5 Nov. 1753; m. John Duncomb.
> Jesse, b. 30 Dec. 1755, bapt. Jan. 1756, bur. 9 Dec. 1813 ae. 58 (Trinity Church rec.); m. Sally Wilson.
> William, b. 29 June 1762, d. at Southbury, 22 June 1841 [Pension Rec.]; m. 23 Nov. 1786, Sarah Hubbell, dau. of Jeremiah, b. 22 June 1770.*
> John, bapt. 29 Apr. 1770; rem. to Ohio; m. 1790, Jerusha Beardsley.

49. **Burr, Justus,** s. of Capt. John.

Born 2 Sept. 1734; d. at Stratfield, 13 July 1766 in 32 yr. (g. s.); m. Hephzibah Nichols, dau. of Elijah, b. at Stratford, 15 Nov. 1732, d. 24 Oct. 1810 ae. 78 (g. s.).

Adm'n granted, 18 Aug. 1766, to Hephzibah Burr. Distribution 28 Apr. 1776: widow Hephzibah and children, Elijah (eldest), Aaron, John, Huldah, Sarah, Comfort, Hephzibah Burr.

Will of Hephzibah of Stratfield, 4 July 1805, proved 26 Nov. 1810; son Aaron (imbecile); son John; daus. Huldah wife of Daniel Curtiss, Sarah wife of David Minott, Comfort Burr, and Hephzibah wife of Philemon Sherwood; children, Elijah, Aaron, John, Huldah, Sarah, Comfort, Hephzibah.

---

* Had eleven children, see Bible Rec. in Vol. III.

Children:

> Elijah, of Bridgeport, d. in 1812; adm'n granted, 23 Sept. 1812, to Deborah Burr, with William Burr as surety; m. Deborah ———, who d. by 1818.*
> Aaron, b. abt. 1757, bur. 24 Aug. 1814 ae. 57 (Trinity Church rec.).
> Huldah, m. Daniel-Mitchell Curtiss.
> Sarah, m. David Minott.
> Comfort, b. abt. 1764, d. at Stratfield, 13 Sept. 1841 ae. 77 (g. s.); m. 3 Jan. 1808, Joseph Strong, of Setauket, L. I.
> Hephzibah, b. abt. 1766, d. 9 Sept. 1848 ae. 82 (g. s.); m. 22 Nov. 1786, Philemon Sherwood.
> John.

50. **Burr, Ozias,** s. of Capt. John.

Born 1 May 1739; d. at Stratfield, 5 Sept. 1836 in 98 yr. (g. s.); m. 1764, Sarah Nichols, dau. of Elijah, b. at Stratford, 15 Jan. 1734/5, d. 2 Sept. 1820 in 82 yr. (g. s.).

Children [dates in part from *Burr Genealogy*]:

> Rebecca, b. 22 Nov. 1765, d. 23 Aug. 1794 in 29 yr. (g. s.).
> Charity, b. abt. 1767, d. 19 Aug. 1794 in 27 yr. (g. s.).
> Amos, b. 26 Dec. 1768, d. at Bridgeport, 20 Nov. 1856; m. at Trinity Church, 18 Apr. 1796, Abigail E. Shelton, b. 17 July 1773, d. 29 Sept. 1840.
> Justus, b. 9 Jan. 1770, d. 1820.
> Ozias, b. 13 Jan. 1773, d. at Worthington, Ohio, 15 Aug. 1845; m. (1) 21 Apr. 1796, Lois Jennings, dau. of Matthew, bapt. 25 Jan. 1776, d. 12 May 1797; m. (2) Elizabeth Couch, dau. of Simon, b. 9 Oct. 1776, d. 21 Feb. 1834; m. (3) Clarissa Thompson, dau. of William, b. 1782, d. 1 Nov. 1864.†
> Nichols, b. 17 Dec. 1774, d. 24 Apr. 1860; m. at Trinity Church, 21 Dec. 1815, Adrea Allen, dau. of Nehemiah, b. at Stratford, 30 Sept. 1776.
> Sarah, b. 10 May 1777, d. 31 Mar. 1862; m. at Trinity Church, 1 May 1806, Seth Couch.
> David, b. 2 Jan. 1779, d. unm.
> Philo, b. 24 Mar. 1781, d. 12 Sept. 1794 in 13 yr. (g. s.).
> Mary, b. 9 Dec. 1783, d. 19 May 1874.

---

* Distribution made, 22 Aug. 1813, to widow Deborah, eldest son William, 2d son Munson, 3d son Lewis, dau. Charity wife of Ezra Hawley, 2d dau. Marietta, 3d dau. Aletia, 4th dau. Ann S. Distribution of the dower of dec'd widow Deborah ordered to the heirs, 2 Apr. 1818: children, William, Lewis, Marietta, Aletia, Ann S., and heirs of Charity Hawley dec'd. Elijah had, bapt. Trinity Church: Charity, 4 June 1786; Munson, 12 Oct. 1788; Lewis, 10 Feb. 1793; Marietta, 15 May 1796.

† Descendants appear in *The "Old Northwest" Genealogical Quarterly*, vol. 6, p. 174.

51. Burr, Wakeman, s. of Capt. John. Ens., 4th Co., 5th Regt., Army, Apr. 1775 (promoted to 1st Lt.); 1st Lt., 1st Co., 1st Batt., Army, June 1776; Capt.

Born 3 Oct. 1743; d. at Fairfield, 9 May 1799 ae. 56 (g. s.); m. Mary ———, b. 1746, d. 26 Oct. 1829 ae. 83 (g. s.).

Children, bapt. Fairfield:

> Justus, bapt. 25 Sept. 1769, d. 10 Oct. 1769 ae. 2 yrs. 8 mos. (g. s.).
> Levi, bapt. 29 Oct. 1769, d. at Fairfield, 27 Sept. 1845 ae. 76-5-25 (g. s.); m. (1) Anna Robinson; m. (2) Anna Darrow, b. 29 Dec. 179[2], d. 23 Jan. 1853 ae. 60 yrs. 29 days (g. s.).
> Abigail, bapt. 5 Jan. 1772, d. at Greenfield, 7 May 1859 ae. 87 (g. s.); m. William Sherwood.
> Mary, bapt. 28 May 1775, d. at Greenfield, 6 Mar. 1845 in 70 yr. (g. s.); m. at Trinity Church, 10 Sept. 1797, Jacob White.
> Catherine, b. [24 Oct. 1780], d. at Westport, 6 Nov. 1805 ae. 25 yrs. 13 days (g. s.).
> Wakeman, b. abt. 1783, d. 26 Oct. 1785 ae. 2 (g. s.).*
> Wakeman, bapt. 16 Nov. 1788; res. Seneca Falls, N. Y.†

52. Burr, Daniel, s. of John.

Born 5 Mar. 1737; d. at Westport, 23 Aug. 1812 ae. 75 yrs. 5 mos. 18 days (g. s.); m. at Westport, 20 Apr. 1769, Abigail Bulkley, dau. of Peter, b. 12 Apr. 1743, d. 28 Jan. 1827 ae. 83 (g. s.).

Will 3 June 1808, proved 9 Sept. 1812; wife Abigail; dau. Elizabeth (unm.); sons Jonathan, Zalmon. Distribution 29 Apr. 1813 by mutual agreement of the widow and three children.

Children, bapt. Westport:

> Jonathan, b. 5 Nov. 1769, bapt. 28 Jan. 1770, d. at Westport, 12 Mar. 1859 ae. 89-3-7 (g. s.); m. 8 May 1791, Sarah Redfield, dau. of Ebenezer, b. [26 Oct. 1772], d. 3 Oct. 1839 ae. 67-11-6 (g. s.).‡
> Zalmon, b. 31 Aug. 1773, bapt. 3 Oct. 1773, d. at Westport, 10 Aug. 1826 (g. s.); m. (1) 15 Jan. 1797, Abigail Hide, dau. of John, b. 12 Sept. 1779, d. 21 Dec. 1798 (g. s.); m. (2) Mary Hanford, who

---

* Wakeman, son of *John* Burr, bapt. at Trinity Church, 4 Sept. 1785.
† Wakeman Burr d. at Albany, N. Y., 20 Aug. 1832 (Miss Treadwell's book).
‡ Children, bapt. Westport: Henrietta, bapt. 26 Feb. 1792. Daniel, bapt. 21 Sept. 1794, d. 21 Mar. 1879 ae. 84-8-9 (g. s.). Elizabeth, bapt. 5 Feb. 1797. Patty, bapt. 2 Feb. 1800, "Martha" d. 10 Dec. 1893 ae. 94 (g. s.); m. Dr. Talcott Banks.

d. 25 Apr. 1846 ae. 65 (g. s.). Adm'n on Zalmon's estate was granted, 12 Dec. 1826, to Ebenezer Beers, with Nathan Beers as surety. Distribution to widow and sons William, Barlow, and Enoch.

Elizabeth, bapt. 18 July 1779, d. at Westport, 17 Feb. 1815 ae. 35 (g. s.).

53. Burr, Talcott, s. of John.

Born 20 Oct. 1746; d. at Westport, 17 Oct. 1802 ae. 56 (g. s.); m. 15 Nov. 1770, Mindwell Banks, b. in 1750. She d. 23 July 1827 ae. 77 (g. s.).

Distribution, 2 May 1804: widow; sons Alva and Talcott; daus. Abigail wife of Ezra Burr, Clarina wife of Eben Beers, and Grace Burr. Adm'n on his estate with will annexed, and on that of Mindwell Burr, was granted, 18 Aug. 1828, to Ebenezer Beers; distribution made to the children as above.

Children, bapt. Westport:

Talcott, bapt. 14 July 1771, d. 15 July 1771.
Elizabeth, bapt. 22 Mar. 1772, d. 23 Mar. 1772.
Mercy, bapt. 22 Mar. 1772, d. 23 Mar. 1772.
Alva, bapt. 4 July 1773, d. in 1825; adm'n granted, 21 Sept. 1825, to Ebenezer Burr, with Seymour Taylor as surety; insolvent; m. 28 Mar. 1803, Almira Taylor.
Abigail, bapt. 25 Aug. 1776; m. 23 Dec. 1798, Ezra Burr, Jr.
Talcott, bapt. 2 Apr. 1780; rem. to Wilmington, N. C.; m. Emily Bernard, dau. of Edward J.
Clarina, b. 6 June 1782 (g. s.), bapt. 28 July 1782; m. 15 Feb. 1803, Eben Beers.
Grace, bapt. 22 Apr. 1787; m. 27 Sept. 1809, Wakeman Burritt.

54. Burr, John, s. of John.

Born 9 Feb. 1751.

He m. at Westport, 18 Oct. 1772, Martha Godfrey, dau. of Nathan, b. 24 May 1752.

Children, bapt. Westport:

Nathan, bapt. 23 May 1773, d. 29 Aug. 1773.
Selleck, bapt. 7 Aug. 1774, d. at Westport, 14 Dec. 1853 ae. 79 (g. s.); Capt.; m. (1) 21 Oct. 1798, Abigail Jennings, dau. of David; b.

208   HISTORY AND GENEALOGY OF

abt. 1774, d. 19 June 1824 ae. 50 (g. s.); m. (2) Sarah Bennett, dau. of Jabez, bapt. 26 June 1785, d. 10 Apr. 1832 ae. 47 (g. s.).*
Esther, bapt. 19 Oct. 1777; m. 7 May 1795, Stephen B. Hanford.
Molly, bapt. 9 Jan. 1780, d. at Ridgefield, 11 June 1866 ae. 87 (g. s.); m. 13 July 1797, Bradley Bulkley.
John, bapt. 27 June 1784.
Martha, bapt. 16 Oct. 1785.
Nathan, bapt. 29 Apr. 1787.
Eleanor, bapt. 25 Nov. 1790.
Priscilla, bapt. 10 Nov. 1793.

55. Burr, Moses, s. of David.

Born 5 Apr. 1744; d. at Weston, 21 Dec. 1836 ae. 93 (g. s.); m. Mabel, prob. dau. of Benjamin Banks, bapt. 13 Oct. 1751; she d. 29 Oct. 1843 ae. 92 (g. s.).

Moses Burr and Mabel his wife of Fairfield conveyed to Hezekiah Banks in 1782.

Children, bapt. Weston:

Ann, bapt. 13 Nov. 1771; ? m. 28 June 1792, Samuel Marvin.
Abigail, bapt. 13 Sept. 1778.
Ellen, bapt. 31 Oct. 1784, d. at Weston, 21 Mar. 1815 ae. 30 (g. s.).

56. Burr, David, s. of David.

Born 29 Sept. 1751; d. at Westport, 22 Dec. 1811 ae. 60-2-23 (g. s.); m. at Weston, 3 Nov. 1776, Jane Banks of Greenfield, dau. of Gershom, b. 8 Aug. 1757, d. 17 Aug. 1838 ae. 80 yrs. 9 mos. (g. s.). She m. (2) 22 Jan. 1814, David Sherwood of Greenfield.

Will 8 Apr. 1808, proved 5 Jan. 1812; wife Jane; sons Aaron, David; gr. children Sally-Burr, Martha-Lorra, and Hezekiah-Morehouse (minors), children of dau. Ann Coley; dau. Mary Bennett; dau. Amelia (a minor).

---

* Children, bapt. Westport: Gershom, bapt. 16 Mar. 1800; Susan, bapt. 15 Mar. 1801; Abigail, bapt. 14 Aug. 1803; Martha, bapt. 31 Aug. 1806; Selleck, bapt. 2 Sept. 1808.

Children (births from Bible rec.), bapt. Westport:

    Aaron, b. 24 Mar., bapt. 6 June 1777, d. at Westport, 24 July 1863 ae. 80 [86?] yrs. 4 mos. (g. s.); m. 3 Apr. 1799, Huldah Morehouse, who d. 12 Jan. 1848 in 69 yr. (g. s.).*
    Ann, b. 1 Mar., bapt. 11 Apr. 1779, d. at Westport, 14 Oct. 1815 ae. 36 yrs. 7 mos. (g. s.); m. 5 Nov. 1797, Hezekiah Coley.
    Moses, b. and bapt. 3 July 1782, d. 4 July 1782.
    Mary, b. 30 July, bapt. 14 Sept. 1783, d. at Westport, 15 Mar. 1826 ae. 42 (g. s.); m. 4 July 1799, James Bennett.
    David, b. 15 July, bapt. 17 Sept. 1786; m. Ann-Maria Hickok, b. 25 July 1802, d. 8 Sept. 1866.
    Moses, b. 11, bapt. 17 Apr. 1790, d. 9 Oct. 1790.
    Amelia, bapt. (as Pamelia) 9 Oct. 1793.

57. Burr, Increase, s. of Joseph.

Born 26 Dec. 1726; d. at Greenfield, 24 Dec. 1793 (Perry Diary and Trinity Church rec.).

He m. (1) 3 Jan. 1753, Jane Bradley, dau. of Francis, b. 21 Apr. 1733, d. 17 Feb. 1768 in 35 yr.

He m. (2) 16 Oct. 1768, Rhoda Burritt, dau. of William, bapt. 24 Oct. 1742, d. at Greenfield, 3 Apr. 1816 ae. 72.

Will 12 Dec. 1793, proved 6 Jan. 1794; wife Rhoda; three sons and five daus. named. Distribution 22 Apr. 1794: Widow; eldest son Increase; 2d son Joseph; 3d son William; daus. Hannah wife of Peter Nichols, Abigail wife of Gould Dimon, Jane wife of Abraham Bulkley, Rhoda wife of Alban Bradley, and Prudence.

He had a son go over to the enemy [Fairfield Town Rec., 18 May 1781].

Distribution of Rhoda's dower, 23 Apr. 1816: son Increase; dau. Prudence Burr; gr. children, heirs of William; dau. Hannah, late wife of Peter Nichols dec'd; dau. Abigail wife of Gould Dimon; son Joseph Burr; dau. Rhoda wife of Alban Bradley; dau. Jane wife of Abraham Bulkley.

Children [by first wife], rec. Fairfield, bapt. Greenfield:

    Hannah, b. 25 Dec. 1754, d. at Easton, 27 Oct. 1845 ae. 91 (g. s.); m. 15 June 1773, Peter Nichols.

---

* Children, bapt. Westport: Mary-Ann, bapt. 2 Mar. 1800; Abigail-Silliman, bapt. 24 Oct. 1801; Aveline, bapt. 18 Feb. 1803; Jane, bapt. 18 Apr. 1808.

Abigail, b. 10 Dec. 1756, d. at Newtown, 10 Dec. 1836 ae. 80 (g. s.);
m. 6 Mar. 1776, Gould Dimon.

Increase, bapt. 22 Apr. 1759, d. at Easton, 17 Nov. 1841 ae. 82 (g. s.);
m. 12 Oct. 1783, Anna Bulkley, dau. of Peter, b. 17 Aug. 1761.*

Jane, bapt. 15 Mar. 1761, d. at Westport, 4 Nov. 1838 in 78 yr. (g. s.);
m. Abraham Bulkley.

Joseph, bapt. 6 Apr. 1763, d. at Greenfield, 24 Mar. 1834 ae. 71 (g. s.);
m. at Easton, Dec. 1790, Sarah Hill, who d. 3 Mar. 1848 ae. 83 (g. s.).

Sarah, bapt. 22 July 1765 (untimely), d. July 1765.

Children [by second wife], bapt. Greenfield:

Rhoda, bapt. 10 Sept. 1769, d. 9 June 1845 ae. 77 (g. s.); m. Alban Bradley.

William, bapt. 14 Aug. 1774, d. at Weston, bur. 20 May 1808 ae. 33 (Trinity Church rec.); will 5 May, proved 6 June 1808;† m. Huldah Goodsell.

Prudence, bapt. 5 July 1778, d. at Greenfield, 25 Feb. 1851 ae. 72 (g. s.).

58. Burr, Abel, s. of Joseph.

Born 8 Sept. 1728; d. in 1779.

He m. 16 Jan. 1751, Sarah Cadwell, dau. of Jacob.

Children, rec. Fairfield:

Abel, b. 19 Dec. 1751, d. at Redding in 1831;‡ m. at Redding, 20 Dec. 1775, Sarah Wood, dau. of Daniel, b. 9 Sept. 1748. His will, 14 Sept. 1830, proved 12 Dec. 1831; wife Sarah; support for bro. Jonathan, deranged for years and destitute; gravestones to be erected for bro. Charles and his wife; Moses, James L., and Abel, sons of nephew David Burr 2d; Polly and Caroline Burr, daus. of bro. David Burr; Delia Burr, dau. of bro. Seth Burr; Seth Burr 2d, sons of bro. Seth; bro. David Burr; nephew David Burr 2d; heirs

---

* Children, rec. Weston, bapt. Trinity Church: Anna, b. 20 Mar. 1784; Abel, b. 18 Mar. 1786; Bradley, b. 6 Apr. 1788; Alfred, b. 7 Mar. 1790, bapt. 22 July 1790; Jesse, b. 31 Jan. 1792, bapt. 18 Mar. 1792, perhaps d. 3 Sept. 1822; Lydia, b. 30 Dec. 1793, bapt. 23 Mar. 1794; Deborah, b. 13 Aug. 1796, bapt. 13 Nov. 1796; Jonathan, bapt. 20 July 1800; Dencey, bapt. 13 June 1802; Horace, bapt. 26 Jan. 1806.

† Wife Huldah; sons David, Nathan; daus. Susanna, Anna. William d. 19 May 1808 (Miss Treadwell's book).

‡ Abel Burr of Redding, a Tory, was imprisoned Jan. 1777, and discharged on parole next month.

of bros. Samuel, David, Jacob C., and Seth; Zalmon S., son of bro. Samuel; bro. David and nephew David 2d and friend Harvey Smith, Exec'rs.*
Jonathan, b. 25 Dec. 1753, living 1830, *non compos mentis.*
Jacob-Cadwell, d. at Redding in 1825; m. Feb. 1787, Eunice Wood.†
Samuel, of Redding; m. Ellen Sherwood, dau. of Nehemiah.
Charles, of Redding; m. Abigail Stevens.
Seth, of Redding; m. 23 Jan. 1788, Elizabeth Lobdell.‡
David, of Ridgefield; m. Sally Lobdell.

59. Burr, Ichabod, s. of Joseph.

Born 1 May 1736; d. at Greenfield, 31 July 1818 ae. 82 (g. s.); m. Grissel Bradley, dau. of Peter, b. 22 Oct. 1739, d. 20 June 1825 ae. 86 (g. s.).

Will 19 July 1814, proved 12 Aug. 1818; wife Grizzel; son Jesse (married); to dau. Rachel Bradley, land in Bradley's farm formerly owned by Elnathan Bradley, also land formerly owned by Ebenezer Bradley dec'd; my right in Est. of Eliphalet Burr.

Will of Grizzel, 25 Dec. 1822, proved 22 Aug. 1825: gr. son David Burr; gr. dau. Grizzel Bradley; children of my gr. dau. Rachel Morehouse, dec'd wife of Abijah Morehouse of Bridgeport dec'd. Nathan Beers of Fairfield was appointed Adm'r with the will annexed. The distribution named the children of Rachel Morehouse as David A. Morehouse, Caroline wife of Moses Sherwood, Mary B. wife of Legrand Bradley, and Jane, George, Frederic, Susan and Elizabeth Morehouse.

Children:
64+Jesse, b. abt. 1756.
Rachel, b. abt. 1760, d. at Greenfield, 25 June 1832 ae. 72 (g. s.); m. 18 Jan. 1784, Joseph Bradley.

* Appeal from probate of will taken by Samuel Burr of Ridgefield and Seth Burr of Redding (brothers of Abel dec'd) and Abel Burr 2d of Redding (son of a bro. of Abel dec'd). They specified the following persons as interested in the estate: David, Polly, Caroline, and Zalmon S. Burr, David Scott and Betsey his wife, Louisa Burr, Nathan Scott and Sally his wife, Nehemiah Mead 2d and Anna his wife, and Noah Taylor and Parmelia his wife, all of Ridgefield; David, Sarah, Jonathan, Moses, James L., Abel, Delia, and John Burr, all of Redding; and David B. Burr of Stamford.

† Jacob-Cadwell's will, 2 Feb. 1824, proved 7 Mar. 1825; wife Eunice; to son Abel, land in Danbury; children, Abel, Sally, David, Anna, Harvey, John, Jacob, Amelia, and Emeline. Children, rec. Redding: Abel, b. 27 Aug. 1787; Sarah, b. 4 Feb. 1789; David, b. 25 Jan. 1791; Ann, b. 19 Feb. 1793; Harvey, b. 13 Feb. 1795; John, b. 15 Sept. 1798.

‡ Children, rec. Redding: Sturges, b. 22 Apr. 1788; Jesse, b. 5 Aug. 1791, d. 9 Feb. 1793; Eli, b. 16 July 1797.

60. Burr, Eliphalet, s. of Joseph.

Born 11 Jan. 1738/9; d. at Greenfield, 2 Mar. 1805 in 67 yr. (g. s.); m. 18 Jan. 1767, Prudence Wheeler, dau. of Thomas, bapt. 14 May 1737, d. 5 May 1816 ae. 79 (g. s.).

Will 2 June 1794, proved 25 Mar. 1805; of Weston; wife Prudence; bros.-in-law Nathan Wheeler and Thomas Wheeler, and sister-in-law Hannah wife of Eliphalet Lyon; Joseph, Increase, William, and Prudence Burr, children of dec'd bro. Increase Burr of Fairfield; Abel, Jonathan, Cadwell, Samuel, Charles, Seth, and David Burr, children of dec'd bro. Abel Burr of Redding; Jesse, son of bro. Ichabod Burr; John and David, sons of bro. Moses Burr of Weston; Eliphalet and Samuel, sons of bro. Samuel Burr of Fairfield. Distribution according to will, 24 May 1816: Increase Burr, Joseph Burr son of Joseph dec'd; Aaron Burr; Seth Burr; Jesse Burr; David Burr son of Moses; David Burr son of Abel dec'd; Abel, Jonathan, Cadwell, Samuel, and Charles, sons of Abel dec'd; Samuel son of Samuel Burr of State of N. Y.; Joseph Burr son of Increase dec'd; Eliphalet Burr son of Samuel; heirs of John Burr; Prudence Burr; heirs of William Burr.

61. Burr, Moses, s. of Joseph.

Born 22 Aug. 1741; d. at Easton, 14 Oct. 1825 in 85 yr. (g. s.); m. at Greenfield, 28 July 1761, Abigail Edwards. [Was she dau. of Thomas, bapt. at Stratfield, 19 Sept. 1736?]. She d. 13 June 1811 in 74 yr. (g. s.), but bur. 14 June 1815 ae. 74 (Trinity Church rec.).

Will 1 May 1820, proved 1 May 1825; two daus. Abigail and Sarah (apparently unmarried); dau. Hannah; heirs of son John Burr dec'd; daus. Rachel Beers and Grizzel Murwin; son David; gr. sons Jesse, Wakeman, Philip, and Eli Burr (sons of said David); gr. sons Moses Burr, Jr., and Jesse Burr, Exec'rs; heirs-at-law. Codicil, 8 June 1821; children of son John Burr dec'd,—Moses, Jr., Betsey wife of Joel Thorp, David, Bradley, and John Burr. The distribution calls Hannah wife of Simeon Fanton, and Grizzel wife of David Murwin.

The estates of Abigail and Sarah Burr of Easton were distributed, 24 Aug. 1852, to heirs of John Burr (Moses Burr, Bradley Burr, Joel and Betsey Thorp); heirs of Hannah Fanton (Burr and Caroline); and heirs of David Burr (one of whom was Willis).

Children, first bapt. Greenfield; others, Easton:

> Abigail, bapt. 17 Oct. 1762, d. before 1852, unm.
> John, bapt. Apr. 1766, d. at sea, 1802 in 37 yr. (g. s., Redding); sea captain; adm'n granted, 15 Dec. 1813, to Moses Burr, Jr., of Weston; distribution ordered to widow, and children,—Moses, David, Bradley, John, Betsey; m. Abigail Davis, of Harpersfield, N. Y., who d. 6 Mar. 1830 ae. 64 (g. s.).*
> David, bapt. 26 June 1768; m. Mary Banks, dau. of Jesse, b. 23 June 1774.
> Grizzel, bapt. Aug. 1771, d. at Easton, 5 June 1843 ae. 70 (g. s.); m. 27 Dec. 1791, David Merwin.
> Rachel, b. [say 1773]; m. 3 Dec. 1791, Sherwood Beers.
> Sarah, d. before 1852, unm.
> Hannah, b. [Feb. 1781], d. at Easton, 16 July 1844 ae. 63 yrs. 5 mos. (g. s.); m. Simeon Fanton.

62. Burr, Samuel, s. of Joseph.

Born 9 Mar. 1745/6; rem. abt. 1770 to Newburgh, N. Y. He m. Sybil Scudder.

Children:

> Eliphalet.
> Samuel, m. Charlotte Case.
> Martha, m. Abraham Tuttle.
> Sybil, m. Robert Gardner.
> Rachel.
> Hannah.

63. Burr, Ebenezer, s. of Timothy. Ens., Greenfield Co., May 1771; Lt., Mar. 1775.

Born 16 Mar. 1732/3; d. at Greenfield, 20 Oct. 1821 ae. 89 (g. s.); m. (1) 17 Jan. 1754, Sarah Sherwood, dau. of Benjamin, b. 13 May 1736, d. at Greenfield, 2 Nov. 1797.

He m. (2) Abigail (Gilbert), widow of John Thorp, b. 19 Dec. 1746. She was prob. the widow Abigail Burr who d. 7 Mar. 1830 (Miss Treadwell's book).

---

* Children, bapt. Trinity Church: Moses and Betsey, bapt. 8 Aug. 1790; David, bapt. 4 Nov. 1792; Bradley, bapt. 28 June 1795.

Will of Sarah, 16 Sept. 1797, proved 26 Dec. 1806; sons Ebenezer, Zalmon; dau. Esther Hawkins; three gr. children, Jonathan, Sarah and Elizabeth Lewis.

Dower was set to his widow, Feb. 1822. A partial distribution, Apr. 1822, named gr. sons Timothy, Rowland, Henry and Lewis Burr; Amanda and Morris, heirs of another gr. son, Morris Burr; gr. sons William and Wakeman Burr.

>Children [by first wife], rec. Fairfield, bapt. Greenfield:
>
>>Esther, b. 29 May 1755, d. at Greenfield, 2 Oct. 1836 ae. 81 (g. s.); m. (1) 17 June 1773, Moses Hill; m. (2) 26 Sept. 1782, Zachariah Hawkins; m. (3) Dea. John Staples.
>>
>>Eleanor, b. 18, bapt. 26 Mar. 1758, d. 22 May 1794 in 37 yr. (g. s.); m. 19 July 1778, Lothrop Lewis.
>>
>>Ebenezer, b. 14 Dec. 1760, bapt. 8 Feb. 1761 (ae. abt. 2 mos.), d. at Greenfield, 20 Feb. 1819 ae. 58 (g. s.); known as Ebenezer, 3d; m. Amelia Goodsell, b. 27 Mar. 1768, d. 3 Mar. 1835 ae. 67 (g. s.).*
>>
>>Zalmon, bapt. 30 Apr. 1769 (ae. 1 week), d. at Greenfield, 1 Mar. 1832 ae. 63 yrs. 10 mos. (g. s.); m. Molly Ogden, dau. of Moses, b. 1 May 1770.†

64. Burr, Jesse, s. of Ichabod.

Born about 1756; d. at Greenfield, 6 Feb. 1837 ae. 81 (g. s.); m. 10 Nov. 1780, Eleanor Ogden, dau. of David, b. abt. 1762, d. 19 Nov. 1835 ae. 73 (g. s.), ae. 77 (Greenfield Church).

Distribution, 15 Aug. 1838; Morris Burr; gr. sons Uriah and David Burr, David A., Frederick, and George Morehouse; gr.

---

* Two distributions, in 1819 and after Amelia's death in 1835, give particulars of the children, who were: Timothy, b. 3 Sept. 1788, bapt. at Easton, 11 June 1791, d. 16 Feb. 1858; m. Sarah Taylor, dau. of Barak of Danbury. Lewis, b. abt. 1790, bapt. 11 June 1791, d. at Greenfield, 26 Apr. 1866 ae. 76 (g. s.); m. at Trinity Church, 28 Feb. 1810, Marietta Bradley who d. 3 Oct. 1876 ae. 83-3-10 (g. s.). Morris, bapt. at Trinity Church, 4 Nov. 1792, d. at Greenfield, 17 Aug. 1816 ae. 24 (g. s.); m. Elizabeth Knapp; had children Morris and Amanda. Eleanor, b. [1794?], d. at Greenfield, 20 Aug. 1867 ae. 71 (g. s.); m. William Bradley. Amelia, bapt. 13 Nov. 1796, d. at Greenfield, 10 Nov. 1862 ae. 66 (g. s.); m. (1) Hezekiah Bradley; m. (2) Samuel Bradley. Betsey, bapt. 20 July 1800; m. Amos-Osborn Sherwood. Henry, b. [18 June 1802], d. at Greenfield, 24 Oct. 1870 ae. 68-4-6 (g. s.); m. Laurinda ———, who d. 12 May 1872 ae. 65-11-11 (g. s.). Sally, bapt. 28 Oct. 1804, d. y. Andrew, bapt. 1 June 1806, d. at Greenfield, 23 Nov. 1815 ae. 10 (g. s.) Wakeman, bapt. 9 July 1809, d. at Greenfield, 25 Jan. 1846 ae. 37-5-15 (g. s.). William, b. 24 Dec. 1810 (g. s.), bapt. 14 July 1811, d. at Greenfield, 1 Nov. 1864 (g. s.); m. Priscilla ———, who d. 10 Feb. 1844 ae. 31 (g. s.). Rowland.

† Children, bapt. Easton: Zalmon, bapt. 11 June 1791, m. Laura Wakeman; Sarah, bapt. Mar. 1793.

daus. Caroline wife of Moses Sherwood, Mary B. wife of Legrand Bradley, Jane S. wife of William Bulkley, Susan wife of Samuel W. Bradley, and Elizabeth wife of Samuel Wickson.

Children, two bapt. Fairfield:

Rachel, b. abt. 1782, d. 1817 ae. 34; m. Abijah Morehouse.
David, bapt. 26 June 1785, d. at Greenfield, 15 Aug. 1825 ae. 41 (g. s.); m. 24 Nov. 1803, Sarah Bulkley, dau. of Turney, bapt. 21 Mar. 1779.*
Uriah, bapt. 26 Nov. 1786, d. at Greenfield, 12 Oct. 1813 ae. 27 (g. s.).
Morris, b. [4 Dec. 1793], d. at Greenfield, 20 Aug. 1853 ae. 59-8-16 (g. s.); m. Arata Bulkley, b. [Aug. 1794], d. 13 June 1881 ae. 86 yrs. 10 mos. (g. s.).

Burr.

MISS SARAH, of Fairfield [dau. of Rev. Aaron], m. 24 June 1773, Mr. Tappan Reeve, of Litchfield.
AARON m. Tamison Bradley, b. 7 Feb. 1765. Aaron was Deputy for Redding, Oct. 1792.
JOSEPH m. Lucinda Bradley, b. 26 Apr. 1773.
PATT [Martha] had a dau. Elizabeth, bapt. 25 May 1788. [Greens Farms Church]
ELIZABETH m. 6 Jan. 1793, Jonathan Middlebrook. [Redding rec.]
LUCY, b. 3 Dec. 1780 m. 10 Apr. 1800, Jonathan Knapp. [Redding rec.]
HANNAH m. 6 May 1804, Isaiah Jennings. [Fairfield Church]
GRIZZEL m. 6 May 1804, Abraham Benson. [Fairfield Church]
MOLLY m. 8 Nov. 1793, Nathan Marvin. [Weston Church]
JOHN had children, bapt. Trinity Church: Anson, bapt. 10 May 1789; Lucretia, bapt. 7 Oct. 1792; Rebecca, bapt. 14 Apr. 1795.
WIDOW ABIGAIL d. 18 May 1833. [Miss Treadwell's book]
SOLOMON had a dau. Mary, bapt. Nov. 1795. [Easton Church]
SARAH m. in 1813, Nathan Wakeman. [Easton Church]

Burritt, William.

Son of Josiah and Mary (Peat), b. at Stratford, 29 Jan. 1709/10; d. at Redding, abt. 1752.

William m. (2) 7 June 1750, Elizabeth Burr; dau. of Stephen, b. 17 Jan. 1728, d. abt. 1779. She m. (2) 11 Oct. 1759, Alexander Bryant, and (3) 19 May 1761, Reuben Squire.

* Adm'n on David's estate was granted, 7 Sept. 1825, to Nathan Beers, with Jesse Burr, surety. Distribution, 1826, to the widow, now Mrs. Taylor, and the sons Uriah and David. Perhaps the wife of David was the Sarah wife of Phineas Taylor who d. at Greenfield, 27 Mar. 1849 ae. 70 (g. s.).

Inv. 22 Oct. 1752. Distribution, 1757; Widow; Mary; Abijah; Rhoda; Sybil; Philip; William.

Children [by first wife], bapt. Redding:

> Mary, bapt. 16 Dec. 1739.
> Abijah, bapt. 18 Jan. 1741.
> Rhoda, bapt. 24 Oct. 1742, d. Apr. 1816; m. 16 Oct. 1768, Increase Burr.
> Sybil, bapt. 19 Feb. 1744; m. by 1769, Joseph Murray, of Danbury.

Children [by second wife]:

> Philip, b. abt. 1750, res. Greenfield, 1771; m. at Redding, 1 Mar. 1774, Rachel Read.* Philip conveyed, 1779, his right from Dea. Stephen Burr, which was distributed to "my mother Elizabeth Burrit" out of the estate of my father William Burrit dec'd.
> William, b. abt. 1752, res. Redding, 1773.

Burritt, Ebenezer.

Son of Joseph and Mary (Wakelee), b. at Stratford, 28 Dec. 1726.

He m. at Redding, 25 May 1757, Elizabeth Platt, dau. of Obadiah, b. 10 May 1739.

Child, bapt. Fairfield:

> Thomas, bapt. 30 Aug. 1772.

Burritt, Isaac.

Born abt. July 1769; d. at Greenfield, 12 Aug. 1808 ae. 39 yrs. 1 mo. (g. s.).

He m. (1) Huldah Redfield, bapt. 28 Jan. 1776, d. 25 Sept. 1798 ae. 22-8-20 (g. s.); m. (2) at Westport, 13 Mar. 1808, Elizabeth Sherwood, dau. of Daniel, b. 24 July 1771, d. 11 Sept. 1826 ae. 55 (g. s.).†

Of Fairfield, will 20 Feb., proved 22 Aug. 1808; Seth Redfield; Isaac Burritt Redfield; residue to wife Elizabeth; William Sherwood, Jr., Exec'r.

Will of Huldah of Fairfield, 21 June 1798, proved 27 Aug. 1799; to husband Isaac, all Est.

---

* Children, bapt. Redding: William, bapt. 9 Apr. 1775; Betty, bapt. 4 May 1777; Abijah, bapt. 21 Mar. 1779.
† For Elizabeth's will, see Daniel Sherwood (50).

Burritt [Unplaced].

ABIGAIL m. 9 Aug. 1744, Timothy Wheeler. [Fairfield rec.]
PHEBE m. 28 Nov. 1797, Salmon Sherwood. [Weston rec.]
WAKEMAN had children, Abigail, Elizabeth, Wakeman, and Stephen, bapt. at Westport, 31 Mar. 1793, of whom Abigail d. 21 Aug. 1793. One Wakeman Burritt, son of Eunice Morehouse, bapt. at Westport, 23 Mar. 1783. One Wakeman of New York m. 27 Sept. 1809, Grace Burr.

Burroughs [Unplaced].

STEPHEN, of Stratfield, m. 27 Mar. 1792, Mary Jennings, of Boston, Mass. [Fairfield Church]

Burton, Solomon.

Son of Benjamin and Bethia (Curtis) Burton, b. at Stratford, 9 Aug. 1718.

He m. (1) Ruth Summers, dau. of Samuel, bapt. 27 June 1719, d. at Stratfield, 9 Nov. 1748 in 30 yr. (g. s.). He m. (2) at Trumbull, 12 Dec. 1749, Hannah Sherman.

Children [by first wife]:

Benjamin, bapt. at Redding, 19 Dec. 1742, d. y.
Ruth, bapt. at Redding, 14 Oct. 1744, d. at Weston, 17 Oct. 1803 ae. 59 (g. s.); m. (rec. Fairfield) 18 Oct. 1764, Hezekiah Osborn.
Solomon, b. abt. 1746, d. at Easton, 1 May 1821 ae. 75 (g. s.); m. Hannah ———, b. abt. 1749, d. 25 July 1835 ae. 86 (g. s.).*
Abigail, b. abt. 1748, the daughter bapt. 26 Oct. 1748, d. at Easton, 20 Feb. 1812; m. Matthew Hubbell.

Children [by second wife]:

Sarah, b. Sept. 1750.
Cyrus, bapt. at Stratfield, 25 Dec. 1754.
? Cyrus, b. (rec. Weston) 24 Feb. 1760, d. at Easton, 12 Apr. 1812 in 53 yr. (g. s.); m. (1) 27 Dec. 1781, Anna Jackson, b. 13 June 1760, d. 19 July 1791 ae. 31-1-6 (g. s.); m. (2) 20 Dec. 1792, Elizabeth Wilcoxson, b. 30 Mar. 1758, d. 7 Jan. 1826 in 68 yr. (g s.).†

---

* Children, bapt. Easton: Ruth, b. 21 Jan., bapt. 25 Mar. 1770: m. 7 June 1789, Gideon Wheeler. Silas-Curtis, b. 2 Sept., bapt. 1 Nov. 1773, d. at Easton, 22 June 1844 ae. 71 (g. s.); m. 30 Sept. 1798, Anne Gregory, b. 21 Apr. 1776, d. 11 Jan. 1836 ae. 60 (g. s.).

† Children by first wife, rec. Weston: Lyman, b. 4 May 1782; David, b. 24 July 1784; John, b. 21 Oct. 1786; Mary, b. 12 Aug. 1788, d. 26 Apr. 1793. Child by second wife: Cyrus W., b. 30 June 1798, d. at Easton, 10 Nov. 1824 in 27 yr. (g. s.).

Burton [Unplaced].

CHARITY, b. 10 Apr. 1760, m. 28 Apr. 1791, Samuel Fairweather. [Weston rec.]

Burwell, Stephen, s. of Samuel.

Born at New Haven, 17 Jan. 1696/7; d. at Newtown, 21 Apr. 1784 ae. 88 (g. s.); m. (rec. New Haven) 26 Dec. 1723, Anna Sherman, dau. of Daniel, b. at Stratford, 3 Dec. 1697.

He was son of Ens. Samuel and Rebecca (Bunnell) Burwell of West Haven. His sister Dinah m. (rec. Stratford) 24 Jan. 1722/3, Samuel Fairchild; another sister, Elizabeth, m. (rec. Stratford) 16 June 1725, Zaccheus Needham, of Rye, N. Y.; and a bro., Nathan, settled in Norwalk. Still another sister, Mary, m. (rec. Newtown) 10 Oct. 1733, Benjamin Glover.

Children, first six rec. New Haven, last two Fairfield:

Sarah, b. 25 June 1725.
Samuel, b. 28 Feb. 1726/7, d. 30 Mar. 1727.
Rebecca, b. 16 May 1728, bapt. at Christ's Church (Prot. Epis.), Stratford, 4 Aug. 1728, d. y.
Ann, b. 6 Nov. 1729, bapt. 2 Jan. 1729/30.
Stephen, b. 10 Apr. 1731, bapt. 16 Apr. 1731, d. 4 Apr. 1803 ae. 72 (called of Newtown, rec. at Trinity Church, New Haven); m. Sarah ———.
Mary, b. 16 Apr. 1733, bapt. 9 May 1733.
Samuel, b. abt. 1737, d. at Newtown, 11 June 1767 ae. 30; m. Rebecca ———.
William, b. 6 May 1740, d. at Newtown, 11 June 1815 ae. 75 (g. s.); m. Phebe ———.
Rebecca, b. 24 May 1741.

Butler [Unplaced].

EPHRAIM and Thankful had: David, bapt. 23 Feb. 1777. [Redding Church]

Byington, John.

He m. at Redding, 16 Nov. 1763, Sarah Gray, dau. of James, b. 19 Apr. 1742.

Children, rec. Redding:

John, b. 17 Sept., bapt. 4 Nov. 1764.
Lucina, b. 4 July, bapt. 10 Aug. 1766.
Reuben, b. 2 May, bapt. 11 June 1769.
Joel, b. 1 Mar., bapt. 28 Apr. 1771; m. 1 Oct. 1795, Deborah Rockwell of Ridgefield.*
Aaron, b. 14 Sept., bapt. 29 Oct. 1775; m. 2 Jan. 1797, Mary Darling, dau. of Benjamin, b. 25 Oct. 1778.
Sarah, b. 22 Apr., bapt. 21 June 1778.
Lucy, b. 19 May 1780 (the "dark day").
Rachel, b. 4 Sept. 1785, d. 26 Jan. 1788.

Cable [Vol. I, pp. 136-138].

```
1 John (    -1682) m. (1) Sarah ——; (2) Ann (——) Betts.
(By 1): 2 John (1641-1673) m. Elizabeth ——.
          3 John (    -1724) m. Abigail Sherwood.
               5 George (1703-1763).
               6 Jonathan (1705-    ).
               7 John (1709-1760).
               8 Andrew (1712-1761).
               9 Daniel (1714-1760).
          4 Joseph (    -1715) m. Abigail Adams.
              10 Joseph (1701-    ).
              11 Samuel (    -1740).
              12 Benjamin (1712-1795).
```

5. **Cable, George,** s. of John.

Born abt. 1703; d. at Westport, 17 Sept. 1763 in 60 yr. (g. s.); m. 17 Feb. 1729, Sarah Shaw, dau. of Nathaniel, bapt. 11 Apr. 1708, d. 29 Jan. 1787.

Will 30 Aug. 1763, proved 26 Sept. 1763; eldest son John; wife Sarah, who received life use of negro girl Phyllis; six sons, John, Jabez, Thomas, Nathaniel, George, Jonathan; five daus. Ann, Abigail, Temperance, Margery, Sarah; John Andrews of Fairfield, Exec'r. Sarah Cable chose mother Sarah guardian, 26 Sept. 1763. Distribution 10 May 1766: six sons as in will; daus. Ann Hanford, Temperance Andrews, Sarah Peach, Abigail Taylor, Margery Squire; widow.

---

* Children, rec. Redding: Belinda, b. 16 Aug. 1798; George, b. 1 Mar. 1802; Mary, b. 28 Apr. 1807.

Children, rec. Fairfield, three youngest bapt. Westport:

    Ann, b. 19 May 1730; m. 15 Sept. 1752, Elnathan Hanford, Jr., of Norwalk.
13+John, b. 15 Aug. 1731.
14+Jabez, b. 14 Apr. 1733; conveyed to bro. George, right in grist mill at Compo, 1766.
15+Thomas, b. 16 Aug. 1735.
    Abigail, b. 19 May 1737, d. 11 Feb. 1803 ae. 65; m. 27 Nov. 1757, Gamaliel Taylor, of Norwalk; they conveyed 1764.
    Temperance, b. 16 Jan. 1739, d. at Westport, 18 Mar. 1819 ae. 79 (g. s.); m. (1) 28 Mar. 1758, John Andrews, Jr.; m. (2) 22 Sept. 1779, Ens. Ebenezer Morehouse.
    Nathaniel, b. 14 Nov. 1740, d. 24 Nov. 1812 ae. 71 (g. s., Westport).
16+George, b. 14 Aug. 1742.
    Margery, b. 1 Jan., bapt. 5 Feb. 1744; m. at Greenfield, 21 Aug. 1766, Seth Squire.
    Sarah, b. July, bapt. 27 July 1746; m. 15 Nov. 1764, William Peck.
    Jonathan, b. Aug., bapt. 1 Sept. 1751; m. (mar. license, N. Y., 16 May 1778), Sarah Ludlow.

6. **Cable, Jonathan,** s. of John.

Born [say 1705].

He m. 3 Sept. 1728, Mary Bennett, dau. of Thomas.

Perhaps he m. (2) at Weston, 30 Sept. 1767, widow Rebecca Chard.

Children, rec. Fairfield:

    Abigail, b. 6 Apr. 1729; m. at Wilton, 21 Feb. 1748/9, John Cole.
    Eunice, b. 4 Nov. 1731; m. 16 Jan. 1749/50, David Sherwood, Jr.
    Sarah, b. 19 Aug. 1734.
    Betty, b. 12 Nov. 1737; m. at Weston, 22 May 1760, John Thompson.
    Margery, b. 1 Oct. 1741, bapt. at Greenfield, 4 Oct. 1741, d. 10 July 1742.
    Damaris, b. 29 Apr. 1745, bapt. at Westport, 16 June 1745; m. at Weston, 3 June 1767, Jabez Sherwood.

7. **Cable, John,** s. of John. Ens., 7th Co., Fairfield, May 1753.

Born [say 1709]; d. at Weston, 24 Mar. 1760.

He m. 26 Sept. 1733, Ann Davis, who d. in 1773.

Est. of Ens. John distributed 4 Apr. 1761: widow Ann; children Nehemiah, William, Isaac, John, Emit, Ann, Elizabeth. Isaac chose George Cable for guardian, June 1760.

Inv. of Widow Ann, 3 Mar. 1773.

Children:
> Emitt, b. 28 June 1734; m. at Greenfield, 8 Aug. 1754, Onesimus Bradley.
> 17+Nehemiah, b. 19 July 1736.
> 18+William, b. 23 Sept. 1739.
> Thaddeus, b. 21 Mar. 1742, bapt. at Westport, 16 May 1742, d. 13 Mar. 1760.
> Isaac, b. 7 Sept. 1744.
> Elizabeth, b. 12 Sept. 1746, bapt. at Greenfield, 23 Nov. 1746; m. at Weston, Apr. 1762, James Disbrow. Elizabeth Disbrow conveyed 1768 land from father John Cable, mentioning sisters Emet and Ann.
> Anna, b. 4 Nov. 1750, bapt. at Greenfield, 19 Dec. 1750, d. at Trumbull, 13 Sept. 1826 in 77 yr. (g. s.); m. at Weston, 4 Apr. 1776, James Bennett.*
> John, b. 29 Apr. 1753.

8. **Cable, Andrew**, s. of John.

Born [say 1712]; d. at Fairfield in 1761; m. Rebecca Wheeler, b. 14 Feb. 1719, d. 23 Feb. 1799 ae. 80 yrs. 9 days (g. s., Stratfield).

Adm'n granted to widow Rebecca, 4 Aug. 1761. Distribution 14 Oct. 1763; widow Rebecca; eldest son Andrew; sons Justus, Wheeler; dau. Olive; dau. Ann had rec'd portion.

Will of Rebecca of Stratfield, 27 Apr. 1791, proved 18 Mar. 1799; daus. Anne Taylor, Olive Vaughn; two gr. children, Catherine and Rebecca Cable, daus. of son Wheeler Cable; bro. Benjamin Wheeler, Exec'r.

Children, three bapt. Westport:
> Olive, bapt. 6 Mar. 1743; m. ——— Vaughn.†
> Andrew, bapt. 2 June 1745, d. in 1768, called of Stratford; adm'n granted to Rebecca Cable, 18 Apr. 1768.
> Justus, bapt. 3 July 1748, d. by 1770, called of Fairfield; adm'n granted to Rebecca Cable, 29 Jan. 1770.
> Ann, m. ——— Taylor.
> Wheeler, b. abt. 1758, d. at Stratfield, 3 June 1782 in 24 yr. (g. s.); m. ———.‡

---

* Abigail Sanford, dau. of Anna Cable, bapt. 14 Aug. 1774.

† Est. of Wheeler C. Vaughn of Fairfield was ordered distributed, Aug. 1807, to bro. and sisters: John Vaughn, Polly wife of Israel Blackman, and Catherine. These were prob. the children of Olive.

‡ One Wheeler Cable m. at Easton, 29 Feb. 1808, Huldah Fairchild.

9. Cable, Daniel, s. of John.

Born [say 1714]; d. at Fairfield in 1760; m. 7 June 1739, Sarah Crane, dau. of Elijah, b. [say 1718].

Inv. 5 May 1761. Adm'n granted to Onesimus Bradley, 10 Mar. 1761; he was chosen guardian by Josiah Cable, 30 Dec. 1760. John Olmstead was chosen guardian by Sarah, and appointed guardian to Abigail, Jan. 1761; John Bradley, 2d, appointed for Elijah, Mar. 1761.

Children, rec. Fairfield:
Abijah, b. 24 June 1742, bapt. Westport, 7 Nov. 1742.
19+Josiah, b. 15 Apr. 1744, bapt. Greenfield, May 1744.
20+Daniel, b. 7 Mar. 1746, bapt. Greenfield, 13 July 1746.
Sarah, b. 10 Jan. 1749, bapt. Greenfield 23 Apr. 1749.
Abigail, b. 22 Nov. 1751; m. at Easton 25 Mar. 1770, David Gorham.
Jerusha, b. 18 May 1753, living 1821; m. at Greenfield, 19 June 1774, Isaac Webb.
Elijah, b. 18 Sept. 1755.

10. Cable, Joseph, s. of Joseph.

Born abt. 1700/1; prob. lived in Salem, Westchester County, N. Y.

Children (hypothetical):
Samuel, res. 1761, Cortlandt, Westchester County, N. Y.; m. at Redding, 7 Jan. 1756, Mary Platt, dau. of Josiah of Norwalk and Redding.
William, was of Salem, Westchester County, N. Y., 1773, when he purchased in Stratford, and doubtless was father of Abner of Monroe (b. at Ridgefield, 6 Dec. 1759), to whom he conveyed his dwelling house. William had children bapt. at Salem: Ruamah, 13 May 1764; Elizabeth, 22 May 1768.*
James, m. at Salem, 15 Apr. 1756, Elizabeth Peat.
Sarah, m. at Salem, 3 Apr. 1759, Abraham Slawson.
Joseph, m. at Salem, 18 Apr. 1764, Martha Cole.
Mercy, m. at Salem, 26 June 1764, Alexander Hubs [Hobby?].

11. Cable, Samuel, s. of Joseph.

He d. at Stratfield in 1740; m. at Stratfield, 27 July 1731, Ann Wheeler, dau. of Timothy, b. 2 Dec. 1713.

---

* Quite likely the wife of William Cable was Anne Wilson, dau. of Thomas of Ridgefield, whose will 1775 called her Anne Cable. This Anne had a bro. Abner Wilson, after whom the son Abner Cable could have been named.

THE FAMILIES OF OLD FAIRFIELD 223

Will 2 Jan. 1739/40, proved 23 May 1740; wife Ann, Exec'x; only son Samuel. The son chose Timothy Wheeler of Fairfield for guardian, 27 Nov. 1749.

Samuel Cable, [Jr.], of Stratfield, conveyed 1755 to Benjamin Wheeler, land set to me in distribution of Est. of grandfather Timothy Wheeler of Stratfield dec'd.

Child, bapt. Stratfield:
21+Samuel, bapt. 8 Sept. 1734.

12. **Cable, Benjamin,** s. of Joseph.

Born abt. 1712; d. at Norwalk in 1795; m. Martha ———.

Will 28 Jan. 1783, proved 10 Sept. 1795; called himself of Norwalk; gr. son Ebenezer Cable, son of dau. Grizzel; sons Abraham, Gershom; daus. Grace, Grizzel Cable.

Children, bapt. Westport:
Samuel, bapt. 7 Apr. 1742, d. y.
Martha, bapt. 31 July 1743, d. 26 Aug. 1746.
Grace, bapt. 4 Nov. 1744, d. at Weston, 1819. Will 8 Oct. 1800, proved 27 Apr. 1819; Sally, Grace, Nabby, and Elizur Cable, children of bro. Gershom dec'd; Benjamin, son of bro. Abraham. Distribution 20 Mar. 1820: Sally wife of Thaddeus Perry, Grace wife of Enos Read, Nabby wife of David Rogers, Elizur Cable.
Grissel, bapt. 30 Mar. 1746.*
Benjamin, bapt. 1 Nov. 1747, d. y.
Abraham, bapt. 19 Aug. 1750; res. Salem, Westchester County, N. Y., 1794, and Poundridge 1796; m. Mary, widow of Thomas Gray.†
Gershom, bapt. 24 June 1753, "hung himself at Norfield," 18 Apr. 1800 (Miss Treadwell's book); Inv. 1 Sept. 1800 (Norwalk); m. at Weston, 23 Feb. 1783, widow Biah Meeker.‡

13. **Cable, John,** s. of George.

Born 15 Aug. 1731; his father placed him in business as a merchant in New York.

---

* Ebenezer, son of "Griswold" Cable, bapt. at Weston, 4 Dec. 1768. Ebenezer Cable chose Squire Adams for guardian, 17 Mar. 1788.

† While living in Weston, he had children bapt. there: Martha, bapt. 19 Apr. 1778; Benjamin, bapt. 10 Sept. 1780; Joab, bapt. 19 Mar. 1786.

‡ Children: Sarah, b. [15 Aug. 1783], d. at Weston, 2 May 1864 ae. 80-8-17 (g. s.); m. 24 Dec. 1806, Thaddeus Perry. Grace, m. Enos Read. Nabby, m. David Rogers. Elizur, b. [1 Mar. 1794], d. at Weston, 15 July 1876 ae. 82-4-14 (g. s.).

He m. at Westport, 3 May 1756, Ann Laborie, dau. of Dr. James, b. at Stratford, Nov. 1731.

In 1771, John Cable, formerly of Fairfield, now of Glastonbury, Conn., released a mortgage.

Children, rec. Fairfield:
> John, b. 27 Feb. 1757.
> Jane, b. 19 Apr. 1759.
> James, b. 1 July 1761.

14. Cable, Jabez, s. of George.

Born 14 Apr. 1733; rem. to St. Johns, N. B.

He m. at Westport, 24 Feb. 1754, Mary Denmore [also called Denbo]; dau. of Salathiel.

Children, first two bapt. at Westport, the others at Weston:
> Jared, bapt. 11 Mar. 1756.
> Molly, bapt. 2 Apr. 1756, bur. 10 Sept. 1776 (Trinity Epis. Church rec., New Haven); m. at New Haven, in 1773, Nathaniel Black.
> Ruth, bapt. 5 Feb. 1758, bur. at New Haven, 25 Jan. 1774.
> Salathiel, bapt. 6 Nov. 1760.

15. Cable, Thomas, s. of George.

Born 16 Aug. 1735; d. abt. 1797.

He m. Rhoda Taylor, dau. of Noah; in 1798 she was of New York City.

Children, bapt. Westport:
> Joseph, bapt. 9 Jan. 1763; res. 1790, Dorset, Bennington County, Vt.
> Thomas, bapt. 9 Sept. 1764; m. 6 Sept. 1786, Charlotte Guire, dau. of Stephen, bapt. 25 Dec. 1768.*
> Samuel, bapt. 2 Apr. 1769, d. at sea, 13 Aug. 1794; m. 13 July 1788, Charity Nash, bapt. 23 Apr. 1769; she m. (2) 4 Aug. 1805, Thomas Sanders, of Weston.
> Lewis, bapt. 12 May 1771; m. 17 Dec. 1793, Sally Bryan.
> William, bapt. 1 Apr. 1773.†
> Nathaniel-Shaw, bapt. 14 May 1775.
> Sarah, bapt. 18 May 1777.

---

* Child of Charlotte Cable: Thomas Guyer, bapt. at Westport, 15 Dec. 1793.

† William B. Cable, a young man, drowned between West Indies and New York, Sept. 1804 (Greens Farms Church).

16. **Cable, George,** s. of George.

Born 14 Aug. 1742, d. at Oxford, 1802.

He m. at Westport, 28 Feb. 1768, Esther Hanford.

Adm'n granted, 14 May 1802, to Isaac Cable of Oxford and Benjamin Morehouse of New Haven.

Children, bapt. Westport:

> Grace, bapt. 29 Jan. 1768; m. at Westport, 16 Nov. 1788, Thomas Nash, Jr.
> Temperance, bapt. 19 May 1771; m. at Milford, 15 Mar. 1795, Benjamin Morehouse.
> Isaac, bapt. 3 June 1773.
> Esther, bapt. 19 Feb. 1775; Esther "of Oxford" m. at Westport, 12 Nov. 1809, Samuel Pearsall.
> Betsey, bapt. 28 July 1776.

17. **Cable, Nehemiah,** s. of John.

Born 19 July 1736; d. 4 Jan. 1813.

He m. at Weston, 22 Feb. 1759, Martha Bradley; dau. of Joseph, b. 2 Sept. 1737; wife of Nehemiah d. 9 Sept. 1808 (Miss Treadwell's book).

Children, bapt. Weston:

> Eunice, bapt. 6 Oct. 1759; m. 8 June 1780, Elias Godfrey.
> Thaddeus, bapt. 29 Aug. 1762, d. at Easton, 12 Dec. 1828 ae. 66 (g. s.). Will 11 Dec. 1828, proved 7 Jan. 1829; sister Hannah Cable; bro. Mahli Cable's dau. Emeline Cable; sister Abigail Morehouse.
> Isaac, bapt. 6 Aug. 1764.
> Hannah, bapt. 9 Nov. 1766, d. at Weston, 23 Apr. 1836, unm. Will 28 July 1834, proved 21 May 1836; bro. Mahli Cable; sister Abigail Morehouse (called of Danbury in the distribution).
> Aaron, bapt. 14 Aug. 1769;* ? m. at Westport, 23 Feb. 1806, Sally Bulkley.
> Anna, bapt. 11 May 1772, living 1809; m. 30 Sept. 1795, Eliphalet Beers.
> Levi, bapt. 20 July 1774.
> Abigail, bapt. 8 Nov. 1778; m. —— Morehouse, of Danbury.
> Mahli, bapt. 6 Oct. 1782, d. at Easton in 1850; m. (1) Rachel ——, who d. at Easton, 6 Mar. 1830 ae. 36 (g. s.); m. (2) Eunice-Maria ——.†

---
* One Aaron d. 27 Feb. 1859 (Miss Treadwell's book).

† Mahli's will, 30 Mar. 1848, proved 22 Mar. 1850; to wife Eunice-Mariah and at her death to her children; dau. Emeline now wife of Joseph Davis, Jr., has had full share.

18. Cable, William, s. of John.

Born 23 Sept. 1739; d. in the Army, 21 Feb. 1778 [Rev. War Rolls]; m. at Greenfield, 1 Feb. 1764, Ruth Merwin, dau. of Daniel, b. 17 July 1741.

Adm'n granted to Ruth, 23 Oct. 1779.

Children, bapt. Weston:

> Leman, bapt. 23 Sept. 1764.
> Esther, bapt. 31 Aug. 1766; ? m. at Weston, 13 Sept. 1792, Nehemiah Bradley.
> Olive, bapt. 31 July 1768; m. at Trinity Church, 23 July 1787, Daniel Coley.
> John, bapt. 20 May 1770, d. y.
> John, bapt. 19 Apr. 1772.
> William, bapt. 17 Dec. 1775.
> Mary, bapt. 9 May 1778 (as child of Widow Ruth); ? m. at Weston, 30 Apr. 1795, Eli Gould.

19. Cable, Josiah, s. of Daniel.

Born 15 Apr. 1744.

He m. at Greenfield, 25 Sept. 1763, Mary Williams, dau. of David, b. 12 Dec. 1741.

Child, first bapt. Greenfield, rec. Weston:

> David, b. 11 Apr., bapt. 20 May 1764 (ae. abt. 5 weeks); rem. to St. Johns, N. B.
> Polly, b. 26 Feb. 1772.
> Hannah, b. 1775.
> Jesse, b. 1775.

20. Cable, Daniel, s. of Daniel.

Born 7 Mar. 1746; d. at St. Johns, N. B., 1818.

He m. at Easton, 22 Nov. 1769, Eunice Turney, dau. of Thomas, b. 19 Jan. 1752.

21. Cable, Samuel, s. of Samuel.

Bapt. at Stratfield, 8 Sept. 1734; bur. there 6 Nov. 1806 ae. 73 (Trinity Church rec.).

He m. (1) Mary Porter, dau. of Daniel, b. at Stratford, 20 Dec. 1738, d. at Stratfield, 7 Dec. 1793 ae. 54 (g. s.).

He m. (2) Jerusha ———.

Dower set to Jerusha, 3 Dec. 1806. Distribution 8 Oct. 1807: eldest child Charity; eldest son Samuel; second son William; youngest dau. Ann wife of James French.

Children [by first wife]:

> Charity.
> Daniel-Porter, b. abt. 1761, d. 20 Apr. 1765 in 4 yr. (g. s.).
> Samuel, b. abt. 1767, bur. 26 June 1817 ae. 50 (drowned in Bridgeport Harbor; Trinity Church rec.); m. at Trinity Church, 20 Oct. 1802, Mary French.
> William; ? m. at Trinity Church, 1 Nov. 1798, Polly French.
> Ann, b. abt. 1771, d. 18 Mar. 1841 ae. 70 (g. s.); m. (1) ——— Beardsley; m. (2) James-Redfield French.

Cable [*Unplaced*].

> EUNICE m. Mar. 1790, Samuel Goodsell. [Easton Church]
> SARAH m. 1 Dec. 1784, Abraham Taylor. [Redding rec.]
> Ebenezer; William Cable of Fairfield appointed his guardian, Mar. 1761. He m. 9 Jan. 1788, Mary Parrott. Children, rec. Weston: Sarah, b. 25 May 1788; Priscilla, b. 13 Apr. 1792. Dower in Est. of Ebenezer of Weston ordered set to widow Mary, 22 Jan. 1807. An Ebenezer had children, bapt. Weston: Ebenezer, Joseph, and Mary-Couch, bapt. 8 Nov. 1795; Deborah, bapt. 13 Nov. 1796.
> RHODA, of New York, m. 20 Mar. 1799, Stephen Gorham. [Greens Farms Church]
> SARAH d. 4 May 1807. [Miss Treadwell's book]

Cadwell, Jacob.

Son of Edward and Deborah (Bunce) Cadwell, b. at Hartford, 22 Feb. 1708/9; grad. Yale Coll. 1729; rem. by 1737 to Fairfield; d. in 1765.

He m. Ann Osborn, bapt. 15 July 1711.

Children:

> Sarah, m. 16 Jan. 1751, Abel Burr.
> Ann, bapt. at Fairfield, 17 July 1737.

Calhoun, Nathaniel.

He m. Abigail ———.

She m. (2) 27 May 1767, Isaac Oysterbanks.

Children, bapt. Westport:
> Eunice, bapt. 8 July 1750; m. at Weston, 21 Dec. 1774, Peter Guire.
> Olive, bapt. 22 Apr. 1753, d. in 1820; m. 20 Sept. 1772, Jonathan Beers, of Weston.

Camp [*Unplaced*].

> CAPT. JONATHAN, of Norwalk, m. 17 Apr. 1766, Miss Abigail Shove. [Fairfield Church]

Campbell, Archibald.

He m. by 1766, Isabel Osborn, dau. of Samuel, b. 1 Feb. 1730/1, d. Dec. 1784 (Perry Diary); they had a dau. Elizabeth, bapt. at Westport, 10 Jan. 1773, who was living unm. at Fairfield in 1792.

Canfield [*Unplaced*].

> PHEBE m. 14 Oct. 1774, Samuel Lyon. [Weston Church]
> HANNAH m. 31 Dec. 1778, Seth Squire. [Weston Church]
> CHLOE m. 25 Oct. 1781, Russell Disbrow. [Weston Church]
> ELIZABETH m. 14 Apr. 1763, Jonathan Robinson. [Greenfield Church]
> EZEKIEL m. 20 Oct. 1773, Ann Jacocks.* [Greens Farms Church]
> ICHABOD m. 18 Aug. 1774, Mary Batterson.† [Greens Farms Church]
> DAVID, of Wilton, m. 23 Nov. 1785, Abigail Godfrey. [Greens Farms Church]
> ELIZABETH m. 8 June 1796, Moses Jerard, of L. I. [Greens Farms Church]
> JOSIAH m. 27 Oct. 1799, Abigail Sanford. Child: Mary, b. 9 May 1801. [Redding rec.]
> SARAH m. 31 Dec. 1781, James Dann, at Wilton. [Weston Church]
> PRUDENCE m. 30 Mar. 1800, Nathan Coley. [Weston Church]

Capers, William.

Of St. Helena, S. C.

He m. 9 Sept. 1789, Abigail Burr, dau. of Gershom, bapt. 9 Sept. 1770.

---

* They had children, bapt. Westport: Josiah, bapt. 5 June 1774; Seth, bapt. 23 Feb. 1776. Children, bapt. Weston: Pruella, bapt. 5 July 1778; Rebecca, bapt. 14 May 1780; Elizabeth, bapt. 19 May 1782; Leman, bapt. 13 Sept. 1789; Molly, bapt. 13 Nov. 1795.

† Widow Mary Canfield had children, Elizabeth and Rachel, bapt. at Westport, 8 Nov. 1777.

THE FAMILIES OF OLD FAIRFIELD 229

Children, rec. Fairfield:
>Charles William, b. 25 Nov. 1794.
>Nathaniel Lothrop, b. 5 Dec. 1798.

Carley, John.

He m. Sarah Sherwood, dau. of David, b. 8 Jan. 1710.
Rem. to the Oblong, Dutchess County, N. Y.; both living 1760.

Carley, Abraham.

He m. Susanna ———.
She m. (2) 28 Feb. 1759, Thaddeus Gray.

Children, bapt. Westport:
>Joel, bapt. 26 June 1748.
>Martha, bapt. 9 Sept. 1750.
>Job, bapt. 24 Feb. 1754.

Carley [Unplaced].

>NANCY m. 24 Nov. 1793, Levi Davis. [Weston Church]

Carson, Walter.

Became school-teacher, 1771 (Perry Diary).
He m. 12 Mar. 1775, Sarah Squire, dau. of Joseph, bapt. 14 Dec. 1755, d. at Fairfield, 20 Nov. 1814 in 59 yr. (g. s.).
Will of Sarah, 25 Jan., proved 2 Dec. 1814; dau.-in-law Elinor Carson; son William Carson; dau. Catherine Gold.

Children, bapt. Westport:
>Catherine, bapt. 21 Oct. 1775; m. at Fairfield, Aug. 1794, Jason Gould.
>William, bapt. 7 Nov. 1779; m. Eleanor ———.

Case [Unplaced].

>FRANCES m. 29 Nov. 1747, Thaddeus Williams. [Greenfield Church]

Chambers, Thomas.

He was bapt. at Fairfield Church, 9 Apr. 1710; m. abt. 1715, Elizabeth (Sanford), widow of Joseph Jackson, and previously of Joshua Jackson. She was dau. of Ezekiel Sanford, b. 6 Sept. 1679.

Children, recorded and bapt. at Stratfield:
Mary, b. 19 July [1716], bapt. 2 Sept. 1716.
Joseph, b. 24(?) Mar. 1718, bapt. 20 Mar. 1718.
Thomas, b. 20 Jan. [1719/20]; rem. to Newtown; m. at Fairfield, 11 Oct. 1742, Mary Bulmore.*
Jemima, b. 22 Feb. 1721/2.
Hezekiah, b. 1[—] Jan. [1723/4].

Chambers [Unplaced].

—— m. Mar. 1773, Naomi Wakelee. [Easton Church]

Chapman, Richard.

Richard of Braintree (d. 1669) and wife Mary were parents of Hope of Westerly (b. 1655), who was father of this Richard, b. 20 Feb. 1687/8.

He m. Sarah Booth, dau. of John and Dorothy (Hawley) Booth,—correct Volume I, page 90, accordingly.

Of Stratford, will 22 Apr. 1741, proved 7 July 1741; wife Sarah; daus. Dorothy White, Sarah Johnson, Elizabeth Salter, Martha French, Mary Curtis, Ann Hawley; sons Hope, Daniel, Benjamin; dau. Ruth Chapman.

On 8 Jan. 1744/5, Sarah widow of Richard Chapman of Stratford, John Salter and Elizabeth his wife, Abner Curtis and Mary his wife, all of Wallingford, Robert Johnson and Sarah his wife of Waterbury, and Samuel French and Martha his wife of Derby, and Ruth Chapman, all in New Haven County, and Hope Chapman of Stratford, conveyed to Joseph Seeley of Stratford a house and shop.

Children:
Dorothy, bapt. at Stratfield as dau. of Richard and Sarah of Stonington, 5 Sept. 1708; m. —— White.
Sarah, b. [say 1710]; m. at Stratford, 21 Mar. 1727/8, Robert Johnson.
Elizabeth, b. [say 1712]; m. John Salter.

---

* Their twelve children were rec. at Newtown, 1743-64.

Martha, b. abt. 1714, d. at Derby, 29 Oct. 1780 ae. near 66; m. (rec. Derby) 17 Dec. 1733, Samuel French.
Hope, b. [say 1716]; m. abt. 1741, Deborah Treadwell, dau. of Timothy.*
Mary, b. [say 1718], d. 24 May 1778; m. 7 Dec. 1738, Abner Curtis.
Ann, b. [say 1720]; m. (rec. New Milford) 12 June 1739, Ephraim Hawley, Jr.
Daniel, b. [say 1722].
Benjamin, b. [say 1724].
Ruth, b. [say 1726].

1. **Chapman, (Rev.) Daniel.**

Son of Dea. Nathaniel and Mary (Collins), b. at Saybrook, 14 Mar. 1688/9; grad. Yale Coll. 1707; minister at Greens Farms (Westport), 1711-41; d. 28 Nov. 1741 in 52 yr. (g. s.); m. Grissel Dennie, dau. of Albert, bapt. 28 Feb. 1696/7, d. 10 June 1754 in 57 yr. (g. s.).

Deed of partition, June 1759, of Phineas, Dennie and Mary Chapman, of land from mother Grizzel Chapman, brothers Daniel and John Chapman, and sister Elizabeth Scott, all dec'd.

Children:

2+Phineas, b. abt. 1715.
    Daniel, b. abt. 1717, d. at Westport, 11 Oct. 1753 in 37 yr. (g. s.); grad. Yale Coll. 1738.
    Elizabeth, m. Joseph Scott, of Boston.
    Albert, b. abt. 1722, d. 28 Oct. 1747 in 26 yr. (g. s.).
    John, b. abt. 1728, d. 2 June 1757 in 29 yr. (g. s.).
3+Dennie, b. abt. 1730.
    Mary, b. abt. 1732, d. at Greenfield, 21 Feb. 1774 ae. 42; m. at Westport, 2 Apr. 1761, Jedediah Hull.

2. **Chapman, Phineas,** s. of Daniel. Lt., 1st Co., west parish, Fairfield, May 1755; Capt., Oct. 1762.

Born abt. 1715; d. at Westport, 20 Nov. 1782 in 66 yr. (g. s.); m. 22 Sept. 1742, Sarah Ketchum, dau. of Nathaniel. She d. 23 Nov. 1812 in 87 yr. (g. s.); 24 Nov. in 88 yr. (church rec.).

---

* Children, bapt. Stratfield: Rachel, bapt. 1744; Reuben, bapt. 1749; Eunice, bapt. 3 Feb. 1750/1; Timothy, bapt. Aug. 1755.

Distribution 8 Dec. 1784; widow Sarah; eldest son Joseph; Albert; James; John; Joshua; gr. son Daniel; Phineas; Mary wife of Moses Bradley; Grissel; Sarah.

Children, rec. Fairfield, bapt. Westport:

4+Daniel, b. 19 Aug., bapt. 30 Oct. 1743.
5+Joseph, b. 29 Aug., bapt. 13 Oct. 1745.
6+Albert, b. 13 Dec., bapt. 10 Apr. 1748.
7+James, b. 8 Apr., bapt. 3 June 1750.
> Molly, b. 10 June, bapt. 16 Aug. 1752, d. at Redding, in 1821; m. (1) 2 Sept. 1770, Moses Bradley; m. (2) John Hull.
> Grissel, b. 16 Apr., bapt. 8 June 1755; m. 4 Dec. 1783, John Bennett; res. Huntington, L. I., 1787.
> John, b. 14 Sept., bapt. 13 Nov. 1757; Deacon; res. Wilton; m. at Norwalk, 26 Mar. 1789, Susan Fitch.
> Sarah, bapt. 8 June 1760; m. Nathaniel Morgan; res. Redding, 1788.
> Joshua, bapt. 8 May 1763, d. 25 Feb. 1831 [Pension Rec.]; res. 1787, Danbury; m. at Weston, 26 Nov. 1788, Lucy Adams, bapt. 5 Oct. 1765, living at Redding, 1851.*
> Phineas, b. 19 Jan. 1766, bapt. 13 Apr. 1766, d. at Westport, 7 Mar. 1823 ae. 57 (g. s.); m. at Weston, 15 Dec. 1796, Ruth Treadwell, b. 15 June 1774, d. 25 July 1844 ae. 70 (g. s.).†

3. **Chapman, Dennie,** s. of Daniel. Ens., west parish company, Fairfield, Oct. 1753.

Born abt. 1730; d. at Westport, 11 Apr. 1793 ae. 63.

He m. 4 Oct. 1750, Desire Lovel. She d. 17 Nov. 1810 ae. 85 yrs. 5 mos. 17 days (Bible record). She was bapt. as his wife, 19 May 1751.

Will 18 Jan. 1783, proved 17 June 1793; wife; Nabbe wife of Simon Couch; dau. Eunice wife of Talcott Banks; two daus. Elizabeth wife of Gershom Bulkley, and Mary wife of Moses Sherwood; four sons, Lovel, Dennie, Daniel, James.

Children, rec. Fairfield, bapt. Westport:

> Elizabeth, b. 12, bapt. 18 Aug. 1751, bur. 26 May 1795 (Trinity Church rec.); m. 3 June 1773, Gershom Bulkley.

---

* Adm'n on his estate was granted, 12 Mar. 1831, to Phineas Chapman. Distribution made to widow Lucy, sons Phineas, David, and Daniel 2d, and daus. Sally wife of Andrew Barnum, Chary wife of Ethel Andrews, Amelia wife of Orson Marchant, Lucy and Mary Chapman.

† Children, bapt. Westport: Lorra, bapt. 16 Aug. 1798. Betsey, bapt. 26 May 1799, d. at Easton, 14 Nov. 1842 ae. 44 (g. s.); m. Hanford Nichols. Ann, bapt. 4 Oct. 1801. Lizur [Eliza?], bapt. 22 Aug. 1802. Matsey, bapt. 15 Mar. 1804. John, bapt. 8 July 1805. Lydia, bapt. 10 June 1807.

Mary, b. 2 May (?), bapt. 29 Apr. 1753, d. 24 Jan. 1784 in 31 yr. (g. s.); m. 20 Feb. 1772, Moses Sherwood.
8+Lovel, b. 14, bapt. 19 Jan. 1755.
Dennie, b. 28 Aug. 1757[1756], bapt. 5 Sept. 1756; m. 26 Nov. 1778, Mabel Godfrey.*
Abigail, b. 10, bapt. 28 Oct. 1758, d. 18 Dec. 1825 ae. 67-2-8 (Bible record); m. 25 Nov. 1779, Simon Couch.
Eunice, bapt. 30 Nov. 1760, bur. at Westport, 26 Mar. 1831 ae. 70 (g. s.); m. 4 Jan. 1781, Talcott Banks.
Daniel, bapt. 1 Aug. 1762; m. (1) 3 Jan. 1785, Deborah Meeker, dau. of Daniel, bapt. 19 May 1765;† m. (2) Elizabeth ———, who d. 6 Feb. 1857 ae. 93 (g. s., Fairfield West Cemetery).
James, bapt. 25 Oct. 1767; hermit, d. unm.

4. Chapman, Daniel, s. of Phineas.

Born 19 Aug. 1743; d. prisoner in N. Y., Revolutionary War.
He m. 12 Jan. 1773, Mary Andrews.
Mary Chapman m. (rec. Redding) 6 Nov. 1777, Benjamin Darling.

Child:

Daniel, b. 28 Nov. 1773, bapt. at Redding, 5 Mar. 1775; m. at Redding, 3 Nov. 1795, Priscilla Bradley, dau. of Moses.‡

5. Chapman, (Dr.) Joseph, s. of Phineas.

Born 29 Aug. 1745.
He m. at Norwalk, June 1771, Elizabeth Taylor, who d. 17 Feb. 1831 (Miss Treadwell's book).

Children, rec. Norwalk, bapt. Westport:

Betty, b. 11 Mar., bapt. 28 June 1772; m. Elijah Jarvis.
Joseph, b. 29 Aug., bapt. 6 Nov. 1774, d. at Norwalk, 1 June 1822 ae. 48; Maj.; m. 2 Jan. 1800, Betsey Hutton, of Stamford, who d. 1 June 1838 ae. 56.
Lydia, b. 21 Feb., bapt. 9 June 1776; m. Col. Enoch St. John.
William, b. 7 May, bapt. 21 June 1778, d. 13 June 1798; student at Yale.

---

* Children, bapt. Westport: Sarah, bapt. 28 Nov. 1779; Mary, bapt. 7 Oct. 1781; John, bapt. 12 Jan. 1783; Eunice, bapt. 10 Sept. 1784; Simon, bapt. 9 Nov. 1788. He had also, Dennie, bapt. at Trinity Church, 5 Apr. 1786.
† Children, one bapt. Westport: Daniel-Meeker, bapt. 28 Jan. 1787. Dennie, bapt. 18 Sept. 1791, d. 22 May 1831. Joseph, bapt. 16 Mar. 1794.
‡ Child, rec. Redding: Harriet, b. 29 Sept. 1796.

Polly, b. 29 Aug., bapt. 25 Nov. 1780; m. Cornelius Brinkerhoff, of New York.
Sally, b. 10 Oct. 1782; m. 8 Sept. 1802, Dea. Samuel Thorp, of Weston; rem. to Camillus, N. Y.
Lucretia, b. 13 Dec. 1784, bapt. 17 Apr. 1785, d. y.
Lucretia, b. 16 Feb. 1787, d. 16 May 1810; m. Fitch Hanford, of Norwalk.
Esther, b. 9 June 1789; m. 3 Nov. 1812, Dr. Samuel S. Noyes, of New Canaan.
Juliana, b. 7 Nov. 1793, d. 24 June 1814.

6. **Chapman, Albert,** s. of Phineas. 1st Lt., 7th Co., 5th Regt., Army, 1775; Capt., Oct. 1776; Major.

Born 13 Dec. 1748; d. at Westport, 27 Dec. 1819 ae. 72.

He m. 25 Feb. 1779, Lydia Ketchum, who d. by 1826.

Will 30 Aug. 1819, proved 22 Jan. 1820; wife Lydia; four children, Albacyndia, Hiram, Sally, William. Distribution 20 Apr. 1826: son Hiram K.; son William R.; dau. Albacinda Comstock; heirs of dau. Sally K. Davis.

Children, bapt. Westport:

Albacinda, bapt. 20 July 1783; m. (1) 24 Jan. 1802, Isaac Hanford; m. (2) ——— Comstock.
Albert, bapt. 30 July 1786, d. 20 Jan. 1796.
Joel, bapt. 27 July 1788, d. 29 July 1788.
Hiram, bapt. 3 Jan. 1790, d. 4 Apr. 1791.
Hiram, bapt. 24 July 1791.
Henry, bapt. 13 Apr. 1794, d. 19 July 1800 ae. 6.
David, bapt. 21 Mar. 1796, d. 18 May 1796.
Lydia, bapt. 11 June 1797, d. 19 Nov. 1804 ae. 8 (idiot).
Sally-Ketchum, bapt. 27 Oct. 1799; m. ——— Davis.
William R., bapt. 13 Jan. 1802.

7. **Chapman, James,** s. of Phineas. Ens., 1777; Lt., 7th Conn. Regt., Oct. 1777.

Born 8 Apr. 1750; d. at Westport, 6 Sept. 1822 ae. 72 (g. s.).

He m. (1) 4 Mar. 1779, Abigail Sherwood, dau. of Jeremiah, b. 6 June 1753, d. 9 Nov. 1801 in 47 yr. (g. s.).

He m. (2) 9 Jan. 1803, Ellen, widow of Samuel Squire and dau. of Abel Gold, bapt. 2 Aug. 1761. She m. (3) 9 Nov. 1829, Aaron Turney.

Will 8 Dec. 1819, proved 14 Sept. 1822; wife Ellen; son Moses S.; children, Jeremiah S., Abigail Coley, James Chapman, Mary Turney, Grizzel Armstrong, Sarah Armstrong, Lucy Chapman, Samuel S. Chapman. Distribution 1823: Widow, Moses S., Jeremiah, James, Samuel S.; Abigail wife of Sturges Coley; Mary wife of Isaac Turney; Grizzel wife of Alexander Armstrong; Sally wife of John Armstrong; Lucy Chapman.

Children [by first wife], rec. Fairfield, bapt. Westport:

Jeremiah-Sherwood, b. 8 Oct., bapt. 24 Dec. 1780.
Abigail, b. 25 Apr., bapt. 2 June 1782, d. at Weston, 23 Aug. 1845 ae. 62 (g. s.); m. 24 Sept. 1805, Sturges Coley.
James, b. 28 Mar., bapt. 9 May 1784; m. ——— Brush.
Mary, b. 25 June, bapt. 6 Aug. 1786, d. at Westport, 1 June 1855 ae. 70 (g. s.); m. 14 Apr. 1805, Isaac Turney.
Grissel, b. 20 May, bapt. 13 July 1788; m. 21 Apr. 1816, Alexander Armstrong, of N. Y. State.
Moses, b. 30 Nov., bapt. 26 Dec. 1790.
Sarah, b. 12 Nov., bapt. 30 Dec. 1792; m. 7 Oct. 1818, John Armstrong, of N. Y. State.
Lucy, b. 1 Apr., bapt 10 May 1795, d. at Westport, 10 July 1865 ae. 70-3-10 (g. s.); m. Alson Banks.
Samuel-Sherwood, b. 15 Oct. 1797 [1796], bapt. 19 Feb. 1797; m. (1) Eunice Banks; m. (2) Sarah Armstrong.

Child [by second wife]:

Ellen-Gold, b. 3, bapt. 11 Feb. 1808, d. 23 Nov. 1810 ae. 3 yrs. 8 mos. 14 days (g. s.).

8. **Chapman, Lovel,** s. of Dennie.

Born 14 Jan. 1755; d. in 1821/2.
He m. (1) 30 Dec. 1779, Eleanor Bulkley, b. 24 July 1759, d. 25 July 1808 ae. 48.
He m. (2) 14 Jan. 1816, Widow Jane Squire.

Children [by first wife], bapt. Westport:

Anna B., b. in 1781, d. 18 Aug. 1807 ae. 26; m. 16 Feb. 1800, Hezekiah Phelps.
James-Lovel, bapt. 24 Oct. 1784; m. 13 June 1807, Susan-Maria Emmons.
Eleanor, bapt. 18 June 1786; m. 7 Apr. 1839, Simeon Wright, of Yorktown, Westchester County, N. Y.

William, bapt. 8 Mar. 1789; supposed slain on Lake Champlain, War 1812.
Elizabeth, b. 25 Dec. 1791, bapt. 10 Apr. 1793; m. 14 June 1817, John Lounsbury.
Dennie, b. 24 Dec. 1793(?), bapt. 10 Apr. 1793; for 33 yrs. in ministry of Meth. Epis. Church; m. (1) 2 Apr. 1820, Ann W. Anderson, who d. 15 Apr. 1839; m. (2) Charity Weeks of N. Y.
Abigail, b. abt. 1795, bapt. 15 Jan. 1798, d. 18 Jan. 1798 in 3 yr.
Charity, b. abt. 1797, bapt. 22 Sept. 1802, d. 29 Sept. 1802 ae. 4.
Abigail, b. 29 Sept. 1799, bapt. 22 Sept. 1802; m. 7 May 1821, William Pugsley, of Peekskill, N. Y.
Joseph, b. 5 Oct. 1801, bapt. 22 Sept. 1802; in 1832 entered ministry of Genesee Conference of Meth. Epis. Church; m. 8 Apr. 1823, Frances Washburn.

Chapman [Unplaced].

NANCY had Eli, bapt. 5 Mar. 1797; Maryan, dau. of Nance, bapt. 1 Sept. 1799. [Greens Farms Church]

Chard [Unplaced].

WIDOW REBECCA m. 30 Sept. 1767, Jonathan Cable.

Chatfield, Samuel.

Born at Derby, 28 Aug. 1699, d. at Oxford, 17 May 1785; son of John and Anna (Harger) Chatfield.

He m. (1) Sarah ———, who d. 15 Apr. 1740 ae. 34.

He m. (2) Ann (Jackson), widow of John Blackman, who d. at Oxford, 17 July 1777 ae. 68.

He m. (3) at Oxford, 4 June 1778, Eunice (Bedell), widow of Thomas Perkins of Enfield.

Children [by first wife], bapt. Redding:

Samuel, bapt. 29 July 1733, d. young.
Daniel, bapt. 31 Aug. 1735, d. at Waterbury, 11 July 1818 ae. 83 (g. s.); m. Prudence Baldwin.
Samuel, bapt. 17 Apr. 1737; res Oxford; rem. abt. 1765 to Waterbury; m. (1) Joanna ———, who d. 20 Aug. 1783; m. (2) Lydia (Pardee), widow of Joseph Peck.
Martha, bapt. 20 May 1739.

Child [by second wife], rec. Derby:

Mary, b. 18 Jan. 1749/50, d. 18 Sept. 1751.

Chauncey, Israel, s. of Rev. Charles [Vol. I, p. 141].

Born 29 June 1693, d. at Stratfield in 1737; m. 2 Feb. 1720/1, Martha Wakeman, dau. of John, b. 24 Sept. 1700.

Adm'n granted to Robert Chauncey, 1 Feb. 1736/7. The daus. Sarah and Abigail chose Robert Chauncey of Stratfield for guardian, 1739, and Peter Hubbell of Newtown was appointed for Rhoda. Eleanor chose Nathaniel Downs for guardian, 1743.

Children, two rec. Stratfield:
> Sarah, b. 26 Oct. [1721], d. at Greenfield, 6 Aug. 1775 in 54 yr.; m. Nathaniel Downs.
> Abigail, b. 9 Apr. [1725], bapt. at Stratfield, 18 Apr. 1725.
> Rhoda, b. abt. 1727; m. at Newtown, 31 Dec. 1754, Ephraim Sherman.
> Eleanor, b. abt. 1729; m. at Redding, 9 Dec. 1747, Gurdon Merchant.
> Mary, bapt. 14 Nov. 1731; m. at Newtown, 1 Apr. 1755, Abraham Botsford.

Chauncey, Robert, s. of Rev. Charles [Vol. I, p. 142].

Born at Stratfield, 30 Oct. 1701; d. there in 1753; m. 6 June 1722, Hannah Wheeler, dau. of Samuel, bapt. 31 Jan. 1703.

Adm'n granted, 25 Aug. 1753, to Robert Chauncey of Fairfield dec'd.

On 25 Dec. 1773, Wolcott Chauncey, David Wheeler, 3d, and Lois his wife, Samuel Patchen and Ann his wife, all of Fairfield, and Hannah Beardsley of Stratford, children and heirs of Robert Chauncey and Hannah his wife of Fairfield dec'd, conveyed to Nathaniel Seeley.

Children:
> Ann, b. 21 Apr. 1723, d. 11 Nov. 1726.
> Hannah, b. 6 Aug. 1725; m. ——— Beardsley.
> Lois, b. 28 Oct. 1727, d. 2 Feb. 1793 (Wheeler Journal); m. 6 Oct. 1749, David Wheeler, 3d.
> Abiah, b. 25 Feb. 1729/30, d. at Stratfield, 10 Nov. 1748 in 19 yr. (g. s.).
> +Wolcott, b. 25 Apr. 1732, bapt. 30 Apr. 1732.
> Ann, b. 29 Mar. 1735, bapt. 30 Mar. 1735, d. at Stratfield, 2 Aug. 1780; m. Samuel Patchen.

Chauncey, Wolcott, s. of Robert.

Born 25 Apr. 1732; d. at Fairfield, 19 Aug. 1805; m. 29 July 1762, Anna Brown, b. at Stratford, 1 Apr. 1741, d. at the Navy

Yard, New York, 27 July 1829;* dau. of Joseph and Parnel (Bostwick) Brown, gr. dau. of Daniel and Mary (Howe) Brown, and gr. gr. dau. of Eleazer Brown by his wife Sarah Bulkley, who was dau. of Thomas Bulkley of Fairfield.

Children (from *Memorials of the Chaunceys*), born at Fairfield:
Parnel, b. 5 Sept. 1763.
Elizabeth, b. 6 Nov. 1764.
Charles-Wolcott, b. 28 Jan. 1767, lost at sea 26 Nov. 1784.
Polly, b. 1 Sept. 1769, d. 16 Jan. 1770.
Isaac, b. 20 Feb. 1772, d. at Washington, D. C., 27 Jan. 1840; the noted Commodore; m. Catharine Sickles.
Robert, b. 8 Nov. 1774.
Lucy Ann, b. 6 Dec. 1778, d. 30 Nov. 1801; m. 10 Apr. 1798, Enoch A. Sanford.
Sally, b. 14 Sept. 1781.
Ichabod Wolcott, b. 18 Jan. 1784, bapt. at Trinity Church, 6 Nov. 1785; Capt., U. S. N.†

Chilson [*Unplaced*].

ASAPH of Middletown, m. 17 Jan. 1762, Lucretia Hanford. [Greens Farms Church]

Chitester [*Unplaced*].

DR. had children bapt. Weston: Rebecca, bapt. 12 Dec. 1779; Hannah, bapt. 2 Sept. 1781.

Chubb [*Unplaced*].

WILLIAM, of Ashford, m. 4 Sept. 1783, Rachel Downs. [Greens Farms Church]
RACHEL m. 20 Dec. 1795, Jabez Gray. [Weston Church]

Churchill, Edward.

Born abt. 1718, perhaps son of Nehemiah Churchill who m. 3 May 1716 Martha Green; and if so, was grandson of Robert and Sarah (Cable) Churchill.

He m. Esther ———.‡

---

* Died at Brooklyn, 30 July 1829 ae. 87, by the *Columbian Register*.
† One Wolcott Chauncey d. 16 Oct. 1814 (Miss Treadwell's book).
‡ Her name has been printed as Hall or Hull, but we find no evidence.

Children, bapt. Westport:
> James, bapt. 25 Dec. 1742.
> John, bapt. 3 June 1744.
> Esther, bapt. 11 May 1746.
> Edward, bapt. 4 Sept. 1748.

Churchill [*Unplaced*].

> CATE d. 11 Apr. 1779. [Greens Farms Church]

Clark, Adam, s. of James, 3d [Vol. I, p. 145].

Born at Stratford, 21 Jan. 1704/5; lived in Redding; rem. to Danbury and d. in 1770; m. Sarah ———.

Will 20 Sept. 1766, proved 6 Mar. 1770; wife Sarah; children, James and John Clark, Abigail wife of Samuel Taylor, Esq., of Danbury, and Sarah Clark.

Children, bapt. Redding:
> Sarah, bapt. 2 Dec. 1739, d. 20 Oct. 1740 ae. 10 mos.
> Abigail, bapt. 1 Aug. 1741; m. Samuel Taylor.
> James, bapt. 29 Jan. 1744.
> John.
> Sarah, b. [10 Feb. 1751], bapt. 19 Feb. 1751, d. at Redding, 31 Dec. 1821 ae. 70-10-21 (g. s.); m. Stephen Betts.

Clark [*Unplaced*].

> MRS. SARAH m. 13 Mar. 1726, Mr. Peter Hepburn. [Fairfield Church]
> ZEPHANIAH m. 31 Oct. 1749, Olive Osborn. [Fairfield Church]

Clift, Wills. Capt., 20th Regt., Jan. 1776; Major, 3d Conn. Regt., Oct. 1778.

Of Fairfield, will 9 June 1808, proved 30 Apr. 1814; my diploma of the Society of the Cincinnati; wife Mary; bro. Lemuel Clift; Willis, eldest son of Lemuel and Sarah Clift; Willis-Clift son of William and Lucy Ripley; Maj. Albert Chapman; residue to eldest child (whether male or female) of my four bros.; my sister's children are amply rewarded for any service they have ever done me.

He d. at Westport, 27 Apr. 1810 ae. 64-11-9 (g. s.); m. (1) Hannah ———, who d. 19 Oct. 1787 ae. 29 (g. s.); m. (2) at Ridgefield, in 1792, Mary, widow of William Henderson, and dau. of John Hazard, b. 21 Nov. 1754, d. at Waterford, Saratoga County, N. Y., 12 Mar. 1847.

Clinton, John.

Son of Thomas and Hope (Downs), b. at West Haven, 8 Nov. 1721; m. (rec. Fairfield) Nov. 1746, Elizabeth Beecher, dau. of Isaac and Elizabeth (Trowbridge), b. at West Haven, 18 Sept. 1729.

Lived in Westport; rem. to Ballston, Saratoga County, N. Y.

Children, rec. Fairfield, bapt. Westport:

David, b. 9 Oct. 1747.
John, bapt. 23 Apr. 1749, d. 5 Feb. 1750.
Phebe, bapt. 24 Mar. 1751, d. 18 Apr. 1751.
John, b. 4, bapt. 10 May 1752.
Elizabeth, b. 10, bapt. 19 May 1754.
Joseph, bapt. 29 Aug. 1756, d. 29 Oct. 1756.
Child, stillborn 26 Oct. 1757.
Francis, bapt. 6 May 1759, d. 11 June 1759.
Sarah, bapt. 29 Aug. 1760, d. 24 Sept. 1760.
Sarah, bapt. 12 Dec. 1762.

Clugston, John, s. of Michael [Vol. I, p. 150].

Bapt. 23 June 1695; d. at Redding, 23 Mar. 1758 ae. 64. He m. (1) at Stratfield, 11 June 1718, Elizabeth Welles, dau. of Samuel; she d. at Stamford, 31 Aug. 1730. He m. (2) at Greenwich, 27 Feb. 1734/5, Elizabeth Peck; she d. at Redding, 1 Sept. 1745. He m. (3) at Fairfield, 24 Mar. 1747/8, Elizabeth Rowlinson; she d. at Redding, 17 May 1759 ae. 55.

On 30 Aug. 1725, Samuel Welles, Sr., of Stratfield conveyed to dau. Elizabeth wife of John Clugston of Stamford.

Inv. 18 Apr. 1758. Distribution 7 Sept. 1759; John Cluckstone; Samuel Cluckstone; Ann Cluckstone; Mary wife of Amos Sanford; Abigail Cluckstone; Elizabeth wife of John Jones; Deborah Cluckstone.

Adm'n on Est. of Elizabeth Clugston granted, 23 Aug. 1759, to John and Samuel Clugston.

Children [by first wife], rec. Stamford:

John, b. 25 Apr. 1719, d. 19 Dec. 1719.
Elizabeth, b. 27 Sept. 1720; m. John Jones, Jr., of Stratfield, with whom she conveyed in 1760.
+John, b. 7 Aug. 1722.
Samuel, d. 24 Apr. 1730.
Ann, b. 3 July 1726; m. between 7 Sept. 1759 and 31 Jan. 1761, Thomas Knowlton, of Ulster County, N. Y.
Deborah, b. 18 Sept. 1729; m. Hezekiah Wood; res. 1765, Old Pound Ridge, Westchester County, N. Y.

Children [by second wife], rec. Stamford:

+Samuel, b. 6 Dec. 1735.
Mary, b. 13 Feb. 1736/7, d. at Sharon, 13 Mar. 1816 ae. 79 (g. s.); m. (rec. Newtown) 13 Jan. 1757, Amos Sanford.
Abigail, b. 22 Mar. 1737/8; m. (rec. Newtown) 11 Feb. 1761, Enoch Pierson.

Clugston, John, s. of John.

Born 7 Aug. 1722; d. at Redding before 1789.

He m. (1) at Redding, 7 July 1760, Eunice Mallory, bapt. 13 Oct. 1736, d. 28 June 1764 ae. 23 or 24.

He m. (2) 20 Nov. 1764, Charity Jennings of Fairfield, who d. in 1800.

Adm'n was granted to Samuel Prince, and after his death, to William Hamilton of Weston, 3 Aug. 1789.

Adm'n on Est. of Charity granted, 16 Sept. 1800, to David Starr, Jr., of Redding. Distribution ordered to her children,— Michael, Eunice and Mary Clugstone.

Children [by first wife]:

? Betty, m. 12 Nov. 1777, Jeremiah Batterson.
? Samuel, b. abt. 1763; enlisted at Sharon 1780; living there 1818.

Children [by second wife]:

Michael.
Eunice, b. abt. 1771, d. at Redding, Mar. 1843 ae. 72 (g. s.).
Mary, bapt. at Redding, 8 Aug. 1779.*

---

* Her mother's name was stated as *Mary* in the baptismal record, evidently in error.

Clugston, Samuel, s. of John.

Born 6 Dec. 1735; d. at Redding abt. 1760.

He m. at Redding, 11 Feb. 1759, Deborah Mallory, bapt. 15 May 1743.

Inv. of Samuel Cluckstone of Redding; Deborah Cluckstone, Exec'x, now wife of Ephraim Osborn, 1 May 1761.

Children, first rec. Fairfield; bapt Redding:
> David, b. 21 Nov. 1759, bapt. 23 Nov. 1759; Deborah Cluckstone guardian, Aug. 1761.

Clugston [Unplaced].
> SARAH m. 1 Jan. 1793, Barnard Keeler. [Redding rec.]

Coggeshall [Unplaced].
> MARY m. 4 Nov. 1756, David Treadwell. [Fairfield Rec.]

Cole, Samuel.

He m. Mary ―――.
Adm'n granted, 2 Dec. 1760, to Jonathan and John Cole.

Children, rec. Stratford, bapt. Stratfield:
> Sarah, b. and bapt. 27 May 1716.
> Timothy, bapt. 12 Jan. 1718.
> Hannah, bapt. May 1719.

Cole, Caleb.

He m. (1) Rebecca Beardsley, dau. of Daniel, bapt. 7 Sept. 1707.

He m. (2) at Wilton, 20 Dec. 1742, Anne St. John.

Children, bapt. Stratfield:
> David (first-born), bapt. 15 Aug. 1731.
> Ann, bapt. 4 Mar. 1732/3.
> Joseph, bapt. 13 July 1735.

Cole, Jonathan. Sergt., Rev. War.

Son of Ichabod and Ruth, b. at Ridgefield, 13 Oct. 1745; d. at Weston, 20 Apr. 1820 ae. 74 (g. s.).

He m. (1) at Fairfield, 15 May 1770, Lois Bulkley, dau. of David, bapt. 27 May 1750.

He m. (2) at Weston, 3 Feb. 1774, Lois Squire, b. abt. 1754, d. at Kent, 28 Oct. 1837.

Will 16 Apr., proved 12 May 1820; wife Lois; children, Daniel, Hezekiah, Jonathan, Morehouse, Betsey, Polly, Abigail, Catherine, and Eunice. Distribution 13 Nov. 1821: wife Lois; son Daniel; daus. Betsey wife of Jabel Sturges, Jr., Polly wife of Eleazer Lockwood, Nabby wife of Andrew Morehouse, Eunice wife of Tillison Gibbs, Catherine wife of Reuben Gibbs; sons Morehouse, Jonathan, Hezekiah.

Children [by second wife], rec. Weston, bapt. Trinity Church:

> Daniel, b. abt. 1775; m. 26 July 1794, Anna Whinkler, bapt. 14 Jan. 1776, d. 17 Nov. 1843 ae. 68-1-2 (g. s.).
> Betsey, b. [say 1777]; m. 5 July 1797, Jabal Sturges, Jr.
> Ebenezer, b. 11 Jan. 1779.
> Hezekiah, b. 28 Jan. 1782; m. 1806, Jerusha Beers.
> Molly, b. 29 Dec. 1783; m. 21 Oct. 1801, Eleazer Lockwood.
> Nabby, b. 18 Nov. 1785, bapt. 15 Feb. 1786; m. Andrew Morehouse.
> Jonathan, b. 30 Apr. 1789.
> Lois, b. 8 Jan. 1792, bapt. 17 Mar. 1792, d. y.
> Morehouse, b. 1 June 1794, bapt. 12 Dec. 1795.
> Catherine, b. 7 Feb. 1796, bapt. 18 June 1796; m. Reuben Gibbs.
> Eunice, b. 24 Apr. 1798; m. Tillison Gibbs.

Cole [*Unplaced*].

> JAMES of Fairfield chose Ephraim Jackson for guardian, 19 Apr. 1764; d. in Army, Apr. 1778. [Greens Farms Church]
> MEHITABEL m. 3 May 1770, Jared Meeker. [Redding rec.]
> ALBIN m. 12 May 1775, Esther Squire. [Weston Church]
> ISAIAH of R. I. m. 30 Jan. 1750/1, Eleanor Nichols of Fairfield. [Greens Farms Church]
> RUTH m. (1) 19 July 1753, Amos Jackson; m. (2) Timothy Platt, of Newtown.

Coley [Vol. I, pp. 153-156].

```
1 Samuel (     -1684) m. Ann Prudden.
  2 Peter (1641-1690) m. Sarah Hide.
    3 Samuel (1664-1713) m. (1) Esther Frost; (2) Mary ———.
      (By 2): 5 Samuel.
              6 John (1706-1775).
    4 Peter (1671-    ) m. Hannah Couch.
      7 Peter (1702-1743).
      8 Andrew (1708-   ).
      9 David (1715-1802).
     10 Jonathan (1717-1810).
```

5. Coley, Samuel, s. of Samuel.

Bapt. 5 Dec. 1703.

He m. Eunice ———.

He conveyed with wife Eunice to Nathaniel Whitehead, right in house where latter lives in the West Parish. The third and last wife of Whitehead was named Eunice, and she may have been mother of Coley's wife.

Samuel of Redding conveyed 1765 to his son Onesimus.

Children, bapt. Redding:

11+Samuel.
12+Gershom.
13 ? Daniel.
   Eunice, d. at Redding in 1823; m. (1) at Redding, 29 May 1754, Isaac Meeker; m. (2) at Redding, 31 July 1803, Ebenezer Sturges, of Stamford, N. Y.*
14+Onesimus.
   Mary, bapt. 5 June 1743. Will of Mary of Redding, 11 Feb., proved 6 May 1805; bro. Onesimus Coley and his wife; nephew Azariah Coley (land in Andrews' Long Lot); niece Elizabeth wife of Ezra Hull.
   Hannah, m. at Redding, 23 May 1771, Justus Bates.
   Ruth, bapt. 15 May 1748; m. 10 Nov. 1773, Henry Whinkler.

6. Coley, John, s. of Samuel.

Bapt. 17 Mar. 1705/6; d. at Westport, 6 June 1775; m. 22 July 1728, Mercy Gregory, dau. of Benjamin; bapt. at Stratfield, 31 Oct. 1708, d. 29 Jan. 1773 in 65 yr. (g. s.).

---

*Will of Eunice Sturges of Redding, 2 Mar. 1814, proved 13 Sept. 1823; estate equally to Ruth wife of Henry Winkley of Weston, Hannah wife of Justus Bates of Redding, and David Coley, Molly Coley, and Azariah Coley, all of Redding; Elias Bates, Exec'r.

"Coley the sow gelder" d. 5 June 1775 (Perry Diary).

Will 14 Feb. 1774, proved 4 July 1775; eldest son John; two sons Hezekiah, Eliphalet; two daus. Mary and Lois, land in Norwalk.

Children, rec. Fairfield, bapt. Westport:

>Mary, b. 13 Aug. 1732, d. in 1814; m. 3 Jan. 1753, John Dikeman.
>Lois, b. 7 Jan. 1736; m. 14 Jan. 1756, Jonathan Taylor, of Norwalk.
>15+John, b. 31 Dec. 1738.
>16+Hezekiah, b. 23, bapt. 25 Apr. 1742.
>17+Eliphalet, b. 3, bapt. 10 Aug. 1746.

7. **Coley, Peter,** s. of Peter.

Bapt. 30 Aug. 1702; d. at Ridgefield in 1743; m. Ruth Treadwell, dau. of Ephraim, bapt. 23 May 1708. She m. (2) James Tongue.

Will 17 Nov. 1742, proved 5 July 1743; wife Ruth; children Ruth, Ephraim, Peter, Benjamin, Joseph; wife and Samuel Olmstead, Exec'rs.

Children:

>Ruth.
>Ephraim.
>Peter, m. Rebecca Bennett, dau. of William, b. 14 Jan. 1736/7.*
>Benjamin, chose his bro. Ephraim for guardian, 18 Mar. 1750/1; m. at Salem, Westchester County, N. Y., 25 Mar. 1759, Elizabeth Truesdale.
>Joseph, chose his father-in-law James Tongue and Ruth his wife for guardians, 2 July 1753.

8. **Coley, Andrew,** s. of Peter.

Bapt. 25 July 1708.
He m. Patience or Thankful ———.
Rem. by 1735 to Woodbury.

---

* Peter had a dau. (unnamed) bapt. at Easton, 18 Mar. 1764; and a dau., Talathacumi, bapt. 12 Dec. 1767. Doubtless the unnamed dau. was Catey Coley, b. 12 Mar. 1764, m. 25 Nov. 1785, Jeremiah Oakley, Jr., and had 4 children rec. at Weston, including a son Peter C. Oakley. Prob. a son was William Coley, b. abt. 1770, d. at Easton, 7 Sept. 1843 ae. 73 (g. s.); m. 20 Dec. 1795, Rachel Johnson, b. 2 Mar. 1772, d. 25 Mar. 1843 ae. 71 (g. s.); they had two children rec. Weston: Laura, b. 16 Apr. 1797, and Eliza, b. 20 Sept. 1798. Laura d. at Easton, 11 Aug. 1849 ae. 52 yrs. 4 mos. (g. s.).

Children, first bapt. Fairfield, the others rec. and bapt. Woodbury:

> Thankful, bapt. 11 Nov. 1733; m. at Fairfield, 13 Mar. 1755, James Baker.
> Andrew, b. 23, bapt. 29 Feb. 1736.
> David, b. Mar., bapt. 12 Mar. 1738.
> Patience, bapt. 25 May 1740.
> Reuben, bapt. 25 Apr. 1742.
> Gideon, bapt. 29 July 1744.

9. **Coley, David**, s. of Peter. Ens., 2d Co., west parish, Fairfield, May 1755; Lt., Norfield Co., May 1765; Capt., May 1768. Justice, 1768-77. Deputy for Weston, Oct. 1788.

Born 29 Jan. 1715; d. at Weston in 1802.

He m. (1) 16 Dec. 1740, Mary Hide, dau. of John, b. 30 Sept. 1720.

He m. (2) 4 Sept. 1774, Ann Morehouse.

Will 14 May 1798, proved 2 July 1802; wife (a second wife); four children living, Ebenezer, David, Rachel, Mary; four gr. children (sons of dau. Abigail dec'd), David, Charles, Joseph and Jamey Prince; sons David Coley, Jr., and William Prince, Exec'rs. Codicil 2 July 1802: gr. daus. Abigail Sanford and Polly Betts. The distribution calls Mary, Betts, and Rachel, wife of Oliver Sanford.

Children [by first wife], rec. Fairfield, bapt. Westport, last bapt. Weston:

> 18+Ebenezer, b. 19 Oct. 1741, bapt. 28 Mar. 1742.
> David, b. 29 July, bapt. 11 Sept. 1743, d. by 1820; dower set to widow Lydia, 24 Feb. 1820; m. 29 June 1786, Lydia Sturges, b. 24 Oct. 1755, d. at Weston, 16 Aug. 1823 ae. 67.*
> Rachel, b. 18 Mar. 1746, d. at Redding, 11 Feb. 1831 ae. 85 (g. s.); m. 9 Apr. 1767, Oliver Sanford.
> Mary, b. 2, bapt. 11 Mar. 1756; m. 27 June 1775, Enoch Betts, of Norwalk, whose will 30 Aug. 1794, proved 27 June 1795, named wife Mary and bro. David Coley, Jr., and five minor children, Elias, Mary, David, Calvin, Isaiah.
> Abigail, b. 29 Apr. 1758, bapt. 11 June 1758, d. at Easton, 1 Nov. 1797 ae. 39-6-2 (g. s.); m. 16 Dec. 1781, William Prince.

---

* David, Jr., accused 1778 of joining enemy on their return from Danbury, Apr. 1777. Children, rec. Weston: Rachel, b. 16 Apr., bapt. 18 Nov. 1787, d. at Weston, 19 Mar. 1819 ae. 31-11-3 (g. s.); m. Samuel Rowland. Mary-Hide, b. 16 Mar., bapt. 20 June 1790, d. 26 Mar. 1871 ae. 81 (g. s.); m. Levi Coley.

THE FAMILIES OF OLD FAIRFIELD

10. Coley, Jonathan, s. of Peter.

Bapt. 30 June 1717; bur. 15 Mar. 1810 ae. 93 (Trinity Church rec.); d. at Weston, 13 Mar. 1810 ae. 93 (g. s.).

He m. 6 Dec. 1739, Lucy Sturgis, dau. of John, b. abt. 1718; the wife of Jonathan bur. 30 Jan. 1795 ae. 77.

Will 5 Sept. 1808, proved 26 Mar. 1810; two sons, Jonathan and Daniel; four daus. Hannah, Sarah, Lucy, Ellen; children of dau. Ann dec'd; son Jonathan and gr. son Robert Downs Exec'rs.

Children, rec. Fairfield:

    Hannah, b. 5 May 1741; m. Robert Downs.
    Sarah, b. 8 June 1743; m. 31 Aug. 1765, John Adams.
    Ann, b. 17 Nov. 1745.
    Ellen, b. 17 July 1748; ?m. at Weston, 6 Apr. 1771, John Whitlock.
    Lucy, b. 26 Jan. 1751.
    Jonathan, b. 21 Sept. 1754, d. at Weston, [9 Apr. 1832 ae. 31 (81?)]; m. at Weston, 28 June 1781, Elizabeth Gilbert, b. 28 July 1758, d. 18 Feb. 1833 ae. 73 (g. s.).*
    Daniel, b. 24 May 1759; ?m. at Trinity Church, 23 July 1787, Olive Cable; dau. of William, bapt. 31 July 1768.

11. Coley, Samuel, s. of Samuel.

He m. at Redding, 17 Sept. 1747, Mary Gray, prob. dau. of Jacob, bapt. 16 Mar. 1728/9.

Children, bapt. Redding:

    Molly, bapt. 8 June 1755.
    Jesse, bapt. 25 Feb. 1759, d. in 1792. Adm'n granted, 15 Aug. 1792, to Capt. Aaron Barlow.
    David, bapt. 19 July 1761; m. (1) 21 Dec. 1788, Tamar† Squire, who d. 17 May 1802; m. (2) 5 Dec. 1802, Parthenia Mead of Wilton.‡

---

* Children, rec. Weston, bapt. Trinity Church: Sturges, b. 16 Nov. 1782, d. at Weston, 18 Nov. 1840 ae. 57 (g. s.); m. 24 Sept. 1805, Abigail Chapman, who d. 23 Aug. 1845 ae. 62 (g. s.). Samuel, b. 18 May 1784. Gilbert, b. 28 June, bapt. 3 Sept. 1786; m. Sarah ———, who d. 2 June 1835 ae. 41 (g. s.). Baley-Stilson, b. 7 Apr., bapt. 23 June 1793. Jonathan, b. 30 June, bapt. 24 Sept. 1797. One Jonathan d. 13 Mar. 1837 (Miss Treadwell's book).

† Perhaps "Tamma" dau. of Thomas Squire, bapt. 4 Aug. 1765.

‡ Children by first wife, rec. Redding: Rebecca, b. 16 Apr. 1789. Elizabeth, b. 4 June 1791, d. 22 Aug. 1794. Henry, b. 16 June 1793, d. 13 Aug. 1794. Samuel, b. 18 Sept. 1795. Zalmon, b. 1 May 1799.

12. **Coley, Gershom,** s. of Samuel.

He d. at Redding, 16 Dec. 1798.

He m. 15 Nov. 1748, Abigail Hull, dau. of Ebenezer, bapt. 28 Sept. 1729.

Adm'n granted, 21 Jan. 1799, to Isaac Coley of Redding; insolvent.

Children, two rec. Fairfield:
> Ebenezer, b. 24 Feb. 1751; m. (rec. Redding) 12 Nov. 1771, Rachel Sturges of Greens Farms, dau. of David, bapt. 26 Jan. 1752; she m. (2) 13 Oct. 1778, Daniel Mallory, and d. 16 June 1791*
> Eunice, b. 26 Feb. 1754, bapt. at Redding, 3 Mar. 1754.
> Isaac, b. (rec. Redding) 5 Sept. 1766, bapt. 31 Aug.(?) 1766; m. at Redding, 8 Sept. 1785, Sarah Griffin, dau. of John, bapt. 3 Oct. 1762.

13. **Coley, Daniel** [s. of Samuel?], Justice, 1771-82, Deputy for Ridgefield, May 1781. [Ens., 8th Co., 16th Regt., Alarm List, May 1777.]

He d. at Ridgefield in 1800.

He m. 16 Apr. 1754, Sarah Sanford, dau. of Lemuel, b. 11 Sept. 1734, d. before 1777.

He prob. m. (2) by 1782, Ann Morehouse, dau. of Nathan, b. 25 Sept. 1741.

He conveyed 1762 to his father Lemuel Sanford. In 1763, then of Ridgebury in Ridgefield, he conveyed to James Sears of Ridgefield, his home in Redding.

Will 24 Dec. 1798, proved 31 Mar. 1800; three daus. Sarah, Rebecca, Eunice; friends Lemuel Sanford, Esq., of Redding, and my two sons-in-law Benjamin Lines and Thomas Boughton, both of Ridgefield, to be Exec'rs.

Children, first rec. Fairfield; two bapt. Redding; last three rec. Ridgefield:
> Stephen, b. 21, bapt. 27 Oct. 1754, d. y.
> Ezra, bapt. 25 Feb. 1759, d. y.
> Sarah, b. 30 Apr. 1765; m. 23 Nov. 1786, Benjamin Lynes.
> Rebecca, b. 17 Jan. 1768.
> Eunice, b. 6 Nov. 1772.

---

* Ezekiel, son of Ebenezer and Rachel, was bapt. at Redding, 14 June 1772. Ezekiel son of Ebenezer chose Daniel Mallory, Jr., of Redding for guardian, 10 Apr. 1786. Adm'n on Est. of Ezekiel was granted, 8 Dec. 1794, to Isaac Coley of Redding. Distribution ordered to Daniel and Eunice Mallory, half bro. and sister.

THE FAMILIES OF OLD FAIRFIELD   249

14. Coley, Onesimus, s. of Samuel.

He d. at Redding, 5 Feb. 1806.

He m. 22 Dec. 1762, Eunice Burr, dau. of Jabez, bapt. 16 Dec. 1739.

Adm'n granted to Azariah Coley and Ezra Hull, 17 June 1806.

Children, rec. Redding:

> Elizabeth, b. 5 May, bapt. 19 June 1763; m. 23 Dec. 1784, Ezra Hull.
> Darius, b. 25 June, bapt. 30 July 1769, d. at Redding, 6 Nov. 1774 ae. 5-4-11 (g. s.).
> Azariah, b. 6 Mar., bapt. 24 Apr. 1776, d. 17 July 1841 ae. 65 (Bible rec.); m. 6 Mar. 1808, Sarah Andrews, dau. of Daniel, b. 1 Sept. 1781, d. 18 Feb. 1857 ae. 75 yrs. 5 mos. (Bible rec.).

15. Coley, John, s. of John.

Born 31 Dec. 1738.

He m. 7 Apr. 1761, Anna Ogden, dau. of Humphrey, b. 2 Nov. 1744.

Of Westchester County, N. Y., 1775, he conveyed to bro. Hezekiah Coley, and 1776 to Humphrey Ogden.

Children, bapt. Weston:

> John, bapt. 6 Oct. 1765; ?m. 13 May 1790, Eunice Morehouse, perhaps dau. of Gideon, b. 8 Jan. 1761.*
> Peleg, bapt. 27 Mar. 1768.
> Anna, bapt. 30 Sept. 1770.
> Rhoda, bapt. 4 Aug. 1776.

16. Coley, Hezekiah, s. of John.

Born 23 Apr. 1742; d. at Westport, 10 Nov. 1791.

He m. Sarah Morehouse, dau. of Jabez, b. 19 Nov. 1746, d. at Weston in 1816.

Will 7 Nov. 1791, proved 20 Feb. 1792; wife Sarah; bro. Eliphalet; son Hezekiah; daus. Mercy, Sarah, Anna.

Will of Sarah of Weston, 2 Jan. 1815, proved 29 Jan. 1816; son Hezekiah for life; Hezekiah's wife Ann and children; two daus. Mercy wife of Nathaniel Wakeman, Sarah wife of Jesup Taylor.

---

*Children, bapt. Westport: William, bapt. 16 Sept. 1792; Eunice, bapt. 11 Aug. 1793. In 1795, John Cooley and Eunice his wife, of Frederickstown, Dutchess County, N. Y., conveyed to John Andrews land in Greens Farms bounded north on land of Temperance wife of Ebenezer Morehouse.

Children, bapt. Westport:

    Mercy, b. 2, bapt. 20 Sept. 1772, d. at Weston, 19 Dec. 1824 ae. 52-3-17 (g. s.); m. at Weston, 22 Mar. 1794, Nathaniel Wakeman.
    Sarah, b. [20 June 1774], bapt. 31 July 1774, d. at Westport, 7 Mar. 1860 ae. 85-8-17 (g. s.); m. 31 May 1798, Jesup Taylor.
    Hezekiah, b. 9 Feb. 1777 (Bible rec.), bapt. 6 July 1777, d. at Westport, 25 Nov. 1834 ae. 57 (g. s.); m. 5 Nov. 1797, Anna Burr, b. 1 Mar. 1779 (Bible rec.), d. 14 Oct. 1815 ae. 36 yrs. 7 mos. (g. s.); had 5 children, rec. Bible.*
    Anna, bapt. 20 Nov. 1785, d. at Weston in 1808. Adm'n granted, 28 Mar. 1808, to Nathaniel Wakeman, with Jesup Taylor as surety. Distribution order, 4 Apr. 1808: bros. and sisters,—Mercy wife of Nathaniel Wakeman, Sarah wife of Jesup Taylor, Hezekiah Coley.

17. Coley, Eliphalet, s. of John.

Born 3 Aug. 1746; at Weston, 12 Nov. 1812.

He m. at Greenfield, 13 Feb. 1770, Eunice Bradley; dau. of Daniel, b. 22 July 1754, d. 25 June 1837.

Will 1 Sept., proved 28 Dec. 1812; wife Eunice; children Rheuamy, Eliphalet, Mary, Sarah. Distribution, 9 Mar. 1813: Widow; Ruhami wife of Samuel Coley; Eliphalet B.; Mary wife of Silliman Fanton; Sarah wife of Ebenezer Andrews.

Children, two bapt. Westport, three Weston:

    Ruhamah, b. [18 Oct. 1770], bapt. 3 Feb. 1771, d. at Weston, 11 Sept. 1855 ae. 84-10-24 (g. s.); m. 23 June 1791, Samuel Coley.
    Eliphalet, b. 9 Dec. 1775 [1773], bapt. 20 Feb. 1774, d. at Weston, 23 Nov. 1841 ae. 68 (g. s.); m. Priscilla Bradley, dau. of David, b. 3 Apr. 1782, d. 25 May 1851 in 69 yr. (g. s.).†
    Mary, b. 20 Sept., bapt. 14 Dec. 1777, d. at Easton, 20 May 1844 in 66 yr. (g. s.); m. 16 Aug. 1798, Silliman Fanton.
    Sarah, b. 17 Sept. 1780 [1779], bapt. 20 Feb. 1780, d. at Redding, 7 Mar. 1854 in 74 yr. (g. s.); m. at Weston, 19 Mar. 1801, Ebenezer Andrews.
    Eunice, bapt. 19 Mar. 1786, d. y.‡

---

* Children, bapt. Westport: Sally-Burr, bapt. 3 June 1798; Mary-Ann, bapt. 20 Apr. 1800; Orra, bapt. 22 Aug. 1802; Hezekiah-Morehouse, bapt. 30 June 1805.

† Eliphalet's will, 4 Sept. 1841, proved 22 Dec. 1841; wife Priscilla and children. Distribution named children: David D., Samuel W., Burr B., and Eunice B. wife of Henry B. Nichols. Adm'n on Priscilla's estate granted 3 June 1851; distribution to Samuel W., Priscilla, Burr B., and David D. Coley, and Eunice wife of Henry B. Nichols.

‡ One Eunice d. 22 Sept. 1805 ae. 29 (Greens Farms Church).

THE FAMILIES OF OLD FAIRFIELD 251

18. **Coley, Ebenezer**, s. of David. Capt., Norfield Co., May 1770.

Born 19 Oct. 1741; d. at Weston, 2 Nov. 1811 ae. 70 (g. s.). He m. (1) at Westport, 11 Aug. 1763* Abigail Morehouse, b. 22 Mar. 1744, d. 3 Feb. 1797; m. (2) 16 Mar. 1797, Mary Godfrey. She was widow of Ebenezer Godfrey, previously of Asher Taylor, and first of Joseph Gorham, and was dau. of Samuel Gray, b. 8 Mar. 1746, d. 25 Sept. 1825 ae. 79 (g. s.).

Will 15 Apr. 1811, proved 7 Nov. 1811; wife Mary; six children; two children of my son Michael. Distribution of Est. of Capt. Ebenezer, 19 May 1814, to the same heirs as named in next paragraph.

Distribution order, estate of Abigail Coley of Weston, 30 Dec. 1811: children,—Ebenezer, Levi, Morehouse, and Samuel Coley, Abigail wife of Shubael Gorham, Mary wife of Abraham Baker, and heirs of dec'd son Michael Coley.

Children [by first wife], rec. and bapt. Weston (except first, bapt. Westport):

Abigail, b. 5, bapt. 29 July 1764; m. Shubael Gorham.
Morehouse, b. 10 Mar., bapt. 20 May 1766, d. at Weston, 6 Oct. 1843 ae. 77 yrs. 8 mos. (g. s.); m. 17 Feb. 1789, Abigail Ogden, bapt. 15 Mar. 1767, d. 4 Jan. 1838 ae. 70 yrs. 10 mos. (g. s.).†
Ebenezer, b. 25 Dec. 1767, bapt. 27 Mar. 1768, d. at Weston, 11 Nov. 1823 ae. 55-10-16 (g. s.); adm'n granted, 24 Nov. 1823, to Walter and David Coley; ?m. 9 Jan. 1788, Mary Parrot [dau. of John, b. 20 Nov. 1767]; m. 2 June 1790, Rachel Goodsell, bapt. 13 Nov. 1768, d. 2 Mar. 1816 ae. 48 (g. s.).‡
Samuel, b. 6 June, bapt. 22 July 1770, d. at Weston, 30 Dec. 1850 ae. 80-6-24 (g. s.); m. 23 June 1791, Ruhamah Coley [b. 18 Oct. 1770], d. 11 Sept. 1855 ae. 84-10-23 (g. s.).§

---

* 5 July, by Weston record.
† Children, rec. Weston, eldest bapt. Westport: John-Hide, b. 11 May 1790, bapt. 14 June 1790, d. at Weston, 11 May 1834 ae. 44 (g. s.); m. Hannah Downs, b. 12 Nov. 1793 (g. s.), d. 21 May 1871 (g. s.). Abigail, b. 9 Nov. 1791, bapt. 7 June 1795, d. 23 Aug. 1867 ae. 75 yrs. 9 mos. (g. s.); m. 31 May 1813, John Gray. Lansing, b. 17 Aug. 1795, d. at Weston, 3 Jan. 1876 ae. 80-4-17 (g. s.); m. Sally Downs, who d. 4 Aug. 1845 ae. 49-10-10 (g. s.). Polly-Morehouse, b. 2 May 1797, d. 3 Nov. 1824 ae. 27 yrs. 6 mos. (g. s.). Polly-Morehouse, bapt. 12 Aug. 1798. Jonathan-Ogden, bapt. 18 June 1800.
‡ Children, rec. and bapt. Weston: Walter, b. 11 Oct. 1791, bapt. 8 Sept. 1793, d. 5 Sept. 1858 ae. 66-10-24 (g. s.); m. Anna Wakeman, dau. of Nathaniel, who d. 1 Oct. 1829 ae. 32-11-21 (g. s.); m. (2) Orra ———, who d. 11 Mar. 1864 ae. 61-11-3 (g. s.). David, b. 5 Nov. 1794, bapt. 12 July 1795. Ebenezer, b. 30 June, d. 5 July 1796. Samuel-Morehouse, bapt. 3 June 1804. Levi, bapt. 23 July 1809.
§ Child, rec. Weston: John, b. 2 Mar. 1798, d. 10 Oct. 1822 ae. 24-7-8 (g. s.).

Michael, b. 6 Sept., bapt. 1 Nov. 1772, d. at Weston, 17 Dec. 1807 ae. 35 (g. s.); m. 13 Jan. 1793, Eunice Hide, dau. of John, bapt. 19 Sept. 1776, d. 22 Sept. 1805 in 30 yr. (g. s., Westport).*

Mary, bapt. 3 Feb. 1775, d. at Weston, 19 Aug. 1775 ae. 11 mos. 16 days (g. s.).

Levi, b. 25 July 1777, bapt. 23 Aug. 1778, d. at Weston, 20 Nov. 1859 ae. 81 (g. s.); m. Mary-Hide Coley, dau. of David, b. 16 Mar. 1790, d. 26 Mar. 1871 ae. 81 (g. s.).

Mary, b. 2 Jan., bapt. 23 Apr. 1780; m. Abraham Baker.

Hide, b. 6 Dec. 1786, bapt. 27 May 1787, d. 23 June 1789.

Coley, Nathan.

He d. at Redding, by 1783.

He m. at Redding, 15 Nov. 1770, Mehitabel Bixby, prob. dau. of Elias. She was prob. the Mabel Coley who m. at Redding, Aug. 1782, Abijah Parsons.

Adm'n granted, 9 June 1783, to Abijah Parsons of Fairfield; insolvent. Dower set 1786 to widow Mabel.

Children, bapt. Redding:

Abigail, bapt. 12 Apr. 1772; ?m. 22 Oct. 1794, Zachariah Stevens, of Ridgebury.

Zalmon, bapt. 9 Apr. 1775.

Nathan, b. [25 Feb. 1778], bapt. 26 Apr. 1778, d. at Easton, 10 Apr. 1853 ae. 75-2-1 (g. s.); m. at Weston, 30 Mar. 1800, Prudence Canfield, who d. 8 Dec. 1844 ae. 68 (g. s.).

Coley [*Unplaced*].

RACHEL m. 13 Oct. 1778, Daniel Mallory, Jr. [Redding rec.]

NATHANIEL m. Mary Davis, b. 2 Nov. 1732, widow of Peter Lyon.

ANN, b. abt. 1763, d. at Easton, 14 Apr. 1813 in 51 yr. (g. s.); m. (rec. Weston) 7 Nov. 1782, Ebenezer Seeley.

Collier, Thomas Langley.

He m. (1) Abiah? Hawley, bapt. Apr. 1752?, d. before 1786.

He m. (2) by 1780, Elizabeth, widow of James Hill, and dau. of Moses Wakeman, b. 15 Mar. 1749/50, d. 14 Mar. 1796 (Trinity Church rec.).

He m. (3) at Trinity Church, 17 Dec. 1797, Catherine Hawley.

---

* Edwin, son of Eunice, bapt. at Westport, 11 Oct. 1795; John-Hide, son of Michael, bapt. 1 Jan. 1797; David, son of Michael and Eunice, bapt. 14 Jan. 1800.

Children:
> Margery, b. abt. 1780, d. at Easton, 6 Oct. 1810 in 31 yr. (g. s.); m. 22 June 1797, Hull Fanton.
> Thomas L., d. at Fairfield, 8 Oct. 1809 (Miss Treadwell's book); m. at Trinity Church, 11 Jan. 1798, Sarah Holmes. Adm'n on his estate was granted, 31 Jan. 1810, to Sarah Collyer, with David Sherwood as surety. Sarah Collyer was appointed guardian to Alanson, Mary, and Sall A. Collyer, 31 Jan. 1811. Hull Fanton was later guardian of Sally-Ann and Mary, but was discharged in 1815 and Daniel Holmes appointed.
> Samuel, bapt. at Trinity Church, 25 Aug. 1791.
> John, bapt. 25 Aug. 1791.

Colwell, John.
Of Fairfield; adm'n granted to Joseph Chapman, 19 June 1786. Insolvent.

Comstock [*Unplaced*].
> JABEZ, of Wilton, m. 16 June 1799, Amelia Ogilvie. [Greens Farms Church.]
> ENOS d. 24 Sept. 1812 ae. 25(?); had children: David, d. 9 Aug. 1796; Charles, bapt. 11 Aug. 1796; David, bapt. 18 Mar. 1798, d. 10 Aug. 1818 in 21 yr.; Louisa, bapt. 5 Oct. 1800. [Greens Farms Church.] Adm'n on estate of Enos was granted, 5 Oct. 1812, to Lewis Raymond.
> BILLY m. 26 Mar. 1797, Rebecca Starr, both of Danbury, and had four children recorded. [Redding rec.] Adm'n was granted on his estate, 12 June 1823, to Eliakim Starr of Danbury and Henry H. Cooley of Redding. Distribution: widow; dau. Cornelia; son Andrew; dau. Sally-Maria; son William-Starr; dau. Betsey; dau. Lavinia.
> DEBORAH m. 21 Oct. 1804, Hezekiah Allen. [Greens Farms Church.]

Cooke, (Rev.) Samuel. Deputy for New Haven, Oct. 1712, May and Oct. 1713, May and Oct. 1714, May 1715, and Clerk of the House the last five sessions. Trustee, Yale College, 1732-46.

Son of Thomas and Sarah, b. at Guilford, 22 Nov. 1687; d. at Stratfield, 2 Dec. 1747 ae. 63 (g. s.); m. (1) at New Haven, 30 Nov. 1708, Anne Trowbridge, dau. of John and Anne, b. at New Haven, 22 July 1688, d. 11 Aug. 1721 in 34 yr. (g. s.).

He m. (2) 3 May 1722, Esther, widow of John Sloss, and dau. of Nathaniel Burr; she d. soon after.

He m. (3)* 28 Sept. 1727, Elizabeth Platt, dau. of Joseph, b. at Norwalk, 2 Dec. 1701, d. 16 May 1732 in 31 yr.

He m. (4) 6 Aug. 1733, Abigail, widow of Rev. Joseph Moss, and dau. of Rev. Samuel Russell.

Grad. Yale Coll. 1705; rector of Hopkins Grammar School, 1707-15; minister of Stratfield Church, 1715-47.

Distribution: Widow Abigail; Samuel, John and William Cooke; Joseph Plat Cooke; Sarah wife of James "Serman"; Anne wife of Mr. Robert Silliman.

Children [by first wife], rec. Stratfield, first four born at New Haven:

    Thomas, b. 1 Sept. 1709, d. y.
    Samuel, b. 22 July 1711, d. at New Haven, 26 Mar. 1788 in 77 yr.; grad. Yale Coll. 1730; Butler, Yale Coll., 1732-34, and Steward, 1734-39; merchant; m. 5 Nov. 1735, Susanna Mansfield, dau. of Moses, who d. 25 Jan. 1789 in 76 yr.
    Sarah, b. 8 June 1713, d. at New Haven, 18 Feb. 1802 ae. 89 (g. s.); m. 17 Jan. 1733/4, James Sherman.
    John, b. 31 Mar. 1715.
    Child, b. and d. 27 Dec. 1716.
    Anne, b. 4 Apr. 1718, bapt. 6 Apr. 1718, d. at Chester, 3 Sept. 1778; m. Robert Silliman.
    William, b. 29 May 1720, d. in service, 23 Aug. 1761; grad. Yale Coll. 1747; Chaplain, 2d Regt., Conn. Troops, 1761.

Children [by third wife]:

    Joseph-Platt, b. 24 Dec. 1729, d. at Danbury, 3 Feb. 1816 in 87 yr.; Deputy for Danbury, about 30 sessions, 1763-83; Assistant, 1784-1803; J. P. from 1764; Col., 16th Regt., 1771; member of Council of Safety, 1778; Member of Congress, 1784-88; Judge of Probate, Danbury District, 1776-1813; m. 22 Nov. 1759, Sarah Benedict, dau. of Capt. Daniel and Sarah (Hickok), b. 10 June 1740, d. 31 Oct. 1822.
    Eliasaph, bapt. 20 Mar. 1731/2, d. 21 Mar. 1731/2 ae. 26 hours.
    Josiah (twin), bapt. 20 Mar. 1731/2, d. ae. 2 hours.

---

* For a family record of Rev. Samuel Cooke and his surviving son by this marriage, see *New Eng. Hist. and Gen. Register*, vol. 63, p. 195. Since this record calls Elizabeth Platt his "4th wife," we must assume that between 1723 and 1727 he had contracted a third marriage and that, despite printed accounts, he had *five* instead of *four* wives in all.

Cooke, John.

Children, first bapt. Stratfield:

+Thomas, bapt. 25 June 1750.
Dorcas, b. abt. 1764, d. 25 July 1854 ae. 91 (g. s.); m. William Wordin.

Cooke, Thomas, s. of John.

Bapt. 25 June 1750.
Of Fairfield, will 22 July, proved 1 Aug. 1814; to wife Ruth, all estate; two daus., of whom one was Anne Lord. Ruth declined trust as Exec'x, and Thomas Brothwell was appointed Adm'r.

Thomas m. [Sarah?] Hall, dau. of James. Wife of Thomas d. at Stratfield, 15 Nov. 1777.

Thomas m. ——— Treadwell, dau. of Josiah.

Copley [*Unplaced*].

DANIEL m. 3 Apr. 1777, Theoda Couch. Children: Calvin, b. 20 Jan. 1791; Theoda-Ann, b. 24 July 1794; Lucy, b. 14 Feb. 1798. [Redding rec.]

EUNICE of Woodbury m. 20 July 1777, Elijah Couch. [Redding rec.]

Corns, George.

He m. at Redding, 12 Nov. 1734, Anna Hall; dau. of Isaac, b. 26 Dec. 1710.

Children, bapt. Redding:

Anna-Aldridge, bapt. 25 May 1735, d. 5 Feb. 1740 ae. 4 to 5.
Elizabeth, bapt. 18 Nov. 1739.
? Sarah, m. 15 Jan. 1765, Samuel Rowley.
? Ann, b. 27 May 1746, bur. 22 Feb. 1822 ae. 76 (Trinity Church rec.); m. 6 Jan. 1768, Jonathan Mallory, Jr.

Couch [Vol. I, pp. 160-164].

```
1 Simon (1633-1688) m. Mary ———.
    2 Simon (    -1713) m. Abigail Sturges.
        4 Thomas (1695-1736).
    3 Samuel (    -1739) m. Edrea Hurlbut.
        5 Samuel (1700-1775).
        6 Benjamin (1702-1748).
        7 Ebenezer (1709-1797).
        8 Solomon (1713-1748).
        9 John (    -    ).
```

4. **Couch, Thomas,** s. of Simon.

Born 9 June 1695; d. at Westport, 1 Apr. 1736 ae. 40 yrs. 9 mos. 22 days (g. s.); m. 7 Dec. 1721, Sarah Allen; dau. of Lt. Gideon, b. 1 Apr. 1697, d. 10 Mar. 1787 ae. 90. She m. (2) 10 Nov. 1736, Timothy Keeler.

Will 6 Dec. 1735, codicil 2 Feb. 1735/6, proved 20 Apr. 1736; wife Sarah; sons Thomas, Simon; daus. Sarah and Ann Couch; negroes; mentions bro. Simon Couch's homelot. Dower in estate of Thomas, Sr., was ordered distributed, 13 June 1765, to his widow, Sarah Keeler of Ridgefield.

Children, rec. Fairfield:

Sarah, b. 1 Dec. 1723, d. 24 Aug. 1773.
10+Thomas, b. 28 Nov. 1725.
11+Simon, b. [5 Apr. 1729].
Ann, m. at Ridgefield, 7 July 1750, Theophilus Stebbins.

5. **Couch, Samuel,** s. of Samuel.

Bapt. 22 Sept. 1700; d. at Westport, 18 May 1775; m. 13 Sept. 1726, Elizabeth Sturges, dau. of John; bapt. 29 Aug. 1708, d. 20 July 1787.

Will 2 Nov. 1774, proved 20 June 1775; wife; daus. Mary Bennett, Elizabeth, Miriam; sons Josiah, Zebulon, Benjamin, Solomon, David, Nehemiah; daus. Abigail, Naomi; three gr. children, Joshua, Elizabeth, and Rachel, children of dec'd son Samuel; son Nehemiah to have care of the property given to Zebulon for the latter's benefit.

Children, rec. Fairfield and Westport:

Miriam, b. 11 Apr. 1727, d. 13 Nov. 1728.
Mary, b. 28 Mar. 1729, d. 27 July 1788; m. 1 Apr. 1754, Thomas Bennett, Jr.
12+Samuel, b. 5 May 1731.
13+David, b. 25 June 1733.
Elizabeth, b. 13 June 1735, d. before 1790; m. 9 Mar. 1756, Timothy Pierson.
Miriam, b. 14 Apr. 1737, d. at Westport, 19 Mar. 1824 in 87 yr. (g. s.); m. Solomon Morehouse.
14+Nehemiah, b. 25 May 1739.
Abigail, b. 10 June 1741; m. 8 Feb. 1778, Isaac Godfrey, of Weston.

15+Josiah, b. Apr., bapt. 1 May 1743.
  Zebulon, b. 28 Aug., bapt. 15 Sept. 1745, d. at Westport, 12 May 1821 ae. 71 [should be 75].
  Benjamin-Solomon, b. 26 Mar., bapt. 2 Apr. 1749, d. at Westport, 26 Feb. 1812 ae. 63.
  Naomi, b. 13 Dec. 1751, bapt. 12 Jan. 1752, d. 15 June 1796; m. 10 Jan. 1773, Benjamin Couch.

6. **Couch, Benjamin,** s. of Samuel.

Bapt. 27 Dec. 1702; d. at Westport, 27 Sept. 1748 in 47 yr. (g. s.); m. Mary ———. She m. (2) 19 Dec. 1749, Moses St. John, of Norwalk.

Agreement 4 June 1751 of Benjamin's heirs; Moses St. John and Mary his wife, of Norwalk; Joseph Couch; Nathan Godfrey and Martha his wife; and Mary Couch ye Second;—all of Fairfield. Dower distributed, 4 Aug. 1769, to Mary St. John, widow of Benjamin Couch.

Children, bapt. at Westport:
16+Joseph, bapt. 17 Sept. 1726.
  Martha, bapt. 16 June 1730/1, d. 31 May 1761; m. 11 June 1747, Nathan Godfrey.
  Mary, bapt. 15 Nov. 1732, d. at Westport, 26 Mar. 1822 ae. 89 (g. s.); m. (1) 27 Nov. 1752, Jabez Gorham; m. (2) 1 Oct. 1766, David Couch.

7. **Couch, Ebenezer,** s. of Samuel.

Bapt. Apr. 1709; d. at Redding, 23 Mar. 1797 ae. 88 (g. s.); m. 18 May 1731, Ann Crane, dau. of Jonathan.

In a deed 30 Sept. 1765, conveying land in Redding, he called himself late of Fairfield, now of Woodbury; but he returned to Redding.

Will 6 June 1796, proved 1 Apr. 1797; three sons, Ebenezer, Jr., Daniel, Elijah; Eunice wife of son Elijah; daus. Theody wife of Daniel Copley, Adah Knap, and Martha wife of James Bosworth.

Children [by first wife], rec. Fairfield, bapt. Redding:
17+Ebenezer, b. 20 Jan. 1733.
18+Jonathan, b. 16 July 1736.

Daniel, b. 20, bapt. 29 July 1739; rem. to Ballston, N. Y.; m. 23 Jan. 1763, Sarah Howes, of Stamford, b. 19 July 1744.*

Adrea, b. 12, bapt. 19 Sept. 1742, d. abt. 1830; m. (1) 27 Aug. 1761, Stephen Crofut; m. (2) —— Knapp.

Martha, b. 25 Dec. 1744; m. James Bosworth.

Elijah, b. 29 July, bapt. 2 Aug. 1747, d. in Sullivan County, 19 Mar. 1816 (family record); m. (1) at New Preston, 5 Nov. 1772, Mary Bosworth; m. (2) at New Preston, 20 July 1777, Eunice Copley, of Washington, b. 7 Dec. 1754, d. 8 May 1845.†

Theoda, b. 24, bapt. 26 Jan. 1755, d. at New Milford, 8 Sept. 1841 ae. 87 yrs. 7 mos. 14 days (g. s.); m. 3 Apr. 1777, Daniel Copley.

8. **Couch, Solomon**, s. of Samuel.

Bapt. 24 May 1713; d. at Westport, 26 Sept. 1748 in 36 yr. (g. s.); m. Deborah Silliman, dau. of Daniel. She m. (2) 11 May 1760, David Bulkley, and d. in 1766.

Adm'n granted to Deborah and John Couch, 1 Nov. 1748. On 4 July 1749, Samuel Couch was appointed guardian to Adrea, Solomon, and Eunice; Widow Deborah Couch was appointed guardian to Deborah, Lydia, Isaac, and Elizabeth, and chosen by Mary; John Osborn appointed guardian to Thankful;—all children of Solomon. Distribution 24 Apr. 1751: Widow Deborah Couch; Solomon, Isaac, Mary, Adrea, Deborah, Thankful, Eunice, and Lydia Couch. Deborah Couch, late Deborah Bulkley, was reported dec'd, 23 Sept. 1766, and distribution of her dower ordered to the children. Distribution of same was made, 30 Sept. 1766, to Solomon and Isaac Couch, Eunice wife of Azariah Lee, Mary wife of Joseph Osborn, Deborah wife of Isaac Bulkley, Lydia Couch, and Adrea wife of David Adams, Jr. In 1775, Solomon Couch, Joseph Osborn and Mary his wife, David Adams, Jr., and Adria his wife, David Morehouse and Thankful his wife, Ebenezer Hubbell and wife Lydia, and Deborah Bulkley, all of

---

* Children, rec. and bapt. Redding: Daniel, b. 22 Apr. 1764; Ira-Howes, b. 29 Sept. 1766; Sally, b. 4 Feb., bapt. 30 Sept. 1770; Mary, bapt. 2 May 1772, d. 11 May 1772 ae. 2 mos. The young Daniel enlisted at Redding, 1781, was pensioned at Milton, Saratoga County, N. Y., 1819, rem. 1835 to Hillsdale County, Mich.

† Children, rec. and bapt. Redding: William, b. 8 Feb., bapt. 10 Apr. 1774; Samuel, b. 29 Jan. 1778; Jonathan, b. 15 Jan., bapt. 5 Mar. 1780, d. at Bethel, Conn., 22 Apr. 1853, m. 10 Feb. 1801, Lydia Hoyt; Elijah, b. 14 Mar. 1782; Mary, b. 20 July 1784; Silas-Crane, b. 8 June 1786; Calvin, b. 14 Aug. 1788; Daniel, b. 15 Dec. 1790; Ebenezer, b. 23 Mar. 1793; Stephen, b. 28 Oct. 1797. Family record adds Harvey, b. 1 June 1800.

Fairfield, and Azariah Lee of Guilford and Eunice his wife, conveyed land in West Parish.

Children, bapt. Westport:

Mary, b. abt. 1735, d. at Greenfield, 14 Feb. 1796 in 60 yr. (g. s.); m. (1) 23 Jan. 1765, Joseph Osborn; m. (2) at Fairfield, 10 Dec. 1778, Jedediah Hull, of Greenfield.
Adrea, b. abt. 1737; m. 10 Nov. 1757, David Adams, Jr.
Deborah, b. abt. 1738, d. at Fairfield, 31 Oct. 1816 ae. 78; m. 18 Nov. 1762, Isaac Bulkley.
Solomon, b. [say 1740].
Thankful, bapt. 6 Feb. 1743; m. 25 Jan. 1764, David Morehouse.
Eunice, bapt. 4 Mar. 1744; m. Azariah Lee, of Guilford; with whom she conveyed 1766 to bro. Solomon Couch.
Isaac, bapt. 20 Oct. 1745, d. in 1771. Adm'n granted to Solomon Couch, 12 Nov. 1771.
Lydia, bapt. 19 Apr. 1747; m. 8 Apr. 1767, Ebenezer Hubbell.
Elizabeth, bapt. 16 Apr. 1749, d. 10 Nov. 1749.

9. **Couch, John,** s. of Samuel.

He m. Sarah ———.

Children, bapt. Redding:

John, bapt. 20 Mar. 1748.
?Sarah, m. 20 June 1769, Ephraim Robbins.
Stephen, bapt. 21 Jan. 1753.
Adrea, bapt. 20 Apr. 1755.
Elizabeth, bapt. 17 July 1757.
Samuel, bapt. 30 Aug. 1758.*
?Abraham, b. abt. 1763, living Redding 1820; m. Abigail ———, b. abt. 1761.
Hannah, bapt. 31 Aug. 1766.

10. **Couch, Thomas,** s. of Thomas. Ens., west parish company, Fairfield, Oct. 1762.

Born 28 Nov. 1725; d. at Westport, 4 Dec. 1764 in 39 yr. (g. s.); m. 22 or 25 Feb. 1749/50, Elizabeth Jessup; dau. of Edward, b. 13 Feb. 1727/8, d. 25 Nov. 1815 ae. 87 yrs. 9 mos. (g. s.).

Thomas chose Elizabeth Couch for guardian, Apr. 1765; and she was appointed for her children, Simon, Mary, Gideon, Stephen, Sarah and Elizabeth.

---

* Mother's name stated as Elizabeth in baptismal record.

Children, rec. Fairfield, bapt. Westport:

19+Thomas, b. 1, bapt. 3 Feb. 1751.
20+Simon, b. 6, bapt. 12 Nov. 1752.
Sarah, b. 30, bapt. 31 Mar. 1754, d. at Easton, 24 Feb. 1815 ae. 62; m. 14 Oct. 1772, Hezekiah Banks.
Elizabeth, b. 23, bapt. 25 Jan. 1756, d. at Westport, 3 June 1780; m. Noah-Taylor Hanford; they conveyed, 1774, right from father Thomas Couch dec'd.
Gideon, b. 14 Sept., bapt. 2 Oct. 1757, d. at Westport, 21 Sept. 1817 ae. 60; m. 26 Dec. 1781, Eleanor Wakeman, dau. of John, b. 30 Jan. 1762, d. 21 May 1846 ae. 84-3-21 (g. s.). His will, 24 Feb., proved 28 Oct. 1817, named wife Eleanor, dau. Charry, three sons Wakeman, Gideon, Eli.*
Mary, bapt. 11 May 1760, d. at Westport, 3 May 1824 ae. 64 (g. s.); m. (1) 5 May 1784, Moses Sherwood; m. (2) 15 Mar. 1801, Aaron Sherwood.
Stephen, bapt. 8 May 1763, d. at Bath, N. H., 21 Apr. 1813 (family rec.); m. 29 Jan. 1784, Ann Edmond, dau. of Robert, b. at Woodbury, 18 Mar. 1764, d. at Bath, 6 Apr. 1813.†

11. Couch, Simon, s. of Thomas. Ens., east company, Redding, May 1767; Lt., May 1770.

Born [5 Apr. 1729]; d. 25 Apr. 1809 ae. 80 yrs. 20 days (Bible record); m. 27 Jan. 1753, Rebecca Nash, dau. of Thomas; b. 18 Nov. 1732, d. at Redding, 12 Jan. 1784.

Children, second rec. Fairfield; two bapt. Westport:

Abigail, bapt. 10 Feb. 1754, d. 3 Mar. 1754.
21+Simon, b. 18 bapt. 25 May 1755.
Thomas-Nash, bapt. at Redding, 21 May 1758, d. at Redding, 3 Jan. 1821; m. 13 Dec. 1787, Abigail Stebbins.‡
Rebecca, bapt. at Redding, 16 Feb. 1761, d. 3 Apr. 1785.

---

* Children, bapt. Westport: Wakeman, bapt. 29 May 1785, d. 3 Oct. 1848 ae. 63 yrs. 7 mos. (g. s.); m. Eleanor Banks, dau. of Isaac. Gideon, bapt. 18 Jan. 1789, d. 31 May 1846 ae. 57-7-12 (g. s.). Eli, bapt. 24 July 1791, d. 3 Sept. 1796. Charry, bapt. 11 Aug. 1793, d. 3 Sept. 1796. Eli, bapt. 26 Nov. 1797, d. 1 Apr. 1876 ae. 78 yr. 5 mos. (g. s.); m. Matilda ———, b. [19 Jan. 1800], d. 29 Jan. 1882 ae. 82 yrs. 10 days (g. s.). Charry, bapt. 2 May 1802.

† Children, first rec. Fairfield: Elizabeth, b. 20 Apr. 1785, bapt. 14 Aug. 1785; Mary, bapt. 18 May 1788.

‡ Will of Thomas N., 23 Dec. 1820, proved 13 Jan. 1821; wife Abigail; dau. Rebecca wife of James Denison; sons Hiram and Nash; Abigail, Jane, James, Jr., William-Thomas, and Mary-Ann Denison, children of dau. Rebecca. Children, rec. Redding: Rebecca, b. 19 June 1788; Hiram, b. 27 July 1791; Nash, b. 17 Oct. 1794.

Abigail, bapt. at Redding, 27 Jan. 1765, d. at Greenfield, 27 Nov. 1815 in 54 yr. (g. s.); m. Thomas Hull.
Lydia, bapt. at Redding, 25 Oct. 1767,* d. 13 July 1820; m. 16 Feb. 1792, Andrew Fairchild, Jr.

12. Couch, Samuel, s. of Samuel, 2d.

Born 5 May 1731; d. 17 Aug. 1760 of smallpox in Army on way to Canada; m. 22 Feb. 1756, Rachel Allen, dau. of Joseph, b. 28 July 1728, d. 23 Feb. 1817 ae. 87 yrs. 7 mos.

Adm'n granted, 8 Dec. 1760, to Rachel Couch. Samuel Couch was appointed guardian to the three children, same date.

Children, bapt. Westport, eldest rec. Fairfield:

Elizabeth, b. 20 Aug., bapt. 10 Oct. 1756, d. at Westport, 25 Apr. 1799 ae. 43; m. 15 Dec. 1776, Andrew Bennett.
Joshua, bapt. 11 June 1758, d. at Westport, 13 Oct. 1841 in 84 yr. (g. s.); Dr.; m. 15 July 1779, Patty Patchen, bapt. 22 Nov. 1761, d. 11 Oct. 1851 in 91 yr. (g. s.).†
Rachel, bapt. 2 Nov. 1760; m. 21 July 1779, Joseph Green, Jr., of Weston.

13. Couch, David, s. of Samuel.

Born 25 June 1733; d. at Westport, 20 June 1816 ae. 83 (g. s.); m. at Weston, 1 Oct. 1766, Widow Mary Gorham, who d. 26 Mar. 1822 ae. 89 (g. s.). She was widow of Jabez Gorham, and dau. of Benjamin Couch, bapt. 15 Nov. 1732.

Of Norwalk, 1781, conveyed with wife Mary, land at Saugatuck.

Children, first two bapt. Weston, next three Westport:

Polly, bapt. 19 July 1767.
Joseph, bapt. 16 June 1769; m. 24 Mar. 1803, Abigail Couch.
Benjamin, bapt. 12 May 1771, d. in West Indies, 23 Dec. 1793.
David, bapt. 20 June 1773, d. 9 Dec. 1773.
Susanna (twin), bapt. 20 June 1773, d. 2 Aug. 1781.

---

* Mother's name stated as Lydia in baptismal record.
† Children, bapt. Westport: Betsey, bapt. 18 Sept. 1785; perhaps the Elizabeth who m. 23 Feb. 1803, Samuel-Sturges Smith of Greenfield. Rachel, bapt. 23 Aug. 1789, d. 19 Nov. 1808 ae. 19-8-4 (g. s.). Samuel, bapt. 4 Mar. 1792, d. 29 Sept. 1793 ae. 2 yrs. less 5 days (g. s.). Joshua, bapt. 6 Oct. 1793, d. 25 Feb. 1869 ae. 75-6-1 (g. s.). Joseph, bapt. 24 Apr. 1796, killed at Lake Champlain, 11 Sept. 1814; ae. 18-8-3 (g. s.). Hezekiah-Allen, bapt. 22 Apr. 1798. Sally-Ann, bapt. 2 July 1802. Mary, bapt. 11 June 1803. Adm'n on Est. of Joseph Couch granted, 9 July 1816, to Joshua Couch, with Benjamin Meeker as surety.

14. Couch, Nehemiah, s. of Samuel.

Born 25 May 1739; d. early in 1823.

He m. 19 Nov. 1780, widow Abigail Baker; widow of Joshua Baker, and dau. of [Eleazer?] Sturges. She d. 9 Aug. 1791.

Child, bapt. Westport:
> Abigail, bapt. 28 Oct. 1781; ?m. 24 Mar. 1803, Joseph Couch.

15. Couch, Josiah, s. of Samuel.

Born Apr. 1743; d. at Westport, 22 Apr. 1821 ae. 78.

He m. at Weston, 21 Apr. 1766, Eunice Frost; dau. of Joseph, b. 16 Sept. 1742.

Children, bapt. Westport:
> Samuel, bapt. 19 Apr. 1767, d. in West Indies, 13 Mar. 1793.
> Adrea, bapt. 30 Apr. 1769.
> Eunice, bapt. 26 Feb. 1775; perhaps d. at Westport, 9 Feb. 1849 ae. 72 (g. s.).
> Josiah, bapt. 20 Nov. 1783.

16. Couch, Joseph, s. of Benjamin.

Bapt. 17 Sept. 1726; Joseph and his son Joseph d. 7 Feb. 1769 between New York and Fairfield, on their passage home.

He m. 7 May 1747, Hannah Sherwood; dau. of David, b. 4 Mar. 1728. Widow Hannah m. at Westport, 21 Nov. 1773, Capt. Gideon Hurlbut.

Adm'n granted, 7 Mar. 1769, to William Bennett, Jr. Dower set to his widow Hannah, 27 Apr. 1770.

Children, rec. Fairfield, bapt. Westport:
> Benjamin, b. 26 Mar., bapt. 3 Apr. 1748, d. 14 June 1777; m. 10 Jan. 1773, Naomi Couch, dau. of Samuel, b. 13 Dec. 1751, d. 15 June 1796.*
> Joseph, b. 5 Feb., bapt. 17 Mar. 1751, d. 7 Feb. 1769.
> Child, stillborn 4 Apr. 1754.
> Hannah, b. 8 June, bapt. 11 July 1756; chose mother Hannah guardian 17 Oct. 1769; m. 23 Sept. 1779, Hudson English.
> Sarah, b. 13 Sept., bapt. 15 Oct. 1758, d. 13 May 1776.

---

* Children, bapt. Westport: Betty, bapt. 1 May 1774; Benjamin, bapt. 11 Sept. 1775. Thomas Bennett was allowed guardian to Benjamin Couch, 7 Feb. 1791.

John, bapt. 19 Oct. 1760; m. 27 Feb. 1782, Rhoda Bennett, dau. of Moses, bapt. 8 May 1763.*
Abraham, bapt. 10 July 1763; m. ———.†
Asa, bapt. 20 Oct. 1765, d. 12 Aug. 1766.
Comfort, bapt. 4 Sept. 1768, d. 10 Feb. 1810 in 43 yr. (g. s.); m. 6 May 1790, John Ogden.

17. **Couch, Ebenezer,** s. of Ebenezer. Ens., 2d Co., 4th Regt., Army, Mar. 1758; 2d Lt., Mar. 1759; 1st Lt., Mar. 1760. Capt. 8th Co., 2d Batt., Army, June 1776.

Born 20 Jan. 1733; d. at Milton, Saratoga County, N. Y., abt Oct. 1800; m. (1) at Greenfield, 27 July 1761, Elizabeth McCarty.

He m. (2) at New Preston, 4 Nov. 1777, Sarah Bostwick. She was widow of Joel Bostwick, and dau. of Jacob Kinney.

Will 17 Aug. 1800, codicil 16 Sept. 1800, proved 8 Nov. 1800; wife Sarah; oldest son John; sons Ebenezer, Jr., Aaron, Joel-Bostwick, Levi; daus. Anna wife of Henry Whitlock, Elizabeth wife of Benjamin Benedict, and Sarah K. Couch. [Surrogate's Court, Saratoga County.]

Children [by first wife], rec. and bapt. Redding:

John, b. 5 May, bapt. 27 June 1762, d. at New Preston, 12 June 1812 ae. 50 (g. s.); m. at New Preston, 9 Mar. 1783, Lois Stone, who d. 8 Jan. 1845 ae. 81 (g. s.).
Levi, b. 25 Aug., bapt. 16 Oct 1763, d. y.
Anna, b. 28 Feb., bapt. 28 Apr. 1765; m. at New Preston, 30 Dec. 1785, Henry Whitlock, of Ridgefield.
Ebenezer, b. 26 Feb. 1768.
Abner, bapt. and d. 24 Mar. 1770.
Aaron, b. 17 June, bapt. 2 Aug. 1772.

Children [by second wife], bapt. New Preston:

Elizabeth, bapt. 30 Apr. 1780; m. Benjamin Benedict.
Joel-Bostwick, bapt. 15 Apr. 1781.
Levi, bapt. 22 June 1783.
Caswell, bapt. 14 Oct. 1785, d. y.
Electa, bapt. 15 June 1788, d. y.
Sarah K.

---

* Children, bapt. Westport: Salome, bapt. 29 June 1783; Charles (son of John and Rhoda of Redding), bapt. July 1785.

† Children, bapt. Westport: Nancy, bapt. 1 July 1786; Joseph, bapt. 10 Feb. 1788.

18. Couch, Jonathan, s. of Ebenezer.

Born 16 July 1736.

He m. (1) at Redding, 15 Aug. 1759, Eunice Griffin; dau. of John, bapt. 22 Oct. 1738.

He m. (2) at Redding, 24 Sept. 1777, Mabel Meeker; prob. widow of Jared Meeker, and née Cole.

Joseph, son of Jonathan of Redding, chose Joseph Frost of Redding for guardian, 3 Aug. 1786.

Children [by first wife], bapt. Redding:

> Lucy, bapt. 8 Apr. 1761.
> Anna, bapt. 17 June 1764.
> Joseph, bapt. 13 Aug. 1769.
> Eli, bapt. 2 Aug. 1772.
> Eunice, bapt. 4 Sept. 1774.

Child [by second wife]:

> Molly, bapt. 31 Jan. 1779.

19. Couch, Thomas, s. of Thomas.

Born 1 Feb. 1751; d. at Redding in 1817; m. 2 Apr. 1772, Sarah Nash, dau. of Jonathan, b. 17 Jan. 1755, d. 1 May 1837.

Distribution, 21 Mar. 1818: widow; heirs of son Thomas, Jr.; sons Jonathan, Nathan, Hezekiah, John; heirs of dau. Sarah; dau. Esther wife of Seth Sanford; dau. Mary wife of Ebenezer Hawley.

Children, bapt. Westport.

> Sarah, b. 9, bapt. 20 Aug. 1773, d. 24 Aug. 1773.
> Thomas, b. 23 Sept., bapt. 30 Oct. 1774, d. 8 Oct. 1805; adm'n granted to Seth Sanford and Mary Couch; m. 25 Sept. 1797, Mary Sanford.*
> Jonathan, b. 13 Feb., bapt. 22 Mar. 1777, d. at South East, N. Y., 4 July 1845.
> Sarah, b. 18 Sept., bapt. 7 Nov. 1779, d. 7 Jan. 1809; m. 8 Oct. 1803, Seth Sanford.
> Nathan, b. 25 Sept. 1781, d. at Natchez, Miss., 9 Sept. 1823.
> Esther, b. 14 Dec. 1783, bapt. 7 Mar. 1784, d. 12 Nov. 1867; m. 28 May 1809, Seth Sanford.
> Moses, b. 2 Oct. 1786, d. 24 June 1796.

---

* Children, rec. Redding: Timothy-Sanford, b. 12 Feb. 1797; Esther, b. 29 Jan. 1799.

Edward, b. 7 Mar. 1789, d. 17 Sept. 1792.
Hezekiah, b. 14 Mar. 1791; res. Patterson, Putnam County, N. Y.
Mary, b. 21 Apr. 1793; m. Ebenezer Hawley, of Ridgefield.
John, b. 28 July 1795; res. Redding.

20. **Couch, Simon, s. of Thomas.**

Born 6 Nov. 1752; d. at Redding, 16 April 1829; m. 7 Jan. 1776, Eleanor Nash, dau. of Jonathan, b. 14 Jan. 1758.

Will 3 Apr. 1828, proved 25 Apr. 1829; son Edward; dau. Eleanor; my son Jessup N. Couch of Chillicothe, Ohio, by will gave to Edward and Eleanor Couch all portion in his mother's estate; children, Elisabeth N. wife of Ozias Burr, Jr., Seth, Eleanor, and Nash Couch, Priscilla wife of Edward Mallery, and Edward Couch; gr. son Simon A. Couch, son of Simon A. late of Ohio dec'd.

Children, rec. Redding, first bapt. Westport, second Redding:

Elizabeth-Nash, b. 9 Oct., bapt. 8 Dec. 1776, d. at Worthington, Ohio, 21 Feb. 1834; m. Ozias Burr, Jr.
Jesup, b. 3 Aug. 1778, bapt. 20 Sept. 1778, d. at Chillicothe, Ohio, 30 June 1821, unm.; grad. Yale Coll.; Judge, Superior Court of Ohio, 1815-21.
Seth, b. 31 Aug. 1780, d. at Brooklyn, N. Y., 30 Apr. 1841; m. 1 May 1806, Sarah Burr, dau. of Ozias.
Eleanor, b. 26 Aug. 1782, d. 8 Dec. 1856, unm.
Simon, b. 2 Dec. 1784, d. 14 Feb. 1794.
Nash, b. 23 Apr. 1787, d. 22 Mar. 1835, unm.; Maj. and Inspector in Militia, N. Y. City.
Priscilla, b. 27 June 1790; m. Edward Mallory, of Worthington, Ohio.
Edward, b. 14 July 1792, d. at Ridgefield, 16 Apr. 1856; Capt.; m. Betsey Marchant, dau. of Joel, b. 6 May 1805.
Simon, b. 6 Dec. 1794; physician, of Marion, Ohio.
Caroline, b. 22 June 1801 (family rec.), d. 8 Mar. 1802.

21. **Couch, Simon, s. of Simon.**

Born 18 May 1755; d. 8 Nov. 1807 ae. 52-5-21 (Bible record); m. 25 Nov. 1779, Abigail Chapman, dau. of Dennie; b. 10 Oct. 1758 (Bible record), d. 18 Dec. 1825 ae. 67-2-8 (Bible record).

Children, rec. Fairfield (also Bible record), bapt. Westport:

Abigail, b. 14 Aug., bapt. Oct. 1782; ?m. 5 Jan. 1800, William Sherwood, Jr.

Simon, b. 16 Oct., bapt. 31 Nov. 1783, d. at Newbern, N. C., 28 July 1819 ae. 35-9-12 (Bible record); m. 2 Nov. 1806, Betsey Hide, dau. of John, b. 5 Feb. 1785, d. 26 Nov. 1863 (g. s.).
William, b. 8 May, bapt. 1 July 1786.

Couch [Unplaced].

WILLIAM m. 26 July 1801, Annis Freeman. [Greens Farms Church.]

Crane, Joseph. Lt., west parish company, Fairfield, May 1731.

Son of Jonathan and gr. son of Benjamin; b. at Windham, 17 May 1696; followed his uncle Elijah to Fairfield; d. 20 Aug. 1781.

He m. abt. 1719, Mary Couch, dau. of Samuel, bapt. 3 May 1696, d. 9 Jan. 1766 ae. 70.

Joseph Crane and Mary his wife, of Dukesfield, Dutchess County, N. Y., conveyed 29 Sept. 1744 to Ephraim Jackson and our son Zebulon Crane of Norwalk, land from Est. of Mary's father Samuel Couch, dec'd. In 1773, suit was brought by Timothy and Abigail Todd of Guilford, Stephen Crane of New Milford, Jonathan Paddock and wife Mary of South Precinct, Dutchess County, N. Y., Joshua Barnum and wife Andrea of the same, and Allen Ball and wife Ann of New Fairfield, against Joseph, David, and Ephraim Jackson, Theophilus Hull and wife Martha, of Redding, and Dan Jackson of Ridgefield [children of Ephraim Jackson dec'd], and Elnathan Sturgis and Martha his wife of Ridgefield.

Children [from Bible record], second bapt. Fairfield:
Zebulon, b. 25 Jan. 1721, d. 24 Jan. 1789.
Joseph, b. 2 Oct. 1722, bapt. 7 Oct. 1722, d. 14 Oct. 1800.
Mary, b. 30 May 1726, d. 17 Mar. 1805; m. Jonathan Paddock.
Thaddeus, b. 27 Mar. 1728, d. 1 Sept. 1803.
Abigail, b. 3 Apr. 1730, d. 30 Sept. 1806; m. 16 May 1751, Timothy Todd.
Anna, b. 12 Apr. 1732, d. 28 Mar. 1805; m. Allen Ball, of New Fairfield.
Stephen, b. 19 May 1734, d. 10 May 1814.
Adrea, b. 25 Oct. 1736, d. 18 Apr. 1810; m. Joshua Barnum.

Crane [Unplaced].

DEBORAH and SARAH, bapt. 25 Jan. 1735/6. [Fairfield Church.]
WIDOW d. 3 Mar. 1761 ae. abt. 90. [Greenfield Church.]

ANN, dau. of Jonathan, m. 18 May 1731, Ebenezer Couch. [Fairfield Rec.]
JABEZ, son of Elijah, bapt. 17 Feb. 1733/4 (the first-born). [Stratfield Church.]
LUCRETIA m. 25 Nov. 1773, Abel Adams. [Easton Church.]

Crawford, Quintin.

He m. Dorothy Newton, dau. of James, b. at Fairfield, 22 Mar. 1681/2.

Children, bapt. Stratfield:
John, bapt. 27 Sept. 1713.
Tabitha, bapt. 27 Sept. 1713.
Israel, bapt. 24 Apr. 1715.
Job, bapt. 24 Mar. 1717.

Crawford [*Unplaced*].

JAMES-LEWIS, b. 20 July 1769. [Redding rec.]
CHARLOTTE, b. 14 Aug. 1763; m. 20 Sept. 1795, Ezra Sanford. [Redding rec.]

Crissey, David.

Son of John and Rebecca (Knowles) (Morehouse) Crissey, b. at Stamford, 12 Sept. 1708.

He m. 26 Mar. 1745, Eunice, widow of Daniel Frost, and dau. of John Sherwood.

They rem. to Cortlandt, Westchester County, N. Y.

Child, bapt. Westport:
John, bapt. 16 Feb. 1746.

Crofut [Vol. 1, pp. 165, 166].
1 Joseph (-) m. Mary Hillier.
  2 Daniel (1670-1707) m. Phebe (————) Lyon.
    3 *Daniel* (1702-1772).
    4 *Joseph* (1704-   ).
    5 *David* (1706-1767).

3. **Crofut, Daniel,** s. of Daniel.

Bapt. 9 Aug. 1702; d. at Redding in 1772; m. Avis Adams, dau. of Nathan, bapt. 29 Nov. 1702.

Adm'n granted to Daniel Crofut, Daniel Beardsley, and James Curtiss, 18 Aug. 1772. Distribution 12 Dec. 1772: Daniel, eldest son, had full portion; Stephen, dec'd, had more than full portion; Stephen, only child and heir to the son John dec'd; dau. Phebe wife of Daniel Beardsley; heirs of dau. Kezia Curtis dec'd; dower of widow "Eves" Crofut.

Children, two rec. Fairfield:

Daniel.
Phebe, m. 10 Nov. 1742, Daniel Beardsley.
6+John, b. 6 May 1735.
7+Stephen, b. 28 Apr. 1740.
Kezia, m. James Curtis.

4. **Crofut, Joseph,** s. of Daniel.

Bapt. at Fairfield, 10 Dec. 1704; m. abt. 1725, Lydia Canfield, dau. of Ebenezer, b. 11 Mar. 1706/7. She was prob. the widow Crofut who d. at New Canaan, 29 Apr. 1794 ae. 89.

Settled in Norwalk; with wife Lydia conveyed 29 Dec. 1725, and 31 Jan. 1727/8, together with other Canfield heirs, being then of Norwalk; lived some years in Ridgefield, but by 1748 rem. to Salem, Westchester County, N. Y.

Children, recorded at Ridgefield:

Samuel, b. 23 Jan. 1727/8.
8+Ebenezer, b. 30 Apr. 1730.
Phebe, b. 3 Feb. 1731/2; m. at Salem, N. Y., 1 Apr. 1757, Benjamin Jones.
Elizabeth, b. 1 July 1734, bapt. at New Canaan, 4 Aug. 1734.
Lydia, b. 13 Dec. 1736, bapt. at New Canaan, 19 Dec. 1736.
Sarah, b. 4 Mar. 1739/40.

Perhaps also:

Rebecca, b. 12 June 1741, d. at New Canaan, 12 Jan. 1792 ae. 50 yrs. 7 mos.; m. 1761, Peter St. John.

5. **Crofut, David,** s. of Daniel.

Bapt. 8 Sept. 1706; d. at Redding in 1767; m. (1) Mary ———; m. (2) Naomi ———. She m. (2) at Trumbull, 14 April 1768, David Welles, of Stratfield.

Will 23 June 1767, proved 7 July 1767; wife Naomi, the estate she brought; gr. children Jemima and Thankful Crofut; dau. Thankful Whitlock; son David, his "birthright"; son James;

gr. son David Crofut; mentioned bro. Daniel Crofut; friend Daniel Hill, Exec'r.

Children [by first wife], one rec. Fairfield:
9+David.
10+James.
  Thankful, m. ―――― Whitlock.
  Nathan, b. 20, bapt. 23 July 1738, d. y.

6. Crofut, John, s. of Daniel.

Born 6 May 1735; d. at Redding in Dec. 1759; m. 16 June 1756, Esther Sanford, dau. of Ebenezer.

Will 24 Dec. 1759, proved 3 Mar. 1760; wife Esther; two sons Stephen and Zalmon; father and mother; father Daniel Crofut, Exec'r.

Children, rec. Redding:
  Stephen, b. 27 Mar. 1757; Ebenezer Sanford of Newtown was appointed his guardian, Apr. 1760.
  Zalmon, b. 16 May 1759.*

7. Crofut, Stephen, s. of Daniel.

Born 28 Apr. 1740; d. at Redding in 1791; m. at Redding, 27 Aug. 1761, Adrea Couch, dau. of Ebenezer, b. 12 Sept. 1742. She m. (2) ―――― Knapp, and d. abt. 1830.

Distribution 27 Apr. 1791: Adra Knap, late widow of the dec'd; Israel Crofut; Ruth Whitlock; Zalmon Crofut; Stephen Crofut; signed also by Ephraim Whitlock.

Adm'n on the part of estate set to the widow Adra as dower was granted, 30 Dec. 1830, to Zalmon Crofut of Redding, with James Denison of Redding as surety; distribution was ordered to the eldest son Israel, Ruth Whitlock, Zalmon Crofut, and Stephen Crofut.

Children:
  Israel, m. (1) 19 Sept. 1784, Annis Sanford; dau. of Samuel, b. at Newtown, 12 Mar. 1766, d. 28 Oct. 1802;† m. (2) 9 June 1803, Elizabeth Stewart.

---

* Children of Zalmon Crofut, rec. Redding: Solomon C., b. 7 May 1779; Ambrose, b. 25 Feb. 1792; Marancy, b. 28 Apr. 1794; Anna-Maria, b. 25 Nov. 1798; Ruth, b. 11 Mar. 1801; Son, b. 13, d. 18 Jan. 1803; Mary, b. 20 Sept. 1809.
† Children, rec. Redding: Josiah-Sanford, b. 30 Dec. 1786; Betsey-Ann, b. 20 Jan. 1793; Joel-Dunning, b. 15 Feb. 1798.

Ruth, m. 15 June 1786, Ephraim Whitlock.
Zalmon.
Stephen.

8. Crofut, Ebenezer, s. of Joseph.

Born (recorded at Ridgefield) 30 Apr. 1730, d. at New Canaan, 30 Mar. 1812; m. (1) 1 Nov. 1749, Sarah St. John, dau. of Jacob, b. 17 Sept. 1733, d. at New Canaan, 3 Oct. 1773; m. (2) Susanna, widow of Hezekiah Green, and dau. of Benajah and Dinah (Smith) Hoyt, bapt. 16 Nov. 1740.

Jacob St. John and wife Experience sold 23 Feb. 1757 land in Norwalk to son-in-law—Ebenezer Crofut.

Children :*

> Joseph, b. 4 Jan. 1751,† d. at New Canaan, 14 Dec. 1831 ae. 79 yrs. 6 mos. 17 days; will 25 Mar. 1829; m. 15 May 1776, Esther St. John, b. 15 May or June 1758, d. 11 Sept. 1838 ae. 80.
> Anne, b. 16 Jan. 1753, d. 10 July 1800 in 46 yr. (g. s., Malta, Saratoga County, N. Y.); m. at Wilton, 11 July 1771, Melatiah Lothrop, who d. 11 June 1826 in 77 yr. (g. s.).
> Joanna, b. 3 Feb. 1755.
> Lydia, b. 9 Nov. 1757; m. at Wilton, 22 Feb. 1778, William Hoyt.
> Sarah, b. 20 May 1759.
> Isabel, b. 31 Aug. 1762, bapt. 26 Sept. 1762.
> Dinah, b. 3 May 1764, bapt. 27 May 1764.
> Phebe, b. 1 Mar. 1766, bapt. 30 Mar. 1766.
> Polly, b. 28 Mar. 1775, bapt. 19 Apr. 1775.

9. Crofut, David, s. of David.

He d. at Redding, 25 Aug. 1802; m. (1) Rachel ———, who d. 17 Feb. 1774; m. (2) at Norwalk, 15 Nov. 1775, Elizabeth ———.

Will 21 May 1799, proved 19 Aug. 1802; wife Elizabeth; two sons, James, Ebenezer; dau. Abigail; heirs of dec'd daus. Sarah and Irena.

Children [by first wife]:

> Sarah, m. ———.
> Irena, d. at Weston 2 Mar. 1792; m. 7 Nov. 1779, Job Curtis.
> James, b. abt. 1761, d. at Preble, N. Y., May 1849; m. by 1786, Eliza-

---

* Baptisms from New Canaan records; births are from a Bible said to have been in possession (before 1900) of Mrs. Hiram Wilkes Crofut of Brookfield.
† Born 26 May 1752, by Bible of his son Ebenezer.

beth Tuttle, dau. of David and Elizabeth (Hickox), b. abt. 1765, d. 4 June 1836.
Abigail.
Ebenezer, b. 7 June 1766, d. at Preble, N. Y., Mar. 1846; m. 23 Feb. 1785, Sarah Raymond, dau. of Benjamin, b. 5 May 1765, d. 28 June 1819.

10. **Crofut, James,** s. of David.

He d. at Ridgefield in 1759; adm'n granted, 13 Apr. 1759, to David Crofoot of Fairfield. Catherine Crofut was appointed guardian to Jemima and Thankful; and David Crofut of Fairfield, guardian to David. The births of the three children of James and Katharine were entered in Fairfield records. David, son of James, chose Mr. Oliver Fairchild of Newtown for guardian, 17 Mar. 1768. Jemima chose Josiah Crofut of Danbury for guardian 8 Nov. 1768; Catherine Crofut asked release from guardianship of Thankful and James Seeley of Danbury was appointed.

Children:
David, b. 21 Oct. 1753.
Jemima, b. 22 Feb. 1755.
Thankful, b. 12 July 1759.

Crofut [*Unplaced*].

—— m. Bethia Squire, dau. of Jonathan, b. [say 1735].
LUCY m. 11 Oct. 1792, Jabez Treadwell. [Weston rec.; also Easton Church.]
NATHAN m. 2 Aug. 1796, Phebe Hendrix. Children: Jonathan, b. 22 Aug. 1797; Silvia, b. 26 Feb. 1799; Peter, b. 16 May 1802 [Redding rec.]
JAMES had children: Elizabeth, bapt. May 1791; James, bapt. 30 Aug. 1794. [Easton Church.]
JOHN had wife Abigail who d. at Redding, 18 Nov. 1843 ae. 80 (g. s.).

Crossman, John. Sergt., French and Indian War.

Born 7 Mar. 1739 (Bible rec.). Called "of Dartmouth," he m. (1) at Westport, 15 Dec. 1756, Ann Allen, b. 20 Dec. 1739 (town rec.) or 19 Jan. 1741 (Bible rec.). They rem. by 1788 to North Salem, N. Y., where he d. 26 Apr. 1812, she 27 Apr. 1806 (Bible rec.). He m. (2) Patty Keeler, a widow.

Adm'n on Est. of John of Ridgefield granted, 4 May 1812, to Ira Crossman of South Salem, Westchester County, N. Y.

Adm'n on Est. of Patty Crossman of Ridgefield, widow of John, granted to Caleb Keeler of Ridgefield, 7 May 1812. Her estate was distributed to her eldest son Silas Keeler, 2d son Gamaliel, 3d son Caleb, 4th son Lewis, 5th son Asa, eldest dau. Abigail, 2d dau. Lurany, 3d dau. Anne.

Children [by first wife], bapt. Westport (births from Bible rec.) :

>Abigail, b. 25 Nov. 1756, d. 19 Apr. 1798; m. 25 Sept. 1776, Elias Bennett.
>John, b. 6 Jan., bapt. 4 Mar. 1759, d. in Army, Apr. 1778 [14 Apr. 1778 by Rev. War Rolls].
>Joseph, b. 10 Jan., bapt. 1 Mar. 1761, d. 15 Apr. 1765.
>Child d. 12 Feb. 1764.
>Amy, b. 12 Oct. 1764, bapt. 27 Nov. 1763; "Rhuama" m. 18 Apr. 1781, Elisha Lincoln.
>Trowbridge, b. 19 Feb., bapt. 11 May 1766, d. at Weston, 12 Mar. 1839 ae. 73 (g. s.) ; m. (1) Pattie Ferris; m. (2) 10 Aug. 1788, Eunice Blatchley, of Norwalk, b. 11 Feb. 1766, d. 5 Feb. 1820 ae. 54 (g. s.) ; m. (3) at Westport, 30 Dec. 1821, Phebe Allen, a widow.*
>Ann, b. 19 Jan., bapt. 12 Mar. 1769; m. 18 May 1788, Gershom Allen.
>Esther, b. 24 Dec. 1771, bapt. 1 Mar. 1772, d. 3 Dec. 1832.
>Ellen, b. 13 May, bapt. 31 July 1774, d. 15 Mar. 1862.
>Jesse, b. 1 May, bapt. 23 June 1776, d. at Weston, 13 Mar. 1852 ae. 75-10-13 (g. s.) ; m. 25 Apr. 1799, Betsey Brown, b. [Dec. 1778], d. 8 Oct. 1867 ae. 88 yrs. 10 mos. (g. s.).
>John Allen, b. 7 Oct., bapt. 6 Dec. 1778.
>Joseph, b. 29 Dec. 1780, bapt. 25 Mar. 1781, d. 12 July 1783.
>Ira, bapt. 18 June 1783.
>Dolly, b. 14 July, bapt. 18 Sept. 1785.

Cullum [*Unplaced*].

>ARTHUR of New York m. 18 Dec. 1803, Harriet Sturges. [Fairfield Church.]

Curtis [*Unplaced*].

>PHEBE m. 25 Dec. 1751, Daniel Morehouse. [Fairfield Rec.]
>MATTHEW, of Newtown, m. 5 Dec. 1759, Abigail Thompson. [Fairfield Church.]
>JOB m. (1) 7 Nov. 1779, Irena Crofut, who d. 2 Mar. 1792. Children: Eliza, b. 9 Oct. 1780; Sarah, b. 25 Feb. 1782; Anna, b. 3 Feb. 1784;

---

* Children, rec. Weston, first two bapt. Westport, others Weston. By first wife: Bradford, b. 20 Aug. 1787, bapt. 30 Nov. 1788. By second wife: Joseph, bapt. 20 Sept. 1789. Hiram, b. 4 Feb., bapt. 8 July 1792. Patty, b. 23 Oct. 1793, bapt. 1 May 1794. Fanny, b. 26 Oct. 1795. John, b. 18 Jan., bapt. 3 Sept. 1798, d. at Weston, 10 May 1885 ae. 87-3-21 (g. s.); m. Nancy Adams, who d. 30 Jan. 1880 ae. 82-4-13 (g. s.). Caroline, bapt. 8 Feb. 1801.

Solomon, b. 15 Apr. 1786; Joseph, b. 3 Apr. 1788; Stephen, b. 8 June 1790; William, b. 25 Feb. 1792. He m. (2) 2 July 1792, Elizabeth Parmelee. Child: Eli, b. 21 May 1793. [Weston rec.]

NEHEMIAH m. 6 Mar. 1787, Ann Beardsley. Children: Lydia, b. 11 June 1787; Lyman, b. 6 Apr. 1795. [Weston rec.]

PHINEAS, of Farmington, m. 29 Sept. 1799, Phebe Toby, of Norwalk. [Greens Farms Church].

GOLD, of Newtown, m. 2 Oct. 1781, Elizabeth Gold, of Fairfield. [Fairfield Church.]

BENJAMIN of Fairfield conveyed, 1767, to son Solomon.

Cutler, Jonathan, s. of David.

Born at Boston, 21 Mar. 1708/9; bur. at New Haven, 29 May 1776 ae. 68; m. Mary MacKenzie, dau. of Dougal, bapt. 10 Oct. 1708, d. at New Haven, 1 Jan. 1792 ae. 83.

They lived in Fairfield, and in New Haven, where he was a member of Trinity Church (Prot. Ep.). He was brought from Boston to New Haven by his mother (Abigail Flagg) and stepfather (Henry Caner, the noted architect). His stepbrother, Rev. Henry Caner, m. his wife's sister (Ann MacKenzie).

Children:

>Richard, b. abt. 1737, d. at New Haven, 20 Mar. 1810 ae. 73 (g. s.); m. 29 July 1767, Hannah Howell, dau. of Thomas, b. 1 Jan. 1744/5, d. 9 Dec. 1827 ae. 83 (g. s.).
>William, b. abt. 1738, d. at New Haven, 3 Aug. 1765 ae. 27 (g. s.), unm.
>Mary, m. John Whittier.
>Benjamin, b. abt. 1746, d. at New Haven, 30 June 1774 ae. 28 (g. s.); m. Mary Beecher, dau. of John, b. abt. 1751, d. 4 July 1786 ae. 35 (g. s.).
>Ann.

Dalley, Cornelius.

Child, bapt. Westport:
>Susanna, bapt. 27 Aug. 1758.

Dann [*Unplaced*].

>JOHN* m. 8 Feb. 1775, Sarah Whitlock. [Weston Church.]
>JAMES m. 31 Dec. 1789, Sarah Canfield, at Wilton. [Weston Church.]
>HANNAH m. 4 Aug. 1795, David Sherwood. [Weston Church.]

---

* His surname was spelled *Tan* in marriage record, *Tean* in a deed. He may not have been a Dann.

Darling, John, s. of John [Vol. I, p. 179].

Bapt. 24 Mar. 1694/5.

He m. Abilene Jessup, dau. of Edward, bapt. 13 Sept. 1696. Their first four children were bapt. at Greenfield, 4 Aug. 1729. Called late of Fairfield, now of Patterson, N. Y., he conveyed, 3 Mar. 1760, to David Darling of Fairfield, land in Norfield.

Children, five bapt. Greenfield:

> John, Ens. of Regt. of Foot, Cape Breton Expedition, Feb. 1745. Adm'n on his estate was granted to his father, 1750.
> James.
> +David.
> Jabez, m. at Wilton, Dec. 1753, ———.
> Elizabeth, bapt. 28 Mar. 1730; m. 1 Mar. 1748/9, Nathan Guire.
> Sarah, bapt. at Redding, 23 July 1738.

Darling, Joseph, s. of John [Vol. I, p. 179].

Bapt. 29 June 1701.

Children, three bapt. Greenfield, four Redding:

> Rachel, b. 28 Jan., bapt. 2 Feb. 1728/9; m. 10 Dec. 1746, Benjamin Sturgis.
> Hannah, bapt. 25 July 1731.
> Grace, bapt. 6 Jan. 1733/4.
> Eunice, bapt. 25 Jan. 1736; m. 25 May 1757, Joseph Dikeman.
> Benjamin, bapt. 15 Apr. 1738; ?m. 6 Nov. 1777, Mary Chapman; widow of Daniel Chapman, née Andrews.*
> Martha, bapt. 11 Jan. 1741;† m. at Redding, 29 May 1778, Austin Baxter.
> Joseph, bapt. 17 Oct. 1743, d. at Ridgefield in 1780; will 3 Mar., proved 13 May 1780, named wife Mary, sons Samuel, John, and Joseph, daus. Elizabeth, Rachel, and Mehitabel Darling; wife and Capt. Ichabod Doolittle, Exec'rs. Samuel chose Daniel Rockwell for guardian, and John and Elizabeth chose Elias Reed, 1787; Rachel chose Samuel Darling, 1788.‡

---

* Children, rec. Redding: Mary, b. 25 Oct. 1778, bapt. 3 Jan. 1779, m. 2 Jan. 1797, Aaron Byington; Joseph, b. 27 July 1780; Elizabeth, b. 24 Feb. 1784; Benjamin A., b. 2 Apr. 1786; Lore, b. 8 Apr. 1788; Sarah, b. 11 Oct. 1791; Selina, b. 27 Dec. 1794. Benjamin A. m. 2 Nov. 1808, Sally B. Odell of Norwalk, and had: Eli-Andrus, b. 12 Oct. 1809; Minott-Odell, b. 22 Apr. 1811.

† John, son of Martha Darling, bapt. 1 Sept. 1771.

‡ Sarah, dau. of Joseph and Mary, bapt. at Redding, 1 Nov. 1772. Joseph, Audra and John, three children, parentage unstated, bapt. at Redding, 11 Mar. 1787 (Trinity Church rec.). The son Joseph m. 1 Jan. 1807, Betsey Ferris of Salem, and had three children, rec. at Redding.

Mary, bapt. 7 May 1749, d. at Redding, 5 Nov. 1773 ae. 24 yrs. 7 mos. (g. s.); m. 12 Mar. 1767, Joseph Meeker.
? Samuel, b. abt. 1754, bur. 1 Sept. 1807 ae. 53 (Trinity Church rec.).*

Darling, Benjamin, s. of John [Vol. I, p. 179].

Bapt. 28 Feb. 1702/3; d. at Ridgefield in 1788.

He m. 6 Jan. 1725/6, Mary Hide; dau. of John, b. 8 Oct. 1705.

Will 8 Mar. 1784, proved 11 Feb. 1788; wife Mary; residue to Benjamin Darling of Redding, the heirs of Joseph Darling of Ridgefield dec'd, and Jonathan Darling of Redding.

Darling, David, s. of John, 2d. Called Ens. at bapt. of child 1758; but no record of appointment is found, and he served as a Private in the Campaign of 1762, French and Indian War Rolls.

He m. 14 Dec. 1756, Sarah Morehouse, dau. of Jehu, b. 24 Oct. 1733.

Of Claverack, N. Y., 1790.

Children, rec. Fairfield:

> Jessup, b. 20 June 1758, bapt. at Westport, 16 July 1758; m. 13 Jan. 1786, Lydia Morehouse, dau. of Solomon, b. 6 July 1763, d. at Westport, 28 July 1814 ae. 51 yrs. 22 days (g. s.).
> Sarah, b. 9 Feb. 1760, bapt. at Greenfield, 17 Mar. 1760.
> Huldah, bapt. at Weston, 22 Mar. 1767.

Darling, (Dr.) Joseph.

Son of Thomas and Abigail (Noyes), b. at New Haven, 1 July 1759, d. there 15 Nov. 1850 ae. 91 (g. s.).

He m. at Fairfield, 24 Mar. 1784, Mrs. Aurelia Mills, of Ripton [Huntington]. She was dau. of Elisha and Mary (DeForest) Mills, b. at Huntington, 14 Dec. 1757, d. at New Haven, 22 Nov. 1846 ae. 89 (g. s.).

He settled in Huntington, 1781, and after a few months rem. to Fairfield, where he was Clerk of Probate and County Courts; in 1787 rem. to North Haven; abt. 1790 settled in New Haven as merchant and druggist, where he was Justice 25 yrs. or more until

---

* Children of Samuel Darling, bapt. Trinity Church: Lois, John, and Mary, bapt. 6 Apr. 1792; Jarvis and Polly Elmira, bapt. 16 Apr. 1796; Lucy and Lucinda (twins), bapt. 2 Dec. 1804. Of these, Mary was bur. 27 Mar. 1796.

1815; frequently Alderman, 1800-17; Treasurer of New Haven County.

Of North Haven, 1789, he conveyed property in Fairfield "where I lately dwelt."

Children, first rec. Fairfield, two North Haven, one New Haven:
   Isaac, b. 21 May 1786, bapt. 20 Aug. 1786; m. Catherine Banks.
   Aurelia, b. 11 Jan., bapt. 9 Mar. 1788, d. Sept. 1813; m. James Dwight.
   Abigail Elizabeth, bapt. 30 May 1790, d. at Brooklyn, N. Y., 9 Jan. 1860 ae. 70 (g. s., New Haven); m. Aretius B. Hull.
   Joseph, bapt. 16 Feb. 1794; m. Zaphira Dana.

Darrow, Jonathan.

Of Norwalk, rem. to Fairfield.

He m. (1) 27 Sept. 1743, Abigail Jackson, dau. of Robert, b. 22 Oct. 1720, d. 20 July 1756 ae. 35 yrs. 9 mos. (Bible record).

He m. (2) 4 Sept. 1758, Grace, widow of Benjamin Lines, and dau. of Samuel Barlow, bapt. 24 May 1724, d. 29 Aug. 1761 ae. 37 yrs. 5 mos. (Bible record).

He m. (3) at Fairfield, 9 Dec. 1761, Elizabeth, widow of Jabez Bulkley, and dau. of Capt. John Osborn, bapt. 28 May 1727.

Children [by first wife], births from Bible record:
   Daniel, b. 15 July 1744, d. 28 Mar. 1754.
   +Jonathan, b. 30 Mar. 1746.
   +Nicholas, b. 11 Feb. 1747/8.
   Abigail, b. 3 Jan. 1749/50, d. 26 Sept. 1772 (Perry Diary); m. at Westport, 15 Feb. 1769, Andrew Bulkley of Greenfield.
   Ann, b. 15 May 1752; m. at Redding, 26 Jan. 1775, Robert Stow.
   Daniel, b. 15 Apr. 1754, d. at Westport, 5 Aug. 1821; m. at Westport, 31 Mar. 1784, Hannah Downs; prob. dau. of Thomas, bapt. 10 Oct. 1760.*
   Sarah, b. 9 July 1756, d. at Thompson, N. Y., in 1841; m. 25 Dec. 1777, Stephen Stratton.

Children [by second wife], bapt. Fairfield, births from Bible record:
   +Benjamin, b. 29 July, bapt. 12 Aug. 1759.
   Grace, b. 25 June, bapt. 19 July 1761; m. 30 Mar. 1779, Samuel Stratton.

---

* Children, bapt. Westport: Betsey, bapt. 15 Feb. 1789; Jonathan and Anne (twins), bapt. 15 Jan. 1792; Eunice, bapt. 8 Oct. 1797; Daniel, bapt. 13 Jan. 1800.

Child [by third wife], bapt. Fairfield, birth from Bible record:
>Thankful, b. 15, bapt. 20 May 1764, d. at Fairfield, 28 Aug. 1848 ae. 84 (g. s.); m. 11 Sept. 1783, Benjamin Sturgis.

Darrow, Jonathan, s. of Jonathan.

Born 30 Mar. 1746; d. a prisoner in New York in 1780.

He m. (1) at Fairfield, 31 Jan. 1771, Elizabeth Bulkley; dau. of Jabez, bapt. 25 Nov. 1750.

He m. (2) 8 Feb. 1778, Molly Thorp; dau. of Eliphalet, b. 16 Aug. 1761, d. at Fairfield, 15 Sept. 1834 ae. 74 (g. s.).

Inv. presented 26 Jan. 1781; Capt. Eliphalet Thorp, Adm'r.

Molly Darrow of Fairfield m. 17 Apr. 1783, William Pike of Roxbury, Mass.

Child [by second wife]:
>Jonathan, bapt. 2 May 1779.

Darrow, Nicholas, s. of Jonathan.

Born 11 Feb. 1747/8.

He m. at Fairfield, 26 Jan. 1775, Elizabeth Beers; dau. of Joseph, b. 28 Apr. 1752.

Children, rec. Stratford:
>Isabel, b. 3 Nov. 1776.
>Abigail, b. 30 Jan. 1780, bapt. June 1780 by the Derby Epis. Rector.
>Polly, b. 10 Jan. 1784.
>John, b. 19 Sept. 1785.
>Sarah, b. 28 Apr. 1787.
>Esther, b. 7 Jan. 1790.

Darrow, Benjamin, s. of Jonathan.

Born 29 July 1759; d. at Fairfield, 5 Mar. 1827; m. at Greenfield, 22 Feb. 1786, Grace Stratton; dau. of John, b. 22 Mar. 1763, living 1848 ae. 85.

Children, from Bible record:
>Betsey, b. 7 July 178[9].
>Anna, b. 29 Dec. 179[2], d. at Fairfield, 23 Jan. 1853 ae. 60 yrs. 29 days (g. s.); m. Levi Burr.
>Sally, b. [—] Aug. 1795.

278 HISTORY AND GENEALOGY OF

Darrow [Unplaced].

WILLIAM, soldier in Putnam's Army, m. 9 Mar. 1780, Ruth Bartram. [Redding Church rec.]
LEVINAH of Stratfield m. 9 Oct. 1784, Gideon Hawley. [Fairfield Church.]
JEMIMA m. 24 Nov. 1785, William Peet. [Trinity Church.]

Dauchy [Unplaced].

Mary m. 24 Feb. 1787, Ebenezer Sanford. [Redding rec.]

Davenport [Unplaced].

MARTHA [of Stamford] m. 21 Jan. 1754, Gold Selleck Silliman. [Fairfield Rec.]

Davern.

Jane m. by 1758 John Wilkinson, a brazier, of Redding. Perhaps by former marriage she was mother of John Davern who m. Lois Knapp, b. 1 Jan. 1743/4 [see DAVID KNAPP].

Davies, (Dr.) Thomas.

He had children, rec. Redding: Thomas F., b. 22 Aug. 1793; Nancy, d. 6 Mar. 1795 ae. 5 yrs. 3 mos. (g. s.).

Davies [Unplaced].

BANKS, offered for baptism by Levi Disbrow, 30 Oct. 1791. [Greens Farms Church.]

Davis [Vol. I, pp. 180, 181].

```
1 John (    -1713) m. Lydia (―――) Waller.
  2 John (1674-1709) m. ―――.
     Probable children:
        4 James (    -1789).
        5 John (  -   ).
        6 Joseph (  -   ).
        7 Benjamin (    -by 1757).
  3 Samuel (1680-1740) m. (1) Elizabeth Banks*; (2) Hannah (―――) Smith.
     (By 1): 8 Jabez (1705-1791).
```

---

* In addition to the information concerning Samuel's children given in Vol. I, it appears from a deed given in 1764 (but not recorded for many years) that his dau. Elizabeth (bapt. 2 June 1723) m. Elias Scribner of Norwalk.

4. **Davis, James** [s. of John, Jr.?].

James, Joseph, John and Benjamin Davis were of age to be bros. or cousins. They have not been identified definitely.

James and Joseph were bapt. as adults at Greenfield, 26 June 1726. James received a conveyance of land in Fairfield from Samuel Bradley, who called him his kinsman, and in selling the land, James called Samuel Bradley his uncle.

He m. (1) 16 July 1729, Hannah Thorp, bapt. 5 Dec. 1702, d. 15 Apr. 1755.

He m. (2) 3 Oct. 1755, Sarah Morehouse (by town rec.); or 12 Oct. 1755, Widow Sarah Hayes (by Greenfield rec.). She was dau. of Nathan Morehouse and widow of ——— Hayes. Mrs. Sarah Davis d. 5 Aug. 1793 ae. 86 (Trinity Church rec.).

Distribution 25 June 1789: James, only son and heir of John Davis, dec'd, who was the eldest son; son Ebenezer Davis; dau. Mary wife of Nathaniel Coley.

Sarah Davis conveyed land to Joseph Morehouse, 1781, in return for support for life.

Children [by first wife], rec. Fairfield, bapt. Greenfield:
9+John, b. 2, bapt. 6 July 1730.
   Mary, b. 2 Nov., bapt. Dec. 1732; m. (1) 13 Dec. 1749, Peter Lyon; m. (2) Nathaniel Coley.
10+Ebenezer, b. 9, bapt. 13 June 1736.

5. **Davis, John** [s. of John, Jr.?].

No record of birth, marriage or death found; nor of probate. He m. Ann Rumsey, dau. of Benjamin, bapt. 2 Nov. 1701, d. at Westport, 28 Feb. 1766.

Will of Ann Davis, 27 Nov. 1753, proved 7 May 1766; sons John and Joseph Davis; dau. Ann Keeler; Isaac Keeler, Adm'r. Adm'n granted, 3 Mar. 1766, to John Davis of Fairfield. Distribution 1766: son John Davis; gr. son Jared* Stebbins and gr. dau. Ann Keeler, children of dau. Ann Keeler dec'd.

Children:
   Ann, m. (1) at Westport, 13 Jan. 1747/8, Ebenezer Stebbins; m. (2) Isaac Keeler, of Ridgefield.
11+John.
   Joseph, d. between 1753 and 1766, apparently s. p.

---
* Or Jeremiah.

6. **Davis, Joseph** [s. of John, Jr.?]

Bapt. at Greenfield 26 June 1726, with James (prob. his bro.). He m. 11 Jan. 1733, Elizabeth Smith, bapt. 2 June 1715.

Children, rec. Fairfield, bapt. Greenfield:

    Eleanor, b. 11 Aug., bapt. Aug. 1733; m. 22 Jan. 1755, Amos Williams.
12+Joseph, b. 16 Feb. 1738.
    Jehiel, b. 31 Mar. 1742.
    Phebe, b. 26 Nov. 1747 [error for 1746], bapt. 25 Jan. 1746/7; m. 23 Jan. 1766, Samuel Goodsell.
    Nathan, b. 25 Mar. 1754.

7. **Davis, Benjamin** [s. of John, Jr.?]

No death or probate found. He m. at Dutch Reformed Church, New York City, 22 Mar. 1734, Abigail Hill, dau. of Capt. Thomas, b. 9 May 1718. She was a widow by 1757; Widow Abigail m. (2) 17 Mar. 1767, David Bulkley. She d. at Amenia, N. Y., 20 June 1807 ae. 89 (g. s.).

The will of Thomas Hill 1769 named his dau. Abigail wife of David Bulkley and referred to her former husband Benjamin Davis. Thomas Davis (son of Benjamin, Jr.) in deeds referred to land "which descended to me from my uncle Thad^s Davis dec^d" (1818), and land "which descended to me from my Grandmother Abigail Bulkley late of Little nine partners deceased" (1808).

Children, rec. Greenfield:

    Samuel, bapt. 8 May 1736.
13+Benjamin, b. [say 1738], bapt. 22 Aug. 1742.
    Thomas, b. [say 1740], bapt. 22 Aug. 1742; chose Abigail Davis for guardian, 11 Oct. 1757; d. (as son of Widow Davis) 12 Nov. 1758 in 20 yr. (g. s.).
    Thaddeus, bapt. 22 Aug. 1742, d. at Amenia, N. Y., 26 July 1812 ae. 70 (g. s.); of Redding 1761.
    Sarah, bapt. 13 Jan. 1744/5; m. at Fairfield, 19 Jan. 1770, George Morehouse.
    Elijah, bapt. in 1748/9, d. in infancy [1748/9].
    Abigail, b. [say 1751], bapt. in childhood, 25 Oct. 1759.
    Ann, bapt. (no date); by family record, b. 15 Feb. 1753, d. 17 Dec. 1839; m. Jesse Dunning, son of Michael and Hannah (Green) Dunning; lived in Dutchess County.

8. **Davis, Jabez,** s. of Samuel.

Born [say 1705], d. at Fairfield in 1791; m. 3 Aug. 1726, Rebecca Rowland; dau. of Israel, bapt. 5 Apr. 1702.

He conveyed, 1761, to dau. Hannah wife of Christopher Sturgis.

Adm'n granted, 6 June 1791, to Nehemiah Phippeny.

Children, rec. Fairfield, bapt. Greenfield:

Hannah, b. 26 May, bapt. 2 June 1728; m. at Westport, 18 Jan. 1749/50, Christopher Sturges, Jr.
Eunice, b. 15 Nov. 1730, bapt. 16 Nov. 1729(?); m. 13 Jan. 1747/8, Peter Thorp.
Experience, b. 29 Aug., bapt. Sept. 1733.
Lydia, b. 19 June, bapt. 17 Aug. 1735; m. 14 Feb. 1771, Nehemiah Phippeny.
Aquila, b. 28 May, bapt. 5 June 1737. [Daughter.]
Grace, b. 25 June, bapt. 1 July 1739.
Betty, b. 29 May, bapt. 23 Aug. 1741.

9. **Davis, John,** s. of James.

Born 2 July 1730; d. in 1760.

He m. 3 Jan. 1752, Elizabeth Meeker; dau. of John, b. 5 Aug. 1732 [1728?].

Adm'n granted 22 Apr. 1760 to Ebenezer Davis and Reuben Olmstead. James Davis appointed guardian to James. Distribution: Widow Elizabeth Davis; only child James.

Children, rec. Fairfield:

Lydia, b. 17 June 1754, d. 15 Sept. 1754.
James, b. 27 July 1755; loyalist.
Hannah, b. 17 Nov. 1756, d. 2 Feb. 1757.
Hannah, b. 3 Dec. 1757, bapt. at Greenfield, 11 Dec. 1757, d. y.

10. **Davis, Ebenezer,** s. of James.

Born 9 June 1736. Eben Davis bur. 14 Dec. 1793 (Trinity Church rec.).

He m. 3 Jan. 1759, Mary Hayes, prob. his stepsister.

Children, bapt. Weston:

Mary, bapt. 27 Oct. 1759.
John, bapt. 12 Apr. 1761.

Nathaniel, b. 13 Mar., bapt. 17 Apr. 1763; m. 7 Mar. 1789, Huldah Dimon; dau. of Benoni, b. 28 Jan. 1765.*
Child, bapt. 1764.
Ebenezer, bapt. 10 Aug. 1766; one Eben Davis d. 13 Nov. 1839 (Miss Treadwell's book); m. 1 Aug. 1789, Mary Dimon; dau. of John, bapt. 17 Oct. 1762.†
Samuel, bapt. 29 May 1768.
Abner, bapt. 14 July 1771.

11. **Davis, John,** s. of John.

He d. at Westport, 19 Apr. 1797; m. 5 Jan. 1763, Olive Jacocks, dau. of William, b. 17 Oct. 1735, d. 5 Oct. 1814 ae. 80.

Adm'n granted, 13 May 1797, to Olive Davis; David and John Davis, sureties.

Adm'n on Olive's estate granted, 10 Jan. 1815, to Jere Davis of Hamden, with Doctor Davis as surety.

Children, bapt. Westport:

David, bapt. 14 Apr. 1765; m. Deborah Bulkley, b. 26 Jan. 1761.‡
John, bapt. 24 Nov. 1765, d. at Easton, 23 July 1824 ae. 48 (g. s.); m. Mindwell Bulkley, b. 22 Aug. 1765, d. 21 Dec. 1834 ae. 70 (g. s.).§
Joseph, bapt. 11 Oct. 1767; ?m. Esther (Burr), bapt. 11 Sept. 1763, widow of Abijah Knapp.‖
Samuel, bapt. 8 Jan. 1769.**
Ann, bapt. 5 May 1771.
Jerry, b. 15 Feb. 1773, bapt. 28 Mar. 1773, d. at Hamden, 23 Jan. 1849 ae. 73 yrs. 11 mos. 8 days (g. s.); m. Martha ———, who d. 18 Aug. 1861 ae. 86 (g. s.).
Daniel, bapt. 27 Aug. 1775; m. 26 Nov. 1801, Ulilly Sherwood.
Doctor, bapt. 14 June 1778.
Sarah (twin), bapt. 14 June 1778, d. at Westport, 19 June 1858 ae. 80 (g. s.).

* Children rec. Weston, bapt. Trinity Church: Justice-Dimon, b. 10 Apr. 1789. Sarah, b. 24 Nov. 1790, bapt. 13 Feb. 1791.
† Children, bapt. Trinity Church: Abigail, bapt. 25 Aug. 1791. Silas, bapt. 17 Mar. 1792, d. 4 Jan. 1827. Betsey, bapt. 15 June 1794. Adm'n on estate of Silas of Weston was granted to Oliver C. Sanford, 12 Jan. 1827, the widow refusing.
‡ Children of David, bapt. Easton: Clarissa, bapt. Sept. 1790; Betsey, bapt. 25 July 1793; Anne, bapt. Apr. 1796. "Clara" m. at Easton, 1 Jan. 1815, Zalmon Gould.
§ Adm'n on John's estate was granted, 27 Sept. 1824, to Nathan Davis. Distribution, 1825; widow Mindwell, daus. Esther B., Sarah, Olive, Bulai, sons John, Joshua. Children, bapt. Easton: Olive, bapt. 27 Dec. 1792, d. at Easton, 4 May 1839 ae. 47 (g. s.); John-Bulkley, bapt. 4 Oct. 1795. One Esther m. at Easton, Mar. 1814, Thomas Treadwell.
‖ Child of Joseph, bapt. Easton: Sarah, bapt. 5 May 1791.
** Adm'n on Est. of Samuel [this Samuel?] granted, 25 Mar. 1816, to John Gray; John Davis, surety. [See Samuel, son of Ebenezer.]

12. Davis, Joseph, s. of Joseph.

Born 16 Feb. 1738; one Joseph, perhaps this man, d. Jan. 1811 (Miss Treadwell's book).

He m. at Greenfield, 21 Mar. 1758, Abigail Bradley; dau. of Francis, b. 20 May 1737.

Children, bapt. Weston [all as children of Joseph, *Jr.*]:
- Hannah, bapt. 5 July 1759.
- Lyman, bapt. 10 Aug. 1760.
- Nehemiah, bapt. 12 June 1762; m. at Easton, 8 Mar. 1789, Ruth Dimon.
- Joel, bapt. 26 Nov. 1763; m. 19 Mar. 1794, Mary Hull, bapt. 17 May 1761.
- Abigail, bapt. 25 May 1766.
- Gershom, bapt. 25 July 1768; m. 3 Feb. 1793, Sarah Sherwood, dau. of Jabez, b. 24 Aug. 1773.
- Rachel, bapt. 27 May 1770.
- Isaac, bapt. 3 Oct. 1771.
- Abel, bapt. 7 Feb. 1775.
- Levi, bapt. 7 Feb. 1775; m. 24 Nov. 1793, Nancy Carley.

13. Davis, Benjamin, s. of Benjamin.

Born [say 1738].

He m. at Redding, 21 May 1758, Eunice Nash, b. 27 Mar. 1737. She m. (2) John Morehouse.

Children, bapt. Westport:*
- Eunice, bapt. 28 Jan. 1759, d. at Westport, 29 Sept. 1803 ae. 44; m. 29 May 1780, Stephen Godfrey.
- Mary, bapt. 28 Dec. 1760;† m. Nathaniel Weeks.
- Abigail, bapt. 6 Feb. 1763, d. at Westport, 6 Dec. 1831 ae. 69 (g. s.); m. (1) Thomas Andrews; m. (2) 14 Feb. 1808, Jeremiah Rowland.
- Thomas, bapt. 25 June 1764, d. at Fairfield, 18 July 1827 [Pension Rec.]; m. 20 Apr. 1786, Abigail Wakeman, dau. of Joseph; she d. at Fairfield, 24 Jan. 1842 ae. 76 (g. s.).‡

---

* Mercy, dau. of Eunice Davis, bapt. 3 Oct. 1773.
† Abigail Bradley, dau. of Mary Davis, bapt. 21 July 1782.
‡ Children, bapt. Westport: Rebecca, bapt. 6 May 1787, d. 27 Oct. 1793; Joseph-Wakeman, bapt. 25 June 1790; Abigail, bapt. 26 Feb. 1792; Hezekiah, bapt. 17 Aug. 1794; Samuel, bapt. 9 Oct. 1796; Rebecca, bapt. 10 Feb. 1799; Mary-Ann, bapt. 15 Mar. 1801; Seth, bapt. 29 Aug. 1803; Thomas, bapt. 10 June 1807.

Davis, John. Ens., west company, Redding, Oct. 1767; Lt., May 1771.

Of Redding, d. by 1777. Connection with other Davis families not ascertained. He m. Sarah ———, who d. by 1791.

Inv. 7 July 1777. Distribution 20 Apr. 1791: eldest son John; Daniel; Stephen; Samuel; eldest dau. Millison Meeker; Sarah, Martha, Eunice, and Esther Davis.

> Children, rec. and bapt. Redding:
>> Millicent, b. 18 Jan., bapt. 10 Mar. 1754; m. 14 Mar. 1775, Seth Meeker.
>> Sarah, b. 4 Jan., bapt. 22 Feb. 1756.
>> John, b. 20 Dec. 1758, bapt. 4 Feb. 1759, d. at Redding, 19 Oct. 1840 ae. 82 (g. s.); m. 21 Oct. 1779, Eunice Gray; dau. of John, b. 15 Mar. 1760.*
>> Daniel, b. 16 Apr., bapt. 24 May 1761.
>> Martha, b. 26 Dec. 1763, bapt. 29 Jan. 1764.
>> Stephen, b. 25 July, bapt. 31 Aug. 1766.
>> Eunice, b. 14 June, bapt. 23 July 1769; m. 19 May 1789, Azariah Meeker.
>> Esther, bapt. 19 Apr. 1772; m. 17 Oct. 1790, John Gray.
>> Samuel, bapt. 25 June 1775.

Davis, Joshua.

Son of David, b. at Brookhaven, L. I., 3 Apr. 1757 (Bible rec.).

Of Long Island, m. at Fairfield, 1 Jan. 1783, Abigail Redfield; dau. of James, bapt. 22 Nov. 1761.

He d. at Greenfield, 25 Jan. 1833 ae. 76 (g. s.); she d. 21 Sept. 1851 ae. 90 yrs. 10 mos. (g. s.).

> Children, bapt. Fairfield:
>> Phebe, bapt. 29 Feb. 1784, d. at Greenfield, 20 Mar. 1840 ae. 56 (g. s.); m. 8 Feb. 1816, Banks-Eliphalet Hull.
>> James, bapt. 7 Jan. 1787.
>> Sarah, bapt. 2 May 1790.
>> Abigail, bapt. 9 Sept. 1792.
>> Spicer, bapt. 26 June 1796, d. at Greenfield, 9 Dec. 1828 ae. 32 yrs. 8 mos. (g. s.).
>> Eunice-Burr, bapt. 20 Apr. 1800, d. at Fairfield, 28 Dec. 1880 ae. 81 (g. s.); m. 31 May 1824, Morris Sturges, of Mill River.

---

* Children, rec. Redding: Daniel, b. 8 Dec. 1783, d. 13 Mar. 1784; Roxey, b. 24 Apr. 1786; Aaron, b. 2 Nov. 1787; Moses, b. 16 July 1792; Hezekiah, b. 19 Feb. 1797.

Davis [Unplaced].

MARY, bapt. 3 May 1747. [Greenfield Church.]
SARAH m. 22 Apr. 1789, Gershom Bradley. [Easton Church.]
PENE m. 24 Nov. 1768, Jehiel Smith. [Weston Church.]
JAMES m. 25 May 1793, Lydia Fitch, at Wilton. [Weston Church.]

Dean, Benjamin.

He m. 6 Dec. 1753, Mary Squire; dau. of Nathaniel, b. 12 Oct. 1735.

Children, rec. Fairfield, first two bapt. Redding:
  Sarah, b. 31 Jan., bapt. 10 Feb. 1754, d. in 1820; m. at Weston, 25 Nov. 1773, Thomas Banks.
  Esther, b. 8 Nov., bapt. 28 Dec. 1755; "Hester" m. at Weston, 27 Aug. 1777, Nathan Whitlock.
  Bradley, bapt. at Weston, 28 June 1761.
  Aaron, bapt. at Weston, 9 Oct. 1774; m. at Weston, 24 Nov. 1793, Huldah Hawley.

Dean, Daniel.

Child, bapt. at Redding:
  Eunice, bapt. 15 Oct. 1738; m. at Redding, 16 Dec. 1757, William Monroe.

Dean, John.

He m. Martha Taylor, dau. of Reuben.

Children, bapt. at Redding:
  Eunice, bapt. 19 June 1763.
  John, bapt. 26 May 1765.
  Lydia, bapt. 15 Feb. 1767.

Dean, Daniel.

He m. at Redding, 29 June 1755, Mary Lee; dau. of William.

Children, bapt. Redding:
  Abigail, bapt. 19 Oct. 1755.
  Hannah, bapt. 5 Sept. 1757.
  Rachel, bapt. 5 Sept. 1757.
  Huldah, bapt. 9 Sept. 1759.
  Rene, bapt. 2 June 1765.

DeForest [Unplaced].

EPHRAIM m. 25 Oct. 1764, Sarah Betts; both of Norwalk. [Redding Town and Church rec.]

DeForest, Nehemiah.

Son of Samuel and Abigail (Peat), b. at Stratford, 24 Jan. 1743; d. at Easton, 9 Dec. 1801 in 58 yr. (g. s.); m. (1) 20 Dec. 1769, Mary Lockwood, dau. of Peter, d. at Monroe, 17 Oct. 1790 ae. 45 (g. s.); m. (2) 28 Aug. 1793, Eleanor Hickock of Southbury, who d. 5 May 1825.

Children [by first wife] :*
    Abby, b. 16 Mar. 1771; m. Legrand-Moss Lewis.
    William, b. 13 June 1773.
    Lockwood, b. 5 Mar. 1775; m. Mehitabel Wheeler, dau. of Nathan and Charity (Beach).
    Polly, b. 27 Apr. 1777; m. Samuel M. Munson.
    Philo, b. 21 July 1779.
    DeLucerne, b. 30 June 1781.
    Betsey, b. 16 Jan. 1785.

Children [by second wife]:
    Charles, b. 28, d. 31 Jan. 1794.
    Charles, b. 10 Aug. 1795.

Denmore, Salathiel.

The name was written "Denbo" in some of the Fairfield records, as well as in New Hampshire, Salathiel having originated at Oyster River in that Province. The standard spelling to-day seems to be Dinsmore.

He m. abt. 1734 Ruth Rumsey, dau. of Benjamin, bapt. 1 Aug. 1709. She divorced him early in 1749, stating that she had married him abt. fourteen years before, and that he deserted her three years before. Ruth Denmore, formerly Rumsey, conveyed in 1758 land laid out to my gr. father Robert Rumsey dec'd, also right from sister Abigail Rumsey dec'd.

Children:
    Mary, m. at Westport, 24 Feb. 1754, Jabez Cable.
    Others?

---

* Combined from Weston rec. and Orcutt's *Hist. of Stratford.*

Dennie, John, s. of Albert [Vol. I, p. 182].

Bapt. 7 Oct. 1694; rem. to Boston, where he was a merchant.
He m. (1) Mary Edwards, dau. of John, bapt. 7 July 1695.
He m. (2) Sarah Webb, dau. of Rev. Joseph, bapt. 30 Jan. 1702/3.

Children [by first wife], bapt. Fairfield:

> Albert, bapt. 4 Nov. 1716; name apparently changed to John, who m. (1) at Boston, 8 Sept. 1743, Sarah Wendell; m. (2) 1 Dec. 1748, Susannah Richardson.
> Mary, bapt. 1 Dec. 1717; m. 18 Oct. 1739, Rev. William Hooper, of Boston.
> Grizzel, bapt. 18 Sept. 1720; m. (1) 30 Nov. 1747, Nathaniel Martin, of Boston; m. (2) 28 Feb. 1753, Dr. Simpson Jones, of Hopkinton.
> Sarah, bapt. May-June 1725; m. 24 Dec. 1747, William Marchant, of Boston.
> William, bapt. 23 Oct. 1726.
> Thomas, bapt. 5 May 1728, d. y.
> Thomas, bapt. 11 Oct. 1730.
> Abigail, bapt. Apr. 1733, living unm. 1758.
> Elizabeth, m. 10 May 1743, William Fletcher.

Dennie, James, s. of Albert [Vol. I, p. 182].

Bapt. 14 Feb. 1702/3; d. at Fairfield in 1759; m. (1) 13 Apr. 1731, Mrs. Eunice Sturgis; dau. of Jonathan, b. 4 Jan. 1708/9, d. 16 Oct. 1740;* m. (2) Sarah Thompson, dau. of David, bapt. 24 May 1724. She m. (2) Dr. Francis Forgue, and d. 24 Jan. 1796 ae. 72 (g. s.).

Adm'n granted, 23 Feb. 1759, to Wm. Samuel Johnson and David Burr, Jr.; Thaddeus Burr, surety. Distribution 1759: widow Sarah; Eunice wife of Thaddeus Burr, land at New Fairfield; Sarah Dennie, youngest dau., land at Litchfield, Salisbury and Cornwall.

Child [by first wife]:

> Eunice, b. abt. 1732, d. 14 Aug. 1805 in 76 yr. (g. s.); m. 22 Mar. 1759, Thaddeus Burr.

Child [by second wife]:

> Sarah, b. 15 Aug. 1757 (Bible rec.), d. at Fairfield, 15 Dec. 1797 ae. 41 (g. s.); m. Rev. James Sayre.

---

* 6 Oct. 1740 in 32 yr. (g. s.).

Dewey [*Unplaced*].

JOSEPH and Elizabeth had: Elizabeth-Eliot, bapt. 30 May 1799; Nancy, bapt. 7 Jan. 1803; Nathaniel, bapt. 20 Jan. 1804. [Fairfield Church.]

Dibble, Henry.

He m. Abigail ———.

Children, two bapt. Westport:

Joseph, bapt. 31 Mar. 1754.
Thomas, bapt. 6 June 1756.
Patrick, bapt. at Weston, 6 Aug. 1758.

Dibble [*Unplaced*].

ELEANOR m. 20 Feb. 1753, Joseph Elwood. [Greens Farms Church.]
ABIGAIL, dau. of Wakefield, of Danbury, and widow of Daniel Starr, Jr., m. 7 Nov. 1774, Job Bartram. [Fairfield Rec.]
SARAH of Ridgefield m. 26 Sept. 1769, Nehemiah Seeley, Jr. [Redding rec.]

Dickinson, Nathaniel, s. of Thomas [Vol. I, p. 184].

Born July 1697.

He m. Susanna Lockwood, dau. of Robert.

Children, three bapt. Stratford:

Sarah, bapt. 5 May 1723; m. Samuel Eastern.
Mary, bapt. 16 May 1725, d. y.
Naomi, bapt. 28 Aug. 1726.
Zadoc, of Redding 1787; m. Nov. 1762, Hannah dau. of Richard and Eunice (Lyon) Waring, of Newtown.*
Benajah, d. at Stratford, 1772; adm'n granted, 19 Aug. 1772, to Judith Dickerson; m. before 1759, Judith ———.†
Nathan, d. at Newtown, 11 Mar. 1772; m. at Newtown, 19 or 20 May 1760, Zilpha Sherman.
Nathaniel, m. at Stratford, 24 Sept. 1754, Catee Church.

---

* Children: Richard, d. at Redding in 1796; adm'n granted, 21 Nov. 1796, to Isaac Higgins of Weston, and distribution made to bros. and sisters. Hannah, m. Isaac Higgins. Daniel. Elizabeth, unmarried in 1796. Thomas.

† Children: Jesse, bapt. July 1759, d. at Stratford in 1783; adm'n granted, 14 June 1783, to Isaac Dickinson of Stratford, and distribution made to the "heirs" who follow. Isaac. Susannah, m. (rec. Derby) 16 Aug. 1780, Edward Harger. Judah [Judith], m. ——— Lamkin. Chloe. Patience. Hannah.

Lockwood, d. in 1760; adm'n granted, 18 Dec. 1760, to Nathan Dickson of Newtown.*
Robert, of Stratford 1766, when he conveyed to Thomas Sharp of Newtown, right in Greens Farms or Norfield.
Abigail, m. John Kinney.

Dickinson, David.†

He m. at Greenfield, 17 Sept. 1781, Mary Redfield; dau. of John, b. 17 July 1758.

David and Mary his wife of Fairfield conveyed 1784 to Benjamin Dickerson of Fairfield, land from estate of her father John Redfield dec'd.

They rem. to Montgomery, Orange County, N. Y.

Children, bapt. Fairfield:
>Sarah, bapt. 14 July 1782.
>Polly, bapt. 24 Oct. 1784.

Dickinson, Benjamin.†

He (called of Long Island) m. at Fairfield, 8 Apr. 1784, Esther Ogden; dau. of Jonathan [q. v.], bapt. 19 Sept. 1762.

They rem. to Montgomery, Orange County, N. Y., by 1791, when he conveyed the property he had purchased from David Dickerson.

Child, bapt. at Fairfield:
>Deborah, bapt. 15 May 1785.

Dickinson [Unplaced].

>DEBORAH, b. 1733, prob. a widow, was entered in Weston records, with Sarah, b. 1764, and Hannah, b. 1769, prob. her daus., and Eliza Lillibridge, b. 1785, prob. a gr. dau. Sarah d. at Weston, 12 July 1834 ae. 72 (g. s.).

Dikeman, John.

He d. at Redding, 28 Apr. 1768 ae. 97.

---

* One of his brothers evidently named a son after him, Lockwood, who is claimed as a Revolutionary soldier of Redding, and was killed 14 Mar. 1782.

† These Dickinsons or Dickersons may be of the tribe of James who m. 8 Dec. 1709, Hannah Rumsey, dau. of Ens. Benjamin; and had two sons rec. Norwalk: John, b. 22 Oct. 1711; and Benjamin, b. 9 Jan. 1713/4. James and Hannah were of Fairfield, 1734, of Courtlandt, Westchester County, N. Y., 1740, and of "'Sciners Farm," Westchester County, 1747.

Dikeman, Cornelius.

Of Norwalk, he conveyed 1770 to dau. Ann wife of Thomas Squire of Fairfield. He conveyed 1783 to dau. Rachel wife of Hezekiah Lyon, and to gr. sons John, Jr., and Daniel Dikeman of Norwalk, land in Fairfield. He conveyed 1770 to dau. Rachel wife of Hezekiah Lyon and her eldest male heir. He conveyed 1767 to son John. He conveyed 1769 to dau. Mary wife of Jabez Canfield and her children. [Fairfield Deeds.]

Cornelius conveyed 1772 to dau. Rachel wife of Hezekiah Lyon of Fairfield, the land to go after her death to her second son Levi Lyon; he conveyed 1772 to son John; he conveyed 1773 to son Daniel Bears and Abigail his wife of Norwalk; conveyed 1782 to grandson John Dikeman, Jr., of Fairfield. [Norwalk Deeds.]

Children:

    Ann, m. at Wilton, 4 Dec. 1748, Thomas Squire.
+John, b. abt. 1729.
    Mary, m. Jabez Canfield; they lived 1812 in Westchester County, N. Y., and conveyed land received by deed from her father.
    Rachel, m. at Weston, 17 Oct. 1760, Hezekiah Lyon.
    Abigail, m. at Weston, 3 Sept. 1760, Daniel Beers.
    Stephen, of Danbury, conveyed 1758 land in Fairfield bounded on land of father Cornelius.

Dikeman, John, s. of Cornelius.

Born abt. 1729; d. at Weston, 16 May 1807 ae. 78 (g. s.); m. 3 Jan. 1753, Mary Coley, dau. of John, b. 13 Aug. 1732, d. 20 Sept. 1814 ae. 83 (g. s.).

Will dated at Norwalk 2 Aug. (no year), proved 8 June 1807, calls him of Weston; sons Eliphalet, Hezekiah; dau. Mary Sturges; son Daniel; wife Mary.

Hezekiah and Eliphalet Dikeman receipted, 12 June 1807, to mother Mary, for portions from Est. of father John dec'd; and on 30 Sept. 1814 to the Exec'r Daniel Dikeman.

Will of Mary of Weston, 13 June 1807, proved 21 Oct. 1814; dau. Mary Sturges; gr. son James Hill Dikeman.

Children, first two bapt. Westport:

    Mary, bapt. 13 Jan. 1754; m. 14 Sept. 1773, James Sturges.
    John, bapt. 9 May 1756, d. at Weston, 1 May 1814 ae. 54(?) (g. s.);

?m. at Redding, 20 Mar. 1780, Sarah Meeker, b. abt. 1757, d. 10 Jan. 1800 ae. 42 (g. s.).*
Eliphalet, bapt. at Weston, 23 Nov. 1760; d. 26 Nov. 1840 ae. 80 yrs. 26 days (g. s.); m. (rec. Weston) 8 May 1783, Huldah Hill; dau. of James.†
Hezekiah, bapt. at Weston, 4 Sept. 1763.
Daniel, bapt. at Weston, 8 Dec. 1765, d. there 2 Feb. 1835 ae. 69 yrs. 3 mos. (g. s.); m. 10 Feb. 1790, Eleanor Godfrey, bapt. 1 Nov. 1767, d. 13 Oct. 1822 ae. 55 (g. s.).

Dikeman, Frederick.

He m. Ann ———.

Children, two bapt. Redding:

Mary, bapt. 3 June 1744.
Ann, bapt. 27 Nov. 1746.
Levi, b. 13 Apr. 1750, d. 2 May 1835 ae. 85-1-9 (Pension rec.); rem. to Norwalk, 1780; m. at Redding, 9 Feb. 1774, Rebecca Lines, dau. of Samuel, b. 11 Apr. 1750.‡

Dikeman, Joseph.

He m. 25 May 1757, Eunice Darling; dau. of Joseph, bapt. 25 Jan. 1736.

Children, bapt. Redding:

Hezekiah, bapt. 26 Aug. 1759, d. at Westport, 13 Jan. 1815; m. at Wilton, 13 Oct. 1785, Esther Scribner, who d. 15 Aug. 1846.
Benjamin, bapt. 24 May 1761.
Joseph, bapt. 8 May 1763.
Aaron, bapt. 20 Sept. 1767.
Peter, bapt. 3 Apr. 1770.

---

* Had two children rec. Norwalk.
† Children: Stephen, b. at Norwalk, 5 Mar. 1781, d. at Weston, 11 Oct. 1826 in 45 yr. (g. s.). James-Hill, b. at Weston, 18 Dec. 1784. William, b. at Norwalk, 16 Mar. 1789, d. at Weston, 14 Nov. 1825 ae. 36 (g. s.); m. at Westport, 7 May 1810, Hannah Gray. John, b. at Weston, 28 Oct. 1794.
‡ Children, from pension records, Redding Church and Norwalk rec.: Samuel, b. 21 Nov., bapt. 4 Dec. 1774; Anne, bapt. 12 May 1776; Zalmon, b. 11 Dec. 1777, bapt. 4 Jan. 1778; Sturges, b. 17 Sept. 1780, killed 25 Apr. 1791; Rebecca, b. 9 Sept. 1782; Levi, b. 6 Oct. 1784; Clara, b. 2 Mar. 1787, d. 28 Nov. 1807; Esther, b. 18 July 1789; Polly, b. 10 Feb. 1792; Aaron, b. 3 Jan. 1796.

Dimon [Vol. I, pp. 184-186].

1 Thomas (-1658) m. ———.
2 Moses (-1684) m. Abigail Ward.
3 Moses (1672-1748) m. (1) Jane Pinkney; (2) Jane (Dirck) Gilbert; (3) Jane (———) Hill.
(By 1): 4 *Moses* (1698-1766).
5 *John* (1700-1764).
6 *Ebenezer* (1705-1746).

4. **Dimon, Moses,** s. of Moses, 2d. Lt., north society company, Fairfield, May 1726; Capt., Greenfield Co., May 1733. Justice, 1745-66.

Born 4 Apr. 1698; d. at Greenfield, 28 Nov. 1766 in 69 yr. (g. s.); m. 27 Apr. 1721, Hannah Gilbert; dau. of Moses, b. 29 Dec. 1700, d. 24 July 1767 in 67 yr.

Deacon, Greenfield Church.

Will 5 Mar. 1765, proved 23 Dec. 1766; wife Hannah; dau. Sarah wife of Samuel Hill; dau. Damaris; son Moses, and after his decease to his children Moses, Ebenezer, Jane, and Anne; son Jonathan. Distribution 2 Dec. 1768: eldest son Moses; Jonathan; heirs of Jane, eldest dau., wife of Gershom Bradley; 2d dau. Sarah wife of Samuel Hill; youngest dau. Damaris wife of Ephraim Bradley.

Children, rec. Fairfield and Greenfield:

Jane, b. 11 Aug., bapt. 7 Oct. 1722, d. 3 Feb. 1755 ae. 32 yrs. 5 mos. 12 days (g. s., Greenfield); m. Dec. [1741], Gershom Bradley.
Sarah, b. 16, bapt. 19 July 1724, d. 15 Apr. 1727 ae. 2 yrs. 9 mos.
David, b. and bapt. 5 July 1726, d. 3 Apr. 1727 ae. 9 mos.
Sarah, b. 6 May, bapt. 2 June 1728, d. at New Milford, 28 Feb. 1797 (g. s.); m. 28 Nov. 1744, Samuel Hill.
Abigail, b. 4 June 1729, d. (unbapt.) "presently after."
Hannah, b. and bapt. 20 Apr. 1730, d. 12 hours after.
Hannah, b. 15 Sept., bapt. 4 Oct. 1731, d. a month after.
Hannah, b. 24, bapt. 27 May 1733, d. 6 weeks after.
7+Moses, b. 2, bapt. 8 Mar. 1734/5.
8+Jonathan, b. 21, bapt. 23 Apr. 1738.
Damaris, b. 23, bapt. 24 Mar. 1744/5; m. 22 Feb. 1764, Ephraim Bradley.

5. **Dimon, John,** s. of Moses, 2d. Lt., 2d Co., Fairfield, May 1741; Capt., May 1745.

Bapt. 17 Nov. 1700; d. at Fairfield, 4 May 1764 in 64 yr. (g. s.); m. 10 May 1727, Elizabeth Wheeler, b. 2 Apr. 1704, d. 8 Feb. 1786 in 84 yr. (g. s.).

Will 25 Feb. 1761, proved 28 June 1764; wife Elizabeth; daus. Hester wife of Joseph Frost, Jr., Grace wife of Moses Dimon, Jr., Elizabeth and Abigail; gr. children Moses and Peter Hull; four sons, John, Thomas, Pinkney, Daniel.

Weston, 2 Apr. 1796; Grace Dimon for £20 assigned to Daniel Dimon her right in legacies given by father John Dimon to Elizabeth and Abigail Dimon, dec'd. Peter Hull receipted, 27 Jan. 1798, to Daniel Dimon, Adm'r of Ests. of Elizabeth and Abigail Dimon.

Children, rec. and bapt. Fairfield:

>Esther, b. 11 May, bapt. 21 July 1728; m. 19 Oct. 1747, Joseph Frost.
>
>9+John, b. 5 July, bapt. 16 Aug. 1730.
>
>Thomas, b. 1, bapt. 16 Apr. 1732, d. at Redding, 24 Dec. 1794 (Perry Diary); m. Esther ———. His will, 24 Nov. 1794, proved 12 Jan. 1795; wife Esther; kinsman, Aaron Dimon.
>
>Ann, b. 12 Apr., bapt. 26 May 1734, d. 9 June 1759 ae. abt. 25; m. 22 Feb. 1753, Peter Hull.
>
>Grace, b. 1 Mar. 1735/6, bapt. 9 May 1736; m. 13 Nov. 1754, Moses Dimon, Jr.
>
>Elizabeth, b. 11 Oct., bapt. 5 Nov. 1738, d. by 1795. Adm'n granted, 23 Feb. 1795, to Daniel Dimon.
>
>Abigail, b. 1 Mar., bapt. 26 Apr. 1741, d. by 1795. Adm'n granted, 23 Feb. 1795, to Daniel Dimon.
>
>Pinkney, b. 12 Sept., bapt. 16 Oct. 1743, d. 7 Sept. 1774 (Perry Diary).
>
>10+Daniel, b. 20 Mar., bapt. 3 May 1747.

6. **Dimon, Ebenezer,** s. of Moses.

Bapt. 18 Mar. 1704/5; d. at Fairfield, 28 May 1746 in 42 yr. (g. s.); grad. Yale Coll. 1728.

He m. Mary Burr, dau. of Col. John, bapt. at Stratfield, 4 July 1708; she m. (2) 4 Jan. 1747/8, Col. James Smedley, and d. 12 Sept. 1766.

Will 1 May 1746, proved 1 July 1746; wife Mary; four daus., Abigail, Deborah, Mary, Sarah; three sons, Ebenezer, William, David; wife and bro.-in-law Capt. John Burr, Exec'rs.

In 1766, Joseph Sturges and Sarah his wife, and Gold Hoyt and Elizabeth his wife (of Norwalk), conveyed to William and David Dimon, their interest in Est. of bro. Ebenezer Dimon. Gershom Bradley and Deborah his wife conveyed 1765 to bro. David Dimon.

Children, bapt. Fairfield:

> Ebenezer, bapt. 10 Jan. 1730/1, d. in 1757. On 17 Feb. 1752, being formerly of Fairfield, late of New Haven, he receipted to John and William Burr, Exec'rs, for £100 under the will of Col. John Burr. Realty ordered distributed, 9 May 1769, to brothers and sisters, William and David Dimon; Abigail wife of Hezekiah Sturges, Deborah wife of Gershom Bradley, Mary wife of Benjamin Osborn, Sarah and Elizabeth.
> Abigail, bapt. 1 Feb. 1732/3, d. 21 Nov. 1803 in 71 yr. (g. s.); m. 21 Nov. 1751, Hezekiah Sturgis.
> Deborah, bapt. 27 Apr. 1735, d. at Easton, 3 Sept. 1832 in 99 yr. (g. s.); m. Gershom Bradley.
> Mary, bapt. 26 June 1737; m. (1) 16 Oct. 1753, Benjamin Osborn; m. (2) Reuben Beers.
> 11+William, bapt. 24 June 1739.
> 12+David, bapt. 23 Aug. 1741; chose David Rowland for guardian, Oct. 1756.
> Sarah, bapt. 18 Dec. 1743; m. 11 Nov. 1762, Joseph Sturges.
> Elizabeth, bapt. 22 June 1746; chose William Dimon for guardian, July 1762; m. 13 June 1765, Gould Hoyt, of Norwalk.

7. **Dimon, Moses,** s. of Moses, 3d.

Born 2 Mar. 1734/5; d. in the Army, 2 Oct. 1778 [Rev. War Rolls].

He m. 13 Nov. 1754, Grace Dimon, dau. of John, b. 1 Mar. 1735/6, d. 4 June 1803.

Children, three bapt. Greenfield:

> 13+Moses, b. [say 1756].
> Jane, bapt. 5 Feb. 1758; prob. m. John Fanton.*
> Ann, bapt. 9 Dec. 1759; prob. m. Lewis Gilbert.*
> Ebenezer, bapt. 30 May 1762 (near 2 mos. old).†
> Noah, bapt. at Weston, 8 June 1766; rem. to Fairfield, Vt.; m. at Weston, 31 Dec. 1788, Molly Marvin.
> Squire, bapt. at Easton, 7 Jan. 1773.

---

* Lewis Gilbert and Anna his wife conveyed 1786 to Nehemiah Fanton, land in Norfield in Dimon's Long Lot, bounded on land of John Fanton and his wife.

† An E. Dimon cut his throat, 22 Nov. 1796 (Wheeler Journal). But an Ebenezer Dimon d. 8 May 1828 (Miss Treadwell's book).

8. **Dimon, Jonathan,** s. of Moses, 3d. Ens., Greenfield Co., Oct. 1767; Capt., Oct. 1770; Maj., 4th Regt., Militia, Oct. 1776; Lt.-Col., May 1777.

Born 21 Apr. 1738.

He m. (1) 12* Feb. 1760 Hannah Rowland, b. 7 Aug. 1742, d. at Greenfield, 6 Dec. 1771 in 30 yr. (g. s.).

He m. (2) 16 Apr. 1775, Elizabeth Wakeman, bapt. 17 Aug. 1752, d. 26 Dec. 1777 in 26 yr. (g. s.).

He m. (3) 11 May 1779, Ruth Bradley; dau. of Joseph, b. 17 July 1751.

Jonathan of "Frederickborough," Dutchess County, N. Y., conveyed land in 1785.

Children [by first wife], bapt. Greenfield:
> Jonathan, b. 14, bapt. 15 Mar. 1761.
> Noah, bapt. 24, d. 25 May 1762.
> Samuel, b. 24 Apr. 1763, bapt. 8 May 1763 (ae. 2 weeks), d. 19 Dec. 1813 (g. s.); m. (1) Abigail Sherwood, dau. of John, who d. before 1792; m. (2) at Trinity Church, 3 May 1794, Sarah Sherwood.†
> Albe, b. 7, bapt. 21 Sept. 1766; res. 1789, New Milford.
> Justus, b. 29 Mar., bapt. 3 Apr. 1768; res. 1789, Warren; m. (1) at New Preston, 19 Aug. 1790, Olive Stone, who d. 13 Mar. 1791 ae. 18-10-14 (g. s., Upper Merryall, New Milford).

Child [by second wife], bapt. Greenfield:
> Richard-Montgomery, b. 21 Jan., bapt. 24 Mar. 1776 [named after Gen. Montgomery].

Child [by third wife], bapt. Greenfield:
> David, bapt. 24 Oct. 1780.

9. **Dimon, John,** s. of John.

Born 5 July 1730; d. at Weston, 1778.

He m. 26 Nov. 1761, Abigail Fanton; dau. of John, b. 15 Feb. 1736/7, d. 2 Oct. 1815 ae. 80 (g. s.).

Distribution of realty, 30 June 1790; widow Abigail; eldest son John; sons Aaron, Pinkney; dau. Mary wife of Ebenezer Davis, Jr.; dau. Elizabeth.

---
* 14 Feb., by town record.
† Children by first wife: Jonathan; Sarah.

Distribution order, part of estate set to his widow Abigail now dec'd, 19 Dec. 1815: Elizabeth wife of Elijah Bradley, and Abigail Dimon, daus. of eldest son John dec'd; children Aaron and Pinkney Dimon, Mary wife of Ebenezer Davis; heirs of Elizabeth late wife of Miles Murwin.

Adm'n on Abigail's estate granted, 20 Nov. 1815, to Nathan Wheeler, with Obadiah Wheeler as surety.

Children, bapt. Weston:

    Mary, bapt. 17 Oct. 1762; m. 1 Aug. 1789, Ebenezer Davis.
    John, b. 11 Oct. 1764, d. at Easton, 7 Dec. 1793 ae. 29 yrs. 26 days (g. s.); m. Dec. 1789, Sarah Thorp, b. 6 July 1768, d. 5 Apr. 1838. Adm'n granted, 17 Mar. 1794, to Sarah Dimon and Samuel Wakeman. Distribution ordered, 26 Mar. 1814, to widow Sarah, now wife of Silvis Jennings, and daus. Elizabeth and Abigail. Distribution 1818; widow, Sarah Jennings, dau. Elizabeth Bradley, dau. Abigail Dimon.*
    Aaron, bapt. 25 Sept. 1766, d. y.
    Elizabeth, b. 22, bapt. 29 May 1768, d. at Easton, 23 Apr. 1808 in 39 yr. (g. s.); m. 20 Dec. 1792, Miles Merwin.
    Aaron, b. abt. 1771, d. at Redding, 12 Jan. 1834 ae. 62 (g. s.); m. 21 Dec. 1796, Urana Beers, bapt. 9 Feb. 1777, d. 6 July 1867 ae. 91 (g. s.).
    Pinkney, bapt. 12 Mar. 1775; m. 31 Oct. 1802, Clarissa Beers; perhaps bapt. 9 May 1779.

10. **Dimon, Daniel**, s. of John. Ens., 4th Co., 4th Regt., May 1776; Lt., May 1779.

Born 20 Mar. 1747; d. at Fairfield, 6 Sept. 1808 ae. 62.

He m. 6 Dec. 1770, Lois Bradley, dau. of Ebenezer, b. Sept. 1751, d. in 1835.

Will 6 Feb. 1804, proved 13 Oct. 1808; wife Lois; daus. Huldah, Anna, Eunice; sons Abel, Bradley; gr. daus. Lucretia and Elizabeth Dimon; gr. sons Robert and John Dimon. Distribution, 18 Feb. 1811: son Abel; children of son Jesse; son Bradley; dau. Huldah Zimmerman; dau. Anna Dimon; dau. Eunice Dimon; the widow.

Will of Lois, 12 May 1825, proved 29 May 1835; dau. Huldah; dau. Eunice wife of Seth Raymond.

---

* What John Dimon had daus. Ruth and Polly, bapt. 30 Mar. 1792?

Children, bapt. Fairfield:

> Jesse, bapt. 27 Oct. 1771, d. at Augusta, Ga., 1 Nov. 1822 ae. 52 (g. s.); m. at Trinity Church, 9 Apr. 1795, Bethia Marquand, b. abt. 1770, d. 13 May 1842 ae. 72 (g. s.).*
> Sarah, bapt. 26 June 1774, d. 22 May 1795; m. 5 June 1794, Ebenezer Burr, 4th.
> Abel, bapt. 23 June 1776, d. 3 Dec. 1779 ae. 3 yrs. 6 mos. (g. s.).
> Huldah, bapt. 7 Mar. 1779, d. 1838; m. John G. Zimmerman.
> Anna, bapt. 14 Jan. 1781, d. 1850; m. 1815, Alfred Perry.
> Eunice, bapt. 12 Sept. 1784; m. Seth Raymond.
> Abel, bapt. 14 Apr. 1787.
> Bradley, b. [Feb. 1789], bapt. 8 Feb. 1795, d. at Fairfield, 6 July 1855 ae. 66 yrs. 5 mos. (g. s.), m. Eliza ———, b. 27 Nov. 1804, d. 4 Mar. 1850 (g. s.).

11. **Dimon, William,** s. of Ebenezer.

Bapt. 24 June 1739; d. at Fairfield, 22 Sept. 1810 in 72 yr. (g. s.); m. 3 Jan. 1765, Esther Sturgis, dau. of Solomon, b. 16 Aug. 1744, d. 2 Dec. 1786 in 43 yr. (g. s.).

Adm'n granted, 20 Oct. 1810, to William B. Dimon and Ebenezer Dimon, Jr., with Miah Perry as surety.

Children, bapt. Fairfield:

> Sarah, b. 29 July, bapt. 3 Aug. 1766, d. Oct. 1778 in 13 yr. (g. s.); or d. 21 Sept. 1778 (town rec.).
> Elizabeth, b. 28 Jan., bapt. 7 Feb. 1768, d. at Fairfield, 15 Apr. 1813 ae. 45; m. 31 Oct. 1787, Miah Perry.
> Esther, b. 10, bapt. 14 Jan. 1770, d. 17 Mar. 1855; m. 29 May 1796, Jessup Wakeman.
> William-Burr, b. 10 Feb., bapt. 28 Mar. 1773, d. at Fairfield, 29 Nov. 1818 ae. 46, or ae. 45-9-6 (Southport g. s.); will 23 Nov., proved 5 Dec. 1818;† m. 12 Sept. 1802, Temperance Andrews; dau. of John, bapt. 18 July 1783, d. 9 Nov. 1870 ae. 86-5-9 (g. s.).
> Abigail, b. 10 Mar.(?), bapt. 26 Feb. 1775; m. 25 Mar. 1804, James Allen, of Sherman.
> Priscilla, b. 2 Apr., bapt. 8 May 1777, d. 15 Feb. 1854 in 77 yr. (g. s.).
> David, b. 28 July 1779, bapt. 28 Jan. 1787.
> Sarah, b. 10 Nov. 1781, bapt. 28 Jan. 1787, d. 1868; m. 11 Aug. 1816, Andrew Bulkley.

---

* Children, bapt. Fairfield: Lucretia, bapt. 24 July 1796; Elizabeth, bapt. 11 Feb. 1798; Robert, bapt. 4 May 1800; John, bapt. 9 May 1802; Isaac-Marquand, bapt. 3 June 1804; Rachel, bapt. 15 June 1806.

† The will named wife Temperance and children, George, William, Delia, Telezon, and Harriet.

Ebenezer, b. 29 Feb. 1784, bapt. 28 Jan. 1787, d. at Southport, 1 Dec. 1857 ae. 73-9-2 (g. s.); m. 19 Aug. 1810, Catherine Sherwood, b. 11 Aug. 1790, d. 19 Dec. 1838 ae. 48 (g s.).*

12. **Dimon, David,** s. of Ebenezer. Ens., 2d Co., Fairfield, May 1771; Lt., Oct. 1773; Capt., Oct. 1774. Capt., 5th Co., 5th Regt., Army, Apr. 1775; Major, May 1776, Oct. 1776; Col.

Bapt. 23 Aug. 1741; Col. David d. in U. S. Army, 18 Sept. 1777 ae. 36 (g. s.); m. 15 Nov. 1762, Ann Allen, b. 28 Sept. 1741, d. 9 Mar. 1812 ae. 70 (g. s.).

Will of Ann, 17 Oct. 1808, proved 20 June 1812; two daus. Mary Whiting, Ann Dimon; son Ebenezer.

Children, bapt. Fairfield:

Ebenezer, bapt. 6 Nov. 1763, d. 9 Dec. 1841 ae. 78 (g. s.); grad. Yale Coll. 1783; High Sheriff, Fairfield County, 1806-19; m. 23 July 1800, Mary-Sherwood Hinman, dau. of Capt. Elisha, U. S. N.; she d. 25 May 1852 ae. 74 (g. s.).†

Mary, bapt. 9 June 1765; m. 29 Oct. 1787, Gamaliel-Bradford Whiting.

Ann, bapt. 30 Aug. 1767, d. at Fairfield, 15 Feb. 1816 ae. 48.

Abigail, bapt. 3 Aug. 1771, d. y.

13. **Dimon, Moses,** s. of Moses, 4th.

Born [say 1756], d. at Fairfield, Feb. 1785 (Perry Diary); m. Grizzel Thorp, dau. of Nathan, b. 18 Apr. 1756. She m. (2) Lyman Bradley, and d. at Easton, 24 Dec. 1821 in 65 yr. (g. s.).

Inv. 2 Sept. 1785; dower set to widow Grizzel; Daniel Banks, Adm'r.

Children:

Abigail, b. [say 1779]; m. —— Thorp.
Sarah, b. [say 1781]; m. —— Barlow.
Thomas, b. abt. 1783, d. 7 Sept. 1859 in 76 yr. (Miss Treadwell's book); m. Rebecca Oakley, b. 27 Sept. 1792.
Moses,‡ b. [say 1785].

Dimon [Unplaced].

RUTH m. 8 Mar. 1789, Nehemiah Davis. [Easton Church.]

---

* They had children rec. Fairfield: Eliza, b. 15 Mar. 1812; Eliza-Perry, b. 8 July 1813.
† A child, Mary-Anne, bapt. 1 Apr. 1804.
‡ Moses, son of "Widow Demon," bapt. at Easton, 20 Oct. 1795.

Dimon, Benoni.

Son of Catherine Gilbert, he was sometimes called *Dimon alias Gilbert*. Born 12 Sept. 1725; d. at Weston, 25 Feb. 1801 ae. 75 (Trinity Church rec.).

He m. (1) at Greenfield, 15 Sept. 1748,* Anna Gold, bapt. 4 Feb. 1727/8, d. 4 Oct. 1761.

He m. (2) (rec. Weston) 14 Jan. 1762, Jerusha Morehouse; dau. of Daniel, b. 1 Nov. 1730.

Will 29 Apr. 1797, proved 7 Mar. 1801; wife Jerusha; son John, residue.

Children [by first wife], rec. Weston (except Benjamin):

> Benjamin, bapt. at Fairfield, 15 Aug. 1749.
> Sarah, b. 27 June 1750, bapt. at Greenfield, 1 July 1750; m. at Easton, Nov. 1772, Aaron Banks.
> Abigail, b. 26 Apr., bapt. at Fairfield, 21 June 1752, d. at Easton, 3 Oct. 1783 ae. 32 (g. s.); m. at Easton, 1 Feb. 1770, Benjamin Bradley.
> Gershom, b. 10 June 1754.
> Gould, b. 5 June 1756, d. at Newtown, 15 Mar. 1842 ae. 86 (g. s.); m. 6 Mar. 1776, Abigail Burr; dau. of Increase, b. 10 Dec. 1756; d. 10 Dec. 1836 ae. 80 (g. s.).†
> Ann, b. 10 June 1758.
> David, b. 16 June 1760, d. 26 Jan. 1761.

Children [by second wife], rec. Weston:

> Catey, b. 24 Dec. 1762, d. 22 Sept. 1793; m. Sept. 1792, James-Adair Merwin.
> John, b. 21 Oct. 1763.
> Huldah, b. 28 Jan. 1765; m. 7 Mar. 1789, Nathaniel Davis.
> Elizabeth, b. 19 Jan. 1768; m. Dec. 1789, James Wakeman.
> Justus, b. 13 July 1770, d. 28 Apr. 1781.

Mercy (Holbridge) Disbrow

Mr. Cyrus S. Bradley, of Fairfield, Conn., has kindly furnished us with a copy of an original letter written in 1696 by Rev. Gershom Bulkeley of Wethersfield to his nephew Joseph Bulkley

---

* 20 Sept. 1749, by Weston rec.

† Children (from a family account): Patty, b. 10 Aug. 1776; Gould, b. 3 July 1778, d. at Newtown, 20 Aug. 1837 ae. 59-1-17 (g. s.); B———, b. 8 May 1781; Betsey, b. 29 Aug. 1783; Charity, b. 9 Sept. 1785; Charlotte, b. 13 Jan. 1788; Sarah, b. 9 Feb. 1791; Gershom, b. 10 Dec. 1792, d. at Newtown, 27 Feb. 1846 ae. 53 (g. s.). m. Lucy Peck; Hannah, b. 11 June 1796.

of Fairfield. This letter is very important, as it contains proof that the noted Mercy Disbrow, who in 1692 was tried for witchcraft, had lived in girlhood in the home of Rev. Gershom Bulkley in New London, and that her maiden name was Holbridge. In our first volume we followed the statement of Winthrop, as copied by Col. Charles E. Banks, to the effect that the name was Holsworth; which suggested that either Holdsworth or Hollingsworth was intended. Both these theories, which were put forward merely as theories, are now definitely disproved, and Mercy must be identified as daughter of Arthur Holbridge of New Haven. The interesting Bulkley letter follows in full.

> Joseph Bulkley's
> letter from his Uncle
> Gershom Bulkley
> June 3ᵈ : 1696
>
> To
> Mʳ Joseph Bulkeley
> in Fairfeild

> Wethersfeild. June 3 1696.

Loving Cousin,

Yesterday, when I was not at home, somebody (I knew not who) left two loose papers at my house, one whereof was a Copy of yoʳ & yoʳ wives testimony, attested by Nathan Gold Clarke, & relating to yᵉ scandall cast upon Mercy Holbridge (now Disborough) by James Redfin; whereby I perceive yᵗ yᵉ matter hath been in Cort. I could wish it had been otherwise, for though I am not insensible that yᵉ slander reflects upon me, as well as upon her, yet had yᵉ case been wholly my own, I should not have troubled yᵉ Cort with it: for as there is a sort of men whose tongues are on slander, so there is a time when such persons onely can be heard, & Innocency must stop its mouth. There is a time to be silent, as well as a time to speake. But being as it is, I shall for yᵉ satisfaction of yoʳ selves & any others that may be in any wise concerned about yᵉ matter, shew you, That this Tale, so far as it concernes Mercy Holbridge, is a most malicious Ly, from yᵉ beginning to yᵉ end of it; & I cañot but wonder at yᵉ bloody malice of some men, who having by a good Pvidance missed theire marke of taking away her life by one Pject,* would now do it, if possible, by another: for I can make no other construction of it, the thing being, though wholly false, as to her, yet so basely repʳsented. for

1. Whereas he sayes, That Mercy Holbridge was with child when she lived with me at N. London: I say this, Viz. That it is true that she did live a

---

* The witchcraft charge is referred to.

while with me at N. London, but that she was with child in that time, I know nothing of it, nor had any reason to suppose any such thing by her: her Conversation while she was with me, was, for ought I could observe, or can remember, as blameless & inoffensive, as of any person (especially of her years) in all ye Colony.

2. Whereas he sayes, That she went to Wethersfeild with me & was there delivered of a child: this is a very great ly. for Mercy went not with me from N. London to Wethersfeild but Elizabeth Walker (a Scotch wench whose time I bought at Boston, & who afterward went for England, intending to go home.) & she indeed was (to my greife) with child while she lived with me at N. London, & went with me to Wethersfeild, & was there delivered of a child: But what is this to Mercy? Redfin is in a great error, his certaine knowledge notwithstanding.

3. Whereas he sayes, That ye child dyed, & a great man being ye father of it, it was smothered up; I answer 1. It is true that Elizabeth Walkers child borne at Wethersfeild did dy; but that it was any way smothered up, is as false, as ye other is true. for she was found to be with child long before her travell, & was assisted by ye midwife & others in her travell: & after ye child was dead, before buryall of it, because we had cause to suspect that she had not dealt so well by it as she ought, I Pcured a Jury to be pannelled, which was done by Capt Wells his order (who was then a Comissioner in Wethersfeild), & ye Jury satt upon ye death of ye child & gave theire Verdict: & this much more I still remember of it, Viz That this was done on a Saturday night, ye case so requiring, & that old Thomas Buxnan* of Hartford, being then in Towne, was taken to be one of ye Jury; ye rest I do not remember.

2. It is possible James Redfin may know ye man whom he accused to be ye father of ye child. I shall spare his name: but he was then no very great man: & was caused to appear at ye next County Cort at N. London, to answer to her accusation, where (as I remember) he denyed ye fact. [Marginal Note: This I suppose, ye Record of ye Cort at N. London will testifye to.] Now if this were a smothering of it up, then Redfin sayes true in that point else not.

4. Whereas he sayes, That ye Country Marshall was sent downe about it; I do not beleive it, nor know any need of it. It is true Capt. Allyn went downe to hold ye Cort there at that time, as well as some other times, & tis Pbable ye Marshall might goe to attend upon him, as he used sometimes to doe; but that he was sent downe upon that account, is (I thinke) a Fiction. [Marginal Note: But if ye Marshall had been sent downe about it, he is beside his marke still, for Mercy Holbridge was not at all concerned in it.]

Lastly, whereas he affirmes ye thing upon his certaine knowledge to be true, I am of opinion that he cañot but know he lyes. For, did he see Mercy goe with me from N. London to Wethersfeild, which she never did? Did he see her delivered of a child there, wch she never was? Was he her Midwife, or other assistant in her travell? Or how is it possible that he living (I know

---

* Buckland?

not where) at ye sea side, should have such certaine knowledge of things done at Wethersfeild? In a word, how should he come to know that to be true, that never was at all? No, no, Redfin hath need to scratch his noddle & bethinke himselfe: to beg forgivenes of ye God of truth, & also of her, & to make good recompense for such an heinous & wilfull wrong.

For my owne part, I value not a thousand such tongues, I am so well privy to my owne Innocency in this matter: & I have other fish to fry than to regard ye Tattle of malice. But it behoves wise men, who would not imbrue theire hands in blood, to take heed how they give eare to such malicious liars, lest they be partakers of theire sin. This I thought good to write for ye satisfaction of freinds; & if it may be any wayes beneficiall, you may shew it to whom you please: I shall stand by it to ye last; let Redfin muster up all ye forces he can to ye contrary.

I have not to adde, but my love & respects to yor selfe & wife, wth my other Cousins & freinds wth you, & so comending you all to God, I am

Yo^r Loving Uncle
Gershom Bulkeley

[Several things are of interest in this manly epistle, the author of which was one of the really great men of his generation in Connecticut. First: that he spelled his own name in the correct English style, *Bulkeley*, a spelling still retained by a few of his descendants, though the Fairfield branches in the second generation had already adopted *Bulkley*. Second: Redfin is of course James Redfin or Redfield. Third: Joseph Bulkley, the recipient of the letter, was son of a stepsister of Mercy Disbrow; or, to put it in a different way, Joseph's maternal grandfather, Rev. John Jones, married Susannah, the mother of Mercy. Finally: it is at last definitely proved that the noted witch, Mercy, was born a Holbridge, and in view of the extreme rarity of the name, we are safe in identifying her as that Mercy who, with her brother John, was baptized at New Haven on 30 June 1650. They were doubtless children of Arthur Holbridge or Halbidge who died in 1648.]

Disbrow [Vol. I, p. 187].

1 Thomas (-1709) m. Mercy Holbridge.
   2 *Thomas* (-1757).

2. Disbrow, Thomas, s. of Thomas.

Born [say 1680-85]; d. at Westport, 30 Sept. 1757; m. Oct. 1708, Abigail Godwin; dau. of Samuel; she d. 19 Apr. 1756.

Adm'n granted to Thomas Disbrow, 4 Oct. 1757. Distribution ordered 1758 to the children, Thomas, Joseph, Nathan, Joshua, Caleb, Sarah wife of Wm. Gray, Jr., and heirs of Susannah wife of Josiah Webb.

Children, rec. Fairfield:
- 3+Thomas, b. 6 Dec. 1710.
- 4+Joseph, b. 15 Dec. 1712.
- 5+Nathan, b. 10 June 1715.
  - Susanna, b. May 1717, d. at Westport, 25 Dec. 1748(?); m. Nov. 1729, Josiah Webb.
- 6+Caleb, b. 1 Aug. 1719.
- 7+Joshua, b. in 1723.
  - Sarah, b. Apr. 1726, d. at Westport, 27 Oct. 1778; m. 25 Jan. 1742, William Gray, Jr.

3. Disbrow, Thomas, s. of Thomas, 2d.

Born 6 Dec. 1710; Capt. Thomas d. at Westport, 11 Oct. 1795. He m. 4 Aug. 1741, Jane Sherwood, dau. of Isaac; she d. 12 Apr. 1778.

Children, rec. Fairfield, bapt. Westport:
- Ann, b. 24 Aug., bapt. 31 Oct. 1742, d. 1 Apr. 1806 in 64 yr.; m. 18 Feb. 1762, Solomon Gray. Her will, 29 Nov. 1803, proved 28 Apr. 1806; sister Sarah wife of Moses Gray; Sally Ann Disbrow, dau. to John, Jr.; Anne Gray, dau. to Seymour Gray; bro. John Disbrow and his sons Thomas, William, Charles, and John; my black boy Ira; tombstone for husband's grave.
- Thomas, b. 24 May, bapt. 28 June 1744, d. Summer 1765.
- Sarah, b. 10 June, bapt. 16 Aug. 1747; m. 19 Mar. 1767, Moses Gray.
- 8+John, b. 22 Oct. 1749, bapt. 1 July 1750.
- Isaac, bapt. and d. 17 Nov. 1751.
- Hannah, bapt. 12 Aug. 1753, d. 8 Apr. 1754.
- Solomon, bapt. and d. 20 Sept. 1757.

4. Disbrow, Joseph, s. of Thomas, 2d.

Born 15 Dec. 1712; d. at Westport, Feb. or Mar. 1777; m. 27 Oct. 1731, Abigail Meeker, dau. of John; bapt. 14 May 1710. Widow Abigail d. 29 Dec. 1795.

Will 24 Feb., proved 17 Mar. 1777; wife Abigail; sons Jabez, Asahel, Elias; dau. Lois; two children of son Noah dec'd (a minor boy and girl); sons Jabez and Joseph, Exec'rs; son Thaddeus.

Abigail Disbrow receipted, 3 Jan. 1794, to Noah and Hannah Disbrow, son and dau. of Noah Disbrow, for part of her dower; Jason Disbrow receipted to Noah Disbrow and Hannah Perkins, gr. children of Joseph Disbrow dec'd.

Children, rec. Fairfield, bapt. Westport:

    John, b. 15 Jan. 1732/3, d. 11 May 1733.
9+Jabez, b. 23 June 1734.
10+Jason, b. 30 Apr. 1736.
    Betty, b. 18 Nov. 1738, d. 12 or 13 Sept. 1748.
11+Noah, b. 8 Feb. 1740/1.
    Lois, b. 29 Jan., bapt. 20 Mar. 1742/3; m. 21 Jan. 1770, Stephen Marvin, of Norwalk.
12+Joseph, b. 28 Feb. 1744/5, bapt. 12 May 1745.
13+Asael, b. 28 Mar., bapt. 31 May 1747.
    Thaddeus, b. 3 May, bapt. 2 July 1749, d. 8 Mar. 1794. Adm'n granted, 21 Mar. 1794, to Stephen Marvin.
14+Elias, b. 26 Nov., bapt. 2 Dec. 1750.

5. **Disbrow, Nathan,** s. of Thomas, 2d.

Born 10 June 1715.

He m. 21 Nov. 1738, Wait Scribner, dau. of Thomas.

He was appointed ferryman and to build a toll bridge between Fairfield and Norwalk at "the Narrows", 1745.

Adm'n on the Est. of Waitee Disbrow was granted, 25 Sept. 1777, to Nathan Disbrow.

Children, rec. Fairfield, bapt. Westport:

    Johanna, b. 6 Jan. 1739/40; m. 9 Sept. 1761, Joseph Adams.
15+Nathan, b. 6 Apr. 1741.
    Patty, b. 31 Aug., bapt. 24 Oct. 1742, d. at Westport, 28 Sept. 1793; m. 23 Nov. 1768, William Thorp.
    Abigail, b. 25 Nov., bapt. 4 Dec. 1743; m. 20 Nov. 1775, Asael Disbrow.
    Ruth, b. 10 Jan., bapt. 17 Mar. 1744/5; ?m. (at First Church, Danbury), 7 Nov. 1771, Stephen Comstock.
    Sarah, b. 19 Feb., d. 22 or 23 Mar. 1745/6.
    Peter, b. 23 Feb., bapt. 8 Mar. 1746/7.
    Wait, b. 10 Oct. 1748.
    Susannah, b. 4 July, bapt. 9 Sept. 1750.
    Andrew, b. 8, bapt. 20 Oct. 1751.
    Jacob, b. 28 Jan. 1753/4 [error for 1752/3], bapt. 1 July 1753.
    Israel, bapt. 12 Apr. 1754, d. 8 Apr. 1761.
    Lydia, b. 1 Apr., bapt. 13 June 1756.
    Solomon, b. 8 July 1757, perhaps the child who d. 23 Aug. 1758.
    David, bapt. 11 Nov. 1758.
    Polly, bapt. 31 Oct. 1760.
    Esther, bapt. 23 Feb. 1766.

THE FAMILIES OF OLD FAIRFIELD

6. **Disbrow, Caleb,** s. of Thomas, 2d.

Born 1 Aug. 1719.

He m. 19 Nov. 1740, Sarah Davis, dau. of Samuel; bapt. 14 May 1721, d. at Westport, 26 Oct. 1802 ae. 82.

Children, rec. Fairfield, bapt. Westport:*

    Samuel, b. 31 Sept. 1741.
    James, b. 24, bapt. 27 Mar. 1743; m. at Weston, Apr. 1761, Elizabeth Cable; dau. of John, b. 12 Sept. 1746. [Elizabeth, dau. of Elizabeth Disbrow, bapt. at Weston, 29 Mar. 1767.]
    Jesse, b. 24 May, bapt. 9 June 1745.
    Damaris, b. 24 June, bapt. 16 Aug. 1747;† ?m. 18 Apr. 1792, Abraham Gregory, of Norwalk.
16+Caleb, b. 10 Dec. 1749, bapt. 2 Sept. 1750.
17+Justus, b. 24 June 1751.
    Asa, b. 13 June 1753, bapt. 13 Oct. 1754; rem. 1819 to Clinton County, Ohio, where he lived in Chester, 1833; m. Charity Platt.‡
    Henry, b. 19 Apr., bapt. 12 Sept. 1756, d. at Medina, Ohio, 15 May 1838; res. 1818, Jefferson, Schoharie County, N. Y.; m. (1) ———; m. (2) at Harpersfield, Delaware County, N. Y., abt. 1 Apr. 1819, Hannah Merriam, a widow, b. abt. 1772.
    Levi, bapt. 4 Sept. 1759.

7. **Disbrow, Joshua,** s. of Thomas, 2d.

Born in 1723; d. at Westport, 13 Jan. 1760; m. 7 June 1743, Mary Gray, dau. of Isaac. She d. 9 Mar. 1760.

Adm'n granted, 12 Apr. 1760, to Samuel Sherwood. Thomas Disbrow was appointed guardian to Joshua and Elizabeth, May 1760. Distribution, 11 June 1761: eldest son Joshua; Isaac; Betty. Susanna wife of Josiah Webb and Sarah wife of William Gray to have right of way on realty. Solomon Gray was appointed guardian of Isaac, May 1767. Joshua chose Thomas Disbrow for guardian, Feb. 1765, and Solomon Gray, April 1767. Thomas Disbrow was appointed for Isaac, May 1760, and he chose Solomon Gray, Aug. 1771.

---

* A grandchild of Caleb Disbrow d. 11 Nov. 1764.
† Rachel Winton, dau. of Damaris Disbrow, bapt. at Westport, 5 June 1774; m. 20 Aug. 1794, Ebenezer Smith, of Norwalk.
‡ Children, rec. Westport: Samuel-Platt, bapt. 11 June 1775, d. (before 7 Oct.) 1776; Olive, bapt. 31 Aug. 1777; Betsey-Platt, bapt. 6 Feb. 1780.

Children, rec. Fairfield, bapt. Westport:

    Joshua, b. 27 Jan., bapt. 17 Mar. 1745, d. 13 May 1747.
    Mary, b. 26, bapt. 30 Nov. 1746, d. 2 Apr. 1760.
    Ebenezer, b. 20 Aug., bapt. 18 Sept. 1748, d. 16 or 17 Sept. 1757.
18+Joshua, b. 29 Sept., bapt. 11 Nov. 1750.
    Betty, b 21 Apr, bapt. 16 June 1754;* "Elizabeth" chose Solomon Gray for guardian, Feb. 1767; m. Ithamar Gregory. Ithamar and Betty, of Ridgefield, conveyed in 1775 to Joshua Disbrow, right from father Joshua Disbrow dec'd.
    Isaac, b. 2, bapt. 30 Aug. 1757, d. in 1819; m. 16 May 1779, Elizabeth Gray, b. 8 Jan. 1755. His will 4 Mar. 1815, proved 29 Apr. 1819; wife Elizabeth; female children of Ithamar and Elizabeth Gregory (said Elizabeth being my sister); Isaac-Disbrow son of Ebenezer Nickerson of N. Y.; Olive Olmsted, the girl that lives with me (under 18).

8. Disbrow, John, s. of Thomas, 3d.

Born 22 Oct. 1749.

He m. 29 July 1773, Jemima Wix.†

Children, bapt. Westport:

    Thomas, bapt. 9, d. 10 Mar. 1776.
    John, bapt. 2 Jan. 1778, d. 8 Sept. 1818 ae. 41; m. 17 Jan. 1799, Priscilla Mallory; dau. of Levi, b. 6 Sept. 1774.‡
    Thomas, bapt. 29 Apr. 1781.
    William, bapt. 27 June 1784, d. 15 Nov. 1819 ae. 36; m. 7 Aug. 1808, Nancy Way.
    Charles, bapt. 7 May 1786; m. ———, who d. in 1819.

9. Disbrow, Jabez, s. of Joseph.

Born 23 June 1734; d. at Westport, 30 Mar. 1797.

He m. 3 Nov. 1754, Mabel Jacocks, dau. of Joshua; b. 21 May 1735, d. 25 Mar. 1792.

Adm'n granted, 1 Apr. 1797, to Jesse Disbrow and Thomas Whitlock, with Asahel Disbrow surety.

---

    * Charity, dau. of Betty Disbrow, bapt. at Westport, 19 Mar. 1775. Charity Disbrow m. Jan. 1793, David Bennett.
    † Prob. Wickes or Weeks.
    ‡ Children, bapt. Westport: Sally, bapt. 2 Mar. 1800; Abigail-Jane, bapt. 26 June 1801; Henrietta, bapt. 21 Aug. 1803, d. 1 Oct. 1819 ae. 17; Caroline-Matilda, bapt. 15 Sept. 1805; Thomas, bapt. 24 Feb. 1808.

THE FAMILIES OF OLD FAIRFIELD 307

Children, rec. Fairfield, bapt. Westport:

19+Russell, b. 20 June, bapt. 17 Aug. 1755.
Betty, b. 10 Nov. 1756, bapt. 13 Feb. 1757;* m. at Weston, 16 July 1793, Thomas Whitlock.
Simon, bapt. 21 Aug. 1758, d. at Stafford, Genesee County, N. Y., 12 Mar. 1833; Ens., Oct. 1781; m. (1) 1 Mar. 1781, Margery ———, who d. 13 Aug. [1788?]; m. (2) at Hubbarton, Vt., 23 Nov. 1790, Philana Ray, b. abt. 1772, living 1839.†
Abigail, bapt. 19 Sept. 1762.
Jabez, bapt. 26 Feb. 1764; m. 19 Mar. 1789, Esther Godfrey; dau. of Nathan, bapt. 17 Sept. 1769.
Mehitabel, d. 6 Jan. 1773.
Moses, bapt. 19 Mar. 1769, d. 8 Oct. 1773.
Deborah, b. [31 May 1771], bapt. 10 Nov. 1771, d. at Westport, 7 Apr. 1840 ae. 68-10-7 (g. s.); m. Benjamin Allen.
Jesse, bapt. 5 Feb. 1775, drowned at sea, near N. C., 26 Aug. 1806; m. 8 May 1800, Abigail Patchen. Children: Samuel, bapt. 7 June 1801; Harriet and Mary, bapt. 27 Nov. 1803; Rebecca-Scott, bapt. 25 May 1806.
Daniel, bapt. 10 Aug. 1777; m. 27 Apr. 1797, Elizabeth-Bulkley Morehouse; perhaps dau. of Peter; she was bapt. at Westport, 15 Nov. 1795. A child, Eloisa, bapt. 10 June 1798.
Polly, bapt. 9 May 1779; Dolly d. 29 Mar. 1781.
Abraham, bapt. 27 July 1783, d. 19 Sept. 1805 ae. 23.

10. Disbrow, Jason, s. of Joseph.

Born 30 Apr. 1736; d. at Westport in 1822 ae. 78.
He m. (1) Mary ———, who d. 10 Aug. 1777.
He m. (2) 26 Aug. 1790, Anna Gray.
Will 6 July 1816, proved 26 Mar. 1822; all estate to wife Anna.

11. Disbrow, Noah, s. of Joseph.

Born 8 Feb. 1740/1; perished in a storm between New York and "here", 5 Dec. 1771; m. ———.
Noah Disbrow of St. Johns, N. B., by power of attorney from Hannah wife of Newman Perkins of St. Johns, sold 1793 to Stephen Marvin of Norwalk, land set to Hannah from her grandfather Joseph Disbrow.

---

* Daniel Ketcham, son of Betty Disbrow, bapt. at Westport, 28 July 1793.
† Children by first wife, bapt. Westport: Lewis, bapt. 16 Dec. 1781; Polly, bapt. 18 May 1783; Moses and Mabel (twins), bapt. 21 Aug. 1785.

Children:

    Noah, res. 1793, St. Johns, N. B.
    Hannah, m. Francis-Newman Perkins, b. at New Haven, 24 Oct. 1770; res. 1793, St. Johns, N. B.

12. **Disbrow, Joseph,** s. of Joseph. Corp., Lexington Alarm List.

Born 28 Feb. 1744/5; d. at New Fairfield, in 1821.

He m. 10 Apr. 1768, Phebe Hendrick; dau. of John, bapt. 28 Oct. 1739, d. at New Fairfield, Feb. 1821.

Adm'n granted, 8 May 1821, to James Platt of New Fairfield. Distribution, 25 Mar. 1822: eldest dau. Polly wife of James Platt; second dau. Rhoda wife of Loyal Pepper; heirs of only son, Joseph, Jr.; third dau. Betsey wife of Abel M. Sherwood.

Children:

    Polly, m. James Platt.
    Rhoda, m. Loyal Pepper.
    Joseph, d. in 1819; adm'n granted, 3 Sept. 1819, to Thomas Hodge and Abel M. Sherwood of New Fairfield; estate insolvent; m.
    Betsey, m. Abel M. Sherwood.

13. **Disbrow, Asael,** s. of Joseph.

Born 28 Mar. 1747 (by later record, 20 Mar. 1746).

He m. 20 Nov. 1775, Abigail Disbrow; dau. of Nathan, b. 25 Nov. 1743.

Children, rec. Fairfield, bapt. Westport:

    Meeker, b. 18 Apr., bapt. 6 July 1777.
    Thomas-Scribner, b. 26 June, bapt. 20 Sept. 1778.
    Wait, b. 5 Aug. 1779, bapt. 11 June 1780.
    Abigail, b. 28 Nov. 1780, bapt. 1 Sept. 1782.
    Asael, b. 17 June 1782, bapt. 1 Sept. 1782.
    George, b. 5 May, bapt. 15 Aug. 1784, d. 1 Aug. 1796.
    Ezra, b. 4 Nov. 1785, bapt. 7 May 1786.
    Anna, b. 4, bapt. 6 Nov. 1787.
    Deborah (twin), b. 4, bapt. 6 Nov. 1787.
    Polly, b. 27 Sept. 1789, bapt. 29 Aug. 1790.

14. **Disbrow, Elias,** s. of Joseph.

Born 26 Nov. 1750; d. at Westport, 12 Jan. 1832 ae. 81; m. (1) Olive Gray; dau. of William, b. 3 Dec. 1748, d. 6 July 1778; m. (2) 17 Jan. 1779, Susanna Green, who d. 15 June 1796.

Distribution, 27 Oct. 1832: Joseph Disbrow; Elias Disbrow; Rhoda wife of Epenetus F. Webb; Sarah wife of Darrow? Betts; Eleanor wife of Joseph Ovitt; heirs of Betsey Olmstead dec'd; Reuben Disbrow.

Children [by first wife], bapt. Westport:

> Reuben, bapt. 24 June 1773; m. at Wilton 24 June 1796, Isabel Olmstead.
> Betsey (twin), bapt. 24 June 1773; m. 9 Aug. 1793, Samuel Olmstead, of Weston.
> Joseph, bapt. 6 July 1778, d. young.
> Olive, b. [17 May 1778], bapt. 6 July 1778, d. at Weston, 12 Dec. 1831 ae. 53-6-25; m. 11 Jan. 1813, Stephen Meeker. Her will, 8 Nov. 1831, proved 1 Apr. 1832; speaks of bodily infirmity; life use to husband; heirs of sister Betsey Olmstead; bro. Reuben Disbrow now living in parts unknown.

Children [by second wife], bapt. Westport:

> Ellen, bapt. 24 Nov. 1782; m. 21 May 1801, Joseph Oviatt of Milford.
> Sarah, bapt. 24 Nov. 1782; m. Darrow? Betts.
> Rhoda, bapt. 17 Oct. 1784; m. Epenetus F. Webb.
> Elias, bapt. 15 July 1787.
> Joseph, bapt. 10 Dec. 1789; m. 26 Feb. 1809, Eleanor Gray, b. [15 Sept. 1791], d. at Westport, 9 Dec. 1837 ae. 46-2-24 (g. s.).
> Esther, bapt. 10 June 1792, d. 23 July 1796.
> Thaddeus, bapt. 5 Apr. 1795, d. 7 July 1796.

15. Disbrow, Nathan, s. of Nathan.

Born 6 Apr. 1741.

Children, one bapt. Westport, next Weston:

> Thomas, bapt. 2 Feb. 1766.
> Thomasin, bapt. 15 Nov. 1767.
> Zalmon, bapt. 8 Nov. 1772.

16. Disbrow, Caleb, s. of Caleb.

Born 10 Dec. 1749.

He m. 8 Oct. 1778, Rhoda Morehouse; dau. of Gideon, b. 16 May 1755. She m. (2) 6 May 1792, Elijah Gray, of Weston.

Child, bapt. Westport:

> Samuel, bapt. 30 Oct. 1779; m. 28 Nov. 1802, Sarah Hanford.

17. Disbrow, Justus, s. of Caleb.

Born 24 June 1751; d. at Westport, 16 Jan. 1840 ae. 88 yrs. 7 mos. (g. s.); m. 30 Sept. 1773, Elizabeth Sherwood; dau. of Jabez, b. 10 Feb. 1750, d. 10 Sept. 1826 ae. 78 (g. s.).

Children, bapt. Westport:
> Sarah, bapt. 29 May 1774.
> Freelove, bapt. 25 Feb. 1776; m. 2 Nov. 1797, Samuel Ressique, of South East, N. Y.
> Justus, b. [say 1778]; m. 25 Sept. 1801, Damaris Baker; dau. of Ebenezer, bapt. 14 June 1778.
> Elizabeth, bapt. 6 Nov. 1781; m. 9 Nov. 1800, Elijah Fillow of Norwalk.
> Caleb, bapt. 27 June 1783.
> Katy, bapt. 15 Jan. 1788.
> Phineas-Sherwood, bapt. 4 July 1790.
> Lucinda, bapt. 14 July 1793.

18. Disbrow, Joshua, s. of Joshua. Sergt.-Major, Revolutionary War.

Born 29 Sept. 1750; living 1820; m. (1) in 1772, Deborah Squire, b. 12 Oct. 1755, bapt. (as his wife) 19 July 1772, d. 19 Mar. 1789; m. (2) 2 Feb. 1792, widow Deborah Jacocks; widow of Jesse Jacocks, and dau. of John Hendrick, b. in 1746, d. 28 Feb. 1807 ae. 60.

Children [by first wife], bapt. Westport:
> Mary, bapt. 11 Apr. 1773; m. 16 Dec. 1792, Thaddeus-Burr Guire.
> Ebenezer-Squire, b. [27 Jan.], bapt. 19 Mar. 1775, d. 13 Aug. 1868 ae. 93-6-16 (g. s.); m. 3 Sept. 1794, Clarina Bulkley, who d. 4 Jan. 1849 ae. 72-9-29 (g. s.).*
> Solomon, bapt. 17 June 1781; m. 26 Oct. 1800, Isabel Bennett.
> James, bapt. 27 June 1784, d. in West Indies, 5 Sept. 1800 ae. 18.
> Lydia, bapt. 16 July 1786; m. 9 Jan. 1803, Hezekiah R. Guire, of Delaware [?County, N. Y.].

19. Disbrow, Russell, s. of Jabez.

Born 20 June 1755.

He m. 17 Aug. 1777, Eunice Godfrey, dau. of Stephen, b. 5 Nov. 1749, d. 3 Jan. 1781.

---

* He was known as Squire Disbrow, and had children bapt. Westport: William, bapt. 22 May 1796, d. in Md., 24 Oct. 1819 ae. 24; Ebenezer-Squire, bapt. 5 Aug. 1798; James, bapt. 12 Mar. 1801, d. 7 Oct. 1819 ae. abt. 19; Clarissa, bapt. 30 June 1805.

THE FAMILIES OF OLD FAIRFIELD 311

Children, bapt. Westport:
> Mabel, bapt. 25 Jan. 1778, d. 26 Jan. 1778.
> Ellen, bapt. 7 Feb. 1779.
> Eunice, bapt. 24 Dec. 1780.

Disbrow [Unplaced].
> DAMARIS m. (30 Nov.?) 1806, William Kissam. [Greens Farms Church.]

Dixon [Unplaced].
> JOSEPH m. 5 Mar. 1772, Susannah Lockwood. [Weston Church.]

Downing [Unplaced].
> ABIGAIL m. 22 Sept. 1796, Daniel Squire. [Weston Church.]

Downs [Vol. I, p. 187].

```
1 John (    -    ) m.
    2 John (1672-1753) m. (1) Mary Perry; (2) Deborah Odell.
    (By 1): 3 Joseph (1703-1783).
            4 David (1706-1759).
    (By 2): 5 Nathaniel (1714-1779).
```

3. Downs, Joseph, s. of John.

Bapt. 21 Mar. 1702/3; d. at Greenfield, 19 Feb. 1783 in 80 yr.; m. (1) Rebecca ———.

He m. (2) Hannah ———, b. abt. 1709, d. 18 Nov. 1783 in 75 yr.

Child [by first wife]:
> Rebecca, bapt. at Fairfield, 16 Aug. 1730, d. at Greenfield, 27 May 1799 in 69 yr. Her will, dated in 1799, proved 3 June 1799, gave a legacy to friend Anne wife of Jesse Wheeler, and residue to friend Bethuel Ogden for life, then to the First Presbyterian Society in Fairfield.

4. Downs, David, s. of John.

Bapt. 3 Mar. 1705/6; d. at Greenfield, 13 Feb. 1759 ae. 53 (g. s.)

He m. 3 Jan. 1733/4, Elizabeth Rowland; dau. of Joseph, b. abt. 1713, d. 12 June 1769 ae. abt. 56.

Will 4 Feb., proved 1 May 1759; wife Elizabeth; dau. Elizabeth wife of Gershom Wakeman; son Seth; dau. Mary; son

David; last two under 20; friend Joseph Bradley, Jr., Exec'r. Gershom Wakeman and Elizabeth his wife, and the widow Elizabeth as guardian of her son David, receipted 1760 to the Exec'r, for the portion given by will to Mary dec'd.

Children, rec. Fairfield, bapt. Greenfield:

6+Seth, b. 10, bapt. 15 Dec. 1734.
    Elizabeth, b. 5 Aug., bapt. Aug. 1737, d. at Greenfield, 29 Mar. 1776 ae. 39 (g. s.); m. 17 Apr. 1757, Gershom Wakeman.
    Mary, b. 9 or 10, bapt. 13 July 1746, d. 29 Oct. 1759 in 14 yr.
7+David, b. 20 or 22, bapt. 26 Aug. 1750.

5. **Downs, Nathaniel,** s. of John.

Bapt. 12 Sept. 1714; d. at Greenfield, 21 Oct. 1779; m. Sarah Chauncey, dau. of Israel, b. abt. 1722, d. 6 Aug. 1775 in 54 yr.

Children, rec. Greenfield:

8+Chauncey, bapt. 9 Jan. 1742/3.
    Sarah, b. 24, bapt. 26 May 1745; ?m. at Weston, 18 Oct. 1765, Nehemiah Gray.
    Martha, b. Aug., bapt. 21 Aug. 1747; m. 15 June 1767, Benjamin Smith, Jr.
    Mabel, b. 26 Aug., bapt. 3 Sept. 1750.
    John, bapt. 27 Aug. 1758, d. 3 Apr. 1831 (Miss Treadwell's book); m. in 1807, Elizabeth Fox.
    Mary, bapt. 5 Oct. 1760 (ae. abt. 4 days); d. young.
    Joseph, bapt. 9 Sept. 1764 (ae. a few days), d. at Weston, 13 Dec. 1842 ae. 78 (g. s.); m. at Westport, 5 May 1804, Elizabeth Downs, b. abt. 1777, d. 25 June 1837 ae. 61 (g. s.).
    Mary, b. 2 Dec. 1768 (family rec.), d. 9 Oct. 1838; m. 24 Jan. 1787, Asa Turney.

6. **Downs, Seth,** s. of David.

Born 10 Dec. 1734; d. in 1777.

He m. 9 May 1753, Hannah Price, dau. of Lemuel, bapt. 25 Nov. 1733.

Will 2 Jan., proved 3 Mar. 1777; wife Hannah; two gr. children left by my daus. Elizabeth wife of Moses Hull, and Hannah wife of Moses Banks; children, sons and daus. surviving; friend David Williams, Exec'r.

Children, rec. Greenfield:

> Hannah, b. in 1755, bapt. 6 Sept. 1755, d. in 1777; m. Moses Banks.
> Elizabeth, bapt. 5 Aug. 1759, d. abt. 1776; m. Moses Hull.
> Seth, bapt. 6 Mar. 1763 (ae. abt. 1 mo.).
> Huldah, bapt. 18 Nov. 1764 (ae. 2 or 3 mos.); ?m. at Westport, 22 Feb. 1789, Nathan Price, of Weston.
> ? Rowland, m. (rec. Weston) 7 Aug. 1793.*
> Polly, bapt. at Easton, Apr. 1768.
> ? Ichabod, bapt. at Easton, 8 Sept. 1771.
> Esther, bapt. at Easton, Oct. 1772.

7. Downs, David, s. of David.

Born 20 Aug. 1750; d. at Greenfield, 19 Feb. 1788 in 38 yr. (g. s.); m. latter part of 1776, Mary Osborn, dau. of David, bapt. 10 June 1753; d. 26 Dec. 1820 ae. 68 (g. s.).

Will 6 Dec. 1786, proved 16 June 1788; wife Mary; two daus. Elizabeth, Lucinda; two sons, David, Levi.

Distribution, 26 Apr. 1797: Widow; son Levi; daus. Lucinda, Elizabeth; son David.

Children:

> Elizabeth, b. abt. 1777, d. at Weston, 25 June 1837 ae. 61 (g. s.); m. 5 May 1804, Joseph Downs.
> David, b. abt. 1779, d. at Greenfield, 14 Apr. 1820 ae. 41; m. 25 Nov. 1816, Betsey Beers; dower set to widow Elizabeth, 15 Nov. 1821.
> Levi.†
> Lucinda.

8. Downs, Chauncey, s. of Nathaniel.

Bapt. 9 Jan. 1742/3; d. at Greenfield, 16 Oct. 1814 ae. 71.

He m. 3 June 1762, Betty Smith; dau. of Benjamin, b. 3 Mar. 1742.

Children, rec. Greenfield:

> Rachel, b. 3, bapt. 27 Feb. 1763; ?m. at Westport, 4 Sept. 1783, William Chub, of Ashford.

---

* Children, rec. Weston: Nabby, b. 7 Apr. 1794; Charlotte, b. 17 Oct. 1795; Betsey, b. 3 Dec. 1797.

† Levi Downs d. 8 May 1855 ae. 69 (g. s., Fairfield West Cemetery); wife Elizabeth d. 3 May 1861 ae. 74 yrs. 10 mos. (g. s.). Levi T. Downs m. at Trinity Church, 14 Jan. 1816, Esther Bulkley, dau. of Abraham; it is said that she was b. 13 July 1789, d. 28 Nov. 1861.

314 HISTORY AND GENEALOGY OF

 Wolcott-Chauncey, bapt. 17 Mar. 1765 (ae. abt. 2 weeks).
 Abel, b. 12, bapt. 28 Dec. 1766, d. at Danbury, 3 Jan. 1857; m. Hannah Whitney, dau. of Samuel, b. 6 Nov. 1768, d. at Weston, 18 Jan. 1824.*
 Sarah, b. 14, bapt. 19 Feb. 1769.
 Betty, bapt. 24 Apr. 1774; ?"Elizabeth" m. at Westport, 31 Dec. 1795, Daniel Meeker.†
 Daniel, bapt. 3 Mar. 1776.
 Pamelia, bapt. 17 May 1778; "of Greenfield" m. at Weston, 25 July 1802, Samuel Bennett.
 Isaac, b. 28 Jan., bapt. 27 Mar. 1780, d. at Easton, 21 Feb. 1853 ae. 74 (g. s.); m. Sarah ———, d. 10 Feb. 1857 ae. 77 yrs. 5 mos. (g. s.).

EDWARD DOWNS FAMILY

1. Downs, Edward.

Was he perhaps a son of ——— and Hannah (Gorham) Downs, and a nephew of Joseph Gorham of Fairfield?

He m. Mercy ———.

Edward, of Norwalk, conveyed 1768 to son William, land in Norfield (Weston). Robert Downs of Norwalk conveyed 1762 to Thomas Downs of Fairfield. [Norwalk Deeds.]

 Children, two rec. Fairfield:

  Thiah, b. [say 1734], bur. 6 Dec. 1804 ae. 70 (Trinity Church rec.); m. in 1752, Jabel Sturges.
2+ ? Thomas, b. [say 1735].
  ? Elizabeth, b. [say 1737]; m. at Weston, in 1759, Jonathan Fanton.
3+ ? Robert, b. [say 1739].
  Hannah, b. 1 Jan. 1741/2, perhaps d. 9 Apr. 1811 ae. 70 (Trinity Church rec.).
  Abigail, b. 24 Jan. 1743/4, d. in 1826, unm. Will of Abigail of Weston, 16 May 1822, proved 10 Nov. 1826, gave whole estate to nephew Eleazer Sturges.
4+William, b. abt. 1746.

2. Downs, Thomas [s. of Edward].

He d. at Norwalk in 1766.

He m. at Weston, 27 Aug. 1758, Eunice Barlow, who d. in 1768.

Adm'n granted, 24 June 1766, to Robert Downs of Fairfield.

---

 * Children, bapt. at Easton: Maria, Morris, and Mabel, bapt. 17 Nov. 1795; Mabel m. at Easton, in 1813, Squire Oysterbanks.
 † One "Betty" m. at Westport, 6 Oct. 1799, Stephen Bradley, and d. at Greenfield as "Elizabeth," 10 Jan. 1820 ae. 42.

Eunice Downs was appointed guardian, 19 May 1767, to Molly, Hannah, Samuel, Eunice, and Huldah Downs.

Distribution, 22 Dec. 1767: Widow; Molly; Hannah; Eunice; Huldah; only son Samuel. Robert Downs was appointed guardian of Samuel, Molly, and Hannah, 5 July 1768. William Downs was appointed guardian, 7 Feb. 1769, of Eunice and Huldah.

Adm'n on Est. of Eunice was granted to Robert Downs, 5 July 1768. Distribution ordered to the son and four daus., Samuel, Molly, Hannah, Eunice, Huldah; 1770.

Children, bapt. Weston:
> Molly, bapt. 21 Feb. 1759; prob. m. at Wesport, 29 Nov. 1781, Abraham Perry, of New Hampshire.
> Hannah, bapt. 10 Oct. 1760; m. at Westport, 31 Mar. 1784, Daniel Darrow.
> Samuel, bapt. 10 May 1762; res. 1794, Salem, Westchester County, N. Y.; m. at Westport, 2 Feb. 1784, Elizabeth Sturges; dau. of John.*
> Eunice, bapt. 25 Dec. 1763; m. at Weston, 8 Dec. 1782, Eliphalet Hull, and rem. to Fredericksborough, N. Y.
> Rebecca, bapt. 10 June 1765, d. y.
> Huldah, bapt. 10 Aug. 1766.

3. **Downs, Robert** [s. of Edward].

He m. Hannah Coley, dau. of Jonathan, b. 5 May 1741.

Perhaps she m. (2) (rec. Redding) May 1785, Daniel Morehouse.

Distribution, 26 Dec. 1783: widow Hannah Downs; son Robert; Eleanor wife of Jeremiah Rowland. In 1783, Benjamin Dean, Robert Downs (a minor, by mother Hannah Downs), and Ellinor Downs now wife of Jeremiah Rowland, the children of Robert Downs of Fairfield dec'd, conveyed land.

Children (births rec. Weston, parentage not stated):
> Eleanor, b. 1 Jan. 1764; m. 27 Jan. 1782, Jeremiah Rowland.
> Robert, b. 7 Nov. 1768, d. at Weston, 24 Jan. 1845 ae. 76 (g. s.); m. 27 Jan. 1792, Betsey Bradley, b. 11 Sept. 1774, d. 11 May 1845 ae. 70 (g. s.). Children, rec. Weston, bapt. Trinity Church: Hannah,

---

* Children, bapt. Westport: Elizabeth, bapt. 12 Dec. 1784, killed by fall of horse, 28 Aug. 1786. Eunice, bapt. 9 Mar. 1788. Esther, bapt. 21 Feb. 1790. Sturges, bapt. 28 Jan. 1792. Betsey (dau. of Samuel of Croton), bapt. 11 Aug. 1794. Thomas [no surname], a child offered by Samuel Downs, Croton River, bapt. 3 Feb. 1793. Thomas (son of Samuel of Croton), bapt. 2 Nov. 1800.

b. 12 Nov. 1793, bapt. 15 June 1794; Sally, b. 24 Sept., bapt. 12 Dec. 1795; Bradley, b. 21 Mar., bapt. 5 Aug. 1798; Child, bapt. 12 Oct. 1800; William, bapt. 5 Sept. 1802; Anna, bapt. 11 Dec. 1803; Harriet, bapt. 16 Aug. 1807; Ebenezer, bapt. 22 Oct. 1809; Mary, bapt. 1 Mar. 1812. The will of Robert, 16 Sept. 1833, proved 23 Apr. 1845; wife Betsey; sons Bradley, William, Charles; daus. Hannah, Sally, Anna, Harriet, Charlotte, Mary. The distribution names the daus. as Hannah Coley, heirs of Sally Coley, heirs of Anna Keeler, Charlotte wife of Charles Crofutt, Harriet wife of Warren Nichols, and Mary Downs.

4. **Downs, William,** s. of Edward.

Born abt. 1746; d. at Weston, 5 July 1804 ae. 58 (g. s.).

He m. (1) 14 Feb. 1769, Hannah Bulkley, bapt. 15 June 1746, d. 10 Feb. 1789, and he m. (2) 12 Mar. 1791, Elizabeth Waterbury, by the Norwalk town rec., but Elizabeth Gray by Weston church rec.

An Elizabeth Downs m. 14 Mar. 1807, John-Silliman Andrews, of Weston, as his second wife.

Children [by first wife], rec. Norwalk, bapt. Weston:

Thomas, b. 4 Oct. 1769, bapt. 14 Jan. 1770, d. at Weston by 1804; m. at Weston, 14 Aug. 1792, Betsey Thorp. Distribution, 4 May 1804, to widow Betty and only son Isaac.*
Isaac, b. 14 Mar. 1772.
Sarah, b. 19 Aug. 1773, bapt. 22 Oct. 1775.
Joseph, b. 13 Dec. 1777, bapt. 1 Mar. 1778.
Ellen, b. 12 Apr., bapt. 13 Aug. 1780.
Rhoda, b. 12 Aug., bapt. 27 Oct. 1782.
William, b. 12, bapt. 17 Jan. 1789.

Downs [*Unplaced*].

ESTHER m. 15 Sept. 1773, Hezekiah Burr. [Easton Church.]
SUSANNAH m. 10 Sept. 1778, Joseph Whitlock. [Weston Church.]

Drew, John.

Born abt. 1724; d. at Redding, 9 Mar. 1819 in 95 yr. (g. s.).

He m. (1) Jan. 1745/6 Mary Northrop, b. 24 Sept. 1727, d. 5 Mar. 1760 ae. 33½.

---

* Isaac d. at Weston, 17 July 1827 ae. 34 yrs. 9 mos. (g. s.). Adm'n granted to David Patchen, 23 July 1827; insolvent; left a widow; realty subject to life use of his mother Elizabeth Downs.

He m. (2) 24 June 1760, Ann Thorp ["Joanna" Thorp, by Redding rec.].

Adm'n granted, 22 Mar. 1819, to Isaac Drew of Redding. Dower set to widow Hannah (also called Johannah), 20 Mar. 1820. Distribution: Asel; Hannah wife of Joseph Morgan; Sarah wife of Gilbert Potter, gr. child to said dec'd and dau. of Sarah Henderson; Daniel; Abel; Anna's heirs; Noah; Samuel; Mary; Isaac; Peter's heirs; John; William's heirs; in equal shares.

Children [by first wife], rec. Greenfield and Redding:

> William, b. 28 July 1746.
> John, b. 16 Dec., bapt. 31 Dec. 1749; m. (1) Deborah Adams; m. (2) Ruth, widow of Stephen Meeker, and dau. of Caleb Lyon, b. 12 Apr. 1745.*
> Isaac, b. 17 June 1752, d. at Redding in 1826; m. Abigail Morehouse, dau. of Zaccheus, b. 1 Aug. 1757.†
> Peter, b. 22 Apr., bapt. 28 Apr. 1754; rem. to Shelburne, Vt.
> Mary, bapt. 9 Apr. 1758.
> Hannah, b. 9 Feb., bapt. 16 Mar. 1760 (ae. abt. 5 weeks); m. Joseph Morgan.

Children [by second wife], first bapt. Greenfield, all rec. Redding:

> Sarah, b. 12 May, bapt. 6 June 1762; m. —— Henderson.
> Daniel, b. 24 Apr. 1764, bapt. at Redding, 27 May 1764.
> Ann, b. 30 Oct. 1765, bapt. at Redding, 19 Jan. 1766.
> Noah, b. 8 Aug. 1768.
> Samuel, b. 21 Mar. 1770.
> Abel.
> Asel, m. at Redding, 25 Nov. 1795, Grissel Wheeler.

Drury(?) [*Unplaced*].

> JOSEPH, of Stonington, m. 16 Sept. 1798, Elizabeth Sturges. [Greens Farms Church.]

---

* Children by first wife: John, b. abt. 1772; Sturgis, b. abt. 1774; Elisha, b. abt. 1779; Isaac; Zerah, b. abt. 1785; Laura; Zalmon; Orrin, b. abt. 1799. Some of these children rem. to Shelburne, Vt.

† Adm'n on Isaac's estate granted, 4 Sept. 1826, to Isaac and Sturges Drew. Distribution: widow Abigail; eldest son Zaccheus; 2d son Isaac; 3d son Levi; 4th son Sturges; eldest dau. Mary, wife of Lyman Munrow; heirs of 2d dau. Sarah wife of Caleb Morgan; 3d dau. Hannah wife of Sturges Drew; 4th dau. Grace wife of Gerry Crofut; 5th dau. Clary wife of Barrit (?) Bearss; 6th dau. Amelia Drew. [The dau. Amelia is said to have m. Hiram Knapp.]

Dudley [Unplaced].

JONATHAN and Deborah had children: Simon and Lena, bapt. 10 Feb. 1754. [Redding Church.]

Duffee, Thomas. [Surname also spelled Durfee, Dorfee, etc.]
He settled in Weston and m. abt. 1765, Elizabeth, widow of Ezekiel Sanford.

Children:
> Eunice, b. 25 Dec. 1766 (Pension rec.), d. at Bridgeport, 31 Dec. 1840; m. 13 Dec. 1781, Thomas Solley.
> Polly, b. 1 Mar. 1769 (Pension rec.); perhaps m. (1) Thomas Burr; m. 30 Dec. 1792, Rowland Fanton.

Duncombe, Charles.

Son of William of Barleyend near Ivinghoe, co. Bucks, Eng., m. (by Rev. Henry Caner) 10 Mar. 1744/5, Elizabeth Hubbard, dau. of Zechariah; b. at Boston, 26 Sept. 1725.

An organizer of the Episcopal Church in New Milford, 1743, where was recorded to him a son b. 28 July, d. 10 Aug. 1745.

Children, rec. Fairfield:
> Charles, b. 24 Apr. 1747; m. at Trumbull (called of Fairfield) 25 Aug. 1768, Mary or Mercy Edwards.
> William, b. 5 Apr. 1749; m. (1) ———, who d. at Stratfield, Dec. 1782; m. (2) 20 Nov. 1785, Sarah Sturges.
> John, b. 18 Apr. 1751; m. Catherine Burr, dau. of John, b. 5 Nov. 1753.
> Elizabeth, b. 23 July 1753; m. Samuel Treadwell, Jr., of Stratford. In 1791, he conveyed to Charles Duncombe use of lands which late wife Elizabeth hired from her father dec'd.
> Thomas, b. Sept. 1756.
> ? Edward, b. abt. 1760, d. at Easton, 12 Nov. 1837 ae. 77 (g. s.); m. Apr. 1783, Anna Hall, b. at Stratford, 30 Apr. 1762, d. 18 June 1848 in 87 yr. (g. s.).*

Duncomb [Unplaced].

NATHANIEL m. 25 Sept. 1803, Nancy Taylor. [Greens Farms Church.]

---

* Adm'n on Edward's estate granted, 21 Nov. 1837, to Isaac Bennett. Distribution: widow Anna; eldest son Zachariah; sons Isaac, Eleazer; daus. Betsey wife of Joseph Taylor, Lydia wife of Eli Hoyt. Adm'n on Anna's estate was granted, 13 July 1848; distribution to son Isaac, heirs of Zachariah dec'd, son Eleazer, dau. Betsey wife of Joseph Taylor, and dau. Lydia wife of Eli Hoyt.

THE FAMILIES OF OLD FAIRFIELD 319

Dunkins, John.

The name is also spelled Dunking, and in the next generation, Duncan.

He d. at Westport, 11 July 1749; m. Mary Lockwood; dau. of Robert. Widow Mary d. 15 Aug. 1749.

Children, three bapt. Fairfield:

>William, incompetent; conveyed 1772, with consent of overseer Daniel Duncan, my brother, land which formerly belonged to Daniel Lockwood.
>Mary, bapt. 9 June 1734, d. Mar. 1816; m. at Westport, 1 Jan. 1751/2, Ebenezer Munroe.
>John, bapt. 12 Sept. 1736.
>+Daniel, bapt. 27 July 1746; chose Nathaniel Adams for guardian, 25 Mar. 1756.

Dunkins, Daniel, s. of John. Ens., 1st Co., 1st Batt., Army, June 1776.

Bapt. at Fairfield, 27 July 1746 (not in infancy, apparently).
He m. (1) at Wilton, 20 Mar. 1758, Sarah Doolittle.
Daniel, Esq., m. 6 July 1799, Elizabeth Williams.

Children, three bapt. Westport, others Weston:

>Jared, bapt. 27 Jan. 1760, d. 1 Feb. 1823 [Pension Rec.]; m. at Weston, 30 Aug. 1780, Dolly Osborn; dau. of William, b. 12 Oct. 1759, d. 19 Mar. 1847.*
>Joseph, bapt. 12 July 1761.
>Tammy, bapt. 26 Sept. 1762, d. at Weston, 7 Nov. 1767 ae. 5-1-23 (g. s.).
>Daniel, bapt. 21 July 1765; m. 2 Nov. 1794, Anna Lockwood.†
>David, bapt. 2 Feb. 1768; m. 26 Sept. 1793, Huldah Smith, bapt. 16 Aug. 1772.
>Samuel, bapt. 3 June 1770; m. Priscilla Smith, bapt. 27 Nov. 1774.
>? Sally, b. abt. 1776, d. at Redding, 19 July 1834 in 58 yr. (g. s.); m. 29 Nov. 1799, John Meeker.

Dunn [*Unplaced*].

>ROGER, a stranger, d. 24 Apr. 1766 ae. abt. 46 [Greenfield Church].

---

* Children, bapt. Trinity Church: William and Daniel (twins), bapt. 10 July 1786; Mary, bapt. 22 Oct. 1791.
† Daniel Duncan had child, bapt. Trinity Church: Hannah, bapt. 11 Nov. 1790.

Dunning, Michael, s. of John [Vol. I, p. 190].

Born at Wilton, 3 June 1726.

He m. at Wilton, 6 Mar. 1744/5, Hannah Green; dau. of John.

Children:
> Thomasin, b. abt. 1750, d. at Westport, 30 Apr. 1808 in 69(?) yr. (g. s.); m. (1) at Weston, 3 Nov. 1768, Samuel Higgins, Jr.; m. (2) 18 Dec. 1792, Dea. Joseph Hide.
> ?Hannah, m. at Weston, 1 Dec. 1768, Jared Marvin.
> Jesse, m. Ann Davis, b. 15 Feb. 1753, d. 17 Dec. 1839.
> James, bapt. at Weston, 26 Feb. 1758; m. Abigail Mallory, dau. of Daniel, b. 12 Mar. 1757.
> Ebenezer, bapt. at Weston, 2 Aug. 1761.
> Betty, bapt. at Weston, 10 Apr. 1763.
> Lewis, bapt. at Weston, 5 May 1765.
> John (twin), bapt. at Weston, 2 Aug. 1767.
> Richard (twin), bapt. at Weston, 2 Aug. 1767.

Dunning [*Unplaced*].
> WILLIAM m. at Redding, 9 Oct. 1776, Sarah Osborn; had child bapt. Weston: Hannah, bapt. 13 Sept. 1778.

Dwight [*Unplaced*].
> TIMOTHY and wife Mary had twins: James, bapt. 5 Dec., and John, bapt. 10 Sept. 1784. [Greenfield Church.]

Edmond [*Unplaced*].
> ANNA, dau. of Robert, m. 29 Jan. 1784, Stephen Couch. [Fairfield Rec.]

Edson [*Unplaced*].
> ADAM m. 3 Dec. 1786, Mercy Hazard. [Greens Farms Church.]

Edwards, William, s. of John [Vol. I, p. 192].

Born [say 1691]; d. before 1754; res. Norwalk and Stratford. He m. 4 May 1713, Abigail Couch, dau. of Simon of Fairfield, b. 31 Jan. 1693/4, d. at Trumbull, Nov. 1747 in 54 yr. (g. s.).

Children, rec. Norwalk:
> William, b. 11 Mar. 1713/4, d. 25 Apr. 1716.
> Abigail, b. 18 Aug. 1716.
> William, b. 17 June 1718, d. at Redding, 20 Mar. 1740 ae. 22.

Mary, b. 13 Sept. 1721; m. 11 Jan. 1749/50, Samuel Turney.
Hannah, b. 22 Sept. 1724; m. 5 Nov. 1747, Nathan-Peat Nichols.
Deborah, b. 12 Feb. 1726/7; m. 28 July 1748, Benjamin Bassett.
John, b. 14 June 1728; m. (1) 11 July 1751, Abiah Lake, dau. of Edward, b. 6 Jan. 1732; m. (2) Huldah [Nichols?].
Couch, b. 22 Apr. 1730; m. at Greenfield, 31 July 1751, Naomi Sherwood; dau. of Daniel, b. 31 Dec. 1731.*
Gershom, b. 28 Jan. 1733, d. in 1753. Adm'n granted, 14 Aug. 1753, to John Edwards of Woodbury.

Edwards, Thomas, s. of John [Vol. I, p. 192]. Capt., North Stratford Co., May 1745.

Born [say 1693].

He m. (1) Sarah ———.

He m. (2) Mary, widow of Joseph Perry, and dau. of Michael Clugston, bapt. at Fairfield, 18 Sept. 1698, d. 8 Nov. 1773.

Children [by first wife] (record incomplete):

Nehemiah, bapt. at Fairfield, 29 Apr. 1722; m. (1) Sarah Sherman, dau. of David, Jr.; m. (2) Anna ———.
Mary, bapt. at Stratfield, 17 Jan. 1725; ?m. (rec. Woodbury) 12 Nov. 1751, James Judson.
Sarah [?m. (1) Samuel Hawley; m. (2) 18 Dec. 1753, Rev. Robert Ross].
Thomas, bapt. at Stratfield 3 Mar. 1734, d. at Trumbull, 20 Jan. 1792 in 56 yr. (g. s.); m. Sarissa Nichols, b. abt. 1737, d. 21 July 1813 in 77 yr. (g. s.).
Abigail, bapt. at Stratfield, 19 Sept. 1736; ?m. at Greenfield, 28 July 1761, Moses Burr.

Edwards, John, s. of John [Vol. I, p. 192].

Bapt. 14 Aug. 1698; d. at Trumbull in 1784; m. (1) Rebecca Porter, dau. of Nathaniel, bapt. 25 Oct. 1702.

He m. (2) Hannah ———.

Will 3 Sept. 1766, proved 2 Feb. 1784; wife Hannah; two daus. Ann wife of John Wheeler and Betty wife of John French; gr. son Agur Edwards, son of dec'd son Albert; two sons David, John.

---

* A son, Samuel, bapt. at Westport, 11 Sept. 1752. He had also, daus.: Abigail, b. 8, bapt. 17 Nov. 1754 (Trumbull rec.); Martha, b. 14, bapt. 17 Nov. 1760 (Trumbull rec.), m. Thomas Stratton.

Children:

    Ann, m. 20 Nov. 1751, John Wheeler.
    Betty, b. abt. 1730, d. at Trumbull, 13 Oct. 1786 in 56 yr. (g. s.); m. abt. 1750, John French.
    Samuel, bapt. 21 Jan. 1733, d. y.
    David, bapt. 16 Feb. 1735, d. at Trumbull, 12 July 1825 in 94(?) yr. (g. s.); m. (1) Mehitabel Treadwell; dau. of Hezekiah, bapt. 17 Oct. 1736, d. 26 June 1767; m. (2) at Fairfield, 23 Jan. 1771, Lydia Osborn, b. abt. 1729, d. 3 Oct. 1812 in 84 yr. (g. s.).
    Albert, d. before 1766; m. ———.
    John, b. [2 July 1744], d. 28 Sept. 1800 ae. 56 yrs. 2 mos. 15 days (g. s., Trumbull); Deacon; m. 3 Nov. 1768, Ruth Beach, b. 5 Mar. 1747, d. 6 May 1817 in 71 yr. (g. s.).

Edwards, Joseph, s. of John [Vol. I, p. 192].

Bapt. 17 June 1705.

He m. at Stratford, 18 Dec. 1731, Prudence Wakelee; dau. of Jonathan, b. 14 Apr. 1715.

He conveyed land in Easton to son Joseph, 1757, and to son Ebenezer, 1765.

Children, first three bapt. Stratfield:

    Prudence, bapt. 16 June 1733; m. 12 Nov. 1752, David Booth.
    Eunice, bapt. 16 Mar. 1735, d. 30 Mar. 1735.
+Joseph, bapt. 18 Apr. 1736.
    Ebenezer, b. abt. 1740, d. at New Milford, 9 May 1806 in 67 yr. (g. s.); m. 29 Sept. 1763, Sarah Peet. A dau., Rhoda, bapt. at Huntington Epis. Church, 15 Jan. 1769.
    Rhoda.
    Justice, m. 16 Nov. 1769, Ann Curtis.
    William, b. abt. 1743, d. 22 Dec. 1808 in 66 yr. (g. s., Huntington); m. (1) 19 Nov. 1767, Charity Beach, b. abt. 1747, d. 18 June 1787 in 40 yr. (g. s.); m. (2) Sarah ———, b. abt. 1748, d. 20 Sept. 1825 ae. 77 (g. s.).
    John.
    Daniel.
    Abel, b. abt. 1753, d. at New Milford, 5 Apr. 1826 ae. 73 (g. s.); m. (1) Lucy Hawley; m. (2) Sarah Mann, who d. 19 Feb. 1842 ae. 83 (g. s.).
    Hanford, d. in 1784. Will 4 Nov. 1783, proved 5 July 1784; mother Prudence Edwards; little nephew Zechariah, son of my bro. Justice Edwards; bros. John, Abel, Daniel, Reuben; bro. David Booth, Exec'r.
    Reuben, bapt. at Huntington Epis. Church, 27 Apr. 1760; rem. to New Milford; m. Mary Burroughs, dau. of John, b. 25 Apr. 1760.

Edwards, Joseph, s. of Joseph.

Bapt. 18 Apr. 1736; lived at Easton, 1757-71; prob. m. Anna Jackson.

Prob. children:
>Rachel, b. 26 May 1757; m. 10 Aug. 1778, Isaac Lyon.
>Isaac, b. 7 Apr. 1762; res. Easton and Redding; m. 22 Dec. 1786, Hannah Hall.*
>Others?

Eggleston [Unplaced].

ELEAZER and Patience had a dau. Everet-Wheeler, bapt. 9 June 1805. [Fairfield Church.]

Eldridge, Abel.

He m. Abigail ———.
He was bapt. as an adult at Redding, 26 Aug. 1753.

Child, rec. Fairfield, bapt. Redding:
>Joseph, b. 2 July 1753, bapt. 26 Aug. 1753.

Eliot, (Rev.) Andrew.

Son of Rev. Andrew, of Boston, D.D.; b. at Boston, 11 Jan. 1743, d. at Fairfield, 26 Sept. 1805 in 63 yr. (g. s.).

His sister Sarah Eliot m. at Boston 5 Oct. 1778, Joseph Squire; and Susanna Eliot m. at Boston, 10 Nov. 1789, Dr. David Hull.

He m. at Cambridge, Mass., 19 July 1774, Mrs. Mary Pynchon, dau. of Hon. Joseph of Boston; b. at Brookfield, Mass., who d. at Fairfield, 10 Dec. 1810 in 62 yr. (g. s.).

Ordained pastor of First Church, Fairfield, 22 June 1774.

Will 18 June 1803, proved 28 Oct. 1808; son Andrew, to have his Greek, Latin and French books; gr. son Andrew Eliot Burr; dau. Eunice Burr Eliot; children.

Children, rec. and bapt. Fairfield:
>Mary, b. 4, bapt. 16 July 1775.
>Elizabeth, b. 29 Oct., bapt. 3 Nov. 1776; m. 15 Oct. 1801, Gershom Burr.

---

* Children, rec. Redding: Zalmon, b. 26 Dec. 1787; Polly, b. 1 Jan. 1791; Benjamin, b. 1 Sept. 1793; Anne, b. 10 Oct. 1795; Lanson, b. 1 Feb. 1799. Trinity Church records give: Elijah son of Isaac Edwards, bapt. 14 Aug. 1785; Thomas son of Isaac, bapt. 19 Aug. 1787; Zalmon son of Isaac, bapt. 6 Apr. 1792.

Eunice-Burr, b. and bapt. 16 Aug. 1778, d. 28 Apr. 1862 ae. 83 (g. s.);
m. 25 Feb. 1821, Dea. Elijah Bibbins.
Andrew, b. 15, bapt. 20 Aug. 1780; m. 17 Sept. 1820, Sophia Wasson, who d. at New Milford, 17 Nov. 1822 ae. 34.
Sarah, b. 2, bapt. 3 Nov. 1782, d. 8 May 1794 in 12 yr. (g. s.).
Ruth-Martha, b. 25, bapt. 31 July 1785.
Susanna, b. 1, bapt. 5 Dec. 1790.

Elsner [Unplaced].

THOMAS m. 23 June 1779, Ann Fillio of Norwalk. [Weston Church.]

Elwell, Samuel.

Son of Samuel and Sarah (Wheadon) of Branford, b. 10 Jan. 1696/7; m. at New Haven, 12 Oct. 1720, Mary Jones, dau. of Isaac, b. 6 Oct. 1698.

They settled in Westport, and Samuel was called of Fairfield in 1734 when granted adm'n on his mother's estate. The following entries may pertain to Samuel's family.

Esther Elwell m. (rec. Fairfield) 11 Dec. 1745, John Finch.

Sarah Elwell d. at Westport, 14 Feb. 1758.

Deborah, dau. of Samuel and Mary, bapt. at Fairfield, 18 Dec. 1743.

Ezra Elwell m. at Weston, 9 Apr. 1779, Mercy Finch, bapt. 4 Jan. 1763; had issue:

> Isaac.
> John.
> James.
> Darius.

Ezra and Mercy of Southeast Precinct, Dutchess County, N. Y., conveyed in 1783.

Jabez Elwell of New Fairfield, Conn., and Franklin, Dutchess County [now Patterson, Putnam County], N. Y., d. in 1810; will named many children and gr. children, including heirs of his son Samuel.

1. Elwood, John.

He d. at Westport, 20 Oct. 1775; he m. Elizabeth Godfrey, who d. 24 Feb. 1764.

Children of John and Elizabeth, rec. Westport:
>   Mary, b. 23 Nov. 1714*; "Molly" d. 8 Jan. 1781.
> 2+Joseph, b. 3 Sept. 1719.
>   Abigail, b. 16 Feb. 1720/1.
> 3+Richard, b. 5 Mar. 1723.
>   Hannah, b. 31 July 1726, d. at Westport, 20 Mar. 1804 in 76 yr.; m. Mar. 1757, John Roberts.
>   Uriah, b. 17 June 1728.
> 4+Hezekiah b. 24 Aug. 1730.

2. Elwood, Joseph, s. of John.

Born 3 Sept. 1719.

He m. at Westport, 20 Feb. 1753, Eleanor Dibble,† dau. of Zachariah, b. at Stamford, 8 June 1731, d. 4 May 1762. They sold land in Stamford 1757, mentioning sister Mary Dibble and bro. Jabez Dibble, and reserving life use to gr. mother Mary Sturges.

> Children, rec. Westport:
>   Uriah, bapt. 17 Mar. 1754.
>   Jabez, bapt. 16 May 1756.
>   Abigail, bapt. 25 Feb. 1759; m. (rec. Norwalk) 4 Nov. 1778, Nathan Hendrick.
>   Joseph, bapt. 10 May 1761.

3. Elwood, Richard, s. of John.

Born 5 Mar. 1723; d. at Westport, 1 Dec. 1800 ae. 78.

He m. 20 Feb. 1742, Rachel Davis; dau. of Samuel, bapt. 2 Aug. 1724, d. 15 Feb. 1789.

> Children, rec. Fairfield, bapt. Westport:
>   Rachel, bapt. 30 Oct. 1743.
> 5+John, b. 15 May, bapt. 2 June 1745.
>   Samuel, b. 14, bapt. 20 Sept. 1747.
>   Eliakim, b. 6 Feb., bapt. 4 Mar. 1750.
> 6+Joseph, b. 15, bapt. 26 Apr. 1752.
>   Thomas, b. 13 July, bapt. 4 Aug. 1754, d. at Fairfield, 29 Sept. 1820 ae. 70; Lt.; adm'n granted, 14 Nov. 1820, to Samuel Rowland; m. 16 Oct. 1777, Susanna Barlow; dau. of David, b. 2 Feb. 1754.‡

---

* Huldah, dau. of Mary, bapt. 11 Mar. 1744; m. 29 May 1768, Grumman Morehouse.

† Olive, dau. of Ellen Elwood alias Dibble, bapt. 20 May 1753.

‡ Children, bapt. Fairfield: John-Barry, bapt. 24 Mar. 1792; John-Barry, bapt. 2 Nov. 1794. Older child, bapt. Trinity Church: Eunice, bapt. 20 Nov. 1785. She was his only surviving child in 1853, and m. 18 Nov. 1804 Benjamin Fairchild of Stratford.

Abraham, b. 19 Dec. 1756, bapt. 16 Jan. 1757; res. 1818, Scipio, Cayuga County, N. Y.; called of Saratoga, he m. 29 Nov. 1787, Sarah Johnson.*
Isaac, b. 19 Dec. 1756, bapt. 16 Jan. 1757, d. 13 Feb. 1757.
7+Isaac, bapt. 25 Feb. 1759.
8+Stephen, bapt. 14 Feb. 1762.

4. Elwood, Hezekiah, s. of John.

Born 24 Aug. 1730; d. at Westport, 12 Apr. 1801 ae. over 70.
He m. Sarah ———, who d. 17 Nov. 1804 ae. 72.
Hezekiah conveyed to son Nathan, 1784.

Children, bapt. Westport:
Nathan, bapt. 25 Feb. 1759, d. 27 Mar. 1761.
Hezekiah, bapt. 27 Apr. 1760; d. 29 Nov. 1776 [Rev. War Rolls].
Nathan, bapt. 9 May 1762, d. at Colchester, Delaware County, N. Y., 19 June 1829 (Pension rec.); m. 29 Dec. 1785, Abigail Smith, dau. of Samuel, b. 22 Mar. 1769 (Pension rec.).†
Elizabeth, bapt. 8 Apr. 1764, living 1839 at Westport, unm.
Abijah, bapt. July 1766, d. at Westport, 18 Sept. 1829 (Pension rec.); m. at Norwalk, 15 Jan. 1789, Susanna Sanders, who d. 5 Jan. 1852 ae. 85 yrs. 5 mos. (g. s.).‡
William, bapt. 4 Aug. 1771.

5. Elwood, John, s. of Richard.

Born 15 May 1745; John Elwood, Jr., d. at Albany, 28 Aug. 1775.
He m. 23 Nov. 1768, Ann Batterson.

Children, bapt. Westport:
Rachel, bapt. 26 Nov. 1769, d. 23 June 1773.
Samuel, bapt. 24, d. 26 Jan. 1772.
Anna, bapt. 10 July 1773.

6. Elwood, Joseph, s. of Richard.

Born 15 Apr. 1752; d. at Weston, 8 June 1826 (Pension rec.).
He m. 3 Oct. 1771, Naomi Batterson; dau. of George, b.

---

* His wife Sarah and son Abraham bapt. at Westport, 12 Sept. 1790; other children: Nathaniel-Brooks and Samuel, bapt. 30 Aug. 1795; John, bapt. 13 Mar. 1796.

† Children, bapt. Westport: Hezekiah, bapt. 13 Aug. 1786; Grumman, bapt. 7 Dec. 1788; Polly, bapt. 13 Mar. 1791; Clarissa, bapt. 23 Sept. 1792; Sally, bapt. 22 Jan. 1798. Nathan was of N. Y. State in 1793, and acknowledged a deed that year before John Quick, a Justice for Westchester County.

‡ Child, bapt. Westport: Rhoda, bapt. 1 July 1798.

THE FAMILIES OF OLD FAIRFIELD 327

19 Mar. 1753. She lived 1837 with a son in Fairfield, Franklin County, Vt.

Children, bapt. Westport:
    Ruhamah, bapt. 22 Feb. 1772 (offered by gr. father Richard Elwood), d. 23 Feb. 1772.
    Urania, bapt. 13 June 1773; m. at Weston, 4 Mar. 1791, Jonah Rockwell.
    Joseph, bapt. 3 Nov. 1776; m. at Weston, 19 Oct. 1796, Charlotte Squire.
    Richard, bapt. 21 Feb. 1779; m. at Weston, 31 Aug. 1800, Sarah Marvin.
    George, bapt. 2 Mar. 1781.
    Naomi, bapt. 29 Aug. 1784.
    Molly, bapt. 15 Apr. 1787;* m. at Weston, 4 Dec. 1806, Joseph Glover.
    Shubael, bapt. 19 Sept. 1790.
    Rachel, bapt. 16 Sept. 1792.
    Esther, bapt. at Weston, 31 Aug. 1794.
    Betty, bapt. at Weston, 8 Oct. 1797.
    Charity, bapt. at Weston, 6 Dec. 1801.

7. **Elwood, Isaac,** s. of Richard.

Bapt. 25 Feb. 1759; res. 1818, Scipio, N. Y.; res. 1832, Mt. Morris, Livingston County, N. Y.

He m. 9 Mar. 1781, Elizabeth Batterson; dau. of James, bapt. 24 June 1759.

Children, bapt. Westport:
    John, bapt. 25 Aug. 1782.
    Pamelia, bapt. 18 July 1784.
    Isaac, bapt. 11 Mar. 1787.

8. **Elwood, Stephen,** s. of Richard.

Bapt. 14 Feb. 1762; d. at Redding (rec. Westport), 13 Apr. 1812 ae. 50; m. 2 Mar. 1780, Betty Batterson; dau. of George, bapt. 18 Mar. 1764, living 1841 at Westport.

Children, bapt. Westport:
    Betty, bapt. 30 June 1782; m. Mar. 1800, Squire Williams.
    Eliakim, b. 24 Oct. 1786 (family rec.), bapt. 11 Feb. 1787, d. at Westport, 26 Apr. 1856 ae. 69-6-2 (g. s.); m. 9 Mar. 1811, Lydia Bennett, b. 22 Sept. 1789, d. 29 Aug. 1849 ae. 59-11-7 (g. s.).

---

* Nathan Lockwood, son of Molly Elwood, bapt. at Weston, 6 July 1806.

Benjamin, bapt. 1 Mar. 1789; m. 5 Dec. 1813, Rhoda Elwood.
Stephen, bapt. 13 Jan. 1793.
Huldah, bapt. 8 Oct. 1797.
Elizur, bapt. 5 Jan. 1800.
Aletheia, bapt. 18 Apr. 1802.
Harriet, bapt. 13 June 1804.
Joseph-Squire, bapt. 2 Feb. 1807.

Elwood [Unplaced].

SALOME, b. [say 1775]; m. at Westport, 9 July 1795, Stephen Godfrey. She was bapt. 1 Jan. 1797; on same date was bapt. EUNICE ELWOOD, b. [say 1777], d. at Fairfield, 1 Dec. 1812 ae. 35, m. 4 Oct. 1801, Samuel Smith.

CHARLOTTE m. 24 Oct. 1804, Silliman Gray. [Weston Church.]

English, Hudson.

He m. at Westport, 23 Sept. 1779, Hannah Couch; dau. of Joseph, b. 8 June 1756.

Children, bapt. Westport:
Joseph-Couch, bapt. 25 Mar. 1781.
Sarah, bapt. Oct. 1782.
Nancy, bapt. 30 Apr. 1784.

Fairchild [Vol. I, pp. 194-198].

1 Thomas (-1670) m. (1) ―――― Seabrook; (2) Katharine Craig.
(By 1): 2 Samuel (1640-1705) m. Mary Wheeler.
    5 *Samuel* (1682-1761).
    3 Thomas (1646-1686) m. Susanna ――――.
    6 *Alexander* (1681-1727).
(By 2): 4 Joseph (1664-1713) m. Joanna Wilcoxson.
    7 *Thomas* (1712-1748).

5. **Fairchild, Samuel,** s. of Samuel. Ens., north company, Stratford, May 1730; Lt., Oct. 1737.

Born abt. 1682, d. at Redding, 28 Feb. 1761 in 79 yr. (g. s.); m. (1) (rec. Stratford), 3 Jan. 1705/6, Ruth Beach, dau. of Thomas, b. at Wallingford, 24 Oct. 1683, d. at Stratford 30 Jan. 1721/2; m. (2) (rec. Stratford) 24 Jan. 1722/3, Dinah Burwell, dau. of Samuel, b. at New Haven, 28 Oct. 1694, d. at Redding, 8 May 1769 in 76 yr. (g. s.).

Adm'n granted, 9 Mar. 1762, to Andrew Fairchild.

Distribution 18 Aug. 1761; widow Dinah; eldest son Samuel of Stratford; son Ephraim of Newtown; son Benjamin; daus. Mary Adams, Abigail Judson; sons Oliver of Newtown, Stephen, Peter, Andrew, Josiah of Redding, Charles of Redding.

Distribution in Land Rec. 15 April 1762: Samuel Fairchild, Esq., Samuel Adams and wife Mary, and John Judson and wife Abigail, all of Stratford, Oliver Fairchild of Newtown, Stephen Fairchild of Danbury, and Benjamin, Peter, Andrew, Josiah and Charles Fairchild of Redding.

Children [by first wife], rec. Stratford:
Anna, b. 12 Oct. 1706, d. 9 Feb. 1721/2.
Mary, b. "27th 1708," d. at Litchfield, 29 Aug. 1803; m. 7 Mar. 1728/9, Samuel Adams.
Samuel, b. 3 Feb. 1710 [1710/1].
Ephraim, b. 28 Aug. 1713; m. Abiah Wakelee, dau. of Nathaniel.
Abigail, b. 15 Dec. 1715; m. John Judson.
Eunice, b. 20 May 1718, d. 21 Apr. 1721.
Benjamin, b. Mar. 1721.

Children [by second wife], bapt. Stratford:
Oliver, bapt. 28 June 1724.
Stephen, bapt. 25 Sept. 1726.
Peter, bapt. Apr. 1729; Deputy for Redding, May 1774; 1st Lt., 10th Co., 5th Regt., Army, Apr. 1775; m. (1) Hannah ———, who d. 4 Feb. 1767 in 34 yr. (g. s.); m. (2) 27 Mar. 1768, Mary Lockwood of Weston; dau. of John, b. 20 Jan. 1743.*
8+Andrew, bapt. 1729.
Josiah, bapt. Aug. 1732.
Charles, bapt. Mar. 1736.

6. **Fairchild, Alexander,** s. of Thomas.

Born Feb. 1680/1; d. at Stratfield in 1727; m. Deborah Jackson, who d. in 1753.

Adm'n granted, 6 June 1727. Deborah was appointed guardian, 5 Mar. 1727/8, to five of her children,—Andrew, Samuel, Stephen, Ruth, and Catherine; and was chosen by Abraham and Hannah.

Capt. Samuel Odell was appointed Adm'r on the estate of Deborah Fairchild, 5 Nov. 1753.

---

* Children by second wife, rec. Redding: Peter, b. 22 Aug. 1768; Hannah, b. 3 Dec. 1769.

Children, bapt. Stratfield:
> John, bapt. 20 Dec. 1702, d. at New Fairfield, 1787; m. Mary Wheeler, dau. of Samuel, b. 22 July 1708, d. in 1790.* The will of Mara Fairchild, 24 Sept. 1788, proved 8 June 1790, named heirs of dau. Hannah Lacey dec'd, dau. Mary wife of John Beardsley, only son Elijah, and dau. Ruth wife of Phineas Beardsley.

9+Alexander, bapt. 2 July 1704.
> Deborah, bapt. 19 May 1706.
> Sarah, bapt. 20 June 1708.

10+Abraham, bapt. 27 May 1711.
> Hannah, bapt. 29 June 1713, d. 11 June 1784 ae. 70 (g. s.); m. David Jackson, of New Milford.†
> Andrew, bapt. 29 Apr. 1716.
> Ruth, bapt. 12 Jan. 1718.
> Samuel.
> Catherine.
> Stephen.

7. Fairchild, Thomas, s. of Joseph.

Born at Stratford, 4 May 1712; d. at Redding in 1748; m. at Fairfield, 22 Sept. 1737, Mary Hall; dau. of Jonathan; she d. in 1748.

Will 20 Dec. 1747, proved 29 Mar. 1748; wife Mary; children, Timothy, Billy, Nathan, Abijah, Sarah, Mary, Rhoda; wife and bro. Lt. Joseph Sanford of Redding, Exec'rs.

Adm'n on Est. of Mary Fairchild granted, 6 Dec. 1748, to Joseph Sanford. Distribution 3 Mar. 1760: Abijah, Sarah, Mary, Rhoda.

Children, first two rec. Fairfield, bapt. Redding:
> Timothy, b. and bapt. 22 Oct. 1738, d. y.
> Billy (twin), b. and bapt. 22 Oct. 1738, d. y.
> Sarah, bapt. 12 Apr. 1741; m. David-Wheeler Morehouse.
> Nathan, bapt. 7 Nov. 1742, d. y.
> Abijah, bapt. 27 May 1744; m. (1) 5 Nov. 1767, Huldah Burr, bapt. 10 Apr. 1747, d. at Redding, 20 Apr. 1774 ae. 27; m. (2) 18 Sept. 1774, Phebe Smith.‡

---

* Children: Elijah, b. 3 Aug. 1730; Hannah, b. 23 Nov. 1734, m. [Seth] Lacy; Ruth, b. 3 Aug. 1736, m. 14 Sept. 1755, Capt. Phineas Beardsley; Mary, b. 22 May 1742, m. John Beardsley. Elijah's estate was distributed, 24 Dec. 1792, to sister Ruth wife of Capt. Phinehas Beardsley; heirs of dec'd sister Hannah "Lessey" of New Fairfield; and heirs of dec'd sister Mary wife of John Beardsley.

† See *N. Y. Gen. and Biog. Record*, vol. 53, p. 135.

‡ Child by first wife, bapt. Redding: Sarah, bapt. 9 June 1771. Child by second wife: Timothy, bapt. 27 Oct. 1776.

Mary, bapt. 23 Oct. 1745.
Rhoda, bapt. 31 May 1747, d. in 1766. Adm'n granted, 13 Sept. 1766, to Abijah Fairchild. Distribution to bro. Abijah, sister Mary Fairchild, and heirs of sister Sarah Morehouse dec'd, late wife of David-Wheeler Morehouse.

8. **Fairchild, Andrew,** s. of Samuel.

Bapt. 1729; d. at Redding, 1806.

He m. 26 Apr. 1752, Abigail Hill; dau. of William, b. 6 May 1734.

Tory, of Redding, imprisoned Jan. 1777, discharged on parole next month.

Adm'n granted, 9 Apr. 1806, to Elihu and Daniel Crofoot of Newtown; and they were appointed the same date to administer the estate of Abigail wife of Andrew. Distribution of the two estates: Andrew Fairchild; Phebe wife of Elihu Crofoot; Rebecca wife of Caleb Northrup; Mary Crofoot; Abigail wife of John Crofoot; Phebe, Betty, Abel, Eliel, and Daniel, heirs of Rhoda wife of Daniel Crofoot and gr. children of the dec'd; Huldah Fairchild.

Children, two rec. Fairfield:
>   Mary, b. 7 Mar. 1754; m. —— Crofut.
>   Phebe, b. 12 Nov. 1756; m. Elihu Crofut.
>   Andrew, m. at Redding, 16 Feb. 1792, Lydia Couch; dau. of Simon, bapt. 25 Oct. 1767, d. 13 July 1820.*
>   Rebecca, m. Caleb Northrup.
>   Abigail, m. John Crofut.
>   Rhoda, m. Daniel Crofut.
>   Huldah.

9. **Fairchild, Alexander,** s. of Alexander. Ens., south company, New Fairfield, May 1749.

Bapt. 2 July 1704; d. at New Fairfield, in 1751.

He m. 24 Feb. 1727, Mary Mallory; dau. of William, bapt. 22 Aug. 1703.

Adm'n granted, 1 July 1751, to widow Mary, who was appointed guardian to Huldah, Christian, Jesse, and Silas. Gershom, Deborah, and Dinah chose their mother guardian, 2 Sept. 1751.

---
* Children, rec. Redding: Simon, b. 29 Sept. 1792; Peter, b. 2 Aug. 1794; Rebecca, b. 13 Aug. 1796; Lydia, b. 3 Mar. 1799.

Distribution was made to the widow Mary, eldest son Alexander, Thomas, Gershom, Jesse, Silas, Grace wife of Samuel Knap of Danbury, Sarah wife of Seth Trowbridge of New Fairfield, Deborah, Dinah, Huldah and Christian.

Children, first four rec. Stratfield:

Grace, b. 27 Sept. 1727, bapt. at Greenfield, 10 Dec. 1727; m. Samuel Knapp, of Danbury.
Alexander, b. 27 Mar. 1729; Ens., New Fairfield south company, Oct. 1765; Deputy, several sessions; ?m. at Stratford, 14 Aug. 1757, Ann Benjamin, dau. of John.*
Sarah, b. 24 Sept. 1730, d. before 1771; m. Seth Trowbridge.
11+Thomas, b. 11, bapt. 21 May 1732.
12+Gershom.
Deborah.
Dinah, d. at Danbury, 1 Feb. 1790; m. 22 Mar. 1758, Samuel Wildman.
Huldah.
Christian.
Jesse.
Silas, perhaps m. at Weston, 11 Jan. 1770, Sarah Goodsell.

10. **Fairchild, Abraham,** s. of Alexander.

Bapt. 27 May 1711; d. at Redding, 9 July 1776.

He m. 7 Nov. 1742, Rachel Scribner; dau. of Benjamin of Norwalk; she d. 23 July 1801.

Children, rec. Fairfield, bapt. Redding; last three rec. Redding:

Abraham, b. 1 Jan. 1745, d. 16 July 1764 ae. 19 (g. s.).
Ezekiel, b. 26 Oct., bapt. 7 Dec. 1746; m. 8 Jan. 1767, Eunice Andrews, b. 31 Aug. 1750.†
Daniel, b. 26 Dec. 1748, bapt. 5 Feb. 1749, d. 15 May 1770 ae. 22 (church rec.) or 20 May 1769 (town rec., in error).
Isaac, b. 6, bapt. 25 Mar. 1751, d. 25 Oct. 1776.
David, b. 10 June, bapt. 8 July 1753, d. 16 May 1777.
Samuel, b. 9, bapt. 12 July 1755, d. at Redding, 6 May 1812 ae. 56 (g. s.); m. 31 Mar. 1785, Abigail Platt b. 9 May 1760, d. 12 Apr. 1833 ae. 74 (g. s.).‡

---

* But one Alexander Fairchild is said to have m. Esther Stevens, dau. of Capt. Ebenezer of New Fairfield.

† Children, bapt. Redding: Sarah, bapt. 6 Dec. 1767, d. at Redding, 22 Apr. 1838 ae. 69 (g. s.); m. 22 Feb. 1782, John Hull, Jr. Abigail, bapt. 29 Apr. 1770, d. at Redding, 25 Apr. 1838, ae. 68 (g. s.); m. Apr. 1790, Lyman Thorp.

‡ His will, 2 May 1812, proved 30 May 1812; wife Abigail; two children, Aaron and Betsey; son-in-law Starr H. Morehouse. Children, rec. Redding: Aaron, b. 9 Oct. 1786, d. 31 May 1787; Betsey, b. 20 Jan. 1789; Aaron, b. 9 Jan. 1792; Uriah, b. 20 May 1794; d. 9 Aug. 1795.

Stephen, bapt. 26 Mar. 1758; m. 30 Dec. 1779, Elizabeth Fitch.*
Rachel, b. 2 Feb., bapt. 21 June 1761; m. 1 May 1782, Seth Andrews.
John, b. 13 Mar., bapt. 20 May 1764, d. at Redding, 30 Oct. 1846 ae. 83 (g. s.) ; m. (1) 6 Jan. 1792, Abigail Wakeman; m. (2) Elizabeth ———, who d. 4 May 1848 ae. 79 (g. s.).†
Ellen, b. 16 Oct., bapt. 13 Dec. 1767.

11. **Fairchild, Thomas,** s. of Alexander. Ens., east company, Redding, May 1771.

Born 11 May 1732.

He m. 17 June 1753, Rachel Sherwood, dau. of John of Newtown, b. 15 May 1732.

Children, rec. Fairfield:
> Alexander, b. 5 Dec. 1753.
> John, b. 26 Jan. 1755; ?m. at Redding, 27 Jan. 1774, Sarah Hull, dau. of Timothy, b. 5 Feb. 1754.‡
> Huldah, b. 20 Apr. 1757.

12. **Fairchild, Gershom,** s. of Alexander.

He m. (1) 19 Nov. 1754, Mary Knapp, dau. of Moses, who d. by 1757.

He m. (2) Abby Morgan, dau. of James, b. 2 Mar. 1738/9.

Child [by first wife], rec. Fairfield:
> Mary, b. 9 Dec. 1756, d. y.

Fairchild, John, s. of John.

Son of John and Ruth (Guernsey) of Durham, b. 1751; d. at Durham, 10 Sept. 1777; m. 17 Feb. 1773, Martha Allen, dau. of Dr. John, b. 1 Apr. 1755, d. at Fairfield, 25 Nov. 1834 in 80 yr.

Child, rec. Fairfield:
> Robert, b. 19 Jan. 1775; grad. Yale Coll. 1793; Marshal of Conn., 1809-21.

---

* Children, rec. Redding: Daniel, b. 20 Oct. 1780, m. 15 Jan. 1801, Betsey Mead; Isaac, b. 27 Jan. 1783, m. 8 Apr. 1802, Rachel Banks; Hezekiah, b. 19 Apr. 1785, m. 25 Oct. 1805, Lois Bennett; Ellen, b. 24 Aug. 1796.
† Children by first wife, rec. Redding: Eli, b. 15 Nov. 1794; David, b. 9 Mar. 1797.
‡ Children, bapt. Redding: John, bapt. 22 Apr. 1774; John, bapt. 12 Apr. 1778; Daniel, bapt. 16 Mar. 1780.

Fairchild, Ephraim.

Of Weston, will 8 Jan. 1794, proved 8 Nov. 1804; wife Hannah; son Ephraim; dau. Ruth wife of Eleazer Russell; dau. Rebecca wife of Zophar Platt; son Nathaniel.

Rebecca m. 2 Feb. 1773, Zophar Platt. [Easton Church.]

Fairchild, Gilbert.

Called of Norwalk, he m. at Westport, 24 June 1779, Hannah Bennett; dau. of Nathan, b. 20 May 1758.

Children, rec. Norwalk, two bapt. Westport:
>Hezekiah, b. 2 Feb., bapt. 16 Apr. 1780, d. at Westport, 1 Sept. 1862 ae. 82 (g. s.); m. 25 Mar. 1801, Rhoda Allen, bapt. 13 July 1777, d. 20 Sept. 1854 ae. 77 (g. s.).
>Eleanor, bapt. 6 Apr. 1783.
>Ebenezer, b. 3 Oct. 1783 [1785?].
>Samuel, b. 2 Aug. 1792.
>Betsey, b. 7 Feb. 1796.

Fairchild.

>HANNAH, dau. of Nathan, lived in Fairfield with her aunt's husband, Samuel Hull; and m. there, 19 Mar. 1750/1, Daniel Kellogg of Norwalk.
>DANIEL m. 25 Dec. 1770, Sarah Lane. [Redding rec.]
>NATHANIEL, b. 5 June 1764; m. 16 Mar. 1786, Esther Wheeler, b. 17 Jan. 1765; children: Isaac, b. 3 Aug. 1786; Huldah, b. 25 Sept. 1787; Ephraim, b. 4 Oct. 1792; Jarvis, b. 3 May 1795, d. 14 Mar. 1796; Esther, b. 25 Oct. 1798. [Weston rec.] Huldah m. at Easton, 29 Feb. 1808, Wheeler Cable.
>PHILO, of Newtown, m. 12 June 1783, Lois Beers, of Weston. [Greens Farms Church.]
>———, of Newtown, m. at Weston, 23 June 1777, Mary Beers. James Fairchild had a child, Amy, bapt. at Weston, 8 Mar. 1778.
>BENJAMIN, of Stratford, m. 18 Nov. 1804, Eunice Elwood. [Fairfield Church.]

Fairweather, John, s. of Benjamin [Vol. I, p. 198].

Born 28 Dec. 1703; d. at Stratfield, in 1749; m. Ann ———,* b. 27 Apr. 1712 (g. s.), d. 24 Sept. 1773 (g. s.).

---

* Possibly dau. of Samuel Bradley, bapt. with her sister Deborah at Fairfield, 25 May 1712.

Adm'n granted, 8 May 1749, to Ann Fairweather and Ezra Hawley. Ann was appointed guardian to the son John, 2 Jan. 1749/50.

Children:
>   Deborah, bapt. 23 Apr. 1732.
>   Sarah, bapt. 3 Nov. 1734.
>   John, bapt. 17 Oct. 1736; m. at Trumbull, 14 Feb. 1760, Abigail Curtis.*

Fairweather, Joseph, s. of Benjamin [Vol. I, p. 199].

Born 4 Nov. 1707, d. at Boston, 3 Sept. 1732 (Stratfield Church rec.); m. Abigail ———.
Will 23 Aug. 1732, proved 5 Dec. 1732; uncle Capt. John Fayerweather of Boston; wife Abigail, Exec'x; only child Hannah. The widow Abigail was appointed guardian to Hannah, 4 Mar. 1734/5; she chose Mr. William Odell for guardian, 20 Jan. 1747/8.

Child, rec. Fairfield:
>   Hannah, b. 30 Nov., bapt. 12 Dec. 1731, d. at Stratfield, 4 June 1815 in 85 yr. (g. s.); m. Joseph Brothwell.

Fairweather, Benjamin, s. of Benjamin [Vol. I, p. 199]. Ens., Stratfield Co., Oct. 1760; Lt., Oct. 1764.

Born 1 Oct. 1717, d. at Stratfield, 20 June 1791 in 74 yr. (g. s.); m. at Fairfield, 7 Jan. 1741/2, Elizabeth Beach; dau. of Nathaniel, b. at Stratford, 10 Mar. 1721/2.

---

* Children:
>   ?Samuel, b. (rec. Weston) 26 Mar. 1761, d. at Upper Stepney, 1848 ae. 87 (g. s.); Capt.; m. 28 Apr. 1791, Charity Burton, b. 10 Apr. 1760, d. 1847 ae. 87 (g. s.). Children, rec. Weston: Lucius, b. 17 Jan. 1792; Stephen, b. 4 July 1793; Daniel-Burton, b. 27 May 1795.
>   Zalmon, b. Mar. 1763, d. at Trumbull, 18 May 1828 ae. 65 (g. s.); m. (1) 25 Jan. 1787, Jerusha Adams, who d. 20 June 1815 ae. 50 (g. s.); m. (2) Eunice ———, who d. 16 July 1830 ae. 59 (g. s.).
>   Joseph, b. Apr. 1765, d. at Weston, by 1821; m. at Weston, 4 Mar. 1787, Rachel Beers. Children, rec. Weston: John-Curtis, b. 20 Dec. 1787; Eunice, b. 10 Nov. 1789; Lucretia, b. 29 Dec. 1793; Anne, b. 18 Mar. 1796; Abigail, b. 16 Apr. 1798; Phebe, b. 8 June 1800; Sally, b. 29 Sept. 1802; Ruthena, b. 18 Mar. 1805; Peter, b. 17 Aug. 1807. Children named in distribution: Polly, Peter, Ruthan and Sally Fayerweather, Phebe Fayerweather dec'd, Abba wife of David Beach, Susanna Fayerweather, Lucretia wife of Elias B. Sanford, Eunice wife of Ebenezer Sherman, John C. Fayerweather; dower to widow Rachel.

Will 4 Feb., proved 27 June 1791; heirs of dec'd dau. Charity, late wife of Samuel Gregory; dau. Elizabeth wife of Benjamin Knapp; two gr. sons James and Daniel Fairweather; gr. dau. Polly Fairweather; son-in-law Ebenezer Sherman, Exec'r.

    Children, rec. Stratfield:
        Charity, b. 27 Aug. 1742; m. Samuel Gregory.
        Katharine, b. 10 Oct. 1744, d. 19 Aug. 1753.
        Elizabeth, b. 20 Apr. 1747; m. (1) John Wilson; m. (2) 13 July 1780, Benjamin Knapp.
        Daughter, b. 12 Sept. 1749, "Liued 2 ours and Died."
        Nathaniel, b. 15 Dec. 1751, but bapt. 16 Dec. 1750, d. of smallpox in New York, 25 Jan. 1779; m. at Trumbull, 14 July 1773, Charity Summers, b. 23 Apr. 1754; she m. (2) Ebenezer Sherman.*

Fanton [Vol. I, p. 199].

1 Jonathan (-1714) m. (1) Mehitabel Staples; (2) Sarah Hide.
(By 2): 2 *Jonathan* (1700-1738).
      3 *John* (1708-1795).

2. Fanton, Jonathan, s. of Jonathan.

Bapt. 22 Sept. 1700; d. in 1738; m. Sarah Hide, dau. of John, 2d, b. 25 Dec. 1703, living 1757.

Inv. Dec. 1738; adm'n granted to John Hide, Jr., and Sarah Fanton. On 23 Sept. 1739, it was reported that the eldest son was now dead, under age, and the remaining children were three sons and four daus.

Sarah Fanton conveyed 1760 to son Zebulon and dau. Ellen Fanton, and 1764 to son Gershom; and a deed of partition was made by Zebulon and Gershom Fanton, Nehemiah Beers and Eunice his wife, Ephraim Beers and Mary his wife, John Sturges and Sarah his wife, and Ellen Fanton; heirs of Jonathan Fanton dec'd; the son Ezra mentioned as dec'd.

    Children:
        Ezra, d. s. p. in 1762; adm'n granted to Zebulon Fanton, 7 Sept. 1762.
        Mary, b. [say 1728], d. at Weston, abt. 1813; m. 24 Dec. 1745, Ephraim Beers.
        Zebulon, b. abt. 1729, d. s. p. 1807; will 26 Mar. 1804, proved 19 June 1807; all to Grace widow of John Goodsell; m. (as a bachelor of

---

* Children of Nathaniel and Charity: James, b. abt. 1774, bur. 16 Sept. 1820 ae. 46 (Trinity Church rec.); m. 16 Mar. 1797, Mercy Burritt. Daniel, m. 8 Mar. 1804, Betsey Smith. Polly, m. William Eaton.

75) 27 Mar. 1804, Grace Goodsell [widow of John], b. abt. 1735, d. at Weston, 16 Apr. 1812 ae. 77 (g. s.). Distribution Nov. 1820: heirs of Gershom Fanton dec'd; heirs of Eunice Beers dec'd; heirs of Mary Beers dec'd; heirs of Sarah Redfield dec'd.

    Eunice, b. [say 1735], d. after 1793; m. 27 June 1753, Nehemiah Beers.
4+Gershom.
    Sarah, m. (1) John Sturgis; m. (2) 4 Nov. 1781, Ebenezer Redfield.
    Ellen, d. unm. abt. 1804. Her will, 18 Sept. 1794, proved 19 Mar. 1804; life use to bro. Zebulon, then to her natural heirs.

3. Fanton, John, s. of Jonathan.

Born 22 Aug. 1708; d. at Easton, 18 Nov. 1795 ae. 90 (g. s.); m. (1) 28 Oct. 1732, Mary Rowland, b. Aug. 1711. He m. (2) at Westport, 28 Feb. 1754 (12 Feb. 1755 by town rec.) Widow Eunice Lyon; widow of Ephraim Lyon, and dau. of John Thorp; b. 18 Mar. 1710, d. 2 Oct. 1762.

    Children [by first wife], rec. Fairfield, bapt. Greenfield:

    Hannah, b. 15 July 1734 [or 1735], d. at Easton, 5 May 1809 ae. 75 (g. s.); m. 1 Mar. 1758, David Merwin.
    Abigail, b. 10 or 15 Feb. 1736/7, d. at Weston, 2 Oct. 1815 ae. 80 (g. s.); m. 26 Nov. 1761, John Dimon.
5+Jonathan, b. 2 Nov. 1738.
    Ann, b. 10 Sept. [or 2 Nov.] 1740.
6+Hezekiah, b. 28 Oct. [or 14 Nov.] 1743.
    John, b. 15 Mar. 1745 (town rec.), or b. 16, bapt. 19 Jan. 1745/6 (church rec.), d. in 1794; m. (1) at Westport, 18 Jan. 1776, Ann Burr;* prob. m. (2) Jane Dimon. Adm'n on estate of John Fanton, Jr., of Weston, was granted to Jane Fanton, 7 Apr. 1794.
7+Nehemiah, b. 10 Jan. 1748.
    Mary, b. 10 Oct., bapt. 3 Nov. 1751; "Molly" m. at Easton, 18 Nov. 1770, Amos Sherwood.
    Esther, b. 10 Oct. 1753, d. at Easton, 17 Aug. 1794 in 41 yr. (g. s.); "Hester" m. 11 Nov. 1774, Peter Oakley.

4. Fanton, Gershom, s. of Jonathan.

He d. 6 Dec. 1810 (Miss Treadwell's book).

He m. at Weston, 18 Jan. 1759, Anna Sturgis; dau. of Jeremiah, b. 3 Feb. 1737.†

---

* Children, bapt. Weston: Aaron-Burr, bapt. 19 May 1782; Ann-Burr, bapt. 31 Oct. 1784. Andrew Bradley of Weston was appointed guardian to these two children, 17 Feb. 1795.

† Gershom Fanton d. 22 Jan. 1804 (Miss Treadwell's book); perhaps intended for Gershom's wife, or for a son of that name.

Adm'n granted, 8 Jan. 1811, to Ebenezer Sherman, with David Wayland as surety.

The two daus. m. at Westport, and were called Fountain.

Children, bapt. Weston:
> Ruhamah, bapt. 13 Apr. 1760; m. 16 Apr. 1786, Isaac Beers.
> Anna, bapt. 28 Mar. 1766; m. 16 Dec. 1784, Peter Thorp.

5. **Fanton, Jonathan,** s. of John.

Born 2 Nov. 1738; d. at Weston, 25 Nov. 1810.

He m. at Weston, [abt. Mar.] 1759, Elizabeth Downs; [? dau. of Edward]; the wife of Jonathan d. 31 July 1803.

Will 16 Feb. 1808, proved 25 Dec. 1810; sons Rowland, Levi, Jonathan, Simeon; daus. Mary, Betsey, Hannah; children of son Abel dec'd.

Distribution 21 Mar. 1811; sons Rowland, Levi, Jonathan, Simeon; heirs of son Abel; daus. Mary wife of Nathan Merwin, Betsey wife of Aaron Hull, Hannah wife of Eli Bradley.

Children, bapt. Weston:
> 8+Abel, b. 19 Mar., bapt. 18 Apr. 1762.
> Mary, b. 9 July, bapt. 3 Sept. 1764, d. at Easton, 15 Jan. 1826 ae. 62 (g. s.); m. 5 Aug. 1784, Nathan Merwin.
> Jonathan, bapt. 29 Jan. 1767; ?m. 7 Feb. 1802, Sally Morehouse.*
> Rowland, bapt. 6 Nov. 1768; m. 30 Dec. 1792, Polly Fanton.†
> Levi, bapt. at Easton, 31 May 1772, d. 28 Aug. 1833 (Miss Treadwell's book); m. at Redding, 26 Feb. 1797, Abigail Beers.
> Betsey, b. 17 Feb. 1784; m. Aaron Hull.
> Hannah (twin), b. 17 Feb. 1784, d. 23 Feb. 1824; m. Eli Bradley.
> Simeon, b. abt. 1782, d. at Easton, 26 May 1839 ae. 57 (g. s.); m. Hannah Burr, dau. of Moses, b. [Feb. 1781], d. 16 July 1844 ae. 63 yrs. 5 mos. (g. s.).

6. **Fanton, Hezekiah,** s. of John.

Born 28 Oct. 1743; d. at Easton, 2 Dec. 1822 in 79 yr. (g. s.).

He m. 14 Jan. 1773, Ruth Merwin; widow of Thomas Merwin,

---

* One Jonathan d. 1 Mar. 1857 (Miss Treadwell's book).

† Children, rec. Weston: Thomas-Burr, b. 16 Apr. 1794; Edmond, b. 24 June 1795; Curtis, b. 20 July 1798. Although Polly was called Fanton in the Weston record, that was her married name, and it may be that she was the Polly left a widow by Thomas (son of Nehemiah) Burr in 1789. She was certainly Polly Duffee, b. 1 Mar. 1769, dau. of Thomas and Elizabeth Duffee, and sister of Eunice Duffee who m. Thomas Solley. See Solley's pension records in Vol. III.

and dau. of Daniel Silliman, b. 1 Mar. 1750, d. 29 May 1817 ae. 67 (g. s.).

Distribution 10 Mar. 1823: son Silliman; Hezekiah; Robert; Priscilla wife of Robert Platt; Abigail wife of Elias Parsons; Ruth wife of Josiah French; Mary wife of Hezekiah Gould.

Children:
>Priscilla, b. [say 1775]; m. (rec. Redding) 31(?) Nov. 1796, Robert Platt.
>Silliman, b. 24 June 1777 (family rec.), d. at Easton, 10 Mar. 1838 in 61 yr. (g. s.); m. 16 Aug. 1798, Mary Coley, dau. of Eliphalet, b. 20 Sept. 1777, d. 20 May 1844 in 66 yr. (g. s.).*
>Abigail, b. [30 Sept. 1779], d. at Easton, 10 Jan. 1837 ae. 57-3-10 (g. s.); m. Elias Parsons.
>Ruth, m. Josiah French.
>Hezekiah, b. 1783, d. at Easton, 1 Nov. 1845 ae. 62 (g. s.); m. Polly ———, who d. 18 Sept. 1851 ae. 66 (g. s.).
>Robert, m. Clarina Banks, dau. of Benjamin.
>Mary, m. Hezekiah Gould.

7. **Fanton, Nehemiah,** s. of John.

Born 10 Jan. 1748; d. at Easton, 11 Apr. 1813.

He m. at Easton, 1 Jan. 1772, Sarah Hull; dau. of Jabez, b. Jan. 1752, d. at Easton, 22 Mar. 1810 ae. 58 (g. s.).

Will 18 July 1812, proved 22 Apr. 1813; sons, Sherwood, Judson, David; children of Hull; Nathan Wheeler, Exec'r.

Distribution, 30 Mar. 1814: son Sherwood; son Judson; son David; children of son Hull,—Langley, John, Betsey, Anna, Huldah, Sarah and Margery Fanton.

Children:
>Hull, bapt. 2 Aug. 1772, d. 22 Aug. 1813; Capt.; m. 22 June 1797, Margery Collier, who d. at Easton, 6 Oct. 1810 in 31 yr. (g. s.).
>Sherwood, of Danbury; m. Thankful Bradley, dau. of Joseph, b. 1775.
>Judson, d. Apr. 1826.
>David, m. 7 Jan. 1806, Eunice Banks.

---

* Children (from family account): Eunice, b. 21 Oct. 1799; m. William Coley. Paulina, b. 4 Aug. 1801, d. 15 June 1806. Eliphalet C., b. 1 Aug. 1806; m. Hannah Silliman. Horace, b. 14 Feb. 1808; m. Katie Dimon. Pauline S., b. 3 Aug. 1817; m. George Godfrey. The heirs of Silliman Fanton assigned their right in his estate, 1839, to their mother Mary; signed by Horace, Eliphalet C., Pollina, and Mary Fanton, of Weston, and William and Eunice Coley of Westport.

8. Fanton, Abel, s. of Jonathan. Capt.

Born 19 Mar. 1762; d. at Easton, 31 May 1805 in 44 yr. (g. s.); m. 2 Feb. 1788, Jerusha Sturges; dau. of Joseph, b. 5 Dec. 1765, d. 18 Jan. 1804 ae. 38 (g. s.).

Will 22 Apr., proved 20 June 1805; children, Sarah D. Sturges, Araty, John, Charlotte, Maria, Altha, Esther; friend Nathan Wheeler of Weston, Exec'r.

Children, first six rec. Weston:
   Sarah-Sturges, b. 4 Feb. 1789, bapt. at Easton, July 1789, d. 6 Jan. 1855; m. Burr Bradley.
   Sturges. b. 21 Dec. 1790.
   Araty, b. 12 Aug. 1792; m. Ezra B. Stevens, of Pembroke.
   John, b. 1 May 1794, d. at New Fairfield, Oct. 1854 (Miss Treadwell's book).
   Charlotte, b. 18 Feb. 1796, d. at Easton, 13 July 1837 ae. 41 (g. s.).
   Maria, b. 4 Mar. 1798; m. Clark Barnum.
   Althea, b. 11 Apr. 1800, d. 1890; m. John W. Sanford, of Redding.
   Esther, b. 12 June 1801; m. Edward Todd.

Fanton, William.

He was of Ripton Parish, Stratford, 1734, and m. Phebe Pierson, dau. of Stephen of Derby, b. prob. by 1704.

Will of William Fanton, 19 Apr. 1764, proved 31 Dec. 1766; wife Sarah; sons Jonathan, Ebenezer; dau. Phebe; mentioned first wife Phebe. Who was he?

The son Ebenezer m. Rebecca Hubbell, dau. of Nehemiah, bapt. 11 May 1755.

Adm'n on Est. of William Fanton of Stratford was granted, 27 Mar. 1788, to Joseph Birdsey. Distribution made 24 Mar. 1795, to widow, son Ebenezer, and dau. Phebe.

Adm'n on Est. of Phebe Phanton of Huntington was granted, 5 Feb. 1798, to Joseph Birdsey.

Ferry, Ebenezer.

Son of Solomon and Lydia (Peck) Ferry of Springfield and Danbury; born [say 1706], d. at Redding in Mar. 1743/4; m. Eleanor Hull, dau. of Cornelius, bapt. 15 Sept. 1706, d. in 1762.

Will 12, proved 22 Mar. 1743/4; wife Ellen; children Charles, Rachel, Sarah, John, Ebenezer; friend Ens. Lemuel Sanford, bro.

Joseph Ferry of Danbury, and wife Ellen, Exec'rs. Distribution 1755 to the five children.

Adm'n on Ellen Ferry's Est. granted, 2 Mar. 1762, to Stephen Gray. Distribution 8 Apr. 1762: Ebenezer, Charles, Hannah wife of Stephen Gray, Rachel wife of Samuel Griffin.

Children, bapt. Redding:

> Charles, b. [say 1728]; served in French and Indian War; m. at New Milford, 18 Oct. 1752, Mary Henry.
> Rachel, b. [say 1731]; m. Samuel Griffin, of Newtown.
> Abigail, bapt. 25 Mar. 1733, d. 7 Dec. 1734.
> Sarah, bapt. 6 May 1739; m. 3 Sept. 1758, Stephen Gray.
> John, bapt. 10 May 1741, d. by 1760; served 1759 in French and Indian War.
> Ebenezer, bapt. 12 June 1743; served in French and Indian War; of Danbury in 1764; prob. rem. to Granville, N. Y.

Ferry [*Unplaced*].

> JOSHUA m. May 1789, Sarah Patterson. [Easton Church.]

Fillio [*Unplaced*].

> ELIZABETH m. Oct. 1742, Jabez Sherwood. [Fairfield Rec.]
> ANN, of Norwalk, m. 23 June 1779, Thomas Elsner. [Weston Church.]
> JOHN, of Norwalk, m. 10 Mar. 1757, Sarah Sherwood. [Greens Farms Church.]

Finch, John, s. of Samuel.

He was gr. son of Nathaniel Nichols; d. at Norwalk in 1799.

He m. (1) at Greenfield, 11 Dec. 1745, Esther Elwell. She was prob. dau. of Samuel; and d. at Westport, 5 Apr. 1751. He m. (2) Mercy ———, who d. at Westport, 15 Jan. 1763. He m. (3) at Weston, 7 Jan. 1779,* Widow Mary Ogden. She was widow of Samuel Ogden, and dau. of Benjamin Banks, bapt. 18 Apr. 1736. She m. (3) 21 Jan. 1801, Shubael Gorham.

John Finch and Mary his wife of Norwalk conveyed, 1792, to Samuel Ogden, right in house where Ogden now lives, reserving liberty to pass through kitchen, etc.

---

* 3 Dec. 1778, by Norwalk rec.

Will 21 Sept. 1793, proved 18 Mar. 1799; wife Mary; dau. Abigail wife of Andrew Sturges; son John Finch; four grandchildren, Isaac, John, James and Darius Elwell, £120 silver money; dau. Chloe wife of Peter Smith; dau. Salomi wife of David Godfrey; dau. Ruany. Codicil states that James Elwell, son of dec'd dau. Mary was dead when will was made, the testator being ignorant of his demise. Distribution May 1799: Widow Mary; dau. Abigail wife of Andrew Sturges; son John Finch; dau. Chloe wife of Peter Smith; son Ichabod Finch; dau. Salome wife of David Godfrey; dau. Ruany Finch; gr. sons Isaac, John and Darius Elwell, children of Mercy Elwell dec'd.

Children [by first wife], rec. Fairfield:

> Abigail, b. 30 June 1746, d. by 1819; m. at Weston, 27 Feb. 1766, Andrew Sturges.
> John, b. 15 Mar. 1748; m. at Westport, 18 Apr. 1789, Huldah Ogden; dau. of Ebenezer.*
> Esther, b. 28 Oct. 1750, d. 25 Mar. 1763.
> Infant, d. Sept. 1751.

Children [by second wife], bapt. Westport:

> Chloe, b. 25 Nov. 1754; m. (1) at Weston, 15 Nov. 1774, Daniel Smith; m. (2) at Greenfield, 27 May 1778, Peter Smith.
> Ichabod, m. Sarah Smith, bapt. 2 Apr. 1758.†
> Salome, b. [June 1760], bapt. 4 Jan. 1763, d. at Weston, 28 Feb. 1843 ae. 82 yrs. 8 mos. (g. s.); m. at Weston, 29 June 1781, David Godfrey.
> Mercy, bapt. 4 Jan. 1763; m. at Weston, 9 Apr. 1779, Ezra Elwell.

Child [perhaps by third wife]:

> Ruamah, b. 1 Sept. 1779 (rec. Norwalk); m. at Weston, 8 Apr. 1800, John Bennett.

Finch [*Unplaced*].

> SARAH m. 17 Oct. 1727, Stephen Adams.
> SARAH m. 28 Oct. 1742, Richard King.
> MARTHA, b. 7 Jan. 1702; m. 5 Dec. 1723, Nathan Hubbell.

---

* Children, two bapt. Westport: Huldah, bapt. 13 June 1790, d. 19 Sept. 1809; m. 24 Apr. 1808, Burr Meeker. Areta, b. [Mar. 1794], d. 1 Oct. 1865; m. 8 Apr. 1810, Burr Meeker. Samuel, bapt. 25 Sept. 1796. Others. Samuel d. 4 Oct. 1854 (Miss Treadwell's book).

† Children (by family account): Budd, b. 13 June 1789; William; John; Daniel; Charlotte; Polly.

Finney [Unplaced].

GARRARD, of Dutchess County, N. Y., m. Sarah Knapp, bapt. 24 Aug. 1712.

WIDOW MEHITABEL m. 9 Feb. 1764, James Gray, Jr., both of Redding [Redding rec.].

JOHN d. in 1761; adm'n granted, 17 June 1761, to Mabel Fenny. She was doubtless his widow, and identical with Mehitabel above.

DINAH, now residing in Newtown, chose Daniel Lyon, Jr., of Redding for guardian, Jan. 1761.

JOSEPH of Stratford chose John Mallery, Jr., of Fairfield for guardian, Dec. 1762.

SARAH m. in 1808, Ezekiel Lyon. [Easton Church.]

Fish [Unplaced].

MARY d. 3 Dec. 1769 ae. 77 (g. s., Greens Farms). [See Noyes.]

Fitch, (Dr.) Asahel.

Dr. Fitch of Redding m. at Wilton, 4 Oct. 1764, Hannah Lockwood of Wilton.

He d. at Redding, 31 Mar. 1793 in 56 yr. (g. s.).

Children, bapt. Redding:

Clarissa, bapt. 21 Oct. 1768.
Hannah, b. 28 Apr., bapt. 1 July 1770.
James-Gale, b. 31 Aug., bapt. 3 Oct. 1773.
Ellis-Abigail, bapt. 8 Sept. 1776.
Abigail-Ellis, bapt. 8 Sept. 1776.
Martha, bapt. 10 Oct. 1779.

Fitch, Hezekiah, s. of (Gov.) Thomas.

He m. 21 Sept. 1767, Jerusha Burr, dau. of Col. Andrew, b. 3 Dec. 1749.

He was of Salisbury, 1774 and 1787.

Children, bapt. Fairfield:

Sarah-Stanley, bapt. 20 Aug. 1769.
Hezekiah, bapt. 27 Mar. 1771.

Fitch [Unplaced].

MARY m. Mar. 1743, Daniel Bradley. [Fairfield Rec.]

ELIZABETH, of Norwalk, m. 9 Apr. 1767, David King. [Greens Farms Church.]

THOMAS, JR., Esq., of Norwalk, m. 28 Apr. 1763, Miss Sarah Hill. [Fairfield Church.]
JOHN m. 6 Nov. 1766, Elizabeth Lockwood. [Weston Church.]
NANCY, of Norwalk, m. 20 Feb. 1782, William Benedict. [Greens Farms Church.]
NANCY, of Norwalk, m. 9 May 1798, Thomas-Hart Taylor, of New York. [Greens Farms Church.]
LYDIA m. 25 May 1793, James Davis, at Wilton. [Weston Church.]
ELIJAH, JR., m. 30 May 1793, Mary Olmstead. [Weston Church.]
MOLLY m. 4 May 1800, Eliphalet Taylor, at Wilton. [Weston Church.]
ELIZABETH m. 30 Dec. 1779, Stephen Fairchild. [Redding Rec.]
ABIGAIL A. m. 13 Sept. 1801, Levi Sanford. [Redding Rec.]

Folliot(?) [Unplaced].

THADDEUS, of Ridgefield, m. 8 Oct. 1797, Olive Bradley. [Greens Farms Church.]
SEABORN, of Norwalk, m. 5 Jan. 1797, Widow Sarah Forbes. [Greens Farms Church.]

Foote, Solomon, [? s. of Daniel].

He m. [say 1715], Elizabeth Osborn; dau. of Capt. John, bapt. 24 May 1696.

Children, bapt. Fairfield:
Sarah, b. [say 1716], bapt. 10 Aug. 1718.
Hannah, bapt. 14 Sept. 1718.
Mary, bapt. 29 Oct. 1721; m. 4 Oct. 1739, Nathaniel Booth.
Abigail, bapt. 12 Jan. 1723/4.
Dorothy, bapt. 13 June 1731, d. before 1760; m. 16 Nov. 1752, Reuben Salmon.

Foote, Nathan.

Son of John and Sarah (Prindle), b. at Newtown, 24 Oct. 1719; bur. 25 Dec. 1796 ae. 77 (Trinity Church rec.).

He m. at Greenfield, 5 July 1750, Abiah Gilbert; dau. of John, b. 6 Dec. 1731.

Adm'n on estate of one Nathan Foote was granted, 10 Oct. 1814, to Turney Foote [see below], with David Hill, Jr., as surety.

Children, rec. Fairfield:
Abiah, b. 15 Jan. 1751.
Hannah, b. 12 May 1754.

Foote [Unplaced].

MARY had a dau. Mary bapt. at Westport, 4 May 1755; and m. 11 Apr. 1757, Benjamin Frost.

EBENEZER m. 29 Aug. 1797, Mabel Banks. [Redding rec.]

TURNEY d. at Easton, 3 Nov. 1825 ae. 41 (g. s.); his wife Jemima d. 5 Nov. 1825 ae. 32 (g. s.). Adm'n granted, 15 Nov. 1825, to Isaac Bennet of Weston, with David Sherwood as surety.

REUBEN d. at Weston, 9 Sept. 1846 ae. 75 (g. s.); m. Mary Sturges, who d. 22 Nov. 1835 ae. 54 (g. s.). Reuben had children, rec. Redding: Peter, b. 4 May 1795; Lucretia, b. 31 Aug. 1802; Phebe, b. 15 July 1806; Frederick, b. 8 June 1811.

BAILEY m. 3 July 1796, Jerusha Glover. [Trinity Church.]

Forbes [Unplaced].

WILLIAM m. 26 Mar. 1795, Salome Baker; he was drowned near New York, Sept. 1796. [Greens Farms Church.]

WIDOW SARAH m. 5 Jan. 1797, Seaborn Folliot(?), of Norwalk. [Greens Farms Church.]

Forgue, (Dr.) Francis. Surgeon, 7th Regt., Army, July 1775.

Born abt. 1730; called "late useful Physician," he d. at Fairfield, 26 Feb. 1783 in 54 yr. (g. s.).

He m. Sarah, widow of James Dennie, and dau. of David Thompson, bapt. 24 May 1724, d. at Fairfield, 24 Jan. 1796 ae. 72 (g. s.).

He was naturalized, May 1774, being called a native of Toulouse, France, now of Fairfield; his son Francis, Jr., was born in this Colony.

Adm'n on Est. of Sarah Forgue was granted, 4 Feb. 1797, to Lewis B. Sturges, with Thaddeus Burr for surety.

Child :*

Mark-Francis, b. 3 Aug. 1767 (Bible rec.).

Forhennere.

MR. had a son William, bapt. 21 May 1749. [Greenfield Church.]

---

* Francis Fogue, illegitimate son of Ann Durand, was bapt. at Derby, 27 Apr. 1766. Dr. Francis Fogue d. at Naugatuck, 27 or 28 Feb. 1825 ae. 58; the church record says of him, "he had imbibed infidel sentiments, made light of death, caused coffin and gravestone to be prepared long before his death and directed that the band of music should play at his funeral. In other respects the solemnity of his funeral was observed in the usual manner."

Fountain, Aaron, s. of Aaron [Vol. I, p. 209].

He d. at Westport, 15 Apr. 1760; m. Elizabeth ———.

Children, rec. Westport:
>Mary, b. 5 June 1722, d. at Westport, 9 Nov. 1780; m. 22 Nov. 1743, David Hendrick.
>Timothy, b. 27 June 1725, d. at Westport, 28 Aug. 1803 ae. 76.
>Hannah, b. 2 Apr. 1729; m. (1) 1 Jan. 1749/50, Abel Sherwood; m. (2) Elisha Perry, of New Fairfield.
>Abel, b. 24 Apr. 1734, d. 4 Dec. 1756.
>Sarah, b. 23 Nov. 1737; m. 24 Nov. 1760, David Raymond.

Fowler, Nehemiah.

He m. at Fairfield, 1 Mar. 1778, Abiah Wheeler; dau. of David, bapt. 2 Dec. 1753. She m. (2) Ammon Johnson.

Children, bapt. Fairfield:
>Esther, bapt. 24 Jan. 1779.
>Sally, bapt. 23 Feb. 1783.
>Julia-Anna, bapt. 11 Feb. 1797.

Fowler, Stephen.

Born [8 Mar. 1756], d. at Fairfield, 24 Mar. 1829 ae. 73 yrs. 16 days (g. s.); m. Mary ———, b. Oct. 1766, d. 13 June 1826 ae. 59-7-25 (g. s.). Children, bapt. Fairfield: Hannah, bapt. 3 Aug. 1788; Joseph-Strong, bapt. 17 Oct. 1790; Lewis, bapt. 17 July 1796; Stephen, bapt. 23 Sept. 1798; William-Henry, bapt. 22 Nov. 1801; Sarah-Ann, bapt. 23 Sept. 1806.

Fox [*Unplaced*].
>AARON m. 14 Mar. 1782, Elizabeth Price. [Fairfield Church.]

Francher [*Unplaced*].
>SILVANUS, of Stamford, m. 28 Apr. 1762, Hannah Gray. [Greens Farms Church.]

Frasier, Daniel.

Born abt. 1731; d. at Westport, 13 Dec. 1804 ae. 74.

He m. 11 Dec. 1764, Eunice Oysterbanks, bapt. 12 May 1745, d. Nov. 1817 in 73 yr.

Child, bapt. Westport:
>Eunice, bapt. 8 Sept. 1770; m. 16 Sept. 1788, John Mills, of Weston.

Fraser [*Unplaced*].
> ELIZABETH m. at Fairfield Church, 21 Feb. 1757, John MacDonald.

Freeman, Isaac.

He d. at Fairfield, 21 May 1732 in 46 yr. (g. s.).
He m. Bethia ———.
She m. (2) 24 Nov. 1735, Job Gorham, of Barnstable.

Children, bapt. Fairfield:
> Isaac, of Marblehead, Mass., with wife Ann conveyed 1766 land in Fairfield lately our father's, Isaac Freeman dec'd.
> Sarah, b. [30 July 1720], d. 7 Feb. 1725/6 ae. 5 yrs. 6 mos. 7 days (g. s.).
> James, bapt. 2 Feb. 1723/4, d. 6 Feb. 1725/6 ae. 2 yrs. 10 days (g. s.).
> Rebecca, bapt. 2 Feb. 1723/4, d. 4 Feb. 1725/6 ae. 2 yrs. 8 days (g. s.).
> Edmund, b. 4, bapt. 9 Jan. 1725/6.
> James, bapt. 10 Nov. 1728.
> David, bapt. 26 July 1730.

Freeman, John.

By wife Elizabeth had children: Anne, b. 21 Feb. 1785; Ebenezer, b. 15 Sept. 1786; Charles, b. 15 Dec. 1790; Thaddeus, b. 15 Feb. 1793; Nancy, b. 5 Nov. 1797.

French, Samuel, s. of Samuel [Vol. I, p. 210].

Bapt. 2 Dec. 1694; d. at Stratfield, 16 Oct. 1773.
He m. Mary Sherman, dau. of Benjamin, b. 24 Feb. 1696/7.

Children :*
> Samuel, prob. rem. to Manchester, Vt.
> John, b. abt. 1721, d. at Trumbull, 31 Aug. 1796 ae. 75 (g. s.); Lt., North Stratford Co., Oct. 1757; Capt., Oct. 1765; m. Betty Edwards, dau. of John, b. abt. 1730, d. 13 Oct. 1786 in 56 yr. (g. s.). Will 5 Dec. 1792, proved 19 Sept. 1796; eldest son David; sons

---

* Mansfield J. French, Esq., Syracuse, N. Y., has collected considerable French data, and kindly given assistance. A descendant of this French family gave the names of the children as David, John, Samuel, Jehiel [should be Jeriel], Benjamin, Abigail, Lucy, Eunice, Mary.

Samuel, John; daus. Rebecca wife of Capt. David Sherman, Joanna wife of Thomas Brothwell, and Lucy French; gr. dau. Mary Stratton; to nephew David, son of bro. Samuel, 100 acres in Vt.
Eunice.
Mary.
Lucy, b. abt. 1729, d. at Stratfield, 28 Oct. 1751 in 23 yr. (g. s.); m. 29 Nov. 1750, Jedediah Welles.
Jeriel, bapt. 30 Jan. 1731/2; m. at Newtown, 8 Jan. 1755, Mary Foote.
Abigail, bapt. 10 Feb. 1733/4, bur. 22 Sept. 1795 ae. 61 (Trinity Church rec.); m. at Fairfield, 19 Dec. 1754, Hezekiah Wheeler.
Benjamin, bapt. 4 July 1736.
Benoni, b. abt. 1738, d. at Stratfield, 20 Dec. 1823 ae. 85 (g. s.); m. 11 Jan. 1763, Mehitabel Booth, who d. 12 Aug. 1814 ae. 71 (g. s.).

French, Ebenezer, s. of Samuel [Vol. I, p. 210].

Bapt. 5 Nov. 1699, lived in Stratfield, d. after 1764.

He m. Eleanor Smith, dau. of Samuel of Fairfield, bapt. 8 Apr. 1711.

Children:

Jehiel, bapt. 5 Nov. 1732; m. (1) at Trumbull, 26 Dec. 1757, Eunice Turney; m. (2) Apr. 1769, Abiah Middlebrook; dau. of David, b. 17 Jan. 1748.
Samuel, bapt. 24 Nov. 1734; res. Brookfield, 1772.
Gamaliel, bapt. 24 Oct. 1736, d. at Newtown in 1811; m. Lucy ———.
Stephen, d. in 1772; will 11 July, proved 13 Aug. 1772; m. Phebe Summers.
? Othniel, m. at Newtown, 15 Aug. 1763, Jerusha Johnson.

French, Gamaliel, s. of Samuel [Vol. I, p. 210].

Bapt. 30 June 1706, d. at Stratfield, 7 Sept. 1783; m. (1) Hannah ———, who d. 10 Oct. 1745 ae. 33 (g. s.); m. (2) at Fairfield, 7 Aug. 1749, Sarah Redfield, dau. of James, bapt. 27 Mar. 1726, d. 27 May 1758 in 32 yr. (g. s.).

Mary, dau. of Mr. French's wife, bapt. at Greenfield, 6 Sept. 1741, was possibly his first wife's child.

Will 12 June 1780, proved 5 Nov. 1783; three sons, James, Gamaliel, Josiah; dau. Deborah Coutong; gr. children, Hannah dau. of said Deborah, the children of dau. Rhoda Mallet dec'd, and the children of dau. Sarah Patterson dec'd.

Children [by first wife]:

Deborah, m. ―― Coutong.
Rhoda, b. abt. 1740, d. 5 Mar. 1777 in 37 yr. (g. s.); m. David Mallett.
Sarah, m. ―― Patterson.

Children [by second wife]:

James R., b. abt. 1752, d. at Stratfield, 14 Jan. 1835 in 83 yr. (g. s.); m. (1) 19 Jan. 1774, Mary Brinsmade, b. abt. Apr. 1757, d. 10 Feb. 1803 ae. 45 yrs. 10 mos. (g. s.); m. (2) Anna Cable, b. 1771, d. 18 Mar. 1841 ae. 70 (g. s.).
Hannah, bapt. 27 Jan. 1754, d. y.
Gamaliel, b. abt. 1756, d. at Stratfield, 28 June 1828 ae. 72 (g. s.); m. 17 Jan. 1782, Susannah Brinsmade, b. 18 Sept. 1760, d. 18 Mar. 1835 ae. 74 (g. s.).
Josiah.

French, Ephraim.

Son of Jehiel and Eunice (Turney), bapt. 31 Dec. 1758. He m. 21 Dec. 1783, Abigail Winton. Children, rec. Weston: Eunice, b. 10 Oct. 1784; Betsey, b. 19 Aug. 1786; Benjamin, b. 16 Apr. 1790; Ephraim, b. 16 Apr. 1790; Asa, b. 3 May 1796.

French, Samuel.

He m. (1) 16 Apr. 1766, Sarah Hall; dau. of Nathaniel; she d. 17 Feb. 1774; m. (2) 4 July 1774, Mary Beardsley.

Adm'n on estate of Samuel French was granted, 19 Dec. 1814, to Joseph Bennett, with Daniel Wheeler, Jr., as surety. Distribution, 1817: widow Mary; son Nathaniel; Samuel French, representative of dec'd son Samuel; sons David, Squire; dau. Sarah wife of Isaac Sturges; daus. Huldah, Mary, Anna, Eunice.

Children [by first wife], rec. Weston:

Nathaniel-Hall, b. 14 Feb. 1767, bapt. at Easton, 19 Apr. 1767.
Wheeler, b. 4 Dec. 1770, bapt. 21 Mar. 1771, d. 10 July 1790.
Samuel, b. 17 Feb. 1774.

Children [by second wife], rec. Weston:

David, b. 28 Apr. 1775, d. 27 Aug. 1775.
David, b. 11 Apr. 1779.
Sarah, b. 20 Jan. 1781; m. Isaac Sturges.
John, b. 22 Nov. 1782, d. 8 Dec. 1782.

Huldah, b. 2 Dec. 1783.
Squire, b. 20 Dec. 1785.
Eunice, b. 22 Mar. 1788.
Mary, b. 17 June 1792.
Anna, b. 17 June 1792.

Frost [Vol. I, pp. 211-213].

1 William (-1645) m. ———.
  2 Daniel (-1684) m. Elizabeth Barlow.
    3 Daniel (-1708) m. Mary Rowland.
      5 *Daniel* (-before 1729).
      6 *Isaac* (1694-1761).
    4 Joseph (-1699) m. Elizabeth Hubbell.
      7 *Joseph.*
      8 *Abner* (1696-   ).

5. Frost, Daniel, s. of Daniel, 2d.

He d. at Westport before 1729; m. Sarah Seeley, dau. of Benjamin, b. [say 1690]; she m. (2) by 1729, Nathaniel Fitch, of Norwalk.

Daniel, son of Daniel, chose his father-in-law Nathaniel Fitch for guardian, 3 Feb. 1728/9; as did Nathan, son of Daniel, 2 Dec. 1729. A delayed distribution was made 12 Jan. 1759 to the heirs of Daniel, the eldest son, Nathan, Benjamin, Sarah, Deborah, Jane and Mary. In 1755, Nathan Frost, John Stewart and Deborah his wife, and Jane Lockwood, all of Norwalk, Benjamin Frost of Fairfield, and William Frost of Courtland's Manor, Westchester County, N. Y., conveyed to Ebenezer Mead, part of Isaac Frost's home. Samuel Abbott and Sarah his wife of Cornwall conveyed 1751 to Ebenezer Mead, right from uncle William Frost.

Children:

  9+Daniel.
    Sarah, b. abt. 1710, d. at Cornwall, 14 Feb. 1773 ae. 63 (g. s.); m. Samuel Abbott, of Norwalk and Cornwall.
    Deborah, m. John Stewart, Jr., of Norwalk.
    Nathan.
    Jane, d. at Westport, 7 Jan. 1774; m. Gershom Lockwood.*
  10+Benjamin.
    Mary, m. 1 Aug. 1744, Ebenezer Mead.

---

* Nathan, son of Jane Frost, bapt. at Westport, 20 Sept. 1748; her Lockwood children were bapt. 23 Oct. 1748.

6. **Frost, Isaac,** s. of Daniel, 2d.

Bapt. 26 Aug. 1694; d. at Westport, 28 Mar. 1761.
He m. Abigail ———, who d. 22 Mar. 1761.
Adm'n granted, 7 Apr. 1761, to Samuel Morehouse.

Children:

    Abigail, b. abt. 1723, d. at Westport, 9 Dec. 1800 ae. 77 yrs. 3 mos. (g. s.); m. (1) 20 Aug. 1743, Samuel Morehouse; m. (2) 24 Aug. 1776, Jabez Raymond, of Norwalk; m. (3) 8 Sept. 1799, Shubael Gorham.

7. **Frost, Joseph,** s. of Joseph.

He m. 27 Aug. 1724, Adrea Couch, dau. of Samuel; bapt. 7 Aug. 1698, d. 23 July 1753.

Children, rec. and bapt. Fairfield:

11+Jabez, b. 4 Aug. 1725.
12+Joseph b. 8, bapt. 13 Nov. 1726.
    Eunice, bapt. 4 July 1731, d. y.
    Grissel, bapt. 4 July 1731, d. y.
    Grissel, b. 24 Oct. 1732, bapt. in 1732, d. in 1823; m. 6 Mar. 1754, Benjamin Wynkoop, Jr.
    Eunice, b. 16 Sept. 1742; m. at Weston, 21 Apr. 1766, Josiah Couch.

8. **Frost, Abner,** s. of Joseph.

Bapt. 16 Feb. 1695/6, living 1760; m. at Stratfield, 24 Sept. 1723, Rebecca Hall, dau. of Francis, b. 23 Nov. 1703.

Of Stratfield, he conveyed 9 Mar. 1722/3, as one of the children of Elizabeth Hull, dau. of Richard Hubbell. Of Elizabeth, Essex County, N. J., he conveyed 18 Mar. 1730/1 one-third of the right in Fairfield commons of his gr. father Daniel Frost.

Children, rec. Stratfield:

    Jedediah, b. 7 May 1724.
    Eleazer, b. 24 Oct. 1725, d. 24 Jan. 1725/6.
    Naomi, b. 20 Nov. 1726.
    Margaret, m. (license 2 Apr. 1751) Stephen Salmon.*
    Others?

---

* His will, 1760, named wife *Hannah*, father Abner Frost, and children Abner and Hannah.

9. **Frost, Daniel,** s. of Daniel, 3d.

He d. at Westport, 21 Nov. 1744; m. Eunice Sherwood, dau. of John; she m. (2) 26 Mar. 1745, David Crissey, with whom she was living, in 1759, in Cortlandt, Westchester County, N. Y.

Adm'n granted, 18 Jan. 1744/5, to Eunice Frost. Distribution 15 Jan. 1758; widow, wife of David Crissey; eldest son William; dau. Lois wife of James Brown; dau. Rebecca wife of Deliverance Purdy; dau. Eunice.

Andrew Brown and Eunice his wife of Westchester County, N. Y., conveyed 13 Feb. 1762, land formerly the right of Mary Frost dec'd; and David Crissey and Eunice his wife quitclaimed their interest in it.

Children:

> William, res. 1755 in Cortlandt, Westchester County, N. Y.
> Lois, m. James Brown; res. 1759, Cortlandt, Westchester County, N. Y.
> Rebecca, m. Deliverance Purdy.
> Eunice, m. by 1762, Andrew Brown, of Westchester County, N. Y.
> Daniel, bapt. 29 Jan. 1743/4, d. y.

10. **Frost, Benjamin,** s. of Daniel, 3d.

He d. at Stratfield, Sept. 1776.
He m. 11 Apr. 1757, Mary Foote.

Child, bapt. Westport:

> Sarah, bapt. 10 May 1761.

11. **Frost, Jabez,** s. of Joseph.

Born 4 Aug. 1725.
He m. 3 Dec. 1746, Deborah King.

Children, rec. Redding, four bapt. Fairfield, the others Redding:

> Adrea, b. 21 Jan., bapt. 6 Mar. 1747/8; m. at Danbury, 15 Nov. 1770, Daniel Comstock, of Danbury.
> William, b. 20, bapt. 24 Dec. 1749.
> Grissel, b. 10, bapt. 13 Oct. 1751; m. at Danbury, 31 Oct. 1771, Ezra Dibble, of Danbury.
> Deborah, b. 5, bapt. 15 Nov. 1753.
> Mary, b. 23 Feb., bapt. 4 Apr. 1756.

Hannah, b. 24 Apr., bapt. 7 June 1761.
Betsey, b. 16 May, bapt. 24 June 1764.
Ezra, b. 21 Aug. 1766; chose Ezra Dibble, Jr., of Danbury for guardian, 1784; m. at Danbury, 7 Sept. 1785, Rebecca Andrus.
Stephen, b. 7 Aug., bapt. 18 Sept. 1768.
Daniel, b. 21 Aug., bapt. 3 Nov. 1771.

12. **Frost, Joseph,** s. of Joseph.

Born 8 Nov. 1726.

He m. 19 Oct. 1747, Esther Dimon, dau. of John; b. 11 May 1728.

Joseph of Redding in 1771 sold all claim by me, my father Joseph or uncle Isaac.

Children, rec. Fairfield:
Sarah, b. 15 Dec. 1747, bapt. 13 Mar. 1747/8; ?m. at Greenfield, 15 Sept. 1777, Philip Mallet.
Joseph, b. 22 May 1755.
Dimon, b. 17 Apr. 1757, d. at Greenfield, 9 Jan. 1777 in 20 yr.

Frost [*Unplaced*].

——— d. 10 Jan. 1781. [Greens Farms Church.]

Fry, Richard.

He d. at Greenfield, 31 July 1818, of old age; m. at Westport, 24 Sept. 1781, Sarah Spears, who d. at Greenfield, 27 Nov. 1820.

Fuller [*Unplaced*].

ABIAH m. 26 Sept. 1787, Francis Newell, at Wilton. [Weston Church.]

Gage [*Unplaced*].

GEORGE m. 7 Sept. 1763, Sarah Adams. [Redding Church]

Gambel, John.

Of Stratfield, will 3 Oct., proved 7 Nov. 1727; estate in Ireland left there some years since, to wife Ann, and children William and Mary; all wearing apparel and "my Millitary armour as Gun sword & belt," to friend Nathan Beardsley of Stratfield; to friend, Dr. Wheeler of Stratfield, £10; Timothy and Anne, children of Timothy Wheeler, Jr.

Gates [Unplaced].

WILLIAM of Long Island m. 24 Feb. 1780, Margaret McRay. [Fairfield Church]

Gerard [Unplaced].

MOSES, of L. I., m. 8 June 1796, Elizabeth Canfield. [Greens Farms Church]

Gibbs [Unplaced].

THOMAS, of Milford, m. 24 Mar. 1742/3, Hannah Allen.

Gilbert.*

Vol. I, p. 217, line 18. Sarah m. Joel *Jenkins*, not *Judkins*.†
Vol. I, p. 218, line 30. Lydia m. (1) *Stephen* Richardson, and (2) Capt. John Chapman.
Vol. I, p. 220, line 6. John was born about *1626*. Of his children,— Thomas m. (2) Bethia Youngs; Amy did not d. y. (though not named in father's will) but m. 19 Aug. 1684, William Clisby of Stonington; and Joseph m. Elizabeth Smith.
Vol. I, p. 220, last two lines. The year of birth of Thomas should be interpreted as 1658/9, that of Henry as 1660/1.
Vol. I, p. 221, line 26. The Josiah who chose Zechariah Blackman for guardian was the son of John, on the next page. The first three children of Moses were born in New York, and bapt. there as follows: Josiah, 6 Nov. 1698; Elizabeth, 16 Dec. 1696; Hannah, 5 Jan. 1700/1.
Vol. I, p. 222, line 1. Sarah was b. 12 Feb. 1705/6, bapt. as stated, and d. 14 Apr. *1767*.
Vol. I, p. 222, bottom of page. This was not the Josiah whose Inv. was exhibited 1777. This Josiah settled in Ridgefield and d. there 20 Oct. 1781; m. (1) Elizabeth Smith, (2) Clemence Northrup.
Vol. I, p. 223, line 2. For 24, read *27*.
Vol. I, p. 223, line 9. Thomas, of Brookfield, Mass., m. (1) Martha Barnes, (2) Mercy (Gilbert) Barnes.
Of the children of Obadiah on p. 223, Elizabeth prob. m. Nathaniel Gray, and Joseph and the second Abigail (p. 224) d. y.
Vol. I, p. 224, line 24. This William m. (1) at Saybrook, 1 Dec. 1709, Lydia Parker, b. 13 Feb. 1690, d. 8 Mar. 1715; m. (2) at Saybrook, 9 Jan. 1717, Frances Woodhouse.

---

* For the following additions and corrections to the early generations, we are chiefly indebted to Mr. Clarence A. Torrey of Dorchester, Mass.

† Manwaring's *Digest* states the name correctly as Jenkins; we erred in following Flagg's *Founding of New England*, p. 265.

Gilbert [Vol. I, pp. 216-224].

1 Thomas (1582-1659) m. Lydia ———.
  2 Josiah (1628-1688) m. (1) Elizabeth Belcher; (2) Mary (Harris) Ward.
  (By 1): 5 Moses (1666-1713) m. Jane Dirck.
      8 *Josiah* (-1760).
  3 Obadiah (-1674) m. Elizabeth (Burr) Olmstead.
    6 Obadiah (-by 1728) m. Abigail ———.
      9 *Benjamin* (1695-).
    10 *John* (1697-1782).
4 Thomas (-1682) m. Catherine (Chapin) Bliss.
  7 John (1657-1709) m. (2) Hannah Canfield.
    11 *Thomas* (1696-1760).

8. Gilbert, Josiah, s. of Moses.

He d. at Fairfield, 4 Dec. 1760; m. 14 June 1722, Sarah Lord; dau. of Robert, bapt. 29 Mar. 1702; she m. (2) William Hill.

Will 4, proved 29 Dec. 1760; wife Sarah.

In 1783 and 1784, receipts were given by Ichabod Gilbert of Simsbury, Moses Gilbert of Nobletown, N. Y., and David Hurlbutt and Mary his wife of Norwalk, to their father-in-law William Hill of Redding, their right from father Josiah Gilbert dec'd and mother Sarah Hill dec'd.

Children, rec. Fairfield:

    Moses, b. 7 Mar., bapt. 14 July 1723; m. Jan. 1745/6, Sarah Gilbert; dau. of Benjamin, bapt. 2 July 1721.
    Richard, b. 14 Oct. 1725 [1724], bapt. 25 Oct. 1724, d. in 1748.
    Mary, b. 11 Nov. 1726; m. David Hurlbut.
    Caleb, b. 12 Mar. 1729.
    Josiah, b. 3 July 1731, d. at Ridgefield, 1774; adm'n granted, 3 May 1774, to his widow Phebe, who was appointed guardian, 7 June 1775, of the only son Ward, with Stephen Hard as surety.
    Phineas, b. 6 Aug. 1734.
    Hannah, b. 16 Apr. 1737, d. 30 Jan. 1740.
    Ichabod, b. 3 June 1741.

9. Gilbert, Benjamin, s. of Obadiah. Lt., Greenfield Co., Oct. 1737.

Bapt. 19 May 1695.

He m. Elizabeth Adams, dau. of Abraham, bapt. 24 Feb. 1694/5.

Children, bapt. Greenfield:

12+Moses, bapt. 4 Aug. 1717.
    Abigail, bapt. 21 June 1719; m. Apr. 1746, Samuel Gregory.
    Sarah, bapt. 2 July 1721; m. Jan. 1745/6, Moses Gilbert.

Benjamin, bapt. 14 Apr. 1723; m. at Wilton, Mar. 1751, Sarah Higgins, dau. of Samuel, b. 1735.*
Elizabeth, b. 11, bapt. 12 Sept. 1731; m. 24 Mar. 1748, Ebenezer Green.

10. Gilbert, John, s. of Obadiah.

Bapt. 23 May 1697; d. 1782 (family rec.).

He m. (1) 29 June 1721, Jemima Williams; dau. of John; she d. at Greenfield, 27 May 1758.

He m. (2) ———; "Wife of John Gilbert" d. at Greenfield, 3 Mar. 1761.

He conveyed, 1770, to son Joseph.

Children, rec. Fairfield, bapt. Greenfield:
13+Thaddeus, b. 5 Aug., bapt. 18 Nov. 1722.
14+Ebenezer, b. 31 Mar., bapt. 24 May 1724.
15+Joseph, b. 14, bapt. 20 June 1726.
    Martha, b. 25 June, bapt. July 1728; [perhaps m. Andrew Winton].
    Abiah, b. 6, bapt. 19 Dec. 1731; m. 3 July 1750, Nathan Foote.
16+John, b. 11, bapt. 17 Aug. 1735.

11. Gilbert, Thomas, s. of John.

Born 16 Apr. 1696; d. at Stratford in 1760; m. (1) 19 Dec. 1717, Jemima Silliman; dau. of Daniel, bapt. 11 Apr. 1697, d. 17 Sept. 1718; m. (2) 18 Dec. 1718, Elizabeth How, dau. of Daniel, b. at Wallingford, 28 Jan. 1699/1700.

Will 26 Mar. 1752, proved 4 Aug. 1760; wife Elizabeth; daus. Jemima wife of Jacob Blackman, Hannah wife of Jonathan French, Betty Gilbert, Ruth Gilbert, Hulda Gilbert; son Thomas Jr.; eldest son John; son Abraham.

Child [by first wife], rec. Stratford:
    Jemima, b. 1 Sept. 1718, d. at Huntington in 1800; m. (1) Daniel Nichols; m. (2) 22 May 1746, Jacob Blackman.

Children [by second wife], bapt. Stratford:
    Hannah, b. abt. 1720, d. at Huntington, 3 Nov. 1802 in 82 yr. (g. s.); m. Jonathan French.
    John, b. [say 1722], d. in 1777; m. 19 Jan. 1748/9, Sarah Marchant, dau. of John.

---
* Son: Ebenezer.

Abraham, bapt. 19 Apr. 1724.
Sarah, bapt. July 1728, d. y.
Betty, bapt. Dec. 1730.
17+Thomas, bapt. Mar. 1733.
Ruth, bapt. Apr. 1736.
Huldah, bapt. Aug. 1743.

12. **Gilbert, Moses,** s. of Benjamin.

Born 4 Aug. 1717; d. at Norwalk, 25 Aug. 1785.
He m. at Greenfield, 11 Mar. 1740/1, Elizabeth Hubbell; dau. of Nathan, b. 11 Nov. 1724.
He settled in Norwalk by 1755.
Adm'n granted, 5 Sept. 1785, to Gershom Gilbert of Norwalk. Insolvent.

Children, two rec. Greenfield:
Obadiah, b. 5, bapt. 11 Feb. 1741/2; m. Beulah Babbitt.
Hannah, b. 16, bapt. 21 Mar. 1742/3, prob. d. y.
Nathan, b. abt. 1746; Capt.; m. Sarah Betts.
Gershom, m. (1) at Westport, 13 June 1771, Rachel Buckingham; dau. of Stephen, b. abt. 1746, d. 13 Sept. 1771 (Perry Diary); m. (2) Eunice Whitlock, dau. of Oliver, bapt. 2 June 1761.
Hannah, m. abt. 1782, Nathan Taylor.
?Moses.

13. **Gilbert, Thaddeus,** s. of John.

Born 5 Aug. 1722; d. at Greenfield, 25 Feb. 1761 in 39 yr.
He m. 7 July 1741, Deborah Winton, dau. of John; bapt. 4 Mar. 1721/2.
Adm'n granted, 24 Mar. 1761, to Joseph and Deborah Gilbert. Andrew chose Ebenezer Gilbert for guardian, Mar. 1761. Deborah Gilbert appointed guardian of Elmer, 24 Mar. 1764; Ruth chose Ebenezer Gilbert for guardian. Distribution ordered to widow, eldest son, and four other children.
Seth and Andrew Gilbert, and Seth Scribner and Ruth his wife, conveyed 8 Mar. 1769 to Obadiah Platt, land in the Burr long lot.

Children, rec. Fairfield, bapt. Greenfield:
18+Seth, b. 31 May, bapt. 6 June 1742.
19+Andrew, b. 10 Oct. 1743.
Ruth, b. 15, bapt. 18 Sept. 1748; m. Seth Scribner.

358 HISTORY AND GENEALOGY OF

Thaddeus, b. 28 Mar. 1753; res. Chautauqua County, N. Y., 1820; Attica, Genesee County, 1822; Elyria, Lorain County, Ohio, 1829; returned to Genesee County, N. Y., 1841; m. Martha Turney, dau. of Thomas.*

Elmer, b. 6 May 1757.†

14. Gilbert, Ebenezer, s. of John.

Born 31 Mar. 1724; d. by 1787.

He m. (1) 18 Apr. 1744, Joanna Northrop; dau. of William, b. 17 June 1724, d. 27 Feb. 1756.

He m. (2) 12 May 1756, Prudence Burr, bapt. 12 Jan. 1731/2. He and Prudence joined the Easton Church, 4 Sept. 1764.

He m. (3) 23 Sept. 1766, Hannah Bennett, b. 11 Dec. 1745 (who was admitted to Easton Church, 12 Jan. 1772).

Adm'n granted to Hannah Gilbert, 19 Feb. 1787. Ezra Gilbert chose Samuel Bennett of Fairfield for guardian, 1787.

Children [by first wife], rec. Fairfield, bapt. Greenfield:

Hezekiah, b. 9, bapt. 16 Dec. 1744; drowned ae. 40.
David, b. 13, bapt. 23 Nov. 1746, d. at Weston, 1813. Adm'n granted, 8 Dec. 1813, to Ezra Gilbert, with David Wakelee as surety. [One David Gilbert is said to have m. Mary Wakeman, dau. of David, bapt. 5 Sept. 1762.]
Joanna, b. 9 May 1748; d. on L. I.; m. David Thompson.
Ebenezer, b. 9, bapt. 30 June 1754. Will of Ebenezer of Weston, 10 Mar. 1798, proved 7 May 1798; wife Ruth; son Pitts; other children; "the Dykman lands" mentioned which he owned.

Children [by second wife], rec. Fairfield; bapt. Redding:

Burr, b. 17 Oct. 1757, bapt. 16 Nov. 1757, d. 6 Mar. 1810 ae. 51 (g. s., Greenfield); Gen; adm'n granted, 17 Apr. 1810, to Nathan Wheeler and Isaac Bennett; estate insolvent. He m. 18 Oct. 1784, Clarissa Johnson; dau. of Rev. James, b. 18 Aug. 1766. She m. (2) 1816, David Turney, and d. 14 Apr. 1844 (Pension rec.).
John, bapt. 16 Mar. 1760.
Huldah.

---

* A Thaddeus m. at Trinity Church, 6 June 1790, Huldah Wheeler. Thaddeus had children, bapt. at Trinity Church: Paulina, bapt. 11 Sept. 1785; Betsey, bapt. 28 Sept. 1794.

† He had children, bapt. Trinity Church: Samuel-Whitney, bapt. 31 Oct. 1790; Andrew-Winton, bapt. 14 July 1793.

Children [by third wife], rec. Weston:

> Zalmon, b. 17 June 1768; m. Sarah ———.*
> Ezra, b. 8 Mar. 1772; m. 3 Dec. 1795, Rebecca Miner.†
> Kate, b. 17 June 1775; "Katharine" m. in 1793, James Parrott.
> Hannah, b. 30 May 1779.

15. **Gilbert, Joseph,** s. of John.

Born 14 June 1726; d. 6 Nov. 1808 ae. 80.

He m. 3 Oct. 1744, Lois Bradley, dau. of John, b. 25 June 1729, d. 28 Dec. (g. s.) and bur. 30 Dec. 1801 ae. 73 (Trinity Church rec.).

He and his wife joined the Easton Church, 25 Aug. 1764.

Will of Lois wife of Joseph, 18 June 1796, proved 4 Mar. 1802; realty to sons Stephen and Reuben, dau. Abigail, and children of dau. Sarah dec'd.

Children, rec. Fairfield, bapt. Greenfield:

> Sarah, b. 29 Mar., bapt. 7 Apr. 1745, d. abt. 1775; m. at Easton, Aug. 1768, Najah Bennett.
> Abigail, b. 19, bapt. 21 Dec. 1746, d. 18 May 1833; m. (1) at Easton, 9 July 1767, John Thorp; m. (2) Ebenezer Burr.
> Stephen, b. 11 Nov. 1749; rem. to Newtown.‡
> Reuben, b. 17 Oct. 1752, d. at Weston, 1823; m. at Weston, Jan. 1776, Lois Mills, b. 25 Mar. 1754; had 8 children rec. Weston.§
> Hannah, b. 13 Apr. 1756.
> Lois, bapt. 19 Oct. 1760; m. Jonathan Robertson.
> Rhoda, bapt. at Easton, 1 June 1766.

16. **Gilbert, John,** s. of John.

Born 11 Aug. 1735; rem. to Fairfield, Vt., prob. in 1782 when he sold the "homestead where I now dwell" in Fairfield, Conn.

He m. 17 June 1756, Lydia Merwin; dau. of Samuel, bapt. 9 Aug. 1730.

---

* Children, bapt. Easton: Anne, Sarah and Ezra, bapt. 22 Feb. 1795.
† Child, rec. Weston: Simeon-Bennett, b. 13 Nov. 1796.
‡ Stephen and wife Molly renewed Covenant and had son Abner bapt. Aug. 1774, Easton Church.
§ Children: Sarah, b. 9 Aug. 1777; Stephen, b. 25 Feb. 1779; Rachel, b. 13 Feb. 1781; John, b. 25 Apr. 1785, bapt. 23 Oct. 1785; Hannah, b. 7 Feb. 1788, bapt. 25 Aug. 1791, d. 31 May 1793; Lydia, b. 9 May 1791, bapt. 25 Aug. 1791; Hannah, b. 13 Mar. 1795; Joseph, b. 9 Nov. 1797. Reuben's will, 7 Mar., proved 14 Oct. 1823; wife Lois; sons Stephen, John, Joseph; dau. Rachel wife of Seth Canfield; dau. Sarah wife of Hezekiah Sherwood; dau. Hannah wife of Charles Thorp.

360 HISTORY AND GENEALOGY OF

Children, eldest rec. Fairfield (Bible record included) :*

    Eunice, b. 16 Apr.† 1757, d. at Greenfield, 26 Jan. 1758 ae. abt. 10 mos.
    Samuel, b. 28 Feb. 1759, d. at Fairfield, Vt., 22 Apr. 1832; m. Sarah ———.
    Eunice, b. 11 Aug. 1761, bapt. at Greenfield, 30 Aug. 1761; m. at Trinity Church, 21 Feb. 1795, David Nichols.
    Lewis, b. 30 Aug. 1763, d. at Fairfield, Vt., 23 Oct. 1848; m. Anna [? Dimon],‡ who d. in Vermont, Oct. 1830 (Miss Treadwell's book).§
    Jemima, b. 15 Aug. 1765, d. 23 Mar. 1767.
    Nathan, b. 29 Aug. 1767, bapt. at Easton, 11 Oct. 1767, drowned at Fairfield, Vt., 10 Sept. 1804; m. Lucy Sherwood, dau. of Nathan and Johanna (Noble).
    Thomas, b. 18 May 1769, bapt. at Easton, 9 July 1769; prob. d. at Bakersfield, Vt., May 1819; m. Feb. 1791, Ann Bennett.
    Albin, b. 17 Aug. 1771, bapt. at Easton, Aug. 1771, d. 26 Aug. [1771?].
    Mary, b. 15 Mar. 1773, d. at Fairfield, 26 Dec. 1863; m. Timothy Hubbell.

17. Gilbert, Thomas, s. of Thomas.

Born 13 Dec. 1735 [Weston record, in error; bapt. Mar. 1733]; d. at Weston by 1808.

He m. 4 Nov. 1756, Mary Booth, b. 19 July 1741.

Dower distributed to his widow Mary, 25 Apr. 1808. Distribution ordered, 1 Aug. 1808, to the children: David, Samuel, Isaac, John, Ephraim, Elisha, the wife of Gideon Wells, the wife of John Peck, Jr.

Distribution, 29 May 1821: Samuel, Hannah, Elisha, David, Isaac, Ephraim, Sally, John.

Children, rec. Weston:

    Benjamin, b. 29 Aug. 1757, d. 14 Feb. 1785.
    Aner, b. 4 May 1760, d. 6 May 1763.
    Samuel, b. 27 Mar. 1763; m. Deborah Lacey, dau. of Edward, bapt. at Easton, Nov. 1770.
    Hannah, b. 9 May 1766; m. (1) ——— Everett; m. (2) Gideon Welles.
    Elisha, b. 26 May 1768, bapt. at Trumbull, 6 July 1768.

---

* Bible dates furnished by Gilbert H. Doane, Esq., of Lincoln, Neb.
† Aug., by Bible record.
‡ See footnote under Moses Dimon (7).
§ Their dau. Jane bapt. at Easton, Aug. 1792.

David, b. 22 Nov. 1771, d. 19 Aug. 1854 (Miss Treadwell's book) ; m.
———, who d. 20 Oct. 1834 (Miss Treadwell's book).
Isaac, b. 17 Sept. 1772, bapt. at Easton, Nov. 1772, d. by 1816. Adm'n granted to Peter Bradley, 27 Mar. 1816; Jesse Morehouse, surety. The wife of Isaac d. 10 Dec. 1809 (Miss Treadwell's book).
Ephraim, b. 16 Aug. 1774.
Sarah, b. 5 Jan. 1778; m. John Peck, Jr.
John, b. 11 Apr. 1780.

18. Gilbert, Seth, s. of Thaddeus.

Born 31 May 1742; d. 14 Oct. 1818 ae. 76.

He m. Jane Gray, dau. of James, b. 20 Apr. 1744; d. 28 Aug. 1816 in 73 yr.

He and his wife owned the Covenant at Easton Church, 17 Mar. 1765. The wife of Seth of Norfield was bapt. at Trinity Church, 11 Nov. 1790.

A descendant states that he was a cooper, of Newtown, and had nine sons and one dau.

Children, two bapt. Easton:
Sarah, b. 24 Apr., bapt. May 1765; m. Nov. 1792, Obadiah Wheeler.
Eliphalet, bapt. 2 Apr. 1769.
Ichabod, d. 4 Aug. 1857; a carpenter, of Newtown; m. Tamar Rowland, dau. of Jabez.
Jonathan, bapt. at Trinity Church, 11 Sept. 1785.
Lewis, bapt. at Trinity Church, 12 Nov. 1790.

19. Gilbert, Andrew, s. of Thaddeus.

Born 10 Oct. 1743; d. 13 Sept. 1803.

He m. 6 [or 10] Sept. 1769, Eunice Wakelee.*

Children, rec. Weston:
Isaac, b. 4 June 1772.
Daniel, b. 21 June 1774.
Justus, b. 22 Dec. 1776.

Gilbert [*Unplaced*].

SUSANNA m. 6 Oct. 1773, [Stephen] son of Reuben Olmstead. [Weston Church]
ELIZABETH, b. 28 July 1758, d. at Weston, 18 Feb. 1833 ae. 73 (g. s.); m. 28 June 1781, Jonathan Coley, Jr.

---

* By Easton Church rec.; *Wheeler* by Weston town rec. Widow of Andrew (this Andrew?) d. 15 Mar. 1839 (Miss Treadwell's book).

PARTHENE of Wilton m. 6 June 1792, Aaron Morehouse. [Weston Church]

JOEL m. 3 June 1772, Widow Mary Guire. [Weston Church]

GILES, soldier in Putnam's Army, m. 23 May 1779, Deborah Hall. [Redding Church]

SARAH m. 6 Apr. 1780, Bela Nash. [Weston Church]

—— m. Mary Banks, dau. of John, and had: Eunice-Banks, Burr, Bradley, and Charlotte.

HULDAH, b. Sept. 1763, d. at Easton, 22 Mar. 1845 ae. 82 (g. s.); m. 19 Oct. 1787, James Silliman. [Pension Rec.]

EBENEZER, b. abt. 1776; of Weston, ae. 18, chose William Griffith of Norwalk for guardian, 7 June 1794; m. 11 Nov. 1798, Betsey Monroe.

THOMAS had a child, bapt. Trinity Church: Nathaniel-Jarvis, bapt. 13 Aug. 1786.

ESTHER m. 7 Apr. 1793, Joseph Bunnell. [Weston Church]

NATHANIEL d. 2 Nov. 1838 (Miss Treadwell's book); m. 17 Mar. 1796, Huldah Monroe. [Weston Church]

SAMUEL d. at Westport, 9 Dec. 1848 in 73 yr. (g. s.); his wife Ann d. 1 Aug. 1850 in 80 yr. (g. s.).

ANNE m. Sept. 1796, Walter Hull. [Easton Church]

TURNEY d. at Redding, 2 Oct. 1807 ae. 28 (g. s.); his wife Susanna d. 25 Feb. 1805 in 26 yr. (g. s.).

Gillet [*Unplaced*].

ANNA m. 22 Nov. 1762, Peter Tuttle. [Weston Church]

Glover, Daniel.

Born [19 Feb. 1743 O. S.]; d. at Stratfield, 8 Nov. 1830 ae. 87-8-6 (g. s.).

He m. 16 May 1765, Sarah Bryan, b. [Apr. 1747], d. 8 Oct. 1804 ae. 57 yrs. 6 mos. (g. s.), bur. 15 Oct. 1804 ae. 57 (Trinity Church).

Will 11 Dec. 1813, proved 23 Nov. 1830; dau. Lucy wife of Samuel Babbitt; dau. Olive wife of Joshua Bailey; dau. Jerusha wife of Bailey Foot; three gr. children, Briant G. Seeley, Maryet Seeley, and Sarah Seeley, children of dec'd dau. Sarah late wife of Ezra Seeley, Jr.; dau. Currance wife of Abel Nichols; dau. Betsey-Ann wife of Wakeman Wilson; only son Daniel-Briant Glover. The children of Currance (Harriet, Laurinda, Clarine and Rufus), and the children of Betsey-Ann (Henry and Silas) received the shares of their respective mothers in the distribution.

THE FAMILIES OF OLD FAIRFIELD 363

Children, rec. Weston:
> Lucy, b. 13 Mar. 1769; m. Samuel Babbitt.
> Olive, b. 22 Jan. 1772; m. Joshua Bailey.
> Jerusha, b. 28 Sept. 1775; m. 3 July 1796, Bailey Foote.
> Sarah, b. 6 Dec. 1778; m. 2 Aug. 1797, Ezra Seeley.
> Daniel-Bryan, b. 16 Sept. 1782, d. at Easton, 7 Sept. 1866 ae. 83-11-22 (g. s.); m. 4 Nov. 1804, Eunice Wilson; dau. of Samuel, b. 17 Aug. 1786, d. 17 Mar. 1873 ae. 86 yrs. 7 mos. (g. s.).
> Currance, b. 7 Aug. 1785, d. at Greenfield, 6 Jan. 1830 ae. 44 (g. s.); m. Abel Nichols.
> Betsey-Ann, b. 15 Feb. 1791, d. at Greenfield, 2 Feb. 1828 ae. 37 (g. s.); m. Wakeman Wilson.

Glover [*Unplaced*].
> LEMUEL m. 29 June 1786, Sarah Meeker; their son Lemuel, b. 26 Apr. 1791. [Redding rec.] Lemuel d. 1 Nov. 1837 ae. 45 yrs. 6 mos. (g. s.).
> JOHN d. 26 Apr. 1802. [Miss Treadwell's book]

Godfrey [Vol. I, p. 226].
> 1 Christopher (1657-1715) m. Ann ———.
>   2 *Christopher* (1686-1758).
>   3 *John* (1699-1745).

2. Godfrey, Christopher, s. of Christopher.

Born abt. 1685/6, bapt. 17 July 1698, d. 20 Aug. 1758 in 73 yr. (g. s., Westport); m. 11 Feb. 1711, Margery Sturgis; dau. of John, b. abt. 1689, d. 4 Nov. 1759 in 71 yr. (g. s.).

Children:
> 4+David, b. 20 Feb. 1713.
> 5+Stephen, b. 8 Sept. 1715.
> Sarah, b. abt. Mar. 1718, d. at Westport, 12 June 1756 ae. 38 yrs. 3 mos. (g. s.); m. 3 Feb. 1742, Gideon Morehouse.
> 6+Nathan, b. 25 Sept. 1719.
> 7+Eleazer, b. 15 Mar. 1721.
> 8+Isaac, b. 25 Dec. 1724.
> 9+Ebenezer, b. 27 June 1727.

3. Godfrey, John, s. of Christopher.

Bapt. 23 Apr. 1699; d. at Westport, 25 Apr. 1745.

He m. Jemima, whose death at Greenfield is entered without date.

Child, bapt. Greenfield:
> 10+John, bapt. 3 Oct. 1736.

4. **Godfrey, David,** s. of Christopher, 2d.

Born 20 Feb. 1713.

He m. 24 June 1738, Mary Silliman, dau. of Daniel, b. [say 1715].

Children, rec. Fairfield, bapt. Westport:

11+Daniel, b. 30 Mar. 1739.
    Ann, b. 16 May 1740; [perhaps the Anna, b. Apr. 1744?, d. at Westport, 30 Oct. 1816 ae. 74 yrs. 6 mos. (g. s.); m. at Weston, 7 June 1780, James Bennett].
    David, b. 1 Sept. 1743, bapt. 30 Oct. 1743.
12+Silliman, b. 1 May 1750, bapt. 3 June 1750.
    Mary, b. 24 Feb. 1752, bapt. 12 Apr. 1752; m. 24 Jan. 1779, Squire Adams.
13+Jonathan, b. 23 Dec. 1754, bapt. 23 Jan. 1754.
    Sarah, b. 12 Feb. 1757.
    ?Mabel, m. at Westport, 26 Nov. 1778, Dennie Chapman, Jr.

5. **Godfrey, Stephen,** s. of Christopher, 2d.

Born 8 Sept. 1715; Dea. Stephen d. at Westport, 22 Mar. 1777.

He m. 11 June 1739, Elizabeth Lewis; dau. of Nathan.

She prob. m. (2) at Weston, 15 Oct. 1781, Ebenezer Abbot.

Will 18 Mar., proved 7 Apr. 1777; wife Elizabeth; son **Stephen** (to sell house where my son Nathan lately lived); daus. **Sarah, Elizabeth, Mary, Eunice, Margery**; gr. son **Seth**.

Children, rec. Fairfield, bapt. Westport:

    Sarah, b. 17 May 1741; m. 7 Feb. 1759, John Hurlbut.
14+Nathan, b. 30 Apr. 1743, bapt. 1 May 1743.
    Eunice, bapt. 18 Nov. 1744, d. 26 Nov. 1744.
15+Stephen, b. 4 Oct. 1745, bapt. 20 Oct. 1745.
    Betty, b. 16 Feb. 1747, bapt. 8 Mar. 1747; m. 3 Mar. 1763, Ebenezer Lewis.
    Child, stillborn 20 Aug. 1748.
    Eunice, b. 5 Nov. 1749, bapt. 24 Dec. 1749, d. 3 Jan. 1781; m. 17 Aug. 1777, Russell Disbrow.
    Mary, b. 12 Nov. 1751, bapt. 15 Dec. 1751, d. 13 Oct. 1833; ? m. 30 Aug. 1770, Jonathan Stratton.
    Child, stillborn 4 Dec. 1753.
    Child, stillborn 8 Sept. 1754.
    Child, stillborn Sept. 1755.
    Child, stillborn 8 May 1757.
    Margery, bapt. Dec. 1759.

6. **Godfrey, Nathan,** s. of Christopher, 2d. 2d Lt., 5th Co., 1st Regt., Mar. 1756.

Born 25 Sept. 1719; d. at Ridgefield in 1800.

He m. (1) 11 June 1747, Martha Couch; dau. of Benjamin, bapt. 16 June 1730/1, d. at Westport, 31 May 1761.

He m. (2) at Westport, 24 Jan. 1764, Sarah Nash; widow of Jonathan Nash, and dau. of John Andrews, b. 6 Aug. 1731, d. at Ridgefield in 1810.

Nathan and Sarah were of Ridgefield, 1795, when they conveyed land in Greens Farms. In 1780, Ebenezer Lockwood and Molly his wife of Norwalk, and John Burr, Jr., and Martha his wife of Fairfield, conveyed land in Greens Farms to Nathan Godfrey, Jr.

Adm'n granted, 13 Feb. 1800, to Andrew Godfrey of Ridgefield; estate insolvent.

Will of Sarah of Ridgefield, 19 Nov. 1801, proved 21 Sept. 1810; to dau. Rhoda, use of estate during life of Caleb for his maintenance, and to herself for life; three daus. Mabel, Rhoda, Esther; three sons Jonathan, Ebenezer, Andrews.

Children [by first wife], rec. Fairfield, bapt. Westport:

16+Abraham, b. 13 May 1748, bapt. 5 June 1748.
    Martha, b. 24 May 1752, bapt. 19 July 1752; m. 18 Oct. 1772, John Burr.
    Nathan, b. 19 Aug. 1754, bapt. 22 Sept. 1754, d. 22 Aug. 1782; m. Mary ———.* Adm'n granted to Mary Godfrey, 3 Apr. 1786; estate insolvent.
    Molly, bapt. 20 Aug. 1758; "Mary" m. (rec. Norwalk) 23 May 1776, Ebenezer Lockwood.
    Benjamin, d. in the army at Albany, 1776 (called son of Lt. Godfrey); died 4 Sept. 1776 [Rev. War Rolls].

Children by second wife:
    Rhoda, bapt. 18 Aug. 1765.
    Jonathan, bapt. Nov. 1766; m. (1) 30 Nov. 1788, Esther Whitehead; dau. of Jehiel, b. [say 1766], d. at Westport, 24 Mar. 1802, in childbed;† m. (2) 26 Oct. 1802, Huldah Parsons.

---

* Children, bapt. Westport: Mary, bapt. 3 Jan. 1779; m. 18 Feb. 1798, Hezekiah Wakeman. Benjamin, bapt. 24 Dec. 1780.

† Children, bapt. Westport: Nathan, bapt. 11 Oct. 1789; Abel, bapt. 27 Nov. 1791, d. 1 Sept. 1811 ae. 20 (in New York); Ebenezer, bapt. 7 July 1793, d. 30 Sept. 1807 in 15 yr.; Elsie, bapt. 30 Oct. 1796; Jonathan, bapt. 2 June 1798; Seth, bapt. 24 Mar. 1802; Esther, bapt. 29 Aug. 1803; Eliza, bapt. 16 Dec. 1806; Ebenezer, bapt. 11 Jan. 1809, d. 9 June 1810 ae. 2½.

Esther, bapt. 17 Sept. 1769; m. 19 Mar. 1789, Jabez Disbrow.
Ebenezer, bapt. 17 Mar. 1772.
Andrews, bapt. 14 Apr. 1776.

7. Godfrey, Eleazer, s. of Christopher, 2d.

Born 15 Mar. 1721; d. at Weston, 1793.

He m. 21 Jan. 1746/7, Rachel Bennett; dau. of Deliverance, b. 11 Oct. 1729.

Will 15 July 1793, proved 15 Feb. 1795; wife Rachel; sons Christopher, Elias, David, Isaac, Moses.

Children, bapt. Westport:

17+Isaac, b. 27 Nov. 1747, bapt. 29 Nov. 1747.
    Moses, bapt. 10 June 1750; m. Esther Prince; dau. of Samuel, b. 20 Aug. 1743; "wife of Moses" d. 17 June 1821 (Miss Treadwell's book).
    Child (twin with Moses), d. 28 Apr. 1750.
18+Christopher, bapt. 10 Feb. 1754.
19+Elias, b. [11 July 1756], bapt. (as "Eleazer") 31 Oct. 1756.
20+David, b. [Mar. 1761].
    Rachel, bapt. 15 June 1765.

8. Godfrey, Isaac, s. of Christopher, 2d.

Born 25 Dec. 1724; d. 20 Nov. 1790 in 67 yr. (g. s., Westport).

Will 25 Oct. 1790, proved 6 Dec. 1790; bros. Ebenezer, Nathan, Eleazer; cousin Stephen Godfrey; bro. David; cousin Richard Elwood; sister Elizabeth Abbot.

9. Godfrey, Ebenezer, s. of Christopher, 2d.

Born 27 June 1727; d. 9 Feb. 1793 in 67 yr. (g. s., Westport).

He m. 25 July 1790, Widow Mary Taylor; she was widow of Asher Taylor, and formerly of Joseph Gorham, Jr., and was dau. of Samuel Gray, b. 8 Mar. 1746; she m. (4) 16 Mar. 1797, Ebenezer Coley of Weston.

Will 7 Feb. proved 19 Mar. 1793; wife Mary; nephew Ebenezer son of bro. Nathan Gray; wife's son Jeremiah Taylor; wife and her son Samuel Gorham, Exec'rs. The following persons were cited to appear in connection with the estate: David and Eleazer Godfrey of Weston, and Ebenezer and Grummon Morehouse and Stephen Godfrey of Fairfield.

THE FAMILIES OF OLD FAIRFIELD

10. Godfrey, John, s. of John.

Bapt. 3 Oct. 1736; d. 23 May 1790 (Perry Diary).

He m. Hannah ———. Perhaps she was the Widow Godfrey who d. at Greenfield, 24 Jan. 1817 (old age).

Children, two bapt. Greenfield, five Fairfield:

> John, bapt. 12 Mar. 1758; m. Eunice ———.*
> Sarah, bapt. 25 Nov. 1759, d. at Greenfield, 1 Mar. 1836 ae. 76; m. 10 May 1787, Jesse Lyon.
> Samuel, bapt. 8 May 1763; m. at New Fairfield, 28 Feb. 1786, Clarine Fairchild.
> Hannah, bapt. 16 June 1765; m. at Fairfield, 29 July 1793, Lebbeus Brown.
> Benjamin, bapt. 16 Aug. 1767.
> Ezra, b. 9 Jan. 1771, 4th son (Perry Diary), bapt. 5 May 1771.
> Lyman, bapt. 31 Oct. 1773;† m. at Westport (he called of Fairfield) 23 Dec. 1800, Rebecca Lockwood.

11. Godfrey, Daniel, s. of David. Capt., 14th Co., 4th Regt., Nov. 1776.

Born 30 Mar. 1739; d. at Weston, 1 Apr. 1808 ae. 68 (g. s.).

He m. at Weston, 22 Mar. 1759, Eunice Bulkley; dau. of David, bapt. 5 Oct. 1740, d. at Weston, 6 Mar. 1831 ae. 91 (g. s.).

Children, bapt. Weston:

> Grace, bapt. 27 Apr. 1760, d. 22 May 1832 ae. 72 (g. s., Weston); m. 12 Apr. 1781, Albert Lockwood.
> Eunice, bapt. 23 May 1762, living 1843 at Weston; m. 6 Mar. 1783 (Pension rec.), Joseph Gray.
> David, bapt. 21 July 1765, d. y.
> Ellen, bapt. 1 Nov. 1767, d. 13 Oct. 1822 ae. 55 (g. s., Weston); m. 10 Feb. 1790, Daniel Dikeman.
> Daniel-Silliman, bapt. 7 Dec. 1777, d. 2 Aug. (?) 1829 ae. 51 (g. s., Weston); m. Rachel Andrews, b. 28 Aug. 1774, d. 30 Dec. 1861 in 88 yr. (g. s.). Adm'n on his estate granted, 18 Apr. 1829, to Erastus Sturges of Wilton; insolvent.
> David-Bulkley, bapt. 7 May 1780, d. 7 Mar. 1861 ae. 81 yrs. 1 mo. 23 days (g. s., Weston); Capt.; m. 4 Oct. 1801, Sarah Bulkley, b. 23 Dec. 1780, d. 8 Feb. 1869 ae. 88 (g. s.).‡

---

* Children, bapt. Fairfield: Zalmon, bapt. 1 Aug. 1790; John, bapt. 20 Oct. 1793; Elbe, bapt. 22 May 1796; Solomon-Curtis, bapt. 28 July 1799; David, bapt. 13 Sept. 1801. One Eunice d. 6 Nov. 1818 (Miss Treadwell's book).

† A Lyman Godfrey d. at Fairfield, 16 Mar. 1819 ae. 60.

‡ A child, Wakeman, bapt. at Weston, 21 July 1805.

12. Godfrey, Silliman, s. of David.

Born 1 May 1750; Dea. Silliman d. at Weston, 1 Mar. 1829 ae. 79 (g. s.); m. (1) Mary Goodsell, dau. of Rev. John, b. July 1751, d. 17 Apr. 1794 ae. 41 (g. s.). He m. (2) 23 Aug. 1795, Mindwell Osborn; dau. of William, b. 18 Mar. 1754, d. at Weston, 12 May 1826 ae. 72 (g. s.).

Children [by first wife], bapt. Weston:
> Sarah, b. 17 Sept., bapt. 8 Dec. 1771; m. 14 Nov. 1792, Burton Osborn.
> Ebenezer, b. 19 Aug. 1773 (Bible rec.), bapt. 10 Oct. 1773, d. 12 Feb. 1844 ae. 70 (Bible rec.), ae. 70-6-23 (g. s.); m. 22 Jan. 1800, Eleanor Andrews, dau. of John-Silliman, b. 11 Aug. 1777, d. 15 Nov. 1867 ae. 90-3-4 (g. s.).*
> Ephraim, bapt. 7 July 1776, d. y.
> Ephraim-Bradley, bapt. 14 Oct. 1779, d. 26 Feb. 1829; m. (1) Mary Wakeman, dau. of Timothy, b. 11 Sept. 1782; m. (2) Lydia ———.
> Silliman, b. [20 Nov. 1781] bapt. 20 Jan. 1782, d. 23 Feb. 1859 ae. 77-3-29 (g. s., Weston); Deacon; m. (1) 6 Oct. 1803, Anna Andrews, b. [7 Oct. 1779], d. 28 Aug. 1848 ae. 68-10-21 (g. s.); m. (2) Elizabeth-Hyde Andrews, who d. 1859.
> Mary, bapt. 31 Oct. 1784, d. 1785.
> Mary, bapt. 19 Mar. 1786; m. Silliman Adams.
> Arity, bapt. 4 Apr. 1790; m. Munson Perry.
> Joseph, b. abt. 1792, d. at Weston, 14 Mar. 1849 ae. 57 (g. s.); will 11 Nov. 1848, proved 14 Apr. 1849;† m. Sarah Sturgis, b. [31 Dec. 1792], d. 20 July 1883 ae. 90-6-20 (g. s.).

13. Godfrey, Jonathan, s. of David.

Born 23 Dec. 1754.

He m. (1) at Weston, 22 Nov. 1778, Mary Rockwell.

He m. (2) Huldah-Ann Bradley.

Children [by first wife], bapt. Weston:
> Hannah, bapt. 18 Apr. 1779.
> Joseph, bapt. 10 June 1781.
> Jeremy, bapt. 1 July 1787.
> Ann, bapt. 30 Aug. 1789.
> Hannah, bapt. 5 Apr. 1795.
> Charity, bapt. 20 Aug. 1797.

---

* His will, 29 Dec. 1835, proved 6 Mar. 1844; wife Ellen; sons Andrews B., William O., Daniel S., Edwin; dau. Rachel A. wife of Joseph Sturges; children of dau. Eunice Fitch (John, Ebenezer, Ephraim, Mary A., Sally J., and Ann Fitch). The distribution calls Mary A. Fitch wife of Peter Smith.

† Named wife Sarah, son Joseph S., dau. Loisa wife of Matthew Bulkley, and dau. Mary B. wife of Miah Perry.

THE FAMILIES OF OLD FAIRFIELD

14. Godfrey, Nathan, s. of Stephen.

Called Jr. to distinguish him from his uncle.

Born 30 Apr. 1743; d. 28 Oct. 1775 in 32 yr. (g. s., Westport); m. at Greenfield, 24 Dec. 1766, Isabel Andrews, b. 20 Sept. 1742, d. 26 May 1772 in 29 yr. (g. s.).

Children, bapt. Westport:

> Seth, bapt. 25 Oct. 1767; res. 1793, Charlton, Saratoga County, N. Y.
> Elizabeth, bapt. 8 Apr. 1770, d. 30 Apr. 1770.
> Nathan, bapt. 9 May 1771, d. 28 Apr. 1772.

15. Godfrey, Stephen, s. of Stephen. Serg., Rev. War.

Born 4 Oct. 1745; living at Fairfield, 1833.

He m. (1) at Westport, 21 Apr. 1768, Abigail Mills; dau. of Beebe, bapt. 12 May 1751, d. 30 June 1772 in 22 yr. (g. s.).

He m. (2) at Westport, 29 May 1780, Eunice Davis, bapt. 28 Jan. 1759, d. 29 Sept. 1803 ae. 44.

Child [by first wife], bapt. Westport:

> Abigail, bapt. 23 Oct. 1768; m. 23 Nov. 1785, David Canfield, of Wilton.
> ?Stephen, m. 9 July 1795, Salome Elwood.*

Children [by second wife], bapt. Westport:

> Mary, bapt. 4 Mar. 1781; ? m. 14 Dec. 1795, Seymour Lockwood.
> Eunice, bapt. 16 Nov. 1783; m. 18 Aug. 1801, Aaron Squire.

16. Godfrey, Abraham, s. of Nathan.

Born 13 May 1748; d. at Westport, 31 Mar. 1784; m. Hannah ———.

Children, all bapt. Westport, 22 Mar. 1783:

> Patty.
> Patience.
> Jinnie.
> Mahew, d. 11 Apr. 1784.

---

* Children, bapt. Westport: Abigail, bapt. 1 Jan. 1797; Charles, bapt. 7 Nov. 1799; Caroline, bapt. 13 Dec. 1801; Eliza, bapt. 13 June 1804; Emily, bapt. 19 Sept. 1807.

17. Godfrey, Isaac, s. of Eleazer.

Born 27 Nov. 1747; d. at Weston, 12 Feb. 1834 ae. 86 (g. s.).

He m. (1) 8 Feb. 1778, Abigail Couch; dau. of Samuel, b. 10 June 1741.

He m. (2) Hannah ———, who d. 7 Jan. 1831 ae. 87 (g. s.).

Children [by first wife], rec. and bapt. Weston:
> Rachel, b. 24 Mar., bapt. 20 June 1779; m. at Weston, 10 Jan. 1802, Lyman Smith.
> Abigail, b. 3 Aug., bapt. 31 Oct. 1784, d. 16 Jan. 1786.

18. Godfrey, Christopher, s. of Eleazer.

Bapt. 10 Feb. 1754.

He m. 12 Sept. 1779, Sarah Ogden; dau. of Samuel, b. 1 Mar. 1757, d. by 1807.

Est. of Sarah wife of Christopher distributed to the six children named below (approved 3 Aug. 1807).

Children, rec. and bapt. Weston:
> Eleazer, bapt. 28 Oct. 1780, d. y.
> Banks, b. 18 Apr., bapt. 15 June 1783.
> Mary, b. 24 Apr. 1785, bapt. 19 Mar. 1786.
> Eleazer, b. 12 Sept., bapt. 9 Dec. 1787.
> Sarah, b. 9 Sept. 1789, bapt. 11 Apr. 1791.
> Priscilla, b. 1 Sept. 1793, bapt. 25 June 1794.
> Christopher, b. 20 June 1798, bapt. 22 Jan. 1799, d. at West Redding, 25 Jan. 1880 ae. 81 yrs. 7 mos. (g. s.); m. Anna A. ———, who d. 21 Aug. 1882 ae. 73-8-4 (g. s.).

19. Godfrey, Elias, s. of Eleazer.

Born [11 June 1756]; d. at Weston, 1 May 1830 (Miss Treadwell's book), or 2 May 1830 ae. 73-9-21 (g. s.).

He m. 8 June 1780, Eunice Cable; dau. of Nehemiah, bapt. 6 Oct. 1759; d. 8 Apr. 1835 ae. 75-7-18 (g. s.).

Will 27 Jan. 1829, proved 17 May 1830; wife Eunice; son Bradley; dau. Milley; son Eli B.

Children, rec. Weston:
> Bradley, b. 14 July 1783, d. at Weston, 12 Aug. 1839 ae. 56 yrs. 1 mo. (g. s.).
> Elias, b. 24 Aug. 1789.
> Milly, b. 11 Apr. 1793; prob. m. Anson Morehouse.
> Eli B., b. 8 Oct. 1796, d. at Weston, 11 Sept. 1844 ae. 47-11-3 (g. s.); his will, 28 Mar., proved 26 Sept. 1844, gave all to wife Sally B.

20. **Godfrey, David,** s. of Eleazer.

Born [Mar. 1761]; d. at Weston, 28 Dec. 1828 ae. 67 yrs. 9 mos. (g. s.); m. 29 June 1781, Salome Finch; dau. of John, b. [June 1760], d. 28 Feb. 1843 ae. 82 yrs. 8 mos. (g. s.).

Will 4 Dec. 1827, proved 27 Jan. 1829; wife Saloma; dau. Mary (unmarried); daus. Nancy and Saloma (rec'd part of portion); the note I gave to Eli B. Godfrey I consider paid in full by my son Joel's services; sons Ahaz and Benjamin.

Children, rec. Weston:
> David, b. 10 Oct. 1781.
> Mercy, b. 18 Dec. 1783.
> Zalmon, b. 4 Aug. 1786, bapt. 11 Feb. 1787; m. Polly Beers, dau. of Anthony of Ridgefield.
> Benjamin, b. 26 Apr. 1789, bapt. 31 Mar. 1790; m. Lydia Beers, dau. of Anthony of Ridgefield.
> Nancy, bapt. 27 Feb. 1793.
> Lewis, b. 7 Apr. 1795.
> Salome-Bennett, b. 6 Aug. 1797, bapt. 29 Nov. 1797.
> Ahaz, bapt. 16 Dec. 1801.
> Joel, bapt. 14 Mar. 1805.

Godfrey [*Unplaced*].
> ANNE Munroe alias Godfrey had son Samuel, bapt. 23 Oct. 1774. [Greens Farms Church]
> ESTHER m. 9 Sept. 1796, Ezra Bennett. [Weston rec.]

Gold [Vol. I, pp. 228-231].

1 Nathan (-1694) m. (1) Martha (———) Harvey; (2) Sarah ———.
(By 2): 2 Nathan (1663-1723) m. (1) Hannah Talcott; (2) Sarah ———.
   (By 1): 3 *John* (1688-1766).
      4 *Nathan* (1690-1761).
      5 *Samuel* (1692-1769).
      6 *Hezekiah* (1695-1761).
   (By 2): 7 *Onesimus* (1701-1773).
      8 *Joseph* (1711-   ).

3. **Gold, John,** s. of Nathan.

Born 25 Apr. 1688; d. at Fairfield, 23 Sept. 1766 in 79 yr. (g. s.); m. Jemima Sherwood, dau. of John, b. 17 Jan. 1696/7.

Adm'n granted to David Allen, 13 Oct. 1766. Distribution 9 Mar. 1767: widow Jemima; Sarah wife of David Allen; Elizabeth widow of Thomas Hawley of Ridgefield. Jemima receipted to son-in-law David Allen, Apr. 1768.

Children, bapt. Fairfield:

> Hannah, b. 20, bapt. 23 Sept. 1716, d. 25 Nov. 1752 ae. 36 (g. s.).
> Sarah, bapt. 1 June 1718, d. at Fairfield, Feb. 1778 in 60 yr. (g. s.); m. 11 Oct. 1739, David Allen.
> John, bapt. 29 May 1720, d. y.
> Nathan, bapt. 2 Feb. 1723/4, d. y.
> Elizabeth, bapt. 24 Apr. 1726; m. (1) 13 Jan. 1747/8, Thomas Hawley, of Ridgefield; m. (2) Ezekiel Wilson, of Ridgefield, with whom she conveyed, 1783, land from her father John Gold.
> Talcott, bapt. 1 Sept. 1728, d. y.
> Mary, b. 4, bapt. 6 June 1731, d. 20 Nov. 1752 ae. 22 (g. s.); m. 8 Nov. 1752, Thaddeus Betts, A.M., of Ridgefield.

4. **Gold, Nathan,** s. of Nathan.

Born 6 Apr. 1690; d. at Fairfield by 1761.*

Adm'n granted, 18 Mar. 1761, to Benoni Dimon. Distribution 28 Sept. 1761: Anna wife of Benoni Dimon; Jabez Hubbell, son of Martha Hubbell dec'd; Mary, Kate, Anna, and Josiah Leavitt, children of Kate Leavitt dec'd.

Children, bapt. Fairfield:

> Kate, bapt. 25 Sept. 1726, d. in 1760; m. 18 Oct. 1742, Jacob Leavitt.
> Anna, bapt. 4 Feb. 1727/8, d. 4 Oct. 1761; m. 15 Sept. 1748,† Benoni Dimon alias Gilbert.
> Nathan, bapt. 24 May 1730, d. y.
> Martha, bapt. 24 May 1730, d. before 1761; m. (1) 5 Feb. 1753, David Hubbell; prob. m. (2) 8 Jan. 1756, John Bulkley.

5. **Gold, Samuel,** s. of Nathan.

Born 27 Dec. 1692; d. at Fairfield, 11 Oct. 1769 in 77 yr. (g. s.); m. (rec. Fairfield) 7 Dec. 1716, Esther Bradley; dau. of Dea. Abraham and Hannah (Thompson) Bradley, b. at New Haven, 14 Mar. 1696, d. in 1776.

---

* Jemima Gold of Fairfield m. 22 May 1764, Jesse Raymond of Middlesex [Darien]. She could not have been widow of his brother John, though she might have been dau. of his brother Joseph. Was she widow of Nathan?

† 20 Sept. 1749, by Weston rec.

Will 1 Oct. 1759, proved 21 Nov. 1769; wife Esther; dau. Abigail Thompson shall have through her widowhood, etc.; sons Abraham, Daniel, Abel; dau. Easter Turney.

Will of Esther, widow of Samuel, 8 Oct. 1773, proved 4 June 1776; sons Daniel, Abel, Abraham; gr. son Isaac Turney; dau. Abigail Curtiss, residue to gr. son Gold Curtiss, but if he die unm. or under 21, then to my dau. Abigail; son-in-law Mathew Curtiss, Exec'r.

Children, rec. and bapt. Fairfield:

9+Daniel, b. 11 July 1717, bapt. 27 Apr. 1718.
    Esther, b. 13 Oct., bapt. 8 Nov. 1719, d. 1 Aug. 1770 (Perry Diary); m. 28 Dec. 1742, John Turney.
    Abigail, b. 27 Apr., bapt. 24 May 1724; m. (1) 19 July 1744, Nathan Thompson; m. (2) at Newtown, 5 Dec. 1759, Matthew Curtis.
10+Abel, b. 14, bapt. 17 Sept. 1727.
    Abraham, b. 12, bapt. 18 Oct. 1730, d. 26 Nov. 1730.
11+Abraham, b. 10, bapt. 14 May 1732.

6. Gold, (Rev.) Hezekiah, s. of Nathan.

Bapt. 17 Feb. 1694/5; d. at Stratford, 22 Apr. 1761 in 67 yr. (g. s.); grad. Harvard Coll. 1719; m. (1) 23 May 1723, Mary Ruggles, dau. of Rev. Thomas of Guilford. She d. 2 July 1750 in 48 yr. (g. s.). He m. (2) Mary ———.

Will 29 Jan. 1761, with codicils, proved 17 June 1761; wife Mary; son Hezekiah; son Thomas at Redding; daus. Anna, Abigail, Rebecca Tomlinson, Huldah Curtiss, Mary Tomlinson. Abraham Tomlinson of Stratford appealed from probate. Adm'n granted, 18 June 1761, to Agur Tomlinson and Mary Gold.

Children [by first wife], rec. Stratford:

    Mary, b. 29 Feb. 1724, d. 23 June 1802 in 79 yr. (g. s.); m. Dr. Agur Tomlinson.
    Catee, b. 31 Aug. 1725, d. 30 Sept. 1742 in 18 yr. (g. s.).
    Jerusha, b. 6 Mar. 1726/7, d. 24 Sept. 1747.
    Sarah, b. 8 May 1729.
12+Hezekiah, b. 18 Jan. 1731.
13+Thomas, b. 8 Jan. 1733.
    Anna, b. Dec. 1734, d. 9 Apr. 1739 ae. 4 yrs. 4 mos. (g. s.).
    Rebecca, b. Sept. 1736, d. 1 Nov. 1774 in 39 yr. (g. s.); m. Dec. 1754, Abraham Tomlinson.

Huldah, b. 15 Apr. 1738, d. 28 Apr. 1765 (g. s.); m. 20 Dec. 1759, Samuel Curtis.
Anna, b. 14 May 1740, d. at New Haven, 13 Feb. 1826 ae. 85 (g. s.); m. Levi Hubbard, of Guilford.
Catherine, b. 15 Oct. 1742, d. 23 Oct. 1743 ae. 1 yr. 7 days (g. s.).
Abigail, b. 4 Nov. 1744.
Elizabeth, b. 15 Aug. 1747.

7. Gold, Onesimus, s. of Nathan.

Bapt. at Fairfield, 19 Oct. 1701; d. at Greenfield, 6 Mar. 1773 ae. over 70; m. Eunice Hubbell; dau. of Samuel, Jr., bapt. 21 Mar. 1703.

Children, bapt. Greenfield:

Rebecca, bapt. 4 Oct. 1724, d. 30 Apr. 1810; m. 5 July 1741, Ephraim Nichols.
14+Nathan, bapt. 17 Sept. 1726.
15+David, bapt. 22 Oct. 1728.
Luther, bapt. 10 Oct. 1731; m. after 1764, Deborah, widow of Ignatius Nichols, Jr., and dau. of Joseph Wheeler, b. 14 June 1731.
Eunice, bapt. Aug. 1733.
Stephen, bapt. May 1736.
Sarah, bapt. 21 Aug. 1737, living 1806; m. 10 Apr. 1760, Ens. Stephen Thorp.
16+Aaron, b. 18 bapt. 25 Jan. 1740/1.

8. Gold, Joseph, s. of Nathan.

Bapt. 21 Oct. 1711; killed in battle at Fairfield, 7 July 1779 (Perry Diary), "a very old man & feeble" (Wheeler Journal). He m. Abigail Barlow, dau. of Samuel, bapt. 5 Aug. 1716.

Children, bapt. Fairfield:

Sarah, bapt. 22 Apr. 1739; prob. m. 6 Oct. 1756, Samuel Lord.
Hannah, bapt. 22 June 1740.
Joseph, m. by 1768, Mary Whittier, dau. of John.*
John, bapt. 21 Aug. 1757.†
?Elizabeth, m. 13 Apr. 1786, Joel Burr, of Redding.

---

* One Joseph had wife Huldah who d. 21 Mar. 1807 ae. 33 (an Episcopalian, but rec. Fairfield Church).

† Perhaps he was the John Gold of Fairfield who m. at New Fairfield, 19 Dec. 1774, Elizabeth Sturdevant. A Martha Gold m. at New Fairfield, 30 Mar. 1780, James Hazard. A William Gold m. at New Fairfield, 20 Sept. 1783, Widow Pitts. A John Gould m. at Easton, Feb. 1808, Esther Whitehead.

9. **Gold, Daniel,** s. of Samuel.

Born 11 July 1717; d. at Redding, 1775.

He m. Grace Burr, dau. of Stephen, b. 12 Dec. 1724, d. by 1776.

Will 15 Aug. 1768, proved 28 Oct. 1775; wife Grace; children, Stephen, Samuel, Hezekiah, Abigail, Esther, Sarah, Hannah, Mary, Elizabeth.

Distribution of Est. of Grace Gold of Redding, 15 Apr. 1776; eldest son Stephen; son Samuel; Abigail wife of Richard Nichols; Esther wife of Nathaniel Northrop; Sarah wife of David Turney; Mary wife of Seth Price; Elizabeth Gold; heirs and legal representatives of Hezekiah Gold dec'd and Hannah Gold dec'd, the other children and heirs of Grace.

Children, all bapt. Redding (except Sarah):

Abigail, bapt. 24 Oct. 1742; m. 2 Dec. 1761, Richard Nichols.

Stephen, bapt. 12 Aug. 1744; Quarter-Master of a Troop of Horse in 3d Regt., May 1781; adm'n on Est. of Capt. Stephen of Redding granted, 1 Apr. 1795, to Samuel Gold.

Esther, bapt. 27 Mar. 1748; m. 10 Nov. 1767, Nathaniel Northrop; res. Newtown.

Sarah, bapt. at Westport, 28 Jan. 1750; m. 4 Nov. 1766,* David Turney.

Hannah, bapt. 20 Oct. 1751, d. 1776. Will 1 Sept. 1775, proved 3 June 1776; sister Betty; Sarah dau. of David Turney; sisters Sarah, Abigail, Esther, Molly; bros. Samuel, Stephen.

Mary, bapt. 27 May 1753; m. 6 Mar. 1771, Seth Price.

Samuel, b. [20 May 1755], d. at Redding, 9 Feb. 1829 ae. 73-8-20 (g. s.); Sergt., Rev. War; m. 9 Apr. 1778, Sarah Platt, b. 26 May 1758, d. 26 Sept. 1844 ae. 87 yrs. 4 mos. (g. s.).†

Hezekiah, bapt. 23 Jan. 1757, d. in 1776.

Elizabeth, bapt. 8 July 1759; m. 18 Dec. 1777, Abel Gold.

---

* 4 Oct. 1766, by town record.

† Children, rec. Redding: Grace, b. 29 Apr., bapt. 15 Aug. 1779, d. 8 Jan. 1798. Sarah, b. 29 July 1782. Hezekiah, b. 30 May 1785, d. at Redding, 19 Jan. 1834 ae. 48 (g. s.); m. Mary ———, who d. 15 Oct. 1870 ae. 78 (g. s.). Polly, b. 12 Jan. 1787. Daniel, b. 20 Feb. 1791. Burr, b. 2 Sept. 1793. Aaron, b. 19 Aug. 1798, d. 10 Jan. 1841 ae. 42 (g. s.); m. Fanny ———, who d. 2 Mar. 1843 ae. 43 (g. s.). Samuel's will, 6 Feb., proved 9 Mar. 1829; wife Sarah; sons Hezekiah, Burr, Aaron; daus. Sally Jarvis, Polly Sanford; gr. sons Edsin (?) and Samuel Gould, and gr. daus. Sally, Fanny, Mary, Malinda, and Delia Gould, children of son Daniel Gould.

10. **Gold, Abel,** s. of Samuel.

Born 14 Sept. 1727; d. at Fairfield, 11 Nov. 1789; m. (1) 19 Dec. 1754, Ellen Burr, dau. of Capt. Samuel, b. Nov. 1736, d. 18 June 1777; m. (2) 18 Jan. 1778, Amelia, widow of Ebenezer Burr, and dau. of Ebenezer Silliman, b. 1736, d. 1794 ae. 58 (g. s.); she d. Oct. 1794 (Perry Diary).

Adm'n on Est. of Ellen Gold granted, 6 Oct. 1790, to Talcott Gold. Distribution, 1791: eldest son Abel of N. Y. State; Talcott Gold; Ellen wife of Samuel Squire; Isaac Gold; Esther wife of William Squire; Nathan Gold; Grissel Gold; Seth-Burr Gold; Hannah Gold. Isaac Gold was made guardian to Seth-Burr Gold, 15 Nov. 1790.

Children [by first wife], rec. and bapt. Fairfield:

> John, b. 2, bapt. 5 Oct., d. 15 Dec. 1755.
> Abel, b. 18, bapt. 24 Oct. 1756; res. Redding, 1783, and N. Y. State, 1791; m. at Redding, 18 Dec. 1777, Elizabeth Gold; dau. of Daniel, bapt. 8 July 1759.*
> Talcott, bapt. 17 June 1759; rem. to Vt.; m. 18 Mar. 1782, Anna Barlow.†
> Ellen, bapt. 2 Aug. 1761, d. 7 Oct. 1845 ae. 84 (g. s.); m. (1) 20 July 1789, Samuel Squire; m. (2) 9 Jan. 1803, James Chapman; m. (3) 9 Nov. 1829, Aaron Turney.
> Samuel, bapt. 27 Nov. 1763; rem. to Canada.
> Isaac, bapt. 23 Feb. 1766; rem. to Delaware County, N. Y.; m. 7 Feb. 1790, Ellen Jennings; dau. of Peter, bapt. 10 July 1768.‡
> Esther, bapt. 8 May 1768; m. 7 May 1789, William Squire; rem. to Delaware County, N. Y.
> Nathan, bapt. 30 Sept. 1770; rem. to Canada.
> Grissel, bapt. 17 Jan. 1773, d. at Fairfield, 28 Feb. 1832 ae. 60 (g. s.); m. 4 Dec. 1791, Seth Sturges, Jr.; with whom she conveyed, 1793, land set to her from estate of her mother Ellen Gold.
> Seth-Burr, bapt. 14 May 1775; rem. to Canada.
> Hannah, bapt. 17 June 1777, d. at Fairfield, 25 Oct. 1819 ae. 42 (g. s.); m. 21 Oct. 1798, John Morehouse.

Child [by second wife], bapt. Fairfield:

> Sally, bapt. 28 Mar. 1779.

---

* Children, bapt. Fairfield: Molly, bapt. 15 Feb. 1779; Samuel, bapt. 21 Nov. 1784; Stephen, bapt. 6 Aug. 1786.
† Children, bapt. Fairfield: Sally and Chary, bapt. 20 Dec. 1789.
‡ Child, bapt. Fairfield: Abel, bapt. 31 Mar. 1791.

11. **Gold, Abraham,** s. of Samuel. Ens., 1st Co., Fairfield, Oct. 1757; Lt., Oct. 1759; Capt., May 1767; Lt.-Col., 4th Regt., Militia, Oct. 1776.

Born 10 May 1732; killed at Ridgefield, 27 Apr. 1777 ae. 44 in defense of his country (g. s.); m. 1 Jan. 1754, Elizabeth Burr, dau. of Capt. John, b. 7 Apr. 1732, d. 5 Sept. 1815 in 84 yr. (g. s.).

Children rec. and bapt. Fairfield:

    Abigail, b. 15, bapt. 17 Nov. 1754, d. at Fairfield, 2 Nov. 1795 ae. 41 wanting 13 days (g. s.); m. 15 Nov. 1770, Isaac Jennings.
17+Hezekiah, b. 9, bapt. 12 Dec. 1756.
    Elizabeth, bapt. 11 Feb. 1759; m. 2 Oct. 1781, Gould Curtis, of Newtown.
    John-Burr, bapt. 12 Apr. 1761, d. at sea, 2 June 1781 ae. 20 (g. s.).
    Deborah, b. 25, bapt. 31 July 1763, d. at Fairfield, 28 July 1785 ae. 22 yrs. 3 days (g. s.); m. 4 Jan. 1785, Daniel Osborn, Jr.
    Abraham, b. 28 Jan. 1766 (Bible rec.), bapt. 9 Mar. 1766, d. at Roxbury, N. Y., 23 Dec. 1823 ae. 57-10-25; res. 1792, "New Stamford," N. Y.; m. 5 Apr. 1789, Anna Osborn; dau. of Eleazer, b. 22 Oct. 1764, d. 27 Mar. 1847 ae. 81-5-5.*
    Ann, bapt. 5 Mar. 1768; m. 9 Jan. 1792, Ebenezer Silliman.
    Jason, bapt. 24 Feb. 1771, d. at Fairfield, 17 June 1810 ae. 39-5-2 (g. s.); will 25 May, proved 26 July 1810; m. Aug. 1794, Catherine Carson; dau. of Walter, bapt. 21 Oct. 1775.†
    Daniel, bapt. 25 Feb. 1776, drowned on coast of France, 28 Dec. 1796 ae. 20 (g. s.). Adm'n granted to Jason Gould, 21 Mar. 1798. Distribution 3 Dec. 1798; bro. Abraham; bro. Jason; sister Betsey wife of Gould Curtiss; sister Anna wife of Ebenezer Silliman; heirs of Abigail dec'd (late wife of Isaac Jennings), viz., Elizabeth, Abigail, Anna, Phebe, Abraham-Gould, Isaac, Seth. The Est. of Daniel showed land in Vt.; mention made of dower of Elizabeth Gould, and of land distributed to Deborah Gould, late wife of Daniel Osborn, Jr.; Deborah dau. of Hezekiah Gould also mentioned.

12. **Gold, (Rev.) Hezekiah,** s. of Hezekiah. Deputy for Cornwall, Oct. 1787.

Born 18 Jan. 1731, d. at Cornwall, 31 May 1790; Yale Coll. 1751; minister of Cornwall, 1754-86; m. (1) 23 Nov. 1750, Sarah

---

* The eldest child, Elizabeth, bapt. at Fairfield, 4 July 1790.
† Children, bapt. Fairfield: Elizabeth-Burr, bapt. 10 May 1795, d. 19 June 1812 ae. 17; William, bapt. 29 Dec. 1799, d. 7 Aug. 1812 ae. 13; John, bapt. 8 Nov. 1801; Catherine, bapt. 9 Feb. 1806. The will named the wife and children Elizabeth B., William and John.

Sedgwick, dau. of Dea. Benjamin and Anna (Thompson); she d. 20 Aug. 1766; m. (2) 11 Oct. 1768, Elizabeth Wakeman, dau. of Joseph, b. 4 Sept. 1745, d. 11 Feb. 1778; m. (3) at Westport, 24 Sept. 1778, Abigail, widow of Jeremiah Sherwood, and dau. of Peter Sturgis, bapt. 21 July 1728, d. 3 Sept. 1804 in 77 yr. (g. s., Westport).

Children [by first wife]:

Thomas, b. 23 Nov. 1759, d. at Pittsfield, Mass., 13 Feb. 1827; grad. Yale Coll. 1778; rem. to Pittsfield 1782; m. abt. 1785, Martha Marsh, dau. of Dr. Perez and Sarah (Williams) Marsh; had 10 children.
Hezekiah, b. 4 May 1761, d. 1765.
Benjamin, b. 25 June 1762.
Thomas-Ruggles, b. 4 Nov. 1764, d. at Whitesboro, N. Y., 24 Oct. 1827; grad. Yale Coll. 1786; lawyer, of Whitesboro, Oneida County, N. Y., 1792; State Senator, 1796-1802; Asst. Att'y-Gen., 1797-1801; Representative to N. Y. Assembly, 1807; Member of Congress, 1809-13, 1815-17; m. abt. 1787, Sarah Sill, dau. of Dr. Elisha, who d. 13 July 1852 ae. 88; had 7 children.
Hezekiah, b. 1 Aug. 1766.

Children [by second wife]:

Joseph-Wakeman, b. 4 Sept. 1769, d. Apr. 1790.
Sarah, b. 15 Aug. 1771, d. 1776.
Mary, b. 1775.

13. **Gold, Thomas,** s. of Hezekiah.

Born 8 Jan. 1733.
He m. at Redding, 13 Feb. 1755, Anna Smith, dau. of Samuel, bapt. 6 July 1740.

14. **Gold, Nathan,** s. of Onesimus.

Bapt. 17 Sept. 1726; d. at Greenfield by 1805.
He m. 2 May 1749, Abigail Burr, bapt. 7 Dec. 1729, d. 13 Apr. 1779 ae. abt. 50.
Distribution order, 8 July 1805: children,—Elizabeth wife of Thomas Wheeler, Abigail Gould, Nathan, Ichabod, Ebenezer, Eldad, Medad, Peter Gould; heirs of Jesse Gould dec'd,—Jesse, Ebenezer, Esther wife of Zachariah Edwards, Joseph, Jonathan, Abel, Sally, Laura.

Children, bapt. Greenfield:

> Elizabeth, b. Dec., bapt. 16 Dec. 1750, d. at Greenfield, 8 Oct. 1822 ae. 71 (g. s.); m. 17 Nov. 1772, Thomas Wheeler.
> 18+Jesse.
> Abigail.
> 19+Nathan, b. May 1756 (Pension rec.), bapt. 25 Dec. 1757.
> Ichabod, bapt. 2 Sept. 1759, d. 9 Apr. 1828; m. Grissel Knapp, dau. of Ebenezer, b. abt. 1761, d. at Greenfield, 11 Dec. 1823 ae. 62.*
> Ebenezer, bapt. 13 June 1762, d. at Greenfield, 6 Dec. 1830 ae. 70 (g. s.); m. at Trinity Church, 24 May 1792, Eleanor Wheeler.
> Eldad, bapt. 26 May 1765, d. at Greenfield, 7 Sept. 1833 ae. 69 (g. s.); m. Huldah ———, who d. 2 May 1846 ae. 74 (g. s.).
> Medad, bapt. 26 May 1765, d. at Fairfield, 16 Apr. 1843 ae. 79 (g. s.); m. 30 Jan. 1794, Elizabeth Jackson, b. abt. 1765, d. 29 July [prob. May] 1852 ae. 87 (g. s.).†
> Peter, b. abt. 1769, d. at Greenfield, 27 Oct. 1852 ae. 83 (g. s.); m. (1) Anna ———, b. [1 Jan. 1778], d. 24 Apr. 1831 ae. 53-3-23 (g. s.); m. (2) ———, who d. 8 Apr. 1835 (Miss Treadwell's book); m. (3) Rachel ———.‡

15. **Gold, David,** s. of Onesimus.

Bapt. 22 Oct. 1728; d. in 1808.

He m. in 1754, Abigail Hill, dau. of Joseph, b. 21 Mar. 1732/3.

Adm'n granted, 1 Dec. 1808, to Gershom Wakeman and David Gould, with Hezekiah Nichols as surety.

David conveyed, 1789, for love to son Dimon.

Children, bapt. Greenfield:

> Mary, bapt. 13 July 1755.
> Sarah, b. abt. 1757, d. at Greenfield, 9 Dec. 1831 ae. 75 (g. s.); m. 19 Feb. 1778, Jesse Gold.
> Hannah, bapt. 22, d. 24 June 1759.
> Abigail, bapt. 26 Sept. 1762, d. Feb. 1846; m. Apr. 1787, Nathan Wakeman.
> Dimon.
> Eunice, bapt. 31 Aug. 1769; m. Samuel Wire, of Milford.

---

* Child, bapt. Fairfield: Burr, bapt. 14 May 1780; possibly m. Polly Lockwood, dau. of Job.

† Children, bapt. Fairfield: Azariah, bapt. 8 Feb. 1795; Maretta, bapt. 7 Feb. 1796; Austin, bapt. 10 Sept. 1797; Eliza, bapt. 6 Oct. 1799; Roderick, bapt. 27 Jan. 1802.

‡ Will of Peter of Easton, 28 June 1850, proved 9 Nov. 1852; wife Rachel; residue to Joseph Osborn of Fairfield in trust for my gr. son Henry S. Gould; after death of wife and gr. son, any residue to the Easton Cong. Church.

Esther, bapt. 31 Aug. 1769; m. Increase Sherwood.
David, bapt. 31 Aug. 1769.
Mabel, b. abt. 1773, d. 30 May 1813 in 40 yr. (g. s.); m. Levi Perry.
Charity.

16. Gold, Aaron, s. of Onesimus.

Born 18 Jan. 1740/1; d. at Greenfield, 2 Oct. 1812 ae. 74(!).
He m. 27 Jan. 1761, Rebecca Scudder, dau. of Peter of Huntington, L. I.; she d. 22 Jan. 1774 in 33 yr. (g. s.).
Will 2 July 1811, proved 16 Nov. 1812; wife Polly; daus. Naomi(?) and Polly Gould; son Samuel and dau. Rebecca wife of Samuel Burdick; dau. Hannah wife of Sanford Haines.

Children, first rec. Fairfield; bapt. Greenfield:

Scudder, b. 27 Mar., bapt. 6 June 1762.
Hannah, bapt. 7 Apr. 1764; m. Sanford Haynes.
Samuel, bapt. 18 May 1766.
Isaac, bapt. 22 Jan. 1769.*
Rebecca, m. Samuel Burdick.
Naomi (?).
Polly.

17. Gold, Hezekiah, s. of Abraham.

Born 9 Dec. 1756; drowned at New York, 30 Oct. 1786† ae. 30 (g. s.); m. 4 Feb. 1786, Ellen Hobart; dau. of Justin, b. 18 Jan. 1764, d. at Trumbull, 27 Mar. 1813 ae. 49 (g. s.). She m. (2) 7 Oct. 1793, Stephen Middlebrook, Jr., of North Stratford.
Adm'n granted, 29 Dec. 1788, to Justin Hobart.

Child:

Deborah, bapt. 9 Dec. 1787, d. at Trumbull, 11 Jan. 1858 ae. 72 (g. s.).

18. Gould, Jesse, s. of Nathan.

He d. before 1805; m. 19 Feb. 1778, Sarah Gold, dau. of David, b. abt. 1757, d. at Greenfield, 9 Dec. 1831 ae. 75 (g. s.).

* An Isaac and Mary had children bapt. Fairfield: Isaac and Bradley, bapt. 27 Nov. 1795; Angelina and Sarah-Couch, bapt. 13 Feb. 1801; Rebecca, bapt. 16 Nov. 1803.
† 1 Nov. 1787, by Perry Diary.

Children:
> Jesse, b. abt. 1778, d. at Greenfield, 5 Mar. 1854 ae. 76 (g. s.); m. Sarah ———, b. abt. 1782, d. 5 Feb. 1859 ae. 77 (g. s.)*
> Ebenezer.
> Esther, m. Zechariah Edwards.
> Joseph.
> Jonathan.
> Abel.
> Sally.
> Laura.

19. Gould, Nathan, s. of Nathan.

Born May 1756 (Pension rec.); d. at Greenfield, 18 Jan. 1827 ae. 71 (g. s.); m. 16 May 1784, Patience Patchen; dau. of Samuel, b. abt. 1764, d. 29 Jan. 1844 ae. 80 (g. s.).

Will 21 July 1826, proved 26 Jan. 1827; wife Patience; daus. Eunice and Pamela, Betsey Burr, Anne; sons Daniel, Eber, Stephen.

Will of Patience of Weston, 24 Nov. 1843, proved 3 Feb. 1844; dau. Anna Gould; gr. son Daniel B. Gould.

Children, bapt. Easton:
> Daniel, bapt. 1 Oct. 1786, d. at Greenfield, 9 May 1833 ae. 47 (g. s.); Col.; m. (1) Phebe Oakley, b. 1 June 1788, d. 22 May 1821 ae. 33; m. (2) Elizabeth ———, who d. 16 Apr. 1868 ae. 82.
> Eunice, bapt. 6 Nov. 1791, d. y.
> Eunice, bapt. 4 Aug. 1793.
> Pamela.
> Eber.
> Betsey-Burr.
> Anna.
> Stephen.

Gold [*Unplaced*].

> ——— m. Elizabeth Knapp, b. 10 Sept. 1753; dau. of Ebenezer whose will 1793 mentioned her heirs.
> ELI m. 30 Apr. 1795, Mary Cable. [Weston Church]
> ABIGAIL,—adm'n granted, 10 Mar. 1812, to Joseph Hyde, Jr., with Isaac Turney of New Fairfield as surety.
> ZALMONT† m. 1 Jan. 1815, Clara Davis. [Easton Church]

---

* Two children of Jesse, poisoned with fennel, d. 28 May 1809 (Miss Treadwell's book).

† Adm'n granted, 14 Apr. 1829, to widow Clarissa. Distribution to widow, daus. Eliza and Catherine, and son Bradley.

1. Goodsell, (Rev.) John.

Born at East Haven, 21 Dec. 1706, son of Thomas and Sarah (Hemingway); d. at Greenfield, 26 Dec. 1763 ae. 57 (g. s.). Grad. Yale Coll., 1724; ordained pastor at Greenfield, 18 May 1726.

He m. 20 July 1725, Mary Lewis, dau. of James and Hannah (Judson), b. at Stratford, 18 May 1706, d. 11 Dec. 1769 in 64 yr. (g. s.).

Will 21 Apr. 1762, proved 21 Feb. 1764; wife Mary; sons John, Thomas; four younger sons, Epaphras, Lewis, Samuel, James.

Nuncupative will of Mary widow of Rev. John, dated 10 Oct. 1769, proved 20 Dec. 1769; dau. Abigail, all estate. Adm'n was granted to Abigail Hicks, 10(?) Dec. 1769.

Children, rec. Greenfield:

    Hannah, b. 9, bapt. 15 Aug. 1726, d. 20 May 1757 ae. 31 yrs. wanting 3 mos.; m. 11 May 1745, Elisha Alvord.
    Mary, b. 29 Nov., bapt. 3 Dec. 1727, d. 16 July 1757 in 29 yr. (g. s.); m. 21 Aug. 1744, Moses Wakeman.
2+John, b. 14, bapt. 19 Apr. 1730.
3+Thomas, b. 4, bapt. 12 Dec. 1731.
    Sarah, b. and bapt. 4 Mar. 1734/5, d. 11 Apr. 1762 ae. 28 (g. s.); m. Oct. 1754, Elnathan Bradley.
    Epaphras, b. 13, bapt. 18 Jan. 1735/6, d. 6 Jan. 1741/2 ae. 6 yrs. less 7 days (g. s.).
    Abigail, b. 8, bapt. 15 Jan. 1737/8, d. at Greenfield, 5 Apr. 1776 ae. abt. 40; m. (1) Feb. 1754, Archibald Blair; m. (2) 28 June 1768, William Hicks.
    Huldah, b. 4, bapt. 6 Apr. 1740, d. 28 May 1765 in 26 yr.; m. 26 Nov. 1761, Silas Hull.
4+Epaphras, b. 23, bapt. 29 May 1742.
5+Lewis, b. and bapt. 23 Oct. 1744.
    Phebe, b. and bapt. 23 Oct. 1744, d. Nov. 1744 ae. 3 wks. less 1 day.
6+Samuel, b. and bapt. 29 June 1746.
    James, b. 19 July 1748, bapt. in infancy, d. 31 July 1748.
7+James, b. 24, bapt. 27 Aug. 1749.

2. Goodsell, John, s. of Rev. John.

Born 14 Apr. 1730; killed by the British in Fairfield, 7 July 1779 (Perry Diary).

He m. (1) 18 Jan. 1748/9, Sarah Bradley, dau. of Ephraim, b. Mar. 1730, d. at Westport, 27 Aug. 1755.

He m. (2) Grace ———. She m. (2) at Weston, 27 Mar. 1804, Zebulon Fanton, "a bachelor of 75 years." The *Conn. Herald* calls the bride 67 yrs. old.

Adm'n on Est. of Grace Fanton of Weston granted, 27 Apr. 1820, to Samuel Rowland.

Sarah wife of John Goodsell in her lifetime owned lands received from her father Ephraim Bradley, which now belong to the three children of John and Sarah: John Goodsell, Silas Fairchild and Sarah his wife, and Silliman Godfrey and Mary his wife. [Fairfield Deeds.]

Children [by first wife], two bapt. Greenfield, one Westport:

> Sarah, b. Sept., bapt. 15 Oct. 1749; m. at Weston, 11 Jan. 1770, Silas Fairchild; res. 1784, Newtown.
> Mary, b. July, bapt. 21 July 1751, d. 13 Apr. 1794; m. Silliman Godfrey.
> 8+John, bapt. 24 June 1753.

Children [by second wife], bapt. Westport:

> Judson, bapt. 13 Nov. 1757.
> Hannah, bapt. 15 June 1760; m. at Westport, 13 Apr. 1780, Nathan Ogden, of Weston.
> Ephraim, bapt. 11 July 1762.
> Grace, bapt. 9 Sept. 1764, d. at Weston, 16 Apr. 1842 ae. 77 (g. s.).
> Rachel, bapt. 13 Nov. 1768, d. at Weston, 2 Mar., 1816 ae. 48 (g. s.); m. (rec. Weston) 2 June 1790, Ebenezer Coley, Jr.
> Abigail, bapt. 5 Aug. 1770, d. 23 Feb. 1772.
> Phebe, bapt. 7 Dec. 1771, d. 12 Dec. 1771.
> Abigail, b. [21 Aug. 1774?], bapt. 12 Dec. 1773, d. at Weston, 6 June 1844 ae. 69-9-16 (g. s.); m. at Weston, 25 Feb. 1798, Robert Sturges.
> Elihu, bapt. 8 Dec. 1776.

3. **Goodsell, Thomas**, s. of Rev. John.

Born 4 Dec. 1731; d. 13 July 1805.

He m. (1) Miriam Bradley, dau. of John, b. 5 Feb. 1736/7, d. 11 Dec. 1781.

He m. (2) Rhoda, widow of Isaac Sturges, and dau. of Benjamin Banks, bapt. 11 Oct. 1741, d. 2 Sept. 1811.

Will 24 Apr. 1805, proved 31 July 1805; wife Rhoda, Exec'x with my bro. Lewis; son Bradley; gr. dau. the wife of William Burr.

Adm'n on Est. of Rhoda granted, 9 Sept. 1811, to Banks Sturges, with Gershom Wakeman as surety.

Children [by first wife], rec. Greenfield:

> Hannah, b. and bapt. 16 Jan. 1758, d. 17 Jan. 1758 ae. 2 days.
> Sarah, b. and bapt. 20 Oct. 1760 ("untimely"), d. 7 Nov. 1760 ae. abt. 20 days.
> Bradley, bapt. 1 Jan. 1764 (ae. abt. 5 wks.), d. 1 Jan. 1816.
> Huldah, bapt. 1 June 1766, d. 28 Apr. 1778 in 13 yr.

4. **Goodsell, Epaphras,** s. of Rev. John.

Born 23 May 1742; bur. 4 Jan. 1801 ae. 58 (Trinity Church rec.).

He m. 5 Dec. 1765, Jane Bradley; dau. of Peter, b. 22 Mar. 1744/5.

Children, rec. Greenfield:

> Milly, bapt. 30 July 1767 (ae. abt. 13 mos., at home, sick), d. 4 Aug. 1767 ae. 13 mos.
> Amelia, b. 27 Mar., bapt. 3 Apr. 1768, d. 3 Mar. 1835 ae. 67 (g. s.); m. Ebenezer Burr.
> Medad, b. 4, bapt. 15 Apr. 1770.
> Ruamah, bapt. 12 July 1772, d. 16 Nov. 1858; m. Eli Wakeman.
> Rachel, bapt. 4 Dec. 1774.
> Epaphras, bapt. 24 May 1777.
> William, bapt. 24 Sept. 1780; m. at Trinity Church, 1 Jan. 1802, Prudence Nichols.

5. **Goodsell, Lewis,** s. of Rev. John. Lt., 8th Co., 4th Regt., May 1777; Capt. by 1793.

Born 23 Oct. 1744; d. at Weston, 22 Aug. 1829.

He m. (1) 2 Mar. 1767, Eunice Wakeman, b. 31 Oct. 1746, d. 11 July 1779 ae. 32 yrs. 9 mos. (g. s.).

He m. (2) 1 June 1780, Widow Sarah Sherwood. She was widow of Noah Sherwood, and dau. of Joseph Banks, b. 26 Dec. 1743, d. at Greenfield, 11 July 1809 ae. 67 (g. s.). For distribution of her estate, see Noah Sherwood (46).

He m. (3) Damaris ———.

Will 22 July 1827, proved 29 Aug. 1829; wife Damaris; to three sons, John, Lewis and Thomas, $80 in lieu of property I received that was their mother's; residue equally to five sons, Joel, George W., John, Lewis and Thomas.

Children [by first wife], rec. Greenfield:

John.
Lewis, b. and bapt. 28 Jan. 1770 (sick); m. 18 Jan. 1796, Debby Jennings, bapt. 20 Oct. 1776.*
Thomas, d. 26 Jan. 1852 (Miss Treadwell's book).
Eunice, bapt. 27 Feb. 1774, d. 25 Nov. 1774 ae. 9 mos.
Joel, bapt. 29 Oct. 1775; m. at Trinity Church, 6 Nov. 1796, Polly Kirtland.†
George-Washington, bapt. 29 Sept. 1777.

Children [by second wife], rec. Greenfield:

Eunice, bapt. Feb. 1781; m. J. Goodyear.
Mary (twin), bapt. Feb. 1781; doubtless the dau. who d. Feb. 1781 in infancy.
Joseph-Banks, bapt. 25 May 1783.

6. **Goodsell, Samuel,** s. of Rev. John.

Born 29 June 1746.

He m. 23 Jan. 1766, Phebe Davis; dau. of Joseph, b. 26 Nov. 1746.

Children, bapt. Greenfield:

Samuel, b. 25 June, bapt. 28 Dec. 1766; m. at Easton, Mar. 1790, Eunice Cable.‡
Stiles, bapt. 22 May 1768 (ae. abt. 1 mo.).
? Huldah, m. William Burr.

7. **Goodsell, James,** s. of Rev. John.

Born 24 Aug. 1749.

He m. 20 Dec. 1770, Esther Adair; dau. of James, b. 2 July 1749.

---

* Children, bapt. Fairfield: Lewis-Burr, bapt. 25 Mar. 1798; Henry, bapt. 5 Oct. 1800; Martha, bapt. 25 Sept. 1803. Wife of Lewis d. 21 June 1817 (Miss Treadwell's book). Wife of Lewis d. 2 Oct. 1831 (Miss Treadwell's book). One Lewis m. at Trinity Church, 18 Mar. 1810, Anna Squire.

† A Polly Goodsell of Redding m. 14 Sept. 1805, Diodate Ambler, of Danbury.

‡ Child, bapt. Trinity Church: Lettice-Lewis, bapt. 10 July 1791.

Children, bapt. Greenfield:*

Paulina, bapt. 16 Aug. 1772, d. 21 Mar. 1775 in 3 yr.
John-McPherson, bapt. 24 Mar. 1776 (named after the aide-de-camp of Gen. Montgomery who fell at Quebec).
James, bapt. 18 Oct. 1778, d. at Weston, 3 Dec. 1855 (Miss Treadwell's book); m. at Weston, 17 Sept. 1801, Mabel Smith of Greenfield.

8. **Goodsell, John,** s. of John, 2d.

Bapt. 24 June 1753; d. at Westport, 20 July 1814 ae. 61 (g. s.). He was called of Derby in 1784 in a Fairfield deed. His wife Anne owned the Covenant at Oxford, 6 June 1779.

Will 2 Feb., proved 27 July 1814; wife Anne; sons Silas, Bradley; daus. Charry Ann wife of Uriah Beers, Sally wife of Hezekiah Hull, Polly wife of Bradley Whitlock, Ellen wife of David Smith, and Harriet wife of Joel Thorp; son John of Weston; son Silas and Gideon Tomlinson, Exec'rs.

Children:

John, b. abt. 1774, d. at Weston, 18 Dec. 1823 ae. 49 (g. s.); m. (1) 17 May 1798, Rachel Meeker, b. [13 Sept. 1774], d. 26 Oct. 1811 ae. 37-1-13 (g. s.); m. (2) Sarah ———, who d. 21 Jan. 1859 ae. 81 (g. s.).†
Charry-Ann, b. [say 1777], bapt. at Oxford, 16 June 1779; m. in 1798, Uriah Beers.
Sarah, b. abt. 1779, bapt. at Oxford, 16 June 1779; d. at Westport, 17 Dec. 1847 ae. 68 (g. s.); m. 28 Feb. 1799, Hezekiah Hull.
Bradley, d. 19 Jan. 1857 (Miss Treadwell's book); m. at Weston, 3 Sept. 1803, Priscilla Ogden.
Polly, bapt. at Westport, 22 Apr. 1787; m. 4 July 1805, Bradley Whitlock, of Weston.
Ellen, bapt. at Westport, 26 Apr. 1789; m. 12 Feb. 1807, David Smith, of N. Y. State.
Silas, b. [15 July 1791], bapt. at Westport, 4 Dec. 1791, d. at Westport, 17 Sept. 1865 ae. 74-2-2 (g. s.); m. Sarah ———, who d. 4 June 1877 ae. 87 yrs. 9 mos. (g. s.).
Harriet, bapt. at Westport, 18 Oct. 1795; m. Joel Thorp.

---

* James Goodsell's boy "Drowned at"—[left blank, entered early in 1792 in Perry Diary].

† Adm'n on John's estate (the widow Sarah declining) was granted, 2 Jan. 1824, to Seth Taylor of Norwalk. Distribution to widow and five children, Ebenezer, Sheldon, John, Ambrose W., and Sally-Ann Goodsell. Children, bapt. Westport: Ebenezer, bapt. 22 Feb. 1801; Sheldon, bapt. 21 Jan. 1807. One Ebenezer d. 26 Dec. 1853 (Miss Treadwell's book).

THE FAMILIES OF OLD FAIRFIELD 387

Goodsell, David.

He d. 23 Apr. 1802.
He m. 27 Jan. 1777, Anna Beers; prob. dau. of Nathan, b. 17 Nov. 1756; wife of David d. 5 Apr. 1810.

Children, bapt. Greenfield:
    Ulilla, bapt. 8 Feb. 1776(?), d. 4 Mar. 1814; m. Stephen Sherwood.
    David, bapt. 20 Jan. 1779, d. 23 Jan. 1779.

Goodsell [Unplaced].

—— m. Elizabeth-Ruth Morehouse, bapt. 10 Nov. 1771.
HANNAH m. Hezekiah Hull of Redding, b. 22 Oct. 1768.
CAROLINE d. 9 May 1823. [Greenfield Church]
ELIZABETH, bur. 13 July 1809 ae. 65. [Trinity Church]
EMILY d. 24 June 1809 (Miss Treadwell's book).

Gorham [Plymouth].

This is the earliest family found which carried a "Mayflower line" into Fairfield.
1. JOHN GORHAM, Capt. in K. Philip's War; res. Plymouth, Marshfield, Yarmouth, and Barnstable; d. 5 Feb. 1675/6 in war service; m. 1643 Desire Howland, dau. of John, Mayflower Pilgrim. Of his children,—
2 James (1650-1707); m. 1674 Hannah Huckins (1653-1728). Children:
    Desire (1675-   ); m. —— Sturgis.
    James (1677-1718); res. Barnstable; m. 1707 Mary Joyce.
    Experience (1678-1733); m. 1697 Thomas Lothrop.
    John (1680-1729); res. W. Yarmouth; m. 1706 Ann Brown.
    Mehitabel (1683-   ); m. 1715 John Oldham; res. Scituate.
    Thomas (1684-1771); res. Barnstable; m. 1707 Rachel Trott.
    Mercy (1686-d. y.).
    Joseph (1689-1762), unm.
  6+Jabez (1691-   ).
  7+Sylvanus (1693-   ).
    Ebenezer (1696-1776); res. Barnstable; m. 1727 Temperance Hawes.
3 John (1652-1716); m. 1674 Mary Otis. One child was:
  8 John (1688-1770); res. Barnstable; m. 1712 Prudence Crocker, and had:
    12+Joseph (1713-   ).
4 Joseph (1654-1726); res. Yarmouth; m. 1678 Sarah Sturgis. One child was:
  9+Joseph (1681-1742).
5 Jabez (1656-1725); m. Hannah (Sturgis) Gray. Children:
    Hannah (1677-1682).
    Samuel (1682-1735).
    Jabez (1684-1745); m. twice.
    Shubael (1686-1734).
    Isaac (1689-1740); founder of New Haven branch.
    John (1690-1717).
  10+Joseph (1692-1773).
    Hannah (1694-   ); m. —— Downs.
    Benjamin (1695-1771/2); m. Bethia Cary.
    Elizabeth (-   ); m. Shubael Baxter.
    Thomas (1701-   ).

6. Gorham, Jabez, s. of James.

Born at Barnstable, Mass., 6 Mar., 1690/1, d. by 1739; settled in Fairfield by 1721; m. Molly ———, with whom he renewed Covenant at Westport Church, 8 Feb. 1733.

David, son of Jabez dec'd, chose Joseph Gorham of Fairfield for guardian, 5 Mar. 1739.

Children, bapt. Fairfield:

11+James.
- David, bapt. 24 Feb. 1722/3; of Plymouth, Mass., conveyed 1769 land in Fairfield; m. at Plymouth, 11 July 1751, Abigail Jackson, dau. of Nathaniel and Rebecca (Poor) Jackson, of Plymouth.
- Jabez, bapt. Oct. 1725, d. at Liverpool, Nova Scotia, 13 Dec. 1806 in 80 yr. (g. s.); of New Liverpool, Queens County, Nova Scotia, conveyed 1769 land in Fairfield; m. at Plymouth, 15 Nov. 1750, Mary Burbank, dau. of Timothy and Mercy (Kempton) Burbank, b. in 1730, d. 11 Sept. 1811 ae. 81 (g. s.).
- John, bapt. 12 May 1728.

7. Gorham, Sylvanus, s. of James.

Born at Barnstable, Mass., 13 Oct. 1693; d. at Stamford in 1747. He lived a short time in Fairfield.

Inv. taken at Stamford, 28 Sept. 1747; George Gorham, Adm'r. Distribution to bros. and sisters or their legal representatives: heirs of James Gorham dec'd; heirs of John Gorham dec'd; Thomas Gorham; Joseph Gorham; heirs of Jabez Gorham; Ebenezer Gorham; heirs of Experience dec'd; heirs of Mehitabel dec'd.

9. Gorham, Joseph, s. of Joseph. Capt.

Born at Yarmouth, Mass., 15 Apr. 1681; d. at Stratford, 24 Apr. 1742 ae. 60 (g. s.).

He m. (1) 9 Nov. 1708, Sarah Kirk, who d. at Stratford, 18 Apr. 1722 in 37 yr. (g. s.).

He m. (2) Temperance Norton, dau. of David, b. 16 Mar. 1697, d. 1743.

Distribution 2 July 1750; to Joseph; to George in his own right and as assignee of John, Samuel, and Hezekiah; to Benjamin.

Children [by first wife], rec. Stratford:
- Mary, m. (rec. New Haven) 27 Apr. 1730, Daniel Munson.
- Joseph, b. 17 Nov. 1712; m. Hannah ———.
- George, m. Hannah, prob. dau. of John and Mary (Judson) Welles, b. 14 Apr. 1718.

Elizabeth, b. 1 Nov. 1716, d. 23 Nov. 1716.
John, b. 20 July 1718.

Children [by second wife], rec. Stratford:

Samuel, b. 15 July 1724; m. 8 Dec. 1747, Ann Greenman, dau. of Jeremiah, b. 21 Mar. 1726.
Hezekiah, b. 29 Mar. 1728.
Benjamin, b. 17 Nov. 1733.

10. **Gorham, Joseph**, s. of Jabez.

Born at Bristol, R. I., 22 Aug. 1692; d. at Westport, 19 Jan. 1773.

He came to Stratford, where he was known as Jr. to distinguish him from Capt. Joseph; there m. (1) 7 Apr. 1715 [or 11 May 1715, by Fairfield rec.], Abigail Lockwood; dau. of Daniel, b. 28 May 1694, d. at Fairfield, 23 Jan. 1724/5 ae. 31 (g. s.). He soon rem. to Fairfield, and m. (2) 13 Jan. 1725/6, Deborah Barlow; dau. of John, b. 10 Jan. 1705/6, d. at Westport, 25 Jan. 1778.

Children [by first wife], first rec. Stratford, rest at Fairfield:

Hannah, b. 10 Mar. 1715/6, d. y.
Daniel, b. and bapt. 10 Nov. 1717, d. 10 Sept. 1787 (Perry Diary), unm. Adm'n granted to Shubael and Joseph Gorham, 1 Oct. 1787. Distribution ordered to the heirs of Jabez Gorham (Martha, Abigail, Rachel, Jabez, Ellen); Lockwood Gorham; and Ichabod Gorham.
13+Jabez, b. and bapt. 22 Mar. 1718/9.
14+Lockwood, b. 1, bapt. 15 Jan. 1720/1.
Joseph, bapt. 25 Feb. 1721/2, d. y.
Shubael, bapt. 15 Sept. 1723, d. y.
15+Ichabod, b. and bapt. 31 Jan. 1724/5.

Children [by second wife], rec. and bapt. Fairfield:

16+Shubael, b. 28 Oct., bapt. 6 Nov. 1726.
Abigail, b. 7, bapt. 28 Apr. 1728, perhaps d. 6 Sept. 1792 (Perry Diary).
17+Isaac, b. 14, bapt. 30 Nov. 1729.
18+John, b. 4, bapt. 16 July 1732.
Hannah, b. 4, bapt. 8 May 1737.
Mary, b. 25, bapt. 30 Dec. 1739, d. at Westport, 19 Aug. 1804 ae. 65; m. (1) at Westport, 24 Mar. 1761, John Sherwood; m. (2) 23 Feb. 1783, William Raymond.
19+Joseph, b. 20 Nov. 1741.
Abigail, b. 7 Apr. 1744, bapt. at Westport, 15 Apr. 1744, d. 1 or 10 Sept. 1789 ae. 45 (g. s.); m. at Westport, 17 Nov. 1763, Daniel Meeker.

11. Gorham, James, s. of Jabez.

He d. 9 Oct. 1748.

He m. at Greenfield, Apr. 1744, Miriam Hull, dau. of Eliphalet, b. 20 Dec. 1724, Widow Miriam Gorham, who d. 4 Aug. 1770 (Perry Diary).

Will of Miriam, 13 June 1770, proved 4 Sept. 1770; son Jabez; dau. Mary. Adm'n was granted to John Hull, 4 Sept. 1770.

Children, rec. Greenfield:

> Mary, b. and bapt. 18 Mar. 1744/5, d. 19 Mar. 1744/5 ae. abt. 24 hours.
> Jabez, b. Apr., bapt. 27 Apr. 1746; chose John Hull for guardian, May 1760; res. 1774 and 1786, Ballston, N. Y.; m. at Westport, 19 Sept. 1771, Mary Oysterbanks; dau. of Isaac, bapt. 10 Dec. 1752.*
> Mary, b. Nov., bapt. 22 Nov. 1747, d. at Greenfield, 22 May 1781 ae. 33 (g. s.); m. 8 Jan. 1766, Joseph Rumsey.

12. Gorham, Joseph, s. of John.

Born at Barnstable, Mass., 25 Aug. 1713, d. at Norwalk in 1760; m. 8 Dec. 1737, Abigail Lovell.

His children Theodate and Rachel were presented for baptism by Joseph Gorham of Greens Farms Parish, as children of Joseph and Abigail dec'd of Norwalk.

Children:

> Theodate, bapt. 29 June 1760.
> Rachel, bapt. 29 June 1760, d. 19 Sept. 1760.
> Others.

13. Gorham, Jabez, s. of Joseph.

Bapt. 22 Mar. 1718/9; d. at Westport, 26 Feb. 1764 in 46 yr. (g. s.); m. 27 Nov. 1752, Mary Couch, dau. of Benjamin, bapt. 15 Nov. 1732. Widow Mary Gorham m. at Weston, 1 Oct. 1766, David Couch, and d. 26 Mar. 1822 ae. 89 (g. s.).

Children, rec. Fairfield, bapt. Westport:

> Martha, b. 13, bapt. 19 Aug. 1753, d. at Westport, 17 Sept. 1788 ae. 35 yrs. 1 mo. 4 days (g. s.).
> Mary, b. 29 Nov. 1754, bapt. 5 Jan. 1755, d. 28 June 1763.

---

* Child of Jabez and Molly, rec. Greenfield: Sarah, b. 1 Jan., bapt. 28 Feb. 1773. Isaac, son of Jabez Gorham of Bealston [Ballston, N. Y.], bapt. at Westport, 27 Nov. 1785.

THE FAMILIES OF OLD FAIRFIELD 391

Lydia, b. 29 May, bapt. 11 July 1756.
Abigail, bapt. 28 May 1758, d. at Greenfield, 5 Sept. 1792 ae. 33 (g. s.); m. 3 July 1791, Joseph Gorham.
Rachel, bapt. 2 Nov. 1760, d. 15 June 1795.
Jabez, bapt. 23 May 1762, d. 25 June 1853; m. (1) 15 Aug. 1784, Sarah Morgan, dau. of James, who d. 9 Mar. 1797; m. (2) 22 May 1797, Hannah Beers.*
Eleanor, b. [7 Feb. 1764], bapt. at Weston, 17 Feb. 1765, d. 28 June 1789 ae. 25 yrs. 4 mos. 21 days (g. s.).

14. Gorham, Lockwood, s. of Joseph.

Born 1 Jan. 1720/1; d. at Fairfield in 1791.
He m. 20 or 21 Sept. 1742, Abigail Meeker, dau. of David, b. 10 June 1725, d. at Greenfield, 28 Aug. 1777.
Adm'n granted to Joseph Gorham, 10 Feb. 1791.

Children, rec. Fairfield and Greenfield:

David, b. 1, bapt. 22 Jan. 1743/4; res. New Fairfield, 1779; ? m. at Easton, 25 Mar. 1770, Abigail Cable; dau. of Daniel, b. 22 Nov. 1751.
Hannah, b. 27, bapt. 29 Sept. 1745; m. 28 Jan. 1768, Gilbert Hunt.
Lockwood, b. 9, bapt. 15 Nov. 1747, d. at Danbury, 3 June 1812 ae. 64; m. Thankful ———, who d. 5 June 1812 ae. 68 (g. s.).†
Elizabeth, b. 4 Jan. 1749/50, d. at Redding, 3 Aug. 1794; m. at Westport, 19 Feb. 1772, Daniel Perry of Redding.
Daniel, b. 9 Oct., bapt. Oct. 1752, d. 14 Jan. 1777.
Joseph, b. 18 June 1755, d. at Greenfield, 18 Oct. 1833 ae. 78 (g. s.); Dr.; m. (1) 3 July 1791, Abigail Gorham of Norwalk, bapt. 28 May 1758, d. 5 Sept. 1792 ae. 33 (g. s.); m. (2) Polly ———.‡
Meeker, bapt. 19 Feb. 1758, d. 11 June 1832 ae. 74; m. 24 Aug. 1780, Elizabeth Hubbell, dau. of Gershom, b. 10 Mar. 1759.
Hezekiah, bapt. 13 July 1760 (ae. abt. 10 days).
Timothy, bapt. 13 Mar. 1763 (ae. abt. 2 weeks), d. 20 Feb. 1766 ae. 3 (wanting a week) (g. s.).
Seth, b. 11, bapt. 17 Nov. 1765.
Abigail, b. 31 July, bapt. 18 Sept. 1768, d. at Westport, 12 Dec. 1849 ae. 81 yrs. 4 mos. (g. s.); m. at Westport, 21 Aug. 1788, Ralph Sherwood.

---

* Children by first wife, rec. Redding: Lydia, b. 26 Nov. 1785; Polly, b. 28 Jan. 1787; Patty, b. 14 Feb. 1790; Jabez, b. 24 Dec. 1793. Children by second wife: Sally, b. 15 Jan. 1798; Marietta, b. 1 Jan. 1800, d. at Greenfield, 12 May 1815; m. 11 Dec. 1814, Lyman Monroe.

† Adm'n granted, 8 June 1812, to Isaac Wilson of New Fairfield. Distribution: eldest dau. Mercy wife of Zar Barnum; youngest dau. Thankful wife of Daniel Barnum.

‡ Joseph, son of Joseph Gorham, bapt. at Westport, 2 Sept. 1793, d. at Greenfield, 30 June 1827 in 35 yr. (g. s.). Joseph's will, 20 Aug. 1833, proved 20 Nov. 1833; legacy to Lydia Redfield; wife Polly; Gershom Wakeman, Exec'r.

15. Gorham, Ichabod, s. of Joseph.

Bapt. 31 Jan. 1724/5; d. at Roxbury, 19 Aug. 1799 ae. 77.

He m. 2 Feb. 1748/9, Sarah Barlow, dau. of George, b. 28 Mar. 1732, d. 17 Nov. 1805 ae. 79.

He bought a farm in Ridgefield, 1757, and sold it 1767, removing to Roxbury. Ichabod of Ridgefield conveyed Fairfield property from deceased mother Abigail, to Lockwood Gorham, 1763.

Children, bapt. Westport:

> Daniel, bapt. 29 Nov. 1749.
> Benjamin, bapt. 24 Dec. 1752; res. Danbury; m. Amy Combs.
> Joseph, bapt. 15 Dec. 1754, d. at Westport, 22 Aug. 1806 ae. 54; m. at Weston, 11 June 1775, Mary Roberts; dau. of John, b. 22 May 1754; prob. d. at Westport, 25 Mar. 1816 ae. 61.
> Phineas, bapt. 17 Apr. 1757, d. 2 Feb. 1842; m. Rachel ———, who d. 16 Sept. 1816.
> Seth, b. at Danbury, 18 Jan. 1762 (his Bible rec.),* d. at West Rutland, Vt., 29 Aug. 1852; m. (1) Amelia Dunks, b. at Danbury, 29 Mar. 1763, d. 17 Oct. 1841; m. (2) in 1842, Louisa Everson.
> Daniel, b. abt. 1766, d. at Roxbury, 25 Jan. 1836 ae. 70.

16. Gorham, Shubael, s. of Joseph.

Born 28 Oct. 1726; d. at Westport, 20 Nov. 1807 in 82 yr. (g. s.); m. (1) 22 Jan. 1746/7, Rebecca Hurlbut, dau. of Gideon, b. abt. 1728, d. 27 Feb. 1799 in 71 yr. (g. s.); m. (2) 8 Sept. 1799, Abigail, widow of Samuel Morehouse and Jabez Raymond; dau. of Isaac Frost, b. [Sept. 1723], d. 9 Dec. 1800 ae. 77 yrs. 3 mos. (g. s.); m. (3) at Weston, 21 Jan. 1801, Mary Finch; she was widow of John Finch, and previously of Samuel Ogden, and dau. of Benjamin Banks, bapt. 18 Apr. 1736.

Lydia (a child born at Shubael Gorham's and left there to be brought up), b. 14 Dec. 1763.

Shubael Gorham of Weston conveyed 1793 for love to dau. Rebeccah, "in part of portion for her present settlement."

Adm'n granted, 21 Mar. 1808, to David Coley, with Hezekiah Nichols as surety.

---

* As it has been given in print; but his pension application gives his birth at New Fairfield, 18 July 1763, states that he enlisted 1777 ae. 14, and that he was ae. 69 in July 1832.

Children [by first wife], rec. Fairfield, bapt. Westport:

    Stephen, b. 19, bapt. 27 Dec. 1747; res. 1787, Lansingburgh, Albany County, N. Y.; m. at Weston, 27 May 1767, Sarah Sturges; dau. of Jeremiah, bapt. 5 June 1748; she m. (2) at Weston, 29 Sept. 1805, Joseph Bennett.

20+Ebenezer, b. 1 Sept., bapt. 29 Nov. 1749.

    Shubael, b. 4 July, bapt. 13 Sept. 1752; m. Abigail Coley, dau. of Ebenezer, b. 5 July 1764.

    Rebecca, bapt. at Weston, 20 Feb. 1759; m. at Weston, 6 Aug. 1775, John Hanford.

17. Gorham, Isaac, s. of Joseph.

Born 14 Nov. 1729; d. at Redding, 14 July 1798 ae. 67-8-10 (g. s.).

He m. 25 July 1752, Ann Wakeman, dau. of Joseph, b. 24 Oct. 1728, d. 11 June 1807 ae. 78 (g. s.).

Will 27 Sept. 1797, proved 17 July 1798; wife Anne; dau. Hannah Andrews; gr. dau. Anna wife of Lazarus Hull; gr. dau. Sally Reed, 2d dau. of Hezekiah Reed; Ulily Read, 3d dau. of Hezekiah; gr. son Hezekiah Read, Jr.; son Isaac.

Will of Anna, 9 Feb. 1799, proved 20 June 1807; son Isaac Gorham; dau. Hannah wife of Ebenezer Andrus; gr. dau. Anna wife of Lazarus Hull; gr. dau. Sarah wife of Sturges Sanford; gr. dau. Lilly Read; gr. son Hezekiah Read, Jr.; gr. son Joseph W. Gorham.

Children, rec. Fairfield, bapt. Westport:

    Hannah, b. 15 Nov., bapt. 3 Dec. 1752, d. in 1826; m. (1) at Redding, 24 Jan. 1773, Lazarus Wheeler; m. (2) June 1781, Ebenezer Andrews; m. (3) James Hubbell.*

    Ann, b. 29 Sept., bapt. 17 Nov. 1754, d. at Redding, 3 Feb. 1785 ae. 31 (g. s.); m. at Redding, 14 May 1775, Hezekiah Read.

    Isaac, b. 15 Nov. 1761, bapt. at Redding, 24 Jan. 1762, d. at Redding, 4 May 1813 ae. 51-5-19 (g. s.); m. 4 Mar. 1780, Sarah Morgan,

---

* The will of Hannah Hubbell of Fairfield, 26 Apr. 1826, proved 13 Dec. 1826; estate to Hezekiah Read, Joseph W. Gorham, Isaac Gorham, Anne wife of Lazarus Hull, Anne wife of Walter Whitlock, Sally widow of Lanson Sanford (and her daus. Eliza and Polly), Hannah wife of Hiram Couch, Polly wife of Nash Couch; Adela wife of Arzy Meeker.

dau. of John, b. 21 Oct. 1763, d. 7 Jan. 1836 ae. 72-2-16 (g. s.). His will, 23 Jan. 1810, proved 19 May 1813; wife Sarah; two sons, Joseph-Wakeman, Isaac; five daus. Anna, Sally, Hannah, Polly, Delia.*

18. Gorham, John, s. of Joseph.

Born 4 July 1732; d. at Kent abt. 1805; m. 5 Oct. 1754, Abigail Wakeman, dau. of Joseph, b. 19 Dec. 1735. She d. at Kent abt. 1810. They rem. to New Fairfield, and 1781 to Kent.

Adm'n granted, 13 Jan. 1806, to Joseph Gorham and Timothy St. John.

Will of Abigail, 2 Oct. 1805, proved 24 Jan. 1811; daus. Deborah, Abigail, Lucy; sons John, James, Seth, Jeremiah [Jared], Wakeman, Hezekiah, Joseph.

Children, two rec. Fairfield, four bapt. Westport:

Deborah, b. 10 Mar., bapt. 27 Apr. 1755; m. Timothy St. John.
John, b. 22 May, bapt. 20 June 1756; res. 1808, Bakersfield, Vt.
James, bapt. 28 May 1758; res. 1808 and 1821, Poultney, Vt.
Seth, b. 6 June 1760 (Pension rec.), bapt. 8 June 1760; res. Castleton, Vt., 1821 and 1833; m. Betsey Thompson, dau. of Eleazer.
Jared, bapt. at Weston, 27 June 1762; res. Ira, 1821.
Wakeman, res. Chittenden, Vt.; m. Polly ———.
Abigail, d. y.
Abigail, b. 19 July 1770, d. 23 Dec. 1842; m. 16 June 1788, Solomon Comstock.
Hezekiah.
Lucy.
Joseph, b. abt. 1780; res. Pa.; m. Lucy Beecher.

19. Gorham, Joseph, s. of Joseph.

Born 20 Nov. 1741; d. at Westport, 8 July 1779 in 40 yr. (g. s.). He was accidentally shot by his own gun, getting over a fence.

He m. 16 Nov. 1763, Mary Gray; dau. of Samuel, b. 8 Mar. 1746, d. 25 Sept. 1825 ae. 79 (g. s.). She m. (2) Asher Taylor; (3) 25 July 1790, Ebenezer Godfrey; and (4) 16 Mar. 1797, Ebenezer Coley.

---

* Children, rec. Redding: Anna, b. 1 Sept. 1782; perhaps m. Walter Whitlock. Sally, b. 20 Sept. 1784; m. 30 Jan. 1815, Alanson Sanford. Joseph-Wakeman, b. 17 Mar. 1788, d. 29 July 1866 ae. 78-4-12 (g. s.); m. Eliza ———, who d. 7 Aug. 1879 ae. 88 yrs. 5 mos. (g. s.). Hannah, b. 17 Aug. 1790; m. Hiram Couch. Polly, b. 4 June 1796; m. Nash Couch. Delia, m. Arza Meeker. Isaac.

Distribution dated 24 Oct. 1787, proved 25 Feb. 1797; relict Mary now wife of Asher Taylor; eldest son Samuel; dau. Abigail Gorham; dau. Mary Gorham; youngest son Joseph-Barlow Gorham. Mary Taylor was allowed guardian to Joseph-Barlow, 15 July 1790.

Will of Mary Coley of Weston, 7 Jan. 1817, proved 6 Oct. 1825; son Samuel Gorham; son Joseph B. Gorham; son Jared Taylor; daus. Abigail and Polly; Seth Taylor of Norwalk, Exec'r.

Children, bapt. Westport:

>Samuel, bapt. 23 June 1765, d. at Westport, 8 Apr. 1842 ae. 76 yrs. 11 mos. (g. s.); m. 21 Nov. 1782, Phebe Buffet, b. [30 Sept. 1766], d. 16 Aug. 1855 ae. 88 yrs. 10 mos. 17 days (g. s.).*
>Abigail, bapt. 24 May 1767, d. at Pawling, Dutchess County, N. Y., 26 July 1850 ae. 83; m. 13 Nov. 1783, Stephen Adams.
>Mary, bapt. 12 May 1771; ? m. at Kent, 20 Dec. 1790, Joshua Converse.
>Joseph-Barlow, bapt. 25 June 1775; m. 16 Nov. 1793, Abigail Stratton; dau. of Cornelius, bapt. 2 May 1773.†
>Son, bapt. 18, d. 19 Aug. 1777.

20. Gorham, Ebenezer, s. of Shubael.

Born 1 Sept. 1749; d. at Westport, 23 Jan. 1807 ae. 58; m. at Weston, 31 Jan. 1770, Martha Lyon; prob. dau. of David, b. 3 Aug. 1751; d. at Westport, 10 Aug. 1822 ae. 73.

Adm'n on Est. of Widow Martha granted, 17 Sept. 1822, to Peter Wynkoop, with Thomas F. Rowland surety.

Children:

>Hannah, bapt. at Weston, 31 Mar. 1771.
>David-Lyon, bapt. at Weston, 16 May 1773, drowned at North River, 16 Aug. 1798 ae. 24.
>Ebenezer, bapt. at Westport, 3 July 1775.‡
>William, bapt. at Weston, 8 Feb. 1778, d. at Westport, 17 Oct. 1802 ae. 25.
>Stephen, bapt. at Westport, 7 May 1780;§ m. 20 Mar. 1799, Rhoda Cable, of New York.

---

* Children, bapt. Westport: Betsey, b. [30 Nov. 1783], bapt. 22 Mar. 1784, d. 4 June 1865 ae. 81-6-4 (g. s.); Samuel, bapt. 20 Aug. 1786; Stephen, bapt. 3 May 1789; Isaac, bapt. 28 May 1791; Phebe, bapt. 6 Apr. 1794, d. 21 Aug. 1804 ae. 10-6-11 (g. s.).

† Children, bapt. Westport: Joseph, bapt. 3 May 1795; Polly, bapt. 5 Mar. 1797.

‡ Child, bapt. Westport: Martha, bapt. 16 Nov. 1800.

§ Stephen L. Gorham, a young man, drowned between West Indies and New York, Sept. 1804 (Greens Farms Church). Samuel, son of Joseph (19) also had a son Stephen.

Rebecca, bapt. at Westport, 18 Aug. 1782; m. 24 Apr. 1803, Elias Betts, of Wilton.
Sarah, bapt. at Westport, 12 Dec. 1784; m. 1 May 1804, David Hutternock.
Lewis, bapt. at Westport, 20 Apr. 1788; m. Anna Lyon, dau. of Ephraim, bapt. 22 Dec. 1790.
Martha, bapt. at Westport, 31 July 1791, d. 8 Dec. 1794.
Abigail, bapt. at Westport, 10 Nov. 1793.

Gorham [Unplaced].

JOB, of Barnstable, m. 24 Nov. 1735, Bethia Freeman.
LYDIA, b. [24 May 1764], d. at Westport, 7 Sept. 1851 ae. 87-5-14 (g. s.); m. 9 Oct. 1783, John Andrews.
JOHN, b. abt. 1777, d. 24 May 1821 ae. 44; m. 10 Mar. 1803, Ruth Ogden. [Greens Farms Church]
POLLY d. 21 June 1813 ae. 21. [Greens Farms Church]

Grant, Darius.

Born abt. 1765; d. at Greenfield, 20 May 1810 ae. 45 (g. s.).

Adm'n granted, 7 June 1810, to Gershom Wakeman, with Buckingham Sherwood as surety.

Widow Esther d. at Greenfield, 23 July 1836 ae. 67 (church record).

Joseph Grant d. at Greenfield, 18 Oct. 1833 ae. 78 (g. s.).

Gray [Vol. I, pp. 232-234].

```
1 Henry (    -1658) m. Lydia Frost.
    2 Jacob (    -1712) m. (1) Joanna Smith; (2) Sarah (———) Bartram.
(By 2): 4 Jacob (1681-1742).
        5 Joseph (1683-    ).
    3 Henry (1653-1731) m. (1) ———; (2) Hannah (Sanford) Gunn; (3) Margaret ———.
(By 1): 6 Isaac (    -1745).
        7 Henry (    -1713).
        8 William (    -1761).
(By 2): 9 Samuel (1704-    ).
```

4. Gray, Jacob, s. of Jacob.

Born 10 Dec. 16[81], d. at Greenfield, 26 Dec. 1742 ae. abt. 61; m. Hannah Seeley, dau. of Lt. Nathaniel, b. 10 July 1683.

Will 21 Oct. 1742, proved 13 Jan. 1742/3; wife Hannah; daus. Hannah, Sarah, Rebecca, and Eunice, £10 each; dau. Mary, £20; son Jacob, west part of dwelling house; sons Nathaniel, John, and

James, the east half of house; wife, and sons Nathaniel and John, Exec'rs. Distribution of lands, 26 Oct. 1743, to the heirs of Nathaniel (one of the sons) and to James, John, and Jacob.

Jacob was bapt. at Greenfield, 5 June 1726, and a week later all the children except the eldest and youngest were bapt. there. The eldest dau. Hannah had been bapt. at Fairfield, 1 Apr. 1722.

Children:
    Hannah, b. [say 1703].
10+Nathaniel, b. [say 1704].
    Sarah, b. [say 1706], d. prob. 17 Nov. 1784 (Perry Diary); m. 1 Jan. 1730, Benjamin Smith.
11+John, b. abt. 1708.
12+James, b. Sept. 1710.
13+Jacob, b. abt. 1712.
    Rebecca, b. [say 1714].
    Eunice, b. [say 1716]; m. William Mallory.
    Mary, bapt. 16 Mar. 1728/9; ? m. 19 Sept. 1747, Samuel Coley.

5. Gray, Joseph, s. of Jacob.

Born [say 1683]; rem. to Newtown; m. Sarah ———.

He, "now of Newtown," was bapt. at Fairfield with the eldest three children, 30 May 1714.

Children, first two rec. Fairfield, all rec. Newtown:
    Joseph, b. 15 Nov. 1706.
    Sarah, b. 10 Sept. 1708.
    Mary, b. 7 Mar. 1713.
    Jonathan, b. 21 Mar. 1715, bapt. at Fairfield, 7 Aug. 1715.
    Ann, b. 14 Feb. 1722/3.

6. Gray, Isaac, s. of Henry.

He d. at Westport, 7 Nov. 1745.

It was prob. his widow or dau. Rebecca who m. at Greenfield, 18 May 1748, Edward Lacy.

Children, four bapt. Fairfield:
    Sarah, bapt. 27 Nov. 1709.
14+Nathan, bapt. 13 Apr. 1712.
    Deborah, bapt. 13 June 1714; m. at Redding, 28 Dec. 1743, Matthew Rowley.
    Rebecca, bapt. 13 June 1714.
    Mary, d. at Westport, 9 Mar. 1760; m. 7 June 1743, Joshua Disbrow.

7. Gray, Henry, s. of Henry, 2d.

Inv. of Est. of Henry Gray, Jr., of Compo, who d. 29 May 1713. Sarah, wife of Henry, Jr., was bapt. at Fairfield, 16 Feb. 1706/7. The probate rec. shows that he left widow Elizabeth and two children, whose birth dates are stated. William Gray was appointed guardian to Benjamin and Elizabeth, 1719. Benjamin of Fairfield receipted 19 Nov. 1728 to uncle William Gray for portion from Est. of father Henry dec'd; and on 28 Apr. 1732, being then of Wallingford, receipted for portion from Est. of gr. father Henry Gray dec'd.

Child [by first wife], bapt. Fairfield:
> Benjamin, b. 28 Apr. 1707, bapt. 1 June 1707; m. at Wallingford, 10 May 1731, Mary Bellamy, dau. of Matthew.

Child [by second wife], bapt. Fairfield:
> Elizabeth, b. 21 May 1711, bapt. 27 Apr. 1712.

8. Gray, William, s. of Henry.

He d. at Westport, 27 Aug. 1761.

He m. (1) 23 Dec. 1714, Abigail Coley; dau. of Samuel; she d. abt. 1715.

He m. (2) 31 Oct. 1716, Elizabeth Meeker; dau. of John, bapt. 29 Mar. 1696, d. 6 July 1772.

Will 5 May 1759, proved 7 Sept. 1761; wife Elizabeth; eldest son Stephen; sons Ebenezer, Jabez, Thaddeus; four sons, William, Joseph, Elisha, Joshua; two of my sons, Joseph and Elisha, are now from Home and supposed at sea and on board a Man of Warr or King's Ship; wife and son William, Exec'rs. A partial distribution, Dec. 1772, was made to son William, heirs of dec'd son Joshua, heirs of Joseph, and son Elisha.

Child [by first wife], rec. Fairfield:
15+Stephen, b. 7 Nov. 1715.

Children [by second wife], rec. Fairfield:
16+William, b. 17 Aug. 1717.
   Abigail, b. 7 May 1719.
   Elizabeth, b. 12 Apr. 1721.
17+Ebenezer, b. 29 Mar. 1723.

18+Jabez, b. 11 Oct. 1728.
19+Thaddeus, b. 27 Oct. 1730.
Joseph, b. 11 Oct. 1732; d. before 1771.
20+Elisha, b. 1 June 1735.
Joshua, b. 22 Sept. 1738; res. Stamford, 1771, when he conveyed to bro. William Gray of Fairfield, right from estates of father William and bro. Joseph; m. at Stamford, 20 May 1766, Elizabeth Dibble.*

9. **Gray, Samuel,** s. of Henry.

Bapt. 25 June 1704.

He m. (1) 24 Oct. 1734, Eleanor Sturgis, dau. of Christopher, b. 19 Oct. 1704, d. 4 Feb. 1762 in 58 yr. (g. s.); m. (2) 19 June 1763, Joanna Stone of Providence, who d. 15 Jan. 1770.

Hezekiah Gray conveyed 1764 to father Samuel Gray, land in Compo for life; also to mother-in-law Johanna Gray for life.

Samuel and Hezekiah Gray of Bedford, N. Y., conveyed land at Compo, 1770.

Children [by first wife], rec. Fairfield, bapt. Westport:

Sanford, b. 23 Sept., d. 23 Nov. 1735.
Hannah, b. 12 Nov. 1736,† m. 28 Apr. 1762, Sylvanus Francher, of Stamford.
21+Hezekiah, b. 14 Nov. 1738.
Samuel, b. 10, bapt. 11 July 1742, d. in New Providence, 3 Nov. 1760.
Sarah, b. 11, bapt. 12 Feb. 1743/4, d. at Bedford, N. Y., 4 Apr. 1814; m. 2 Mar. 1763, Gabriel Higgins, of Bedford, N. Y.
Mary, b. 8, bapt. 16 Mar. 1746, d. at Westport, 25 Sept. 1825 ae. 79 (g. s.); m. (1) 16 Nov. 1763, Joseph Gorham, Jr.; m. (2) Asher Taylor; m. (3) 25 July 1790, Ebenezer Godfrey; m. (4) 16 Mar. 1797, Ebenezer Coley, of Weston.

10. **Gray, Nathaniel,** s. of Jacob, 2d.

He d. at Redding, 2 Jan. 1742(?).

He m. Elizabeth Gilbert, dau. of Obadiah, bapt. 8 Sept. 1700; she m. (2) —— Porter, of Danbury.

Will of Nathaniel of Redding, 27 Apr. 1741, proved 1 Aug. 1743; wife Elizabeth; children Ebenezer, Obadiah, Elizabeth, Abigail; bro. John Gray of Norwalk, and wife, Exec'rs. Distri-

---

* Child, rec. Stamford: Abigail, b. 9 Feb. 1769.
† John Nott, son of Hannah Gray, bapt. 25 Dec. 1757.

bution 4 Jan. 1744/5; widow; Ebenezer; Obadiah; Elizabeth Gray. A later additional distribution was made to Ebenezer and Obadiah Gray (minors) and Elizabeth wife of Thomas "Pary" of Danbury.

Elizabeth Porter of Danbury, with eldest son Ebenezer Gray of Fairfield, conveyed 1761.

Children, first three bapt. Greenfield:

> Elizabeth, bapt. 29 Jan. 1729/30; m. Thomas Perry, of Danbury, with whom she conveyed 1756 to Ebenezer Gray, land from gr. father Jacob Gray dec'd.
> Abigail, bapt. 5 Aug. 1731, d. at Greenfield, Mar. 1745. Adm'n granted to James Gray, 28 Jan. 1752.
> Ebenezer, bapt. 4 May 1735; conveyed 1761 (as did also Thomas and Elizabeth Perry of Danbury) to mother Elizabeth Porter, their right in her dower from estate of their father Nathaniel that was distributed to bro. Obadiah Gray dec'd.
> Obadiah, bapt. at Redding, 9 Mar. 1740; chose James Gray for guardian, Apr. 1755; d. before 1761, unm.

11. **Gray, John,** s. of Jacob, 2d.

Born abt. 1708, d. at Redding, 16 May 1755 ae. abt. 47; m. 19 Sept. 1730, Hannah Scribner; dau. of Benjamin of Norwalk.

Will of John of Redding, 27 Mar., proved 9 June 1755; wife Hannah; dau. Ann to be equal with other daus.; children, John, Stephen, Abraham, Hezekiah, Nathaniel, Hannah, Abigail, Joseph, Eunice; eldest son John and son Stephen, Exec'rs. It was reported, Apr. 1759, that the child Eunice had died; and the widow Hannah receipted for her dower.

Children, rec. Fairfield, first four bapt. Greenfield, others Redding:

> Ann, b. 2, bapt. 6 Aug. 1732, living 1800; m. 14 Dec. 1749, Timothy Hull.
> 22+John, b. 17, bapt. 24 Feb. 1733/4.
> 23+Stephen, b. 7, bapt. 14 Dec. 1735.
> 24+Abraham, b. 22 June, bapt. 24 July 1737.
> Hezekiah, b. 1 Oct. 1738; res. New Fairfield 1761, when he conveyed land from the Est. of his father John Gray.
> Nathaniel, b. 20 July 1741; chose Thomas Judd of Danbury for guardian, Aug. 1759.
> Hannah, b. 25 June, bapt. 1 July 1744.

Abigail, b. 28 Dec. 1745, d. at Danbury, 7 Mar. 1807; m. (rec. Danbury) 7 Dec. 1767, Eliphalet Stevens.
Joseph, b. 7, bapt. 15 July 1753, d. at Ridgebury, 7 Oct. 1833; Corp., Rev. War; rem. to Ridgebury, 1767, to Stockbridge, Mass., 1774, returned soon to Ridgebury; m. 1 Apr. 1777, Lydia Keeler.
Eunice, b. 21 Dec. 1754, bapt. 2 Jan. 1755, d. 2 Sept. 1755.

12. Gray, James, s. of Jacob, 2d.

Born Sept. 1710; d. at Danbury, abt. June 1778.

He m. at Greenfield, 15 July 1733, Sarah Gilbert; dau. of Obadiah, b. 20 Dec. 1711.

Of Danbury, 1771; his son Ichabod then recently dec'd; had land at Redding [Conn. Col. Rec. 13: 457].

Will 25 May, proved 6 July 1778; wife Sarah; children, James Gray, Sarah wife of John Byington, Jane wife of Seth Gilbert; gr. children, Phebe, Ithiel, Sarah, Nathaniel, children of dec'd son Ichabod.

Children, four rec. Greenfield:

James, b. 18 Feb., bapt. Feb. 1735/6; m. (1) at Redding, 27 Mar. 1760, Asena Taylor, who d. 6 Nov. 1760; m. (2) 9 Feb. 1764, Mabel Phinney.*
Ichabod, b. 30 Mar., bapt. 1 Apr. 1739, d. at Newtown, 1770; adm'n granted to John Byington, 13 Sept. 1770; estate insolvent; m. ———, who survived him. Ethel and Sally Gray, children of Ichabod, chose Abraham Kimberly for guardian, 17 Aug. 1781; Nathaniel, son of Ichabod, chose Abraham Kimberly, 4 Apr. 1786.
Sarah, b. 19 Apr. 1742, bapt. in infancy; m. at Redding, 16 Nov. 1763, John Byington.
Jane, b. 20 Apr., bapt. 6 May 1744, d. 28 Aug. 1816 in 73 yr.; m. Seth Gilbert.
"Liffy," bapt. at Westport, 28 Jan. 1750, as son of James and Sarah of Redding; "Eliphalet" d. at Redding, 7 July 1768 ae. 19.
Jacob, bapt. at Redding, 10 Feb. 1754, d. y.

13. Gray, Jacob, s. of Jacob, 2d.

Born abt. 1712; d. at Greenfield, 22 Apr. 1776 in 64 yr.

He m. (1) Naomi Thorp, b. 18 Jan. 1717/8, who d. at Greenfield, 22 Oct. 1759 in 42 yr.

He m. (2) 27 July 1760, Abigail, widow of Beebe Mills.

---

* Children, rec. and bapt. Redding: Jerry, b. 11 Jan. 1766 [1765], bapt. 14 Apr. 1765, d. 14 Jan. 1788 in 24 yr. (g. s.); Mabel, b. 29 Nov. 1768 (?); Betsey, b. 9 Oct. 1773.

HISTORY AND GENEALOGY OF

Children [by first wife], rec. Greenfield:

25+Seth, bapt. 8 Jan. 1738/9.
    Child, bapt. 14 June 1741.
    Jacob, bapt. 10 June 1744.
    Reuel, b. 4, bapt. 16 Aug. 1747; m. Naomi Wheeler, dau. of Timothy, b. 4 Aug. 1751.*
    Son, d. Sept. 1751.

Children [by second wife], rec. Greenfield:

    Daniel, bapt. 2 May 1762 (ae. abt. 3 mos.).
    Naomi, b. 8 Jan., bapt. 4 Mar. 1764 (ae. abt. 2 mos.), living 1849; m. Dec. 1783, Ebenezer Smith.
    Jacob, bapt. 2 Oct. 1768 (in infancy); m. at Trinity Church, 25 Jan. 1792, Susan Thorp.

14. Gray, Nathan, s. of Isaac.

Bapt. 13 Apr. 1712; d. at Weston in 1794.

He m. 24 July 1735, Mary Hurlbut, dau. of Gideon, b. [say 1719], d. 29 July 1800.

Adm'n granted, 13 Feb. 1795, to John Gray.

Children, rec. Fairfield, bapt. Westport:

26+Nathan, b. 29 Sept. 1737. He conveyed in 1783, as Nathan, Jr., of Fairfield, to Daniel Gray of Stamford, land at Kettle Creek, Weston, which formerly belonged to "my Aged Father."
27+Isaac, b. 7 May 1739.
28+Solomon, b. 21 Apr. 1740.
29+Thomas, b. 7 Dec. 1742, bapt. 6 Mar. 1743.
    Daniel, b. 29 Oct., bapt. 11 Nov. 1744; m. at Stamford, 15 Nov. 1765, Prudence Waterbury; for seven children recorded there, see Huntington's *Stamford Registration,* p. 38.
    Mary, b. 11 Mar. 1745/6, d. abt. 1775; m. 20 Jan. 1771, Jonathan Squire.
30+Elijah, b. 16 Nov. 1747, bapt. 24 Jan. 1748.
31+John, b. 3 Sept., bapt. 13 Dec. 1749.
32+Gideon, b. 7 Mar., bapt. 5 May 1751.
    Eliphalet, b. 4 May, bapt. 1 July 1753, d. at Amherst, Mass., abt. 10 Oct. 1810 (Pension rec.); m. at Warren, Mass., 28 Nov. 1784, Lydia Munson, who d. 4 July 1846.

---

* One Reuel had a son Charles, b. 5 Mar. 1796 (rec. Redding). One Reuel had children, rec. Trinity Church: Clarissa, bapt. 14 Aug. 1785; Irena, bapt. 16 Mar. 1788; Timothy-Wheeler, bapt. 12 Sept. 1790.

Joseph, b. 9 Nov. 1754, bapt. 11 Mar. 1756; perhaps m. at Ridgebury, 1 Apr. 1779, Lydia Keeler.
Eunice, b. 19 Jan. 1756; m. 15 Nov. 1778, Robert Harris.
Benjamin, bapt. at Weston, 30 Dec. 1759, d. unm. in 1788. Adm'n granted, 17 Mar. 1788, to David Silliman. [But one Benjamin m. at Wilton, 25 Nov. 1779, Elizabeth Waterbury.]

15. Gray, Stephen, s. of William.

Born 7 Nov. 1715.

He m. Eunice Bennett, dau. of Deliverance, b. 24 Oct. 1718.

Of Ridgefield 1749, he conveyed land from mother Abigail dau. of Samuel Coley.

They lived in New Milford, 1762. In 1774, being of "New Canaan," Albany County, N. Y., he conveyed to William Gray of Fairfield, all right from Joseph Gray dec'd which he had from his father William Gray dec'd.

Children (record incomplete):

Eunice, bapt. at Westport, 18 Sept. 1743.
Stephen, bapt. at Redding, 10 May 1747.

16. Gray, William, s. of William.

Born 17 Aug. 1717; d. at Westport, 30 Aug. 1793; m. 25 Jan. 1742, Sarah Disbrow; dau. of Thomas, b. Apr. 1726, d. 27 Oct. 1778.

Will 16 July, proved 3 Sept. 1793; sons Moses and Elias of New Fairfield; dau. Elizabeth wife of Isaac Disbrow; son Amos; gr. son William, son of Elias Gray.

Order to distribute Est. of Sarah wife of William Gray, 4 Apr. 1794; Moses, Elias, and Amos Gray; Elizabeth wife of Isaac Disbrow; heirs of Olive wife of Elias Disbrow; heirs of Lydia Gray; heirs of Sarah Gray.

Children, rec. Fairfield, bapt. Westport:

33+Moses, b. 11 Aug., bapt. 11 Sept. 1743.
34+Elias, b. 4 Apr., bapt. 11 May 1746.
Olive, b. 3, bapt. 18 Dec. 1748, d. 6 July 1778; m. Elias Disbrow.
Sarah, b. 3 Apr., bapt. 2 June 1751, d. at Westport, 26 Apr. 1792.

404   HISTORY AND GENEALOGY OF

    Amos, b. 17 Mar., bapt. 3 June 1753, d. s. p. at Westport, 25 Mar. 1803 ae. 50; m. 22 Dec. 1793, Mary Burr. His will, 17 Mar., proved 4 Apr. 1803; wife Mary; my late father William Gray; two bros. Moses and Elias Gray.

    Elizabeth, b. 8 Jan., bapt. 27 Apr. 1755, living 1815; m. 16 May 1779, Isaac Disbrow.

    Lydia, b. 18 Jan., bapt. 24 Apr. 1757, d. at Westport, 31 Dec. 1786.

17. Gray, Ebenezer, s. of William.

Born 29 Mar. 1723; d. at Fairfield in 1777.

He m. at Wilton, 26 Dec. 1757, Ann Lockwood of Greens Farms; dau. of John, b. 18 Apr. 1734.

Will 4 Sept., proved 15 Dec. 1777; wife Ann; five sons, Justus, Gilead, Joseph, Ebenezer, Jabez; three daus. Anne, Abigail, Esther.

Children:

    Justus, m. (1) at Redding, 10 Jan. 1780, Rachel Weed, who d. 4 Dec. 1795; m. (2) at Wilton, in 1799, Mary Belden.*
    Ann.
    Gilead.
    Joseph, b. at Oblong, N. Y., 19 Nov. 1758 (Pension rec.), d. at Weston, 10 Oct. 1840; m. 6 Mar. 1783, Eunice Godfrey; dau. of Daniel, bapt. 23 May 1762, living 1843.†
    Abigail.
    Ebenezer.
    Jabez, ? m. at Weston, 20 Dec. 1795, Rachel Chubb.
    Esther, ? m. at Weston, 7 Aug. 1793, Ebenezer Hubbell.

18. Gray, Jabez, s. of William.

Born 11 Oct. 1728; d. in Maryland of smallpox, 31 May 1760.

He m. at Westport, 17 Jan. 1753, Betty Jacocks; dau. of Joshua, b. 20 Dec. 1731, d. 26 Mar. 1760.

Adm'n granted, 2 Aug. 1760, to Thaddeus Gray; and 19 Jan. 1762, to Jabez Disbrow.

---

* Children, rec. Redding: Mary-Levine, b. 29 Jan. 1781, bapt. at Weston, 20 Jan. 1782; Hannah, b. 23 Aug. 1782; Rachel, b. and d. 13 Apr. 1784; Sally, b. 12 June 1785; Eli, b. 28 June 1787; Rachel, b. 18 July 1789; Edward, b. 25 July 1791; Alford, b. 15 Sept. 1793; Betsey, b. 25 Oct. 1795. One Justus Gray of Redding, by will 14 Nov. 1821, proved 17 Dec. 1822, left all to wife Grissell.

† Children, bapt. Weston: Sally, bapt. 25 Apr. 1784; David, bapt. 19 Mar. 1786; Ellen, bapt. 21 Sept. 1788; Levi, bapt. 16 Oct. 1791; Aaron, bapt. 13 Nov. 1795; Daughter, bapt. 23 Jan. 1799; Munson, bapt. 26 Jan. 1803; Prissa, dau. of Eunice Gray, bapt. 25 Apr. 1784.

Children, bapt. Westport:

> Nabby, bapt. 23 Feb. 1755; "Abigail" m. at Fairfield, 28 Dec. 1775, Jabez Hubbell; they conveyed 1777 to William Gray, one-seventh of homelot that belonged to William Gray dec'd.
> Polly, bapt. 24 Apr. 1757, d. 20 Mar. 1760.
> Infant, d. 18 Mar. 1760.

19. Gray, Thaddeus, s. of William.

Born 27 Oct. 1730; d. 26 Nov. 1761.

He m. 28 Feb. 1759, Susanna Carley. She was widow of Abraham.

Adm'n granted, 21 Dec. 1761, to Joseph Couch.

Children, bapt. Westport:

> Polly, bapt. 27 Apr. 1760; res. 1781, Fredericksburgh, N. Y., when she conveyed to William Gray of Fairfield, land in Compo, in said William's homestead.
> Lois, bapt. 19 July 1761, d. 27 Apr. 1762.

20. Gray, Elisha, s. of William.

Born 1 June 1735; d. at Westport, 30 Nov. 1774.

He m. at Greenfield, 31 July 1766, Widow Ellen Hill. She was widow of Thomas Hill, and dau. of Peter Sturgis, bapt. 21 Mar. 1735/6.

Children, bapt. Westport:

> Joseph, bapt. 11 Oct. 1767.*
> Mary, bapt. 30 Dec. 1768, d. at Southport, 8 Sept. 1851 ae. 82 (g. s.); m. at Trinity Church, 20 Sept. 1789, David Beers.

21. Gray, Hezekiah, s. of Samuel.

Born 14 Nov. 1738; d. at Bedford, N. Y., by 1784.

He m. 24 Apr. 1760, Abigail Waterbury, dau. of Capt. David of Stamford; perhaps b. 14 May 1743. Hezekiah Gray and Abigail his wife of Fairfield conveyed 1764 to brother David Waterbury 3d, land in Stamford.

---

* Children of Joseph, bapt. Westport: Mary, bapt. 13 Nov. 1793, d. 25 Mar. 1795. Eleanor and Charlotte, bapt. 24 June 1798. Mary-Ann, bapt. 7 June 1801. Joseph, bapt. 22 Oct. 1804.

Of Bedford, he conveyed in 1770 land which his father Samuel gave him by deed in 1763.

Adm'n granted, 5 Mar. 1784, to Samuel "Banett," of Bedford, and Abigail his wife, late widow of Hezekiah Gray.

Children, first rec. Fairfield; bapt. Westport:

> Abigail, b. 22 May, bapt. 9 Aug. 1761.
> Lucy, bapt. 15 May 1763.
> Ellen, bapt. 23 June 1765.
> Hezekiah, bapt. 3 May 1767.

22. **Gray, John**, s. of John. Capt., 9th Co., 4th Regt., Jan. 1778.

Born 17 Feb. 1733/4; d. at Redding, 25 Oct. 1793 ae. 59 (g. s.); m. 7 Aug. 1759, Ruhamah Barlow, dau. of Samuel, b. 22 Jan. 1737, d. 2 June 1813 ae. 74 (g. s.).

Adm'n granted, 26 Nov. 1793, to Ruhamah, Joel, and John Gray. Agreement, 1806, of widow Ruhamah, Joel Gray, John Gray, and John and Eunice Davis, all of Redding, only heirs of Capt. John Gray.

Children, two rec. Fairfield; bapt. Redding:

> Eunice, b. 15 Mar., bapt. 19 Apr. 1760; m. 21 Oct. 1779, John Davis.
> Joel, b. 27 July, bapt. 11 Sept. 1763; d. at Redding, abt. June 1826; m. 18 Mar. 1784, Phebe Smith.*
> John, bapt. 5 May 1771; m. 17 Oct. 1790, Esther Davis; dau. of John, bapt. 19 Apr. 1772.†

23. **Gray, Stephen**, s. of John.

Born 7 Dec. 1735; d. at Redding, 26 Feb. 1796 ae. 60 (g. s.); m. 3 Sept. 1758, Sarah Ferry, dau. of Ebenezer, bapt. 6 May 1739.

Will 12 Sept. 1792, proved 10 Mar. 1796; wife Sarah; son Stephen; three daus. Huldah wife of Zalmon Read, Jr., Hannah wife of Ezekiel Jackson, and Sarah.

---

* Joel's will, 26 May 1826, proved 27 June 1826; wife Phebe; son Samuel S.; heirs of dau. Eunice dec'd. The distribution called Eunice, *Holmes*. Children, rec. Redding: Eunice, b. 24 Feb. 1785; Samuel-Smith, b. 1 Aug. 1797.

† Children, rec. Redding: Sally, b. 3 Sept. 1791; Laura, b. 24 Apr. 1794; Joel, b. 3 Feb. 1796.

Children, first rec. Fairfield; bapt. Redding:

> Huldah, b. 9 Nov., bapt. 14 Dec. 1760, d. at Redding, 27 June 1810 ae. 49-7-18 (g. s.); m. Nov. 1780, Zalmon Read, Jr.
> Hannah, bapt. 3 Oct. 1762, d. 8 June 1805; m. 30 Apr. 1786, Ezekiel Jackson.
> Sarah, bapt. 17 June 1764.
> Stephen, bapt. 23 Oct. 1768, d. at Redding in 1831; adm'n granted to Jonathan R. Sanford, 28 Nov. 1831; estate insolvent; m. 1 Nov. 1792, Annis Boughton.*

24. Gray, Abraham, s. of John. Lt., 8th Co., 16th Regt., Oct. 1774; Capt., 7th Co., 5th Regt., Army, Apr. 1775; Capt., 8th Co., 16th Regt., Oct. 1775.

Born 22 June 1737; d. at Ridgefield, in 1776; m. Mary ———.

Of Ridgefield, conveyed 1764 to bro. John of Redding, land from father John's estate.

Adm'n granted, 19 Nov. 1776, to Mary and John Gray. Dower set to widow Mary, 1777.

Distribution to the heirs, accepted 12 Apr. 1828, of the part of Abraham's estate which had been set to his widow Mary as dower. The heirs named were: Joseph, Nathaniel, Hezekiah, Abigail, Stephen, John, Anna, Hannah.

25. Gray, Seth, s. of Jacob.

Bapt. 8 Jan. 1738/9.

He m. 23 June 1762, Sarah Mills; dau. of Beebe, bapt. 23 Mar. 1746.

A widow Sarah Gray d. at Greenfield, 20 Apr. 1823.

Children, bapt. Greenfield:

> Naomi, bapt. 2 Dec. 1762 (sick, at home), d. 3 Dec. 1762.
> Sarah, bapt. 26 Feb. 1764; ?m. 15 Feb. 1778, Jonathan Spears.
> Seth, bapt. at Easton, 31 Aug. 1766.
> Joseph, bapt. 16 Aug. 1772.
> Abigail, bapt. 5 Oct. 1777.
> Huldah, bapt. 23 July 1780.

---

* Children, rec. Redding: Uriah, b. 8 June 1793; Anne, b. 4 Mar. 1797.

26. Gray, Nathan, s. of Nathan.

Born 29 Sept. 1737; d. in 1787.
He m. 4 May 1780, Eunice Bulkley; [? dau. of James, bapt. 17 June 1759].
Adm'n granted, 6 Aug. 1787, to James and Eunice Gray.

Children, bapt. Weston:

> Mary, bapt. 5 Aug. 1781; ? m. at Westport, 11 Nov. 1804, Benjamin Stevens, of New Fairfield.
> Nathan, bapt. 14 May 1787.

27. Gray, Isaac, s. of Nathan.

Born 7 May 1739.

Children, first bapt. Weston:

> Isaac, bapt. 26 Feb. 1763.*
> Elijah, bapt. at Redding, 16 Aug. 1772.

28. Gray, Solomon, s. of Nathan.

Born 21 Apr. 1740; d. at Westport, 1 Mar. 1799 in 58 yr. (g. s.).
He m. 18 Feb. 1762, Ann Disbrow, b. 24 Aug. 1742, d. 1 Apr. 1806 in 64 yr.
Will 21 Feb. 1798, proved 18 Mar. 1799; wife Anne; nephews Elijah and Zalmon Gray, sons of bro. Isaac dec'd; brothers and sisters living,—Daniel, Elijah, John, Joseph, Eliphalet, Eunice; children of dec'd brothers and sisters,—Nathan, Isaac, Thomas, Gideon, Mary; mother living.
Distribution Mar. 1800; Widow Ann; John, Daniel, Eliphalet, and Joseph Gray; heirs of Mary Squire dec'd; Elijah Gray; heirs of Nathan Gray dec'd; heirs of Thomas Gray dec'd; Eunice Harris; heirs of Isaac Gray dec'd; heirs of Gideon Gray dec'd.
John Disbrow was appointed Adm'r of the intestate part of Ann Gray's estate, 1 Feb. 1808.

---

* Adm'n on Est. of an Isaac Gray of Brookfield was granted, 25 Mar. 1818, to Thaddeus Gray of Brookfield. Dower set to widow Susanna.

29. Gray, Thomas, s. of Nathan.

Born 7 Dec. 1742.

He m. at Weston, 1 Mar. 1767, Mary Mills; doubtless dau. of Beebe, b. [say 1743].

Elijah Gray of Weston was appointed guardian of Beebe Gray, 5 Oct. 1789.

Children, bapt. Weston:

> Silliman, bapt. 25 Oct. 1767; "of Greenfield," m. (1) at Fairfield, 20 Dec. 1789, Anna Hubbell; m. (2) at Weston, 24 Oct. 1804, Charlotte Elwood.
> John B., bapt. 28 Oct. 1770, d. at Weston, 15 Mar. 1861 ae. 91 yrs. 8 mos. (g. s.); m. Mehitabel ———, who d. 22 June 1853 ae. 82 yrs. 11 mos. (g. s.).*
> Beebe, bapt. 6 Oct. 1772, d. y.
> Beebe, bapt. 16 Oct. 1774, d. 18 Sept. 1852 (Miss Treadwell's book); m. 27 Sept. 1798, Eleanor Sherwood, b. [22 June 1777], d. at Weston, 7 July 1843 ae. 65 yrs. 15 days (g. s.).
> Mary, bapt. 12 Jan. 1777 (as child of Widow Mary); perhaps m. (at Weston, rec. Fairfield Church) 26 Oct. 1800, Lockwood Adams.

30. Gray, Elijah, s. of Nathan.

Born 16 Nov. 1747; d. at Weston, 16 Nov.(?) 1827 ae. 80 (g. s.).

He m. (1) 10 Sept. 1769,† Esther Sturges, bapt. 12 Apr. 1752, d. 10 Oct. 1791 ae. 40 (g. s.).

He m. (2) 6 May 1793 [1792 by church rec.], Rhoda Disbrow, b. 20 Dec. 1740 [Weston rec.], d. 3 Jan. 1797. She was widow of Caleb Disbrow, Jr., and dau. of Gideon Morehouse, b. 16 May 1755.

He m. (3) 19 Feb. 1797, Lydia Taylor, b. 29 Feb. 1764, d. 22 Aug. 1826 ae. 62 (g. s.).

Adm'n granted, 17 Sept. 1827, to Alva Gray of Fairfield and Solomon Gray of Weston. Distribution, Nov. 1828: heirs of son Sturges dec'd; sons Jeremiah, Elijah, Walter; heirs of Samuel; sons Solomon, Hezekiah; daus. Widow Esther Morehouse, Rhoda M. Gray, Abigail wife of David Lockwood, Temperance Gray.

---

* Child, bapt. Weston: Alva, bapt. 26 June 1796.
† 20 Sept. 1770, by Weston Church rec.

Adm'n on Est. of Esther Gray [the first wife] was granted to Alva Gray, 19 Mar. 1828; and distribution was made to the five surviving sons and heirs of the two dec'd sons.

Children by first wife, rec. and bapt. Weston:

Sturges, b. 15 Apr., bapt. 5 June 1774, d. in 1815; adm'n granted, 3 Apr. 1815, to Elizabeth Gray, with Samuel Wood as surety; m. at Westport (called of Lansingburg) 4 Dec. 1800, Betty Wood.
Jeremiah, b. 20 July, bapt. 23 Sept. 1778.
Elijah, b. 21 Mar., bapt. 27 May 1781.
Samuel, b. 13 Mar., bapt. 13 Apr. 1783; m. at Westport, 1 Oct. 1806, Hannah Ogden of Norwalk.
Walter, b. 15 Dec. 1785, bapt. 19 Mar. 1786, d. 6 Oct. 1857 ae. 71 yrs. 10 mos. (g. s.); m. Anna ———, b. [5 Aug. 1790], d. 16 Apr. 1844 ae. 53-8-11 (g. s.).
Solomon, b. 31 Mar. 1788, d. at Weston, 23 Mar. 1834 ae. 46 (g. s.); m. Abigail H. ———, who d. 29 Sept. 1862 ae. 65 (g. s.).*
Hezekiah, b. 15 July, bapt. 19 Sept. 1790.

Child by second wife, rec. Weston:

Esther, b. 7 Sept., bapt. 25 Oct. 1795; m. ——— Morehouse.

Children by third wife, first rec. Weston, three bapt. Weston:

Rhoda Morehouse, b. 3 May 1798, bapt. 12 Aug. 1798.
Gamaliel, bapt. 6 July 1800, d. y.
Abigail, b. 3 Jan. 1802 (Bible rec.); bapt. 3 May 1802; m. David Lockwood.
Temperance, b. 26 May 1805 (Bible rec.), d. 12 Jan. 1864; m. 5 Dec. 1830, Hezekiah M. Coley.

31. **Gray, John,** s. of Nathan.

Born 3 Sept. 1749; d. at Weston, in 1817.

He m. 4 Feb. 1774, Eunice Morehouse, b. 26 Aug. 1753, d. at Weston, 24 Apr. 1838 ae. 84.

Will 5 Mar. 1812, proved 8 Mar. 1817; wife Eunice; son John; daus. Anna, Deborah; etc.

Distribution, 24 May 1817; Widow; John Gray; Morehouse Gray; Alva Gray; Deborah wife of Samuel Meeker; Anna wife of Joseph Rowland.

---

* Solomon's estate was distributed to his widow Abigail and children Eliphalet, Esther-Burr, Mary, Abigail-Augusta, and Ellen-Wakeman Gray.

Children, rec. and bapt. Weston:

> Deborah, b. 5 Aug. (?), bapt. 14 May 1775, d. at Westport, 2 Oct. 1839 ae. 64 (g. s.); m. 5 Mar. 1798, Samuel Meeker.
> Mary, b. 14 May, bapt. 20 June 1779, d. 13 Mar. 1785.
> Anna, b. 13 Feb., bapt. 13 Apr. 1783, d. at Weston, 6 Aug. 1844 ae. 61-5-23 (g. s.); m. 5 Dec. 1812, Joseph Rowland.
> John, b. 1 Sept. 1785, bapt. (rec. Westport as son of Lt. John of Norfield), 20 Nov. 1785, d. at Weston, 21 Dec. 1875 (g. s.); m. 31 May 1813, Abigail Coley; dau. of Morehouse, b. 9 Nov. 1791, d. 23 Aug. 1867 ae. 75 yrs. 9 mos. (g. s.).
> Morehouse, b. 22 Dec. 1787, bapt. 10 Feb. 1788, d. at Little Egg Harbor, Aug. 1825; m. 4 May 1817, Clarissa Hoyt.
> Alva, b. 4 May 1796; m. 17 Feb. 1823, Sarah-Coley Wakeman.

32. Gray, Gideon, s. of Nathan.

Born 7 Mar. 1751; d. at Westport, 7 June 1792.

He m. Ann ———.

In a deed in 1778 he called himself of Stamford.

Children, first two bapt. Westport, two Weston, last two Westport:

> Ebenezer, bapt. 7 Jan. 1776.
> Ellen, bapt. 7 Jan. 1776.
> Gideon, bapt. 26 Apr. 1778; on 17 Jan. 1793, ae. 15, chose Solomon Gray for guardian.
> Betty, bapt. 31 Oct. 1784.
> Esther, bapt. 21 June 1789.
> Charles, bapt. (as child of Widow Anna) 5 Aug. 1792.

33. Gray, Moses, s. of William, 2d.

Born 11 Aug. 1743; rem. to New Fairfield, and d. in 1811.

He m. 19 Mar. 1767, Sarah Disbrow, dau. of Thomas, b. 10 June 1747, d. abt. 1831.

Of New Fairfield, he conveyed in 1772 to father William of Fairfield.

Adm'n granted, 28 Oct. 1811, to Nathan Bulkley of Danbury and Solomon Gray of New Fairfield. Dower set to widow Sarah. Distribution 1812: eldest son Gabriel; heirs of 2d son Thomas; 3d son Seymour; 4th son Solomon; youngest son Jesse. Distribution 9 Sept. 1831 of realty that had been set to the widow for dower, was made to the same heirs.

Children, bapt. Westport:
> Gabriel, bapt. 14 Feb. 1768.
> Thomas, bapt. 17 Nov. 1768.
> Seymour, bapt. 4 Aug. 1771.
> Child of Moses and Sarah of New Fairfield, bapt. 22 Aug. 1775.
> Solomon.
> Jesse.

34. Gray, Elias, s. of William, 2d.

Born 4 Apr. 1746; rem. to New Fairfield.

He m. (1) at Greenfield, 27 Nov. 1766, Eunice Allen; dau. of John, b. 4 May 1748.

He m. (2) ———.

Of New Fairfield, he conveyed 1794 to sister Elizabeth wife of Isaac Disbrow, right from mother dec'd, also from sister Lydia dec'd.

Children by first wife, two bapt. Westport:
> William, bapt. 8 Nov. 1767.
> Huldah, bapt. 16 July 1769; m. Moulthrop Nickerson.
> Allen.
> Sarah, m. Nathan Wheeler.

Children by second wife:
> Olive, d. at New Fairfield in 1829. Adm'n granted, 13 Apr. 1829, to Russel Gray. Distribution 1830; sister Eunice wife of Joseph Sherwood; sister Polly wife of Cyrus Gray; bro. Russel; heirs of half-sister Huldah wife of Moultrop Nickerson; half-bro. Allen; half-bro. William; heirs of half-sister Sarah wife of Nathan Wheeler.
> Eunice, m. Joseph Sherwood.
> Polly, m. Cyrus Gray.
> Russell.

Gray, Nehemiah.

He d. 17 Apr. 1810 (Miss Treadwell's book).

He m. at Weston, 18 Oct. 1765, Sarah Downs; prob. dau. of Nathaniel, b. 24 May 1745.

Children, bapt. Greenfield:
> Esther, b. abt. 1766, bapt. 3 Apr. 1768 (ae. abt. 2).
> Nehemiah, bapt. 4 Dec. 1768.
> Noah, bapt. 11 Sept. 1774; m. at Trinity Church, 16 Mar. 1800, Rebecca Nichols.
> Eli, bapt. 25 May 1783.

Gray [*Unplaced*].

JAMES, s. of Daniel [David?], bapt. at Redding, 15 May 1743. Mary wife of David (?) d. there 21 Oct. 1741.
LOCKWOOD; adm'n granted to Joseph Gray, 15 Jan. 1787.
JAMES m. 5 Nov. 1789, Elizabeth Osborn. [Weston rec.] He d. at Weston, 19 June 1819 ae. 54-5-6 (g. s.); Elizabeth d. 20 Nov. 1825 ae. 55 (g. s.). Children, rec. Weston: Hannah, b. 5 July 1790; Lewis-Benedict, b. 7 Sept. 1793; Clarissa, b. 11 June 1795; Molly, b. 16 Sept. 1797.
MABEL m. 23 Jan. 1791, Daniel Lyon. [Trinity Church]
REBECCA m. 23 Apr. 1772, Gideon Beebe. [Greens Farms Church]
SARAH m. 2 Feb. 1793, Elijah Welles. [Weston rec.]
JOHN, b. at Fairfield, 5 Jan. 1776 (Pension Rec.), lived Westport 1847; m. 19 Oct. 1800, Lucinda Gregory, dau. of Josiah.
ANNA m. 26 Aug. 1790, Jason Disbrow. [Greens Farms Church]
SALLY m. 9 Jan. 1810, Orrin Boughton. [Redding Rec.]
ELIZABETH m. 12 Mar. 1791, William Downs. [Weston Church]
MARY of New Fairfield m. 2 May 1748, Nathan Noble of New Milford. [New Fairfield]
MRS. ESTHER d. at Greenfield, 27 June 1850 ae. 86 (g. s.).
AARON, b. abt. 1780, d. at Greenfield, 10 Dec. 1857 ae. 77 (g. s.); m. Eunice Bulkley, dau. of Turney, bapt. at Greenfield, 1 Oct. 1780, d. there 1869 (g. s.).
SALLY d. 23 Aug. 1802; Eleanor d. 28 Apr. 1804. [Miss Treadwell's book]
EUNICE of Weston, will 31 Aug. 1832, proved 13 Apr. 1835; sons Eli B. Gray, Bradley Gray; dau. Milly wife of Aaron Morehouse.

Green, John, s. of John [Vol. I, p. 236].

Born [say 1690], d. at Norwalk in 1752;* m. Rebecca Gregory, dau. of Thomas, b. abt. 1691.

Will 10 Mar. 1752, proved 8 May 1752; wife Rebecca; eldest son Joseph; sons Ebenezer, William; eldest dau. Rebecca; dau. Hannah Dunning; dau. Tomasin; my bro.-in-law Ebenezer Gregory of Norwalk, and my son Ebenezer, Exec'rs.

Children:

+Joseph.
+Ebenezer, b. 25 Oct. 1723.
Rebecca, m. at Wilton, 4 June 1754, William Sterling.
Hannah, m. Michael Dunning.
Thomasin, m. at Wilton, 16 July 1765, Daniel Sterling.

---

* A John Green d. at Greenfield, 9 Sept. 1751. It may have been this John who m. 7 Apr. 1720, Ann Hull, dau. of Theophilus, bapt. at Fairfield, 26 Aug. 1694. Their son Thomas was bapt. at Fairfield, 15 Jan. 1720/1. The Greens, though not numerous, are among the most difficult of Fairfield families.

414   HISTORY AND GENEALOGY OF

Green, Joseph, s. of John.

He m. at Wilton, 15 May 1746 (?), Sarah Beers.
One Joseph d. at Westport, 17 Jan. 1792.

Children, bapt. Weston:

>Joseph, bapt. 21 Aug. 1757; m. 21 July 1779, Rachel Couch; dau. of Samuel, bapt. 2 Nov. 1760.*
>William, bapt. 2 Mar. 1759.
>Samuel, bapt. 2 May 1762; m. at Westport, 15 Mar. 1787, Tamason Batterson; dau. of James, bapt. 4 Apr. 1762.†
>Ebenezer, bapt. 1 July 1770.

Green, Ebenezer, s. of John.

Born 25 Oct. 1723.

He m. at Wilton, 24 Mar. 1747/8, Elizabeth Gilbert, dau. of Benjamin, b. 11 Sept. 1731 (rec. also Fairfield).

Children, rec. Fairfield:

>Hannah, b. 14 Sept. 1749.
>Mary, b. 8 Aug. 1751; m. at Redding, 2 Oct. 1768, Peter Bulkley.
>Thomas, b. 11 May 1753.‡
>William, b. 12 Apr. 1755; ? m. at Weston, 10 Nov. 1779, Huldah Squire; dau. of Thaddeus, bapt. 3 June 1759.
>Ebenezer, b. 16 Apr. 1757.

Green, James.

Child, bapt. Redding:

>Mary, bapt. 21 Jan. 1753.

Child, bapt. Westport:

>Eunice, bapt. 16 July 1758.

Children, bapt. Redding:

>James, bapt. 8 Sept. 1775.
>Jonah, bapt. 8 Sept. 1775.

---

* Children, bapt. Westport: Samuel, bapt. 24 Sept. 1780; Andrew, bapt. 23 Feb. 1783; Joshua, bapt. 20 Apr. 1785. Children of Rachel Green: Kezia, bapt. 5 Nov. 1787; John, bapt. 19 Sept. 1790; James, bapt. 27 Oct. 1793; Sarah, bapt. 20 Sept. 1795; Ebenezer, bapt. 21 Oct. 1798.

† Children, bapt. Westport: Rachel, bapt. 16 Dec. 1787; Sarah, bapt. 5 Sept. 1790; Lydia, bapt. 6 Apr. 1794.

‡ A Thomas had a child bapt. Trinity Church: Charles, bapt. 11 Sept. 1785.

Green [Unplaced].

SUSANNA m. 17 Jan. 1779, Elias Disbrow. [Greens Farms Church]
REBECCA m. 24 Mar. 1785, William Allen. [Greens Farms Church]
MARY-MOREHOUSE of Fairfield m. 20 July 1805, John Sniffin of L. I. [Fairfield Church]
HULDAH m. 5 Jan. 1797, Jonah Rockwell. [Weston Church]

Greenell [Unplaced].

CATHERINE wife of CAPT. JOHN d. 25 Nov. 1780. [Greens Farms Church]

Gregory, Thaddeus, s. of Samuel [Vol. I, p. 240].

Bapt. at Stratfield, 13 July 1701, d. there 30 Dec. 1777 in 77 yr. (g. s.); m. Rebecca Smith, dau. of Samuel, b. at Fairfield, 20 Mar. 1704.

Distribution of Est. of Thaddeus of Stratford, 6 Feb. 1786; heirs of Thaddeus of Stratford; Mary wife of John Burroughs of Stratford; Sarah wife of Daniel Hubbel of Fairfield; Jemima wife of Nathaniel Sherman of New Stratford; Rebecca wife of Samuel Summers of New Milford; Beulah wife of David Seeley of Stratford.

Children, rec. Stratford, bapt. Stratfield:

Mary, b. 8 Mar. 1725, d. 17 Apr. 1726 in 14 mo. (g. s.).
Mary, b. 5 Nov. 1726; m. John Burroughs.
Sarah, b. 26 July 1728, d. at Stratfield, 11 Apr. 1801 in 73 yr. (g. s.); m. 28 Dec. 1749, Daniel Hubbell.
Jemima, b. 28 Mar. 1730, d. at Stratfield, 10 Feb. 1806 in 77 yr. (g. s.); m. 29 Aug. 1784, Nathaniel Sherman. Will 19 Apr. 1804, proved 12 Mar. 1806; nephews James and Selah Gregory; sisters Mary widow of John Burroughs, Rebecca widow of Samuel Summers, Beulah wife of David Seeley; three surviving children of late sister Sarah Hubbell, viz.: Onesimus, Thaddeus and Sarah Hubbell; gravestones for her father Thaddeus Gregory and herself.
Selah, b. 5 Nov. 1732, d. 15 Sept. 1758 in 28 yr. (g. s.).
Rebecca, b. 12, bapt. 15 Sept. 1734; m. Samuel Summers, of New Milford.
Beulah, b. 16, bapt. 21 Mar. 1736; m. David Seeley.
Thaddeus, b. 15 Nov. 1738, d. at Stratfield, 13 Aug. 1777; Huldah Gregory, Adm'x, 21 Nov. 1777; m. Huldah Hawley, dau. of James.*

---

* Children: James; Seeley. Other children d. 26 and 31 July, and 9 Aug., 1777.

Gregory, Enoch, s. of Samuel [Vol. I, p. 240].

Bapt. at Stratfield, 28 Dec. 1707, d. there 23 Dec. 1776; m. Esther Smith, dau. of Samuel, bapt. at Fairfield, 22 May 1709, d. 16 July 1791 in 83 yr. (g. s.).

Will 23 Jan. 1764, proved 12 Jan. 1777; eldest son Samuel; sons Enoch, Gilead, Ebenezer; dau. Peninah Jackson and her children; dau. Miriam Sherman; dau. Esther Beach and her children; dau. Ann Hawley; dau. Deborah Seeley; wife Esther Gregory. Distribution 21 June 1777: Widow; eldest son Samuel; 2d son Gilead; 3d son Enoch; dau. Peninah wife of Samuel Jackson; dau. Deborah wife of Nathan Seeley; 4th son Ebenezer; dau. Anna wife of Thomas Hawley; dau. Esther Beach; dau. Miriam wife of Josiah Sherman.

Will of Esther Gregory, 28 Mar. 1788, proved 29 July 1791; four sons Samuel, Gilead, Enoch, Ebenezer; five daus. Peninah widow of Samuel Jackson, Miriam wife of Josiah Sherman, Esther wife of Josiah Brinsmade, Ann wife of Thomas Hawley, Deborah Seeley.

Children, bapt. Stratfield:

+Samuel, b. abt. 1727.
  Gilead, b. [Feb. 1730], d. at Stratfield, 25 Aug. 1733 ae. 3½.
  Peninah, bapt. 26 Dec. 1731, living in Weston, 1791; m. in 1749, Samuel Jackson.
  Miriam, bapt. 12 May 1734; m. Josiah Sherman; res. Weston, 1791.
  Esther, bapt. 28 Dec. 1735, living in Weston, 1791; m. (1) Thomas Beach; m. (2) Josiah Brinsmade.
  Gilead, living in 1791, when Daniel Gregory was his conservator; m. (1) at New Haven, 10 Apr. 1765, Mary, widow of Ebenezer Ives, dau. of Stephen Atwater, b. 7 Mar. 1735/6, d. at Trumbull, 30 Nov. 1772 in 37 yr. (g. s.); m. (2) Sarah ———.*
  Enoch, d. at Trumbull abt. 1812; Ephraim Sterling was his conservator in 1791; m. Phebe ———. Distribution, 27 Feb. 1813: Silas, Josiah, Elijah, and Joseph Gregory, Sarah wife of Daniel Wheeler, Anna wife of S. C. Burton, Phebe wife of D. Jennings, Esther wife of Curtiss [sic], and Mary wife of Monson Curtiss.†

---

* Children, by first wife, rec. Trumbull Church: Stephen-Atwater, b. Aug., bapt. 13 Sept. 1767, d. at New Haven, 6 July 1774 ae. 7 (g. s.); Ebenezer-Ives, b. Dec., bapt. 4 Mar. 1770, d. at New Haven, 19 Aug. 1787 ae. 18 (g. s.). Children by second wife: David, bapt. 7 May 1775; Mary, b. Oct., bapt. Dec. 1776; Enoch, b. 1 Feb., bapt. 21 Mar. 1779; Cornelius Hamlin, b. June, bapt. 13 Aug. 1780; Lewis, b. Aug., bapt. 15 Sept. 1782; Ruth, b. 2 Feb., bapt. 23 Mar. 1785.

† Children, rec. Trumbull Church: Son, bapt. 18 June 1769; Josiah, bapt. 15 Sept. 1771; Phebe, bapt. 19 Apr. 1778.

Anna, m. Thomas Hawley.
Deborah, b. abt. 1743, d. at Stratfield, 22 Sept. 1811 in 69 yr. (g. s.); m. Nathan Seeley.
Abijah, bapt. 14 Dec. 1747, d. s. p. before 1764.
Ebenezer, bapt. 23 Dec. 1750, living in 1791; perhaps m. Huldah Lacy, bapt. 17 June 1750; with wife Huldah he conveyed to Benjamin Lacy in 1772.

Gregory, Ithamar, s. of Benjamin [Vol. I, p. 241].

Bapt. 8 Oct. 1710.

Children, two bapt. Greenfield:
Nathan, bapt. 26 Jan. 1734/5.
Thomasin, bapt. 13 June 1737.

Gregory, Samuel, s. of Enoch.

Born abt. 1727; d. at Trumbull, 9 Nov. 1808 in 82 yr. (g. s.); m. Naomi Burritt, dau. of Charles, who d. 10 Apr. 1810 ae. 82 (g. s.).

Will 26 Dec. 1801, proved 5 Dec. 1809; sons Stephen, Daniel, Abijah, Samuel, William, Aaron, Benjamin; daus. Sarah, Mary, Esther, Patience; gr. son Philo, son of Philo and Hannah; dau.-in-law Hannah Gregory; wife Naomi.

The estate of Naomi distributed, 5 Nov. 1810, to Stephen Gregory; Daniel Gregory; heirs of Abijah Gregory; Samuel Gregory; William Gregory; heirs of Aaron Gregory; Benjamin Gregory; Sarah Sherwood; Mary DeForest; Esther Judson; Patience Seeley.

Children, rec. Stratford and Trumbull Church:
+Stephen, b. 3 Dec. 1751.
Daniel.
Abijah, prob. the child bapt. 10 July 1757 (by Mr. Ross of Stratfield).
Sarah, b. Aug., bapt. 8 Oct. 1758; m. —— Sherwood.
Mary, b. 12 Aug., bapt. 30 Sept. 1760; m. 1 Feb. 1781, Isaac DeForest.
Samuel, b. June, bapt. 25 July 1762.
William, bapt. 8 July 1764.
Aaron, b. 15, bapt. 21 Sept. 1766.
Benjamin.
Esther, m. —— Judson.
Patience, b. [17 Mar. 1774], d. at Easton, 20 Feb. 1863 ae. 88-11-3 (g. s.); m. Elijah Seeley.

Gregory, Stephen, s. of Samuel.

Born 3 Dec. 1751 (Stratford rec.) or 4 Dec. 1752 (Weston rec.); d. at Weston by 1818.

He m. at Easton, 26 Mar. 1772, Rhoda Hall, b. 12 Jan. 1754, d. by 1833.

Agreement 3 Nov. 1818 of widow Rhoda and the heirs: eldest dau. Naomi wife of Joseph Bennett; son Abel; 2d dau. Rhoda wife of Stephen A. Gregory; 2d son Stephen; youngest son Alvah. The widow's dower was distributed to the heirs, 1833.

Children, rec. Weston:

> Naomi, b. 5 Sept. 1772, d. at Easton, 30 Jan. 1845 ae. 72 (g. s.); m. 10 Mar. 1791, Joseph Bennett.*
> Abel, b. 2 June 1775, d. at Easton, 23 Jan. 1823 ae. 48 (g. s.); m. Lydia ———, who m. (2) Aaron Sherwood, and d. 21 Nov. 1859 ae. 84 yrs. 7 mos. (g. s.). Will 9 Jan., proved 22 Feb. 1823; wife Lydia; bros. Stephen and Alva; sisters Naoma, Rhoda.
> Rhoda, b. 21 Feb. 1781; m. Stephen A. Gregory; res. 1824, Liberty, Sullivan County, N. Y.
> Stephen, b. 19 May 1788, d. at Easton, 22 Dec. 1832 ae. 44 yrs. 7 mos. (g. s.); res. 1824, Trumbull; m. Huldah ———, who d. 23 Nov. 1846 ae. 58 (g. s.).
> Alvah, b. 10 Dec. 1797.

Gregory, William.

He m. 11 Jan. 1787, Polly Sherwood. Children: Eunice, b. 2 Apr. 1788; William S., b. 9 Feb. 1790; David, b. 24 Oct. 1796; Polly, b. 8 Sept. 1798. [Weston rec.]

Gregory [*Unplaced*].

> SAMUEL m. Apr. 1746, Abigail Gilbert. [Greenfield Church]
> ABIJAH m. 18 Jan. 1776, Molly Thorp. [Greenfield Church]
> ISAAC m. 12 Sept. 1776, Sarah St. John. [Redding Church]
> SILAS, of Norwalk, m. 14 Mar. 1781, Sarah Bennett. [Greens Farms Church]
> ANNE, b. 21 Apr. 1776, m. 30 Sept. 1798, Silas C. Burton. [Weston rec.]

---

* The will of Naomi wife of Joseph Bennett, 21 Apr. 1843, proved 10 Feb. 1845; Baptist Church of Weston; to bro. Alva Gregory, land in Trumbull; Charles Patterson of Weston; Naomi B. Stewart of Liberty, N. Y., dau. of my niece Fanny Stewart; sister Rhoda Gregory and her children Abel, Burrit, Ives, Alva, Bennett, Fanny, Theresa, Emeline, and Huldah; Edson Gregory, son of bro. Alva.

POLLY m. 2 May 1805, Peter Silliman. [Weston rec.]
SAMUEL, of Norwalk, m. 27 Nov. 1789, Rhoda Ogden. [Greens Farms Church]
ABRAHAM, of Norwalk, m. 18 Apr. 1792, Damaris Disbrow. [Greens Farms Church]
ABRAHAM, JR., of Norwalk, m. 10 Apr. 1798, Polly Allen, 2d. [Greens Farms Church]
CLARA, of Stratfield, m. 19 Feb. 1789, John-Walker Odell, of Stratfield. [Fairfield Church]
MATTHEW had children rec. Redding: Rebecca, b. 11 May 1789; Matthew, b. 10 Apr. 1791.*
BENJAMIN m. 14 Nov. 1797, Abigail Sanford; child, Walter, b. 4 Feb. 1798. [Redding rec.]
Wife of SETH d. 11 Oct. 1772; Widow d. 5 Jan. 1786; Wife of Samuel d. 31 Aug. 1786. [Stratfield Bill of Mortality]

Griffin, John, [s. of John?].

He m. abt. 1732, Sarah Nash, dau. of Capt. Thomas, b. 20 Mar. 1712.

In 1741 he, called late of Norwalk now of Fairfield, bought land in Redding from Samuel Smith, 3d.

Children, bapt. Redding:

    Sarah, bapt. 9 May 1736; m. 22 Nov. 1755, Jehu Burr, Jr.
    Eunice, bapt. 22 Oct. 1738, d. by 1777; m. 14 Aug. 1759, Jonathan Couch.
    +John.
    +Joseph.
    Jonathan, bapt. 23 Nov. 1746; res. Danbury.
    Elizabeth, m. Jeremiah Sherman.

Griffin, John, s. of John.

He m. 23 Dec. 1761, Widow Katherine Johnson [widow of Joseph].

Will of Catharine, 7 Mar. 1815, proved 13 Sept. 1815; dau. Sarah wife of Isaac Cooley; heirs of dau. Huldah Sanford dec'd; heirs of dau. Mary Burr dec'd; sons Eli and Uriah Griffin; son John had rec'd portion.

---

* Matthew d. 20 Feb. 1835 ae. 86; wife Eunice d. 2 Nov. 1828 ae. 76 (gravestones, Weston).

Children, bapt. Redding :*

    Sarah, bapt. 3 Oct. 1762; m. 8 Sept. 1785, Isaac Coley.
    Huldah, bapt. 20 May 1764; m. 1 May 1788, Joel Sanford.
    Molly, bapt. 31 Aug. 1766; m. 19 Feb. 1787, Stephen Burr.
    John, bapt. 25 Sept. 1768.
    Esther, bapt. 26 Aug. 1770.
    Eli.
    Uriah.

Griffin, Joseph, s. of John.

He m. 18 Sept. 1766, Esther Hall.

Children, rec. Redding:

    Esther, b. 16 Apr. 1767, d. in Chemung, N. Y., 1835; m. (1) William Read, Jr.; m. (2) 18 Mar. 1790, John Wynkoop.
    Ebenezer, b. 21 Aug. 1768.
    Hannah, b. 4 Aug. 1770.
    Joseph, b. 9 Nov. 1774; m. 25 Jan. 1798, Eunice Hamilton; dau. of Benjamin.†
    Eunice, b. 25 Mar. 1777 [1776?], bapt. 16 June 1776.
    Hannah, b. 29 Apr., bapt. 21 June 1778.
    Ebenezer, b. 24 Aug. 1781.
    Eunice, b. 4 Sept. 1784.

Griffin, Elnathan.

He m. 26 Nov. 1750, Patience Burr, dau. of Jehu, bapt. 9 Mar. 1728/9.

Children, rec. Fairfield, bapt. Redding:

    Sarah, b. 8 Sept. 1751.‡
    Hezekiah, b. 30 Aug. 1753.
    Huldah, b. 26 Dec. 1755.
    Aaron, bapt. 2 July 1758.
    Abigail, bapt. 24 May 1761.
    Samuel, bapt. 26 Feb. 1764.

---

* Who was the Abigail Griffin of Redding, on whose estate Isaac Coley was appointed Adm'r, 24 May 1808? Her estate was ordered distributed to her bros. and sisters and the representatives of any who were dead.
† Child, rec. Redding: Seley, b. 17 Mar. 1799.
‡ Greenfield records say, b. 10, bapt. 22 Sept.

Griffin or Griffith, Nathaniel.

He m. at Wilton, 5 Aug. 1746, Molly* Noble.

Nathaniel Griffith sold land at Redding to Silas Griffith, which the latter sold in 1765.

Children:

> Hephzibah, b. 17 Aug. 1747, d. 4 Aug. 1826; m. 2 Nov. 1762, Joseph Sanford.
> Solomon, bapt. at Redding, 16 Oct. 1757.

Griffin [Unplaced].

ELLEN m. 27 Feb. 1783, Isaac Summers. [Weston rec.]

Griffith [Unplaced].

WILLIAM m. 16 Oct. 1791, Betsey King. [Weston Church]

Guire [Vol. I, p. 248].

```
1 Luke (    -     ) m. Mary Adams.
  2 Luke (    -1699) m. Rebecca Odell.
    3 Luke (1689-1751).
```

3. Guire, Luke, s. of Luke.

Born abt. 1689; d. at Westport, 10 May 1751; m. abt. 1711, Mary Adams, dau. of Nathan, who d. in 1767.

Distribution 6 Dec. 1751: widow Mary; son Ebenezer; Nathan; John; Luke; Stephen; Sarah Rayment; Hannah Lee; Mary Wood; Rebecca, Abigail, and Ruth Guire.

Distribution ordered 11 June 1767 of the part set out as dower in the Est. of Luke Guire: heirs of eldest son Ebenezer; heirs of Sarah late wife of Lemuel Raymond of Norwalk; heirs of Ruth late wife of Daniel Sturges of Fairfield; Nathan, John, Luke, and Stephen Guire; Mary wife of Daniel Wood; Hannah wife of Enos Lee; Abigail wife of Nehemiah Seeley; Rebecca wife of Abel Seeley.

On 9 July 1756, Ebenezer, Nathan, John, and Luke Guire, Enos Lee and Hannah his wife, Nehemiah Seeley and Abigail his wife, and Rebecca Guire, all of Fairfield, and Daniel Wood and Mary his wife, of Ridgefield, conveyed to Daniel Sturgis, Jr.

---

* Or Mable?

Will of Mary, 14 Apr. 1767, proved 10 June 1767; son Stephen (Exec'r); daus. Abigail, Rebecca, Joanna, Mary; sons Nathan, John, Luke, Stephen; children of dec'd son Ebenezer.

Children, three bapt. Fairfield:

> Sarah, bapt. 23 Nov. 1712; m. in 1730, Lemuel Raymond, of Norwalk; lived in New Canaan. Land set to the children of Lemuel Raymond of Norwalk was mentioned in 1773 in a deed given by Abel and Rebecca Seeley to Peter Guire.
> 4+Ebenezer, bapt. 27 Apr. 1718.
> Joanna, bapt. 28 Feb. 1719/20, d. in 1798; m. 1 Oct. 1740, Enos Lee.
> Mary, m. by 1748, Daniel Wood, of Ridgefield.
> 5+Nathan.
> 6+John.
> Rebecca, d. 19 Nov. 1808; m. Abel Seeley.
> Ruth, d. 29 Sept. 1755; m. 11 Dec. 1752, Daniel Sturgis, Jr. Adm'n granted to John Guire, 29 June 1756. Her Est. distributed 1756 to: Ebenezer Guyer; Hannah Lee; Mary Wood; Nathan Guyer; Rebecca Guyer; Abigail Seeley; John Guyer; Luke Guyer; and Stephen Guyer (Mary Guire his guardian). Another distribution made Oct. 1769 to: Nathan Guyer; heirs of Ebenezer Guyer; heirs of Abigail wife of Nehemiah Seelye; Mary wife of Daniel Wood; John Guyer; Stephen Guyer's heirs; Luke Guyer; Rebecca wife of Abel Seeley; and Johanna wife of Enos Lee.
> 7+Luke.
> Abigail, m. 12 Apr. 1755, Nehemiah Seeley, Jr.
> 8+Stephen.

4. Guire, Ebenezer, s. of Luke.

Bapt. 27 Apr. 1718; d. by 1765.

He m. 20 Apr. 1742, Sarah Beers, dau. of Ephraim. She was bur. 5 May 1807 ae. 88 (Trinity Church rec.).

Distribution according to will, 23 May 1765: Jesse; Peter; Ebenezer; Betty wife of Benniah Monroe; Susanna; Sarah; Widow. Ebenezer chose Jesse Guire for guardian, Mar. 1765. Robert and Susanna Whitlock conveyed, 1770, to Peter Guire, land in Norfield from her father Ebenezer Guire dec'd.

Children, rec. Fairfield:

> Jesse, b. 3 Feb. 1743, d. at Weston, in 1768; will 23 Apr., proved 21 June 1768, named wife Mary, dau. Ann, and bro. Peter; m. at Weston, 20 Nov. 1765, Mary Squire. She m. (2) 3 June 1772, Joel Gilbert.

Peter, b. 6 Apr. 1744; m. at Weston, 21 Dec. 1774, Eunice Calhoun; dau. of Nathaniel, bapt. 8 July 1750.
Ann, b. 17 May 1746, d. y.
Betty, b. 15 Feb. 1748; m. at Weston, 1 Feb. 1764, Benaiah Monroe.
Ebenezer, b. 16 Jan. 1750, d. at Weston, 17 Sept. 1821 ae. 71 (g. s.). Will 26 June 1816, proved 10 Oct. 1821; sister Sarah; nephew Peter Guire of Weston.
Susanna, b. 31 July 1752; m. 9 Apr. 1770, Robert Whitlock.
Infant, d. at Westport, Feb. 1754.
Daniel, b. 27 Aug. 1755, d. y.
Sarah, b. 1 Aug. 1759, d. at Weston, 2 Aug. 1837 ae. 78 (g. s.).

5. Guire, Nathan, s. of Luke.

He m. at Westport, 1 Mar. 1748/9, Elizabeth Darling.
He, of Redding, conveyed in 1773.

Children, rec. Fairfield, bapt. Westport:

John-Darling, b. 16 Mar., bapt. 1 Apr. 1750; m. at Redding, 29 Nov. 1768, Rebecca Hill; prob. dau. of Ezekiel, b. 13 Mar. 1751.*
Nathaniel, b. 9 Nov., bapt. 15 Dec. 1751, d. prob. by 1793.†
Mary, b. 4 Aug. 1754.
Lazarus, b. 12 Apr. 1757.

6. Guire, John, s. of Luke.

He m. 22 Nov. 1750, Sarah Brinsmade, who d. at Redding, 16 June 1795.
He, of Redding, conveyed 1771.

Children, rec. Fairfield:

Luke, b. 27 Oct. 1751.
Thaddeus, b. 22 Oct. 1753; m. Rebecca Lee, b. 2 Apr. 1754.‡
Joseph, b. 11 Nov. 1755; res. Redding; m. (1) Eunice Meeker, dau. of Benjamin; m. (2) at Westport, 24 May 1780, Polly Burcham, of Norwalk.§
? Ruth, d. 23 Oct. 1796; m. 11 Mar. 1778, Billy Morehouse.

---

* John, son of Darling Guire of Redding dec'd, ae. abt. 17, chose Seth Hull of Redding for guardian, 11 Feb. 1794.
† Anne, ae. abt. 12, dau. of Nathaniel Guire of Newtown (he supposed dec'd), chose Clark Baldwin of Newtown for guardian, 9 Jan. 1794.
‡ Child, bapt. Trinity Church: Silas, bapt. 14 June 1786.
§ Child by first wife, bapt. Redding: Eunice, bapt. 25 Nov. 1775.

7. Guire, Luke, s. of Luke.

He m. 14 Apr. 1757, Elizabeth Bedient, dau. of John, b. 30 Oct. 1731, and they settled in Wilton. In 1818 Elizabeth was living in Wolcott, Orleans County, Vt., and testified that Seth Hubbell, a pension applicant, had married her daughter during the Revolutionary War. At Wilton we find the record that Seth Hubbell m. 27 Aug. 1779, Elizabeth Guire. Presumably there were other children, rem. to Vt. Luke Guyer and "Zeth" Hubbell were listed in Wolcott, Vt., 1790.

8. Guire, Stephen, s. of Luke.

He m. at Westport, 21 Feb. 1764, Rebecca Burr; dau. of Peter, b. abt. 1740.

Children, bapt. Westport:
> Nathan, bapt. 1 Mar. 1767; m. at Fairfield, 7 Jan. 1795, Elizabeth Jennings.
> Charlotte, bapt. 25 Dec. 1768; m. 6 Sept. 1786, Thomas Cable, Jr.
> Infant, d. 19 Sept. 1771.
> Thaddeus-Burr, bapt. 22 Sept. 1771, d. 17 Nov. 1853; m. 16 Dec. 1792, Mary Disbrow, dau. of Joshua, b. 17 Feb. 1773, d. 5 Mar. 1854.*
> Thomas, bapt. 18 Sept. 1774.
> Jeremiah-Wadsworth, bapt. 28 Sept. 1777.
> John-Lord, bapt. 5 Sept. 1779.
> Hezekiah-Ripley, bapt. 10 Feb. 1782.

Guire, Samuel, Jr.

He m. Ann ———.†

Children, bapt. Fairfield:
> Samuel, bapt. 27 Aug. 1775.‡
> Ann, bapt. 27 Aug. 1775.

Guire [Unplaced].

> JOHN m. 22 Jan. 1794, Huldah Whitlock. [Weston Church]

---

* Children, bapt. Westport: Stephen, bapt. 15 Dec. 1793. Gershom-Burr, bapt. 6 May 1795, d. at Westport, 7 Dec. 1875 ae. 80 yrs. 8 mos. (g. s.); m. 29 Apr. 1817, Fanny B. Smith, b. [20 Oct. 1796], d. 2 Feb. 1868 ae. 71-3-12 (g. s.).

† A Samuel Guire m. at Weston, 27 Nov. 1792, Rebecca Bennett.

‡ Samuel, b. abt. 1760, d. at Redding, 24 Apr. 1793 in 33 yr.; m. 24 Mar. 1782, Elizabeth Burlock(?). Adm'n granted to Elizabeth Guire, 10 June 1793. Children, rec. Redding: John, b. 7 Sept. 1782; Esther, b. 2 Jan. 1784; Charity, b. 2 Mar. 1787; Joseph-Benjamin, b. 7 Nov. 1791.

Hall [Vol. I, pp. 249-256].

```
1 Francis (    -1690) m. (1) Elizabeth ———; (2) Dorothy (Smith) Blackman.
(By 1): 2 Isaac (    -1714) m. Lydia Knapp.
            4 Isaac (1667-1741) m. Jane Burgis.
                9 Samuel (1695-by 1730).
               10 Burgis (1701-1749).
               11 Asa (1706-1771).
               12 Joshua (1708-1789).
            5 Francis (1676-1761) m. Margaret Stites.
               13 Francis (1705-1735).
               14 Richard (1713-1768).
            6 John (1680-1749) m. Abigail Summers.
               15 Elnathan (1711-1774).
               16 John (1717-    ).
            7 Jonathan (1684-1718/9) m. Mary [Lacy?].
               17 Ichabod (    -1800).
         3 Samuel (    -1694) m. (1) Mary ———; (2) Hannah ———; (3)
            Susannah ———.
(By 3): 8 Samuel (1692-1768) m. Sarah Silliman.
           18 Nathaniel (1720-1761).
           19 Ebenezer (1723-1805).
           20 David (1728-    ).
           21 Abel (1730-1809).
```

9. Hall, Samuel, s. of Isaac.

Born 2 Oct. 1695; d. by 1730; m. Hannah Guire, dau. of Luke, bapt. 18 Apr. 1697. She m. (2) Jonathan Squire.

Distribution 18 Mar. 1730: widow; four surviving children,— Ebenezer, Johanna, Jemima, Rebecca.

Children, two bapt. Stratfield:

Jesse, bapt. 2 June 1717, d. y.
Joanna, bapt. 31 Aug. 1718; m. 28 Feb. 1737, Peter Mallory.
Jemima.
Rebecca.
Ebenezer.*
Joseph, bapt. 21 June 1734, d. y.

10. Hall, Burgis, s. of Isaac.

Born 8 Nov. 1701; d. at Bordentown, Burlington County, N. J., in 1749; m. Abigail ———. She was prob. the Abigail Hall of New Jersey who m. (2) (rec. Redding) 12 Apr. 1761, Dea. Stephen Burr.

---

* Wife of Ebenezer, d. at Stratfield, 30 Nov. 1778.

Will 27 Sept. 1748, proved 31 Aug. 1749; wife Abigail; daus. Martha French, Ruth, and Abigail.

Children:
> Martha, m. [Benjamin] French, of Bordentown.
> Ruth.
> Abigail.

11. Hall, Asa, s. of Isaac.

Born 9 Feb. 1706; d. at Danbury in 1771; m. Rachel Meeker, dau. of Daniel.

He with wife Rachel, of Danbury, conveyed 1750 land from her father Daniel Meeker.

Adm'n granted to Timothy Lyon, 22 Apr. 1771. Distribution 30 Apr. 1771: eldest son Samuel; Isaac Hall; Asa Hall; Miriam wife of Timothy Lyon; Eunice wife of John Silliman; "being the Children and all the Children of the s^d dec^d."

Children:
> Elizabeth, b. abt. 1729, d. at Redding, 28 Aug. 1736 ae. 7.
> Miriam, m. 1 July 1752, Timothy Lyon.
> Eunice, m. John Silliman.
> Samuel.
> Isaac.
> Asa.

12. Hall, Joshua, s. of Isaac. Capt., east company, Redding, May 1754.

Born 4 Nov. 1708; d. at Redding in 1789; prob. m. (1) ——— Williams, dau. of Thomas. In 1755 and 1786 his wife was Anna Lane, dau. of Charles.

Joshua of Redding conveyed to sister Anne Corns, 15 Jan. 1744/5. Joshua conveyed 1762 to son Joshua; and 1765 to son Burges. Burges Hall of Redding conveyed 1765 to bro. Thomas-Williams Hall, half of land he purchased of father Joshua.

Adm'n granted, 25 Sept. 1789, to William Hall of Newtown. Estate insolvent.

Children, bapt. Redding:
> ?Lydia, b. abt. 1729, d. at Winchester, 24 Feb. 1824 ae. 95; m. Capt. Timothy Benedict.
> Deborah, b. abt. 1731, d. 3 Sept. 1736 ae. 5.

Elizabeth, bapt. 8 July 1733.
Millicent, bapt. 24 Nov. 1734.
Mabel, bapt. 13 June 1736.
Joshua, b. [say 1738].*
William,† b. 1741, d. 1824; res. Hartford, N. Y.; m. at Newtown, 10 Jan. 1764, Sarah Peck.
Burges, b. [say 1743]; m. at Redding, 23 July 1767, Eunice Whitehead; they res. 1791, Cambridge, Albany County, N. Y.

13. Hall, Francis, s. of Francis.

Born 24 Aug. 1705; d. at Stratfield, 26 Feb. 1734/5 in 30 yr. (g. s.); m. Ann Seeley, dau. of James, b. 20 Jan. 1707. She m. (2) 7 Oct. 1736, Zechariah Sanford, and d. 21 Sept. 1779.

Ann Sanford, formerly Hall, widow of Francis Hall of Stratfield, was appointed guardian in 1738 to James, Eleazer, and Sarah Hall, children of dec'd; Zachariah Sanford gave bond.

Children, rec. Fairfield:

Francis, b. 7 Mar. 1730.
Eleazer, bapt. 19 Mar., 1731/2; m. at Trumbull, 27 Dec. 1756, Mary Lake; dau. of Joseph, b. 30 June 1737.‡
Sarah, b. 10 July 1734, bapt. 21 July 1734.
22+James, b. 7 Mar. 1736(?).

14. Hall, Richard, s. of Francis.

Born 9 Apr. 1713; d. at Stratfield abt. June 1768; m. (1) 30 June 1731, Hannah Booth; dau. of Joseph, Jr.; m. (2) Hannah ———, who was living in 1769. Widow Hannah Hall d. 22 May 1775.

He conveyed 1765 to dau. Hannah wife of Lemuel Bangs.

Will 27 May, proved 14 June 1768; wife Hannah; son Benjamin; children, Mehitabel Hubbell, Rebecca Hall, Margaret Lacy, Hannah Bangs, Lois Hall, Huldah Hall. Adm'n on the intestate part of his estate granted, 14 June 1768, to Benjamin Lacy. Distribution made to widow and children. Benjamin was guardian, 1771, to Huldah (under 18). The estate of Hannah Hall was

---

* Elnathan, son of Joshua and Naomi Hall, bapt. at Huntington Epis. Church, 17 Dec. 1769.
† Was he identical with Thomas-Williams Hall mentioned in deeds?
‡ Children: Deborah, b. 16, bapt. 19 Feb. 1758 (Trumbull rec.). Francis, b. 14, bapt. 27 Jan. 1760 (Trumbull rec.). Anna, b. 30 Apr., bapt. 16 May 1762 (Trumbull rec.); m. Apr. 1783, Edward Duncombe of Easton. Eunice, bapt. June 1769 (Easton Church).

distributed, 14 July 1768, to her son and six daus. (same as in Richard's will); Abel Hall of Stratford had been appointed Adm'r on her estate, 14 June 1768.

> Children [by first wife], bapt. Stratfield:
> Jedediah, bapt. 27 Feb. 1732, d. y.
> Mehitabel, bapt. 7 Oct. 1733; m. Gershom Hubbell.
> Rebecca, bapt. 28 Dec. 1735, d. at Trumbull, 11 Jan. 1810 ae. 74 (g. s.); m. 6 Sept. 1751, Abel Hall.
> Margaret, b. abt. 1741, d. at Stratfield, 1 Sept. 1792 in 52 yr. (g. s.); m. Benjamin Lacy.
> Hannah, bapt. 30 Jan. 1742/3, d. at Stratfield, 9 Sept. 1771; m. Lemuel Bangs.
> Benjamin, m. Ellen Morehouse, dau. of Abijah, bapt. 9 Feb. 1745/6.*
> Lois.
> Huldah, b. abt. 1753, d. 17 Aug. 1773 in 20 yr. (g. s.); Benjamin Hall was appointed her guardian, 1769.

15. Hall, Elnathan, s. of John. Ens., south company, New Fairfield, May 1752; Lt., May 1757; Capt., May 1761. Deputy for New Fairfield, Oct. 1764, Oct. 1765.

Bapt. 19 Aug. 1711; d. at New Fairfield in 1774; m. (1) 28 Dec. 1732, Hannah Hawley, who d. 9 Apr. 1741 in 26 yr. (g. s., Stratfield); m. (2) Hannah ———.

Adm'n granted, 7 June 1774, to widow Hannah. Estate insolvent.

Tirza and Martha, daus. of Elnathan Hall, chose Cornell Smith of New Fairfield for guardian, 14 Aug. 1786. A Mary Hall m. at Danbury, 13 Apr. 1780, Eliud Taylor, and named a son Elnathan-Hall Taylor.

> Children [by first wife], bapt. Stratfield:
> Elizabeth, bapt. 28 Oct. 1733; ? m. 24 Oct. 1750, Joseph Benedict, of Danbury.
> Abigail, bapt. 27 July 1735; ? m. at New Fairfield, 9 Dec. 1756, Samuel Gregory.
> Ephraim, b. [19 Apr. 1738], d. 22 Apr. 1739 ae. 1 yr. 3 days (g. s.).
> Ephraim, b. [18 June 1740], d. 2 July 1740 ae. 14 days (g. s.).
>
> Children [by second wife], bapt. Stratfield:
> Hannah, bapt. 29 Oct. 1749.
> ?Huldah, b. (rec. Danbury) 17 Nov. 1753; m. at Danbury, 30 Jan. 1777, Hezekiah Benedict, Jr.

---

* Children of Benjamin d. 5 Aug. 1770, 2 Feb. 1774, and 19 and 25 Sept. 1778.

16. **Hall, John,** s. of John.

Bapt. 19 May 1717.

He m. (1) Sarah ———, who d. 6 Apr. 1739 ae. 26 (g. s., Stratfield).

He m. (2) Martha Hall, dau. of Samuel, bapt. 9 Apr. 1717, d. 8 June 1802 ae. 85 (Trinity Church rec.).

17. **Hall, Ichabod,** s. of Jonathan.

Will 15 Nov. 1793, proved 12 Apr. 1800; dau. Abigail wife of Amos Beardslee; wife to have residue for life, and then to son William Hall.

Children, bapt. Stratfield:
> William, a Methodist minister in Greenfield by family tradition; m. Anna Williams.*
> Abigail, m. Amos Beardsley.
> Hannah, bapt. 19 Mar. 1748/9, d. y.

18. **Hall, Nathaniel,** s. of Samuel.

Born 3 Nov. 1720; d. at Stratfield in 1761; m. Rebecca Wheeler, who apparently d. by 1774. The will of Ebenezer Wheeler, 1744, named his dau. Rebecca Hall. Did she m. (2) at Greenfield, 23 June 1768, David Thorp, as his third wife? If so, she was b. abt. 1724 and d. 17 Feb. 1781 in 57 yr.

Nathaniel Hall and Rebecca his wife of Stratfield conveyed 1748 land at Long Hill, Stratford, bounded on land of heirs of Ebenezer Wheeler.

Adm'n granted, 15 June 1761. Mabel Hall chose Rebecca Hall for guardian, May 1766. Ebenezer Hall had been appointed guardian of Mabel and Rebecca, Sept. 1762. Sarah chose Daniel Silliman for guardian, June 1762.

Distribution 6 Dec. 1762: widow Rebecca; only son Daniel; eldest dau. Sarah Hall; 2d dau. Mabel Hall; youngest dau. Rebecca Hall. Distribution of the dower which had been set to the widow Rebecca, 9 Apr. 1774: Daniel Hall; heirs of Sarah late wife of Samuel French of Fairfield; Rebecca Hall; Mabel wife of Isaac Wildman of Danbury.

---

* Children (by a family account): Charity; Annie; Lyman; LeGrand; Willis; George-Washington, bapt. at Trumbull, 4 Feb. 1780, m. Lois Bulkley, dau. of Turney. William Hall, b. abt. 1739, d. 1830 ae. 91, was Lt. in Revolution, and father of Lyman Hall of Kent (see affidavit of latter in pension file of Gideon Wells). Lyman Hall m. after 1807, Sarah (Nichols), widow of Jabez Hill.

Children:

    Sarah, d. 17 Feb. 1774; m. (rec. Weston) 16 Apr. 1766, Samuel French.
    Mabel, m. Isaac Wildman, Jr., of Danbury.
    Rebecca, bapt. at Stratfield, 25 Dec. 1754.
    Daniel, had Abel Hall appointed for his guardian, Sept. 1762.

19. Hall, Ebenezer, s. of Samuel.

Born 12 Mar. 1723; d. 10 Apr. 1805 (Private rec.).

He m. (1) 19 May 1747 (Private rec.), Tabitha Hubbell; dau. of Daniel, b. 22 Oct. 1722; d. 30 Nov. 1778 (Private rec.).

He m. (2) abt. 1780/1, Elizabeth, widow of Thaddeus Bennett, and dau. of Joseph Wilson; bapt. 2 Apr. 1732, d. in 1815.

Had been inimical to U. S.; gave bond of £1000, Jan. 1777, not to depart from bounds of Fairfield and Stratford, and declared himself now convinced of justice of American cause.

Will 20 July 1799 (?), proved 29 Apr. 1805; wife Elizabeth; my five children, Seth, Esbon and Daniel Hall, Esther wife of Hezekiah Treadwell, and Mary wife of Isaac Silliman. Distribution to the widow and five children, 1805.

Children [by first wife]:

23+Seth, b. 9 May 1749.
    Daniel, bapt. at Stratfield, 19 Aug. 1750, d. y.
24+Ezbon, b. 20 Mar. 1753.
    Esther, b. abt. 1755, living 1845 in East Franklin, N. Y.; m. Hezekiah Treadwell.
    Mary, b. 13 Mar. 1757 (family record), living 1855 in Stamford, N. Y.; m. 18 May 1780, Isaac Silliman.
25+Daniel, b. 9 Nov. 1758.

20. Hall, David, s. of Samuel.

Born 20 June 1728.

He m. at Trumbull, 23 Aug. 1754, Lydia Wildman.

Children (perhaps others):

    Matthew, b. ———; res. Roxbury.
    David, m. at Weston, 17 Apr. 1782, Ann Jackson.*
    Martha, b. 3 Dec. 1760; m. 28 Feb. 1782, Thaddeus Bennett.

---

* Children, rec. Weston: Aaron, b. 10 Apr. 1783; David, b. 24 Feb. 1785; Levi, b. 22 Apr. 1787; Wildman, b. 7 Nov. 1789; Lydia, b. 4 Nov. 1791; Alva, b. 13 Feb. 1794; Cyrus, b. 9 Feb. 1796; Truman, b. 9 Dec. 1798.

Wildman, b. at Fairfield, 23 Apr. 1765, bapt. at Easton, 23 June 1765, d. at Easton, 10 July 1851 in 86 yr. (g. s.); m. at Weston, 8 Nov. 1786, Alice Blackman, b. 28 Sept. 1767, d. 20 Jan. 1843 ae. 78 (g. s.).*
Ann, bapt. at Easton, 12 Sept. 1767.
?John, b. 28 Feb. 1770; m. at Easton, 7 Mar. 1791, Hannah Wheeler, b. 20 Jan. 1767.†

21. **Hall, Abel,** s. of Samuel. Ens., east company, North Fairfield and North Stratford, May 1762; Lt., May 1763; Capt., Oct. 1771.

Born 12 July 1730; d. at Trumbull, 7 Mar. 1809 in 79 yr. (g. s.); m. 6 Sept. 1751, Rebecca Hall, dau. of Richard, b. abt. 1735, d. 11 Jan. 1810 ae. 74 (g. s.).

Will 23 Aug. 1808, proved 11 Apr. 1809, calls him of Weston; wife Rebecca; son Aaron, 100 acres in Township No. 3, Tioga County, N. Y.; son Samuel; son Abel, land near dwelling house lately owned by sister Munson (?), dau. Rhoda wife of Stephen Gregory; dau. Olive, land at Tashua in Trumbull; dau. Hannah wife of Isaac Edwards, land adjoining land where said Hannah and Isaac now dwell; dau. Rebecca wife of John Winton; two gr. daus. Sarah and Susannah Fairchild; dau. Clara wife of James M. Bulkley; son Benjamin.

Adm'n on Est. of Rebecca Hall was granted, 15 Jan. 1810, to Abel Hall, with Samuel Edwards as surety.

Distribution order, estate of Rebecca Hall of Weston, 1 Aug. 1810: children,—Aaron Hall, Rhoda Gregory, Olive Mallet, Samuel Hall, Hannah Edwards, Rebecca Winton, Clara Bulkly, Abel Hall, Benjamin Hall.

Children, rec. Stratford:
Aaron, b. 13 Dec. 1751; m. 18 Feb. 1773, Rebecca Summers.‡
Rhoda, b. 12 Jan. 1754; m. 26 Mar. 1772, Stephen Gregory.

---

* Children, rec. Weston: Levi, b. 5 May 1787; Lewis, b. 1 July 1789; Ezra, b. 25 June 1792, d. at Easton, 3 Nov. 1876 ae. 84 (g. s.), m. Esther ———, who d. 3 Jan. 1873 ae. 74 (g.s.); Burr, b. 15 Jan. 1795; Isaac, b. 30 Jan. 1798, d. at Easton, 29 Oct. 1874 ae. 76-3-8 (g. s.), m. Polly Gould, dau. of Aaron, who d. 16 Nov. 1880 ae. 74 (g. s.). Adm'n on estate of Polly Hall [dau. of Wildman?] granted 6 Apr. 1852; distribution to Lewis Hall, Ezra Hall, Burr Hall of Michigan, Isaac Hall, Nathan E. Hall, Lorinda, wife of Alanson Banks of State of New York, and Catherine E. Burritt of Newtown.

† Children, rec. Weston: Mira, b. 24 July 1791; Wheeler, b. 22 Oct. 1793, d. 10 July 1796; Lambert, b. 21 June 1797.

‡ Children, rec. Weston: Sarah, b. 6 Dec. 1775; Mary, b. 22 Feb. 1778; Rebecca, b. 9 Apr. 1780; Aaron, b. 1 June 1782, d. at Easton, 9 Nov. 1837 ae. 55-5-8 (g. s.), m. Hannah Lyon; Jedediah, b. 10 Apr. 1784; Lyman, b. 3 May 1786; Clara, b. 12 Sept. 1792; Anne, b. 5 Oct. 1795.

Jedediah, b. 27 Apr. 1756, d. y.
Olive, b. 26 Aug. 1758; m. ——— Mallett.
Nathaniel, b. 27 Apr. 1761, d. y.
Samuel, b. 14 July 1763.
Hannah, b. 19 Nov. 1765; m. 22 Dec. 1786, Isaac Edwards.
Rebecca, b. 29 Dec. 1767; m. John Winton.
Clara, b. 18 May 1770; m. James M. Bulkley.
Abel, b. 2 Aug. 1772, d. at Easton, 30 Dec. 1836 ae. 64 (g. s.); m. at Easton, Nov. 1792, Sarah Sherwood, dau. of John, b. 4 Nov. 1771, d. 31 Dec. 1855 ae. 84 (g. s.).*
Benjamin, b. 13 Aug. 1775.

22. Hall, James, s. of Francis.

Born 7 Mar. 1736; perhaps d. at Westport, 6 Aug. 1793.

He m. 3 Apr. 1755, Abigail Beers; dau. of James, b. 2 Apr. 1731.

Children, first rec. Fairfield:

Sarah, b. 8 Feb. 1756, bapt. at Stratfield, 15 Feb. 1756; ? m. Thomas Cook.
Olive, b. 29 Oct. 1760 (Pension rec.), living 1840 at Bethel, Sullivan County, N. Y.; m. 15 Apr. 1779, David Jackson.
James-Seeley, b. abt. 1768, d. at Stratfield, 29 Apr. 1770 in 2 yr. (g. s.).
Prob. others.

23. Hall, Seth, s. of Ebenezer.

Born 9 May 1749; res. Weston to 1805; res. Fairfield 1805-31; living in Danbury 1832.

He m. 11 May 1769, Lois ———.

He was a pensioner for Revolutionary service. Probably earlier he had been inclined to the loyalist side, like his father; for a Seth Hall, a Tory, was released on bond, Feb. 1777.

Children, rec. Weston:

Ebenezer, b. 20 Aug. 1770; m. at Easton, 26 Oct. 1791, Lydia Booth.
Gideon H., b. 3 May 1772, d. at Easton, 22 Jan. 1826 ae. 53 (g. s.); m. Ruth Hubbell, dau. of Nathaniel, b. abt. 1771, d. 20 Mar. 1859 ae. 88 (g. s.).

---

* Probate records show that Abel left widow Sarah and had a dau. Sally who d. unm. by 1837; a dau. Mabel who left a child Eliza G. Summers; and a son Abel, Jr., who d. by 1837, leaving widow Polly and children Abel S., Francis M., Charles W., and Henry S. In 1855, Eliza G. Summers was wife of Charles W. Everett; Abel, Charles and Henry Hall were of California, Francis Hall of Bridgeport.

Betsey, b. 7 Apr. 1774, d. 11 Apr. 1792.
Molly, b. 3 Sept. 1776; m. Timothy Wildman, of Brookfield.
Richard, b. 7 Mar. 1779, d. at Stratfield, 23 Sept. 1826 ae. 47 (g. s.); adm'n granted, 24 Oct. 1826, to widow Sally; m. Sally ———, b. abt. 1779, d. 12 Mar. 1840 ae. 61 (g. s.).
Philo, b. 27 Apr. 1784.
Lucy, b. 9 Jan. 1788.
Clarissa, b. 6 Jan. 1791.
Esther, b. 13 Feb. 1793.
Rebecca, b. 1 Nov. 1795.

24. **Hall, Ezbon,** s. of Ebenezer.

Born 20 Mar. 1753; d. at Easton, 15 Aug. 1833 ae. 80 yrs. 6 mos. (g. s.); m. 4 May 1775, Rhoda Brinsmade, b. 9 Apr. 1755, d. 5 Apr. 1850 ae. 95 (g. s.).

Adm'n granted, 3 Oct. 1833, to James Baldwin; estate insolvent.

Adm'n on estate of Rhoda Hall was granted, 28 Aug. 1850; distribution to Josiah B. Hall, Rhoda Hall, Pamela wife of Sherman French, Joseph B., Isaac, and heirs of Sarah Wheeler.

Children, rec. Weston, three bapt. Easton:

Josiah B., b. 30 Mar. 1776, d. at Easton, 17 Apr. 1858 ae. 82 (g. s.); m. 13 Nov. 1794, Elizabeth Burr; dau. of Daniel, b. 24 July 1775, d. 24 Jan. 1848 ae. 72 yrs. 6 mos. (g. s.).*
Naomi-Bennett, b. 8 July 1778, d. 20 Mar. 1794.
Gershom-Odell, b. 18 Sept. 1780, d. 16 June 1782.
Sarah, b. 1 Dec. 1782, d. at Easton, 12 Feb. 1846 ae. 64 (g. s.); m. Jesse Wheeler.
Isaac, b. 23 Sept. 1784; m. Polly ———, who d. at Easton, 16 Dec. 1841 ae. 47 (g. s.).
Almon, b. 25 Sept. 1787, d. 20 Mar. 1798.
Priscilla, b. 9 Aug., bapt. 12 Dec. 1790, d. at Easton, 25 Sept. 1815 ae. 25 (g. s.); m. Peter C. Oakley.
Joseph-Bennett, b. 12 Feb., bapt. Apr. 1793, d. at Easton, 6 Dec. 1866 in 74 yr. (g. s.); m. abt. 1814, Cornelia Baker.
Pamela, b. 4 May 1795, bapt. June 1795; m. Sherman French.
Rhoda, b. 12 Mar. 1798, d. at Easton, 10 Feb. 1888 ae. 89 yrs. 11 mos. (g. s.).
Philemon, b. 28 Feb. 1802, d. in 1837. Adm'n granted, 19 June 1837, to Zenas Johnson. Distribution made to bros. and sisters: Josiah B. Hall; Sarah widow of Jesse Wheeler; Isaac Hall; Joseph B. Hall; Permila wife of Sherman French; Rhoda Hall.

---

* Child, rec. Weston: Ebenezer-Silliman, b. 11 Dec. 1795, d. at Easton, 13 Apr. 1881 ae. 85 (g. s.); m. Eliza Coley, who d. 11 Apr. 1880 ae. 81 (g. s.).

25. Hall, Daniel, s. of Ebenezer. Ens., 12th Co., 4th Regt., Alarm List, Jan. 1780.

Born 9 Nov. 1758; d. at Trumbull, 1 Apr. 1849 in 91 yr. (g. s.); m. 30 Apr. 1782, Jemima Turney; dau. of Thomas, b. 8 May 1762, d. 24 Jan. 1821 in 59 yr. (g. s.).

Children, rec. Weston:
>Tabitha, b. 17 June 1783.
>Mabel, b. 10 Oct. 1786.
>Thomas-Turney, b. 13 Feb. 1789.
>Daniel-Alanson, b. 25 Sept. 1790, d. at Trumbull, 18 June 1863 ae. 73 yrs. 9 mos. (g. s.); m. Sophia S. Edwards, who d. 4 Jan. 1862 ae. 66 (g. s.).
>Zalmon, b. 13 June 1795,* d. at Trumbull, 13 Feb. 1884 (g. s.); m. (1) Rhoda Beach, b. 9 May 1795 (g. s.), d. 24 Aug. 1827 (g. s.); m. (2) Apr. 1829, Hannah-Melinda Bennett, b. 30 Dec. 1804 (g. s.), d. 3 Apr. 1865 (g. s.).
>Alben, b. 20 Oct. 1798, d. at Trumbull, 28 Oct. 1865 ae. 67 (g. s.); m. (1) Huldah Taylor, dau. of Hiram of Brookfield; m. (2) Lola Turner, dau. of Enoch of New Haven.
>Benjamin, m. Hannah M. ———.

Hall, Lyman. Signer of Declaration of Independence; Governor of Georgia.

Son of John and Mary (Street), b. at Wallingford, 12 Apr. 1724; d. in Ga., 19 Oct. 1790 ae. 67; grad. Yale Coll.; settled in Fairfield as a physician.

He m. (1) 20 May 1752, Abigail Burr, dau. of Thaddeus, b. 24 Mar. 1729, d. 8 July 1753 ae. 24 (g. s.); m. (2) Mary Osborn, dau. of Samuel, b. 8 Aug. 1736; her will dated 10 Oct. 1793, Burke County, Ga.

No issue survived.

Hall [*Unplaced*].
>ABIAH, bapt. 14 Aug. 1743. [Greens Farms Church]
>ESTHER m. 18 Sept. 1766, Joseph Griffin. [Redding rec.]
>EUNICE m. 28 Apr. 1779, Jesse Belknap. [Redding Church]
>DEBORAH m. 23 May 1779, Giles Gilbert. [Redding Church]
>HEZEKIAH m. Sarah Bradley, dau. of Francis, b. 18 Apr. 1763.
>ABIGAIL m. 17 Oct. 1773, Samuel Platt. [Redding Church]
>OLIVE m. Oct. 1791, Ezekiel Robertson. [Easton Church]

---
* One Dr. Zalmon H. Hall d. at Easton, 25 July 1867 ae. 72 (g. s.).

THE FAMILIES OF OLD FAIRFIELD 435

Hamilton, Benjamin.

Children, bapt. Redding:
> ? Benjamin.
> Esther, bapt. 28 May 1733.
> Seth, bapt. 4 May 1735.
> Deborah, bapt. 2 Jan. 1737.
> Amelia, bapt. 23 Apr. 1738; m. 21 May 1760, Ebenezer Whitlock.

Hamilton, Benjamin [? s. of Benjamin].

He m. 6 Apr. 1754, Hannah Bulkley, dau. of Daniel, bapt. 21 Nov. 1731.

Will 5 Oct. 1793; wife Hannah; daus. Hannah Marchant, Tabitha, Molly Bartram, Miriam Durant, Eunice Hamilton; sons Isaac, Seth, Benjamin. Inv. 11 Nov. 1793.

Children, rec. Fairfield, bapt. Redding:
> Isaac, b. and bapt. 22 Sept. 1754, d. at Redding in 1830; will proved 10 Nov. 1830;* m. 28 Aug. 1774, Eunice Platt, bapt. 30 May 1756, d. at Redding, 27 Jan. 1829 ae. 76 (g. s.).
> Hannah, b. 28 Nov., bapt. 1 Dec. 1755, d. at Redding, 25 Aug. 1804; m. 19 May 1773, Chauncey Merchant.
> Tabitha, bapt. 24, d. 26 Apr. 1757 ae. 1 mo.
> Tabitha, bapt. 16 Apr. 1758, living at Sharon, 1839; m. 13 Nov. 1778 (Pension rec.), John Merchant.
> Seth, bapt. 11 Jan. 1761, d. 18 June 1761 ae. 6 mos.
> Molly, b. abt. 1764, living at Sherman, 1839; m. Isaac Bartram.
> Miriam, b. abt. 1768, living at Danbury, 1839; m. (1) ―― Durant; m. (2) ―― Hoyt.
> Seth.
> Benjamin.
> Eunice, m. 25 Jan. 1798, Joseph Griffin, Jr.

Hamilton [*Unplaced*].

> ALEXANDER m. by 1768, Ann Jennings, dau. of Nathan.
> WILLIAM m. 3 June 1766, Martha Prince. [Redding Church rec.]
> JAMES m. Rhoda Morehouse, dau. of Abijah, bapt. 21 Sept. 1740. In 1763, James in a deed was called now Sergeant in his Majesty's 48th Regt. of Foot; in 1770, res. Stratford.

---

* The will gave $1000 to Urilly wife of David Canfield of Batavia, N. Y., and the residue to David and Urilly Canfield and to Lydia wife of Isaac H. Bartram of Redding.

Hamlet [Unplaced].

ANNA, of Norwalk, m. 7 Mar. 1781, Richard West, of L. I.

Hancock [Unplaced].

HON. JOHN m. 28 Aug. 1775, Miss Dorothy Quincey, both of Boston. [Fairfield Church]

Hanford, Eleazer, s. of Eleazer [Vol. I, p. 258].

Born abt. 1720.

He m. Dec. 1745, Ann Taylor, dau. of Noah; she d. 1802.

Children:

    Sarah, b. 1746; m. 3 Apr. 1761, David Morehouse.
    Noah-Taylor, d. at Westport, 15 Feb. 1783; m. (1) Elizabeth Couch, dau. of Thomas, b. 23 Jan. 1756, d. 3 June 1780; m. (2) 12 Nov. 1780, Hannah Morehouse; dau. of Gideon, b. 12 Oct. 1753, d. 18 Mar. 1784.*
    Eleazer.
    Rhoda, m. 4 Mar. 1784, Aaron Adams.
    Ozias, d. at Fairfield, 8 Jan. 1806 (Pension rec.); will 23 Dec. 1805, proved 27 Jan. 1806, named nephew William Hanford and my wife Elizabeth; m. at Wilton, 20 Mar. 1783, Elizabeth Fitch, b. abt. 1763; she m. (2) 3 Dec. 1807, Dr. Joseph Crane, who d. 28 Nov. 1825.
    Anna, m. Gideon Wilcoxson.
    Lewis, m. Susanna Gregory.
    Matthew, d. Sept. 1783 (Pension rec.); m. 11 Mar. 1779, Betsey Lyon; dau. of David, bapt. 19 Nov. 1758, living 1837.†

Hanford, Elnathan, Jr.

He m. at Westport, 15 Sept. 1752, Anna Cable of Fairfield; dau. of George, b. 19 May 1730.

Child, bapt. Westport:

    Susanna, bapt. 11 Feb. 1754;‡ ? m. 18 Dec. 1788, Jonathan Poor.

---

* Children of Noah and Elizabeth, bapt. Westport: Ebenezer, bapt. 26 Feb. 1775; Hezekiah, bapt. 6 June 1777. Child [by second wife]: Joseph, bapt. 11 Nov. 1781; idiot, living 1828.

† Child of Matthias and Elizabeth, bapt. Westport: Sarah, bapt. 3 Aug. 1783; perhaps m. at Westport, 28 Nov. 1802, Samuel Disbrow.

‡ Annah Beebe, dau. of Susanna Hanford, bapt. 9 Apr. 1786.

Hanford [Unplaced].

LUCRETIA of Fairfield m. 17 Jan. 1762, Asaph Chilson, of Middletown. [Greens Farms Church]
ESTHER m. 28 Feb. 1768, George Cable. [Greens Farms Church]
ELIZABETH m. 16 May 1771, Simon Andrews. [Greens Farms Church]
ANN m. 8 Mar. 1770, Joseph Hollister, of Glastonbury. [Greens Farms Church]
JOSEPH m. 20 Sept. 1772, Abigail [Adams] Bradley.* [Greens Farms Church] [Joseph of Fairfield went to Long Island and put himself under protection of the enemy, 1779.] Hains, son of Joseph, d. 12 July 1787. [Greens Farms Church]
HAINS d. 18 Sept. 1798 ae. 82. [Greens Farms Church]
JANE, wife of JOSEPH of Fairfield, by will 29 Mar., proved 21 Apr. 1815, gave all to husband.
JOHN m. 6 Aug. 1775, Rebecca Gorham. [Weston Church]
POLLY m. 29 Apr. 1779, John S. Pearsall. [Greens Farms Church]
GEORGE m. 30 Apr. 1786, Elizabeth Wright. [Greens Farms Church]
RUTH m. 10 Sept. 1764, Preserved Taylor. [Redding rec.]
LEWIS m. 12 Nov. 1793, Mary Betts, at Wilton. [Weston Church]
ISAAC, b. abt. 1780, d. 28 Aug. 1805 ae. 25; m. 24 Jan. 1802, Albacinda Chapman. [Greens Farms Church]
WIDOW ELIZABETH d. 11 Sept. 1807 ae. 86. [Greens Farms Church]
WIDOW MARY d. 27 Mar. 1808. [Greens Farms Church]

Harper [Unplaced].

MARY, dau. of John of Martha's Vineyard, m. 22 Aug. 1754, John Squire.

Harris, Robert.

Of Weston, m. (1) at Fairfield, 26 Oct. 1775, Mary Bulkley, of Fairfield; possibly dau. of James, b. 3 Apr. 1757, d. in 1779 ae. 22 (g. s.).†

He was bapt. at Weston, 12 July 1777, with his son Stephen.

He m. (2) at Weston, 15 Nov. 1778, Eunice Gray; dau. of Nathan, b. 19 Jan. 1756.

A son of Robert, unnamed, was bapt. at Easton, Aug. 1789.

---

* They had: Jonathan, d. at Westport, 12 Oct. 1793; Stephen-Bradley, who m. at Westport, 7 May 1795, Esther Burr. "Bradley" Hanford had children, bapt. Westport: Jonathan, bapt. 26 Nov. 1797; Abigail-Adams, bapt. 20 Apr. 1800; Esther, bapt. 1 Sept. 1803.

† The year date seems to be in error, if this Mary was the one who married Harris.

Hawkins [Unplaced].

ZACHARIAH, of L. I., m. 26 Sept. 1782, Esther Hill.

Hawley, Thomas, s. of Samuel [Vol. I, p. 265].

Born at Stratford, 30 July 1678; d. at Stratfield, 6 May 1722 ae. 44 (g. s.); m. Oct. 1701, Johanna Sherwood, widow of John. She was dau. of Ephraim Booth, b. Sept. 1678, d. 28 Jan. 1761 in 84 yr. (g. s.).

Deacon, Stratfield Church.

Between 1761 and 1765, several receipts were given to William Bennett, Exec'r on the estate of Joannah Hawley, by the following heirs; son Ezra Hawley; gr. children Joseph and Elizabeth Benedict; Hannah Sherman; Abigail Gregory; gr. dau. Joanna Peet; children Joseph and Esther Sterling; dau. Eunice Hawley of Stratfield; and children John and Jemima Gold of Fairfield. [Jemima was dau. of Johanna by her first husband.]

Children, rec. Stratford, bapt. Stratfield:

Ebenezer, b. 11 (?), bapt. 6 June 1703; m. ———.
Mary, b. 11 Sept., bapt. 14 Oct. 1705, d. y.
Elizabeth, b. 5 Nov., bapt. 22 Dec. 1706, d. 12 July 1731 ae. 25; m. 29 Nov. 1727, Isaac Judson.
Thomas, b. 7 Jan., bapt. 27 Feb. 1708/9.
Ezra, b. 15, bapt. 20 May 1711, d. at Stratfield, 27 Apr. 1773 in 62 yr. (g. s.); Capt.; m. 30 Jan. 1734/5, Abigail Hall; dau. of John, b. [late in 1715], d. 18 Apr. 1786 in 71 yr. (g. s.).
Mary, b. 16, bapt. 25 Jan. 1712/3; m. 28 Feb. 1732/3, Peter Walker, of Woodbury.
Hannah, b. 15 May 1715, d. at Stratfield, 9 Apr. 1741 in 26 yr. (g. s.); m. 28 Dec. 1732, Elnathan Hall.
Hester, b. 30 June, bapt. 17 July 1717, d. at Trumbull, 27 Apr. 1773 in 56 yr. (g. s.); m. Joseph Stirling.
Samuel, b. 15 Apr., bapt. Apr. or May 1719, at Stratfield, 11 Sept. 1749 ae. 31 (g. s.); m. Sarah Edwards, who d. 10 Oct. 1772; she m. (2) 18 Dec. 1753, Rev. Robert Ross.*
Katharine, b. 19 Feb. 1721/2, d. at Easton, 22 July 1809 in 88 yr. (g. s.); m. 3 Dec. 1744, William Bennett.

---

* Their only child, Molly, d. at Stratfield, 4 Apr. 1765 ae. 17 (g. s.). Her personal estate was set to [her half-sister] Sarah dau. of Rev. Robert Ross; her realty to Ezra Hawley, Catherine wife of William Bennet, Hester wife of Joseph Sterling, heirs of Ebenezer Hawley dec'd, heirs of Elizabeth Judson dec'd, heirs of Hannah Hall, heirs of Mary Walker.

Hawley, Joseph, s. of John [Vol. I, p. 267].

Bapt. at Stratford, 27 Apr. 1707; d. at Redding, 12 Dec. 1771 ae. 66; m. 25 Jan. 1727/8, Hannah Walker, dau. of John, b. abt. 1710, d. 16 July 1769 ae. 59.

Children, first six rec. Stratford, four Fairfield (bapt. Redding):

Tabitha, b. 5 Apr. 1730, d. at Redding in 1783; m. (1) at Redding, 18 Dec. 1746, John Read, Jr.; m. (2) 25 Feb. 1759, Elias Bates.
Ezekiel, b. 29 Aug. 1731, d. at North Salem, N. Y., 6 Feb. 1788; ? m. at Redding, 20 Dec. 1770, Huldah Lyon. [If he was her husband, they were divorced.]
Sarah, b. 2 Aug. 1733; m. 11 Dec. 1753, William Read.
Hannah, b. 4 Dec. 1734, d. at Redding, 13 Mar. 1805 in 70 yr. (g. s.); m. 7 Sept. 1755, Hezekiah Sanford.
+William, b. 24 Mar. 1738.
John, b. 24 Sept. 1739; m. 21 Dec. 1762, Abigail Sanford; dau. of Samuel, bapt. 13 Jan. 1742/3.
Mary, b. 2, bapt. 7 Feb. 1742; m. 19 Sept. 1756, Paul Bartram.
Samuel, b. 2, bapt. 5 Aug. 1744, d. abt. 1785; Ens., east company, Redding, Oct. 1773;* m. 6 July 1779 (divorce record), Catherine, widow of Eliphalet Wakeman, and dau. of Dea. William Bennett, b. 7 Apr. 1751; she divorced him after he deserted her in 1783.
Ruth, b. 26 Oct., bapt. 5 Nov. 1746; m. 22 Apr. 1767, Elnathan Sturges.
Eunice, b. 6 Sept., bapt. 25 Oct. 1750; m. 27 Apr. 1773, Elijah Burr.

Hawley, William, s. of Joseph. Deputy for Redding, May and Oct. 1774, Mar., Apr., May, July, Oct., and Dec. 1775, Oct. 1779, Jan. and Apr. 1780, May and Oct. 1781, May 1786; 1st Lt., 10th Co., 5th Regt., Army, 1775 (apparently declined); 2d Lt. in Army, May 1776; 1st Lt., June 1776; Capt., 8th Co., 4th Regt., Alarm List, May 1780; Justice, 1775, '76, '77, '81.

Born 24 Mar. 1738; d. at Redding, 16 Feb. 1797 in 59 yr. (g. s.); m. at Westport, 12 July 1758, Lydia Nash; dau. of Capt. Thomas, b. 26 Mar. 1740, d. 26 Apr. 1812 ae. 72 (g. s.).

Adm'n granted, 15 Mar. 1797, to Hezekiah Hawley.

---

* Samuel gave bond, Dec. 1776, to remain on farm of his dec'd father, but joined the enemy at time of Danbury raid; was pardoned on returning and taking oath of fidelity, Jan. 1778.

Children, rec. Redding; all except first bapt. Redding:

Lydia, b. 6 Sept., bapt. at Westport, 7 Oct. 1759, d. 5 Dec. 1761.
Joseph, b. 3 June, bapt. 4 July 1762; m. 3 Aug. 1785, Chloe Rogers; prob. m. (2) Hannah Meeker, dau. of Jonathan, b. 24 Apr. 1770.*
Lydia, b. 13 Dec. 1763 (?), bapt. 16 Dec. 1764, d. 5 Dec. 1766 ae. 2 yrs. 3 mos. (g. s.).
William, b. 1 Jan. 1766, bapt. 19 Jan. 1766, d. 20 Jan. 1766.
Billy [William], b. 9 Feb., bapt. 12 Apr. 1767, d. at DeRuyter, Madison County, N. Y., 16 June 1854; grad. Yale Coll. 1787; lawyer, settled 1798 in Woodbury, which he represented in the Conn. Assembly, May 1802, Oct. 1802, Oct. 1805; rem. to Oswego, N. Y.; m. 24 Dec. 1794, Sarah Marshall, dau. of Rev. John-Rutgers Marshall; she d. at Oswego, 24 June 1845 in 74 yr.
Hezekiah, b. 10 Mar. 1772(?), bapt. 19 May 1771; m. 4 Apr. 1796, Rebecca Sanford.†
Lemuel, bapt. 18 Sept. 1774, d. 22 Mar. 1846 ae. 74 (g. s., Easton); m. 19 July 1794, Elizabeth Lyon, b. 22 May 1778, d. 27 Aug. 1856 ae. 78 (g. s.).‡

Hawley [Unplaced].

WOLCOTT m. 29 Nov. 1764, Ellen Osborn. [Fairfield Church]
HULDAH m. 24 Nov. 1783, Aaron Dean. [Weston Church]
LT. GIDEON d. at Fairfield, 11 Sept. 1784 ae. [—] (g. s.); Gideon, s. of Gideon and Hannah, bapt. 21 Nov. 1784, d. 6 Jan. 1788 ae. 3 yrs. 6 mos. (g. s.). Gideon of North Stratford had m. at Fairfield, 18 Jan. 1784, Hannah Penfield; she m. (2) 20 Feb. 1791, Ezekiel Lovejoy.
GIDEON of Stratfield m. 9 Oct. 1784, Levina Darrow. [Fairfield Church]
THOMAS of Ridgefield m. 13 Jan. 1747/8, Elizabeth Gold. [Fairfield Church]
REBECCA m. 23 Sept. 1792, Nathan Thorp. [Weston rec.]
LYDIA m. 2 Nov. 1780, Aaron Sanford. [Redding rec.]

Hawley, Ephraim.

Son of Daniel and Elizabeth (Brinsmade), and gr. son of Ephraim and Sarah (Welles) Hawley [Vol. I, p. 266]; b. at Stratford, 1 June 1711; settled on Fairfield side of Stratfield, and d. there in Mar. 1786. He m. 24 May 1738, Sarah Watkins, dau. of Samuel.

---

* Children, rec. Redding: Lemuel, b. 8 Dec. 1785; Maria, b. 16 Mar. 1788; Uriah-Rogers, b. 14 June 1790; Joseph C., b. 23 July 1792; Aaron, b. 1 Nov. 1794; James-Rogers, b. 18 Sept. 1797.

† Children, rec. Redding: Sarah-Sanford, b. 31 Jan. 1797; William, b. 9 Jan. 1799; Hezekiah and Rebecca (twins), b. 10 Aug. 1801.

‡ A child, rec. Weston: Eli-Lyon, b. 1 Nov. 1797.

Will 2 Mar., proved 20 Mar. 1786; dau. Elizabeth wife of Nehemiah Buddington; dau. Isabel Hawley; dec'd daus., wives of David Hawley and Thomas Langley Collier; dau. Charity; wife Sarah; son Silas; friend Ozias Burr, Exec'r.

Children, rec. Stratford:

>Frederick, b. 16 Jan. 1738/9.
>William, b. 11 Oct. 1740, d. at Stratfield, Jan. 1783 ae. 47 (?) (g. s.), or 23 Feb. 1784 (Mortality List).
>Elizabeth, b. 13 Nov. 1742; m. Nehemiah Buddington.
>Sarah, bapt. Apr. 1745; ? m. David Hawley. [Capt. David Hawley's wife d. 8 Feb. 1781, by Stratfield Mortality List.]
>Ephraim, bapt. Mar. 1746, d. at Stratfield, 11 Apr. 1777 ae. 30 (g. s.). Will 8 Apr., proved 30 June 1777; calls himself of Fairfield; sister Abiah's eldest son; sister Isabel Hawley; bro. Silas Hawley; father and mother living; friend, Thomas Langley Collyer of Fairfield, Exec'r.
>Silas, bapt. Sept. 1749.
>Abiah, bapt. Apr. 1752; ? m. Thomas-Langley Collier.
>Isabel.
>Charity.
>Ann, d. at Stratfield, 30 June 1778.

Hayes, Abraham.

Son of Martha Patchen, bapt. 26 Nov. 1727; Abraham *Hayes alias Patchen* was mentioned 1758 in a deed. He m. Mary Adams, dau. of Stephen, b. 18 Oct. 1728, d. by 1793.

Children:

>Ann.
>John, m. at Fairfield, 18 Oct. 1781, Sarah Adams.
>+Joseph, b. 29 June 1756 (Pension rec.).
>Stephen.
>Irene, m. at Fairfield, 7 Nov. 1781, George Squire.
>Nehemiah, m. at Fairfield, 20 Feb. 1790, Eunice Wilson; dau. of Nathaniel, bapt. 25 Jan. 1776.
>Sarah.
>Nathan-Adams, m. at Fairfield, 15 Feb. 1787, Phebe Sturges; dau. of David.*
>William, m. at Fairfield, 22 Dec. 1789, Jane Redfield; dau. of James, bapt. 6 Dec. 1767.†
>Elizabeth.

---

* Children, bapt. Fairfield: Meliora, bapt. 31 Mar. 1791; Elizabeth, bapt. 17 Mar. 1793.

† Children, bapt. Fairfield: Samuel, bapt. 17 June 1792; Nancy, bapt. 2 June 1793.

Hayes, Joseph, s. of Abraham.

Born 29 June 1756 (Pension rec.); d. at Greenfield, 29 Sept. 1843 ae. 87 yrs. 3 mos. (g. s.); m. (1) Sarah ———; m. (2) at Fairfield, 22 Nov. 1795, Grizzel Burr, bapt. 10 Nov. 1765, d. 22 June 1846 in 81 yr. (g. s.).

Will 29 Dec. 1841, proved 24 Oct. 1843; wife Grizzel; gr. gr. son Joseph Hays Morehouse, son of William B. Morehouse; gr. dau. Mary-Burr Hays Morehouse wife of William B. Morehouse.

Children [by first wife], bapt. Fairfield:

> Sarah, b. [14 May 1784], d. at Greenfield, 26 Oct. 1808 ae. 24-5-12 (g. s.).
> Mary, bapt. 18 June 1786, d. at Greenfield, 30 Aug. 1815 in 29 yr. (g. s.); m. Burr Lyon.
> Joseph, bapt. 11 Jan. 1789, d. at Greenfield, 17 Dec. 1811 ae. 23-4-12 (g. s.).

Hayes [*Unplaced*].

> ——— m. Sarah Morehouse, dau. of Nathan, b. abt. 1707; she m. (2) 3 Oct. 1755, James Davis.
> MARY m. 3 Jan. 1759, Ebenezer Davis. [Weston Church]
> JOHN m. 23 Apr. 1782, Sarah Bradley. [Greens Farms Church]

Haynes, Silas.

Born 22 Nov. 1745; killed in battle at Fairfield, 8 July 1779; called of North Stratford, he m. at Greenfield, 3 Nov. 1768, Amy Whitney, b. 6 June 1747.

Children, rec. Weston, bapt. Easton:

> Molly, b. 15, bapt. 25 Dec. 1769.
> Amy, b. 12 Nov., bapt. 29 Dec. 1771; m. Dec. 1790, Nathaniel-Freeman Seeley.
> Sarah, b. 7 Mar. 1774, d. 15 Aug. 1794.
> Ruth, b. 25 Feb. 1776; m. 3 Jan. 1798, Nehemiah Lyon.
> Silas, b. 8 Dec. 1779; chose Nathaniel F. Seeley for guardian, 1794.

Hazard, John.

The will of Mary Fish, last of Jamaica, L. I., 24 July 1769, proved 2 July 1771, gave all her estate to son John Hazard of Fairfield.

He d. at Westport, 29 Mar. 1771 ae. 52 (g. s.); m. 9 Apr. 1752, Mary Wakeman, dau. of Joseph, b. 5 Jan. 1731/2. She m. (2) 15 Mar. 1773, Moss Kent, of Dutchess County, N. Y., and d. at Westport, 13 Sept. 1822 ae. 91 (g. s.).

Will 2 June 1770, proved 24 Apr. 1771; wife Mary; sons, Joseph, Samuel, John; daus. Mary, Mercy, Anne, Abigail. The widow was Mrs. Kent in the distribution.

Will of Mary Kent of Fairfield, 27 Dec. 1817, proved 8 Oct. 1822; dau. Mary widow of Wills Clift; dau. Mercy Edson; son John Hazard; dau. Abigail Henry, widow.

Children, rec. Fairfield, bapt. Westport:

>Joseph, b. 13, bapt. 25 Mar. 1753, d. 7 Jan. 1775 ae. 22 (g. s.).
>Mary, b. 21, bapt. 24 Nov. 1754; living 1839, Clarkson, Monroe County, N. Y.; d. at Waterford, Saratoga County, N. Y., 12 Mar. 1847; m. (1) abt. Mar. 1775, William Henderson of "Philips Town," N. Y.; m. (2) Wills Clift; no issue.
>Samuel, b. 3, bapt. 7 Nov. 1756, d. 24 July 1794 ae. 38 (g. s.). Adm'n granted, 23 Aug. 1794, to Wills Clift and John Hazzard of Half Moon.
>Mercy, bapt. 15 July 1759, d. 1 Nov. 1761.
>Mercy, bapt. 29 Nov. 1761; m. 3 Dec. 1786, Adam Edson; res. 1791, Saratoga County, N. Y.
>Anna, bapt. 30 Sept. 1764; m. 3 Apr. 1782, Rev. John Avery; res. 1791, Stamford, Conn.
>Abigail, b. abt. 1766; living 1792, Lansingburgh, N. Y.; 1839, Clarkson, N. Y.; m. Dr. Michael Henry.
>John, bapt. 4 Sept. 1768; res. 1791, Saratoga County, N. Y.; m. Hannah Van-Schoonhoven.*

Hedge [Unplaced].

>BARNABAS, of Plymouth, Mass., m. 9 Sept. 1789, Eunice-Dennie Burr. [Fairfield Church]

Hendrick [Vol. I, pp. 270-272].

>1 Henry (-1684) m. Hannica ———.
>   2 Henry (-1741) m. Elizabeth Bennett.
>   3 *John* (1695-by 1785).
>   4 *Henry* (1699-1734).
>   5 *David* (1717-1756).

---

* Children, bapt. Westport: Susanna, bapt. 7 Dec. 1800; John-Van-Schoonhoven, bapt. 21 Nov. 1802; Jane-Ann, bapt. 15 Sept. 1805.

3. **Hendrick, John,** s. of Henry.

Bapt. 31 Mar. 1695; d. at Westport, before 1785.

He m. in 1728, Phebe Coe, who d. at Westport, 21 Apr. 1752 ae. 50 (g. s.). She was called dau.-in-law [stepdau.] in will of William Proboy of Rye, 1731/2.

In 1768 he conveyed to Mary wife of son Samuel, right in estate of my bro. James Hendrick which I purchased 1758 from Daniel Jennings and Hannah his wife.

Adm'n was granted, 5 Dec. 1785, to Wright White [a gr. dau.'s husband]. He left a will, appointing his daus. Sarah and Deborah Executrices; they did not give bond.

In 1771, Samuel, John, Jr., and Peter Hendrick, Joseph Disbrow, Jr., and Phebe his wife, David Sturgis, Jr., and Elizabeth his wife, and Deborah Hendrick, sold right from John Hendrick that was our bro. James Hendrick's decd.

Children, rec. Fairfield: six bapt. Fairfield, three Westport:

6+John, b. in 1730, bapt. 15 Dec. 1734.
7+Andrew, b. in 1732, bapt. 15 Dec. 1734.
8+Samuel, b. in 1734, bapt. 15 Dec. 1734.
   Sarah, b. in *1736*, bapt. 26 Jan. 1734/5, d. at Bedford, N. Y., after 1802; m. 17 Mar. 1757, Rowland Hughes.
9+Peter, b. in *1738*, bapt. 22 May 1737.
   Phebe, b. in *1740*, bapt. 28 Oct. 1739, d. at New Fairfield, Feb. 1821; m. 10 Apr. 1768, Joseph Disbrow, Jr.
   James, b. in 1742, bapt. 18 July 1742, d. in 1766. Adm'n granted to Samuel Hendrick, 10 July 1766. Distribution 17 Jan. 1771; Samuel and Peter Hendrick; Elizabeth wife of David Sturgis, Jr.; Phebe wife of Joseph Disbrow, Jr.; Deborah Hendrick; John Hendrick, Jr.; Sarah Hughes; heirs of Andrew Hendrick dec'd.
   Elizabeth, b. in 1744, "Betty" bapt. 5 Jan. 1745; m. David Sturges, Jr.
   Deborah b. in 1746, bapt. 22 Nov. 1747, d. at Westport, 28 Feb. 1807 ae. 60; m. (1) 3 Aug. 1777, Jesse Jacocks; m. (2) 2 Feb. 1792, Joshua Disbrow.

4. **Hendrick, Henry,** 3d, s. of Henry.

Bapt. 15 Oct. 1699, d. in 1734; m. Elizabeth Luff, dau. of John of Stratford.

Adm'n granted to John Hendrick, 21 June 1734. On 7 Apr. 1736, Henry Hendrick was appointed guardian to Hannah, Ebenezer, Daniel, and Nehemiah, children of Henry, Jr.

Children:

> Hannah, m. at Trumbull 14 June 1753, Hezekiah Bennett; as his widow, she conveyed 1762 right in estate of uncle James Hendrick.
> Ebenezer, of Norwalk 1762, conveyed right in estate of uncle James Hendrick; m. at Wilton, 30 Apr. 1751, Mary Sturdevant.
> Daniel, of Norwalk 1762, conveyed right in estate of uncle James Hendrick; of Kent 1774, conveyed to Samuel Hendrick a right in the estate of Peter (?) Hendrick.
> Nehemiah.

5. Hendrick, David, s. of Henry.

Bapt. 20 Jan. 1716/7, d. 5 Nov. 1756 on way home from army (rec. Westport); m. at Westport, 22 Nov. 1743, Mary Fountain; dau. of Aaron, b. 5 June 1722, d. at Westport, 9 Nov. 1780.

Adm'n granted, 19 Apr. 1759, to Mary Hendrick; Samuel Sherwood surety on her bond. All given to widow to support two orphan children, who were aged 3 yrs. 4 mos. and 15 mos. at his death. Andrew chose Phineas Chapman for guardian, 30 Sept. 1765.

Children, rec. Westport:

> Abigail, bapt. 31 Mar. 1745.
> Ann, bapt. 30 Mar. 1746; m. 2 Nov. 1772, Moses Allen.
> Infant, d. Sept. 1747.
> David, bapt. 9 Oct. 1748; living 1820, New Canaan; d. 27 Mar. 1828 (family rec.); m. at Wilton, 25 Sept. 1774, Anne Westcott, who d. 3 Oct. 1827.*
> Andrew, bapt. 17 June 1753; rem. to Washington; living 1818, Middletown, Susquehanna County, Pa.; m. at Wilton, 2 Sept. 1779, Elizabeth Gaylord, b. 24 Oct. 1755.
> Mary, bapt. 22 July 1753; ? m. at Redding, 17 Mar. 1779, John Lines.†
> Tammy, bapt. 3 Aug. 1755; ? m. 5 Mar. 1779, Joseph Batterson, Jr.

---

* They had children, bapt. at Wilton: Hannah, bapt. 30 Dec. 1775; Sabra, bapt. 23 July 1777; David, bapt. 30 Oct. 1780. Children (from family rec. furnished by Mrs. Mary North Shepard, Alhambra, Calif.): Hannah, b. 29 Apr. 1774 [1775]; Sabra, b. 18 Nov. 1776; David, b. 8 Sept. 1778; Salome, b. 15 Dec. 1780, d. at Redding, 7 June 1866 ae. 85-5-22 (g. s.), m. Isaac Perry; Abigail, b. 15 June 1783; Betsey, b. 10 May 1785, d. 10 May 1864, m. ——— Seeley; Henry, b. 17 Apr. 1787; Anne, b. 24 Feb. 1790, d. at DeWitt, N. Y., 2 Mar. 1861, m. 22 June 1809, Charles Lewis. One David d. 19 Feb. 1831 (Miss Treadwell's book).

† According to the *Whitney Genealogy*, by Phoenix, John Lines m. Mary Bennit.

6. Hendrick, John, s. of John.

Born in 1730, d. at Fairfield, Vt., 6 Feb. 1807; m. 13 Nov. 1753, Eunice Bradley, dau. of David, b. 15 Mar. 1731/2, d. at Sherman, 6 Feb. 1790.

Children rec. Fairfield, bapt. Westport:
> Phebe, b. 5 Nov. 1754, bapt. 24 Nov. 1754, d. 3 Apr. 1836; m. Jeremiah Wakeman.
> Justus, b. 20 Jan. 1757, bapt. 15 May 1757, d. 18 Oct. 1758.
> Eunice, bapt. and d. 22 June 1759.
> John, bapt. 10 Aug. 1760; is said to have d. at East Highgate, Vt., 7 June 1851; m. at New Fairfield, 15 Apr. 1785, Amy Barnum.*
> Damaris, bapt. 17 July 1763; m. Moses† Wanzer.
> Betty, bapt. 13 Apr. 1766; m. 3 Apr. 1786, Ebenezer Wanzer.
> Peter, bapt. 19 Feb. 1769.
> Mary, bapt. at Sherman, 9 May 1773; m. 29 Jan. 1792, Samuel Hollister, of Fairfield, Vt.
> Ellen, b. [bapt. ?] 8 Jan. 1776, d. at Wilkes-Barre, Pa., 6 Aug. 1872; m. (1) 11 Jan. 1801, Moses Wadhams; m. (2) 15 June 1807, Joseph Wright, of Plymouth, Luzerne County, Pa.

7. Hendrick, Andrew, s. of John.

Born in 1732; by a family tradition d. on a voyage to Africa, supposed thrown overboard for his money; m. Susanna ———.

Children, bapt. Westport:‡
> Hanny, bapt. 10 Apr. 1754.
> Coe, b. 26 Aug. 1752 (Pension rec.), bapt. 8 Dec. 1754; rem. to Kent or New Milford, 1770, and 1775 to New Haven, where he lived 1832; m. Nancy ———.§

8. Hendrick, Samuel, s. of John.

Born in 1734, d. at New Fairfield, 25 May 1797; m. (1) 30 Aug. 1759, Mary Rumsey, dau. of Benjamin, b. 28 July 1734, d. 22 Aug. 1788. He m. (2) Martha Crane.

Children, all but youngest rec. Fairfield:
> Samuel, b. 22 May 1761, bapt. 12 July 1761, d. 24 July 1802; m. 2 Oct. 1788, Mary Pardee. She m. (2) Dec. 1806, Silas Abbott.

---
* The account written by Samuel-Hendrick Pardee states that John m. Elizabeth Beardsley.
† Nicholas, by account of Samuel-Hendrick Pardee.
‡ Lucy, dau. of Susanna Hendrick, d. 9 Aug. 1775.
§ They had children bapt. at Second Cong. Church, New Haven: Son, bapt. 12 Oct. 1788; William, bapt. 18 May 1789; Nancy, bapt. 1 Jan. 1792.

Benjamin, b. 24 May 1763, bapt. 10 July 1763, d. 2 Feb. 1843; m. in 1789, Cynthia Gregory, b. 18 Nov. 1768.
Nancy, b. 14* Apr. 1765, bapt. 12 May 1765, d. at Windham, Ohio, 29 Dec. 1841; m. 13 Apr. 1786, Asher Pardee.
James, b. 27 Mar. 1767, bapt. 29 Mar. 1767, d. 4 Aug. 1812; m. Jan. 1793, Elizabeth Wheeler, b. 22 June 1773, d. 2 Sept. 1819.
Joseph, b. 14 Sept. 1769, bapt. 3 Dec. 1769, d. at Westport, 14 Aug. 1773.
Andrew, b. 15 Oct. 1771,† bapt. 10 Nov. 1771, d. 8 Sept. 1839; m. in 1799, Rena Leach, b. 25 May 1775, d. 14 Sept. 1842.
Mary, b. 16 Aug. 1775‡, bapt. 25 Sept. 1774, d. 2 Feb. 1845; m. 20 Oct. 1796, Stephen Pardee.

9. **Hendrick, Peter.** Lt., 1st Co., Fairfield, Oct. 1774. 1st Lt., 4th Co., 5th Regt., Army, Apr. 1775.

Bapt. 22 May 1737, d. at Ballston, N. Y.

He m. (1) ———, who d. of smallpox, 13 July 1775 (Perry Diary).

He m. (2) at Fairfield· Church, 11 July 1776, Sarah Allen; perhaps the dau. of David, b. 23 July 1745.

He m. (3) at Norwalk, 19 May 1785, Mary Thatcher, dau. of Josiah, b. 3 Dec. 1753, d. 30 Aug. 1796.

He bought land in Norwalk 1786, sold it in 1792, and rem. to Ballston, N. Y.

Child [by third wife]:

Burr, d. at Saratoga Springs, N. Y., 7 Apr. 1829.

Hendrick or Hendrix [*Unplaced*].§

SARAH chose Moses Gray for guardian, 5 Aug. 1771; Andrew Hill had been appointed her guardian, May 1767.
NATHAN m. 4 Nov. 1778, Abigail Elwood. [Hall's *Norwalk*, p. 268, *q. v.* for children.]
PHEBE m. 2 Aug. 1796, Nathan Crofut. [Redding rec.]
MARY m. 18 Oct. 1752, Charles Ferry of Redding. [New Milford Church rec.]
JEMIMA d. 27 Apr. 1759 in 20 yr. [Greenfield rec.]
ANNA wife of NATHANIEL d. 30 Sept. 1828 ae. 83 (g. s.).

---

* 13 by family record, written by her son, Samuel-Hendrick Pardee.
† 27 Oct. 1773 by family record.
‡ By family record.
§ The name was also spelled Henry or Henries. Some of these unplaced individuals prob. belonged to the family which follows.

HENDRICK (SECOND FAMILY)

1. Hendrick or Henry, ———.

Identity not established; his son Samuel's family adopted the spelling Henry, Henries or Hendrix; the Wallingford branch used the spelling Hendrick.

Children:

> Mary, d. abt. 1712; m. Ebenezer Canfield, of Norwalk. His Inv. 20 Jan. 1715 [1715/6]; names of children and ages stated: Patience, 20, 15 of last Oct., Mary, 18, 5 of last Aug.; Ebenezer, 16, 24 of last Aug.; Timothy, 14, 16 of last Sept.; Elizabeth, 12, 5 of last June; Jabez, 11, 20 of last Oct.; Lydia, 8, 11 of last Mar.; Matthew, 7, 12 of last Oct.; Ezekiel, 5, 16 of last Nov.; and David, 3, 14 of last Apr.*

2+Samuel.

> Francis, d. at Wallingford, 3 Sept. 1733; m. Martha How, dau. of Jeremiah, b. 2 Aug. 1684. His will named wife Martha; four children of sister Mary Canfield, viz. David, Ezekiel, Elizabeth, Lydia; John and William, sons of dec'd bro. William; Francis, son of bro. Samuel of Newtown.

> William, d. at Wallingford in 1726; m. at Springfield (rec. also at Wallingford) 7 Jan. 1707/8, Abigail Sikes, b. at Springfield, 16 Mar. 1676/7; had issue.†

2. Henry, Samuel, s. of ———.

He m. Phebe, dau. of Elizabeth (Dickerson) (Knapp) Wake, perhaps by her last husband (Wake).

Children, five born at Stratford, two at Chestnut Ridge, last at Newtown (eight rec. Newtown), first five bapt. Stratfield:‡

> Nathaniel, b. 7 Feb. 1704 [1704/5], bapt. 22 Apr. 1705.
> Roger, b. 14 Aug. 1705 [Apr. 1706?], bapt. 16 June 1706.

3+Samuel, b. 15 Mar. 1707 [1707/8], bapt. 25 Apr. 1708.

> Francis, b. 1 Apr. 1709 [1710], bapt. 7 May 1710, d. at Newtown, 1759; adm'n granted to James Hard, Jr.

---

* Possibly the first four of these children were by a former wife, since they were not named in the will of Mary's brother Francis. Ebenezer Canfield had a last wife, Sarah, named in the probate.

† For descendants, see *Families of Ancient New Haven*, vol. 3, p. 737.

‡ One of the above sons prob. m. Mary Knapp, b. 7 Mar. 1711/2.

Benoni, b. 31 Jan. 1711/2, bapt. 9 Mar. 1712, d. at Newtown, 1761; adm'n granted to Roger Hendryx, 3 Feb. 1761. Roger was appointed guardian to Benoni's son Eleazer, and gave bond with Abel Prindle.
Obed, b. 28 Apr. 1714, bapt. at Fairfield, 2 Oct. 1715; Obed Henrys d. at Woodbury, 26 Jan. 1738; m. 20 Jan. 1737, Elizabeth Thomas.
Elizabeth, bapt. 2 Oct. 1715.
David, b. 1 Jan. 1716/7.
Aaron, b. 25 May 1720.

3. **Hendrix, Samuel**, s. of Samuel.

Born 15 Mar. 1707/8; d. in the French War, 22 Sept. 1760; m. Deborah ———.

Adm'n granted, 6 Jan. 1761, to widow Deborah. She was appointed guardian to the son Abner, and gave bond with Asa Hall of Danbury. The son Samuel chose Seth Hull of Redding for guardian, 24 Feb. 1762.

Children (perhaps others), prob. born at Newtown:

Beulah, m. (rec. Fairfield) 2 Sept. 1754, Samuel Bulkley.
4+Samuel, b. before 1748.
Abner, m. at Greenfield, 17 Nov. 1774, Sarah Thorp; dau. of Gershom; she m. (2) at Weston, 30 June 1791, Ebenezer Monroe.

4. **Hendrix, Samuel**, s. of Samuel.

He d. at Weston, 27 Nov. 1811 (Miss Treadwell's book).
He m. Catherine Jennings, dau. of Zachariah, b. in 1747.*

Children:

Esther, d. before 1840; m. ——— Gilbert.
Parthena, b. abt. 1769, d. at Easton, 24 May 1849 ae. 72 (g. s.); m. at Trinity Church, 31 Mar. 1791, Stephen Wheeler.
Catharine, b. abt. 1777, d. at Easton, 22 May 1840 ae. 63 (g. s.). Adm'n granted to Obadiah Hendrix and Sherwood Lyon. Distribution to brothers and sisters: Obadiah Hendrix; Asahel Hendrix; Alson Hendrix; Parthena Wheeler; Deborah Robertson; Sarah Lyon; Priscilla Hoyt; Jacob B., Jerome B., and Susan Hendrix, children of dec'd bro. Samuel Hendrix; heirs of dec'd sister Esther Gilbert.

---

* "Mrs." Hendrix hung herself, 6 Apr. 1815 (Miss Treadwell's book). Isaiah d. 16 Mar. 1813; Abner d. 28 May 1822 (same source). These were prob. children of Samuel or of his brother.

450   HISTORY AND GENEALOGY OF

    Samuel, d. before 1840; m.
    Sarah, b. 15 Dec. 1782, d. 9 Jan. 1862 ae. 79; m. Hezekiah Lyon.
    Obadiah, b. 7 July 1784, d. at Easton, 8 Jan. 1855 ae. 70 (g. s.); m.
      (1) Abigail G. ———, who d. 13 June 1836 ae. 52-10-8 (g. s.); m.
      (2) Esther ———, who d. 19 Apr. 1864 ae. 79 yrs. 9 mos. (g. s.).*
    Asahel, b. abt. 1774, d. at Butternuts, N. Y., 3 Mar. 1855 ae. 81.
    Deborah, m. ——— Robertson.
    Priscilla (twin), b. at Weston, 31 Jan. 1792; m. ——— Hoyt.
    Alson (twin), b. 31 Jan. 1792, d. in 1854; m. Cynthia Bunnell.

Hepburn [Unplaced].

    MR. PETER m. 13 Mar. 1726, Mrs. Sarah Clark. [Fairfield Church]

Herns, William.

He m. Elizabeth Thorp, dau. of John, b. 11 June 1708.

Children, bapt. Greenfield:

    Naomi, bapt. Sept. 1728.
    Gilead, bapt. in 1729.
    Thomas, bapt. Nov. 1731.
    Sarah, bapt. 25 Nov. 1733.
    Naomi, bapt. in 1735.
    Najah, bapt. 14 Aug. 1737.

Heron, William.
Deputy for Redding, May 1778, Oct. 1779, Jan. and Apr. 1780, May 1781, Oct. 1784, May 1785, Oct. 1786, May and Oct. 1787, May and Oct. 1788, May and Oct. 1789, May 1790, Oct. 1795, May and Oct. 1796.

Born in City of Cork, Ireland, in 1742, d. at Redding, 8 Jan. 1819 (g. s.).

He m. at Greenfield, 8 Mar. 1767, Mary Jennings; dau. of John, b. 5 Dec. 1743, d. 16 July 1819 ae. 74 (g. s.).

Will 27 July 1818, proved 2 Feb. 1819; wife Mary; sons William and John-Maurice; dau. Susanna Peck; dau. Betsey; daus. Lucy and Aloisa; gr. child William Judd.

Will of Mary, 27 July 1818, proved 17 Aug. 1819; dau. Sally(?) Sanford; dau. Susanna Peck; dau. Margaret Judd (she having no

---
    * Adm'n on Obadiah's estate granted, 11 Jan. 1855, to Stephen Wheeler of New Haven; dower set to widow Esther. Henry B. Hendrix appointed guardian to Minot T. Hendrix.

abiding place of her own); sons William, Jr., and John-Maurice; daus. Lucy and Aloisa Heron; poor dau. Betsey, $20 for her use, she being provided for in my husband's will.

Children:
> Mary, b. 3 Nov. 1768, d. at Redding, 6 Dec. 1832 (g. s.); m. 1 Jan. 1795, Lemuel Sanford, Jr.
> Susanna, b. abt. 1771, d. at Westport, 20 Jan. 1853 ae. 82 (g. s., Redding); m. Dr. Thomas Peck.
> William, b. abt. 1773, d. at Redding, 3 Feb. 1859 ae. 86 (g. s.).
> Elizabeth, b. abt. 1777, d. at Redding, 11 Apr. 1847 ae. 70 (g. s.).
> Margaret, m. ―――― Judd.
> Lucy, b. abt. 1781, d. at Redding, 8 Nov. 1859 ae. 78 (g. s.).
> Elosia, b. abt. 1784, d. at Redding, 19 Jan. 1860 ae. 75 (g. s.).
> John-Maurice, bapt. at Trinity Church, 15 June 1786; grad. Yale College.

Hibbard, Nathaniel.

He m. 24 Apr. 1740, Abigail Couch, bapt. 4 Sept. 1715, d. 15 Nov. 1776.

Children, rec. Fairfield, bapt. Westport:
> Abigail, b. 22 Feb. 1741, d. 15 Nov. 1776.
> Mary, bapt. 10 Apr. 1743, d. 28 Nov. 1746.
> +Elisha, b. 20 May, bapt. 29 June 1746.
> Deborah, b. 7 Sept., bapt. 27 Nov. 1748.
> Grissel, b. 20 Feb., bapt. 5 Apr. 1752.
> Sarah, b. 24 Feb., bapt. 14 Mar. 1756.

Hibbard, Elisha, s. of Nathaniel.

Born 20 May 1746.

He m. 5 Nov. 1767, Elizabeth Osborn; perhaps dau. of Nathan, bapt. 21 Nov. 1742.

Children, bapt. Westport:
> Molly, bapt. 18 Dec. 1768.
> Sarah, d. 6 Nov. 1776.

Hickock [*Unplaced*].

> ABIGAIL, dau. of Benjamin, m. Aug. 1733, William Bennett.

Hicks, William.

He m. 28 June 1768, Abigail, widow of Archibald Blair, and dau. of Rev. John Goodsell; b. 8 Jan. 1737/8, d. 5 Apr. 1776 ae. abt. 40.

Will of Abigail Hix, 3 Apr., proved 20 May 1776; dau. Abigail; residue to Phebe and Hannah; bro. Lewis Goodsell, Exec'r.

Children, one bapt. Greenfield:

>William, bapt. 16 Apr. 1769 (ae. abt. 1 yr. 4 mos.), d. 1 May 1769 ae. 16 mos.
>Abigail.
>Phebe.
>Hannah.

Hide [Vol. I, pp. 275-277].

>1 Humphrey (-1684) m. Ann ———.
>2 John (-1689) m. Elizabeth Harvey.
>3 John (1668-1744) m. Rachel Rumsey.
>4 *John* (1692-1761).

4. Hide, John, s. of John, 3d.

Born 6 Oct. 1692; d. at Westport, 15 Jan. 1761 (g. s.); Deacon; m. (1) 22 Apr. 1718, Rachel Holmes, who d. 30 Sept. 1736 in 37 yr. (g. s.); m. (2) 22 Mar. 1737, Abigail, widow of David Adams, and dau. of Daniel Silliman; she d. in 1775.

John and Eunice Wilson receipted, 14 Apr. 1761, to John and Joseph Hide, Exec'rs of father John Hide; so also, Ebenezer and Sarah Banks, David and Mary Coley, Samuel Jr. and Rachel Sherwood, and the widow Abigail Hide (her marriage covenant dated 22 Mar. 1736/7).

Children [by first wife], rec. Fairfield:

>Eunice, b. 10 Feb. 1719, d. at Fairfield, 25 Dec. 1793 in 75 yr. (g. s.); m. 27 Feb. 1740, John Wilson.
>Mary, b. 30 Sept. 1720, d. before 1774; m. 16 Dec. 1740, David Coley.
>5+John, b. 25 Nov. 1724.
>Sarah, b. 27 Nov. 1727, d. at Greenfield, 20 Mar. 1796 in 69 yr. (g. s.); m. 17 or 18 June 1746, Ebenezer Banks.
>6+Joseph, b. 5 Dec. 1729.
>Rachel, b. 29 Feb. 1736, d. at Weston in 1811; m. 6 June 1754, Samuel Sherwood.

THE FAMILIES OF OLD FAIRFIELD 453

5. **Hide, John,** s. of John.

Born 25 Nov. 1724; d. s. p. at Westport, 6 Sept. 1792.
He m. 21 Jan. 1748, Abigail Ogden, dau. of David, b. 9 Feb.
1729/30, d. at Westport, 15 Oct. 1817 ae. 88 (g. s.).
Will 10 Feb. 1789, proved 1 Oct. 1792; wife Abigail; the Presbyterian Society, Greens Farms; nephews John Hide, Jr., and Joseph Hide, Jr., sons of my bro. Joseph.
Will of Abigail, 19 Sept. 1806, proved 21 Oct. 1817; Abigail Hide Ogden, dau. of my nephew Jonathan Ogden, and John, son of the same; Abigail wife of Morehouse Coley of Weston; residue to nephew Jonathan; Joseph Adams of Fairfield, Exec'r.

6. **Hide, Joseph,** s. of John.

Born 5 Dec. 1729; d. at Westport, 28 Aug. 1814 ae. 86 (g. s.);
Deacon; m. (1) 1 Aug. 1753, Betty Sherwood, dau. of Samuel, b.
14 Feb. 1732, d. 13 June 1785 ae. 53 yrs. 3 mos. 20 days (g. s.);
m. (2) 18 Dec. 1792, Thomasin, widow of Samuel Higgins, Jr.,
and dau. of Michael Dunning, b. abt. 1750, d. 30 [or 3] Apr. 1808
in 69 (?) yr. (g. s.).
Will 4 Apr. 1804, proved 5 Sept. 1814; wife Tamasin; daus. Elizabeth wife of Daniel Andrews, Jr., and Rachel wife of Joseph Wakeman; children of dec'd dau. Salome wife of Nathaniel Adams; son John; gr. son Joseph Hide 3d; son Joseph Hide, Jr.

Children [by first wife], rec. Fairfield, bapt. Westport:*

Elizabeth, b. 15, bapt. 30 Dec. 1753; "Betsey" m. 27 May 1778, Daniel Andrews, of Weston.
John, b. 17, bapt. 24 Aug. 1755, d. at Westport, 14 Jan. 1836 (g. s.); m. 7 Apr. 1776, Abigail Jennings, b. 1 Jan. 1756, d. 30 Apr. 1823 (g. s.).†
Salome, b. 30 Aug., bapt. 4 Sept. 1757, d. at Westport, 15 May 1802 ae. 44-8-15 (g. s.); m. 21 Dec. 1775, Nathaniel Adams, Jr.

---

* Priscilla, dau. of ——— Hide, bapt. at Westport, 13 Aug. 1769; d. at Greenfield, Mar. 1841 ae. 73.
† Children, bapt. Westport: Eunice, bapt. 19 Sept. 1776, m. 13 Jan. 1793, Michael Coley; Abigail, bapt. 7 Nov. 1779, m. 15 Jan. 1797, Zalmon Burr; Betty, bapt. 17 Apr. 1785, m. 2 Nov. 1806, Simeon Couch, Jr.

Joseph, b. 3 Jan., bapt. 22 Feb. 1761, d. at Westport, 3 Dec. 1850 (g. s.); m. 16 Dec. 1790, Arite Jessup, dau. of Ebenezer, b. 22 Mar. 1770, d. 24 Dec. 1844 (g. s.).*

Rachel, b. 30 Oct., bapt. 26 Dec. 1762, d. 12 May 1840; m. 25 Jan. 1786, Joseph Wakeman.

Hide [Unplaced].

PETER had Annis, bapt. 6 Mar. 1795; Elsie, b. abt. 1799, d. 10 Apr. 1817 ae. 18. [Greens Farms Church]

Higgins, Samuel, s. of Abraham [Vol. I, p. 278].

Bapt. 20 Sept. 1708, d. at Norwalk in 1789; m. Miriam Belden, dau. of William, b. 11 Nov. 1714, d. at Weston, 23 Apr. 1800 ae. 89 (g. s.).†

Will 24 Mar. 1788, proved 7 Dec. 1789; wife Miriam; gr. son Uriah Rockwell; children of dec'd son Samuel; three children now living and gr. children; dau. Sarah the now present wife of Benjamin Gilbert, the land where they now live, and one acre to Ebenezer, son of Benjamin Gilbert; dau. Abigail wife of John Hurlbut; dau. Martha wife of Isaac Osborn; children of dec'd dau. Miriam late wife of John Rockwell; children of dec'd dau. Mary late wife of Jonah Rockwell. Distribution 6 Apr. 1790: widow Miriam; gr. sons John, Abner, Abraham, Michael, and Samuel Higgins; eldest dau. Sarah wife of Benjamin Gilbert; dau. Abigail wife of John Hurlbut; dau. Martha wife of Isaac Osborn; gr. sons Justice and William Rockwell; gr. daus. Mary Bedient and Ann wife of Lyman Rowe; gr. son Uriah Rockwell; gr. dau. Dorothy Bowen; gr. sons Jonah and Noah Rockwell; gr. son Ebenezer Gilbert; heirs of Samuel Higgins of Weston dec'd.

Children:

Sarah, b. abt. 1735; m. at Wilton, Mar. 1751, Benjamin Gilbert.
Miriam, b. 1738; m. at Wilton, 15 Feb. 1758, John Rockwell.
Abigail, bapt. at Westport, 6 Mar. 1743; m. John Hurlbut.

---

* Children, bapt. Westport: Arite, bapt. 26 Feb. 1792, d. 26 Nov. 1811 in 20 yr. (g. s.). Eleanor, b. 17 June 1793 (g. s.), bapt. 11 Aug. 1793, d. 9 Aug. 1857 (g. s.). John, bapt. 22 Mar. 1795, d. 9 Aug. 1806 in 12 yr. (g. s.). Myrinda, bapt. 5 Feb. 1797, d. 10 Dec. 1882 ae. 86 (g. s.). Joseph, bapt. 4 Nov. 1798, d. 27 Dec. 1824 in 27 yr (g. s.). Rev. Ebenezer-Jesup, b. [28 July 1800], bapt. 7 Sept. 1800, d. 12 Aug. 1801 ae. 1 yr. 15 days (g. s.). Rachel, bapt. 8 Aug. 1802. Edward, bapt. 6 May 1804. William-Swift, bapt. 15 Jan. 1806.

† Called Marian on stone.

Martha, b. 28 Sept. 1745, d. at Weston, 25 Dec. 1823 ae. 78-2-14 (g. s.) ; m. at Wilton, 22 Sept. 1763, Isaac Osborn.
+Samuel, b. 14 Apr. 1747.
Mary, b. abt. 1749; m. at Wilton, 5 Aug. 1766, Jonah Rockwell.
William, bapt. 17 May 1752.

Higgins, Abraham, s. of Abraham [Vol. I, p. 278].

Bapt. 24 July 1715.

He m. May 1739, Mary Allen; dau. of Gideon of Compo.

In 1760, then of Bedford, N. Y., he conveyed to Samuel Higgins of Norwalk, land in Fairfield.

Children, rec. Fairfield, bapt. Westport:

John, b. 5 Mar. 1740.
Gabriel, b. 16 Mar. 1741, d. at Bedford, N. Y., 1 Aug. 1809 ae. 57; Ens., 1775; Lt., 1778; m. 2 Mar. 1763, Sarah Gray, b. 11 Feb. 1743/4, d. 4 Apr. 1814 ae. 70 yrs. 12 days.
Phebe, b. 23 Sept., bapt. 30 Oct. 1743.
Ebenezer, b. 12, bapt. 15 Dec. 1745.
Moses, b. 1 Mar., bapt. 5 Apr. 1747, d. at Bedford, N. Y., 7 Oct. 1832 ae. 87-7-7 (g. s.) ; m. 5 Oct. 1769, Elizabeth Holmes, dau. of David, b. 9 Sept. 1749, d. 26 Nov. 1848 ae. 99-2-17 (g. s.).
Elisha, bapt. 27 Nov., d. 1 Dec. 1748.
Joseph, b. 4 Apr., bapt. 12 May 1751.
Elijah, bapt. 27, d. 31 Jan. 1754.

Higgins, Samuel, s. of Samuel.

He m. at Weston, 3 Nov. 1768, Tamasin Dunning; dau. of Michael, b. abt. 1750; Widow Tamasin m. at Weston, 18 Dec. 1792, Dea. Joseph Hide; and d. at Westport, 3 or 30 Apr. 1808 in 69(?) yr.

Will 25 Nov. 1787, proved 25 Feb. 1788; wife Tamasin; sons John, Abner, William, Michael Dunning, Samuel. Tamasin Higgins was appointed guardian of Michael and Samuel, 3 Sept. 1792. John Higgins was allowed guardian of William and Michael, 1795.

In 1798, Tamasin Hyde, widow of Samuel Higgins of Weston, sold land in Norwalk to son John Higgins.

Children, bapt. Weston:

John, bapt. 3 Dec. 1769, d. at Hillsdale, N. Y., 24 Mar. 1854; m. Sarah ———, b. 20 Oct. 1768, d. 17 May 1841.*

---

* Children, bapt. Weston: Anna and Bradley, bapt. 3 June 1795; Tamasin, bapt. 12 Jan. 1797; Dunning, bapt. 9 Apr. 1799.

Abner, bapt. 12 July 1772; said to have settled in New York City; m. ———.

Hannah, bapt. 2 Oct. 1774, d. y.

William, bapt. 14 Dec. 1777; rem. to Hillsdale, N. Y.; m. 1802, Judith Spencer.

Michael-Dunning, bapt. 8 Oct. 1780; rem. to New York City; m. Sarah Stuart, dau. of Isaac and Olive, b. at Wilton 1781, d. 6 Apr. 1805.

Samuel, b. 17 Feb. 1783, d. 3 Sept. 1832; res. Spencertown, Columbia County, N. Y.; m. at Westport, 21 Sept. 1804, Elizabeth Bulkley, b. 28 Mar. 1785, d. 23 Oct. 1866.

Higgins, Abraham.

On 6 Apr. 1756, Samuel Odell was appointed guardian to Abraham Higgins, a minor who lately belonged to Eastchester, N. Y.

He m. (1) ———.

He m. (2) 12 Mar. 1777, Martha ———.

Will 20 June 1800, proved 27 Apr. 1811; wife Martha; son Isaac; dau. Molly; sons John, Dennis; daus. Sally, Ruth.

Distribution 23 Mar. 1812: widow Martha; John; Sally; Ruth; Dennis. The part set to the widow was distributed to the four heirs, 24 Oct. 1818.

Children [by first wife]:

Isaac, b. 7 Aug. 1764, d. in 1811; m. Hannah Dickinson, dau. of Zadoc. Adm'n on Isaac's estate was granted, 26 Aug. 1811, to Deodate Silliman, Esq., with Nathan Wheeler as surety; insolvent.

Molly.

Children [by second wife] rec. Weston:

John, b. 5 May 1778, d. at Weston in 1821; m. Hannah Lacey, dau. of Zachariah, b. 11 Feb. 1782. Will 26 Jan., proved 1 Mar. 1821; eldest son Eli; to wife Hannah, the residue.*

Sally, b. 8 June 1780, unm. 1818.

Ruth, b. 17 Jan. 1783, unm. 1818.

Dennis, b. 26 July 1785.

---

* It is said that a son Lacey, b. at Easton, m. Priscilla Silliman, settled in Roxbury, and d. 1892 ae. 78.

HILL FAMILY (WILLIAM)

Hill [Vol. I, pp. 278-283].

1 William (-1650) m. Sarah Jourdain.
  2 William (-1684) m. Elizabeth Jones.
    3 William (1661-1739) m. (1) Abigail Osborn; (2) Sarah ———; (3) Sarah (Hide) Fanton.
    (By 1): 6 *Joseph* (1699-1797).
       7 *William* (1702-1787).
    4 Eliphalet (-1695/6) m. Esther (Ward) (Hawley) Nichols.
      8 *William* (1692-1775).
    5 John (-1727) m. Jane ———.
      9 *John* (1707-1759).

6. **Hill, Joseph**, s. of William.

Born 1 Apr. 1699; d. at Greenfield, 6 Mar. 1797 in 98 yr. (g. s.); Deacon; m. 30 Mar. 1731, Abigail Dimon, dau. of Moses, bapt. 17 Aug. 1707, d. 25 Apr. 1774 in 67 yr. (g. s.).

Will 9 Nov. 1787, proved 20 Mar. 1797; far advanced in life; son Ebenezer; Sarah wife of William Wakeman; Dimon, David Jr. and Sarah Gould, Eunice Wier, Abigail, Esther, Mabel, and Charity Gould, children of dec'd dau. Abigail wife of David Gould; Sarah, John and Moses Hill, children of dec'd son Jabez; William and Abigail Hill, children of dec'd son Moses.

Distribution 30 Nov. 1797: eldest son Ebenezer Hill; Sarah wife of William Wakeman; gr. son William Hill and Abigail wife of Elihu Staples (sister of William Hill); gr. children, heirs of Abigail Gould dec'd and of Jabez Hill dec'd; gr. dau. Sarah wife of Jesse Gould; Esther wife of Increase Sherwood; gr. son David Gould, Jr.; gr. dau. Charity Gould; gr. son Dimon Gould; gr. dau. Mabel wife of Levi Perry; Eunice wife of Samuel Wires; gr. dau. Abigail wife of Nathan Wakeman; gr. son Moses Hill; gr. son John Hill; Sarah wife of Timothy Platt. (Abigail Staples was dau. of Moses Hill dec'd.)

Adm'n on Est. of Abigail Hill granted, 20 Mar. 1797, to Ebenezer Hill; William Wakeman, surety. Distribution, Apr. 1799: eldest son Ebenezer; dec'd son Moses; dec'd son Jabez; dau. Abigail Gould; dau. Sarah Wakeman.

Children, rec. Fairfield, bapt. Greenfield:

    Abigail, b. 21 Mar. 1732/3, bapt. 14 May 1732 (?); m. in 1754, David Gold.

458   HISTORY AND GENEALOGY OF

 Sarah, b. 21 Aug. 1735, bapt. 30 Sept. 1733 (?), d. 29 Apr. 1803; m. 21 June 1753, William Wakeman.
 David, b. 22 Apr., bapt. 22 May 1737, d. 26 Mar. 1760 in 23 yr. (g. s.).
10+Ebenezer, b. 26 Feb. 1741/2.
11+Jabez, b. 17 June, bapt. 1 July 1744.
12+Moses, b. 11, bapt. 18 Jan. 1748/9.

7. **Hill, William,** s. of William. Cornet, Troop of Horse, 4th Regt., May 1744.

Born 16 May 1702; d. at Redding in 1787.

He m. (1) 28 Apr. 1725, Hannah Morehouse, dau. of Daniel, bapt. 24 Sept. 1704, d. 10 Aug. 1729; m. (2) 28 Feb. 1730, Rebecca Sanford, dau. of Ezekiel, b. 21 Nov. 1710, d. abt. Nov. 1730; m. (3) 6 May 1731, Mary Ogden; perhaps dau. of Joseph; m. (4) after 1760, Sarah (Lord) Gilbert, widow of Josiah Gilbert and dau. of Robert Lord, bapt. 29 Mar. 1702, d. before 27 Mar. 1783.

Will 13 July, proved 28 Aug. 1787; son Ezekiel; three daus. Hannah Bulkley, Abigail Fairchild, Mary Sherman; son Daniel; negro girl Patience to have freedom and a legacy; son Daniel and son-in-law Andrew Fairchild, Exec'rs.

Children [by first wife], rec. Fairfield:

13+Daniel, b. 26 Jan. 1726 [1726/7], bapt. at Greenfield, 19 Mar. 1726/7.
 Hannah, b. 25 June 1728 [1729], bapt. at Fairfield, 17 Aug. 1729, d. at Greenfield, 7 Dec. 1809 ae. 82 (g. s.); m. (1) 31 Oct. 1744, David Meeker, Jr.; m. (2) 18 Mar. 1759, Daniel Bulkley, Jr.

Child [by second wife], rec. Fairfield:

 Rebecca, b. 9 Nov. [1730], d. 22 Mar. 1749.

Children [by third wife], rec. Fairfield:

14+Ezekiel, b. 16 Feb. 1732.
 Abigail, b. 6 May 1734; m. 26 Apr. 1752, Andrew Fairchild.
 Mary, b. 13 Feb. 1739; m. ―――― Sherman.

8. **Hill, William,** s. of Eliphalet.

Born 17 Nov. 1692; d. at Greenfield, 25 Apr. 1775 ae. over 80; m. (1) abt. 1716, Abigail Barlow, dau. of John, b. 30 June 1697, d. 16 Apr. 1743 ae. 47 (g. s.); m. (2) Esther, widow of Benjamin Lines, and dau. of Joseph Sturges, bapt. 2 Mar. 1700/1.

Will 25 Feb. 1773, proved 16 May 1775; son Ward William Hill; sons Eliphalet, Augustus, James, Samuel; daus. Ruhamah, Elizabeth, Frances, Anna, Sarah, Mary, Catherine; gr. dau. Esther Parruck.

In 1784, Samuel Hill, and John McEwen and Elizabeth his wife, of New Milford, and Zalmon Wheeler of Pownal, Vt., conveyed right in William Ward's home lot given to Samuel Hill, Elizabeth McEwen and Francis [sic] Wheeler by their father William Hill dec'd.

Children [by first wife], four bapt. Fairfield:

    Catherine, bapt. 2 June 1717, d. before 1768; m. 4 Jan. 1739, Hezekiah Bulkley.
15+Samuel, bapt. 27 Apr. 1718.
    Ann, bapt. 28 Feb. 1719/20, d. at Westport, 11 Apr. 1795 ae. 76 (g. s.); m. 9 Apr. 1740, Peter Bulkley.
    Mary, bapt. 25 Mar. 1722, d. by 1818; m. 22 Nov. 1750, Elnathan Parruck.
    Elizabeth, m. (rec. New Milford) 30 Apr. 1754, John McEwen, of New Milford.
16+Eliphalet, b. abt. 1727.
    Sarah, b. abt. 1729, d. 8 July 1816 ae. 87 (Trinity Church rec.); m. Dec. 1756, John Sherwood.
    Augustus, res. Fairfield, 1783; perhaps m. at Easton, 24 Nov. 1773, Susannah Lyon.
17+Ward-William, b. abt. 1736.
    Frances, b. abt. 1737, d. 30 July 1805 ae. 68; m. Joseph Wheeler; they, of Pownal, Bennington County, Vt., conveyed 1784 to Zalmon Wheeler of Pownal, all right in estate of William Hill.
18+James.
    Ruhamah.

9. Hill, John, s. of John.

Bapt. 29 June 1707; d. at Fairfield, 17 Dec. 1759 in 53 yr. (g. s.); m. 27 Jan. 1729, Esther Bulkley, dau. of Joseph, bapt. 20 Dec. 1713. She m. (2) 9 May 1764, Stephen Adams.

Will 7 Dec. 1759, proved 15 Jan. 1760; wife Esther; five children, Nathan, Isaac, Joseph, Esther, Sarah; friend Nathan Bulkley, Exec'r.

Nathan Hill conveyed 1774 home bounded on land of mother (now wife of Stephen Adams) and on land of my children Aaron, Stephen and Sarah. Isaac conveyed 1775 to bro. Nathan of

Amenia, N. Y., right set to mother Esther Adams in estate of father John Hill. Joseph, called Jr., of Fairfield, conveyed 1791 land which was part of Esther Adams' dower in estate of her first husband John Hill.

Children, rec. and bapt. Fairfield:

19+Nathan, b. 9 Oct. 1731, bapt. 21 Feb. 1741/2.
John, bapt. 15 May 1741, d. y.
Esther, bapt. 11 Aug. 1736, d. y.
Esther, b. 21 Apr. 1738, bapt. 21 Feb. 1741/2; m. 28 May 1761, Daniel Wakeman.
Rachel, bapt. 15 July 1741, d. y.
Sarah, b. 28 Apr. 1742, d. 6 Feb. 1832; m. 17 June 1762, George Wakeman.
Isaac, b. 25 Sept. 1745;* chose Nathan Bulkley for guardian, May 1760.
Joseph, b. 2 May 1752; chose Isaac Hill for guardian, Oct. 1766. He was bapt. as an adult at Trinity Church, 20 Nov. 1791, with his four children, Rachel, Huldah, Polly, and Nathan.
John, bapt. 25 Sept. 1755, d. y.

10. **Hill, Ebenezer,** s. of Joseph. Ens., Greenfield Co., Mar. 1775; 2d Lt., 4th Co., 5th Regt., Army, Apr. 1775 (resigned); Lt. (acting Capt.), 1st Co., 7th Regt., Army, July 1775; Capt., 8th Co., 4th Regt., May 1777.

Born 26 Feb. 1741/2; d. at Greenfield, 27 Mar. 1798 in 57 yr. (g. s.); m. 17 Jan. 1765, Mabel Sherwood, dau. of Benjamin, b. 6 Jan. 1745/6, d. 26 Oct. 1820 in 75 yr. (g. s.).

Adm'n granted, 5 Apr. 1798, to Mabel and David Hill. Distribution, 1800: widow; sons David, Ebenezer, Seth, Joseph, Jabez.

Will of Mabel, 5 Oct., proved 7 Dec. 1820; three sons, David of Fairfield, Ebenezer of Redding, Seth of Weston; children of dec'd son Joseph of State of New York; gr. dau. Esther Hill, dau. of dec'd son Jabez.

Children, rec. Greenfield:

David, bapt. 20 July 1766; m. Eleanor Staples, dau. of John, b. 21 Nov. 1769.
Ebenezer, bapt. 6 Mar. 1768; m. May 1791, Sarah Barlow, dau. of Nathaniel, b. 16 Jan. 1770, d. 11 Apr. 1845.†

---

* Elizabeth wife of Isaac Hill d. at Amenia, N. Y., 20 June 1810 ae. 53 (g. s.).

† A dau., Mabel, bapt. at Easton, July 1792. Children, rec. Redding: Mabel b. 17 Dec. 1791; Barlow, b. 23 [Dec.?] 1793; Gershom, b. 10 Mar. 1796; Ebenezer, b. 11 Oct. 1797.

Seth, bapt. 31 Dec. 1769, d. at Easton, 10 Dec. 1821 ae. 52 (g. s.);
m. (rec. Weston) 26 Oct. 1793, Cynthia Banks, b. 16 Nov. 1772,
d. 3 Jan. 1839 ae. 66 (g. s.). Will 20 Nov. 1821, proved 22 Jan.
1822; wife Cynthia; sons Joseph, Wakeman, Edward; dau. Polly D.*
Dimon, bapt. 28 June 1772 (ae. abt. 6 mos.), d. 5 Dec. 1793 in 23 yr.
(g. s.).
Joseph, bapt. 10 July 1774, d. 6 May 1816 (Miss Treadwell's book);
Capt.; m. Sarah Banks, dau. of Hezekiah, b. abt. 1776, d. in Sullivan
County, N. Y., 8 Sept. 1868 in 93 yr.
Mabel, bapt. 5 Dec. 1776, d. July 1779 in 3 yr.
Ellen, bapt. 8 Nov. 1778, d. y.
Jabez, b. [13 June], bapt. 21 Aug. 1780, d. 2 Aug. 1807 ae. 27 yrs. 1
mo. 19 days (g. s.); dower distributed to widow Sarah, 6 Dec. 1807;
m. 25 Nov. 1806, Sarah Nichols, dau. of Ebenezer, b. [Nov. 1777],
d. 3 Oct. 1863 ae. 85 yrs. 11 mos. (g. s.); she m. (2) Lyman Hall,
with whom she petitioned 1819 as mother of Esther Hill, dau. of
Jabez dec'd.
Esther, b. [Oct. 1785], d. 27 Aug. 1804 ae. 18 yrs. 10 mos. (g. s.).

11. **Hill, Jabez,** s. of Joseph. Cornet, 2d Troop, 4th Regt., May 1769; Capt., May 1774; Major, 3d Regt., May 1777 (resigned May 1779).

Born 17 June 1744; d. at Easton, 19 Oct. 1779 ae. 35 (g. s.); m. 10 May 1772 (Perry Diary), Sarah Read, dau. of Col. John, b. 27 Nov. 1751, d. at Redding, 14 July 1809 ae. 57-7-17. She m. (2) 26 Feb. 1782, Capt. Theophilus Munson, b. 4 Jan. 1747, d. 30 Mar. 1795, who grad. Yale Coll. 1768.†

Jabez and his wife admitted to full communion, Easton Church, 26 Sept. 1773.

In the Danbury raid, he sent Samuel Thorp, Jr., on Hill's own horse to warn the inhabitants, and lost horse, saddle and bridle, for which he was allowed £60.

Inv. 2 June 1784. Distribution, 17 Mar. 1788: widow; eldest son John; 2d son Moses; dau. Sarah.

Ebenezer Hill was appointed guardian to John, Moses and Sarah Hill, 3 Sept. 1787.

Children:

Sarah, b. [20 Aug. 1772], d. at Redding, 6 Nov. 1842 ae. 70-2-16
(g. s.); m. 8 Feb. 1793, Timothy Platt.
Mabel, bapt. at Redding, 19, d. 20, Apr. 1774.‡

---

* One child, Polly, b. at Weston, 5 Mar. 1795, and bapt. Easton, Nov. 1795.
† See *The Munson Record*, vol. 2, p. 828.
‡ The record calls her dau. of Cornet and Sarah Hill.

John-Read, b. 26 Apr. 1775, d. at Redding, 29 July 1851 ae. 76-8-5 (g. s.); m. (1) 23 Mar. 1799, Betsey Sanford; dau. of Aaron, b. 5 Oct. 1781, d. 29 July 1818 (g. s.); m. (2) 1 Sept. 1819, Deborah Read; dau. of Hezekiah, b. 23 May 1790, d. 16 June 1860 ae. 70 yrs. 24 days (g. s.).*

Moses, b. [say 1777]; chose Nathan Wheeler for guardian, 14 Apr. 1794; m. abt. 1805, Phebe Robertson. dau. of Thomas and Elizabeth (Soper), b. at Huntington, L. I., 3 Feb. 1788, d. there 8 Feb. 1837; she m. (2) ―――― Clark; left issue.

12. Hill, Moses, s. of Joseph.

Born 11 Jan. 1748/9; d. at Greenfield, 13 Oct. 1777 in 29 yr.; m. 17 June 1773, Esther Burr, b. 29 May 1755, d. 2 Oct. 1836 ae. 81 (g. s.). She m. (2) at Westport, 26 Sept. 1782, Zachariah Hawkins of Long Island, and (3) Dea. John Staples.

Children, rec. Greenfield:

William, b. 30 Apr. 1774 (family rec.), bapt. 10 July 1774, d. at Greenfield, 6 July 1808 in 35 yr. (g. s.); Capt.; adm'n granted, 15 Aug. 1808, to Betsey Hill and Elihu Staples; m. Betsey Barlow, dau. of Nathaniel, b. 2 Aug. 1778, d. 9 Sept. 1864.†

Abigail, b. 14 Oct. 1774 (Weston rec.), bapt. 6 Jan. 1776; m. Elihu Staples.

Esther, b. 17 June, bapt. 20 July 1777, d. y.‡

---

* Children by first wife rec. Redding: Aaron-Sanford, b. 23 Mar. 1800, d. at New Haven, 15 July 1893; m. (1) 9 Oct. 1822, Phebe Hunt, dau. of Rev. Aaron, who d. 1827/8; m. (2) abt. 1833, Abia-Ann Judson of Cornwall, who d. at New Haven 17 or 27 Sept. 1875 ae. 71. Moses, b. 5 Feb. 1802, d. at Redding, 2 Apr. 1870 ae. 68-1-27 (g. s.); m. 28 Mar. 1826, Julia Fanton, b. 29 Dec. 1802, d. 17 Nov. 1881 ae. 79 (g. s.). William-Hawley, b. 29 Mar. 1804, d. at Redding, 30 Dec. 1830 ae. 26 yrs. 9 mos. (g. s.); m. at Newtown, 12 Dec. 1828, Emma Clark, b. at Newtown, 11 Nov. 1806, d. at Brooklyn, N. Y., 6 Feb. 1886. Betsey, b. 6 Mar. 1806, d. 25 Jan. 1849 ae. 42-10-19 (g. s.). John-Lee, b. 15 June 1810, d. at Redding, 18 Jan. 1852; m. (1) 26 May 1837, Hester-Ann Sanford, dau. of Hezekiah, who d. 18 Dec. 1838 ae. 19-5-25; m. (2) 4 May 1840, Harriet-Newell Duncomb, b. 29 Apr. 1820, d. 27 Apr. 1893 ae. 72-11-28. Morris, b. 6 Oct. 1812, d. at New Haven, 5 Apr. 1902; Rev.; m. 14 May 1837, Rhoda-Ann Smith of Bristol, b. 6 May 1810, d. 5 Feb. 1890. Lydia, b. 26 Mar. 1815, d. 24 Dec. 1835 (g. s.). Joseph, b. 21 Aug. 1817, d. at Redding, 31 Dec. 1909; m. 11 May 1842, Chloe-Margaret Sperry.

† William's Est. was ordered distributed, 26 June 1809, to widow Betsey, children Bradley, Abby, Horace, Burr, William. The distribution, 1814, omits Burr and calls the dau. Abigail Hill. Children (from family record): Bradley, b. 9 Sept. 1798. Abigail, b. 23 Nov. 1800. Horace, b. 15 Dec. 1802, d. 9 Mar. 1877; m. (1) 7 Jan. 1830, Eleanor Lyon, b. 27 Feb. 1807, d. 27 Feb. 1842; m. (2) 27 Sept. 1843, Almira Ogden, b. 10 Nov. 1808, d. 16 Apr. 1900. Burr, b. 23 Dec. 1804. William, b. 6 Oct. 1807. Bapt. at Greenfield: Bradley, Abbey and Horace, on 4 Sept. 1803.

‡ Greenfield records state that Abigail, dau. of ye widow Hill, d. July 1779; but apparently it was Esther.

13. **Hill, Daniel,** s. of William. Lt., east company, Redding, May 1766; Capt., May 1770.

Born 26 Jan. 1726/7; Capt. Daniel d. at Redding, 11 July 1805 ae. 78 yrs. 5 mos. 15 days (g. s.); m. (1) 31 Oct. 1748, Phebe Beach, dau. of Rev. John, b. 1729, d. 9 May 1751 in 22 yr. (g. s.). He m. (2) Apr. 1752, Elizabeth Lane, b. 27 Apr. 1734, d. 19 Feb. 1808 ae. 74 yrs. 9 mos. 19 days (g. s.).

Will 21 Sept. 1798, proved 10 Aug. 1805; wife Elizabeth; son Abel; son Andrew L.; dec'd son Daniel; daus. Hannah, Betty; gr. son John Hill.

Adm'n on estate of Widow Elizabeth granted, 22 Mar. 1808, to Andrew L. Hill. Distribution: Andrew L. Hill; John Hill; Sarah wife of Eli Sanford; Betty wife of Eli Lyon.

Child [by first wife], rec. Fairfield:

Abel, b. 10 Jan. 1750; m. at Easton, 11 May 1773, Anna Lyon, dau. of Peter, b. 1 Apr. 1757, d. 22 Jan. 1827 ae. 69 yrs. 10 mos. (g. s.).*

Children [by second wife], rec. Fairfield:

Hannah, b. 27 Feb. 1753, d. 27 Sept. 1755 in 3 yr. (g. s.).

Andrew-Lane, b. 14 Dec. 1755, d. at Redding, 17 Oct. 1813 in 58 yr. (g. s.); Deputy for Redding, Oct. 1790, May and Oct. 1791, May 1792, May 1793, Oct. 1795, Oct. 1798, Oct. 1800, May 1801, May 1802, May and Oct. 1803, May 1804, May 1805, May and Oct. 1806, May 1807, May 1808, May and Oct. 1809, May and Oct. 1810, Oct. 1811, May and Oct. 1812; m. 23 Apr. 1775, Hannah Lyon; dau. of Henry, b. abt. 1757, d. 13 Apr. 1845 in 88 yr. (g. s.).†

Hannah, b. 25 Sept. 1758; m. 2 June 1775, Asahel Lyon.

Daniel, b. 12 Apr. 1761, d. at Redding, 7 Aug. 1793 ae. 32-3-26 (g. s.); m. Elizabeth ———. Will 8 May 1792, proved 3 Sept. 1793; wife Elizabeth; son John; wife and bro. Andrew-Lane Hill, Exec'rs.‡ Widow [Elizabeth] m. 27 Dec. 1796, Hezekiah Morgan.

Sarah, b. 24 Mar. 1764, d. 19 June 1764 in 1 yr. (g. s.).

Betty, b. Sept. 1777, d. at Redding, 30 Mar. 1853 ae. 75 yrs. 6 mos. (g. s.); m. 26 Apr. 1795, Eli Lyon.

---

* Children, rec. Redding: Beach, b. 2 Apr. 1777; Lucy, b. 4 Mar. 1783, d. 9 Mar. 1794.

† Children, rec. Redding: Hannah, b. 7 Jan. 1776, m. 26 Sept. 1797, Isaac Beach; Clarry, b. 24 Aug. 1788, d. 16 Dec. 1808 ae. 20-3-23; Daniel, b. 1 Sept. 1793, d. 2 Aug. 1814 in 21 yr. (g. s.); Fanny, b. 18 Sept. 1798. The will of Andrew L. Hill, 2 Oct. 1813, proved 20 Nov. 1813; wife Hannah; son Daniel; dau. Hannah Beach; dau. Fanny; son-in-law Isaac Beach. The distribution, 1814, called Fanny wife of Aaron Sanford, Jr. Adm'n on Est. of Daniel Hill granted, 18 Aug. 1814, to Isaac Beach and Aaron Sanford, Jr.; distribution to two sisters.

‡ His son John d. at Redding 3 Aug. 1826 ae. 41 yrs. 11 mos.; adm'n granted to Aaron Sanford, Jr., 8 Aug. 1826. Distribution: widow Sally; son Daniel; dau. Eliza; son George; son Andrew; dau. Mary Hill; son John; dau. Mabel Hill.

464   HISTORY AND GENEALOGY OF

14. **Hill, Ezekiel,** s. of William.

Born 16 Feb. 1732; d. at Redding by 1801.

He m. 3 June 1750, Elizabeth Morehouse; dau. of Stephen, b. 1 Nov. 1728, d. in 1811.

Dower in Ezekiel's estate set to his widow Elizabeth, 28 Aug. 1801.

Adm'n on Est. of Elizabeth widow of Ezekiel was granted, 3 Dec. 1811, to Thomas Starr of Redding.

Children, rec. Fairfield (perhaps others):

> Rebecca, b. 13 Mar. 1751; ? m. at Redding, 29 Nov. 1768, John-Darling Guire.
> Ann, b. 19 Jan. 1754; ? m. at Redding, 7 Dec. 1773, Daniel Read.
> David, b. 11 Mar. 1757, d. at Hampton, Washington County, N. Y., 1 Jan. 1813; m. at Redding, 15 June 1782 (Pension rec.), Chloe Beebe; she m. (2) at Hampton, 25 Dec. 1814, Elijah Blackman, who d. at Warsaw, N. Y., 15 June 1828; she was living at Wethersfield Springs, Wyoming County, N. Y., 1862 ae. 96.
> Elizabeth, m. at Redding, 15 Dec. 1789, Thomas Starr.

15. **Hill, Samuel,** s. of William. Lt., Greenfield Co., Oct. 1759.

Bapt. 27 Apr. 1718; d. at New Milford, 1 Dec. 1811 ae. 94 (g. s.).

He m. at Greenfield, 28 Nov. 1744, Sarah Dimon, b. 6 May 1728, d. 28 Feb. 1797 (g. s.).

He bought land in the Upper Merryall district of New Milford from Thaddeus Peet in 1765, and in 1766 sold his Fairfield property to Peet. He, with his sons Samuel and Jonathan, were members of St. Andrew's Church, Marbledale.

Samuel and Sarah his wife, of New Milford, conveyed in 1772 land in Fairfield.

Children:

> Samuel, b. abt. 1748, d. at New Milford, 12 Jan. 1832 ae. 84 (g. s.); m. (1) Anna ———, b. abt. 1754, d. 18 Apr. 1812 ae. 58 (g. s.); m. (2) Eunice ———, b. abt. 1761, d. 21 Mar. 1823 in 62 yr. (g. s.).
> Jonathan, b. 8 Apr. 1755; m. at New Milford, 25 May 1782, Mary Coady, b. 11 June 1759.
> Others?

16. **Hill, Eliphalet,** s. of William.

Born abt. 1727; d. 18 July 1821 ae. 94 (Greenfield Church rec.), bur. 18 July 1821 ae. 94 (Trinity Church rec.).

He m. at Greenfield, 8 Jan. 1758, Isabel Burr; dau. of James, b. 8 Jan. 1733, d. 24 Jan. 1806.

Children:
>Mary, b. abt. 1756, d. at Easton, 14 Mar. 1848 ae. 92 (g. s.); m. John Nichols.
>Eleanor, b. abt. 1759, d. at Easton, 31 Oct. 1843 ae. 84 (g. s.); m. Joseph Wilson.
>Eliphalet.
>A son, rem. to Vermont.
>Sarah, b. abt. 1765, d. at Greenfield, 3 Mar. 1848 ae. 83 (g. s.); m. Dec. 1790, Joseph Burr.

17. **Hill, Ward-William,** s. of William.

Born abt. 1736; d. at Greenfield, 5 Oct. 1801 [1800] in 66 yr. (g. s.), bur. 6 Oct. 1800 ae. 66 (Trinity Church rec.); m. at Westport, 26 Aug. 1770, Grace Hull, b. 16 July 1736, d. 17 Feb. 1813 in 77 yr. (g. s.).

Child:
>Abigail, b. abt. 1772, d. at Greenfield, 30 July 1828 in 56 yr. (g. s.); m. Nov. 1792, Jesse Nichols.

18. **Hill, James,** s. of William.

He m. at Greenfield, 13 July 1766, Elizabeth Wakeman; dau. of Moses, b. 25 Mar. 1749/50.

He d. of smallpox by inoculation, Apr. 1777 (Perry Diary); she m. (2) Thomas-Langley Collier, and d. 14 Mar. 1796 (Trinity Church rec.).

Distribution, 27 June 1780; widow Elizabeth, now wife of Thomas-Langley Collier; eldest son Wakeman; dau. Huldah Hill.

Children:
>Wakeman, d. at Norfolk, Oct. 1800; m. 3 Aug. 1787, Sarah Sturges; ? dau. of Peter, b. 11 July 1766.*
>Huldah, m. (rec. Weston) 8 May 1783, Eliphalet Dikeman.

---

* Children, rec. Weston: Huldah, b. 14 Mar. 1789; James, b. 26 May 1790. Distribution 24 Nov. 1801 to widow Sarah, dau. Huldah, and son James-Wakeman. Huldah m. at Westport, 7 Jan. 1805, Joseph Nash of Norwalk.

19. **Hill, Nathan,** s. of John.

Born 9 Oct. 1731; rem. to Amenia, N. Y.; d. before 1794; m. (1) 3 July 1753, Eunice Wakeman, dau. of Stephen, b. 31 Jan. 1734/5, d. 29 Jan. 1765; m. (2) 26 Aug. 1765, Martha Wakeman, dau. of Samuel; bapt. 15 Aug. 1736, d. 9 Mar. 1766; m. (3) Dec. 1766, Elizabeth Whitehead, dau. of Gershom; b. Apr. 1747.

Aaron Hill of Saratoga, N. Y., and Stephen Hill of Tioga County, N. Y., heirs to Nathan Hill, once of Fairfield, late of Amenia, Dutchess County, conveyed 1794 to Stephen Adams. John Hill of Nine Partners, N. Y., conveyed 1794 to Stephen Adams, land from father Nathan Hill dec'd.

Children [by first wife], rec. and bapt. Fairfield:

Eunice, b. 5 June, bapt. 8 Sept. 1754, d. y.
Aaron, b. 12 Dec. 1755, bapt. 8 Feb. 1756, d. in Saratoga County, N. Y.; m. 15 Sept. 1777, Hannah Fiske; had 11 children.*
Rebecca, bapt. 22 Oct. 1758, d. y.
Sarah, b. 17 Nov. 1760.
Stephen, b. 16 Nov. 1762; res. 1794, Tioga County, N. Y.

Child [by third wife], rec. Fairfield:

John, b. 5 June 1767; res. 1794, Nine Partners, N. Y.

HILL FAMILY (THOMAS)

Hill, Thomas, s. of Thomas [Vol. I, p. 283]. Quarter-Master, Fairfield County Troop, Oct. 1722; Capt., Fairfield Co., May 1726. Deputy for Fairfield, May, Sept., and Oct. 1756, May 1757. Justice, 1764-70.

Born [say 1692]; d. at Fairfield, 31 July 1770 (Perry Diary); m. (1) 9 Dec. 1715, Mary Burr, dau. of John, b. [13 Oct. 1694], d. at Fairfield, 19 Dec. 1763 ae. 69 yrs. 1 mo. 26 days (g. s.); m. (2) 13 Apr. 1764, Hannah ———.

Will 27 Dec. 1769, proved 10 Aug. 1770; wife Hannah, mentioning marriage covenant dated 13 Apr. 1764; dau. Mary wife of Josiah Burnham, formerly wife of Merritt Smith dec'd, her dau. Elizabeth and six other children; dau. Sarah wife of Thomas Fitch, Jr.; gr. son Ebenezer Wakeman; gr. dau. Esther Rowland;

---

* According to *Western New York Genealogies* (Lewis Hist. Pub. Co., 1912), p. 335.

gr. son Thomas Merritt Smith; gr. son Thomas Hill, son of dec'd son Thaddeus Hill; gr. son Thomas Hill, son of dec'd son Andrew; gr. dau. Grace wife of Bela Hubbard of New Haven; dau. Abigail wife of David Bulkley, formerly wife of Benjamin Davis; gr. dau. Mary wife of Wakeman Burr; Abigail widow of son Andrew dec'd.

Children [by first wife], rec. Fairfield and Greenfield:

> Abigail, b. 9 May 1718, bapt. 5 June 1720, d. at Amenia, N. Y., 20 June 1807 ae. 89 (g. s.); m. (1) at New York, 22 Mar. 1734, Benjamin Davis; m. (2) 17 Mar. 1767, David Bulkley.
> +Thaddeus, b. 19, bapt. 26 June 1720.
> Mary, bapt. 11 Nov. 1722, d. y.
> Mary, b. 5, bapt. 9 Aug. 1724; m. (1) Merritt Smith; m. (2) 14 Apr. 1763, Capt. Josiah Burnham, of Kensington. With her second husband, then of Charlestown, Cheshire County, N. H., she conveyed in 1786, all right in Greens Farms which formerly belonged to Capt. Thomas Hill.
> Elizabeth, b. 27 Dec. 1726, bapt. 1 Jan. 1726/7, d. 18 July 1753; m. 14 Feb. 1749/50, David Rowland.
> Ann, b. 6, bapt. 11 May 1729, d. 31 July 1749; m. 4 Sept. 1748, Ebenezer Wakeman.
> Thomas, b. 20 Nov., bapt. 12 Dec. 1731, d. at Westport, 25 July 1765; m. 20 Jan. 1757, Ellen Sturgis; she m. (2) 31 July 1766, Elisha Gray. They had an infant who d. 20 Dec. 1759.
> Sarah, b. 2 July, bapt. 25 Aug. 1734, d. at Norwalk, 27 Jan. 1795 in 61 yr.; m. 28 Apr. 1763, Thomas Fitch, Jr.; Yale Coll. 1746. They conveyed, 1787, one-seventh of realty that her father gave in his lifetime to her bro. Thomas Hill.
> +Andrew, b. 22, bapt. 28 Oct. 1739.

Hill, Thaddeus, s. of Thomas.

Born 19 June 1720.

He m. Elizabeth Isaacs. She was prob. the "Widow Elizabeth Hill" of New Haven who conveyed Fairfield land in 1793.

Children:

> Thomas, b. abt. 1745, d. at Fairfield, 8 Mar. 1781 in 36 yr. (g. s.); Dr.; m. Elizabeth Thatcher, dau. of Josiah of Norwalk; she m. (2) at Stratford, 6 May 1783, John Blackleach.* Thomas Hill, grandson of Thomas Hill, Esq., chose David Rowland for guardian, Mar. 1762.

---

* John and Elizabeth Blackleach were Adm'rs on Est. of Thomas Hill of Fairfield, 17 July 1787.

Grace-Dunbar, b. at Antigua, W. I., abt. 1748, d. at Farmington, 27 Apr. 1820 ae. 72; m. (at Fairfield, rec. also Trinity Church, New Haven) 15 May 1768, Rev. Bela Hubbard.

Hill, Andrew, s. of Thomas.

Born 22 Oct. 1739; d. 25 Oct. 1769; Yale Coll. 1759; m. 1 Dec. 1763, Abigail Lewis, dau. of Nathaniel, of Barnstable. She m. (2) 9 Jan. 1771, Samuel Sturgis, and d. 29 Nov. 1818 ae. 76 (g. s.).

Will 22 Oct., proved 5 Dec. 1769; wife Abigail, all estate. Abigail Hill of Fairfield was appointed guardian of Thomas Hill, Jr., 6 Sept. 1770.

Child, rec. Fairfield, bapt. Westport:

> Thomas, b. 13 Jan., bapt. 13 Apr. 1766, d. at Westport, 26 Oct. 1821 ae. 59 (g. s.); m. at Fairfield, 20 June 1784, Catherine Jennings; dau. of Moses, bapt. 24 Feb. 1765, d. 27 Nov. 1832 ae. 68 (g. s.). Adm'n on his estate granted, 15 Nov. 1824, to Nathaniel L. Hill, with Catherine Hill as surety. Distribution 1825: Widow Catherine; Andrew; Thomas; Nathaniel L.; Abigail Hill; Catherine wife of Peter Jennings; Hezekiah son of Anna Phillips dec'd. Catherine's dower was ordered distributed, 15 Feb. 1833, to the children: Nathaniel L.; Catherine wife of Peter B. Jennings; Abigail Hill; Thomas; and the gr. son Hezekiah, son of Anna Phillips, dec'd.*

Hill [Unplaced].

> EDWARD, of Fairfield; adm'n granted, 14 Feb. 1726/7, to William Hollins.
> WIDOW BETSEY of Greenfield m. 20 Oct. 1814, Ebenezer Seeley of Weston.
> JOSEPH d. at Albany, N. Y., 20 Aug. 1832. [Miss Treadwell's book]
> BENAJAH m. in 1794, Molly Jackson. [Easton Church]

Hillard [Unplaced].

> ISAAC and Sarah had: Betsey, b. 11 Sept. 1780. [Redding rec.]
> ZOA m. 15 June 1783, John Read, Jr. [Redding rec.]
> THURSTON m. 1 June 1790, Eunice Jackson. Children: Charles, b. 24 July 1791; Anne, b. 31 July 1793; Henry, b. 28 Sept. 1795. [Redding rec.]

---

* Children, bapt. Westport: Abigail, bapt. 16 July 1786, d. Feb. 1867 ae. 82 (g. s.). Anna, bapt. 15 Apr. 1787, d. 8 Apr. 1816 in 29 yr.; m. 2 Oct. 1811, Hezekiah Phillips. Andrew, bapt. 12 Oct. 1788. Thomas and Lewis, bapt. 22 Jan. 1791; the latter d. 24 Jan. 1791. Nathaniel-Lewis, bapt. 3 Nov. 1793; m. Maria Wakeman. Samuel, bapt. 18 Dec. 1795, d. 3 Jan. 1796. Catherine, bapt. 18 Nov. 1798.

THE FAMILIES OF OLD FAIRFIELD

Hilton, Adkinson.

He was prob. son of ———— and Mary (Morehouse) Hilton. The Weston (Norfield) church record calls him Sergt. at baptism of his child, 1777.

He m. Mary Allen, dau. of John, b. 1 Sept. 1742.

Adm'n granted to Daniel Wakeman, 18 Apr. 1814, with Josiah Bennett and Allen Hilton on bond.

Children, bapt. Weston:
> Sarah, b. abt. 1761, bapt. 26 Feb. 1764, d. at Westport, 23 Oct. 1834 ae. 73 (g. s.); "Sally of Norfield" m. 19 Apr. 1781, Joseph Meeker.
> Nathan, bapt. 26 Feb. 1764; m. ————.*
> Mary, bapt. 31 Aug. 1766; m. 13 Sept. 1789, Josiah Bennett.
> Rhoda, bapt. 15 July 1770.
> Silva, bapt. 17 Aug. 1772.
> Joseph, bapt. 11 Mar. 1774.
> John, bapt. 12 July 1777.
> Allen, bapt. 18 June 1780; m. at Westport, 14 Apr. 1805, Dolly Bennett.

Hobart, (Rev.) Noah. Preached Election Sermon, 1750.

Born at Hingham, Mass., 2 Jan. 1705/6; d. at Fairfield, 6 Dec. 1773; m. 22 Sept. 1735, Ellen Sloss; dau. of John, bapt. 1 Oct. 1710, d. 19 Aug. 1753; in 43 yr. (g. s.). He m. (2) in 1757, Mrs. Priscilla Lothrop, of Plymouth, Mass.

He was grad. Harvard Coll., 1724; ordained pastor at Fairfield, 7 Feb. 1732. He was son of David and Joanna (Quincy) Hobart, and gr. son of Rev. Peter Hobart.

Will 6 Dec. 1773; son John-Sloss Hobart, £100, Chambers' Dictionary, London Magazines, and all clothing except great coat which I give to my bro. David; to wife, all she brought with her, also use of my house as long as she has a mind to stay here, with the negro boy Dauphin, and five vols. of Dodridge's Works; to Justin Hobart, his note, he balancing his book account against me; to Priscilla Burr, the negro child Toney; the rest of my estate to dau. Ellen Lothrop.

Children, rec. and bapt. Fairfield:
> John-Sloss, b. 6, bapt. 7 May 1738, d. 5 Feb. 1805; m. (license 22 June 1764) Mary Greenill; no issue. Grad. Yale Coll. 1757; settled in Huntington, L. I.; Deputy from Suffolk County to First, Second,

---
* Children, bapt. Weston: Hester and Priscilla, bapt. 14 Sept. 1782.

Third, and Fourth Provincial Congresses of N. Y., 1775-76, and a leader in the State Convention, 1776; member of Council of Safety; Associate Judge of N. Y. Supreme Court, May 1777; member of N. Y. Convention for adoption of Constitution, 1788; appointed U. S. Senator, 1798 (resigned); Judge of U. S. District Court for N. Y., 1798-1805.

Ellen, b. 15, bapt. 18 Oct. 1741, d. at Plymouth, Mass., 1 July 1780; m. 10 May 1768, Mr. Nathaniel Lothrop, of Plymouth; no issue.

Noah, b. 18, bapt. 19 June 1743, d. 4 Oct. 1756 in 49 yr. (g. s.).

Hobart, Justin.

Son of Nehemiah, b. at Hingham, Mass., 1731; d. at Fairfield, 7 Apr. 1809 ae. 78 yrs. 2 mos. (g. s.); m. 18 Mar. 1762, Hannah Penfield, dau. of Peter, b. 10 Nov. 1737, d. 7 Jan. 1809 ae. 71 yrs. 2 mos. (g. s.).

Adm'n granted, 22 June 1809, to Justin Hobart, with Joseph Allen as surety.

Children, rec. and bapt. Fairfield:

Ellen, b. 18 Jan., bapt. 4 Mar. 1764, d. at Trumbull, 27 Mar. 1813 ae. 49 (g. s.); m. (1) 4 Feb. 1786, Hezekiah Gold; m. (2) 7 Oct. 1793, Stephen Middlebrook, Jr., of North Stratford.

Mary, b. 21, bapt. 29 Dec. 1765, d. 15 June 1845 ae. 79 (g. s.).

Jerome, b. 26 Feb., bapt. 6 Mar. 1768, d. 2 (?) Mar. 1768 (g. s.).

Noah, b. 23, bapt. 26 Mar. 1769.

Justin, b. 26 Mar., bapt. 7 June 1772, d. 3 June 1830 ae. 58 (g. s.); m. 1 July 1804, Desire Burr, b. 19 Feb. 1782, d. 22 Feb. 1872 ae. 90.*

Lydia, b. 12 Mar., bapt. 3 July 1774; m. 21 Dec. 1796, Stephen Beers.

Hannah, b. 7 Nov. 1777, bapt. 15 Feb. 1778, d. 6 May 1827 ae. 49 yrs. 7 mos. (g. s.). Will 27 Apr. 1825, proved 4 June 1827; nieces Rebecca and Hannah Hobart, daus. of Justin Hobart; sister Mary Hobart; niece Mary Beers, dau. of Stephen Beers; niece Deborah Gould.

John Sloss, b. 12 Feb., bapt. 4 Mar. 1781, d. in New York, 10 Aug. 1803 ae. 22 yrs. 6 mos. (g. s.).

Hobart [Unplaced].

Joseph of Fairfield chose John Finch for guardian, Apr. 1762.

---

* Children, rec. Fairfield: Rebecca, b. 22 Oct. 1806; Jane-Ann, b. 2 Feb. 1809; Peter, b. 8 Oct. 1811; Edmund, b. 29 July 1814; Hannah, b. 18 Dec. 1817.

Hodgdon, William.

Settled in Stratfield.

Will 1 Dec. 1749, proved 8 Jan. 1753; sons David, Timothy; daus. Mehitabel and Hannah Hodgdon; wife Margery.

Will of Margery, 9 Apr. 1755, proved 28 Mar. 1760; sons David, Timothy; daus. Mehitabel Mead, Hannah Hodsden; son-in-law Nehemiah Mead, Exec'r.

Children:
>Mehitabel, m. 18 July 1750, Nehemiah Mead.
>+David.
>Timothy, m. at Trumbull, May 1750, Mary Beach, dau. of Benjamin.
>Hannah.
>Sarah, bapt. 10 Feb. 1731/2, d. y.

Hodgdon, David, s. of William.

He m. 7 June 1750, Sarah Lacy, dau. of John.

Child, rec. Fairfield:
>Benjamin, b. 24 Dec. 1750, bapt. at Stratfield, 3 Feb. 1751.

Hoile [*Unplaced*].

>JOHN had Elizabeth, bapt. 11 July 1714. [Fairfield Church]

Holberton, John.

He d. at Stratfield, 21 June 1750.

He m. Mary Fairweather, dau. of Benjamin, bapt. 4 Mar. 1716.

Will 2 June 1750, proved 26 June 1750; wife Mary; three children, Thomas, William, Mary; estate both in this Colony and in Great Britain; friend Theophilus Nichols, Exec'r. His widow was living when distribution was made 1759.

Children:
>+Thomas, b. abt. 1739.
>William, b. abt. 1740, d. 12 Dec. 1797 ae. 57 (Trinity Church rec.); m. Dec. 1769, Eunice Burr, dau. of John, b. 5 Oct. 1750, d. in 1837.
>Mary, b. abt. 1744, d. at Stratfield, 12 Jan. 1824 ae. 80 (g. s.); m. Stephen Summers.

Holberton, Thomas, s. of John.

Born abt. 1739; d. 9 Sept. 1822 ae. 83 (Trinity Church rec.).
He m. (1) 31 May 1770, Ruth Wilson, dau. of Robert, b. 5 Oct. 1744, d. 25 May 1785 (Wheeler Journal).
He m. (2) 23 Oct. 1786 (Wheeler Journal), Mary Wakeman, who d. 3 Jan. 1792 (Trinity Church rec.).
He m. (3) 15 Nov. 1795, Bathsheba Peet, who d. 14 Apr. 1824 (Wheeler Journal).

Children [by first wife], eldest rec. Fairfield:

> John, b. 13 Oct. 1770.
> George, b. [Jan. 1776], d. at Stratfield, 5 Oct. 1777 ae. 20 mos. (g. s.).
> Ruth, m. at Fairfield, 6 Nov. 1796, Job Bartram.
> Catherine, m. at Fairfield, 21 Aug. 1799, John Wheeler.

Hollings, William.

Came to Fairfield with wife Joan, who m. (2) 3 Dec. 1728, Edward Webber. He was Adm'r on estate of Edward Hill, 1727, and six months later made a mutual "will" with Edward Webber; and did not long survive.

Hollingsworth, Joseph, s. of Richard, 3d [Vol. I, p. 290].

Bapt. 14 Jan. 1712/3; d. at Fairfield in 1776; m. (1) 4 Nov. 1734, Ann Jennings, bapt. 12 Mar. 1703/4; m. (2) Ruth ———; Widow Hollingworth d. 20 July 1782 (Perry Diary).

Inv. 1776. Distribution 10 Dec. 1777: widow Ruth; Sarah wife of Abel Jennings; Mary; Ruth; Abigail; Ann; Elizabeth. Each of the unmarried daus. received one-fifth of the house.

Children [by first wife], rec. Fairfield:

> Sarah, b. 31 Mar. 1736, d. at Fairfield, 9 June 1816 ae. 80; m. 16 Aug. 1758, Abel Jennings.
> Mary, b. 26 June 1737, d. 25 Aug. 1826 ae. 89; adm'n granted, 12 Sept. 1826, to Grizzel Jennings.*
> Ruth, b. 6 June 1741, d. in 1802, unm. Her will, 28 Mar. 1800, proved 28 June 1802; legacies to Ephraim-Seeley Sherwood and Sally, Mary and Ruth Sherwood, children of Samuel Sherwood; Robert

---

* The estates of Abigail and Mary Hollingsworth were ordered distributed to the children of Sarah Jennings (their sister) now living, viz. Noah, Abel, Grizzel, Eunice, Anna, and Ruth, and also one-seventh to Lois Turney and Laura Johnson, daus. of Abijah Jennings dec'd. The distribution called Eunice wife of Jonathan Wilson, and Lois wife of Levi Turney.

son of sister Sarah Jennings; Ethan, son of said Samuel Sherwood; sister Sarah wife of Abel Jennings; four sisters, Mary, Abigail, Anna, and Elizabeth Hollingsworth.

Abigail, b. 16 Jan. 1743, bapt. at Fairfield, 4 Aug. 1749, d. in 1826; adm'n granted, 12 Sept. 1826, to Grizzel Jennings.*

Ann, b. 9 Dec. 1744, d. by 1823; prob. the "Miss Hollingsworth" who d. at Fairfield, Aug. 1821. Adm'n granted, 2 May 1823, to Abel Jennings, with Anson Jennings as bondsman.

Elizabeth, b. 18 Jan. 1748, d. in 1820. Adm'n granted to Abel Jennings, 24 Apr. 1820, with Mary Hollingsworth on bond. Distribution, 7 May 1821: Abigail Hollingsworth; Mary Hollingsworth; Ann Hollingsworth; Abel Jennings; Noah Jennings; Eunice wife of Jonathan Willson; Ruth, Grizzel, Ann, and Joseph Jennings.

Hollister [*Unplaced*].

Joseph, of Glastonbury, m. 8 Mar. 1770, Ann Hanford.

Holmes [*Unplaced*].

Rachel m. 22 Apr. 1718, John Hide. [Fairfield rec.]

Daniel, b. abt. 1755, d. at Easton, 4 Apr. 1828 ae. 73 (g. s.); m. (1) ———; m. (2) 29 Dec. 1783, Mary Jennings, perhaps dau. of Nehemiah, b. 25 Nov. 1754; she d. 29 Apr. 1813 in 58 yr. (g. s.). Children by first wife: Sarah, b. 26 Jan. 1777; Lois, b. 14 Feb. 1779; Anna, b. 3 Nov. 1781. Children by second wife: Mary, b. 26 Dec. 1784; Mabel, b. 22 Feb. 1786. [Weston rec.]

His estate was distributed, 15 Oct. 1829, to heirs of Sarah Fanton; Sally-Ann wife of Cornelius Miller; Mary Collear (?); Margery Fanton; Lois wife of Thomas Lyon; Polly Hill; and Mabel wife of Peter Lyon.

Honeywell [*Unplaced*].

Israel of Westchester had son Israel, bapt. 3 June 1716. [Fairfield Church]

Hopkins, Henry.

He, called "a stranger," m. at Redding, 26 July 1769, Hannah Burr; dau. of Jabez.

Children, bapt. Redding:

Jabez, bapt. 28 Mar. 1773.
Francis, b. [Nov. 1771], d. 25 Dec. 1771 ae. 1 mo.
Mary, bapt. 30 Mar. 1773.
Huldah, bapt. 24 July 1775.

---

* See footnote on page 472.

Howes [Unplaced].

SARAH of Stamford m. 23 Jan. 1763, Daniel Couch. [Redding rec.]

Hoyt, Daniel.

He m. at Easton, 10 June 1773, Sarah Wheeler; dau. of Jabez, b. 19 Feb. 1754. She m. (2) at Weston, 14 Jan. 1779, Daniel Treadwell.

Daniel and wife Sarah joined the Easton Church, 6 Sept. 1774.

Of Fairfield, distribution 29 Sept. 1778: widow Sarah; son Isaac; dau. Clarina.

Children:

> Isaac-Wheeler, bapt. 6 Sept. 1774.
> Clarina.

Hoyt [Unplaced].

> JACOB, of Salem, [N. Y.], m. 16 Apr. 1761, Sarah Sturges. [Greens Farms Church]
> GOULD, of Norwalk, m. 13 June 1765, Elizabeth Dimon. [Fairfield Church]
> RUTH m. 30 Dec. 1797, John Sanford. [Redding rec.]
> ISAAC W. m. 8 Oct. 1796, Hannah Banks, and had child, Charles, b. 2 Oct. 1797. [Redding rec.]
> MOLLY m. 17 Nov. 1788, William Mead. [Redding rec.]
> JOHN m. 1 Nov. 1764, Hannah Treadwell. [Easton Church]
> WILLIAM d. at Greenfield, 8* Sept. 1820 ae. 49. [Fairfield Church]
> WILLIAM and Sarah had: Henry, bapt. 12 Apr. 1778. [Redding Church]

Hubbard, Zachariah.

He m. (1) at Boston, Mass., 15 May 1722, Mary Hobby, dau. of Sir Charles and Elizabeth, b. 19 Feb. 1702 [1702/3].

He m. (2) at Boston, 18 May 1732, Sarah Kingsman.

He d. at Greenfield, 31 Mar. 1769 ae. between 70 and 80.

Now of Fairfield, will 27 Nov. 1768, proved 6 June 1769; negro servant James to have freedom and tools for hatter's trade; residue to gr. dau. Susannah Pond of Milford; Joseph Bradley, 2d, of Fairfield, Exec'r.

---

* 7 by Greenfield Church records.

Samuel Pond, a minor late of Milford now of Fairfield, chose gr. father Zachariah Hubbard for guardian, 21 May 1766.

Children [by first wife], rec. Boston:

    Mary, b. 5 Mar. 1722 [1722/3], d. at Milford, 16 June 1761 in 37 yr.; m. abt. 1739, Peter Pond.
    Elizabeth, b. 26 Sept. 1725; m. 10 Mar. 1744/5, Charles Duncomb.
    Susannah,* b. abt. 1727, d. 15 Oct. 1745 in 19 yr. (g. s.); m. 27 Dec. 1743, David Barlow.
    Zechariah, b. 24 June 1728.
    Charles-Hobby, b. 16 Oct. 1730.

Hubbard [Unplaced].

PHILIP m. 21 Feb. 1780, Amarillis Morehouse. [Fairfield Church]

Hubbell [Vol. I, pp. 300-306].

  1 Richard (1627-1699) m. (1) Elizabeth Meigs; (2) Elizabeth Gaylord; (3) Abigail (Prudden) Walker.
(By 1): 2 John (1652-1690) m. Patience Nichols.
        9 *Richard* (1685-1758).
       10 *Josiah* (1688-1752).
  3 Richard (1654-1738) m. (1) Rebecca Morehouse; (2) Hannah Swillaway.
(By 1): 11 *Peter* (1686-1780).
      12 *Ebenezer* (1687-1761).
      13 *Jonathan* (1692-1766).
(By 2): 14 *Zachariah* (1694-   ).
      15 *Richard* (1696-1787).
      16 *Eleazer* (1700-1770).
  4 Samuel (1657-1713) m. (1) Elizabeth Wilson; (2) Temperance (Nichols) Preston.
(By 2): 17 *Daniel* (1691-1735).
      18 *Ephraim* (1694-1780).
      19 *Stephen* (1696-1792).
      20 *David* (1698-after 1757).
      21 *Joseph* (1702-1777).
(By 2): 5 Samuel (-) m. Elizabeth Burr.
      22 *Nathan* (1699-1761).
      23 *David* (1711-1753/4).
      24 *Samuel* (1714-1760).
  6 James (1674-1777) m. Patience Summers.
      25 *Andrew* (1706-1777).
      26 *Elnathan* (1717-1788).
(By 3): 7 John (1691-1774) m. Ann Welles.
      27 *Benjamin* (1717-1793).
      28 *John* (-1739).

---

* Susannah was called dau. of Zachariah at marriage, but her birth is not found; a Susanna dau. of John and Elizabeth Hubbard was b. at Boston, 13 July 1726.

9. **Hubbell, Richard,** s. of John. Lt., Ripton [Huntington] Co., May 1728; Capt., May 1737.

Born at Stratford, 20 Jan. 1684/5; d. 27 Nov. 1758 ae. 74; m. 11 Dec. 1707, Abigail Thompson, dau. of William, b. at New Haven, 18 Oct. 1685.

Will 3 Dec. 1751, proved 2 Jan. 1759; wife Abigail; sons John, William, Nathan; daus. Mary Shelton, Abigail Hurd, Mehitabel Curtis, Hannah Smith; gr. son Richard Hubbell.

Children, rec. Stratford.

> Mary, bapt. (at Stratford, rec. Stratfield) 3 Apr. 1709; m. 12 Aug. 1727, Daniel Shelton.
> John, b. 20 Feb. 1709/10, d. at Huntington, 7 May 1782 in 73 yr. (g. s.); will 12 Mar. 1776, proved 18 June 1782; m. Hannah Wheeler, dau. of Robert, b. 19 Nov. 1719, d. 2 Nov. 1797 ae. 78 (g. s.).*
> Abigail, b. 3 Dec. 1711, d. 1 July 1756 in 45 yr. (g. s.); m. at Trumbull, 26 Jan. 1731/2, Ebenezer Hurd.
> Mehitabel, b. abt. 1713, d. 1790 ae. 77; m. Hezekiah Curtis.
> William.
> Nathan, b. abt. 1719, d. at Huntington, 27 May 1788 in 69 yr. (g. s.); m. Patty Nichols.†
> Timothy, b. abt. 1719, d. at Huntington, 11 Feb. 1739/40 in 20 yr. (g. s.).
> Hannah, m. (1) ―― Smith; m. (2) Hezekiah Booth.‡

10. **Hubbell, Josiah,** s. of John.

Born abt. 1688; d. at Stratfield in 1752; m. 18 June 1713, Martha Ufford, dau. of Samuel, b. 28 Sept. 1695.

---

* Children (arranged from probate of John and Hannah and other sources): Timothy, b. abt. 1740, d. at Huntington, 12 Jan. 1808 in 68 yr. (g. s.); m. Abigail Lake, dau. of David, b. 23 May 1737, d. 31 Aug. 1830 ae. 94 (g. s.). Sarah, m. Abel Thompson, rem. to Vt., and d. before 1791. Gideon, m. Lucy Beardsley. Hannah, b. [26 Feb. 1748], d. at Huntington, 24 Oct. 1819 ae. 71-7-15 (g. s.); m. 31 Dec. 1772, Samuel Patterson. Richard, res. Oxford; m. Mercy Bennett. John, b. abt. 1751, d. at Huntington, 18 Sept. 1822 in 71 yr. (g. s.); m. 28 June 1773, Sarah Curtis, who d. 4 Nov. 1841 ae. 92 (g. s.). Elisha, b. abt. 1754, d. at Huntington, 7 June(?) 1828 ae. 72(?) (g. s.); m. Kezia Curtis, who d. 23 Jan.(?) 1832 ae. 72 (g. s.). Abigail, b. abt. 1758, d. at Oxford, 29 Sept. 1805 ae. 47 (g. s.); m. Abel Hull, of Oxford. Ann, m. Zachariah Bostwick, of New Milford.

† Nathan's will, 5 Mar. 1787, proved 19 June 1788; wife Martha; Nathan Jr., son of Gideon Hubbell; sister Hannah wife of Hezekiah Booth; Clarissa Beard; Hannah wife of Samuel Patterson; Abigail wife of Abel Hull; remainder to Timothy, Gideon, Richard, John and Elisha Hubbell.

‡ Unless Booth is a misreading for Smith.

Will 12 July 1752, proved 1 Sept. 1752; wife Martha; daus. Elizabeth Wilcoxson, Hannah Brinsmade; eldest son Samuel; sons Ebenezer, John, Josiah; dau. Martha Hubbell.

Children, rec. Stratford:
>
> Elizabeth, b. 15 Mar. 1713/4; m. 18 June 1735, Josiah Wilcoxson.
> Samuel, b. 23 Feb. 1715/6, d. at Stratford, May or June 1784;* m. Elizabeth Booth, dau. of James.
> Abiah, b. 18 Apr. 1718, d. y.
> Hannah, m. ——— Brinsmade.
> Ebenezer, m. Mary Brooks, dau. of Benjamin, bapt. 13 Oct. 1723, d. 18 Sept. 1790 ae. 67 (g. s.).
> John.
> Martha.
> Josiah, m. (1) 30 Oct. 1760, Sarah Edwards, dau. of Gershom, b. June 1735, d. 9 Mar. 1790 ae. 56; m. (2) Katharine Curtis.

11. Hubbell, Peter, s. of Richard, 2d.

Born 10 Aug. 1686; d. at Newtown in 1780; m. (1) at Stratfield, 19 Jan. 1709/10, Katharine Wheeler, dau. of Ephraim, b. 20 Mar. 1693/4, d. 16 Mar. 1742 in 49 yr.; m. (2) Sarah ———.

Will 1 May 1770, proved 22 Feb. 1780; wife Sarah; eldest son Ephraim; sons Peter, Ezra, Jedediah, Matthew, Gideon; dau. Sarah's heirs; daus. Katharine, Mary; sons Comfort, Enoch, Silas. Distribution 1780: Widow Sarah; Ephraim; Peter; Jedediah or his heirs; Ezra or his heirs; Matthew or his heirs; Gideon; Sarah Bryan or her heirs; Katharine Birch; Mary Beardsley; Comfort; Enoch; Silas.

Children [by first wife]:
>
> Ephraim, b. 21 Dec. 1712 [1711], bapt. at Stratfield, 13 Apr. 1712, d. at Sherman, 17 Dec. 1795; Dea.; Deputy for New Fairfield, May 1764, May 1766, Oct. 1768, Jan. 1769, May 1771, May and July 1775, May 1776, May 1778; Justice, Fairfield County, 1757-80; m. (1) 25 Dec. 1735, Joanna Gaylord of New Milford, who d. 17 May 1781 ae. 64; m. (2) Alice Hatch.
> Peter, b. 15 Apr. 1715; res. New Milford; Ens., Newbury [Brookfield] Co., Oct. 1762; Lt., Oct. 1763; m. Hephzibah Botsford, dau. of John, bapt. at Milford, 30 June 1717.
> Ezra, b. 28 Feb. 1717; sea Capt.; m. [prob. Katharine Hubbell, dau. of Ephraim, b. 21 Jan. 1721/2]; had a son Isaac.

---

* His will, 17 May, proved 17 June 1784; wife Elizabeth; daus. Eunice wife of Judson Burton, Sarah wife of Elisha DeForest, Elizabeth wife of John Uffoot, and Martha wife of Samuel Lampson; son Samuel.

HISTORY AND GENEALOGY OF

    Sarah, b. 27 Feb. 1719; m. Alexander Bryan.
    Jedediah, b. 22 Aug. 1720, d. in 1819; rem. to Lanesborough, Mass.;
      m. (1) 20 Aug. 1748, Abigail Northrup; m. (2) 18 Oct. 1759,
      Susannah Hickock; m. (3) Mary Hurlbut; m. (4) 20 Nov. 1782,
      Eunice Johnson, of Middletown, who d. in 1806 ae. 75; m. (5) Mrs.
      Chloe Bemen, of Wethersfield, who d. in 1821 ae. 85.
    Matthew, b. 4 Sept. 1723; rem. to Lanesborough, Mass.; m. 6 Dec.
      1743, Abiah Hawley.
    Gideon, b. 28 Apr. 1726.
    Comfort, b. 10 Nov. 1729, d. at Newtown abt. 1797; will 23 Apr. 1797;
      Capt.; m. (2) Susannah ———.
    Katharine, b. July 1732; m. 27 Sept. 1750, William Burch.
    Enoch, b. 10 Aug. 1735, d. at Hubbell Hill, Delaware County, N. Y.,
      3 Oct. 1827; m. Sarah ———.
    Silas, b. 24 Feb. 1738, d. at Norwich, Mass., 27 Aug. 1805; m. (1) 16
      June 1763, Elizabeth Edmond, who d. 7 July 1783 in 41 yr.; m. (2)
      in 1785, Hannah (French) Wheeler.

Children [by second wife], rec. Newtown:

    Rhoda, b. 31 May 1745, d. 3 Oct. 1746.
    Mary, b. 21 Nov. 1746; m. ——— Beardsley.
    Phebe, b. 21 Feb. 1748, d. 1 Feb. 1756.

12. Hubbell, Ebenezer, s. of Richard, 2d.

Born 19 or 20 Sept. 1687; d. at Easton, 6 Mar. 1761 in 74 yr. (g. s.); m. Sarah Titherton, b. 31 Jan. 1696/7, d. 20 May 1788 in 93 yr. (g. s.).

Adm'n granted, 12 Mar. 1761, to Ebenezer Hubbell. Distribution, 17 Aug. 1761, Stratfield: wife; Ebenezer (double portion); Jeremiah; Timothy; Abijah; heirs of Patience dec'd; Rebecca; Hannah.

Children:

    Patience, m. ———.
    Rebecca, b. [say 1721], d. at Easton, 16 Feb. 1773 in 52 yr. (g. s.); m.
      at Fairfield Church, 14 Jan. 1747/8, Nathaniel Seeley.
29+Ebenezer, b. abt. 1723.
    Jeremiah, b. 22 Feb. 1725, d. at Monroe, 9 Feb. 1801; m. 13 Dec. 1750,
      Abigail Wakelee, b. 14 Apr. 1725, d. 27 Jan. 1790.
    Hannah.
30+Timothy, b. abt. 1732.
    Abijah, b. abt. 1737, d. at Dunham, Missisquoi County, Canada East, in
      1822; m. ———.

13. Hubbell, Jonathan, s. of Richard, 2d.

Born 25 Mar. 1692; d. at Newtown, 6 Sept. 1766 ae. 73; m. at Stratfield, 18 Nov. 1713, Peaceable Silliman; dau. of Daniel.

Adm'n granted, 15 Oct. 1766, to son-in-law John Griffin, at request of eldest and youngest sons, Daniel and Joseph Hubbell. Distribution order and the distribution mention: eldest son Daniel; Ichabod; Richard; Hannah wife of Samuel Weed; Elizabeth wife of Benjamin Weed; Jemima wife of Joseph Smith; Hephzibah wife of David Welles; Beulah wife of John Griffin; Jeptha; heirs of Ithamar; heirs of Silliman.

See *Hubbell Genealogy* for this branch.

14. Hubbell, Zachariah, s. of Richard, 2d.

Born 26 Aug. 1694.

He m. at Stratfield, 26 Jan. 1713/4, Abigail Bennett; dau. of James, b. abt. 1691.

Children, rec. Stratfield (record incomplete):

    Phinehas, b. 30 Oct. 1715, bapt. 25 Mar. 1716.
    Mehitabel, b. 19 Aug., bapt. 1 Sept. 1717.
    Hannah, b. 2 Dec. 1720.
    Lewis, bapt. 17 Mar. 1733.
    Glorianna, bapt. 28 Nov. 1736.

15. Hubbell, Richard, s. of Richard, 2d.

Born 20 Oct. 1696; d. at Stratfield, 27 June 1787 in 93 yr. (g. s.); m. 9 Dec. 1725, Penelope Fairweather, bapt. 24 Feb. 1705/6, d. 29 Aug. 1791 in 87 yr. (g. s.). He was Deacon of Stratfield Church, 30 yrs.

Will 23 June 1787, proved 7 Mar. 1788; wife Penelope; son Benjamin; son Amos, Exec'r.

Children, rec. Fairfield, bapt. Stratfield:

    Benjamin, b. 11 May 1726, d. 17 Sept. 1788 in 62 yr. (g. s.).
31+Hezekiah, b. 24 Feb. 1728.
    Christopher, b. 6 July 1729.
    Penelope, b. 22, bapt. 30 July 1732.
    Grizzel, b. 12 Aug. 1733, bapt. 20 Oct. 1734; m. Edward Burroughs.

480   HISTORY AND GENEALOGY OF

 32+Walter, bapt. 14 Nov. 1736.
  Mary, b. abt. 1738, d. at Stratfield, 15 Jan. 1786; m. (rec. Fairfield) 1 Sept. 1757, Isaac Youngs.
  Christian, b. abt. 1740, d. 27 Feb. 1805 (Wheeler Journal); m. 14 Oct. 1762, Joseph Silliman.
 33+Richard, b. abt. 1742.
 34+Amos, b. 3 Dec. 1746.

16. **Hubbell, Eleazer,** s. of Richard, 2d. Capt., Willington Co., Oct. 1734; Lt., north company, New Fairfield, May 1746; Capt., Oct. 1750. Deputy for New Fairfield, May and Oct. 1764, Oct. 1765, May 1766.

Born 15 Aug. 1700; d. at New Fairfield, 3 Sept. 1770; m. 25 May 1727, Abigail Burr; dau. of Col. John, bapt. 16 Mar. 1701, d. 6 Apr. 1780.

He rem. to Willington, and by 1738 to Newtown; rem. to New Fairfield.

Children:

 Mary, b. at Willington, 18 June 1735; perhaps the Molly of Stratfield who m. at Greenfield, 3 May 1759, John Smith.
 Eleazer, b. at Newtown, 14 Feb. 1739, d. at Jericho, Vt., 14 Apr. 1810; m. 30 Jan. 1765, Anna Noble, b. 27 July 1749, d. 8 June 1818.
 Dennis, b. at New Fairfield, 5 Feb. 1743.

17. **Hubbell, Daniel,** s. of Lt. Samuel. Lt., Stratfield Co., May 1729; Capt., Oct. 1731.

Born 8 Aug. 1691; d. at Stratfield, 11 Dec. 1735 in 45 yr.; m. 17 May 1716, Esther Beach; dau. of John, b. 3 May 1694. Widow Esther d. at Stratfield, 12 Dec. 1772.

Will 24 Feb. 1734/5, proved 12 Jan. 1735/6; wife Esther; three sons, Daniel, Abel, Gideon; daus. Mary, Tabitha, Abiah; bro. Ephraim Hubbell, Exec'r.

Children, rec. Stratfield:

 Mehitabel, b. 26, bapt. 29 Sept. 1717, d. 12 Oct. 1717.
 Hannah, b. 30, bapt. 31 Aug. 1718, d. 20 Sept. 1718.
 Mary, b. 13 Jan. 1719/20, d. at Stratfield, 1 Apr. 1810 in 91 yr. (g. s.); m. John Lacy.

Tabitha, b. 22 Oct. 1722, d. 30 Nov. 1778 (Private rec.) ; m. 19 May 1747 (Private rec.), Ebenezer Hall.
35+Daniel, b. 22 Aug. 1724.
Abiah, b. 22 Mar. 1725/6.
36+Abel, b. 30 May 1728.
Gershom, b. 17 June 1729, d. 10 Dec. 1729.
Gideon, b. 18, bapt. 21 Nov. 1731, d. in 1808; will 28 Mar. 1798, proved 22 Dec. 1808, gave all to wife Anna, with Josiah Strong an Exec'r; m. (1) by 1755, Abigail Meeker, dau. of Nathan, living in 1778; "wife of Gideon" d. at Stratfield, 7 Sept. 1785; m. (2) Anna ———.

18. **Hubbell, Ephraim,** s. of Lt. Samuel. Ens., Stratfield Co., Oct. 1731; Capt., Kent Co., May 1745. Deputy for Kent, Oct. 1765, Oct. 1769, Oct. 1771, May and Oct. 1773, Jan., May and Oct. 1774, Mar. and Apr. 1775.*

Born 11 Oct. 1694; d. at Kent, 4 Nov. 1780; m. 17 Oct. 1717, Abigail Bradley; dau. of John, b. abt. 1695, d. 22 Apr. 1772.

Children, rec. Stratfield:

Samuel, b. 2, bapt. 4 Oct. 1718; Ens., 1st Co., Kent, Oct. 1753; Lt., May 1755; served in French War, 1757, as Lt. of Capt. Samuel Dunham's Co.
Jehiel, b. 22 Nov. 1719.
Katharine, b. 21 Jan. 1721/2; [prob. m. Capt. Ezra Hubbell].
Ezbon, b. 15 Aug. 1724, d. in 1752; m. Mary ———; no issue. His will, 17 Jan. 1751, proved 9 Jan. 1753, calls him of Stratford, about to leave on a voyage; to wife Mary, house and lot of four acres, also 100 acres at Kent, and moveables, except £50 to my "niece" Isaac Hubbell, son of Capt. Ezra Hubbell of the town aforesaid; friends Capt. Ezra Hubbell and Mr. Ezra Hawley, Exec'rs.
Mehitabel, b. 14 Oct. 1726; m. at Kent, 14 Apr. 1743, Sylvanus Comstock.
Ephraim, b. 20 Feb. 1728/9; Deputy for Kent, May and Oct. 1764, May 1765, May 1769, May and Oct. 1772, May and July 1775, May 1777; Justice, Litchfield County, 1775-80.
Jedediah, b. 16, bapt. 18 July 1731, d. at Cleveland, Ohio, 11 June 1813; res. Newburgh, Cuyahoga County, Ohio; m. 25 Dec. 1754, Lucy Noble, who d. 26 May 1813.
Abigail, bapt. 28 Sept. 1735.
Abijah, b. 1 Feb. 1739, d. at Kent, 19 Nov. 1819; m. 4 Feb. 1768, Fear Sturdevant, b. 17 Dec. 1745.

---

* Possibly the services as Deputy belonged to his son, but we have assigned to the father those where "Jr." was not specified.

19. Hubbell, Stephen, s. of Lt. Samuel.

Born 16 Feb. 1695/6; d. at Stratfield, 29 Apr. 1792 in 98 yr. (g. s.); m. 10 Jan. 1720/1, Abigail Squire; dau. of Jonathan, bapt. 11 Nov. 1694, d. 1 Aug.* 1777 in 84 yr. (g. s.).

Will 16 May 1780; children of dec'd son Nehemiah; son Jabez; children of dec'd son Gershom; son Jabez, and Daniel Lacy, Exec'rs.

Children, first rec. Stratfield:
- 37+Nehemiah, b. 19 May 1722.
- 38+Jabez.
- 39+Gershom.
    - Rebecca, bapt. 4 July 1736, d. at Stratfield, 9 Nov. 1754 in 19 yr. (g. s.).

20. Hubbell, David, s. of Lt. Samuel.

Born 1 July 1698; m. Eunice Sanford, dau. of Thomas, bapt. 26 Aug. 1705.

David and Eunice his wife, late of Fairfield, now of Courtland Manor, N. Y., sold 1757 right in estate of father Thomas Sanford.

Children, bapt. Stratfield:
- David, bapt. 6 Aug. 1732.
- Temperance, bapt. 3 Mar. 1733/4.
- Seth, bapt. 30 May 1736.
- Eunice, bapt. at Trumbull, 14 May 1747.

21. Hubbell, Joseph, s. of Lt. Samuel.

Born 29 Oct. 1702; d. at Stratfield, May 1777.

He m. Kezia Hall, dau. of Jonathan. Widow Kezia d. at Stratfield, 24 Oct. 1778.

In 1780, Eunice Seeley of Fairfield conveyed to Joseph Hubbell, right in estate of father Joseph Hubbell; and Joseph Hubbell of Fairfield conveyed to Eunice Seeley, right from mother Keziah Hubbell.

Children, one bapt. Stratfield:
- Eunice, m. Nathan Seeley.
- Onesimus, bapt. 30 July 1732, d. at Stratfield, 3 Dec. 1754 in 23 yr. (g. s.).

---

* Perhaps misread; 1 Oct. by mortuary list.

Joseph, b. 2 Nov. 1744, d. at Ballston, N. Y., 4 Apr. 1792 ae. 48-5-2; of Bennington, Vt., 1780, when he conveyed land inherited from father Joseph; m. Ruth ———, b. [12 Feb. 1733], d. 4 Sept. 1798 ae. 65-6-22.*

22. Hubbell, Nathan, s. of Samuel, Jr.

Born 1 Dec. 1699; d. at Wilton, 6 Feb. 1761; m. at Greenfield, 5 Dec. 1723, Martha Finch, b. 7 Jan. 1702, d. at Wilton, 1 Dec. 1755 ae. 53.

Will 3 Feb. 1761; wife Sarah; sons Thaddeus, Nathan, Gershom, John, Peter, Abraham; daus. Mary Bates, Elizabeth Gilbert, Martha Patchen.

Children, rec. Greenfield (first four bapt. Fairfield):

 Elizabeth, b. 11, bapt. 15 Nov. 1724; m. 11 Mar. 1740/1, Moses Gilbert.
 Thaddeus, b. 12, bapt. 13 Mar. 1725/6, d. at Wilton, 8 Apr. 1806; m. (1) 25 Dec. 1753, Ruth Betts, b. abt. 1733, d. 16 May 1773; m. (2) 24 Nov. 1774, Mrs. Phebe Squire; widow of Seeley Squire, and dau. of Joshua Sears.
 Nathan, b. 26 Apr., bapt. 28 May 1727, d. at Wilton in 1801; Capt., Wilton Co., Oct. 1762; m. 2 Aug. 1753, Ann Wakeman, bapt. 8 Aug. 1726.
40+Gershom, b. 17, bapt. 20 July 1729.
 Martha, b. 18 June, bapt. July 1731, d. 2 Oct. 1816; m. 9 Aug. 1749, Daniel Patchen.
 Sarah, b. 10 Dec. 1732, bapt. 17 Feb. 1732/3, d. y.
41+John, b. 31 July 1734, bapt. in infancy.
 Abijah, b. 13 May, bapt. May 1736, d. Sept. 1760.
 Sarah, b. 28, bapt. 30 Apr. 1738, d. y.
 Mary, b. 14, bapt. 29 Apr. 1740; m. ——— Bates.
 Peter, b. 10, bapt. 18 Apr. 1742, d. at Wilton, 1826; m. 7 Jan. 1764, Sarah Stewart, dau. of Robert.
 Abraham, b. 26, bapt. 27 Jan. 1745/6, d. at Boston, Mass., 5 May 1783; res. Wilton and Stratford; m. (1) 25 Oct. 1768, Sarah Wakeman, b. 6 Feb. 1748,† d. 23 Apr. 1772; m. (2) 17 July 1776, Eunice Sterling, b. 1 Aug. 1751, d. 4 Sept. 1794, in 38 yr. (g. s., Stratfield).‡
 A dau. by first wife, Eunice, b. at Wilton, 30 Sept. 1770, m. at Fairfield, 8 Mar. 1792, Daniel Young, Jr., of Stratfield.

---

* Prob. Ruth's age was misstated. Children: Onesimus, b. 28 Sept. 1769, d. 28 Aug. 1837; res. Ballston; m. Charity Lacy, b. 8 Apr. 1773, d. 4 May 1855. Eunice, b. 23 Dec. 1772, d. 6 May 1852; m. 12 Mar. 1792, Nathaniel Jennings. A child of Joseph d. at Stratfield, 27 Sept. 1774.

† New Style date, prob. from Bible record; 26 Jan. 1747/8, by town record.

‡ The will of Eunice, 29 Aug. 1794, proved 13 Oct. 1794; sons Levi and Isaac; dau. Sarah Hubbell. The will of the dau. Sarah, 15 Oct. 1799, proved 4 Feb. 1799; estate distributed to Eunice wife of Daniel Young, Jr., and to Levi Hubbell.

23. Hubbell, David, s. of Samuel, Jr.

Bapt. 2 Sept. 1711.

He m. (1) Martha Middlebrook, dau. of Jonathan, bapt. 11 Jan. 1718/9.

He m. (2) 5 Feb. 1753, Martha Gold, dau. of Nathan, bapt. 24 May 1730. She prob. m. (2) 8 Jan. 1756, John Bulkley, and d. soon after; she certainly d. before 1761.

Distribution, 2 May 1765: Aaron, Ebenezer, David, Jabez, and Sarah wife of John Parret.

Children [by first wife], bapt. Fairfield:
  Jabez, bapt. 18 Mar. 1738/9, d. y.
  Sarah, bapt. 18 Mar. 1738/9; m. 17 Jan. 1752, John Parrot.
  42+Aaron, bapt. 27 Dec. 1741; Anthony Annabel was appointed his guardian, Apr. 1755.
  43+Ebenezer, bapt. 18 Nov. 1744; chose Jonathan Middlebrook for guardian, Mar. 1761.
  44+David, bapt. 20 Mar. 1747/8.

Child [by second wife], bapt. Fairfield:
  45+Jabez, bapt. 11 Nov. 1753.

24. Hubbell, Samuel, s. of Samuel, Jr.
Ens., 1st Co., Fairfield, Oct. 1752. 1st Lt., 3d Co., 3d Regt., Army, Aug. 1755; 1st Lt., 5th Co., 1st Regt., Mar. 1756; 1st Lt. (served as Capt.), 5th Co., 4th Regt., Feb. 1757; Capt., 7th Co., 4th Regt., Mar. 1758; Capt., 5th Co., 3d Regt., Mar. 1759; Capt., 7th Co., 3d Regt., Mar. 1760.

Bapt. 30 May 1714; d. by 1760; m. Abigail ———, who d. in 1793.

Adm'n granted to Widow Abigail, 24 Nov. 1760.

Distribution of Est. of Capt. Samuel of Fairfield ordered 2 May 1775: widow Abigail; eldest son Isaac; other children, William, Abel, Mary, Grace, Elizabeth, Grizzel, Abigail.

Will of Abigail, 9 Apr., proved 6 May 1793; dau. Grissel Hubbell, all estate.

Children, bapt. Fairfield:
  Isaac, bapt. 4 Oct. 1741; [Lt., Conn. Line, 1777-81]. [Wife of Capt. Isaac d. at Stratfield, 21 May 1786.]
  Mary, bapt. 4 Oct. 1741; ? m. 11 Feb. 1756, Nathan Adams.

William, bapt. 3 July 1743, bur. 20 Sept. 1805 ae. 60 (Trinity Church rec.); chose Daniel Sterling for guardian, Apr. 1761.
Grace, bapt. 24 Mar. 1744/5.*
Abel, bapt. 20 Mar. 1747/8.
Samuel, bapt. 10 June 1750, d. y.
Elizabeth, bapt. 12 Apr. 1752; ? m. 21 Jan. 1768, Isaac Turney.
Grizzel, bapt. 7 July 1754.
Abigail, bapt. 12 Dec. 1756.

25. Hubbell, Andrew, s. of James.

Born 22 June 1706; d. at Stratford in 1777; m. (1) Sarah Parruck, dau. of John, bapt. 19 June 1709, d. 20 July 1736; m. (2) 2 Dec. 1736, Mary Welles.

Will 3 July, proved 5 Aug. 1777; wife Mary; son Elijah; dau. Jerusha Seeley; heirs of dau. Hannah Beers; daus. Abiah Woodcock, Mary Northrup, Rhoda Bennett; son Matthew; gr. son Gideon Summers Hubbell; residue to sons Parruck and Matthew, Exec'rs.

Children [by first wife], rec. Stratford:

Elijah, b. 9 May 1727.
Jerusha, b. 19 May 1729, d. at Trumbull, in 1809; will 5 Aug. 1809, proved 6 Nov. 1809; m. (1) Joseph Seeley, of Stratford; m. (2) Jonathan Tongue.
Parruck, b. 22 Jan. 1730/1; Ens., Alarm List Co. in bounds of 6th Co., 16th Regt., May 1777; m. by 1757, Sarah Barnum, dau. of Samuel.
Hannah, b. 12, bapt. 26 Nov. 1732; m. 14 June 1750, Ebenezer Beers.
Sarah, b. 5 Aug., bapt. 8 Sept. 1734, d. y.

Children [by second wife], rec. Stratford:

Gideon, b. 6 Oct. 1737, d. y.
James, b. 6 Nov. 1738, d. y.
Andrew, b. 7 Feb. 1740, bapt. at Stratfield (by Rev. R. Miner of Trumbull), 10 Feb. 1740, d. y.
Sarah, b. 19 Nov. 1741, bapt. 22 Nov. 1741 (Trumbull Church rec.).
Matthew, b. 17 Apr. 1745, d. at Easton, 12 Apr. 1812 ae. 67 (g. s.); m. Abigail Burton, b. abt. 1748, d. 20 Feb. 1812.
Abiah, m. —— Woodcock.
Mary, b. May, bapt. 4 June 1749 (Trumbull Church rec.); m. 17 Dec. 1767, Isaiah Northrup.
Rhoda, m. 4 Jan. 1773, Daniel Bennett.

---

* A Grace Hubbell renewed her Covenant with Fairfield Church, 20 July 1766, and had dau. Ann bapt. same date.

26. **Hubbell, Elnathan,** s. of James. Chairman of Committee of Safety, Bennington, Vt., 1778.

Born 22 Sept. 1717; d. at Bennington, Vt., 21 July 1788 ae. 71 (g. s.); m. (1) Mehitabel Sherwood, dau. of Lemuel, b. 21 Feb. 1719/20, d. at Bennington, 24 Sept. 1770; m. (2) Abigail Higgins.

Children [by first wife], first rec. Stratford, last six at Trumbull Church :*

> Elnathan, b. 26 Jan. 1742 [1742/3], bapt. at Stratfield, 30 Jan. 1742/3; d. 9 Mar. 1801; prominent Green Mountain Boy; served in the Revolution in Col. Herrick's Regt. and Col. Walbridge's Regt., and was in the Battle of Bennington; m. Isabella Breakenridge, b. at Colrain, Mass., 3 Nov. 1749.
> Mehitabel, b. [say 1745]; m. 23 Sept. 1762, Samuel Brinsmade.
> Patience, b. [say 1747]; m. ——— Hine.
> Experience, b. 7, bapt. 10 Sept. 1749, d. at Bennington, 25 Apr. 1774; m. Nathaniel Holmes.
> Huldah, b. 20, bapt. 24 May 1752; m. John Stewart.
> Lemuel, b. 2, bapt. 6 Apr. 1755, d. at Burlington Flats, Otsego County, N. Y., 11 Apr. 1845; served in the Revolution; m. Rebecca Clark, dau. of Nathan, b. 3 Aug. 1754, d. 13 Feb. 1837.
> Aaron, b. 18, bapt. 25 Sept. 1757, d. at Bennington, 26 Dec. 1844; Dea.; J. P.; Lt., served in the Revolution; m. (1) 27 June 1782, Sarah Dewey, dau. of Capt. Elijah, who d. 18 Apr. 1797; m. (2) 11 Mar. 1798, Lucinda Moody, b. 15 Jan. 1770, d. at Sharon, Conn., 3 Oct. 1864.
> Beulah, b. 25 May, bapt. 5 June 1760; prob. d. young.
> Bildad, b. 22 Aug., bapt. 5 Sept. 1762; d. at Cambridge, Vt., 3 Dec. 1840; served in Revolutionary War; m. (1) Hannah ———; m. (2) Polly Fay, dau. of Dr. Jonas; m. (3) Susannah Follett.

Children [by second wife] :†

> Almerin, b. 2 Jan. 1776; d. at Berne, Albany County, N. Y., 12 Apr. 1822; Dr.; Surgeon in N. Y. Militia; m. Maria Elizabeth Weidman.
> Experience, b. 4 Mar. 1779.

27. **Hubbell, Benjamin,** s. of John.

Bapt. 6 Oct. 1717; d. at Stratfield, 24 Feb. 1793 in 76 yr. (g. s.); m. Mary Porter, b. abt. July 1721, d. 29 Aug. 1813 ae. 92 yrs. 1 mo. (g. s.).

---

* On Elnathan Hubbell and his children, we are specially indebted for information to James F. Hubbell, Esq., Utica, N. Y.

† Recorded at Dutch Reformed Church, Schaghticoke, N. Y.

Children:

> John, b. [19 Oct. 1744, O. S.], d. at Stratfield, 7 Feb. 1808 ae. 63 yrs. 3 mos. 7 days (g. s.); m. Elizabeth Brothwell, dau. of Joseph, b. 2 Feb. 1751, d. 13 Mar. 1840 in 90 yr. (g. s.).
> Anna, b. abt. 1747, d. at Stratfield, 9 May 1770 in 23 yr. (only dau. of Benjamin) (g. s.).

28. Hubbell, John, s. of John.

He m. Patience ———, and d. in Nov. 1739; and had a posthumous son, John, b. 17, bapt. 25 Feb. 1739/40. In entering this baptism in the Trumbull Church records, Rev. Richardson Miner stated that the child's father was deceased, having been killed by an accidental shot out of a gun in the hands of his only brother last November.

29. Hubbell, Ebenezer, s. of Ebenezer.

Born abt. 1723; d. at Trumbull, 21 Mar. 1800 ae. 77 (g. s.); m. (1) Lydia ———; m. (2) Tamar ———.

Dower in Est. of Ebenezer of Weston set to widow Tamar, 31 May 1800.

Children (record incomplete):

> Seth, b. abt. 1748, d. at Weston, 23 Jan. 1827 ae. 79; m. (1) at Easton, 1 Nov. 1771, Lois Jackson; dau. of John, bapt. 10 Nov. 1745, d. at Trumbull, 23 Mar. 1806 in 61 yr. (g. s.); m. (2) Lucy (Beardsley), widow of Gideon Hubbell of Huntington.*
> Sarah, bapt. at Stratfield, 15 Apr. 1750; m. (rec. Weston) 1 Oct. 1768, Nathan Summers.
> ?Mary, b. [say 1752]; m. 1 July 1773, Daniel Blackman.

30. Hubbell, Timothy, s. of Ebenezer.

Born abt. 1732; lived in Weston; bur. 7 Aug. 1812 ae. 80 (Trinity Church rec.).

He m. (1) Ann Bennett, dau. of Dea. William, b. Nov. 1738, d. by 1778.

He m. (2) Ann Adams, dau. of Stephen, b. 10 Aug. 1742, living 1793.

---

* Children, rec. Weston: Lois, b. 20 Apr. 1779. Sarah, b. 10 Nov. 1781. Lucinda, b. 8 Oct. 1784. Mary, b. 28 May 1790. Jeremiah, b. 11 Apr. 1795, d. at Trumbull, 4 Jan. 1870 ae. 74 (g. s.); m. Lucy Crawford.

Distribution, 17 June 1813, to his children, Timothy and Daniel Hubbell, Hannah Watkins, Rebecca Allen; to John and Ethan Parrit, Anne Platt, Ellen Mallory, and Rebecca Mead, children of Patience Parrit, dau. of Timothy Hubbell; and to the heirs of Rhoda Cardwell, dec'd dau. of Timothy.

Children [by first wife] :

    Patience, m. ——— Parrott.
    Rhoda, m. John Cardwell.*
    Rebecca, m. (1) ——— Lyon, of Vt.; m. (2) by 1813, ——— Allen.
    Hannah, m. William Watkins.
    Zachariah, b. abt. 1769, d. at Easton, Apr. 1808 ae. 39. Will 3 Feb., proved 9 May 1808; nephew Ethan Parrott, nephew John, and niece Rebecca Parrott, children of dec'd sister Patience Parrott; bro. Timothy Hubbell and sister Rebecca Lyon of State of Vt.; bro. Daniel; sister Hannah wife of William Watkins; father Timothy Hubbell; children of dec'd sister Rhoda Cardwell.

Children [by second wife] :

    Timothy, res. in Vt.; m. Mary Gilbert, dau. of John, b. 15 Mar. 1773.†
    Daniel.
    Ann, living 1793, prob. d. s. p. before 1808.

31. **Hubbell, Hezekiah,** s. of Richard. Ens., Stratfield Co., Oct. 1766. Justice, 1779-82. Deputy for Fairfield, Oct. and Nov. 1780, Feb., May and Oct. 1781, Oct. 1782.

Born 24 Feb. 1728; d. at Stratfield, 19 July 1784 ae. 56 yrs. 4 mos. 12 days (g. s.); m. 14 May 1752, Anna Patterson, dau. of William, b. at Stratford, 3 July 1731. She d. by 1818.

Will 8 June 1784; wife Anna; children, William, Asa, Aaron, Hezekiah, Ezra, Anna, Parthenia wife of Thomas Hubbell, and Charity Hubbell. The distribution, 6 Feb. 1786, called Charity wife of Isaac Youngs.

Order to distribute the dower right of his widow Anna to the heirs, 14 Apr. 1818: eldest son William Hubbell; heirs of dec'd sons Asa, Ezra, and Hezekiah, and of dec'd dau. Anna Keeler; dau. Parthena Hubbell; heirs of dec'd dau. Charity. Distribution,

---

* Timothy-Hubbell, son of John Cardwell, bapt. at Trinity Church, 21 Aug. 1791.
† Children, bapt. Trinity Church: Sarah, bapt. 10 Mar. 1793; Eunice, bapt. 15 Jan. 1797.

24 Apr. 1818: eldest son William; 2d son Asa; 3d son Aaron; heirs of 4th son Ezra; heirs of 5th son Hezekiah; heirs of eldest dau. Anna Keeler; heirs of 2d dau. Parthenia Hubbell; heirs of 3d dau. Charity Young.

Children, first three rec. Fairfield:

>Ann, b. 6 Mar. 1753, bapt. at Stratfield (Trumbull Church rec.), 21 Mar. 1753; m. ―――― Keeler.
>William, b. 24 July 1755, bapt. at Stratfield, June (?) 1755, d. near Georgetown, Ky., in 1830; m. Margaretta Gano.
>Asa, b. 9 Jan. 1757, drowned in Hudson River, 5 July 1801; rem. Spring 1787, to Hillsdale, Columbia County, N. Y.; m. Miriam ――――.
>Parthenia, m. Thomas Hubbell; they res. Stratford, 1787.
>Aaron, b. 10 Oct. 1762, d. at Stratfield, 13 Oct. 1848 ae. 87 (g. s.); m. 9 Sept. 1787, Sarah Silliman, dau. of Joseph, b. 22 Dec. 1766, d. 15 Mar. 1851 ae. 84 (g. s.).
>Ezra, lost at sea, Jan. 1805; a sea captain; m. in 1795, Mary-Alice Lewis, dau. of David, who d. 26 Jan. 1805.*
>Hezekiah, perhaps d. in 1793; adm'n on estate granted, 12 Aug. 1793, to Ezra Hubbell.
>Charity, m. abt. 1785, Isaac Youngs.

32. Hubbell, Walter, s. of Richard.

Bapt. 14 Nov. 1736.
He m. Ruth ――――.

Children:

>Josiah, b. [July 1764], d. at Stratfield, 14 Oct. 1765 ae. 15 mos. (g. s.).
>Joel, res. 1791, New Milford; m. Charity Hubbell, dau. of Josiah, b. 3 June 1766.
>Walter.
>David, b. [14 Mar. 1776], d. 1 Oct. 1777 ae. 16 mos. 17 days (g. s.).

33. Hubbell, Richard, s. of Richard.

Born abt. 1742; d. at New York City, 16 July 1829 in 87 yr. (g. s., Stratfield); m. Roxanna Burritt, b. abt. 1746, d. 28 Dec. 1805 in 60 yr. (g. s.).

---

* Adm'n granted, 23 Feb. 1805, to Josiah Lacey and Aaron Hubbell. Distribution to only son William D., eldest dau. Catherine-Maria, youngest dau. Mary-Ann.

Children:

>Richard, lost at sea in 1811; m. in 1804, Sarah Tomlinson, dau. of Agur.
>Philo, bapt. 29 Apr. 1770, d. 13 Feb. 1774 ae. 4 (g. s.).
>Penelope, b. abt. 1772, d. 21 Feb. 1864 ae. 92 (g. s.).
>Pamela, m. Capt. Robert-William Wetmore.
>Eli.
>Polly, m. Asa Hurd.
>Charles, b. [8 June 1785], d. 15 June 1786 ae. 1 yr. 7 days (g. s.).

34. Hubbell, Amos, s. of Richard.

Born 3 Dec. 1746; d. at Stratfield, 2 July 1801 ae. 55 (g. s.); m. (1) 4 Jan. 1770, Catherine Wilson; dau. of Robert, b. 6 Feb. 1750/1, d. 4 Jan. 1776 in 23 yr. (g. s.); m. (2) 17 Dec. 1776, Eleanor Hubbell, dau. of Nathan, b. 3 June 1755, d. 11 Feb. 1833.

He was allowed to transport flax on the *Sally*, Sept. 1780, in exchange for merchandise needed by inhabitants of Fairfield.

Will 13 June, proved 6 July 1801; wife Eleanor; sons Anson and Charles-Benjamin; gr. dau. Julia-Ann Hubbell; dau. Catherine.

Children [by first wife]:

>Amos, b. 2 Oct. 1770, d. 10 Sept. 1777 in 7 yr. (g. s.).
>Wilson, b. 7 Apr. 1773, d. at sea 5 Apr. 1799 ae. 26 (g. s.); m. 17 Aug. 1797, Pamela Hubbell, dau. of John, bapt. 15 May 1773, d. 1 Sept. 1798.*
>Catherine, b. 27 Dec. 1775; m. 17 Jan. 1796, Ezekiel Hubbell.

Children [by second wife]:

>Amos, b. 12 May 1780, d. at Havana, Cuba, 15 Oct. 1798 ae. 18 (g. s.).
>Eleanor, b. 12 June 1784, d. 22 Mar. 1786 ae. 1 yr. 9 mos. 10 days (g. s.).
>Anson, b. 8 Feb. 1787, d. 9 Sept. 1819 ae. 32 (called of New York, recorded Fairfield Church).
>Charles-Benjamin, b. 20 Mar. 1789, d. at Bridgeport, 12 May 1873; m. Elizabeth Thompson.

35. Hubbell, Daniel, s. of Daniel.

Born 22 Aug. 1724; d. at Stratfield, 4 Mar. 1801 in 77 yr. (g. s.); m. 28 Dec. 1749, Sarah Gregory, dau. of Thaddeus, b. 26 July 1728, d. 11 Apr. 1801 in 73 yr. (g. s.).

---

* Their dau. Julia-Ann, b. 25 May 1798.

Distribution, Est. of Sarah, 11 Nov. 1808: eldest son Onesimus Hubbell; 2d son Thaddeus Hubbell; eldest dau. Sarah Hubbell; 2d dau. Esther Hubbell; Huldah and Mary Bennet, children of dau. Mercy late wife of Joseph-Wilson Bennet.

Children:

> Daniel, bapt. 25 Nov. 1750, d. at Stratfield, 12 Jan. 1778 in 28 yr. (g. s.); m. Ann ———. His will, 15 Sept. 1777, proved 15 Feb. 1778; wife Anne; two bros. Onesimus and Thaddeus.
> Onesimus, bapt. 16 Nov. 1755, d. at Stratfield, 14 Sept. 1824 in 69 yr. (g. s.). Adm'n granted, 27 Sept. 1824, to Thaddeus Hubbell.
> Rebecca, b. abt. 1757, d. 8 May 1796 in 39 yr. (g. s.).
> Sarah, b. abt. 1761; living unm. 1833.
> Thaddeus, b. 15 Oct. 1764, d. at Stratfield, 30 Nov. 1849 ae. 85 (g. s.); m. Eunice ———, b. abt. 1770, d. 1 May 1838 ae. 68 (g. s.).
> Esther, b. abt. 1766, d. 7 Nov. 1802 in 36 yr. (g. s.).
> Mercy, m. Joseph-Wilson Bennett.

36. Hubbell, Abel, s. of Daniel.

Born 30 May 1728; d. at Stratfield, 6 Jan. 1832 ae. 103 yrs. 6 mos. 26 days (g. s.); m. (1) Martha Beardsley, dau. of John, b. 22 Mar. 1728; m. (2) Sarah ———, b. abt. 1761, d. 9 Oct. 1842 ae. 81 yrs. (g. s.).

Child [by first wife], bapt. Stratfield:

> Eunice, bapt. 12 Nov. 1750; it is said she m. before 1773, Zebulon Platt.*
> ?James, b. abt. 1757, d. at Stratfield, 15 Sept. 1827 ae. 70 (g. s.); m. (1) ———; m. (2) Hannah (Gorham), widow of Ebenezer Andrews and previously of Lazarus Wheeler, b. 15 Nov. 1752, d. in 1826.†

37. Hubbell, Nehemiah, s. of Stephen.

Born 19 May 1722; d. at Fairfield in 1785.
He m. Hannah Treadwell, perhaps dau. of David.
Adm'n granted to Nathan Seeley of Fairfield, 4 Apr. 1785.

---

* *The Conn. Magazine*, vol. 5, p. 494.
† His will, 29 May 1810, proved 22 Mar. 1828; son Abel; daus. Sally wife of Ephraim-Seeley Sherwood, Eunice and Polly Hubbell. Distribution: Abel Hubbell, Jr.; Alven(?) and Mary-Ann Sherwood, children of Ephraim S. and Sally Sherwood dec'd; Eunice wife of Walker Lyon; Polly wife of Roswell Seeley. The children were all by his first wife; the son Abel m. 12 June 1803, Sally Turney, dau. of Peter. Abel d. Dec. 1821 ae. 42 (Fairfield Church).

Children:

46+Stephen, b. 10 Oct. 1744.
47+Nathaniel, b. in 1747.
    Abigail, bapt. 7 Oct. 1750; m. at Easton, May 1773, Stephen Turrel.
    David, b. Dec. 1752, d. 5 Apr. 1820; m. 15 Oct. 1777, Abiah Leavenworth, b. 6 July 1758.
    Rebecca, bapt. 11 May 1755; m. Ebenezer Fanton.
    Isaac, b. 8 Sept. 1755, bapt. Jan. 1756, d. 5 May 1842; m. 5 Dec. 1783, Mabel Beach, b. 22 Sept. 1757.
    Huldah, b. 1758, d. 25 Jan. 1853; m. 1781, Philo Curtis.
    Billy, b. 1759, d. at Monroe, 2 Apr. 1848; m. Mary Booth, who d. 10 Mar. 1810 ae. 49.
    Hannah, m. Silas Dayton.
    Nehemiah, b. 7 Apr. 1764, d. at Painted Post, Steuben County, N. Y., 21 June 1835; m. 5 Oct. 1797, Jemima (Hayden) Patterson, b. 24 Feb. 1764, d. 27 May 1842.
    Rachel, m. Enoch Jennings.

38. **Hubbell, Jabez,** s. of Stephen.

He m. (1) 28 June 1750, Sarah Seeley, dau. of Nathaniel, bapt. 20 Aug. 1732, d. at Stratfield, 12 Jan. 1754 in 22 yr. (g. s.).

He m. (2) Sarah Rowland; dau. of Henry, bapt. 27 May 1733.

He would seem to be the Jabez of Ballston, Albany County, N. Y., who conveyed land in Fairfield, 1775, to Walter Hubbell. Jabez, late of Fairfield, now of Ballston, conveyed in 1774 land in Stratfield bounded east on land of Stephen Hubbell.

Nathaniel Seeley conveyed for love in 1782 to gr. dau. Tabitha Lacy.

Children [by first wife]:

    Tabitha, bapt. at Stratfield, 17 Mar. 1751, d. at Stratfield, 9 Aug. 1814 in 64 yr. (g. s.); m. Daniel Lacy.
    Sarah, d. at Stratfield, 27 June 1770.

Children [by second wife]:

    Clarissa, b. 21 Apr. 1767, d. 9 July 1848; m. Felix Benedict.
    Abiah, bapt. at Stratfield, 20 May 1770.

39. **Hubbell, Gershom,** s. of Stephen. Capt., North Stratfield and North Stratford Co., Oct. 1758.

He m. Mehitabel Hall, dau. of Richard, bapt. 7 Oct. 1733.

Gershom Hubbell, "Jr.," and Mehitabel his wife conveyed, 1768, to Rebecca wife of Abel Hall, one-seventh of land at Bluff Hill, which came by will from Richard Hall dec'd.

Children:
- Lois, bapt. at Stratfield, 21 Apr. 1754.
- Ezbon, b. 1757, d. 1820; res. Ballston, Saratoga County, N. Y.; m.
- Benjamin.
- Enos.
- Ephraim.
- Richard, b. 4 July 1766, d. at Cincinnati, Ohio, 1830; res. Ballston, N. Y.; m. Anna Trowbridge.
- Gershom, b. 4 July 1766, d. at Springfield, Ohio, 1833; res. Ballston, N. Y.; m.
- Abigail.

40. **Hubbell, Gershom,** s. of Nathan. Ens., Greenfield Co., Oct. 1765; Lt., Oct. 1767. Justice, 1777, '81.

Born 17 July 1729; d. at Greenfield, 14 Apr. 1802 ae. 72 (g. s.); m. (1) 2 May 1754, Mary Bradley, b. 21 June 1733, d. 3 [23 by town rec.] Feb. 1756 ae. 22 yrs. 7 mos. (g. s.); m. (2) 3 Nov. 1756, Sarah Wakeman, dau. of Samuel, bapt. 31 Oct. 1731, d. 18 Jan. 1769 ae. 38 (g. s.); m. (3) 30 Nov. 1769, Sarah St. John, b. 15 Apr. 1746, d. 6 Sept. 1842 ae. 96 (g. s.).

Will 1 Apr., proved 6 May 1802; wife Sarah; five youngest children, Moses, Priscilla, William, Uriah, Abraham.

Child [by first wife]:
- Mary, b. 10 July, d. 27 Dec. 1755.

Children [by second wife], bapt. Greenfield:
- Mary, b. 15 Aug. 1757; m. 22 Oct. 1779, Zadok Hubbell.
- Elizabeth, b. 10 Mar. 1759, bapt. 27 May 1759 (ae. abt. 2 mos.); m. 24 Aug. 1780, Meeker Gorham.
- Abijah, b. 27 Feb. 1761, bapt. 1 Mar. 1761 (ae. 3 days), d. at Canandaigua, N. Y., 24 Oct. 1843; res. Ballston, N. Y.; m. 16 Nov. 1788, Clarissa Fitch, b. at Redding, 25 Sept. 1768, d. at Pulaski, N. Y., 6 July 1841.
- Gershom, b. 17, bapt. 20 Mar. 1763, d. at Greenfield, 3 Jan. 1782 ae. 18 yrs. 10 mos. (g. s.).
- Sarah, b. 11 Apr. (?), bapt. 5 Mar. 1765, d. 26 Feb. 1815; m. —— Kellogg.
- Walter, b. 17, bapt. 23 Aug. 1767, d. at Brooklyn, N. Y., 9 Sept. 1803; m. (1) Mary Ventris; m. (2) 4 Sept. 1797, Anne Law, dau. of Chief Justice Richard Law.

Children [by third wife], bapt. Greenfield:

> Moses, b. 25 Jan. 1771, d. 26 Oct. 1851; m. 25 Nov. 1792, Anna Silliman, bapt. 1 Nov. 1772, d. 10 May 1849.
> Priscilla, b. 22 Jan., bapt. 28 Feb. 1773, d. at Greenfield, 2 May 1868 ae. 95 yrs. 3 mos. 11 days (g. s.).
> William, b. 1 Dec. 1775, bapt. 17 Mar. 1776.
> Uriah, b. 3 May, bapt. 12 July 1778, d. at Greenfield, 25 Aug. 1828 ae. 50 (g. s.); m. Mabel Hull, dau. of John, who d. 18 Feb. 1847 ae. 70 (g. s.).
> Susanna, b. 15 Nov., bapt. 31 Dec. 1780, d. 13 Sept. 1783.
> Gershom, b. 13 Jan. 1783, d. Feb. 1783.
> Abraham, b. 27 Mar. 1786; m. Esther B. Williams, b. 21 Oct. 1792.

41. Hubbell, John, s. of Nathan. Lt., 2d Troop, 4th Regt., May 1769.

Born 31 July 1734; d. at Southeast, Putnam County, N. Y., 10 Mar. 1810; m. (1) 30 Mar. 1758, Eleanor Burr, dau. of Timothy, b. 30 July 1738, d. at Greenfield, 20 May 1773 in 35 yr.

Lt. John m. (2) at Greenfield, 24 Oct. 1773, Elizabeth Bradley. She was widow of Reuben Bradley, and dau. of Thomas Nash, b. 23 Aug. 1734.

Children [by first wife], bapt. Greenfield:

> John, bapt. 26 Aug. 1758 (at home, sick), d. July 1780 ae. 22.
> Rachel, bapt. 13 Apr. 1760, d. at Greenfield, 15 Jan. 1819 in 60 yr. (g. s.); m. Jan. 1780, Dr. Hosea Hulbert.
> Eleanor, bapt. 11 Apr. 1762, d. at Poughkeepsie, N. Y., [15 Jan. 1819]; m. 2 June 1779, Joseph Bulkley.
> Esther, bapt. 26 Aug. 1764 (ae. abt. 8 days), d. 5 June 1851 in 87 yr. (g. s.); m. Wakeman Lyon.
> Hannah, b. 20 July, bapt. 3 Aug. 1766, d. 4 May 1847; m. Isaac Wilson.
> Ezekiel, b. 5, bapt. 17 Apr. 1768, d. at Bridgeport, 1 Apr. 1834; m. 17 Jan. 1796, Catherine Hubbell, dau. of Amos, b. 27 Dec. 1775, d. 2 Mar. 1850.
> Jonathan, bapt. 15 May 1773 (immediately after birth), d. at Nankin, Wayne County, Mich., 12 Aug. 1852; m. (1) 5 Feb. 1801, Anna Bird, dau. of Ebenezer, b. abt. 1780, d. 5 Oct. 1807 ae. 27; m. (2) 8 May 1809, Elizabeth Delia Prudden, b. in 1779, d. in 1859.
> Amelia* (twin), bapt. 15 May 1773, d. 1 Sept. 1798; m. 17 Aug. 1797, Wilson Hubbell.

---

* Also called Pamela.

THE FAMILIES OF OLD FAIRFIELD

42. **Hubbell, Aaron,** s. of David.

Bapt. 27 Dec. 1741.

He m. 29 Nov. 1761, Mary Burr, dau. of Nathaniel, b. 13 June 1740, d. 9 Sept. 1775 (Perry Diary).

Dower distributed to widow of Aaron, Feb. 1807.

Children, rec. and bapt. Fairfield:

> Martha, b. 2 May 1762, bapt. 27 Aug. 1775; as "Patty," she m. (rec. Weston) 29 Sept. 1780, David Seeley.
> David, b. 1 Aug. 1763, bapt. 27 Aug. 1775.
> Mary, b. 2 July 1767, bapt. 17 Sept. 1768, d. 26 Oct. 1768.
> Mary, b. 29 Jan. 1769, bapt. 19 Aug. 1775. [Child d. Aug. 1775 by Perry Diary.]

43. **Hubbell, Ebenezer,** s. of David.

Bapt. 18 Nov. 1744.

He m. at Weston, 8 Apr. 1767, Lydia Couch, dau. of Solomon, bapt. 19 Apr. 1747.

Ebenezer Hubbell was allowed guardian of Isaac-Couch Hubbell, 26 Feb. 1791; and of Aaron, son of Ebenezer, 5 Feb. 1795.

Children, bapt. Fairfield:

> Ebenezer, bapt. 27 Mar. 1768; ? m. at Weston, 7 Aug. 1793, Esther Gray.
> Jabez, bapt. 25 Mar. 1770, d. in 1794. Adm'n on Est. of Jabez, Jr., granted 20 Oct. 1794 to David Hubbell.
> Lydia, bapt. 16 May 1773.
> Isaac-Couch, bapt. 25 June 1775; ? m. at Weston, 14 June 1801, Hannah Rowland.
> Aaron, bapt. 25 Oct. 1778; m. 30 Jan. 1799, Betsey Jennings; perhaps dau. of Ezra, bapt. 30 July 1777; Elizabeth, widow of Aaron, d. 8 June 1850 ae. 85 (g. s.).*

44. **Hubbell, David,** s. of David. Capt.

Bapt. 20 Mar. 1747/8; d. at Greenfield, 22 Dec. 1814 ae. 66 (g. s.), or ae. 66 yrs. 11 mos. (church rec.); m. 28 Feb. 1773, Sarah Perry; dau. of Joseph, b. 25 July 1744, d. 6 Feb. 1826 ae. 81 (g. s.).

---

* Children, bapt. Fairfield: Elizabeth, bapt. 7 Apr. 1800; Susan, bapt. 19 July 1801.

Children, bapt. Greenfield:

    Sarah, bapt. 22 May 1775, d. 22 Sept. 1777 ae. 2 yrs. 8 mos. (g. s.).
    David, bapt. 28 June 1778, d. 23 Oct. 1806 ae. 28 yrs. 5 mos. (g. s.).
    Sarah, bapt. 24 June 1781.
    Samuel, bapt. 5 Oct. 1782, d. 2 May 1789 ae. 6 yrs. 7 mos. (g. s.).
    Harriet, b. 11 May 1786, d. 12 Oct. 1842 (g. s.); m. William Hoyt.

45. Hubbell, Jabez, s. of David.

Bapt. 11 Nov. 1753; d. at Fairfield, 29 May 1817 ae. 64; m. (1) 28 Dec. 1775, Abigail Gray; m. (2) 24 June 1779, Rhoda Osborn; widow of Stratton Osborn, and dau. of Jabez Patchen. The widow of Jabez Hubbell d. 22 June 1833 ae. 76 (Wheeler Journal).

Will 3 Jan. 1798, proved 7 July 1817; wife Rhoda; son James; dau. Sarah.

Adm'n on estate of Rhoda Hubbell granted, 23 July 1833, to Charles L. Mills and David Mallory. Distribution, 1835, to gr. children, Emily Bulkley, David Mallory, Sally-Ann West, Harriet West, Caroline Gilbert, James H. Mallory, George Mallory, Elizabeth Mallory, and Simeon Mallory.

Child [by first wife], bapt. Fairfield:

    Abigail, bapt. 5 Nov. 1777, d. y.

Children [by second wife], bapt. Fairfield:

    Sarah, bapt. 28 Jan. 1781, d. 5 Mar. 1833 ae. 52 (g. s.); m. 14 Dec. 1799, Andrew Mallory.
    James, bapt. 3 Nov. 1782.

46. Hubbell, Stephen, s. of Nehemiah.

Born 10 Oct. 1744; d. at Easton, 27 Feb. 1836 ae. 91 (g. s.); m. 27 Jan. 1765, Rhoda Middlebrook, b. 16 Apr. 1743, d. 15 Aug. 1826 ae. 83 (g. s.).

Children, rec. Weston:

    Joseph, b. 28 May 1765, d. 1828; m. Eunice Hooker, dau. of Nathaniel, b. abt. 1771, d. 9 Dec. 1851 ae. 80.
    Eunice, b. 29 Oct. 1766; m. 28 Nov. 1783, Reuben Judd.
    Ezra, b. 2 Sept. 1768, d. 2 Nov. 1768.
    Elizabeth, b. 4 Sept. 1769, d. 29 Mar. 1850 ae. 80; m. 25 Apr. 1793, Theophilus Middlebrook.

THE FAMILIES OF OLD FAIRFIELD 497

Abigail, b. 6 Dec. 1770; m. Thaddeus Jennings.
Rhoda, b. 11 Sept. 1772; m. 16 Nov. 1796, Josiah-Beach Sherman.
Olive, b. 25 Sept. 1774; ? m. Henry Bennett.
Abiah, b. 16 Sept. 1776, d. 23 Sept. 1776.
Hannah, b. 6 Dec. 1777; m. Lewis Mallett.
Stephen, b. 19 Sept. 1779.
Rachel, b. 28 May 1781; m. Joseph Seeley.
Billy, b. 10 May 1783; m. Eunice Preston.*

47. **Hubbell, Nathaniel**, s. of Nehemiah.

Born in 1747; d. at Easton, 27 May 1837 in 91 yr. (g. s.); m. at Easton, 15 Oct. 1766, Sarah Burton, who d. 8 Dec. 1835 ae. 85 (g. s.).

Children:

Ruth, b. abt. 1771, d. at Easton, 20 Mar. 1859 ae. 88 (g. s.); m. Gideon H. Hall.
Zalmon.
David S., b. abt. 1775, d. at Easton, 26 Nov. 1847 ae. 72 (g. s.); m. (rec. Weston) 20 Dec. 1794, Phebe Silliman; dau. of David, b. 3 Nov. 1772, d. 1 Jan. 1844 ae. 72 (g. s.).†
Huldah, b. 9 July 1780, d. 12 Feb. 1867; m. 28 Feb. 1798, Hiram Taylor, of Brookfield.
Sarah, b. abt. 1785, d. at Easton, 24 Feb. 1809 in 24 yr. (g. s.); m. Squire Terrell.

Hubbell [*Unplaced*].

ISAAC, b. abt. 1747, d. at Stratfield, 22 May 1787 in 40 yr. (g. s.); Lt., Conn. Line, 1777-81; Capt.; m. Frances ———, who d. 21 May 1786 in 34 yr. (g. s.).
ANNA of Fairfield m. 20 Dec. 1789, Silliman Gray of Greenfield. [Fairfield Church]
WIDOW d. of smallpox, 12 Apr. 1793 (Perry Diary).
MARY m. 21 Nov. 1790, Thomas Whelpley. [Weston Church]
CATE m. Dec. 1790, Abraham Bennett. [Easton Church]
——— m. by 1768, Abigail Sackett, dau. of Richard of Greenwich.

Hubbert [*Unplaced*].

EUNICE m. Oct. 1795, Burr Silliman. [Easton Church]

---

* One William d. at Greenfield, 6 Apr. 1813 ae. 30 (g. s.). Eunice m. at Easton in 1813 (name of bridegroom omitted).

† Children, rec. Weston: Catey, b. 27 May 1795; Isaac, b. 21 Jan. 1797, d. at Easton, 22 Apr. 1873 ae. 76 yrs. 6(?) mos. (g. s.).

Hughes, Rowland.

He d. at Westport, 19 Aug. 1758; m. 17 Mar. 1757, Sarah Hendrick, bapt. 26 Jan. 1734/5, d. at Bedford, N. Y., after 1802. Sarah Hughs of Fairfield sold in 1774, land my father John Hendrick conveyed to Rowland Hughs.

Child:

>Esther, b. abt. 1758, d. at Fairfield, 15 May 1832 ae. 73; m. 10 June 1779, Wright White.

Hulbert, (Dr.) Hosea.

Born abt. 1745; d. at Greenfield, 5 Apr. 1825 in 80 yr. (g. s.); m. at Fairfield, Jan. 1780, Miss Rachel Hubbell of Greenfield; dau. of John, bapt. 13 Apr. 1760, d. 15 Jan. 1819 in 60 yr. (g. s.).

Children:

>?Sally, m. 12 Jan. 1800, Joseph Nichols, of Newtown.
>Fanny, b. abt. 1784, d. at Greenfield, 2 June 1851 ae. 67 (g. s.).

Hull [Vol. I, pp. 307-312].

```
1 George (    -1659) m. (1) Thomasin Mitchell; (2) Sarah (———) Phippen.
(By 1): 2 Cornelius (1627-1695) m. Rebecca Jones.
          3 Samuel (    -1720) m. (1) Deborah Beers; (2) Elizabeth (Hubbell)
                  Frost; (3) Jane ———.
    (By 1): 6 Samuel (1696-1787).
    (By 2): 7 Josiah (1702-1740).
          4 Theophilus (    -1710) m. Mary Sanford.
             8 Theophilus (1697-1748).
             9 Eliphalet (1701-1737).
            10 John (1704-1761).
            11 Jabez (1706-    ).
          5 Cornelius (1655-1740) m. Sarah Sanford.
            12 George (1686-1769).
            13 Nathaniel (1695-1749).
            14 Ebenezer (1697-    ).
            15 John (1703-1741).
            16 Cornelius (1710-1787).
```

6. **Hull, Samuel,** s. of Samuel.

Bapt. 26 Apr. 1696; d. at Fairfield abt. 1787.

He m. (rec. Fairfield) 3 Feb. 1727, Joanna Fairchild, dau. of Joseph, b. at Stratford, 2 Feb. 1696/7, d. at Fairfield, 4 Nov. 1789 ae. 93 yrs. 8 mos. (Wheeler Journal).

He was appointed guardian, 2 Feb. 1730/1, to Hannah Fairchild, dau. of Nathan [his wife's niece]. She receipted to him for her portion, 25 June 1747.

Will 13 Mar. 1765, proved 8 Mar. 1787; wife Joanna; nephew Samuel Hull, Jr.; niece Elizabeth wife of David Patchen; friend, Gold Selleck Silliman.

7. **Hull, Josiah,** s. of Samuel.

Bapt. 12 Apr. 1702, d. at Stamford, in 1740/1; m. at Norwalk, 27 July 1727, Hannah Prindle, dau. of Eleazer of Milford.

Will 5 Dec. 1740, proved 8 Jan. 1740/1; wife Hannah; children Hannah, Josiah, Eleazer, Elizabeth; bro. Samuel Hull of Fairfield, Exec'r.

Children, first four rec. Norwalk, last two at Stamford:

> Eleazer, b. 29 Dec. 1728, d. 28 Mar. 1729.
> Hannah, b. 9 Apr. 1730, d. at Waterbury, 22 Aug. 1756; m. (rec. Waterbury) 14 July 1752, Obadiah Scovill.
> Josiah, b. 19 June 1732; chose uncle Samuel Hull of Fairfield for guardian, 2 Feb. 1747/8; m. at Stamford, 11 Nov. 1754 [1751?] Esther Seeley. Children: Hannah, b. 22 Sept. 1752; Esther, b. 29 Oct. 1754.
> Eleazer, b. 31 July 1734, d. at Stratford in 1756. Adm'n granted, 2 Mar. 1756, to Samuel Hull. Distribution: Samuel Hull, Jr., of Fairfield; Hannah wife of Obadiah Scovel of Waterbury; Elizabeth wife of David Patchin of Fairfield; heirs of Josiah Hull of Stamford, dec'd.
> Elizabeth, b. 7 June 1737; m. David Patchen.
> Samuel, b. 2 Mar. 1740/1 (posthumous) ;* res. 1789, Coxsackie, N. Y., and conveyed land which the will of Samuel Hull dec'd divided (after death of widow Joanna) between himself and Elizabeth wife of David Patchen.

8. **Hull, Theophilus,** s. of Theophilus.

Bapt. 23 May 1697, d. at Redding, 7 Oct. 1748 (g. s., which contains only the initials T. H.); m. abt. 1719, Sarah Sherwood, dau. of Samuel, bapt. 29 Mar. 1696.

He and wife Sarah renewed Covenant at Fairfield Church, 26 Feb. 1720/1; adm. to Greenfield from Greens Farms, 18 May

---

* He had a son Eleazer, bapt. at Fairfield Church, 19 Nov. 1769.

1726; they were original members of Redding Church, 1729, adm. from Greenfield. Deacon 1733.

Will 7 June 1748, proved 31 Oct. 1748; wife Sarah; son Theophilus; dau. Lydia wife of Samuel Smith; bro.-in-law Samuel Sherwood, wife and son, Exec'rs.

Children, rec. and bapt. Fairfield:

    Lydia, b. 31 Dec. 1720, bapt. 26 Feb. 1720/1, d. at Redding, 8 Feb. 1776 ae. 55-1-8 (g. s.); m. at Redding, 25 Aug. 1736, Samuel Smith.
    Mary, b. 12 Sept. 1723, bapt. 22 Sept. 1722, d. at Redding, 18 Sept. 1741 (g. s., which contains only the initials M. H.).
17+Theophillus, b. 21 Feb. 1725/6.

9. **Hull, Eliphalet,** s. of Theophilus.

Born 5 Feb. 1700/1, d. at Greenfield, 14 Mar. 1737 ae. 36 yrs. 1 mo. 9 days (g. s.); m. Sarah Barlow, dau. of John, 3d, b. 27 Feb. 1703/4, d. 28 Nov. 1767 in 64 yr. (g. s.); she m. (2) 1 Nov. 1738, Capt. David Banks.

Will 9 Mar. 1736/7, proved 22 Mar. 1736/7; wife Sarah; daus. Miriam, Sarah, Ruth, and Mary Hull; sons Seth, John, Daniel; lands in New Fairfield; wife Sarah, bro. John Barlow, and Mr. Joseph Wakeman, Exec'rs.

Adm'n on Est. of Sarah, late wife of David Banks and formerly wife of Eliphalet Hull, was granted to Daniel Hull, 31 Jan. 1791. Distribution: Daniel Hull; heirs of Seth Hull; heirs of John Hull; Mary wife of James Redfield; Ruah wife of Francis Bradley; heirs of Eliphalet Banks; heirs of Miriam Gorham; heirs of Sarah Bradley.

Children, rec. Greenfield:

    Miriam, b. 20 Dec. 1724, bapt. in infancy, d. 4 Aug. 1770 (Perry Diary); m. Apr. 1744, Jabez Gorham.
    Sarah, b. 10 May 1726, bapt. 29 May 1726, d. 20 Nov. 1770 (Perry Diary); m. Ebenezer Bradley.
18+Seth, b. 23 Feb. 1728/9, bapt. 18 Mar. 1728/9.
    Ruth, b. 27 Mar. 1730, bapt. 5 Apr. 1730, d. 6 Jan. 1806 ae. 76 (g. s.); m. 21 Feb. 1749/50, Francis Bradley.
19+John, b. 28 Mar. 1732, bapt. 9 Apr. 1732.
20+Daniel, b. 15 May 1734, bapt. 18 May 1734.
    Mary, b. 28 Mar. 1736, bapt. 18 Apr. 1736, d. at Greenfield, 10 Oct. 1814 ae. 78 (g. s.); m. (1) 13 Mar. 1754, Seth Jennings; m. (2) in 1758, James Redfield.

10. Hull, John, s. of Theophilus.

Bapt. 2 Apr. 1704, d. at Newtown, 28 May 1761; m. Elizabeth Adams, dau. of Freegrace.

Adm'n granted to Elijah and Eliphalet Hull of Newtown, 22 June 1761. On 20 Apr. 1764, Simeon and Mary Shepard receipted to the Adm'rs for portion from our father John Hull dec'd.

Children, rec. Newtown:

> Ebenezer, b. 5 Oct. 1729, d. in 1756; adm'n granted, 6 Sept. 1756, to Mary and John Hull of Newtown, and Mary was appointed guardian to her son Abel, who is only son to Ebenezer Hull.
> Elijah, b. 24 Mar. 1734, d. at Newtown, 14 Mar. 1811 ae. 78 (g. s.); m. 31 Jan. 1760, Rebecca Summers.
> John, b. 13 Nov. 1735; m. Sarah Hepburn.
> Eliphalet, b. 1 Jan. 1737/8; m. 30 Oct. 1765, Rebecca Baldwin.
> Mary, b. 5 Mar. 1743; m. by 1764, Simeon Shepard.

11. Hull, Jabez, s. of Theophilus.

Bapt. 10 Feb. 1705/6.

He m. Mary Thorp, dau. of John, b. 17 Feb. 1705/6.

Children, rec. Westport:

21+Jabez, b. 14 June 1729.
> Hezekiah, b. 23 July 1731, d. at New York 27 Dec. 1755 (buried at Westport). Adm'n granted, 6 Jan. 1756, to Jeremiah Sherwood of Fairfield. Distribution to Jabez Hull, Jr., Nathan Hull, Isaac Hull, Sarah Hull.
> Mary, b. 16 Apr. 1734, d. at Greenfield, 17 Sept. 1762 in 29 yr.; m. 5 June 1755, Oliver Whitlock.
> Eunice, b. 19 July 1736; m. 9 Nov. 1756, Eli Taylor, of Norwalk.
> Sarah, b. 3 Feb. 1739.
> Eliphalet, bapt. 1 Aug. 1741, d. 9 Jan. 1756.
> Nathan, bapt. 13 May 1744.
> Isaac, bapt. 17 July 1748.

12. Hull, George, s. of Cornelius.

Born abt. 1686, d. at Redding, 9 Feb. 1769 ae. 83; m. abt. 1711, Martha Gregory, dau. of Samuel, b. [say 1690].

Adm. with wife Martha to Greenfield Church, 18 May 1726; original member of Redding Church, and Deacon.

Adm'n granted, 18 Feb. 1769, to Seth Hull. Distribution: son George; Seth had portion; dau. Rebecca Hull; dau. Martha Bixby; Gershom, John, Peter, and Seth Squire, and Bethia Crofut, children of Mary Squire of Redding dec'd, a child of George Hull.

Children, five bapt. at Fairfield, two at Greenfield, two at Redding:

>Abigail, bapt. 1 June 1712, d. 27 Apr.(?) 1712.
>Mary, bapt. 12 July 1713; m. Jonathan Squire.
>Joseph, bapt. 9 Oct. 1715, d. y.
>Abigail, bapt. 4 June 1721, d. at Redding, 17 Dec. 1760.
>Thaddeus, bapt. 14 Apr. 1723, d. abt. 1761. Adm'n was granted, 17 June 1761, to Seth Hull, Jr. Distribution, 1 Jan. 1763: George Hull, Jr.; Mary wife of Jonathan Squire; Martha wife of Jonathan Bixby; Seth Hull; Rebecca Hull.
>George, bapt. 24 Sept. 1727.
>Martha, bapt. 22 Sept. 1731; m. 4 July 1752, Jonathan Bixby.
>22+Seth, bapt. 29 July 1733.
>Rebecca, bapt. 25 May 1735.

13. **Hull, Nathaniel,** s. of Cornelius.

Born Mar. 1695, d. at Greenfield, 16 July 1749 ae. 54 (g. s.); m. 29 Nov. 1716, Elizabeth Burr, dau. of Daniel, b. 12 Apr. 1696, d. at Redding, 11 Nov. 1760 ae. 64.

Will 13 July 1749, proved 8 Aug. 1749; wife Elizabeth; eldest son Stephen; daus. Elizabeth Burr, Hester Barlow, Hannah Hull; sons Stephen, Nathaniel, Peter, Ezekiel, David, Silas; wife to have use of portions of minor children until they come of age; wife Elizabeth, bro. Cornelius Hull, and son Stephen, Exec'rs.

Elizabeth Hull resigned as guardian to children Ezekiel, David, and Silas, 28 Mar. 1750, only reserving the use of Hannah's estate for three years. David chose Lockwood Gorham for guardian, same date; Stephen Hull was appointed for Silas and Hannah; and Ezekiel chose Cornelius Hull.

Adm'n on Elizabeth's Est. was granted to Stephen Hull, 3 Dec. 1760.

Children, rec. Greenfield:

>Sarah, b. 8 Nov. 1717, bapt. 9 Feb. 1717/8, d. y.
>Elizabeth, b. 2 Aug. 1719, bapt. 20 Sept. 1719, d. at Redding, 16 Nov. 1760 ae. 41 (g. s.); m. Jabez Burr.

Esther, b. 11 June 1721, bapt. 16 July 1721, d. at Redding, 28 Aug. 1775 ae. 54 (g. s.); m. 7 Aug. 1744, Samuel Barlow.
23+Stephen, b. 25 July 1724, bapt. 2 Aug. 1724.
24+Nathaniel, b. 20 Feb. 1726/7, bapt. 26 Feb. 1726/7.
25+Peter, b. 15 Nov. 1728, bapt. 17 Nov. 1728.
Sarah, b. 20 Dec. 1730, bapt. in infancy, d. 2* Oct. 1748 in 18 yr. (g. s.).
26+Ezekiel, b. 12 Oct. 1732, bapt. Dec. 1732.
David, b. 10 Dec. 1734, bapt. 15 Dec. 1734, d. 20 Aug. 1758 in 24 yr. (a gentleman of liberal education).
Aaron, b. 11 Sept. 1736, bapt. 3 Oct. 1736, d. 13 Oct. 1748 ae. 13 (g. s.).
27+Silas, b. 15 June 1739, bapt. 10 (?) June 1739.
Hannah, b. 20 Jan. 1740/1, bapt. 25 Jan. 1740/1, d. by 1761. Adm'n granted, 7 Feb. 1761, to Ezekiel Hull. Distribution to Stephen, oldest bro.; Nathaniel, 2d bro.; children of Peter dec'd; Ezekiel, 4th bro.; Silas, 5th bro.; heirs of Elizabeth Burr dec'd; sister Esther wife of Samuel Barlow.

14. **Hull, Ebenezer,** s. of Cornelius.

Bapt. 20 June 1697.

He m. Martha Bradley, dau. of Daniel, bapt. 4 Oct. 1702.

Prob. he m. (2) Grace Williams, dau. of Thomas, b. 1 Aug. 1722.

With wife Martha he conveyed 1723 land from the Est. of her father.

Children:

28+Daniel, bapt. at Fairfield, 15 Sept. 1723.
29+Ebenezer.
Abigail, bapt. at Greenfield, 28 Sept. 1729; m. 15 Nov. 1748, Gershom Coley.
Nehemiah, bapt. at Redding, Apr. 1743, d. there by 1796; Lt., 9th Co., 4th Regt., Jan. 1778; m. (1) 5 Feb. 1767, Grissel Perry, dau. of Daniel, b. 20 Feb. 1745/6; m. (2) Sarah ———, who m. (2) Eli Sherwood.†

15. **Hull, John,** s. of Cornelius.

Born abt. 1703, d. in Cuba, where he went with the Provincial troops, in 1741. He m. (1) ———; [perhaps m. (2) at New

---
* 21 Oct., by Greenfield rec.
† Adm'n granted, 18 Jan. 1796, to Sarah Hull. Abigail, ae. 17, dau. of Nehemiah, chose Daniel Perry, Jr., for guardian. Sally Hull was appointed guardian to Betsey-Sally, ae. 3, and Sally-Betsey, ae. 3. Distribution, 1797: Widow Sarah, now wife of Eli Sherwood; Abigail; Sally-Betsey; Betsey-Sally. Children by first wife: Ezekiel, bapt. 7 Mar. 1768, d. same day; Abigail, bapt. 3 Jan. 1779.

Milford, 1 Nov. 1737, Abigail Gillet. She was widow of Abraham Gillet, and dau. of Samuel Prindle, b. 30 Dec. 1711. If so, the son John was b. at New Milford, 28 May 1738.]

Will of John of Redding, 16 Sept. 1740, proved 15 Sept. 1741; wife Abigail; daus. Anna, Abigail, Esther, all under 18; three sons, Timothy, James, John; bro. Dea. Stephen Burr of Redding, and wife, Exec'rs. One-third of his farm was distributed to his eldest son Timothy, 20 Nov. 1751.

Adm'n on estate of Abigail Hull of Redding granted, 13 Mar. 1801, to Stephen Jackson; insolvent. [Perhaps refers to the widow of John or to their dau.]

Children [by first wife]:

30+Timothy, b. 4 Sept. 1726, bapt. at Greenfield, 11 Sept. 1726.
James, d. at Redding, 20 Feb. 1805. Will 26 Apr. 1799, proved 26 Feb. 1805; Polly wife of Jesse Benedict; heirs of her sister Abigail Sanford dec'd; residue to bro. John Hull, Exec'r.
Anna, b. abt. 1732, d. at Redding, 23 Apr. 1805 ae. 72 (g. s.); [? m. Moses Ward, Jr.].
Abigail, bapt. at Redding, 31 Mar. 1734.
Esther, bapt. at Redding, 25 July 1736; m. 18 Apr. 1758, Daniel Sanford.

Child [perhaps by second wife]:

John, d. at Redding in 1820; m. (1) at Redding, 3 Feb. 1763, Molly Andrews, dau. of Ebenezer, b. 15 June 1746; m. (2) Mary (Chapman), widow of Moses Bradley, b. 10 June 1752, d. in 1821.*

16. **Hull, Cornelius,** s. of Cornelius.

Bapt. 14 May 1710, d. at Greenfield, 26 Dec. 1787 ae. 78 (g. s.); m. 24 Aug. 1731, Abigail Rumsey, dau. of Robert, bapt. 4 Mar. 1710/1, d. 7 June 1776 ae. 66 (g. s.).

Will 9 June 1775, proved 31 Dec. 1787; wife Abigail; sons Eliphalet, Jedediah; four daus. Grace wife of William Hill, Abigail wife of Cornelius Stratton, Sarah wife of David Allen, Jr., and Rue Hull; Sarah, Levi, Eliphalet, Alvin, and Hull Bradley, children of dec'd dau. Eunice wife of Seth Bradley. Codicil 21 Dec. 1787: wife and dau. Rue are dec'd; Rue left three children,

---

* Children, rec. and bapt. Redding: Ellen, b. 3 Dec. 1763, bapt. 22 Jan. 1764, m. Theophilus Goodyear, of Hamden; Molly, b. 3, bapt. 15 Feb. 1766. The will of John, 24 June 1815, proved 18 Oct. 1820; wife Mary, mentioning marriage contract; gr. son John Goodyear, and his two sons and one dau., naming the son Hull Goodyear.

Abigail, Peter, and Rue, of whom son-in-law Capt. David Allen is to be guardian.

Distribution 24 Mar. 1790: Jedediah Hull; Eliphalet Hull; Grace wife of Ward W. Hill; heirs of Eunice Bradley dec'd,—Sarah, Levi, Eliphalet, Alvin, and Hull Bradley; Sarah wife of David Allen; Abigail wife of Cornelius Stratton; heirs of Ruami dec'd,— Peter, Abigail, and Ruami.

Children, rec. Fairfield, bapt. Greenfield:

31+Jedediah, b. 24 July 1732, bapt. 30 July 1732.
    Eunice, b. 6 Mar. 1734/5,* bapt. 24 Mar. 1734/5, d. at Greenfield, 28 Sept. 1770 ae. 36 yrs. 7 mos. 22 days (g. s.); m. 8 Sept. 1755, Seth Bradley.
    Grace, b. 16 July 1736, bapt. July 1736, d. at Greenfield, 17 Feb. 1813 in 77 yr. (g. s.); m. at Westport, 26 Aug. 1770, Ward William Hill.
32+Eliphalet, b. 18 Apr. 1738, bapt. 23 Apr. 1738.
    Abigail, b. 26 Apr. 1742, bapt. 2 May 1742, d. at Westport, 21 Feb. 1813 in 74 yr. (g. s.); m. 15 Aug. 1764, Cornelius Stratton.
    Sarah, b. 15 Apr. 1745, bapt. 21 Apr. 1745, d. at Fairfield, 30 Aug. 1804 in 60 yr. (g. s.); m. 10 Nov. 1768, David Allen, Jr.
    Ruhamah, b. 16 Dec. 1751, bapt. 25 Jan. 1752, d. 19 May 1784 (Perry Diary); m. (as "Rhue") 7 Dec. 1779, Jonathan Andrews.

17. Hull, Theophilus, s. of Theophilus.

Born 21 Feb. 1725/6, d. at Redding, 5 Dec. 1785 in 60 yr. (g. s.).

He m. at Redding, 25 Jan. 1759, Martha Betts. She was widow of ──── Betts, and dau. of Ephraim Jackson, b. 8 Sept. 1731, d. 10 Apr. 1785 in 52 yr. (g. s.).

Will 1, proved 19 Dec. 1785; son Zalmon; two daus. Sarah and Lydia Hull; Zalmon to be Exec'r with my friend David Jackson of Redding.

Children, bapt. at Redding:

Zalmon, b. 22 Apr. 1759 (Pension rec.), bapt. 13 May 1759, living 1834; m. 4 Mar. 1784, Eunice Belden.†
Sarah.
Lydia, bapt. 7 May 1769, d. 13 Jan. 1818 ae. 49; m. 8 Jan. 1792, William Sanford.

---

* 1733 by town record.
† Children, rec. Redding: Sarah, b. 20 June 1784; Theophilus, b. 5 Nov. 1785; Hezekiah, b. 20 Nov. 1788; Lydia, b. 28 Dec. 1790; Henry, b. 25 Dec. 1794. Theophilus B. d. at Redding, 17 Apr. 1830 ae. 44-5-12 (g. s.); m. Sally B. ────, who d. 22 Feb. 1834 ae. 41-2-16 (g. s.).

18. **Hull, Seth,** s. of Eliphalet.

Born at Greenfield, 23 Feb. 1728/9.

He m. 24 Dec. 1747, Hannah Rumsey, dau. of Robert, bapt. 31 Mar. 1728.

Settled near Saratoga, N. Y.

Children, rec. Fairfield; all except first bapt. Redding:

> Eliphalet, b. 4 Dec. 1749, bapt. at Greenfield, 4 Feb. 1749/50; prob. m. at Wilton, 24 Nov. 1768, Huldah Patchen.
> Seth, b. 12, bapt. 23 Feb. 1755.
> David, b. 5, bapt. 17 Dec. 1760.

19. **Hull, John,** s. of Eliphalet. Ens., Greenfield Co., Oct. 1770; Lt., May 1771.

Born at Greenfield, 28 Mar. 1732, d. there 2 May 1791 ae. 60 (g. s.).

He m. 11 Jan. 1759, Eleanor Sherwood; dau. of Benjamin, b. 6 Aug. 1740, d. 16 Oct. 1822 ae. 81 (g. s.) [10 Oct. by church record].

Will 8 Sept. 1788, proved 6 June 1791; wife Eleanor; eldest son John; sons, Benjamin, Eliphalet, Lyman, Seth; three daus. Eleanor, Sarah, Mabel.

Will of Eleanor, 18 June 1821, proved 16 Nov. 1822: two daus. Sally and Mabel Hull; son Eliphalet Hull, land in Greenfield; children of dec'd dau. Eleanor Banks; sons John, Eliphalet, Lyman; son Benjamin had his share, nothing left to his children.

Children of John and Eleanor, bapt. Greenfield:

> Ellen, b. 14 Jan. 1761 (Bible rec.), bapt. 15 Feb. 1761, d. at Greenfield, 16 Nov. 1791 in 31 yr. (g. s.); m. 19 Nov. 1778, Joseph Banks.
> John, bapt. 7 Aug. 1763, d. 29 Nov. 1830 ae. 67 (g. s.); m. at Westport, 1 Apr. 1798, Elizabeth Price, dau. of Hezekiah, b. 30 Nov. 1772, d. 25 Dec. 1856 (g. s.).*
> Sarah, bapt. 26 June 1766; "Sally" d. at Greenfield, 17 Mar. 1825 in 59 yr. (g. s.). Her will, 27 July 1824, proved 30 Apr. 1825; sister Mabel wife of Uriah Hubbell for life; bro. Eliphalet Hull's four sons (John, Burr, Wakeman, Edwin); bro. John Hull; nephew Alfred Hull's children.

---

*John's will, 28 Jan. 1726, proved 9 Feb. 1831; wife Betsey; five daus. of dec'd bro. Lyman Hull, viz. Eliza, Amelia Eleanor, Sally Bradley, Delia Meriah and Mary Catherine; bro. Eliphalet Hull for life, then to his chidren, John, Sally, Burr, Wakeman, and Edwin Hull.

Benjamin, b. 22 Apr. 1769, bapt. 30 Apr. 1769, d. 8 Apr. 1820 ae. 50 (g. s.); m. Pamelia Wakeman, dau. of Gideon, bapt. 6 Oct. 1771.
Mabel, b. [1771?], d. at Greenfield, 18 Feb. 1847 ae. 70 [76?] (g. s.); m. Uriah Hubbell.
Lyman, b. 21 [or 22, by Bible rec.] Aug. 1773, bapt. 17 Oct. 1773, d. 11 Oct. 1822 ae. 48 (g. s.); adm'n granted, 26 Mar. 1823, to John Hull, with Nathan Burr as surety; m. (1) 22 Oct. 1797, Amelia Bulkley, b. Aug. 1775, d. 19 Aug. 1815 in 40 yr.;* m. (2) 14 Mar. 1816, Sarah Hill.
Eliphalet, bapt. 6 Jan. 1776, d. 15 Nov. 1842 ae. 70 (g. s.); Capt.; m. at Westport, 16 Feb. 1800, Eunice Burr, of Greenfield; dau. of George, bapt. Mar. 1777, d. 14 Aug. 1845 ae. 67 (g. s.).
Seth, bapt. 10 Feb. 1778, d. 5 Feb. 1794 ae. 16 (g. s.).

20. **Hull, Daniel**, s. of Eliphalet.

Born at Greenfield, 15 May 1734, d. there 26 Feb. 1809 ae. 74 (g. s.); m. 11 Apr. 1759, Betty Bradley, dau. of Ephraim, b. abt. 1733, d. 3 May 1809 ae. 77 (g. s.).

Will 27 Jan. 1804, proved 27 Mar. 1809; gr. son Charles William, son of dau. Rachel; wife Betty; three sons, Daniel, Hezekiah, Banks Eliphalet; seven daus. Molly, Sarah, Hannah, Betsey, Abigail, Rachel, Deborah.

Est. of Betty Hull distributed, 28 May 1819, to Hezekiah Hull, Betsey wife of Aaron Thorp, Molly wife of Joel Davis, Abigail wife of Hezekiah Meeker, Rachel wife of Peter Thorp, Deborah wife of Increase Sturges, Widow Sarah Murwin, Widow Hannah Dickinson, Banks E. Hull, and heirs of Daniel Hull dec'd.

Children, two bapt. Greenfield, the rest Westport:

Molly, bapt. 17 May 1761; m. at Weston, 19 Mar. 1794, Joel Davis.
Daniel, bapt. 19 June 1763, d. in 1810; adm'n granted, 22 Dec. 1810, to Aaron Sherwood, Esq., Samuel Meeker surety; distribution made, 21 Dec. 1812, to widow Sarah, sons Hezekiah D., John; daus. Sarah, Abigail, David.
Sarah, bapt. 29 Dec. 1765, d. after 1814; m. 21 Feb. 1788, Meeker Merwin.
Hannah, bapt. 8 May 1768; m. ——— Dickinson.

---

* Children by first wife (from Bible rec.): Benjamin S., b. 25 May 1798, d. 10 Sept. 1859 in 62 yr.; Eliza, b. 11 Sept. 1800, d. 16 Jan. 1883 ae. 82, m. Simon Sherwood; Amelia-Eleanor, b. 9 Dec. 1802, d. 3 Dec. 1839, m. Joseph Jennings; Sally-Bradley, b. 27 Oct. 1806; Delia-Maria, b. 24 Dec. 1809, d. 10 May 1851, m. Joseph Jennings; Mary-Catherine, b. 20 Aug. 1813; m. 29 Oct. 1833, William-Webb Wakeman.

Hezekiah, bapt. 19 Jan. 1772, d. at Westport, 29 Dec. 1847 ae. 77 (g. s.) ; m. 28 Feb. 1799, Sarah Goodsell, dau. of John, b. abt. 1779, d. 17 Dec. 1847 ae. 68 (g. s.).
Betsey, bapt. 21 Aug. 1774, d. at Easton, 7 Apr. 1863 ae. 89 (g. s.); m. 26 Nov. 1798, Aaron Thorp, of Weston.
Abigail, bapt. 25 May 1777, d. at Weston, 22 Apr. 1862 ae. 85-1-11 (g. s.) ; m. 30 Nov. 1806, Hezekiah Meeker.
Rachel (twin), bapt. 25 May 1777, d. at Easton, 10 Dec. 1863 ae. 86-3-8 (g. s.) ; m. 30 Apr. 1799, Peter Thorp.
Eliphalet-Banks [known as Banks E.], bapt. 19 Mar. 1780, d. at Greenfield, 11 Apr. 1860 ae. 79 yrs. 3 mos. 26 days (g. s.) ; m. 8 Feb. 1816, Phebe Davis, dau. of Joshua, who d. 20 Mar. 1840 ae. 56 (g. s.).
Stephen, bapt. 30 June 1783.
Deborah, bapt. 25 July 1784, d. at Greenfield, 19 Mar. 1842 ae. 58 (g. s.) ; m. 25 Oct. 1803, Increase Sturges.

21. Hull, Jabez, s. of Jabez.

Born at Westport, 14 June 1729, d. in 1777; m. at Greenfield, 30 May 1751, Grace Sherwood, dau. of Joseph, b. 20 Oct. 1731.

Will of Jabez of North Fairfield, 15 Feb. 1777, proved 2 June 1777; wife Grace; eldest dau. Sarah wife of Nehemiah Fanton; dau. Eunice; eldest son Hezekiah; son Eliphalet.

The widow Grace was of Weston, 1793; and of Carmel, Dutchess County, N. Y., 1805.

Children, rec. Greenfield:

Sarah, b. Jan. 1752, bapt. 25 Jan. 1752, d. at Weston, 22 Mar. 1810 ae. 58 (g. s.) ; m. at Easton, 1 Jan. 1772, Nehemiah Fanton.
Hezekiah, bapt. 13 July 1755; res. 1784, Fredericksborough, N. Y.; m. at Greenfield, 28 Oct. 1779, Sarah Merwin; dau. of Daniel, b. 12 Mar. 1758.*
Eunice, bapt. 18 Mar. 1759.
Eliphalet, bapt. 24 May 1761; res. 1784, Fredericksborough, N. Y.;† m. at Weston, 8 Dec. 1782, Eunice Downs; dau. of Thomas, bapt. 25 Dec. 1763.

22. Hull, Seth, s. of George.

Bapt. 29 July 1733; d. at Redding, 5 Apr. 1795 ae. 61-9-13 (g. s.) ; m. Elizabeth Mallory, b. 11 Dec. 1738, d. 22 Feb. 1795.

---

* One Hezekiah Hull had a dau. Sarah bapt. at Easton, Oct. 1794.
† One Eliphalet Hull d. 1 Aug. 1813 (Miss Treadwell's book).